Loving Christ and Fleeing Temptation

Loving Christ and Fleeing Temptation

Select Sermons of Andrew Gray

edited by

Joel R. Beeke and Kelly Van Wyck

REFORMATION HERITAGE BOOKS

Grand Rapids, Michigan

Published by

Reformation Heritage Books
2965 Leonard St., NE
Grand Rapids, MI 49525
USA
616-977-0599 / Fax 616-285-3246
e-mail: orders@heritagebooks.org
website: www.heritagebooks.org

ISBN 978-1-60178-018-8

Library of Congress Cataloging-in-Publication Data

Gray, Andrew, 1633-1656.
[Selections. 2007]
Loving Christ and fleeing temptation: select sermons of Andrew Gray / by Andrew Gray; edited by Joel R. Beeke and Kelly Van Wyck.
p. cm.
ISBN 978-1-60178-018-8 (hardcover : alk. paper)
1. Church of Scotland--Sermons. 2. Sermons, English--17th century. I. Beeke, Joel R., 1952- II. Van Wyck, Kelly, 1981- III. Title.
BX5330.G7L68 2007
252′.052--dc22

2007014495

For additional Reformed literature, both new and used, request a free book list from Reformation Heritage Books at the above address.

CONTENTS

Biographical Preface ix
Original Preface xv

1. God's Love to Sinners Manifested in Bruising His Own Son 1
2. The Necessity and Excellency of Delighting in God 9
3. The Sinfulness and Loss of Not Calling on God 19
4. Christ's Mournful Visit to Obstinate Sinners 28
5. The Mansions of Glory Prepared for Believers. 36
6. Christ's Royal Priesthood, Sufficient Encouragement for Faith. 44
7. Christ's Continual Intercession in Heaven, Efficacious for His Members on Earth 53
8. Christian Diligence: The Way of Attaining Comfortable Assurance (1) 62
9. Christian Diligence: The Way of Attaining Comfortable Assurance (2) 70
10. Christ's Remarkable Condescension for the Confirmation of His People's Faith 78
11. Jesus Christ's Preciousness to Believers (1) 88
12. Jesus Christ's Preciousness to Believers (2) 98
13. A Call to Improve the Brevity of Human Life 104
14. The Christian's Case and Exercise in the Night of Desertion 111
15. The Time of Life: A Time of Trouble 117
16. The Believer's Love to an Unseen Christ 127
17. Hope Producing Holiness 140
18. The Blessedness of Forgiveness. 155
19. The Constant Necessity of Christian Watchfulness 162
20. The Sinner's Extremity, God's Opportunity 168

21. A Christian's Exercise under Desertion 177
22. The Intercourse of Divine Love between Christ and His Church 183
23. The Appropriating Nature of Saving Faith 198
24. The Sincere Christian, God's Peculiar Favorite 205
25. Overcoming Believers Crowned with Glory 217
26. The Great Efficacy of the Grace and Duty of Prayer 226
27. A Solemn Charge to Hearken to the Voice of the Son of God 239
28. Humility: The Christian's Best Ornament 253
29. How to Prevent Spiritual Pride During Special Manifestations (1) 266
30. How to Prevent Spiritual Pride During Special Manifestations (2) 281
31. How to Prevent Spiritual Pride During Special Manifestations (3) 297
32. How to Prevent Spiritual Pride During Special Manifestations (4) 310
33. How to Prevent Spiritual Pride During Special Manifestations (5) 322
34. Singular Temptations Call for Fervent and Frequent Supplications (1) 338
35. Singular Temptations Call for Fervent and Frequent Supplications (2) 353
36. Singular Temptations Call for Fervent and Frequent Supplications (3) 370
37. Singular Temptations Call for Fervent and Frequent Supplications (4) 396
38. The All-Sufficiency and Seasonableness of Divine Grace Manifested in the Return of Prayer: God's Time and Way of Answering Prayer Always Best, Though Different Than Our Expectations (1) 422
39. The All-Sufficiency and Seasonableness of Divine Grace Manifested in the Return of Prayer: God's Time and Way of Answering Prayer Always Best, Though Different Than Our Expectations (2) 439
40. Precious Remedies against Satan's Devices (1) 456
41. Precious Remedies against Satan's Devices (2) 471
42. Precious Remedies against Satan's Devices (3) 489

43. The Christian in Complete Armor; or, The Devil Resisted and Put to Flight (1) 507
44. The Christian in Complete Armor; or, The Devil Resisted and Put to Flight (2) 524
45. The Christian in Complete Armor; or, The Devil Resisted and Put to Flight (3) 536
46. Strangers Called to Behold Christ (1) 548
47. Strangers Called to Behold Christ (2) 565
48. The Necessity and Advantage of Looking unto Jesus 574
49. The Comfort and Blessedness of a Pardoned Sinner 587
50. The Indispensable Duty of Giving the Heart to Christ 597

A Word of Exhortation before the Communion of Glasgow 615

BIOGRAPHICAL PREFACE

The Life and Writings of
Andrew Gray (1633-1656)

Andrew Gray was born in Lawnmarket, Edinburgh, to Sir William of Pittendrum, a merchant and staunch royalist, and Egidia Smyth. He was the fourth son and eleventh child in a family of twenty-one. As a child, he was convicted of the sin of ingratitude by unexpectedly witnessing a beggar pour out his heart to God in a field near Leith. Before long, Gray was brought to rest in the finished work of Christ for his distraught soul.

Gray felt called to the ministry already as a boy. That gave impetus to his studies at Edinburgh and St. Andrews universities. He earned a Master of Arts degree in 1651 and at age nineteen was declared a candidate for the ministry. He was ordained in the Outer High Kirk in Glasgow by the Protestors on November 3, 1653, despite the objections of Robert Baillie and other Resolutioners who opposed his appointment for political reasons.

Gray was regarded as a burning light by thousands who heard him preach. William Blaikie, author of *The Preachers of Scotland,* wrote, "His knowledge of Christian experience was wonderfully extensive and minute; he knew well the joys and troubles, the helps and hindrances, the temptations and elusions of the Christian life. He had a remarkable power of probing the conscience; as James Durham remarks, 'he could make men's hair stand on end.'"

Both in preaching and in his personal life, Gray exhibited the need for holiness. He was a genuinely pious man. George Hutcheson spoke of him as "a spark from heaven."

That spark did not stay lit for long. Gray often preached of and longed for glory. When he was twenty-two, he expressed the desire that he would meet his Master in celestial bliss before his next birthday. Six months later, after a few days of fever, God granted that wish. Gray died on February 8, 1656, after contracting "purple" fever. He left behind a God-fearing wife, Rachel Baille (who later married George Hutcheson), and two children, Robert (who would soon die as a child) and Rachel. Gray's body was interred in Glasgow Cathedral.

"We may safely say that never in the history of our country did a man of his years make so deep a mark," said Blaikie. God used Gray mightily in his twenty-seven months of ministry.

With the exception of a few scarce sermons, Gray's corpus has been collected in three volumes, all of which are now reprinted and available. Here is a summary of each of them:

The Works of Andrew Gray (Soli Deo Gloria; 505 pages; 1992). Most of Gray's sermons were taken down in shorthand. These sermons were first published from a student's notes but contained numerous errors. Later, they were revised from additional sets of notes, including those owned by Gray's wife, and issued by Robert Traill and John Stirling. Printed as short books (*The Mystery of Faith Opened* [1659]; *Great and Precious Promises* [1669]; *Directions and Instigations to the Duty of Prayer* [1669]; *The Spiritual Warfare* [1671], etc.), Gray's written sermons proved as popular as his preaching, not only in England, Scotland, and North America, but also in the Netherlands. Most of his works were translated into Dutch and are still being reprinted today.

For more than a century these short books passed through numerous editions until they were collected and printed in 1762 in Glasgow as *The Works of the Reverend and Pious Mr. Andrew Gray*. This work also went through several printings, the most notable being the definitive 1839 edition published by George King in Aberdeen, from which the 1992 reprint is taken.

Since Gray's writings are sermons rather than treatises, they do not offer exhaustive treatments of each subject. They do not offer precise language, either, since Gray did not have the opportunity to edit his own sermons. On the other hand, Gray's sermons were "studied with prayer, preached with power, and backed with success." Moreover, his profound insights, poignant statements, and succinct summaries on various truths are priceless. Gray's gifts are not in propounding new theological insights but in presenting "old truth" in fresh ways.

For example, when explaining assurance of faith, Gray offers the following evidence: (1) the lives of biblical saints that showed assurance; (2) "the great scope of many scriptures, to show how Christians may attain unto assurance"; (3) "commands in Scripture for Christians to be serious in searching after assurance," most notably, 2 Peter 1:10; (4) "the blessed end of God's oath in the everlasting covenant that a Christian might get assurance" (5) "the ends of the sacraments, that our assurance may be confirmed"; and (6) the very exercises of divine graces that affirm the necessity of assurance. None of these points are new, but no one prior to Gray had compiled such a list.

Gray's writings will warm your soul, convict you of slothfulness, and urge you to godliness. They are full of spirit and life. Unlike many collections of *Works*, Gray is thoroughly readable from the opening series of sermons on the mystery of faith to the closing letter addressed from his deathbed to Sir Archibald Johnston.

A Door Opening Into Everlasting Life: An Essay Tending to Advance Gospel Holiness, and to Establish the Hearts of True Believers against Their Many Doubts and Fears (Netherlands Reformed; 220 pages; 1989). Reprinted for the first time since 1810, this volume (not included in Gray's *Works*) is Gray's major work on the doctrine of sanctification. Gray uses a five-pronged approach to spur believers onward in holy living. First, he shows why Christians should pursue sanctified lives. Second, he provides directions for "living holily." Third, he describes marks of grace evidenced in the lives of God's people. Fourth, he answers fears, doubts, and objections raised by those who feel the poverty of their own sanctification. Fifth, he encourages the children of God by showing the privileges and happiness of those who follow after Christ.

Loving Christ and Fleeing Temptation: Select Sermons of Andrew Gray (Reformation Heritage Books; 640 pages; 2007). These fifty sermons, of which only a few are in Gray's *Works,* show why Gray was so popular as a preacher. They make doctrine intelligible and practical. They powerfully speak to the mind and the conscience, comforting the regenerate, arresting the backslider, inviting the unsaved, and unmasking the hypocrite. Above all, they seek to win souls to Christ. As William Tweedie wrote, "Christ was the beginning, the middle, and the end of all his sermons."

Loving Christ and Fleeing Temptation was first published as *Select Sermons* in 1765 from handwritten manuscripts obtained by Gray's former wife from a friend in northern Scotland. A second edition was printed in 1792 by Patrick Mair in Falkirk. The present edition is freshly typeset and edited from the more accurate 1792 edition. (A selection of twelve sermons from this volume was reprinted as *Twelve Select Sermons* by Westminster Standard in Gisborne, New Zealand, in 1961.)

Select Sermons includes the following:

- Five sermons on how to fight spiritual pride (2 Cor. 12:7a)
- Four on praying against temptation (2 Cor. 12:8)
- Three on God's way of answering prayer (2 Cor. 12:9)
- Three on precious remedies against Satan's devices (2 Cor. 2:11)
- Three on resisting the devil (James 4:7)
- Two on beholding Christ (Isa. 65:1)
- Two on the role of Christian diligence in obtaining assurance of faith (2 Pet. 1:10)
- Two on Christ's preciousness to believers (1 Pet. 2:7)
- Several on Communion occasions
- A variety of individual sermons

Some of the more remarkable individual sermons include "The Necessity and Excellency of Delighting in God" (Ps. 37:4), "The Mansions of Glory Prepared for Believers" (John 14:2), "The Christian's Case and Exercise in the Night of Desertion" (Song of Sol. 3:1), "The Intercourse of Divine Love Between Christ and His Church" (Song of Sol. 2:1-2), and "The Necessity and Advantage of Looking Unto Jesus" (Isa. 45:22).

Regrettably, Andrew Gray never had a chance to edit his sermons in this book, so even the improved 1792 edition had many rough spots. The editing of this volume proved to be a major undertaking. Though it still does not read as smoothly as we could wish, we trust that it is vastly more readable now, and pray that God may abundantly bless its contents to many. I wish to thank Kelly Van Wyck for co-editing this book with me, Gary and Linda den Hollander for their typesetting and proofreading, and Amy Zevenbergen for her cover design.

—Joel R. Beeke

Puritan Reformed Theological Seminary
Grand Rapids, Michigan

ORIGINAL PREFACE

Dear Christian Reader,

That the following discourses are the genuine works of the reverend, pious, and learned author whose name they bear will be indisputable by comparing them with his other works, which it may be believed are as universally known through Scotland as any sermons that were ever yet published.

No doubt they will be found to labor under the many disadvantages that usually attend posthumous pieces which the authors never designed for the press, and on this account may not be so pleasant to the critic as to the serious reader; yet, as the whole scope and strain of them breathe such a warm and affectionate concern for the exaltation of free grace in the salvation of sinners, it is presumed that their publication at this time may be both necessary and useful.

May it not be thought more especially needful in such a degenerate age as this, both to publish and peruse such sermons as are so well calculated, under the divine blessing, to propagate the interest of pure and undefiled Christianity? May not the reading of such sermons, under the influence of the Spirit of all grace (which there is much ground to believe accompanied their preaching), be a means to impress the consciences of guilty and carnally secure sinners with an awakening and humbling sense of their deplorable state by nature, and the necessity of a better righteousness than their own for justification in the sight of a holy God, and to establish and build up believers in their most holy faith?

May it not be allowed a proper season for emitting sermons that are so rich with gospel truths, when error in doctrine so universally prevails? How affecting must it be to any serious Christian to observe that instead of the doctrines revealed in the divine oracles, there is little more heard through a multitude of churches than a carnally devised jingle of what goes under the name of wit or fine composition, which rather appears to be an imitation of Socrates or Plato than the doctrine of the cross of Christ!

To repeat all that has been said in commendation of this singularly eminent author by the various prefacers of his formerly published collections, would here be both tedious and unnecessary; only it may be observed, in a few words, what some of them notice: "That the Lord had endued this His young servant with special graces, extraordinary gifts and experiences, called him to the ministry when scarce twenty years old, and enabled him to improve and employ his talents so faithfully, arduously, and successfully, with so much humility, gravity, wisdom, diligence, and authority, as might have been a great conviction to many then in the ministry. One thing is desiderate by tender Christians: the author's mind was in accordance with the Public Resolutions, seeing he entered the ministry in the fourth year of that fifty-seven year-old, and yet growing apostasy.[1] Whatever his zealous contendings in public were, it is credibly reported that he had debated against these defections with his learned colleague Mr. Durham, who asked him on his deathbed what he thought of these things. Mr. Gray answered that he was of the same mind against them as he had formerly heard, and did regret he had been so sparing in public against these woeful resolutions, speaking so gravely and pathetically of their sinfulness, and of the public calamities and wrath they would procure, that Mr. Durham, contrary to his former practice, dared never after speak in defense of them."[2]

Another prefacer of Mr. Gray's sermons mentions, "No sooner were the notes of his sermons first seen abroad, but almost all the presses thro' the nation fell a-laboring about them; so that (if we mistake not) in less than two or three months' time, three or four impressions were cast off."

A late prefacer of another collection of his sermons, says, "His great advancement and progress in the short time he lived made him the wonder of the age he lived in. He was a burning and a shining light, of very uncommon gifts and experiences in Christianity; he was so admired and followed by serious Christians, far and near, that any who could write short hand were greedy to catch every

1. Now a hundred and fifteen years old.

2. The author's opinion regarding the nation's apostasy, appears in his Letter to my Lord Wariston.

word which dropped from his lips. It would seem that there was scarce ever a sermon that this youth preached, at home or abroad, but was thus written and preserved as a precious memory of him. His sermons show that he had great acquaintance with the Holy Scriptures and the practical part of religion; he had both a lively faith and a lively imagination about things spiritual and heavenly, and he improved greatly in spiritual and experimental preaching. He had a noble evangelistic turn in preaching Christ and recommending Him to his hearers in every exigency; he understood rightly how to divide the Word of truth, to separate between the precious and the vile, the converted and the unconverted, the sincere and the hypocrite, and to give each of them their proper share. His expressions are very warm, rapturous, and heavenly, and well adapted to affect the hearts of his hearers or readers, especially such as believe the gospel."

He adds, "Oh, how will this holy, active, and diligent youth rise up in judgment against the vain, negligent, and slothful men of our day, who misspend and waste the days of youth, their best time, in folly and things that cannot profit them, forgetting their Creator, and the things which belong to their peace! Yea, how awakening, convincing, and reproving, may the example of this very young minister be to many ministers of the gospel, who have been many years in the vineyard, but fall far short of his labors and progress! God thinks fit, now and then, as it were, to raise up a child to reprove the sloth and negligence of many thousands of advanced years, and show that He can perfect His own praise out of the mouth of babes."

Mr. Gray's contemporaries in the ministry witness to his gifts and great capacity. They say, "He was a scholastic genius, and had made considerable progress in reading and study for the few years he lived, though he was far from any affectation of learning in the pulpit; and his sermons were accompanied with remarkable power and success."

If any should object against these sermons of Mr. Gray's because of some defects or imperfections they may think they labor under, such are desired to consider that they are all supposed to have been only written from his mouth in the pulpit; and the writers, possibly, might not be so careful to note down the critical explications of the texts or truths which he handled, as other things which they might judge more edifying. No doubt, in writing they have lost both words and sentences, which, in sundry places, would have rendered the connection more natural, the construction more easy, and the sense more clear. Besides, it should be adverted to, what vast alterations have been made in the English language since that time. But to serious and experienced Christians, who regard matter rather than words, especially those who have perused the author's other sermons; it is presumed that they will be very accepting, as his dialect is so plain, familiar, and engaging, and so well calculated to the capacity of the weakest reader.

As truth, in its own native simple dress, has been frequently attended with the most remarkable and convincing evidence, even to its stoutest adversaries, so we find an inspired apostle express himself to this purpose: "And I, brethren, when I came to you, came not with excellency of speech or of wisdom, declaring unto you the testimony of God. For I determined not to know any thing among you, save Jesus Christ, and him crucified" (1 Cor. 2:1-2). But it is presumed that the character which this eminent author sustained, among the seriously religious, will very justly supersede any encomium that can be made on his performances, his name being so savory in the churches of Christ; and who, though being dead, yet speaks.

It may be asked why these sermons were never published until now. It is answered that the persons into whose hands they have been, for a great number of years, had never had any proper application for their publication, but still kept them for their own private use. If it should be further asked, how these manuscripts were procured, and in whose custody they have been so long detained, to this it is answered that one of the manuscript volumes, which contains besides what are here, a good number of the author's other sermons long ago published, was procured, first from Mrs. Hutcheson,[3] by a friend of hers in the North. They were kept in her custody until late, when eleven sermons were published out of it in 1746. The other volume, which likewise contains several of the author's sermons formerly published, was obtained from a gentlewoman in Preston-

3. This Mrs. Hutcheson was spouse, for some short time, to the reverend author, and was afterwards married to Mr. George Hutcheson, minister at Irvine. For a further account of which gentlewoman, together with the worthy author, the reader is referred to the prefaces affixed to his formerly published sermons.

pans, whose husband, of a well-known religious character, lately deceased, kept it by him for a good number of years.

There are no manuscript sermons left unprinted, so far as is known, belonging to the author.

It was judged proper to annex three of the sermons already printed[4] in their proper places, for the sake of connection, being on the same texts that are more fully handled here. There are also the other three sermons preached at the communion at Bothwell, which were already printed, that are not contained either in the collection, which of late goes under the name of his works, or in the collection published in 1746, by Mess. Lumisden and Robertson. Together with some discourses at communion tables, and his letter on his deathbed to my Lord Wariston, which, though they have been often printed, yet may be agreeable to such as have not had an opportunity of seeing them before—these additions have swelled the book considerably above what was proposed.

The respect subscribers discover to the memory of the worthy author is very observable, in their favoring this publication, which comes out with very little alteration, even as to words from what they stand in the manuscript, unless in some grammatical inaccuracies of the transcribers.

It was once proposed to have left unpublished some sermons that appear incomplete; yet, on the other hand, as all his sermons are no more than notes taken from his mouth in the pulpit, it is not to be supposed that any of them could be so full as delivered, or as if finished with his own hand. Therefore, it was thought better to take them just as they were than leave out any, or attempt either making up or remodeling them any manner of way; lest, in deviating from his own words, the sense of the author should have been impaired. The words of the late Mr. Hervey may, with propriety, be used here: "Only," says he, "let candor, not rigor, fill the chair; and interpret an unguarded expression, or a seemingly inconsistent sentence, by the general tenor of the discourse. We are not to expect much pathos of address, or any delicacy of composition. Here the gospel-diamond is set, not in gold, but in steel; not where it displays the most sprightly beam, or pours a flood of brilliancy, but where it may do the most signal service, and afford a fund of usefulness."

4. Sermons 12, 32, 48.

That the following sermons may be seriously perused by many, and by none without much spiritual profit; and that the God of all grace, who can render reading as well as hearing, an effectual means of salvation, may vouchsafe His rich and efficacious blessing, is our sincere desire.

Falkirk, May 20, 1792
The Publishers

SERMON 1

God's Love to Sinners Manifested in Bruising His Own Son

Yet it pleased the Lord to bruise him, he hath put him to grief: When thou shalt make his soul an offering for sin, he shall see his seed, he shall prolong his days, and the pleasure of the Lord shall prosper in his hand.

—Isaiah 53:10

It is, without all debate and controversy, the great and cardinal mystery of godliness, that God was manifested in the flesh; He who was the eternal Son of God became the Son of man, that we might become the children of God. He contracted affinity with this lower house by taking on Himself our nature, that so we might contract affinity with that higher house by becoming partakers of His divine nature. Rendering this mystery more wonderful is the unspeakable highness and excellence of that person who did condescend, and the unspeakable lowness and wretchedness of those for whom He did condescend. If we were asked how much we owe to Christ for this, we could not answer; but, upon serious consideration and search, we should respond that the more we search, the more we see our obligation to Him.

We may here see, or behold, that infinite wisdom of God, who contrived such a noble and precious way for making up such a distance and breach between Him and us by bruising such a person, the very Son of God. If God had summoned angels and men to sit down and do counsel about this way of our salvation, in what a confusion and silence would they all have remained! Surely this should have the general vote of that meeting and assembly: *non liquet,* or they could not tell. But when human wisdom fell, then His divine wisdom began and answered.

We may likewise see here the love that He has manifested toward wretched sinners, and that perfect justice that He has manifested toward His Son. Oh, did ever angels or men see such a spectacle, that a most loving father should command that sword of justice to awake and smite an obedient Son! And, when that knife was coming down on that blessed sacrifice of His soul, there was none in heaven or in earth that cried, "Hold Thy hand!" Oh, stand astonished and wonder at that blessed condescension of Jesus Christ, that He who was God, equal to the Father, should have made Himself of no reputation, and taken upon Him the shape of a servant! Oh, to see how rigorously spotless justice dealt with spotless innocency! I suppose, if all the redeemed had seen Him hanging upon a tree, and these beautiful lips growing pale, and had seen how He was bruised between these two millstones of God's wrath and indignation, the justice and the omnipotence of God, we might have said as David in 2 Samuel 24:17, "Lo, I have sinned," but what has this spotless Lamb done? That saying cannot be considered with awe enough, in John 18:8, when they were seeking to betray Christ: "Jesus answered, I have told you that I am he: if therefore ye seek me, let these go their way."

We may likewise here behold the spotless justice of God, that though He was a person in whose lips was no guile, yet, by the imputation of our sin upon Him, we conceive justice did punish Him as if He had been the greatest reprobate in the world. Justice delivered Him up until He had paid the utmost farthing of our debt; and we doubt not but there are some here today for whom He satisfied the Father's wrath. Woe is to them eternally who are not among these for whom He satisfied! Oh, but they shall be an excellent and glorious company, when they shall be all together—when all these children shall be as olive plants planted about His table! Shall not that be an excellent day, when we shall eat and drink, and shall remember our poverty no more? Oh Christians, comfort yourselves in the hope and expectation of the approaching of this day, when you shall rejoice for evermore, and all sorrow and sighing shall flee away from your eyes. Oh, shall not we rejoice, when all the redeemed of the Lord shall be brought together to that place, and be brought to the King in garments broidered with needlework? Shall it not be a pleasant day, when they shall come from every corner of the earth, and shall sit down in heaven together with Abraham, Isaac, and Jacob; when all your enemies shall be cast into that lake that burns with fire and brimstone, whose worm never dies, but their smoke ascends forever and ever? Oh, remember on that day, when you shall behold Him face to face, and all your shadows shall flee away, and you shall have the immediate and naked sight of God, and shall rejoice and delight yourselves in Him through all the ages of eternity, and God shall delight Himself in you for evermore. Shall not that be an excellent day, when such things shall be? But we shall speak of these things in the words of our verse.

You have in them that fountain from whence the redemption of man flows. Certainly there was nothing in us that caused our redemption, but only infinite love in Him. Grace, no doubt, was the presses of that council when such an excellent purpose and decree was brought forth. Oh, He is an excellent rule to Himself! Our redemption would have been lain by, if Christ had stayed in heaven until He had found something in us to be a cause in our redemption.

The greatness of Christ's suffering is held forth under these two words: "he was bruised" and "put to grief." The initial word displays the pain of His body—"he was bruised"; and oh, what a sight was it to see these blessed hands that never wrought iniquity, to be pierced through; and His precious feet, the sound whereof was never heard in the paths of unrighteousness, to be thrust through; and that blessed side of His, pierced with a lance! Oh, what a sight it was to see the infinite and eternal Son of God so handled for our cause! Christians, stand astonished at this! Second, "he put him to grief." This comprehends all the sufferings of the soul of Christ. Was it not the insupportable burden of our iniquity which was laid on His blessed back? Further, when He was drinking the cup, infinite grace subjoined, "I delight to do thy will, O my God" (Ps. 40:8)! But that which makes it mysterious is that which is in the beginning of our text: "Yet it pleased the Lord to bruise him." Oh, might not the law of nature and of love have entered a protest against this? "Yet it pleased the LORD to bruise him." It was so that He was bruised; it behooved Him so to be.

The most precious and excellent promises that the Father gives to the Son are the execution of the ancient covenant of redemption. These three promises are expressly set down in the words: first, that he should "see his seed"—that He should behold His offspring and generation. The second promise is that He should "prolong his days"—He should once have that triumphant song put in His mouth, "O death, where is thy sting? O grave, where is thy victory?" (1 Cor. 15:55). Thus He is now prolonging His days. And the third promise is that "the pleasure of the Lord should prosper in his hands." We think there has been a blessed concurrence and holy harmony among all the Persons of the blessed Trinity to accomplish this blessed and admired work of man's redemption and eternal salvation. Is redemption purchased for lost mankind not glad tidings from a far country? Ought it not to be as cold water to a thirsty soul? Is it not a great wonder to see sinners sleeping at this news, for whom this redemption is purchased and bought with such a price, even the blood of Jesus Christ, who is the eternal Son of God, incarnate and made manifest in the flesh? What love He had for us, that He should have condescended so far as to come down from heaven to earth; that He could not be happy alone in heaven, but He would come down and be miserable on earth that we might be happy in heaven?

Paul sounded out a fourfold dimension of this love of God to sinners. There are three of them ordinary: the length, and the breadth, and the depth; but there is also the height of that love, and oh, what a love must that be! Let us point at some considerations that may commend this blessed and precious love of our Lord Jesus Christ in undertaking the design of our redemption and eternal salvation.

First, consider the unspeakable highness of that Person who suffered such pain. Was it not the Son of God, who was equal with the Father? If it had been an angel who suffered those things, it would not have been so admirable and wonderful; but that He was an all-sufficient and self-sufficient Being, who stood not in any need of us, that He should have been bruised for us! Oh, what an admiration may this be to men and angels! That He who is the eternal God, the Creator of the ends of the earth, should have ever conceived such a thing as to take upon Him our nature and pay our debt; that He should have laid down His life for us; that He should have done this, when we were cast out to the loathing of our persons—oh, stand astonished, marvel, and wonder at this, that ever such a thing should have been! Have you ever seen two such unequal persons joined together in so near a bond that such wretched sinners should be married to Him and be advanced to such a high dignity and privilege that we should be espoused to that excellent One, even our Creator? Certainly we may say with Abigail, "We are going to be married to the King." Oh, less dignity would have satisfied me; yet, seeing it is the King's will, I will heartily concur with it. He has taken us off the dunghill, and has clothed us, and will yet clothe us, with the garments of His righteousness. Is not this a divine and matchless mystery? Christians, what do you think of this great love? Has not Christ been very considerate that He should ever have taken such wretches as we are to be His companions and bride? I confess, I wonder that men and women are not swallowed up in a sea of wonder at this matchless consideration of the highness and transcendent excellence of the Person who suffered such things for them.

Let us consider, in the second place, the greatness of the pains that He underwent for us. He was "bruised" for us; or, as the word may be rendered, he was *brayed in a mortar*. Oh, what pain do you think that would be? What horrible pain made Him "sweat...as it were great drops of blood," (Luke 22:44) and when He was forced to cry out, "My God, my God, why hast thou forsaken me?" (Matt. 27:46). What a painful experience was that which made Him so cry out? That Jesus Christ, who is the eternal begotten of the Father, should have been forsaken for us! He was forsaken for a moment, so that we might not be forsaken eternally. Oh, what would have become of us if Christ had not condescended so far as to take upon Him our nature, to satisfy the divine justice of God, and come under the Father's wrath? Certainly we would never have been able, through all the ages of eternity, to satisfy the least point of the justice of God; we would have lain eternally under the stroke of the naked sword of the justice of God without any hope of redemption; but blessed be He eternally, that such a gracious purpose and design should have entered into His blessed breast as to redeem mankind, who were utterly lost, and to redeem them by His own precious and worthy blood. Oh, our redemption was bought for us at a dear rate! It was not purchased with gold or silver, or with any corruptible thing, but with the incorruptible blood of Jesus Christ. It behooved Him to be "bruised" and "grieved" before our redemption could be purchased for us; His shame was His greatest pain, that even the sun, against the course of nature, did cast a veil over its face, and, as it were, thought it shame to see its Creator put to such an open shame, hanging between heaven and earth upon a tree. I confess this can never be wondered at enough, that He who was infinite and of Himself all-sufficient, that He should have stooped so low, from heaven to earth, and have suffered the shameful death of the cross! This was so wonderful a spectacle and sight that the very souls who were departed rose and saw it, and the rocks and mountains did lament; yea, they brake and burst asunder at such a sight, and then the sun did not shine, nor did the moon give her light. Seeing, however, that all this was done to purchase redemption and salvation to sinners, oh, what shall become of those who neglect this great salvation? Seeing justice dealt so with Jesus Christ, who was but the cautioner of the debt, what shall it extort from you, when you are gnashing your teeth and wailing in the bitterness of your souls? What shall it exact from you, who are the full and principal debtors, when you are lying tormented forever in that lake that burns with fire and brimstone that shall never be quenched? What shall become of you, for whom this satisfaction was not made, and for whom this redemption and everlasting salvation was not purchased? What shall it make you do, when it caused Jesus Christ to cry out, "My soul is exceeding sorrowful, even unto death" (Matt. 26:38)?

The third consideration that does commend the blessed and precious love of our Lord Jesus Christ in undertaking this most noble and excellent design of our redemption and eternal salvation, is to consider the infinite wretchedness of those for whom He underwent such sore and unspeakable pain. Was it for an excellent creature that He was pleased to undertake this immense pain? No, it was for the lost and miserable seed of poor mankind. Two things make this subject most mysterious. First, it is unthinkable that He should undergo these pains and torments for the very dust of His feet. Might not Christ have created other creatures more excellent and more spiritual in their walk and conversation, letting us go our own way, for we are running the highway to destruction? Oh, blessed of the Lord, do you not think that a Christian is much indebted to Christ for this? I confess it is a great mystery that Christ did not create, or think it good to create, other creatures better than we were. The second thing that makes this a mystery and wonder is that He condescended to undergo these unspeakable pains for men and not for angels. If He had done it for angels, and not for us, we might have sunk through the earth with heaviness when we thought upon the days of eternal torment that were approaching to us. But blessed be God forever, that He has purchased a redemption for us rather than for fallen angels: "For verily he took not on him the nature of angels, but he took on him the seed of Abraham" (Heb. 2:16). When angels were falling, He let them go; but when we were falling, He went in between us and the depth.

The fourth consideration that may commend the precious love of Christ to us for undertaking the great design of our redemption is that it would have been woefully impossible for us to have obtained everlasting life without His suffering for us, and His coming down from heaven to earth. But there was a threefold impossibility wherewith we were clothed: (1) The impossibility of the weakness of the law (2) The impossibility of the weakness of nature (3) The sinfulness of our nature. We read in Romans 5:6, "For when we were yet without strength, in due time Christ died for the ungodly." These blessed and precious arms did sweetly dissolve these impossibilities; He rent asunder, and made a new and living way to enter into the holiest of all.

There is a fifth consideration, which commends to us the precious love of Christ, by undertaking this blessed design of our redemption. There was but one in heaven or in earth that could undertake this business; this makes it most mysterious. If there had been multitudes of persons to have done it, His love would not have been so singular; but there was only one, the second Person of the blessed Trinity; He alone was able and willing. Oh, what a wonder that there was even a consultation among the Persons of the blessed Trinity about this work of our eternal redemption! It is easier to take up all the mysteries of nature than the mystery of how our redemption was brought about; it is easier to take up all the languages of the earth than this fact.

The sixth consideration concerning the precious love of Christ in undertaking our redemption is that although many affronts were put on Him, yet He condescended to satisfy justice for us. Oh, what blessed news was this to our forefather Adam, who had this promise held out to him, that the seed of the woman would bruise the head of the serpent! When he was expecting that God would arm all the beasts of the field against him, he met with a blessed disappointment of his expectation.

In further prosecuting of this, we shall speak of some advantages from the consideration of Christ's sufferings and humility. First, it provokes Christians to the grace of love: "Herein is love, not that we loved God, but that he loved us, and sent his Son to be the propitiation for our sins" (1 John 4:10). Love takes fire and kindles best at love, and when the love of God and of the creature shall be brought to one, we shall be taken up to the third heaven. The second advantage is that it keeps the grace of God eminently in exercise: "Wherefore henceforth know we no man after the flesh; yea, though we have known Christ after the flesh, yet henceforth know we him no more" (2 Cor. 5:16). Oh, may we not blush that we should solace ourselves in the paths of iniquity, and He to have done this for us! Third, considering Christ's sufferings keeps the grace of humility eminently in exercise: "For if they do these things in a green tree, what shall be done in the dry?" (Luke 23:31). A fourth advantage is this: by this consideration, you may be distinct in the knowledge of sin. Oh, what a cruel and monstrous thing must sin be! Yet, to know it is a most excellent thing. Finally, through considering the sufferings of Christ, we may behold much of God in this mystery of our redemption.

Oh, Christians, we desire you to be much in the consideration of this glorious mystery, which is so astonishing that we are told the angels themselves "desired to look into it" (1 Peter 1:12). However, at present we must cease from speaking any more concerning this; but, I am persuaded that it is the exercise of those that are now above not to search, but to admire at the boundless mystery of our redemption. Do you desire to know the tenor of their praise? It is this: "Blessed be the Lamb who was slain from the foundation of the world, that He should have taken the crown of thorns and put it on His head, to cause us to have a crown of immortal glory." Oh, Christians, we shall surely be humbled on that day, when we shall put that threefold crown upon us, the crown of joy, the crown of righteousness, and the crown of immortal glory; then, when we have that triple crown upon our head, then we shall fall down at His feet, and cry out in admiration, "Thou alone, O Lord, art worthy of honor and glory!" Amen.

SERMON 2

The Necessity and Excellency of Delighting in God

Delight thyself also in the Lord; and he shall give thee the desires of thine heart.
—Psalm 37:4

It was one of the most high and wonderful steps of the condescension of Christ Jesus, that before the mountains were brought forth, or ever the cornerstones of the world were laid or the blessed morning stars did shout, Christ was rejoicing in the habitable places of the earth. Ought not this to be a motive and incentive for us to delight in God? May we not say to the commendation of precious Christ—how pleasant and how fair art Thou? Is it not most certain that there is advantage to delighting in God, without any mixture of loss; joy, without any mixture of sorrow? There is beauty, without any mixture of imperfection or spot to be found in Him. All joy and delight for evermore is with Him, and all beauty and comeliness is in Him. He is altogether lovely, white and ruddy, the chief among ten thousand, and at His right hand are pleasures for evermore. Certainly, that matchless One can never be overvalued, and He can never be too loved; we can never commend nor praise Him too much.

Let us consider the words of our text. The psalmist, in the first part of this psalm, considers the doctrine of patience and submission of spirit, as he beholds the prosperity of the wicked. When he sets down the command in the first seven verses, he suggests many ways by which one may win an excellent frame of spirit under all trials and cross dispensations. In this text, we may observe several worthy points.

First, a most precious and excellent command is given: "Delight thyself in the Lord." In these words are three excellent considerations to press home the importance of obedience to that command. First, consider the object in which a Christian's consolation is to be found: "in God." Second, consider the most ample and comprehensive promise that is given: "and he shall give thee the desires of thine heart." Third, there are several properties of this most excellent promise. This promise is described by the fountain from whence it comes, that is, the Lord. Also, notice the freedom of this promise: He shall give you the desires of your heart, freely. Last, observe the extent and comprehensiveness of this promise, held forth in the word "desires."

Now, let us look closely at the text, which is the most excellent and precious command, "Delight thyself in the Lord." Let us consider five points concerning these words.

1. It is the duty of every Christian, and of everyone within the visible church, to delight and solace himself in God.

2. Believing, and putting our conscience in Him, is an excellent help to a soul under trouble.

3. After a soul has closed by faith with God in Christ, there is still an *also* to be done: trust in God, and delight thyself also in the Lord.

4. A soul delighting and solacing itself in God is a most excellent, noble, and spiritual way for a Christian to win a patient and silent frame of spirit under all crosses and afflictions that he may meet with; this we gather from the scope.

5. Last, there is a promise that the meek shall delight themselves in an abundant peace. From the consideration of these two verses, observe that the most substantial and excellent duties of the covenant of grace are turned over into promises, as the duty of beholding Christ is turned over into a promise: "They shall look upon me whom they have pierced, and they shall mourn for him, as one mourneth for his only son" (Zech. 12:10). The duty of hearkening unto Him is turned over into a promise.

Here we come to the first observable point concerning the command. It is the duty of every Christian to delight and solace himself in God. This duty is made clear in Isaiah 55:7, which says, "Let the wicked forsake his way, and the unrighteous man his thoughts: and let him return unto the LORD, and he will have mercy upon him; and to our God, for he will abundantly pardon." A similar command is stated in Matthew 22:37: "Thou shalt love the Lord thy God with all thy heart, and with all thy soul, and with all thy mind." Now what is delight in God but to love Him, and to add high degrees to our love? But I shall clarify that it is the duty of a Christian to delight in God from these three things:

1. Does not this relationship between Christ and believers make it clear that it is their duty to delight in Him? Is Christ your husband, and your eldest brother? Ought you not then to delight yourselves in Him? Is Christ your husband, and are you His wife? Is it not then most convenient and suitable for the wife to delight herself in and love her husband?

2. The second thing that clarifies it is the most precious and excellent names that Christ has taken to Himself. One of these names is "the desire of all nations." Is that Christ's name? Then certainly it is our duty to delight in Him. Another name is "noble plant of renown." Is that Christ's name? Further, there is "the bright morning star." Then delight yourselves in Him! Has He not taken the name, "the Lord our righteousness"? Is He not called, "the root and offspring of David," "the lion of the tribe of Judah," and, "the beginning of the creation of God"? Is He not also named the Father of eternity? He is altogether holy, and in Him is no spot at all. Oh then, delight in Him, for all these precious and most excellent names of Christ call for you to delight yourselves in the Lord.

3. The third thing that makes clear the duty of Christians to delight in God is the transcendent comeliness, excellent beauty, and overcoming perfection that is in the face of Christ. Oh, if once you got a sight of Christ in His beauty, you would become His captives, and would delight yourselves in Him. Never a soul had a sight of Him but was constrained to cry out, "Oh, who would not love thee, oh

King of nations!" Is not this a sufficient ground to know that it is our duty to delight in God?

Before we go further, we shall consider the following question: what is it to delight in God? To delight in God consists of the following things: first, a soul should be much taken up in the exercise of the grace of love. To delight in God is to have love smoking in a Christian's heart towards God. Love is but a bruised reed; but delight is love coming up to perfection. Second, a soul delighting in God has a high esteem and account of Christ. One whose delight is in God will have a matchless estimation and high considerations of Him. Third, the soul that delights in God has all its thoughts running towards God, and is exercised upon Him. His thoughts are only terminated on Him; He is the object of them all. Now, oh Christians, on what are your thoughts fixed? Is it not certain that they are all confined within this rivulet and span-length of time? Has not the world your first thoughts in the morning and your last thoughts at night? Then certainly, your delight is not in God. Fourth, one who delights in God is consumed with desire for communion and fellowship with God. Then try yourselves by this test: if it is not your main desire to have fellowship with God, your delight is not in Him, for if God is the object of your delight, you will strongly desire communion with Him, and it will also be refreshing to you. Fifth, such a soul will often lament and grieve the absence of Christ. Certainly, if your delight is in God, His absence will be your greatest cross, and His presence will be your main joy and pleasure. Finally, the person who delights in God will study and endeavor in all things to please and give satisfaction to God; for if we delight in any person, certainly we will attempt to please Him in all things. Now this may be a trial and evidence as to whether we delight in God; our main design and endeavor will be to please Him in all things.

To further prosecute this truth, we have proposed to you six things wherein we believe this delight in God rests, which may be as so many trials and evidences to us, whether or not God is the subject of our delight. We shall speak a little concerning these considerations by which all may be enforced to set about the noble exercise of delighting in God.

First, dear Christians, do you desire to have the exercise, or do you desire to win the exercise of these noble exercises that are above, around the throne? Then delight yourselves in God. To delight in

God is the only exercise of the saints above; but I shall point out three differences between the saints in heaven and the saints that are below on earth.

1. The saints above are in the higher room, and we are in the lower room.

2. The souls of the saints above are in a higher degree of love than we are; their praise is higher than ours; they are now delighting themselves in and praising Him through all eternity.

3. Those above are enjoying Christ by sight and fruition, but we on earth enjoy Him through the veil of faith. They have the immediate sight of God, and behold Him face to face; but we behold Him darkly as through a glass. Oh, Christians, if you desire to delight yourselves in God, you would bring down heaven upon earth; for what is heaven, but a soul's delighting itself in God, and God delighting Himself in the soul?

Second, be persuaded to delight yourselves in God for it is an exceedingly commendable pursuit. I would commend delight in God in four ways.

1. What is it to delight in God? It is the soul of a Christian embracing the soul of Christ by the two arms of love and desire. Is not that an excellent thing which may commend it unto you?

2. The soul of a Christian that delights in God is more where it loves than where it lives; it is more where its object is, than where its own abode is.

3. By delighting in God, a Christian achieves three acts of admiration. First, Christian, you shall say, "Oh, how far is Christ above the report that I have heard of Him!" You shall be constrained to remark, "The half was never heard of Him that now I see." Second, you will then experience and remark, "Oh, how far is Christ above the love that I have had to Him! He is far above it." Third, you will be forced to say, "Oh, how far is Christ above the admiration and amazement that I have had of Him!" Now, if your

delight is in God, you will be put to these acts of admiration and astonishment.

4. By delighting in God, the soul is helped to a spiritual walk and holy conversation. Who are the persons that have the moon under their feet? Only those that have their hope and delight in God. But I fear there are many of us here that have the moon on our heads, and not under our feet; certainly such have not their delight in God.

The third consideration to enforce your delight in God is that this delight in God makes all duties pleasant and heart-warming; for without delight in God, all duties of religion will be most unpleasant and burdensome (Job 22: 26-27). There are four advantages in the exercise of duty that waits on delighting in God. These four advantages are as follows:

1. He that has his delight fixed on God has boldness to speak to Him: "For then shalt thou have thy delight in the Almighty, and shalt lift up thy face unto God" (Job 22:26).

2. Delight in God will help a Christian to multiply his prayers: "Thou shalt make thy prayer unto him" (v. 27).

3. Delight in God will help to much fervency in prayer. The word rendered *prayer* may also be rendered as "many strong prayers."

4. The fourth advantage in duty that attends delighting in God is that it will help a Christian to tell all his mind to Him: "Thou shalt make thy prayer unto him, and he shall hear thee, and thou shalt pay thy vows" (Job 22:27).

The fourth consideration for pressing home this duty of delighting in God is that it will bring a Christian to a patient bearing of any cross or affliction that he encounters; this is clear from the scope of the text. It will be an excellent help and guard against fretting at the prosperity of ungodly men.

Fifth, consider the excellence of the object of the Christian's delight, which is the Lord. He is the most excellent object of delight; He is the fountain from which all our streams come. Oh, then delight in Him who is excellent and majestic!

The sixth and last consideration is this: if you delight yourself in God, surely He will give you the desires of your heart. I say, they shall lack nothing that is for their own welfare and God's glory. If you delight yourself in God, you shall lack nothing that is fitting for you. Oh then, be persuaded to give obedience to this most soul-concerning commandment of delighting in God. Christians, it is of your everlasting concern. Oh, do it while it is still being offered. Do not neglect this excellent work any longer. Oh, do not delay any longer, for delays are dangerous, especially in the matter of our eternal salvation.

Now we must point out the things that influence a Christian's lack of delight in God. We conceive that there are these seven things that have a main influence on a Christian's lack of delight in God.

1. Hosea 4:11 shows us that when our idols have the preeminence in all things—when our idols sit often upon the throne of our hearts—Christ stands behind the door. Oh, beware lest Christ depart from you, and you perish from the way; seeing our idols have so much of our hearts, it cannot be that our delight is fixed on God.

2. The second thing that has influence on our not delighting in God is that we are too worldly minded. All our delight is in this present life, and not upon God. Our worldly mindedness, as it were, has eaten up all our love to God and has consumed all the delight that we had in Him. We read in 1 John 2:15, "Love not the world, neither the things that are in the world. If any man love the world, the love of the Father is not in him." It was the prayer of a religious person, "Lord, never make me a servant of the creatures." But oh, I suppose, if the world were taken away from many of us, we would cry out, as in Judges 18:24, "Ye have taken away my gods which I made, and the priest, and ye are gone away: and what have I more?" Oh, but our hearts cleave fast to the things of this life and make them our gods; our hearts do not remember that these are all but vanity and vexation of spirit, and shall be found one day to be so! All your idols, in which you now take so much pleasure and delight, shall one day become as tasteless and savorless to you as they have been savory,

or as the white of an egg; you shall have no consolation at all in them.

3. There is this third thing that we conceive has influence on your seldom delighting yourselves in God: we too often fall away from that lively and near communion and fellowship that we once had with God. This is clear from Song of Solomon 1:16, "Behold, thou art fair, my beloved, yea, pleasant." What is it that makes Christ so fair and pleasant? It is that "our bed is green"; that is, the bride had a secret fellowship and correspondence with her love; we must have the same correspondence with God. It is likewise clear from Song of Solomon 2:3, where we read, "As the apple-tree among the trees of the wood, so is my beloved among the sons." What was the reason of her commending Christ so? It is because she sat down under His shadow, and His fruit was sweet to her taste; He brought her to the banqueting house, and His banner over her was love. It is likewise clear from Psalm 73:23, where we read, "Nevertheless, I am continually with thee; thou hast holden me by my right hand." Then, in verse 25 the psalmist says, "For whom have I in heaven but thee? and there is none upon earth that I desire besides thee." I suppose there are many of us that are here that may complain, "It is thirty days since I saw the king's face." Yea, many I fear may say, it is thirty months since I saw Him. Oh, but there is often a great distance between Christ and us, and yet without much grief and sorrow!

4. We too little delight in God because of the cursed formality that we have in going about duties of prayer. Do not our tongues go before our hearts? In our prayers to God, a Christian should pray as David in Psalm 45:1; his heart should be indicting a good matter—"my tongue is the pen of a ready writer." But formality and indifference in duties makes one extremely weary in duty: "But thou hast not called upon me, O Jacob; but thou hast been weary of me, O Israel" (Isa. 43:22).

5. Neglect of duty has great influence on our little delighting ourselves in God. We read in Isaiah 43:23, "Thou hast not brought me the small cattle of thy burnt offerings; neither hast thou honoured me with thy sacrifices."

6. Our little delight in God is also due to our lack of faith. Nothing will bring delight in God more under a consumption and decay than lack of faith; faith is the good spy of the soul, and it draws aside the veil, so that a Christian may have a clear sight of Christ, and may delight in Him.

7. Wrong apprehensions and misconstructions of the ways of God obstruct our delight in God. Nothing quenches love more than jealousies and suspicions; and nothing quenches delight more than misapprehensions and misconstructions of God's excellent ways. Dear Christians, I would desire you to stop your pursuit after the things of the world. Consider what you are doing, and what the end of your pursuit shall be! I will say to you what Abner said to Joab: "Shall the sword devour for ever? knowest thou not that it will be bitterness in the latter end?" (2 Sam. 2:26). Certainly you shall find it to be bitterness, when it shall not be in your offer to amend and help it. Oh, then delight in God. I would only say this, delight in God, for it is commanded; and certainly, if there were no more to press it on you but the fact that it is His command, that should be more than sufficient to provoke you to it. If the question that king Ahasuerus asked Haman should be directed to us: "What shall be done unto the man whom the king delighteth to honour?" (Esther 6:6), we should answer it thus: "He shall have the desires of his heart, and what can be asked more?" Yea, I may say unto you that which Saul's servant said to David: "The king desireth not any dowry, but an hundred foreskins of the Philistines" (1 Sam. 18:25); so Christ desires no more with you, but that you give Him the foreskins of your idols, that He may be avenged on your enemies.

I would ask you six questions, dear Christians, which, if you are not able to answer, will tell you that you are yet in the gall of bitterness and bonds of iniquity. First, what has most of your delights? What has most of your thoughts? Has the world or your idols? Then you are yet in the bonds of iniquity. Is it not certain that the world has most of your thoughts? Then you are yet in the gall of bitterness. Second, what is the thing you endeavor most to keep, and are most afraid to lose? Is it Christ? I fear few can answer the question so. Oh, is the world the main thing we endeavor to keep, and the thing we are most afraid of losing? Then we are yet in the gall of bitterness. Third, what is the thing that has most of your heart? Is it Christ or your idols? If it is not Christ, you are cursed; for as yet you are in the gall of bitterness. The fourth question is this: do you value Christ and the things of eternal salvation and life, above all other things in the world? Then you are safe, for if Christ is the object of your delight, you will value Him most. Fifth, is it your endeavor to please Him in all things? If it is not, then certainly you are yet in the gall of bitterness and bonds of iniquity. Last, is it your desire, or could you ever say that it was your desire above all things to have communion and fellowship with God? Was that ever your main desire, and the thing for which you labored most? If not, then certainly you are still in the gall of bitterness and bonds of iniquity. I shall say no more to you at this time, but it is like many of you to not pose these questions to your consciences, or think how you shall answer them; for if many of you did, could you not but say that you are in the gall of bitterness? Oh Christians, delight yourselves in the Lord, and He shall give you the desires of your heart. Amen.

SERMON 3

The Sinfulness and Loss of Not Calling on God

And there is none that calleth upon thy name, that stirreth up himself to take hold of thee: for thou hast hid thy face from us, and hast consumed us, because of our iniquities.

—Isaiah 64:7

Are there not most certain and undeniable symptoms and evidences of a spiritual consumption that is among us? Is it not certain that the strength of our idols has brought us to the gates of spiritual death? We must take up this lamentation, that we have sold ourselves to commit iniquity. Are you not afraid that that day is approaching when you shall curse the day that you took on the profession of godliness? Do you not fear the day when religion shall be ashamed of you, and you of your religion; when Christ shall propose that sad challenge to your consciences, saying, "For which of all my good works take ye up stones to stone me?" Let us discuss the six evidences of spiritual consumption and decay.

The first is that we are more covetous to seem to be religious than truly to be so. It is our great design that our names might be written in the writing of Israel. I conceive there are some that are Christians in their tongues, and not so in their hearts. Is this not a monstrous thing that one should begin to speak before they begin to live? But such are many Christians in these days; they can speak of God before they live for God. The second evidence is our little time spent in the exercise of secret prayer; we thus prove the words of the text, "there is none that calleth upon thy name." Is it not certain, dear beloved of the Lord, that you pray less in secret than you once did? Is it not certain that your secret groanings because of your absence from God, are not so bitter now as they were before? I conceive that if any could hear most of us pray in secret, they would bear witness that we often desire not the thing which we seek. The third evidence of our spiritual decay is our lack of spiritual fervor in the exercise of the duties of religion; thus, we take up these words in the text: "There is none…that stirreth up himself to take hold of thee." Is it not certain that we go about our duty in a most lazy way, and that our affections in prayer are not lively? Is it not true that we do not endeavor to shake off that spirit of slumber that is poured on us? The fourth evidence is that we are under the mighty strength of our idols; neither are we much in prayer that the lawful preys may be taken from the mighty. The fifth evidence is that we do not exercise such divine actions of the grace of love that we were once accustomed to do. The last evidence of our spiritual consumption is the little pains we take to pursue after an absent Christ. Christ retires Himself from us, and we never ask, "Whither dost Thou go?" or, "When wilt Thou return?" This despondency is an evidence that speaks of our decay.

But you also see the sad condition that the people of God were under; we conceive that this time was when they were under the Babylonian captivity. We may observe two things in our text: first, the sad affliction that the people suffered while they were in bondage. There are two branches that set out their condition: first, that the exercise of the grace of prayer was much neglected and slighted, and second, there was none that stirred up himself to take hold upon God. This proves that they did not use divine fervor and seriousness in the exercise of prayer.

The second thing in the words is the aggravation of their sad condition. God had withdrawn Himself from them, and yet there was none that called on Him. This is evident in the words, "For thou hast hid thy face from us"; meaning, "although Thou hast hid Thy face from us, yet we do not call upon Thee." Also, although they were under much outward affliction ("although thou hast consumed us"), yet they did not stir themselves up to call upon God. Although they were under the power of their idols, they called not on Him.

As for the second branch of their condition, there was none that called on God. We conceive it is not to be understood that there was not any amongst the people of Israel that prayed, or sought, God; but rather that those that neglected the duty of prayer were so many, that those that made conscience of it were none in comparison. We shall not insist long on this matter, only consider three points. First, this was a time of great affliction. We may remark three times that God does take a special notice of the carriage of His people under affliction: "Why should ye be stricken any more? ye will revolt more and more" (Isa. 1:5). God does not only take notice of these things that are amiss in His people in their affliction, but likewise of the exercise of their graces in affliction: "In all this Job sinned not, nor charged God foolishly" (Job 1:22). Now the grounds why He takes such special notice of the carriage of His own under their afflictions, may be this: if a Christian carries himself well under the cross, he exceedingly glorifies God. For example, "If ye be reproached for the name of Christ, happy are ye; for the spirit of glory and of God resteth upon you: on their part he is evil spoken of, but on your part he is glorified" (1 Peter 4:14). "Wherefore glorify ye the LORD in the fires, even the name of the LORD God of Israel in the isles of the sea" (Isa. 24:15). The second ground is that a cross and times of affliction are times that are exceeding discovering. Difficult times reveal in a Christian many unmortified corruptions which still remain within, as is shown in Genesis 42 and Job 13:26, "Thou writest bitter things against me, and makest me to possess the iniquities of my youth." We conceive that a Christian under the cross will know the weakness of his faith, the weakness of his love, and his lack of growth in mortification, which he could not well understand in prosperity. The third ground is that the times of affliction will try the sincerity of our graces. There are some that will love Christ when He has thousands following Him; but bring Him to Caiaphas's hall, and many will desert Him. Certainly it is not much to love a prospering Christ; but it is much to love a persecuted Christ. The fourth ground is that the time of affliction is a time when the Christian is in a most swift motion to heaven.

I would only say these three things concerning enjoyments: first, that the enjoyments of God that a Christian encounters under the cross are not so readily abused as those that he encounters under prosperity. Second, the enjoyments that a Christian meets with in ordinances are not so readily abused as those he meets with in prayer; and there is this reason for it: in the enjoyments we meet with in prayer, we seem to be more active in having them, and they seem to be more immediate, and so we cut off the boasting we have of the enjoyments in prayer. Third, there is a greater difficulty for a Christian to be mortified to his public enjoyments than his private enjoyments. Finally, you should remark that God takes special notice of the neglect of prayer in affliction: "All this evil is come upon us: yet made we not our prayer before the LORD our God, that we might turn from our iniquities, and understand thy truth" (Dan. 9:13).

Now the second notion or consideration under which you may take up the words is this: you may take them up as a step of the calamity to come on them. The saddest thing in affliction is to have the spirit of prayer withdrawn. There are six bad attendants that accompany the neglect of prayer.

1. Neglect of prayer shows a Christian that has forgotten what he is. When you neglect prayer, you turn into independent Christians: "We are lords (say they) we will come no more unto thee" (Jer. 2:31).

2. A second bad attendant that accompanies the neglect of prayer is that the neglect of prayer is an evidence that they cast off fear: "Thou castest off fear, and restrainest prayer before God" (Job 15:4). This is a bad attendant, for the grace of fear is the door by which Christians have access to God.

3. A third bad attendant of neglect of prayer is the loss of delight in God. These two are evidences one of another: delight in God, and calling on His name.

4. The neglect of prayer shows a person who is much given up to a spirit of delusion. Prayerless Christians are deluded in three aspects: first, respecting themselves; second, respecting God, in that they do not have a right apprehension of God; and third, respecting the duty of prayer itself.

5. A fifth bad attendant of the neglect of the duty of prayer is that it shows that one is much under the power of his idols.

6. The last bad attendant is that there is not a sin but it may assault the Christian, and there is not a grace of the Spirit but it is under decay. In this state, it is impossible for a Christian to grow and not to pray.

Continuing with the study of the verse, "There is none that stirreth up himself to take hold on God," we may understand these words as the complaint of Christians. Take notice that it is the duty of a Christian not only to regret his condition, but to lament it before the Lord. The second branch which we intended to speak of is their lack of fervency. We conceive that their lack of fervency appeared in these four things, all of which are seen in the words "take hold."

1. It vented itself in their prayer.

2. They lack seriousness in the exercise of faith, as "who have fled for refuge, to lay hold upon the hope set before us" (Heb. 6:18).

3. They lack seriousness in the exercise of entertaining communion and fellowship with God.

4. They had no fervency, venting itself in their not exercising love. Now take notice that the lack of seriousness in the duties of religion is a curse, but possessing it is blessedness. We shall shortly speak a little concerning these things.

It is a Christian's duty to be serious in the action of religion. Christians are commanded to be "continuing instant in prayer" (Rom. 12:12). These words show that a Christian should wrestle in prayer with all his might, and that a Christian should never cease praying until he obtains an answer. It is clear: "Strive to enter in at the strait gate" (Luke 13:24), or contend as in an agony. Second, it is clear that the lack of seriousness obstructs our enjoyment of God. God clearly says, "Then shall ye find me"; but when shall we find Him? "When ye shall search for me with all your heart" (Jer. 29:13). Thirdly, it is evident that prayer is a thing much commended of God. It is commended in Jacob, when as a prince, he wrestled with God; also in Colossians 4:12, we read, "Laboring for you fervently in prayer."

We will also speak about what it is to be serious; being serious comprehends these things:

1. A Christian should be importunate in prayer and other duties; for example, at the close of Matthew 21, as well as in Matthew 15:22 and following, we read the description of the woman that came to Christ.

2. A Christian should take pains to engage his heart in those duties to which he is called. He should endeavor to overcome all difficulties that lie in the way of the performing of his duty.

3. A Christian should be constant in the duties of religion.

Third, we shall point out the impediments of the duty of seriousness, especially in prayer. We are not under a sensible impression of our needs and wants. Would you like to know why? We are so indifferent; we pray not from a principle of pressing necessity. I would press this on the Christian, that if we would desire to pray seriously, we must endeavor to have our necessities on our hearts. I conceive that if we were needier, we would not so much slight it as we do; we are not poor in our own eyes. The second hindrance of seriousness in prayer is that our hearts are too much engaged in the things of this present world. If a Christian desires to strive, he must be temperate in all things. The third impediment is that our own spirits are not under the impression of the greatness and dreadfulness of the majesty of God. In prayer, do you not speak to God as to your companions? You must take notice of two evils. First, there are some that worship an unknown God. Is it not a wonder that God does not destroy you while you are engaged in the very act of prayer? Second, study to keep a divine distance from God in prayer. A fourth impediment that hinders our seriousness is that we do not exercise faith in God's ability and willingness to help us. The greatest enemy to seriousness is discouragement, for it answers his prayer before he prays. There is a fifth impediment, and it is this: we know not the matchless excellence of the thing for which we pray. Finally, we do not watch over our hearts while we are about the duty of prayer. A Christian should watch before prayer, in prayer, and after prayer. Is it not certain a Christian will be serious the first ten words he speaks to God, and yet ere the end he will be dead as a stone? Now what is the reason for this? Certainly it is that you do not watch over your hearts. I would only say that in his prayer a Christian changes his fear into presumption; at the beginning he will be afraid, but, before the end, he will grow presumptuous, because he does not watch over his heart.

Furthermore, many mistake seriousness for something else. There are four things that they put in the place of their seriousness.

First, when he has a swift venting of himself in prayer, he takes that for seriousness. I would only say to you that the enlargement of gifts is more often in public than in private; there may be much gifts and enlargements, though there be no heart in the enlargements. A second thing that passes for seriousness is this: when you obtain some tickling of affection to the duty of prayer, you conclude that to be seriousness. I will give you these three evidences by which you may distinguish the seriousness of a Christian from the seriousness of a hypocrite.

1. The seriousness of a Christian is exceedingly humbling; but the hypocrite, when he inclines to seriousness, especially in public, it is impossible for him to be humble.

2. Suspect that seriousness which is experienced with little difficulty. I know there are some who, when they have made defection from God, then they begin to seek Him again. Their hearts begin to flow within them, and that makes them cry out when they are under the power of their idols, "I will shake myself as at former times!" I say, beware, lest God depart from you.

3. They differ in their source. The source of a Christian's seriousness is God; but a hypocrite's seriousness rises from certain circumstances. For example, when he is under a cross, then he will attempt seriousness, or, the applause and approbation of the world will be the rise of a hypocrite's seriousness. Ultimately, the rise of a hypocrite's seriousness is but from a natural spirit.

Now there is a third thing that is mistaken for seriousness: upon receiving an answer to prayer, the hypocrite may conceive that he was serious in that prayer. However, a hypocrite may have an answer to prayer in temporal things, yet not be serious in his prayer.

Fourthly, a hypocrite may have something in his sorrow that looks like seriousness; he may have sorrow in prayer for things which are not approved of God. Now we shall only say these words, by which you may know if your seriousness is true. Is it not certain that you are more serious in the pursuit after things in the world than after these things which are for your everlasting benefit? Also, is it not certain that the loss of the things of the world has troubled you more than the loss of Christ and His fellowship? Finally, do you not take a greater delight in the things of the world than you ever did in God, or communion with Him? Has the addition of anything to your worldly condition affected you more than communion with God? What does this reveal? It reveals a heart void of love toward God. You may also know that you are not serious in responding to this question: is it not certain that the most part of the pains you take are for the things in this present world? "The people shall labour in the very fire, and the people shall weary themselves for very vanity" (Hab. 2:13). It is certain that you spend your labor for that which is nothing, and which does not profit, yet you slight and undervalue the matchless and noble Plant of renown.

I shall close with these three thoughts. Be persuaded that one moment of the enjoyment of Christ is worth ten thousand eternities of the enjoyments of the choicest things in the world, if it could be possible there were so many eternities. What comfort shall the choicest idol afford you in the day when you shall be standing before the tribunal and judgment seat of Christ? Second, it is impossible to receive satisfaction in anything but in Christ. Some say, "If I had such things in the world, so many thousands, and some lands, then I would rest and be satisfied"; but I tell you that if you had ten times more than that which you desired, your lust would be no more mortified than before. There is nothing besides Jesus Christ that can afford any satisfaction to the soul. All the idols in which you now delight yourselves shall in that day be a torment unto you. Third, I should think it better to have the enjoyment that is suitable to a predominant lust than to want it as long as the lust is not mortified. There is a greater disadvantage in wanting the idol than in having it. Ahithophel, while he lacked the enjoyment of his idol, went and hanged himself. However, I say, a Christian may pray against his lust when he prays not against his idol; a covetous person will pray for the mortification of the lust of covetousness, but will not want to quit the idol.

I shall say no more at this time; but oh, that in this day you might be serious! Oh, know it, and be persuaded of it, that there are many thousands out of heaven today for the lack of seriousness. "Strive to enter in at the strait gate: for many, I say unto you, will seek to enter in, and shall not be able" (Luke 13:24). Therefore, there must be wrestling and striving before you can obtain that prize. Certainly there are thousands of damned souls in hell today because they have not striven to enter into heaven. Know it of a certainty, those whose seed-time is in sin, their harvest shall be in hell. Oh, be afraid, and stand in awe to sin, lest that unawares He come upon you and tear your "soul like a lion, rending it in pieces, while there is none to deliver" (Ps. 7:2). "It is a fearful thing to fall into the hands of the living God" (Heb. 10:31); therefore know it is for your everlasting concern to be serious. Amen.

SERMON 4

Christ's Mournful Visit to Obstinate Sinners

And when he was come near, he beheld the city, and wept over it, saying, If thou hadst known, even thou, at least in this thy day, the things which belong unto thy peace! But now they are hid from thine eyes.

—Luke 19:41-42

There are two great and wonderful mysteries which may occasion much divine admiration and holy astonishment to angels and men. First, there is that unsearchable mystery of the condescending grace of Christ, that He should expose Himself to so much toil and labor, even to the pouring out of His soul, that He may purchase our love, which is but a small thing when it is purchased, and that He should entertain peace between sinners and Himself. Secondly, there is a mystery which is no less mysterious, and it is man's impertinent refusal of these precious offers that grace does propose to us; we cast them behind our backs and embrace the offers of idols. This sin is aggravated when, even after frequent convictions of the vanity of our idols, we embrace them and find solace for ourselves in them. It is a difficult question to determine whether the first or second of these is most mysterious, but they both make up a matchless mystery. The first is His doing, and the second is our doing, which ought to be detestable to us. Heaven and earth may wonder at such folly—that we refuse that delicious feast of the gospel, which is full of marrow and fatness. Ought we to reject His wise counsels? Yet we have rejected the counsels of Jesus Christ, of Him who is wiser than any among the sons of men. How we have rejected Jesus Christ, set His counsels at naught, and cast Him behind our back! Oh, what a dreadful indignity is that which we put upon Him! Dear

Christians, while yet it is today, harden not your hearts, but embrace this offer of Jesus Christ, which is freely extended to you. Now all of you suppose that if Jesus Christ Himself would come and preach this doctrine unto you, "Come unto me, and have life," would there be any so impudent as would not receive His offer? Yet I suppose if He would preach that doctrine to us, thorns and briers would arise after His preaching. He preached this to the people in the days of Isaiah, and yet what is His report of them? "I have laboured in vain, I have spent my strength for nought" (Isa. 49:4). In John's time, see what report He gives: "He came unto his own, and his own received him not" (John 1:11). He could not persuade them because of their impenitence and hardness of heart. No doubt you will condemn this refusal for impenitence, the offer being given by so excellent a messenger, Jesus Christ, the eternal Son of God, whose feet bring "glad tidings of great joy."

Oh, I fear that Christ has often times labored in vain amongst us, who have had the offers of this blessed gospel presented to us, and we would not hear it; then eternal woe shall be unto us! Oh, you who slight the precious offers of Jesus Christ in this blessed gospel, and who still continue to disregard it, are you not afraid that Christ shall depart from you, and shall also remove His blessed ordinances from you? Do you not fear that you shall be made to seek Him, but shall not find Him, nor yet know where to seek Him? Oh slighters, and cursed undervaluers of Jesus Christ, stand in awe to slight Him any more, lest He consume you from heaven! Oh, people who slight Jesus Christ, what shall be the latter end of this? I am persuaded that it shall be bitterness to you at last. What would you answer God if He were pleased to call you in this very hour? What would you answer Him for all your dreadful abominations? Would you be able to answer the sad challenges of your conscience that you will experience in that day? It is a sad thing to live and die slighters of these blessed offers. If you will not embrace them now, know that it is not long when God shall cease to reprove you, "and these things which now belong to your peace shall then be hid from your eyes." Oh, then embrace precious Christ, and delay not any longer.

Now let us consider the words of our text. Although Christ is precious, yet here is a people refusing Him; but as He departs from them, He weeps. He began to weep, desiring an invitation to stay. Oh, did ever angels or men behold such a spectacle, that Christ should weep for the destruction of sinners, and especially that He should weep for the destruction of those sinners who would have destroyed Him! Have you ever seen such a wonder? We are sure that Christ did not walk after the rule of men in so doing, but after the rule of His infinite love. Oh, what wonderful love, that He should have wept for the destruction of those who would deliver Him up to be crucified! Here He gives us a blessed confirmation of the everlasting covenant of redemption; He delights not in the death of sinners, but rather that they would live, repent, and turn to Him: "If thou hadst known, even thou, at least in this thy day, the things which belong unto thy peace! but now they are hid from thine eyes." Certainly they might have sung here that blessed song that He dealt not with them as they deserved, or according to their iniquities. I am persuaded that Christ weeps more for the ruin of men than they do for themselves. If Christ had done with us according to our iniquities, or according to our merits, surely we would have long ago found ourselves in the pit, without any redemption.

Now we have here the infinite compassion of Christ, that "when he drew near the city," beholding such a multitude of persons hastening to destruction, He wept for them. Oh, what a sight it must have been to see Christ weeping for sinners—sinners who were not weeping for themselves! He expresses His grief in verse 42, wishing that they had known the things that belonged to their peace.

In this verse, there are three things to notice:

1. That they would know their infinite obligation to the glory of God; in short, that they would be convinced of their misery and things which belong to their peace.

2. That they would be convinced of their utter inability to satisfy the justice of God of their own selves.

3. That they would have recourse to Him, the blessed Lamb of God who saves the elect world from all their iniquities.

Now these three points, of which we must be convinced, are our own misery, our own inability to save ourselves and satisfy the justice of God, and the remedy for how to satisfy the justice of God. These are the whole substance of the law and of the gospel; for the law is of the first and second, and the third is comprehended in the gospel. I confess that we shall never be able to tell our obligation to God. Oh, if our understandings were enlightened, and we might see how much we are bound and obliged to God for this very ordinance of His! Might He not have given it to another people, who would have made better use of it, and profited more by it than we have done? Might He not have allowed you to have continued on your own way, even to your own destruction? Is this not a great and matchless wonder, seeing that Christ has given us His ordinances and invited us to receive His offers that are freely offered to us in the gospel? If you will not receive the gospel, or embrace this offer of Jesus Christ, the day is coming when you will know that it was a work of soul-concern to have embraced the offers of salvation that were offered to you in the gospel. The day will arrive when you will curse the day of your birth. Therefore, study to make the law of God your meditation, and the rule of your walk. No doubt it would certainly be to our advantage to be conversing between Moses and Christ, between the law and the gospel, and to have our walk and conversation mixed with the gospel. Oh, but Christ rejoices and greatly desires that we would come unto Him; therefore, dear Christians, come and embrace this offer of your eternal salvation. We confess, if the joys of heaven were founded, as it says in Luke 15:7, on the repentance of sinners, we are constrained to say that there would not be much joy in heaven these days. When was a song sung in heaven for the conversion of a sinner in this city? I fear there be many days of thanksgiving kept by the devil and his angels, for the success of his kingdom in this city. Let us discuss the following considerations, which render Christ's compassion most mysterious.

First, let us consider the person who did thus weep and lament; it was Jesus Christ, the eternal Son of God. Is not that a mystery? How may we be astonished, that the second person of the blessed Trinity should weep and lament for the destruction of sinners! If an angel or a saint in heaven had done this, it would not have been nearly as wonderful; but that He who is equal with the Father, He who is infinitely exalted above the creatures' goodness or evil, should weep for our ruin and destruction—certainly this is a wonder that shall never be appreciated enough! Christ rejoices as much at our conversion, as if there were some profit redounding to Him by it; but He also weeps as much for our ruin and destruction as if He had a disadvantage or prejudice by it. He is so infinite a Being, and all-sufficient of Himself, that even with all the honor and glory we can give unto Him, nothing can be added unto His glory. Furthermore, despite the dishonor He receives from us, there can be nothing diminished from His glory. Oh, what a wonder and matchless mystery! Even He who is so infinite and self-sufficient should have stooped so far beneath Himself as to take on Himself our nature, and undergo our punishment which was justly due to us for sin! The thought of this may be wonderful to us! We may wonder when we look over the pains that He has taken upon Himself for our cause; we may wonder what it was that moved Him to it. Certainly, it was nothing in us; it was His own free love that put Him to it.

A second consideration of the mystery of Christ's compassion arises when we consider the time that He wept for them. It was after He had been greatly honored, and garments were spread on the ground before Him; His disciples had just sung the song, "Blessed is he that cometh in the name of the Lord" (Matt. 21:9). Is it not a great mystery that then Christ should have wept for the destruction of sinners, at a time when people were applauding and honoring Him? Certainly His compassion under that consideration is most mysterious and wonderful. Oh, Christians, consider your own vileness and wretchedness; Jesus Christ, who is altogether holy, and wholly free of all the pollutions of the world, wept at our destruction!

A third consideration that renders Christ's compassion most mysterious is that the time of His compassion was fifteen days before He was to encounter devils, principalities, and powers. Now then you may conceive that the thoughts of His approaching death might have so taken Him up, that He might have forgotten the pitying of any other person. He might rather have pitied Himself than us, so to speak; but this is a mystery, and matchless wonder of the love of Christ! He not only pitied such unworthy creatures, but He wept over their destruction, especially over the destruction of those who would soon cry out, "Crucify him, crucify him" (Luke 23:21). Oh, admire this infinite, patient, and boundless love of Christ towards the most wretched and miserable of mankind! What a wonder may it be to men and angels, that our redemption and eternal salvation was brought about in such a way, that by His stripes we should be healed, and that He should have borne the iniquity of us all upon His blessed back! Dear Christians, let this urge you to fix all your love and delight upon Him. Let not your idols of the world any longer be your delight; but let God have the preeminence in your mind and heart.

We shall continue by discussing the reason for Christ's lamentation and weeping. This weeping arises because of the contempt of the gospel, and the disregarding of the glorious messenger of peace. This reason is clearly shown in these words: "but now they are hid from thine eyes." We confess that all sins, compared to this sin of unbelief, seem to be little sins. It is a wonder to us that there should be so much access to preach upon the subject of the contempt of the gospel, and of that glorious messenger Jesus Christ, who publishes peace, and whose feet bring glad tidings of great joy. Now we shall sum up the condemners of the gospel in these two sorts:

1. There are some that condemn the gospel with civility. We see such in Luke 14:18-20; all of them say, "I have bought a piece of ground, and I must needs go and see it: I pray thee have me excused. And another said, I have bought five yoke of oxen, and I go to prove them: I pray thee have me excused. And another said, I have married a wife, and therefore I cannot come." What necessity exists that could hinder us from receiving Jesus Christ? There are many of us who pretend an impossibility; we have married our idols, and after them we will go, so we cannot come.

2. There are some that refuse Him more absolutely and absurdly, which is shown in Matthew 22:6: "And the remnant took his servants, and entreated them spitefully, and slew them." They may have had reason if Christ and his messengers had come to denounce wrath against them; but coming to pronounce peace and salvation to them—oh, it is a most irrational thing.

Now we shall, in the third place, speak concerning the impediments of their not embracing the gospel. The first impediment is the lack of the faith of the truth of the gospel. The gospel is a real thing, and not a fancy, says the apostle in 2 Peter 1:16: "For we have not followed cunningly devised fables." A second impediment obstructing our embracing the gospel is the lack of solid faith of these unspeakable dignities that come to any by embracing the offers of the gospel.

We are not only advanced to great communion and fellowship with God, which indeed is a thing of most excellent nature; but we are made the adopted children of God. What can be desired more than that? A third obstacle is the fact that we have no solid conviction of our misery and desperate estate, wherein we are by nature. We are sure that, were we studying the law more, the gospel should get better employment by us. A fourth impediment is that we are not convinced of our inability to satisfy the justice of God; yet people are "going about to establish their own righteousness" (Rom. 10:3), being ignorant of the justice of God. A fifth obstacle is that there are some who, out of the strong convictions of their own unworthiness, have found themselves transgressors from the womb, who think it presumption to receive these offers; and that hinders them. To such persons, I would propose these thoughts:

1. You must understand how serious the sin of unbelief is. We conceive that the lack of strong convictions of the sin of unbelief makes us fruitless.

2. We would have you know that unbelief hinders our liberty in conversing with God.

3. When we set about the exercise of faith with unbelief, we encounter many trials. We would say to them that encounter such trials that if they obtain victory over these trials, they will find great joy and deep root in the Holy Ghost.

4. You must consider the excellent things that unbelief causes us to quit; it causes us primarily to abandon our interest in and love to God. Furthermore, you should consider the free and complete proposal of the gospel: "And whosoever will, let him take the water of life freely" (Rev. 22:17).

Let us end our discourse with this thought. We conceive that if Christ would come down, He would no doubt preach to you on this text; He would desire you to know the things that belong to your peace. Surely if Christ were coming here today, as He drew near and beheld the Jews, He might weep over Glasgow. Certainly, the despisers of this gospel shall be in that row that shall be summoned to depart from Him; and no doubt both their condemnation and their pain shall be aggravated by the knowledge that there was a way of salvation for them, but "they would not." Oh, people, know "in this thy day, the things which belong unto thy peace"; in this your day, the time is not long until these things shall be hidden from your eyes. Oh, when will you beware and know your own misery? When shall that day come? Dear Christians, you are like those that sleep on a top-mast, and are not aware of the danger that awaits them! "Be not deceived; God is not mocked: for whatsoever a man soweth, that shall he also reap" (Gal. 6:7). Oh beware, and stand in awe before sin, lest God with His justice pursue you, and also shall overtake you. Be persuaded, if you have sown iniquity, you shall also reap the whirlwind; but if you have sown your seed with tears, be comforted knowing that you have a joyful harvest day approaching, when you shall go forth to gather your vintage, and shall return with great joy and gladness, and your sheaves on your shoulders. What a joyful harvest day shall that be for those who have waited on their Redeemer! We confess that it shall be a day of joyfulness and great mirth.

We shall say no more to you at this time; but let your soul wait with expectation until that day shall spring. Let that blessed and most excellent harvest day come, and let all other harvest days pass away. Amen.

SERMON 5

The Mansions of Glory Prepared for Believers

In my Father's house are many mansions: if it were not so, I would have told you. I go to prepare a place for you.
—John 14:2

It is a great difficulty for Christians to have their spirits submissive unto every dispensation that God does carve out unto them; it is much easier for a Christian to give unto God a negative vote in carving out his lot and condition than to be content sweetly to be regulated and guided by Him, whose name is "Wonderful Counselor." Such is the pride and arrogance of our spirits; we love to be co-ordinate with God, and not subordinate to Him, in the carving of any dispensation, lot, and condition to us.

Studying the text a little closer, we find that Christ had in the former chapter spoken to the disciples of His removal and departure from them, saying that He was now to go to the Father, from whence He came, and was to sit down as a strong victor after He had "spoiled principalities and powers" (Col. 2:15), and "spiritual wickedness in high places" (Eph. 6:12). This blessed Sun of righteousness, after He had run His race, as a strong man, entered into the holiest of all, and was there advanced to sit down upon the throne on the right hand of the majesty of God, and shall remain there until He shall appear again and take His own into heaven with Him.

Now, lest His disciples should be too discouraged and affected by the withdrawal of Christ's presence, He proposes some arguments and grounds to remove and take away their discouragements and anxieties. His first argument is in verse 1, where He presses them to faith in Himself, saying, "Ye believe in God, believe also in me" (John 14:1). Faith is that grace which can give to a Christian a resemblance and representation of Christ in the saddest and most afflicting dispensation. Faith is one of the most excellent graces that a Christian can possess. Faith can read love in Christ's heart, when sense cannot read love in His face. Faith, when it is absent and distant from God, can draw by the veil, and get a sight of the beauty and excellence that is in the face of Jesus Christ.

The second argument says that Christ proposes to remove their discouragement and anxiety, in the latter part of verse 2: "I go to prepare a place for you." It is as if Christ had said, "My removal and departure from you is so much for advantage and gain, that you need not be a whit affected and discouraged with it; for if I go My way from you, I go to prepare a place for you in heaven with Myself, that where I am, there you may be also. Then let this comfort your hearts under My absence, I will, ere it be long, come again, and take you to Myself; I am now to go away from you, as a forerunner, to prepare a place for you." He was going as a general quartermaster, as it were, to take up quarters and possessions for them in heaven. So that this argument might take root in the disciples' hearts, He describes heaven unto them in the first part of verse 2. He calls it His Father's house: "In my Father's house are many mansions." He was calling God His Father, as He was mediator; likewise, such divine fellowship and correspondence that should be entertained between the Father and the Son, and the Father and believers through the Son. Furthermore, He holds out to the disciples their interest in this communion and correspondence. He likewise points out the permanence of this, saying that there are many mansions in His Father's house. There are many mansions; therefore, they need not fear, for they would get a place of eternal abode with Christ and the Father. Thus Christ delivers a pressing argument and ground why the disciples should neither be affected by nor discouraged with His departure from them, but shows them that they should have interest in His departure. He then points forth the reality of His statement, that there were many mansions in His Father's house, when He says, "If it were not so, I would have told you." If there were not such an excellent thing as heaven, and such excellent mansions in heaven, "I would have told you of it." If it were not so, I would not feed you with golden dreams and fancies. I who am the faithful witness, in whom all the promises of the everlasting covenant are yea and amen, can speak nothing but that which is real truth; and no doubt that might persuade the disciples not to be anxious or discouraged with Christ's leaving and departing from them.

Likewise, you may behold the method and divine order that Christ keeps in proposing His arguments and grounds. The first argument is that they should believe in Him; the next is that He went to prepare a place for them. It shows us that to reap any joy and satisfaction in the consideration of heaven is first to believe; faith is the most noble and excellent grace which most discovers to us the sweetness of heaven; so that, before we believe, it is impossible for us to take up the excellence of that inheritance and glorious possession. It is impossible for us to receive much joy and consolation in the consideration of heaven without the exercise of the grace of faith. Let this commend the worth of the grace of faith unto you: it is the grace by which you may receive joy in the darkest night of your affliction. Be encouraged to mind the excellence of heaven, whereof every subject is a king. What shall it be to sit down at the mouth of that river, and drink of the comfortable and inexhaustible pleasures and wells of consolation! We are here admitted only to taste of the springs that flow from that higher house; but there, we shall be admitted to sit down at the mouth of that ocean and river of everlasting pleasures! Oh, Christians, what do you suppose it shall be, when we shall be set down together in heaven with all the redeemed of the Lord, and shall delight ourselves in Him forever and ever throughout all eternity! Oh, what an exercise do you suppose that shall be, to embrace Him who smells of the rose of Sharon and of the lily of the valleys! What an exercise that shall be, to embrace Him, who is that excellent One, the Ancient of days, the Root and Offspring of David, the Lion of the tribe of Judah! I confess it is a mystery for us to believe that such a day is approaching, when these tongues of ours shall be made as the pen of a ready writer, fit to express the praises of the Lord; and when we shall be made to enjoy Him no more through the dark veil of faith, but we shall enjoy Him by sight; and so we shall have the immediate sight of Jesus Christ.

Dear Christians, long for the excellence of that glorious place. I think that which makes Christians rejoice so little in the expectation of the excellence of that inheritance and possession is this: we walk under a woeful uncertainty of our interest in that blessed estate. Certainly if our interest were in these precious things, undoubtedly our affections would be bent and set more upon them than they are. If only we were persuaded of the precious excellencies of that estate that the saints above are now enjoying! They are freed from all their labor and toil, and their reward follows them. We must long for that blessed estate! They are eternally happy that shall have their portion, where all joy and delight is to be found, and where all manner of pleasures are; for at His right hand are pleasures evermore. There is no darkness there; there is no need of the sun to give light by day, nor the moon to give light by night, for the Lamb is the light thereof. It must be a heartsome and glorious place, where Jesus Christ is the light thereof! There is no sorrow there, but joy perpetual, and consolation for evermore: all sorrow shall flee away from them, and all tears shall be gone.

Dear Christian, long for the day when you shall be once advanced to that blessed estate. Long for the day when you shall be advanced to communion and fellowship with Jesus Christ, who is that excellent one, the desire of nations, who is fairer than any among the sons of men. Long for the day when you shall delight yourselves in Him, who is most beautiful and desirable, who is altogether lovely; He is white and ruddy, the chief among ten thousand. Certainly it shall be thought an excellent thing to have delighted ourselves in Him, and to have had all our desires and affections set upon Him, in the day when He shall appear to repay His vengeance on the earth. In that day, He shall sit down on His white throne to judge the whole tribes of the earth, and the hypocrites in Zion shall tremble and be afraid. Oh, then, consider in time these things which belong to your peace, lest before long they be hid from your eyes.

But, as for the argument that He uses and proposes to divert them from the discouragement and anxiety that they might have had through His departure and removal from them, we shall not discuss in what respect Christ has gone to prepare a place for them, but we know that He has not gone there as a single person for Himself only, but He has gone there for us and the whole body of believers: "Whither the forerunner is for us entered, even Jesus, made an high priest for ever" (Heb. 6:20). It is certain that Christ has entered into heaven as an intercessor for us, to plead at the bar of the divine justice of God: "For Christ is not entered into the holy places made with hands, which are the figures of the true; but into heaven itself, now to appear in the presence of God for us" (Heb. 9:24). That is the continual exercise that Jesus Christ has before the throne of God; He is interceding for us at the right hand of the Father in heaven, and therefore Christ may be said to have gone before us in this respect—He is preparing us and making us fit to come there. He is making us fit for heaven, and He is making also heaven fit for us. Is that not an excellent exercise, that Christ should be fitting us for the time we come there unto Himself? "Who hath delivered us from the power of darkness, and hath translated us into the kingdom of his dear Son: in whom we have redemption through his blood, even the forgiveness of sins" (Col. 1:13, 14). Then we must be made fit certainly before we depart while we are here below, otherwise we cannot at all be made fit when we go hence. Then how is it said that Christ goes to prepare a place for believers, since it is said that these places were created before, when they shall inherit the kingdom prepared for them before the foundation of the world (Matt. 25:34)? But we believe that Christ has made manifest and clear the way to heaven; for the way to heaven was darker before He went up to heaven than it is now; likewise, Christ's going to heaven was the fitting of His disciples for heaven, and also fitting heaven for them; might not that be a very great comfort to them?

Let us pay particular attention to the words of the text. We see that there are precious advantages that a Christian may reap by the consideration of Christ's going to heaven. First, we know that Christ has wholly triumphed over all spiritual enemies before He ascended into heaven. This is clear from Ephesians 4:8, "Wherefore he saith, When he ascended up on high, he led captivity captive, and gave gifts unto men." The second advantage that one may have by the consideration that Christ has ascended into heaven is that one may go unto God with boldness in the day of his need. This is clear from Hebrews 4:16, where we read, "Let us therefore come boldly unto the throne of grace, that we may obtain mercy, and find grace to help in time of need." Christians, is it not much for our advantage then that we have One in heaven to intercede for us, who is a great courtier, and can plead our cause at the bar of the justice of God? Believe it, it is unspeakably for our advantage, that ever Christ did condescend so far as to take upon Him our nature, plead our cause, and intercede for us before God. The third advantage of this consideration is that you may be persuaded that Christ is gone to prepare a place for you—that is the reason why He went to heaven. What a wonder that Jesus Christ, who is blessed forever and exalted far above all creatures, should have taken such a low employment as to have been the harbinger of such poor things; but love has determined these things. Then certainly it is our part only to admire, and not curiously inquire into, the causes of these things. It is a matchless mystery that Christ should have been so condescending toward us, but we can say nothing. The only cause of it was His infinite and free love.

A fourth advantage that one may have by this consideration is that when He appears, they shall be taken up with Him in the clouds; for mystical Christ shall be incomplete until all the members be complete in Him. Then, dear Christians, long for that day when Christ shall be complete with all His members. The fifth advantage one may have is this: it is a sweet evidence and token, yea, and a divine confirmation, that we at last shall obtain victory over all our spiritual enemies, for the scripture says, "Thou hast put all things in subjection under his feet. For in that he put all in subjection under him, he left nothing that is not put under him. But now we see not yet all things put under him" (Heb. 2:8). This was the fact that comforted Paul in this place. Then there is this sixth advantage that a Christian may have by considering that Christ has ascended into heaven: Christ, by His going to heaven, does now stand as a high priest to make intercession for us. "For Christ is not entered into the holy places made with hands, which are the figures of the true; but into heaven itself, now to appear in the presence of God for us" (Heb. 9:24). There is a strange word in Hebrews 8:4, "For if he were on earth, he should not be a priest"; we understand this to mean that if He had remained on the earth, He could not have been a priest. Thus, His going to heaven capacitates Him to be a priest for us.

Now we come to that which is the foundation of this argument: it would hold out that divine thoughts of heaven are an holy diversion from our thoughts on earth. Likewise, a Christian that is much in consideration of heaven may sweetly solace himself knowing that his trouble shall eventually cease and have an end. Furthermore, thoughts and considerations of heaven are suitable to remove the anxious thoughts of the vexing world, or those we have by want of anything here below, that he shall soon be made up, even by that glorious place, heaven. If a Christian is groaning under outward trouble and vexation of spirit; if groaning under a body of sin and death, he may comfort himself in the fact that heaven is called a rest from our labors and redemption from all our troubles and anxieties. Then, Christians, let this comfort you under your saddest afflictions—before long all your afflictions shall come to a close, and all your wants shall be made up, when you will enter in that holy city, whose streets are paved as with transparent gold. Long for that day; if you be under reproach and calumny here, you may comfort yourselves, that before long you shall receive the excellent approbation of Jesus Christ, the second person of the blessed Trinity, the Judge of all the tribes and families of the earth, when we shall be ever with the Lord. A Christian may likewise receive much joy and satisfaction from the consideration of the excellence and blessedness of heaven, when he remembers the greatness of his toil and labor, and when he thinks that once he shall be freed of all that ere long. Now then, let even the thoughts of the approaching of that day help you to bear your afflictions with patience. There is a precious and immense hope set before you that may remove all the bitterness of afflictions. The consideration of heaven may remove, I say, all the bitterness and anxiety in this time; it will cast a divine smell on all the crosses that we encounter in this life. A soul that is filled with the joy of heaven cannot be much anxious for the lack of anything here upon earth.

Finally, we shall only speak a little to the permanence of that estate, and the reality of it, seen in the word *mansions*, opposite to this transient and shortly passing dwelling that is here below, which shall, before long, decay and perish. Those above shall not need to loose the pins of their tabernacle, for it shall be a sure and firm dwelling, never to be removed through all the ages of eternity. It shall be a steadfast habitation; those who have been walking up and down the earth in sheep and goat skins shall then have a sure habitation, a sure dwelling place, and a durable state of life. Know that the day is at hand when the people of God shall lose all hope of change, when they shall be made pillars fixed in the temple of our God, to go no more out at all.

But, Christians, believe it, there is not such a facility in believing this truth, of the shortness of our time and of our change, as we do suppose; therefore, be persuaded, Christians, of the reality of this truth. There is a heaven and a hell, and an eternity of pain and an eternity of joy; for if these truths were certainly believed, surely they would have more effect upon us. Be persuaded of the matchless excellence that is in that state and blessed condition which is above. Believe it—it is no fancy. Certainly they have a blessed life that are now above, far from all the troubles and crosses of this wicked world; and they, no doubt, could best speak and declare what a life that is, who know it by experience. We only know it by report; but no doubt it is an excellent and blessed life, and shall be once known to be so. But it is suitable and convenient for us to wait until He instructs us in the reality of the blessedness of that estate and condition, when faith and hope shall vanish and flee away, and sense shall sit down and solace itself most sweetly in the victories of faith. Oh, that day, when these graces shall make a sweet and blessed change! When faith shall pass into fruition, and hope into possession! We can say nothing of it; but no doubt it shall be a glorious and most excellent day, when love and delight on both sides shall increase more and more. We shall say no more; but oh, that you might be persuaded to long for that blessed day, when all your shadows shall be gone, and you shall see Him face to face as He is. Now let that blessed day come and let all other days pass away. Amen.

SERMON 6

Christ's Royal Priesthood, Sufficient Encouragement for Faith

Seeing then that we have a great high priest, that is passed into the heavens, Jesus the Son of God, let us hold fast our profession.

—Hebrews 4:14

Our blessed High Priest has the names of believers engraven on three parts of His precious person. He has them engraven in His heart, which points out His infinite love and boundless condescension. This corresponds to that which was typified of Him by the high priests under the law, who had the names of the twelve tribes of Israel engraven on their breast-plates of onyx-stones. Christ also has the believers' names engraven on His shoulders, which displays His strengthening and supporting them in all their temptations and assaults of the devil that they encounter. This corresponds to that which was typified of Him by the high priest under the law, of having the names of the twelve tribes engraven on their shoulders, to be a memorial before the Lord. Christ has the names of believers engraven on the palms of His hands; this points out His everlasting remembrance of them. No doubt this respect ought to engage our hearts; when Christ cannot catch by force, He will catch us by deceit. Christ's love has not only an omnipotence, but also a divine deceit and guile: "Therefore, behold, I will allure her, and bring her into the wilderness" (Hos. 2:14); or, as the word may be rendered, "I will deceive her in the wilderness."

There are three parts of Christ's office: His kingly, priestly, and prophetical office. His kingly office points out His absolute dominion and infinite sovereignty. His prophetical office points out His infinite wisdom in teaching sinners, and His priestly office points out His boundless compassion and goodwill towards us. There is a great difference between our high priest and the high priests under the law, between the high priest under the New Testament and the Old Testament; for our high priest was both the sacrifice and the sacrificer. You know that Christ got and bought all the lives of the believers, on His promise and bond before God dealt so with them, that He should suffer for them. Justice suffered Him a little, but at last He perfected His work. Is there any difference between them that were born under the law and them that are born under the gospel? For you know that under the law, there are sacrifices in Adam's time, in Noah's and Abraham's times; and for four thousand years there were sacrifices. The fire upon the altar drank up the blood of lambs and goats; yet divine justice was never satisfied until that spotless Lamb sacrificed Himself. Justice delayed Christ four thousand years, but at length He came and perfected the work of our redemption.

There is a great difference between man's first and second creation. We confess there was much love and wisdom manifested in man's first creation, but that was all accomplished by a word of command. In the second creation, there was not only infinite love, wisdom, and power, but much suffering and acting in this creation. But blessed be His name, for He has now perfected our redemption, and is now requiring that all these for whom He has laid down His life and paid that ransom, may be in heaven with Him.

However, we intend primarily to speak concerning Christ's priestly office. We do not intend to prosecute these words any further; however, they give us ground to speak concerning this part of Christ's office, which is the foundation of religion. First, we will discuss what Christ's priestly office comprehends, and how He executes it. Secondly, we shall speak about the properties of our great high priest, Jesus Christ. Thirdly, we will discuss what advantage the Christian receives from Christ's priestly office. Finally, we shall speak a little of the properties and qualifications of Christ's priesthood.

In the first place, Christ's priestly office comprehends two things. The first is that Christ offers Himself as a spotless sacrifice for our sins. We see this in Hebrews 5:7, which says, "Who in the days of his flesh, when he had offered up prayers and supplications with strong crying and tears unto him that was able to save him from death, and was heard in that he feared." Second, His offering up Himself for us imports that He has taken upon Him the high priest, blameless and harmless, and is made higher than the heavens: "Who is made, not after the law of a carnal commandment, but after the power of an endless life" (Heb. 7:16). From this, Christ is called the Prince of peace in purchasing that precious peace between God and sinners; for in the day that there was a woeful diversion made between God and sinners, Christ then began His peace and reconciliation between God and us. Now that which we shall discuss concerning this may make this act of Christ most mysterious to you. Furthermore, there are more mysteries in this one act; though we had eternity to make a commentary on it, we could not well explain it.

Let us first consider that divine harmony and sweet consent that was among all the persons of the blessed Trinity, that Christ should accomplish this work of dying for sinners; there was not one negative aspect to this. Was not the Father, the first person of the blessed Trinity, most willing for this? Hence it is called the Father's will: "I delight to do thy will, O my God" (Ps. 40:8); and in Hebrews 10:7, "Then said I, Lo, I come (in the volume of the book it is written of me,) to do thy will, O God." There are these three things that may evidence the Father's consent to this blessed work: first, that God the Father manifested much love to His Son, because of His doing this work, as we see in John 10:17: "Therefore doth my Father love me, because I lay down my life, that I might take it again." It is as if Christ had said, "The Father loved Me; and the reason why He loved Me, is, because I lay down My life for My sheep." The second thing that speaks the Father's consent to the work are the great promises given to Christ in the covenant of redemption, if He would lay down His life an offering for sin, such as, "He shall see his seed, he shall prolong his days, and the pleasure of the LORD shall prosper in his hand" (Isa. 53:10). The last thing that points out the Father's consent to this work is the great reward that He gave to the Son after the accomplishment of this great work. In Philippians 2:9-10 we read, "Wherefore God also hath highly exalted him, and given him a name which is above every name: that at the name of Jesus every knee should bow, of things in heaven, and things in earth." Likewise, this is clear from Hebrews 2:9, "But we see Jesus, who was made a little lower than the angels, for suffering of death, crowned with glory and honor."

Was not the Son, the second person of the Trinity, most willing to accomplish this work? We hope none will dispute His willingness; for oftentimes He says, speaking about this work, "I delight to do thy will." In Luke 12:50, we read, "But I have a baptism to be baptized with; and how am I straitened till it be accomplished?" As it were, He could not tell the pain He was in until He was in pain; He longed to be lifted up between heaven and earth, and to have it said, "It is finished." Also, was not the third person of the blessed Trinity most willing and content? Yes, He does evidence His willingness, not only in that He furnished Christ with all gifts for this work: "Behold my servant, whom I uphold; mine elect, in whom my soul delighteth; I have put my spirit upon him" (Isa. 42:1); but likewise He manifested His will in this, that when Christ was under His sorest exercises, He was comforted by the consolation of the Spirit of God.

Let us also consider the mysteriousness of the act of Christ offering up Himself by considering the loftiness of this person and the depth of His sufferings. Put these two together, and you will fall into a sea of wondering. Beloved, was not this a mighty condescension, that He who was clothed with light as with a robe and with the garments of immortal glory, should have clothed Himself with that clothing of the nature of man? Is it not a wonder that He who was dwelling in light inaccessible, should now dwell in the tents of mortality? Is it not a mystery that He should descend into hell that we might ascend into heaven? He lay three days in the grave, that we might live with Him in heaven through all the ages of eternity! Is not that a mystery that the Ancient of days, the Father of eternity, should become a child, and know an end of life and a beginning of days? Oh, Christians, bathe yourselves in the sweet thoughts of God incarnate; and if any of you come to plumb this deep, you shall be like the shipmen (Acts 27:28); the farther you go into this deep, the more wonders you shall see there.

In our last consideration of that which makes this act of Christ more mysterious, we ask this: what was the end of Christ's coming into the world and offering Himself up for us a sacrifice? It is set down in Romans 8:3, "God sending his own Son in the likeness of sinful flesh, and for sin, condemned sin in the flesh." Christ might have come to condemn sinners; but here is infinite love! He came to condemn that which condemned us. Shall neither the conquering grace of Christ, the restraining grace of Christ, nor the pardoning grace of Christ, provoke you to love Him?

Second, we must point out the advantage that flows to a Christian from Christ's priestly office, which is His dying for us. There is a further advantage: Christ's death is the evidence of our justification, the cause of our sanctification, the pledge of our glorification, the hope of our eternal and complete victory, and the door of hope that shall make you sing, "O death, where is thy sting? O grave, where is thy victory?" (1 Cor. 15:55). We are brought to paradise by four streams: His justification, whereby He justifies us; His sanctification, whereby we that lay among the pots are made white as a dove; His wisdom, whereby we are conducted to heaven; His redemption, by His complete victory (1 Cor. 1:30). For the first, is it not clear that Christ's death was an evidence of our justification? "Neither by the blood of goats and calves, but by his own blood he entered in once into the holy place, having obtained eternal redemption for us" (Heb. 9:12). Also, we read in verse 26, "But now once in the end of the world, hath he appeared, to put away sin by the sacrifice of himself." We may answer all objections by the solid faith of Christ's death. If you could multiply objections throughout eternity, you could have no answer but this: Christ died, and is risen again. His resurrection is a great pillar of justifying faith: "Being justified by faith, we have peace with God through our Lord Jesus Christ" (Rom. 5:1). All objections are answered in the fact that Christ has died and risen again: "Who is he that condemneth? It is Christ that died, yea rather, that is risen again, who is even at the right hand of God, who also maketh intercession for us" (Rom. 8:34). "When we were enemies, we were reconciled to God by the death of his Son" (Rom. 5:10). Faith's great pillar, whereon it is founded, is Christ's resurrection. Is not Christ's death the cause of our glorification? "How much more shall the blood of Christ, who, through the eternal Spirit, offered himself without spot unto God, purge your consciences from dead works to serve the living God?" (Heb. 9:14). Speaking of the cross of Christ, Paul says, "The world is crucified unto me, and I unto the world" (Gal. 6:14). "Forasmuch as ye know that ye were not redeemed with corruptible things, as silver and gold, from your vain conversation received by tradition from your fathers; but with the precious blood of Christ" (1 Peter 1:18-19). For, "If one died for all, then were all dead: and that he died for all, that they which live should not henceforth live unto themselves, but unto him which died for them, and rose again" (2 Cor. 5:14-15). Likewise, is not Christ's death the pledge of your glorification? Did not Christ wear a crown of thorns, so that you might wear a crown of immortal glory? Did He not wear a purple robe, that you might wear that robe of His righteousness? If Christ ascended up, then certainly He will draw all His members after Him. Likewise, Christ's death is the door of hope through which you may overcome your lusts. This fact speaks Christ's victory; He has in His person overcome principalities and powers, and has made an open show of them. He has likewise overcome death and the grave; that is an evidence of your victory and overcoming, for there is a great correspondence between the head and the members.

The second advantage that comes to believers from Christ's death is a strong argument to embrace and entertain Christ. It may stir us up to the duty, saying, "Open to me, my sister, my love, my dove, my undefiled: for my head is filled with dew, and my locks with the drops of the night" (Song 5:2). If Christ has died and is now risen again, will not that persuade you to love Him? What arguments will do with you? Do not the five wounds of His blessed body preach this doctrine—to love Him?

The third advantage is that if the sufferings of Christ were believed, it would be a compendious way to bring your souls under the constraining power of His love, "For the love of Christ constraineth us" (2 Cor. 5:14). There is a sweet constraint of His love that lies upon the judgment and the affections. Christ's love lays a constraint on the Christian's judgment, that he thinks Him alone to be excellent; it lays a constraint on his affections, making them burn within him, for love to enjoy the person loved.

Likewise, the fourth advantage is that the way to heaven is now made manifest through the sufferings of Christ: "I will make a new covenant with the house of Israel and with the house of Judah: not according to the covenant that I made with their fathers" (Heb. 8:9). Believe it, dear Christian, there was a greater difficulty for Christians to go to heaven under the Old Testament dispensation than under the New. Christ is now crucified before your eyes, so that we are not to exercise faith in Christ as yet to come, but as already come; and certainly the sin against the gospel shall be greater than it was under the law.

The fifth advantage is that once you believed that Christ died for sinners, your unbelief would be put to an end. "This is a faithful saying, and worthy of all acceptation, that Christ came into the world to save sinners" (1 Tim. 1:15), and then he subjoins, "Of whom, I am chief." The great ground on which we stand is this: once you believe that Christ came over that infinite distance between Him and man, how easily do you think He will come over that infinite distance between you and Him? There is this ground likewise, that Christ's love will bring your souls to the necessity of this love, and the impression of the preciousness of Christ, who has perfected the work of your redemption.

The last advantage that comes to the person from Christ's death is that it is an excellent way for a Christian to bring his soul to a divine detestation and hatred of sin. "And that he died for all, that they which live should not henceforth live unto themselves, but unto him which died for them, and rose again" (2 Cor. 5:15). "Forasmuch then as Christ hath suffered for us in the flesh, arm yourselves likewise with the same mind: for he that hath suffered in the flesh hath ceased from sin" (1 Peter 4:1). There are two things in Christ's death that make sin most hateful to you. First, if you look to the burden of sin, do you not think that it was a heavy burden that made Him cry out, "My soul is exceeding sorrowful unto death" (Mark 14:34)? Was it not an infinite weight that made Him say, "If it be possible, let this cup pass from me" (Matt. 26:39)? Second, that which may make sin hateful to you is to look on these sufferings on account of sin. Do you not suppose that the justice of God was highly offended? "Yet it pleased the LORD to bruise him" (Isa. 53:10).

Now, to close up our discourse, we shall say to you these things. First, Christ dying is the immediate object of justifying faith. The grounds of this assertion are these: first, that which formally justifies a sinner must be the proper object of faith: Jesus Christ who died to justify sinners. The second ground is that Christ, in His relative excellence, is the object of faith more than in His absolute excellence; that is, Christ is God to us in this excellence more than the excellence in Himself.

There is a second thing that I would say, and it is this. To consider the eternal design of Christ's dying, one should sincerely consider the depth, height, length, and breadth of this design, that, before the mountains were brought forth, it was decreed in heaven that Christ must die. Would you know what was Christ's exercise before the world was made? You may see it in Proverbs 8:30-31: "Rejoicing in the habitable parts of the earth; and his delights were with the sons of men." Believing this would bring us to the faith of these two things: the faith of the infiniteness of His love, and the freeness of His love. Likewise, consider the height and the depth of His love; that shows itself in Christ fixing such desires of His on such wretches as we are. Do you not think that if Christ should come a-suiting, He should have wooed such as were more fit than we were? But that He should have pitched His love on us who were clothed with sinfulness and necessity, having only these two ornaments to commend us to Him, who were wallowing in the mire: "thou hast increased and waxen great, and thou art come to excellent ornaments: thy breasts are fashioned, and thine hair is grown, whereas thou wast naked and bare. Now when I passed by thee, and looked upon thee, behold, thy time was the time of love; and I spread my skirt over thee, and covered thy nakedness" (Ezek. 16:7-8). Then consider the breadth of His love, which vents itself in this, that He should have chosen us of all nations to be His firstborn, and to set His delight upon us.

Now we shall end with these three questions:

1. Were you ever, through the consideration of His death, constrained to sit down and put your mouth in the dust?

2. Were you ever, on consideration of Christ's death, constrained to love Him, and cry out, "His love to us has been wonderfully great, passing the love of women"?

3. Were you never constrained to wonder at that union between Him and us? Was the death of Christ ever an effectual means to unite you to Christ by the two chains of faith and love?

Furthermore, there is a difference between faith and love uniting to Christ. First, faith is the nail that unites the soul of a Christian to the soul of Christ, and love is the hammer that drives home and fastens that nail. The second difference is that faith draws the first lineaments and image of Christ upon a soul, but love perfects this image. The third difference is that faith is the grace that is most sober in its actions, but love is most impatient in its actions. Faith may be called a rational grace. Believe it, it is no blind bargain to take Christ upon implicit faith. We shall give you this description of love. Love sets the soul in a sweet traveling towards God, as the center and sweet rest of all. Love can find no rest in anything besides God.

The last difference is that faith is the grace that first reveals the excellence of Christ to a Christian, but love solaces itself in these discoveries. Love is born blind, and it knows nothing of itself; but when faith has discovered the excellence of Christ, and cries forth, "It is good for me to be here, and to make a tabernacle," then love subscribes and seals that with an oath. Love has two idols, impatience and desire; it is impatient until it may enjoy, and desires when it is enjoyed. Love is like the horse-leech; it cries, "Give, give"—it knows not what it is to be satisfied.

Would you like to know when the first day of love's satisfaction shall be? Certainly it shall be in that day when we shall be standing within the gates of the new Jerusalem. That day shall be the first day of love's satisfaction. This is clear from Psalm 17:15, "I shall be satisfied, when I awake, with thy likeness." That shall be when faith passes into possession, and hope into fruition and enjoyment of Jesus Christ. Faith and hope shall flee away and be no more; we shall be made to walk by sight and vision, and not by faith. Christ was content to live thirty-three years amongst us, so that we might live an eternity with Him.

When they were going to make Christ a king, He fled unto the mountains; but when they were going to put a crown of thorns upon His head, how willing He was! With what a divine submission and delight He endured it! Yet, how we slight and undervalue Christ! Did we not woefully undervalue Him when we sold Him for thirty pieces of silver? I fear there are many here that would sell Him for thirty pieces; yea, I fear many would sell Him for less. I would say to such, beware and stand in awe anymore to slight Jesus Christ. Oh, slighters and undervaluers of God, beware lest your destruction and everlasting desolation be suddenly approaching and drawing near. Dear Christians, shall Christ ever be accounted precious by us? Blessed be the person whose portion and lot is Christ, and let all the congregation say, Amen! But cursed be that person by whom Christ is not accounted precious, and let all the congregation say, Amen.

SERMON 7

Christ's Continual Intercession in Heaven, Efficacious for His Members on Earth

"Seeing he ever liveth to make intercession for them."
—Hebrews 7:25

Our blessed Lord Jesus, who is our everlasting High Priest, has most precious crafts of infinite wisdom and unspeakable grace engraven upon all His actions and dispensations; we conceive that this divine action of Christ's interceding at the right hand of God for sinners, is that in which a sinner may behold much spotless condescension and much boundless compassion. What a wonder it is to behold infinite majesty standing as a suppliant before the throne of God! I am persuaded that Adam and Abraham, the twelve patriarchs, and the twelve apostles have majestic conceptions and precious uptakings of Jesus Christ; do not these ten thousand times ten thousand of holy angels, and the souls of just men made perfect, do they not with much melodious harmony sing these everlasting songs of praise to Him that sits on the throne? Moses, who once complained that he was of a slow speech, his tongue is now as the pen of a ready writer; and Jeremiah, who said he could not speak, has now obtained the tongue of the learned.

Before I speak anything concerning the text, I would propose these two considerations to elevate your souls to hear of a crucified Christ.

First, let us consider that this Ancient of days, the Lord Jesus Christ, in all His motions and actions, proposes our advantage as the ultimate end and upshot of them all. Look on His birth, and becoming flesh of our flesh; was it not for our advantage? Look upon Christ's death and His stretching forth of His precious hands and feet upon the cross; was that not for our advantage? "Who was delivered for our offences, and was raised again for our justification" (Rom. 4:25). "I am come that they might have life, and that they might have it more abundantly" (John 10:10). "And for their sakes I sanctify myself, that they also might be sanctified through the truth" (John 17:19). Look on Christ's resurrection and rising again from the dead; was not that also for our advantage and gain? "Who was delivered for our offences, and was raised again for our justification" (Rom. 4:25). Look to Christ's leaving of the world, and going to heaven to His Father; was not that also for our advantage and gain? "It is expedient for you that I go away; for if I go not away, the Comforter will not come" (John 16:7). And is not Christ's presence in heaven for our advantage? The texts are abundantly clear: "Seeing he ever liveth to make intercession for them" (Heb. 7:25). "Whither the forerunner is for us entered, even Jesus, made an high priest for ever" (Heb. 6:20).

Second, consider the infinite delight that Christ takes in the enjoyment of believers: "Thou shalt also be a crown of glory in the hand of the LORD, and a royal diadem in the hand of thy God" (Isa. 62:3). He holds the crown and diadem in His hand because of the delight He takes in them, that His eyes may be ravished. Oh, wonder and stand astonished at that matchless goodwill of the Ancient of days towards us! "As the lily among the thorns, so is my love among the daughters" (Song 2:2). "As the apple tree among the trees of the wood, so is my beloved among the sons" (v. 3), she says, because His fruit was sweet unto her taste.

But we intended to speak today on the second part of Christ's priestly office. At the last occasion we spoke about the first part of Christ's priestly office, which was His offering up Himself for us a sacrifice; the second part is His continual intercession at the right hand of the Majesty of God for sinners.

First we shall speak of the properties of Christ's intercession. The first property of it is that Christ intercedes successfully for sinners: "But I know, that even now, whatsoever thou wilt ask of God, God will give it thee" (John 11:22). It is wholly impossible for Christ not to receive a sweet return of all His desires that He presents to the Father. Now, we may see the successfulness of it if we look to that precious knot of union that is between the Father and Christ;

there, we may be brought to see that, "If any man sin, we have an advocate with the Father, Jesus Christ the righteous" (1 John 2:1), interceding for us. That speaks the success of it, that ancient promise that was given to Christ; whatever He should ask He should receive it, "By grace are ye saved through faith; and that not of yourselves: it is the gift of God" (Eph. 2:8). "The pleasure of the LORD shall prosper in his hand" (Isa. 53:10). There is this likewise that may give us assurance of Christ's success: that precious delight that the Father carries in the behalf of the prosperity of sinners will give us a sure proof of the success of His intercession for us. "At that day ye shall ask in my name: and I say not unto you, that I will pray the Father for you: for the Father himself loveth you" (John 16:26, 27). This points to the great delight that the Father has in doing good to sinners. Lastly, we may have a sure proof of Christ's success in His intercession for us because of that infinite power which rests in Him who is our advocate and intercessor: "All things are delivered unto me of my Father" (Matt. 11:27). It is likewise clear from John 3:35 that "the Father loveth the Son, and hath given all things into his hand." Now, seeing all power is delivered to Christ of the Father, it may be a clear evidence and manifestation of His success in His intercession for us.

The second property of Christ's intercession for us is this: He intercedes with a great deal of brotherly affection and sympathy for us. In all our straits Christ speaks that word oftentimes to believers, saying, as it were, "All thy wants be on Me." "For we have not a high-priest which cannot be touched with the feelings of our infirmities; but was in all points tempted like as we are, yet without sin" (Heb. 4:15). Christ is more affected with the miseries of His own than they themselves are. "For thus saith the LORD of hosts; After the glory hath he sent me unto the nations which spoiled you: for he that toucheth you toucheth the apple of his eye" (Zech. 2:8). What a noble consideration of love this is, that He should be affected so with all our infirmities!

Finally, Christ's intercession is constant. He intercedes constantly at the right hand of the Father for us, as these words of our text prove: "Seeing he ever liveth to make intercession for us." Christians, what is the great end of Christ's being in heaven? It is to make intercession for us. We conceive that this consideration may sweetly engage our souls to Christ, that when you are all asleep in the silent watches of the night, Christ is standing at the right hand of the Father, making intercession for you.

Now the second aspect that we shall consider concerning Christ's intercession shall be to speak to these things, and hold them out, in which Christ's intercession reveals itself. We conceive there are the following three parts.

First, when a believer is compassed about with temptations, Christ intercedes for him, as we see in Luke 22:31:32: "Satan hath desired to have you, that he may sift you as wheat: but I have prayed for thee, that thy faith fail not." "I pray not that thou shouldest take them out of the world, but that thou shouldest keep them from the evil" (John 17:15). I would only say to you concerning this, lay more strength on Christ's intercession than on your own prayers. Were you never convinced that all strength that comes to you to mortify even one lust is by Christ's intercession? I confess that there are many works that Christ does for us, for which we do not at all acknowledge Him.

Next, Christ's intercession for us with the Father shows itself when believers are under the spirit of discouragement; it is then that Christ prays for their consolation. "And I will pray the Father, and he shall give you another Comforter, that he may abide with you for ever" (John 14:16). Is it not Christ's great design to have His own refreshed in a strange land?

The third way Christ's intercession shows itself toward us is that He stands at the throne of grace, pleading for the acceptance of the prayers and petitions that believers send up to God. Is not that an excellent design of His intercession, to be an holy priesthood, to offer up spiritual sacrifices, acceptable to God through Jesus Christ (1 Peter 2:5)? Further, in Revelation 8:3-4, John saw an angel standing at the altar, which is understood to be Jesus Christ; and there was given unto Him much incense, which represents His merits, making the prayers of His people to be accepted; He offered the incense with the prayers of the saints before God.

I desire then to mention the three works that Christ performs concerning the prayers of believers.

1. Christ sweetly takes away the superfluities and redundancies that are in our prayers. Christ puts all the prayers of believers in a new frame, and He cuts off all these

expressions that may render our prayers unsavory to God. Is that not an excellent work?

2. Christ takes our prayers and supplications and presents them to the Father.

3. Christ stands continually before the throne of God, pleading for an answer and return to our prayers. Do you know the reason why Christians get so few answers and returns of their prayers? It is because they do not make use of Christ's intercession surely, otherwise they would get answers to their prayers. He has promised that whatsoever you will ask in My name, that is, through My intercession, you shall receive it.

The fourth aspect wherein Christ's intercession vents itself is that when sinners are taken and ensnared in sin, He intercedes for their pardon, "If any man sin, we have an advocate with the Father, Jesus Christ the righteous" (1 John 2:1). He answers all the charges that are laid against us and intercedes for oblivion with the Father for all our offences done against Him. He is praying today that our sins may be buried in that immense sea of everlasting forgetfulness; we see this in Zechariah 3:2-3: "And the LORD said unto Satan, The LORD rebuke thee, O Satan; even the LORD that hath chosen Jerusalem rebuke thee." Christ answers all the challenges of the devil against believers.

There is a fifth aspect wherein Christ's intercession shows itself. When believers are under the long and sore exercise of troubles, Christ prays that they may have exemption from that case. This is clear, as we read, "Then the angel of the LORD answered and said, O LORD of hosts, how long wilt thou not have mercy on Jerusalem and on the cities of Judah, against which thou hast had indignation these threescore and ten years?" (Zech 1:12). In this passage, Christ as a priest is making intercession for believers; there is an apology made to Christ in verse 15 of that chapter: "For I was but a little displeased, and they helped forward the affliction."

The sixth, or last aspect in which Christ's intercession reveals itself, is this: He intercedes with the Father, that all those for whom He died should be once where He is, to partake of the everlasting depths of that precious felicity and blessed happiness that is above. We see this in the prayer of Christ recorded in John 17:24: "Father, I will that they also whom thou has given me may be with me, where I am; that they may behold my glory which thou hast given me." We do not know whether that looks like a prayer or command, but certainly it is a most imperious prayer. Christ longs for believers to come where He is.

A third part of Christ's priestly office, His offering up Himself, is to point out why people make so little use of the intercession of Jesus Christ, and so seldom employ Him. I ask you that profess yourselves to be heirs of that grant of life: when were you put to it to make use of Christ's intercession for you? We shall give you three reasons why believers make so little use of Christ's intercession.

First, most of us do not believe in the power of the spiritual virtue of Christ's intercession. It is a mystery to us, and we conceive that it is a great mystery even to a Christian's faith to believe the virtue of Christ's intercession for them. Second, we are not living under a spiritual conviction of the absolute necessity of the things we seek in prayer. We confess that Christians not praying from a principle of necessity makes formality abound in prayer. Third, and last, we are not deeply convinced of the sweet delight of that which we are seeking from God in prayer; therefore, we seek with much coldness of affection. I would only say to you that never knew what it was to make use of Christ's intercession in prayer: be afraid that Christ never interceded for you at the right hand of the Father.

We shall briefly name these sorts of persons for whom Christ does not pray. First, He does not pray for unbelievers. Is it not a most sad and desperate thing to be outside of the reach of Christ's intercession at the right hand of the Father in heaven? I am persuaded that there are many that live in this generation who pretend they have a right to Christ's intercession, for whom Christ has never interceded. A second group of persons for whom He never interceded are those who make the world their god: "I pray not for the world, but for them which thou hast given me; for they are thine" (John 17:9). Third, Christ does not intercede for those that never knew what it was to pray unto Christ. Certainly such shall never know what it is to have Christ interceding for them in heaven.

Finally, to end our discourse, we shall point out some advantages that come to a Christian by Christ's intercession for you in heaven. First, it is the great pillar of justifying faith: "Who is he that condemneth? It is Christ that died, yea rather, that is risen again, who is even at the right hand of God, who also maketh intercession for us" (Rom. 8:34). There are four pillars of justifying faith: Christ's death, His resurrection, His ascension, and His intercession. But there is a second advantage that comes to a Christian by Christ's intercession—an evidence that Christ shall finish the work of your salvation, and shall once lead you within the borders of eternity; for Christ will save to the utmost all them that through faith come to Him. This may seem impossible, but Christ will perfect your salvation. The third advantage that comes to a Christian by the intercession of Jesus Christ is that Christians are persuaded and convinced of Christ's infinite love towards them. Christians, is it not a consideration that overcomes you, that Christ should have taken so low an office as to intercede with God for wretched sinners? He does not, as the priests under the law, enter once a year to make atonement before the Lord, but He stands continually before God making intercession for us. Fourth, the advantage that comes to a Christian by Christ's intercession for them is that it is an excellent encouragement to go to the Father and pray to Him. It will greatly help the exercise of prayer: "Seeing then that we have a great high priest, that is passed into the heavens, Jesus the Son of God, let us hold fast our profession. For we have not an high priest which cannot be touched with the feeling of our infirmities; but was in all points tempted like as we are, yet without sin. Let us therefore come boldly unto the throne of grace, that we may obtain mercy, and find grace to help in time of need" (Heb. 4:14-16). Oh, sinners, I would ask you two questions. First, what love is this, that He should undertake the work of our redemption? What love is this, that Christ came from heaven to die for you? Christ was willing to be three days in the grave so that we might be through all the ages of eternity in heaven. Christ was willing to wear a crown of thorns so that we might wear a crown of precious and immortal glory. He was willing and content to wear a purple robe that we might once be clothed with His righteousness as with a garment. Christ was content to drink of the wrath of God that we might drink of divine consolation of the Holy Ghost when we come to the blessed city of the new Jerusalem. Christians, what marvelous and matchless condescension was in Him, that He who was God, equal with the Father, should undergo such things for miserable and wretched sinners like us! A second question that I would ask you, sinners, is this:

what would have become of you, if Christ had died for fallen angels and not for you? Surely we might have spent our days in the bitterness of our spirits. The angels in heaven may laugh at our folly in undervaluing and slighting of Jesus Christ, who has perfected the work of our redemption and has bought it with a dear price—His precious blood. There is a final advantage that comes to a Christian by Christ's intercession for them, and it is this: it is a door of hope that you shall one day have a complete victory over all the lusts and temptations that now you encounter.

Dear Christians and those who expect heaven, are you not longing for that blessed day when you shall sing that triumphant song: "O death, where is thy sting? O grave, where is thy victory?" (1 Cor. 15:55). Do you not seek to see the day when the Spirit shall say, "Come," and the bride shall say, "Come,"; and shall not we, the poor wearied prisoners of hope, put in our word also—"Come blessed Lord Jesus, come quickly"? Oh, be much in longing for that day, when there shall be thousands crying, "Come," and ten thousands crying, "Delay." Oh, let the sweet thoughts of that day approaching, when you shall enter your eternal possession in that blessed city that is above, comfort your hearts. We confess we are put to a nonplus in this—what shall be a Christian's thoughts when first he shall behold that spotless one, Jesus Christ? Shall He love more, rejoice more, wonder more, or praise more? I know not which of all these shall most be a Christian's exercise, when he shall be advanced to that high state of dignity, being with Jesus Christ in heaven forever; but this I know—they will have a most sweet and precious exercise. They shall have a precious and excellent exercise in heaven, forever to behold the Lamb, who was slain from the foundation of the world. I know not whether love shall be their exercise, when they shall be admitted to solace themselves, and to have their eyes delighting themselves in the precious sights and visions of Him who is fair and altogether lovely; or whether they shall be most in the exercise of joy and admiration. You shall wonder that you were so ignorant of Him while you were here, who are now made fully to understand and take Him up, and have so high and majestic thoughts of Him. Or, perhaps you shall be most in the exercise of praise, when joy and light shall be flowing in, and praise and admiration flowing out. We shall not determine this question; but certainly all these exercises being put together make up a divine exercise of the saints, when they shall be admitted of Him to drink of these rivers of the consolations of the Holy Ghost, and shall enjoy all manner of pleasures forever with Christ, and enjoy His fellowship eternally. We shall say no more; but be persuaded to long for that blessed day when Christ shall come, and shall receive you unto Himself. Now let that blessed day come, and let all other days flee away. Amen.

SERMON 8

Christian Diligence: The Way of Attaining Comfortable Assurance (1)

Wherefore the rather, brethren, give diligence to make your calling and election sure; for if ye do these things, ye shall never fall.
—2 Peter 1:10

It was decreed in the eternal counsel of the three persons of the blessed Trinity that man should once be lost, and that his soul should be separated from his body, in recompense of his breaking that tie and knot of union that was between God and him. Had man not broken that blessed knot of love, the covenant of works, that blessed knot of subordination, there would not have been such a thing as death, or the breaking of the "golden bowl," as Solomon calls it (Eccl. 12:6), but herein may we have comfort and strong consolation—Christ has purchased unto us an everlasting hope. He came from the bosom of the Father to restore these that were strangers to God, so that these that were far off might be made near by a new knot of union, through His blood. Furthermore, there is such a thing as everlasting hope, which has been purchased unto us; since there is such infinite advantage in this, should we not preach this to you that you should give all diligence to see whether or not your right to this hope is sure? Examine yourselves to see whether or not your right to this hope be founded on a sure foundation. I dare say Christians are neither positive concerning their reprobation, nor concerning their salvation and effectual calling; but I must say that a Christian that is ignorant about his estate, and is not anxious about it, may believe that his grace is either growing old as a wound, and may be groaning within him with the wounds of a mortally wounded man; or else he may think that he has not been begotten to a lively hope, and has not been elected. I would ask you all that are here, Christians: when have you spent one hour in the trial and examination of your own state and condition? We are, for the most part, void of the grace of love; and the thing that causes us to be void and so far distant from that love is that we are not frequent and earnest in making our calling and election sure.

Let us focus a little more particularly on the words of our text. After the apostle has pressed the doctrine of growth in grace, he proposes the two disadvantages that follow the persons that do not grow in grace. First, such a person is "blind and cannot see afar off." Secondly, "he has forgotten that he was purged from his old sins." He does, in this tenth verse, draw a divine conclusion from the former doctrine that men should endeavor, by all diligence, to make their calling and election sure. This has a natural dependence on the former verse. We spoke on another occasion of growing in grace; for the apostle had been first stamping that on their hearts; now we shall speak to the words themselves, as in them you have this great duty concerning the soul pressed upon you, that you should endeavor to "make your calling and election sure." We shall not stop to debate why calling is put before election, for election is before effectual calling. The apostle presses this exhortation on them to whom he writes, not only from the argument that Christians, if they did set about this excellent work, would find it a compendious way to attain perseverance: "If ye do these things, ye shall never fall." But likewise, he presses on them from this argument and ground that the making of their calling and election sure is a most effectual means for growth in grace. Before we speak to the exhortation here pressed, we shall propose these things.

First, there is a faith of evidence as well as a faith of adherence. The faith of evidence is building upon the conditional promise of the book of life, and the faith of adherence is when a Christian lays hold upon the absolute promises of the gospel for salvation. Certainly there was nothing in us that moved Him to prepare this salvation for us, but it was His own infinite and free love. Next, there must be direct acts of faith and reflex acts of faith. There may be direct acts of faith without assurance; these direct acts of faith are shown when a Christian closes with the offers of the gospel for salvation, and embraces Christ in them. The reflex acts of faith are those by which a Christian understands that he is in the state of grace and believes that he has passed from death to life. Third, there is a difference between the grace of faith and the joy of that grace; sometimes a Christian may believe, and yet not have much strength for going about his duties; therefore, sometimes it is joined to faith: "Now the God of hope fill you with all joy and peace in believing" (Rom. 15:13).

Likewise, you should consider that there is an objective certainty of salvation and a subjective certainty of salvation. That which we call an objective certainty is God's eternal electing of a Christian to save him; and that which we call a subjective certainty of salvation is when a Christian is convinced that he is in a gracious state and condition. There is a difference between eternal election and vocation, by the power of which we are able to bring sin under foot, and strive for righteousness forever.

Now, in speaking about this excellent exhortation that is pressed here for making your calling and election sure, we need not stop long to prove that it is a Christian duty. It is clear from 2 Corinthians 13:5 that Christians are to "examine yourselves, whether ye be in the faith; prove your own selves." It is likewise clear from 1 Corinthians 11:28, "But let a man examine himself, and so let him eat of that bread, and drink of that cup." "But let every man prove his own work, and then shall he have rejoicing in himself alone, and not in another" (Gal. 6:4). By which words we conceive that men should not rest upon the testimony and applause of others, but that they should prove their own works; only then they shall have rejoicing in themselves. Neither shall we insist on proving the necessity of the duty of your self-examination, and making your calling and election sure. We conceive that if there were no more to point forth the necessity of this duty but these two, it would yet be abundant and more than sufficient.

First, the heart of man that will go his own ways is desperately woeful. It is certain that delusion and mistake has such influence on some that they will not quit it. Christians, I would have you seriously consider your own estate, so that you do not deceive yourselves. I am persuaded there are many idle Christians in these days wherein we live, who have eyes and see not, ears and hear not, hands and handle not, feet and walk not.

Second, one thing that may press you to do the duty and exercise of this grace of self-examination is the precious advantage that results to a Christian from the knowledge of the reality and certainty of his condition. What a delight it will it be for a Christian to have engraven on his spirit the assurance of his state and condition! What pleasure will it be for a Christian to die with the hope of being with Him, the righteous Judge of all the tribes of the whole earth! We shall not speak much about the fact that there is a possibility of attaining this assurance of our interest in God. I think that a Christian so-called by name, who has taken up religion before religion took up him, will not be much in trial and examination of himself and of his interest in God.

The first advantage is that such a Christian, who lives under the sight of his interest in God, has most majestic thoughts and divine conceptions of God and of Jesus Christ. This is clear from 1 Peter 2:7, "Unto you therefore which believe, he is precious." Faith makes Christ very precious to a Christian. Sense will not make Him so precious, but faith is building on Him, and He is the proper object of faith; therefore, it will make Him more precious to the soul than sense. Here are four grounds why faith renders Christ more precious to the soul than sense.

1. Faith receives Christ's excellence, and shows Him to the soul, as "God-Made-Man" in one person, but sense lets a Christian see Christ in His goings and in His actions.

2. Must not faith, which is the fountain, make Christ more precious to the soul than sense, which is but the stream? Faith is a most understanding grace; therefore, it can show forth more of Christ's excellence than sense can do.

3. Faith looks into the love that is in Christ's heart, but sense looks into the love that is in His face; for faith goes into the heart, and there solaces itself.

4. Finally, faith is a more durable grace than sense; therefore, Christ is more precious to the soul by faith than sense. Faith can prophesy much good of Christ when He is under a cloud, when sense can say nothing.

There is this second advantage that comes to those who live within sight of their interest: such people are much in the exercise of prayer: "They shout for joy, they also sing" (Ps. 65:13). Often, you shall see these two linked together, living within sight of their interest, and the grace of prayer; and it must be so, for he that believes takes up what is in Him, with whom he has to do. There is nothing that so much breaks the neck and cuts off the life of diligence in prayer as unbelief; it turns diligence into desperateness. Oh, how much sin we commit in the duty of prayer because of our lack of diligence and lack of assurance of our interest!

A third advantage that comes to one by having his interest made sure in God is that knowing your calling will keep the grace of love most eminently in exercise. In Ephesians 3:17-19, we read, "That Christ may dwell in your hearts by faith; that ye, being rooted and grounded in love, may be able to comprehend with all saints what is the breadth, and length, and depth, and height and to know the love of Christ, which passeth knowledge, that ye might be filled with all the fulness of God." This is also presented in 1 John 4:19, where we read, "We love him because he first loved us." Also, Psalm 63:1-3: "O God, thou art my God; early will I seek thee: my soul thirsteth for thee, my flesh longeth for thee in a dry and thirsty land, where no water is; to see thy power and thy glory, so as I have seen thee in the sanctuary, because thy lovingkindness is better than life." A believing Christian has most lovely affections towards Jesus Christ. The grace of love in a Christian's heart mounts up with wings, in admiration at Him, who should have ever loved him, and given Himself for him. I know not whether it be the greatest wonder of love, that He should have loved us, or that He should have given Himself for us; but certainly these two, being put together, make up a matchless mystery.

There is a fourth advantage that comes to one by living within sight of his interest in God: it keeps the grace of humility eminently in exercise. What is the murderer of pride? It is faith and humility: "Be not drunk with wine, wherein is excess; but be filled with the Spirit" (Eph. 5:18). "But I labored more abundantly than they all: yet not I, but the grace of God which was with me" (1 Cor. 15:10).

The fifth advantage is that the assured Christian attains the most mortification over his lusts: "And every man that hath this hope in him, purifieth himself, even as he is pure" (1 John 3:3). Fellow Christians, why are we so little subject to mortification? It is because of our unbelief.

A sixth advantage that comes to one that is convinced of his interest in God is that such a Christian is most diligent in the use of means, and attains to most grace: "And besides this, giving all diligence, add to your faith virtue, and to virtue knowledge, and to knowledge temperance, and to temperance patience, and to patience godliness" (2 Peter 1:5-6). In this passage, faith is put first.

The last advantage is that this is the way to keep a Christian under most patient submission, despite every dispensation or affliction that he encounters; you can read in Hebrews 11:36-39, where they met with hard experiences: "They were stoned, were sawn asunder, were tempted, were slain with the sword"; yet in the 39th verse it is said that through faith they obtained a good report. Further, compare Romans 5:1 with verses three and four: "Therefore, being justified by faith, we have peace with God"; we further have patience, experience, and hope, and "we glory in tribulation," knowing that they work patience.

Now, let us discuss the reasons that Christians debate their own interests so often. There are four mistakes that Christians commit; but first, we shall name some grounds why we do hesitate about our effectual calling.

First, we desire rather to evidence the reality of our grace by the degrees of it than by the sincerity of it; for certainly our Lord has a higher respect unto the sincerity of our grace than unto any other thing. Second, Christians, being under bonds when they go to pray, are not hardened, but they are put to exile from the presence of the Lord. But certainly, the reason why His dew comes not down, and lies not on our branches, is because we are not in capacity to receive it by reason of our unbelief; and certainly, when we go to prayer under bonds, we are not fit for prayer: "And where the Spirit of the Lord is, there is liberty" (2 Cor. 3:17). Thus we are not in a fit frame that His dew may lie upon us, for His new wine would burst these old bottles of ours. Third, Christians question while beholding their growth in mortification and their conformity to God: "Every man that hath this hope in him, purifieth himself, even as he is pure" (1 John 3:3). "If any man be in Christ Jesus, he is a new creature" (2 Cor. 5:17). A fourth reason is this—that woeful remissness, slackness, and formality in going about prayer, or any other spiritual exercise. Faith is an excellent grace, and it cannot be kept in exercise except all other inferior graces be kept up and moved. The last reason why we dispute and debate our interest so often is because a Christian entertains a predominant lust within him, which does occasion God's withdrawing of His presence. It is the advantage of a Christian under a desertion, to have His presence, though the Christian may not see Him.

Now, to conclude our discourse, we desire that you may be much in the trial and examination of yourselves, and that faith may be entertained to go about your duties. You who never knew what it was to dwell forty days on Mount Sinai with Him, you may doubt much if you ever came to Mount Zion; you may question your happiness. There are many that embrace the gospel before the law; yet certainly, if your hope is in Christ, you will find little difficulty to entertain the law. That which was a mystery to Isaac, and which was a mystery to nature, to bring forth and travail without pain, may be a mystery to us in this respect: how can we attain and maintain our hope with so little difficulty and labor?

I must say that the Christian that attains and maintains this hope easily certainly may question the reality of his hope. Furthermore, the way of living by faith is exceedingly more commendable than the way of living by sense. Faith is an excellent grace that must carry the Christian through dark valleys; faith is the most excellent piece of a Christian's armor, by which we must buckle and wrestle with the temptations of the devil. The devil is most earnest in assaulting us when the grace of faith is out of exercise; therefore, labor to be much in the study and exercise of faith, so that Satan may not prevail against you with his assaults and temptations. When the strong man keeps the house, all is at peace; and when Christ comes in and begins to put out Satan, then he begins to double their hearts and makes them hard as a stone. Labor to keep the grace of faith in exercise; but let this comfort Christians who are now living in the dark: the day is coming when disputing and questioning shall be put to a close. Then you shall not at all dispute or question your interest in heaven; then you shall be no more in the dark, and under a cloud, but you shall see Him face to face, as He is. The day is coming when these two volumes shall be folded up, the great volume of the creation and the volume of the Scriptures; then, we shall have to read that volume of His incomprehensible essence and being, and shall be admitted to inquire into those things.

Let us long for the day when we shall be admitted to behold that spotless Lamb who sits upon the throne, who was slain from the foundation of the world, to purchase redemption and eternal salvation unto His people. Let us long for that day when you shall enjoy all delights, and all manner of pleasures above with Himself; where you shall delight yourselves in Him, and He shall delight Himself in you eternally; when all our misconceptions and our misconstructions of Him shall vanish; when we shall no more be under ignorance at all, but shall live in the midst of light; when we shall not only have the immediate sight and vision of Jesus Christ, but high and precious conceptions and majestic thoughts of Him. He is all their meditation and delight. But the Christians who studied nothing while here but a bare profession of godliness, let them know that they are put among the first rank of those that are excluded from that blessed and everlasting rest above, prepared for those that are heirs; unbelievers shall be excluded, and have no portion of that excellent and precious inheritance. It is of your everlasting benefit to know these things which belong unto your peace before they be hid from your eyes. It is your eternal advantage to search and try yourselves, lest you be deceived. Study more the exercise of the grace of self-examination; examine yourselves and find whether or not you have the faith of those things. We shall say no more; but, "give diligence to make your calling and election sure." Amen.

SERMON 9

Christian Diligence: the Way of Attaining Comfortable Assurance (2)

Wherefore the rather, brethren, give diligence to make your calling and election sure; for if ye do these things, ye shall never fall.
—2 Peter 1:10

It is certain that when Christians reflect upon the woeful and impious actions of the mystery of iniquity that is within them, they may be constrained to put on their mourning apparel, and to walk with the spirit of heaviness. We confess that it is a great mystery that we can walk with so much peace and contentment under the chains of our iniquity, as if they were chains of gold, and fetters of fine gold. Certainly, that which darkens a Christian's hope and obscures his interest in Christ is his entertaining a body of death in his company. However, we would say to such people that it is suitable for a Christian to assent to the assertions of unbelief concerning our iniquities; but they must deny the conclusion from such assertions drawn by sense. We confess this is not good logic, but precious divinity—"Iniquities prevail against me" (Ps. 65:3); but there is a sweet conclusion in answer to such an assertion: "But as for our transgressions, thou shalt purge them away." We would say to those that are under the power and dominion of their lusts that they may make an argument with God from the multitude of their iniquities to obtain pardon from God. In Psalm 40:11-12, we read, "Withhold not thou thy tender mercies from me, O LORD: let thy lovingkindness and thy truth continually preserve me. For innumerable evils have compassed me about: mine iniquities have taken hold upon me, so that I am not able to look up; they are more than the hairs of mine head: therefore my heart faileth me." We confess that this argument would not hold in schools, but we may make it our argument to plead for pardon from God. We conceive it is suitable that one dwelling under the conviction of a body of sin and death would be thus in proposing that desire, that He whose hands are soft as oil, and will not bruise your head, may reprove you, and cause you to walk in the paths of righteousness.

You may remember that we were speaking concerning the advantages that a Christian has by living under the solid faith and certain persuasion of his interest in God. Now we shall propose to you the Christian's disadvantage when he walks under the uncertainty of his interest, and of his calling and election being made sure.

The first disadvantage is that one that is much under the exercise of unbelief, walking under the uncertainty of his interest in God, will eventually develop that woeful evil of hardness of heart and stupidity. Hebrews 3:12-13 reads, "Take heed, brethren, lest there be in any of you an evil heart of unbelief, in departing from the living God. But exhort one another daily, while it is called today; lest any of you be hardened through the deceitfulness of sin." The deceit of unbelief is most singular, not only because it is so spiritual, but because it walks under the visor of the holiness of God. But be persuaded that if unbelief is entertained, it will procure and entertain hardness of heart, because unbelief is the sin that interrupts the lively action of the grace of prayer. The unbelieving Christian cannot at all be a diligent Christian in duties; it is impossible that diligence and unbelief can be companions. Is not that a notable disadvantage and prejudice?

A second disadvantage that comes to a Christian when he lives under uncertain faith in God is that he can much less mourn for the absence of Christ than these who are under the exercise of faith. This is clear not only from Song of Solomon 3:1-2, where the spouse is said still to seek Him, though she could not find Him. There the bride's faith and anxiety are conjoined together; the Bridegroom was absent, and she sought Him, but she could not find Him. It is likewise clear from John 20:12-13, where Mary misses Christ; she saw two angels standing, "And they say unto her, Woman, why weepest thou? She saith unto them, Because they have taken away my LORD, and I know not where they have laid him." Certainly it must be that faith puts a Christian to the pursuit after Jesus when He is away; for it is this grace that makes known to Him these visible perfections that are in Christ. Faith is a most intelligent grace, and therefore it is called *understanding*: "That their hearts might be comforted, being knit together in love, and unto all riches of the full assurance of understanding" (Col. 2:2). Likewise it must be so, because such a one that has that grace of faith takes up that infinite solace and advantage which is found in conversing with God. Faith cries out, "One day with Christ is better than a thousand elsewhere!" Love comes in, and seals that assertion with an oath, and it says, "That is most true; it is better to be a door-keeper in the house of God, than to dwell in tents of sin." Love lays hold on the heart of Christ, and Christ's heart, as it were, melts in the hands of love, and faith lays hold on the word of promise.

The third disadvantage that comes from uncertain faith in God is that such a one lays an impediment in the way between himself and the enjoyment of Jesus Christ. Dear Christians, what makes us so often cry out, "Why art thou as a sojourner, and a way-faring man, to turn in but for a night?" It is clearly the lack of faith: "That Christ may dwell in your heart by faith" (Eph. 3:17). This is likewise clearly shown in 1 Peter 1:8, "Whom having not seen, ye love; in whom, though now ye see him not, yet believing, ye rejoice with joy unspeakable and full of glory." It is the exercise of the grace of faith that makes a Christian rejoice with unspeakable joy; likewise, we may see this in Matthew 13, at the close: "He could not do many" things or works there because of their unbelief. Do you suppose that Christ can rest with you who have so many jealousies and suspicions of Him?

A fourth disadvantage is that a person living in uncertainty cannot be much in the exercise of love; though Christ gave never so many signs of His favor, unbelief calls them all delusions. Unbelief is an evil thing; nothing puts so great a price on precious Christ as faith does. It is certain that unbelief keeps love at a very low exercise; likewise, unbelief hinders the grace of mortification. I can hardly believe that a Christian under the practice of unbelief can attain the mortification of any lust because he cannot take hold of Him in whose strength only will his lusts be mortified.

The last disadvantage that comes to a Christian living under the uncertainty of his interest in Jesus Christ is that his unbelief does exceedingly impede the grace of repentance. Be persuaded, you who take such delight in this evil of unbelief, that your uncertainty hinders any divine sorrow for sin and contrition of spirit. It is a folly when Christians lose their feet, that they should lose their hands also. Be persuaded that the point of conviction is away when the grace of faith is out of exercise. Therefore a Christian, in condemning himself, speaks these words: "If it had been an enemy that had done this evil, you might have allowed it; but it is by one whom you dealt familiarly with, and with whom you had sweet fellowship; that he should rise up against you, that it is a transgression that cannot be soon done away." So the Lord, when He presses repentance, holds out Himself in the lowest degree, "Return, ye backsliding children, and I will heal your backslidings" (Jer. 3:22). When did the conviction of your sins make you go in your mourning apparel and clothe yourselves with sackcloth, weep seven days in the bitterness of your souls, causing you to put your mouths in the dust?

Now, the second thing we shall discuss is this: what is the most compendious way to attain this certainty and assurance? We conceive the best way to make our calling and election sure is in these ways. First, a Christian desiring to attain this certainty should be much in prayer. We conceive that prayer is the grace from which most Christians get their assurance as well as the intimation of their interest in God. When was it that Daniel got (we shall not say intimation, but) confirmation? It was when he was praying, the angel said unto him, "I am come to shew thee; for thou art a man greatly beloved" (Dan. 9:23). A second way in which a Christian gets assurance of his interest in God is this: one that would attain this should be much in the exercise of fear: "The secret of the LORD is with them that fear him, and he will shew them his covenant" (Ps. 25:14). The secret of the Lord here, we conceive, is for one to have the intimation of their election. The following words say, "He will shew them his covenant," which is but explicatory to the former; this does comprehend high thoughts and apprehensions of the majesty of God.

A third way in which a Christian gets intimation and assurance of his peace and interest with God is this: one who would attain to this would be much in the mortification of iniquity, as we read in Psalm 85:8: "I will hear what God the LORD will speak: for he will speak peace unto his people, and to his saints: but let them not turn again to folly." This is likewise clear in the passage reading, "Every man that hath this hope in him purifieth himself, even as he is pure" (1 John 3:3). Their hope and mortification are linked together. But the most ordinary way folk attain to this assurance and intimation of their interest and peace with God is either by sense, by holy reason, or by the grace of faith. They attain to this assurance by sense when Christ condescends to let them taste of the sweetness of His love. Then, on the communication of His signal love, or signal tokens of His love, a Christian's faith begins to grow. Faith that is built upon sense may be compared to a house that is built on the sand, which will fall by the wind; therefore, it will be to your advantage to build upon the Word of promise. They that attain to assurance of their interest in God do so when they are comparing some characters of grace with their own way. Finding some of those characters in themselves, they presently conclude that they have passed from death to life. Those that attain their assurance by faith do so because there is no place else to fly; but when a sinner is so convicted that he knows not where to go, then faith, the forlorn hope, comes in and strengthens the Christian, saying, "Why art thou cast down, O my soul? and why art thou disquieted in me? hope thou in God" (Ps. 42:5). Faith has a holy magnanimity and courageousness; it will hold to that which it asserts.

A third topic we will discuss is the difference between faith's actions on a promise and faith's resting on a promise. We conceive that one may believe the truth of a promise, even with some conviction, and yet not rest upon the promise. It is certainly a work of the Holy Spirit that must bring one to quietness in resting on the promises. There are three reasons why promises, even those of our eternal salvation, when believed, do not quiet our consciences.

1. A Christian believes not the truth of these promises as he ought to do; if he did believe the truth of these promises, he would retire and turn back, and mourn over his believing.

2. A Christian that believes a promise but finds no satisfaction in it must learn that it is not an easy thing to quit unbelief and to cast it away from us. Leaving unbelief will take as much mortification as any other sin.

3. If a Christian can believe a promise, yet not find quietness in it, we conceive it proceeds from the fact that he

is not convinced of the absolute necessity of closing with such a promise. Further, we say that "necessity has now law"; for if we were brought to a necessity, we would not wait on these ceremonies. It may proceed also from the fact that a Christian lacks the knowledge of the freedom of the promise. Furthermore, free grace is the rule of the necessity of the promise, and Christ is the rule for application to the promises.

A last point we would discuss is this: what is the most fit and compendious way for a Christian to maintain his interest in God, once he has attained it? It is said, *Non minor est virtus, quam querere, partatueri*: "it is no less art, or virtue to keep the things that are purchased, than to purchase them." But the best way for a Christian to maintain his interest in God is to often entertain communion and fellowship with God—this is a great means to preserve our faith, and keep it in exercise. This is clear from Psalm 119:167, 169, which says, "I have kept thy precepts," therefore, "let my cry come near before thee"; and "give me understanding." It is certain that our communion and correspondence with God is a most effectual means to preserve our interest in Jesus Christ. A Christian that converses often with God through prayer receives most sweet and precious manifestations of His love, which keep faith in exercise. On the contrary, faith that is without communion and is not entertained and kept in exercise thereby, is but a golden dream and a night vision that quickly passes away and is gone; but where communion and fellowship with God is entertained and kept in exercise, sense may then read love in Christ's face and in His hands, and faith is permitted to read love in Christ's heart.

A second way a Christian may study and endeavor to maintain his interest in Christ Jesus is to endeavor to keep his conscience unspotted, without blemish and offence towards God and man. The excellent and precious grace of faith can lie on no bed but the bed of a pure conscience. A challenging conscience and the grace of faith cannot continue together, for when a Christian is challenged in his conscience, then the grace of faith begins to languish and decay.

The third way a Christian should study and endeavor to maintain his interest in Christ is through strengthening the grace of experience. This is clear from Romans 5:3-5, which says, "And not only so, but we glory in tribulations also: knowing that tribulation worketh patience; and patience, experience; and experience, hope: and hope maketh not ashamed." It would certainly be to your advantage to conclude the reality and maintain these enjoyments, so that when temptation or unbelief may call them into question, you may have a decree passed on them already.

The fourth way we would prescribe that you entertain the reality of your hope is to be much in the spirit of tenderness. One that has a holy reluctance to stretch out his hand to any forbidden fruit is where Christ will maintain his interest longest. Look at every difficulty and impediment that lies in the way of the exercise of your faith, and remove it. This will teach you to maintain the exercise of the grace of your faith, the reality and certainty of your interest in Jesus Christ, and your peace with God. Christians, study in all your actions to have your peace made with God, and to make your calling and election sure. Oh, be persuaded no longer to delay this excellent business, which is of great concern to your soul. Know it—it is not long until all these shadows shall flee away, and the voice of the archangel, with the sound of his trumpet, shall be heard in heaven, saying, "Arise ye dead, and come to judgment." Do you not think that you shall have a sad entrance into eternity if you pass the borders of this span-length of time with an uncertainty of your interest and peace with Jesus Christ?

I am afraid that there are many who live in this generation who are under an exceedingly woeful and dangerous delusion; who suppose that they are going to heaven, and that they are in the highway that leads to that blessed and precious city; yet they are going to hell and eternal torments, and posting to their own destruction. Oh, try and examine your own estates and condition, lest you go to the grave with a lie in your right hand and to hell with a delusion in your bosom; woe eternally shall be to you if so be! "Be not deceived; God is not mocked: for what a man soweth, that shall he also reap" (Gal. 6:7). Dear Christians, what may most of us expect to reap of all our labors, but the wearying of our souls? Have we not sown iniquity; shall we not then reap the whirlwind? Dear Christians, endeavor to walk answerably to your calling and election. What infinite love appears in this, that He should have put His desires on you, before you desired Him! "I am found of them that sought me not: I said, Behold me, behold me, unto a nation that was not called by my name" (Isa. 65:1). Know it—the first offer came on His side, not on your side; for when we were sleeping as on the top of a mast, He sweetly capitulated for our souls. I think, Christian, if you seriously meditate on the freedom of the infinite love manifested in making a difference between you and others, it might provoke you to a holy admiration and astonishment to consider how you were chosen in His election, while so many thousands were passed by. Surely there is no cause or reason of such love, but love.

I would say to those that are yet strangers to Him, be persuaded of this: you who never knew what it was to embrace this precious offer and exhortation, "Come unto me," the day is coming when Christ shall with equity retaliate—He shall render unto you as you did unto Him. You shall call upon Him to open, but He will not hear. To others of us, may the beauty of Christ overcome us to long for the day when He shall be admired and glorified by all His saints, and by all them that believe in Him. Amen.

SERMON 10

Christ's Remarkable Condescension for the Confirmation of His People's Faith

Then saith he to Thomas, Reach hither thy finger, and behold my hands; and reach hither thy hand, and thrust it into my side; and be not faithless, but believing.

—John 20:27

There are two great and wonderful mysteries of God. The first is His unsearchable love; despite all our provocations, He does not take advantage of our infirmities. The second mystery is the low condescension of God, in that He should be content to stoop so low as to come from heaven to earth and take our nature upon Himself; furthermore, what a great mystery, that He was touched with the feeling of our infirmities, yet without sin. What a matchless mystery, that Jesus Christ, who is God, equal with the Father, should condescend to such toil and infinite labor for us! Here Thomas would not believe, except he thrust his hand into Christ's side; at this miscarriage, the Lord does not punish him as he deserved, but condescends and submits unto him. We may observe from this action that our blessed Lord Jesus is of a very condescending nature towards sinners. That which He said of Himself may be fitly and eminently said of Him—in Him alone dwelleth all goodness and all excellent properties; was not His condescension an excellent property? Let us take notice of these points concerning Christ's condescension.

In the first point, consider the person who thus condescended; it is our blessed Lord Jesus. It was He who was the infinite God, eternal and all-sufficient. It was not a finite man, but the eternal God who did thus condescend.

The second point of His condescension is that He condescended to one man. Had there been a nation of them, there might have been somewhat of a reason for it; but this is a wonderful and admirable mystery, that He should so deal with one person and condescend so low. It is certain that there was a blessed necessity lying on precious Christ to gain to Himself all that the Father had given unto Him. The passage of John 4:4, where it is said that He "must needs go through Samaria," implies that it behooved Him to go through Samaria; there was a blessed necessity lying on Him to accomplish that duty.

There is a third point concerning the condescension of Christ: consider that He did sweetly and freely come over Thomas's unbelief. He condescends so far to him to renew him and to bring him out from under all the plagues and curses of God. What marvelous love and condescension is in that blessed step of His! His love is unsearchable. Now, Christians, and expectants of the crown, let us exalt Him together, who has remembered us and delivered us from the gates of death. Do not at all distrust Him!

The fourth point of His condescension is that He overcame Thomas's unbelief, which was so great, and of such a high and eminent degree that it seems unreasonable. Was it not an unreasonable thing for him not to believe God until he had thrust his fingers into His side? Besides all this, Thomas had the promise of everlasting life. He had the testimony of Him who is a faithful witness, in whom all the promises are yea and amen; and still, he did not believe God! Yet, our blessed Lord Jesus does condescend to him, and comes over all the difficulties and mountains of his unbelief, which certainly was marvelous and wonderful. Now, we shall say no more of that, but love sees no impediments before it in its exercise; mountains of difficulties are nothing in its sight.

The fifth point of Christ's condescension is that He made use of the remedy to recover Thomas from his unbelief, which Christ despised. Thomas's unbelief could not be satisfied—it was so peremptory that except it saw Christ's side and beheld the print of the nails, Thomas would not believe; and lo, Christ condescends unto Thomas!

The sixth point is that the remedy which Christ used was made effectual for curing Thomas's unbelief. Many of us are so peremptory and strict in our unbelief that Christ may say to us, "Except ye see signs and wonders, ye will not believe" (John 4:48); yet, herein is His love manifested to us, that these means are made effectual for our recovery, to bring us back again.

There is a seventh point of Christ's blessed condescension. Christ overcomes Thomas's unbelief, which was of great continuance, for He was under it eight days, as appears from the previous verse; yet Christ overcomes it. Is not that matchless condescension?

The last point of the blessed condescension of Christ is this: Christ was content to live many days upon the earth after He had risen from the dead so that He might confirm Thomas's faith, as well as the faith of the rest of the apostles, and so they might strengthen their faith and confidence in Him. That was a great act of condescension. Now, what is the reason for this wonderful condescension? It is the prerogative of Jesus Christ and it brings Him glory so to do.

But there are two main grounds and reasons why it is so. First, He has great love for sinners. The second reason is His faithfulness, for it is an article of the covenant of redemption that He delights not in the death of sinners. Now for use of this, you would profit much by studying His free grace in His matchless condescension towards you. Now this act is a blessed mystery; it passes all knowledge. We must study to know the unsearchableness of this condescension, and study to know the reason for Christ's condescension. Certainly there is no cause in us for Christ to be so condescending toward us. The only reason for this condescension was free love; love was the cause of love, and love had no other root than love!

We shall briefly answer two questions from the text. First, why did Christ show Thomas His hands and His side? We conceive that there are three reasons for it. First, Christ desired to cure Thomas's unbelief, which had great power over him. Secondly, it was to convince Thomas himself of his unbelief. He condescended so far to us that He was content to be bruised for our iniquities, that by His stripes we might be healed. The third reason was that Thomas might be persuaded that it was to Christ's eternal glory and honor that He was now risen from the grave.

Secondly, why does Christ bid Thomas believe? We think there are two reasons. First, Christ desires to convince him of his own weakness and inability to believe and to teach Thomas not to believe or trust upon his own strength. The second reason is because there is strength in His commands, which will abundantly furnish a person to obey them, as is shown in John 11:43, where He commands Lazarus to rise out of the grave. There was such strength in the command that it made the man who was dead for four days rise and live again. He bade Lazarus come forth, and Lazarus obeyed Him. This is likewise clear from Matthew 15:28, where He raised the woman's daughter by His word: "Be it unto thee even as thou wilt."

A second observation is that our blessed Lord Jesus does most wisely apply remedies and cures to every disease wherewith a Christian is afflicted: "A bruised reed shall he not break, and smoking flax shall he not quench" (Matt. 12:20). He is an excellent physician; He alone must cure all our diseases. There are two branches of this. First, His omniscience may be seen in this act of His condescension; He beholds all things, even the darkest things that are done in secret. This may afford much consolation unto a Christian for several reasons. We may stand in awe of Him, being such a one who condescends so low to us that even He who is as comely as the "tents of Solomon," and in whom there is no spot at all, should condescend so low.

Let us also be comforted that we may freely go to Him with all our diseases and distempers, with the confidence that as He knows us so well, He will so answer. If there is any groaning and disquiet in you, go to God for a remedy for that disquiet; He knows our hearts better than we know ourselves. Does it not comfort you that in your distress, you have a Physician to visit—One who knows your diseases better than yourselves? Finally, you may find consolation in the knowledge that since there is to be found in Christ remedies for all your diseases, let nothing be grounds for delay in coming unto Him; nothing can be an impediment to Christ curing your diseases. Furthermore, Christ can apply a remedy and cure unto every disease perfectly well; "The Lord GOD hath given me the tongue of the learned, that I should know how to speak a word in season to him that is weary: he wakeneth morning by morning, he wakeneth mine ear to hear as the learned" (Isa. 50:4).

Third, it is our duty to believe and to strengthen our faith and confidence in God. A Christian may have many advantages by strengthening confidence in God. First, it ensures that we will always have His dew lying on our branches; thereby we may remain green and full of sap and fatness. Also, to have our faith strengthened in God is the most compendious way to keep our hearts in the precious thoughts and estimation of Christ's love to us: "Unto you therefore which believe he is precious" (1 Pet. 2:7). It is a most excellent and compendious way for a Christian to have a constant joy, satisfaction, and delight, while he is in the world, to have his faith strong in God. To them that believe, the command is given, "Rejoice evermore" (1 Thess. 5:16).

On this subject, some questions arise. First, what influence does sense have upon the strengthening of our faith? I would answer that sense lets a Christian see that God is near at hand to him, and will be near unto all that trust in Him. No doubt this will exceedingly strengthen a Christian's faith in Him. Sense also has influence on the strengthening of our faith in God as it discovers the infiniteness of His precious love toward us. Furthermore, sense strengthens faith in God by revealing to us the great delight and pleasures that are to be found in conversing with God. If this were on foot, no doubt we would long after Him more, and delight and solace ourselves in His fellowship more than we do. Sense also reveals unto us the exceeding freeness of His love. Was there any cause in us that moved Him to this love, that He should have lain down His life for us? Surely there was no cause in us! His love was exceedingly free towards us. May not this encourage us to believe and to place our confidence in God?

Finally, sense strengthens our faith in God by making the Christian despise and fall out of conceit with all other lovers besides Jesus Christ. It reveals unto the soul the matchless beauty and excellence that is in Christ, which makes the believers become dead to all things here below, and to place their confidence God alone. Oh, Christians, was there ever so much of Christ's excellence revealed unto you that you were made to cry, "What have I to do any more with idols?" (Hos. 14:8), and to cast them from you, as a menstruous cloth "to the moles and to the bats" (Isa. 2:20)? Oh, study to live under the deep impression and apprehension of the excellence of this grace of faith, that it may reveal unto you the precious excellence of Jesus Christ.

Now for a second question that arises. How may a Christian know whether the enjoyments that he receives are real, and that they are for the strengthening of his confidence in God? We propose this question because there are many things which a Christian encounters that look like enjoyments of God, that in reality are nothing but fancies and delusions. There are several marks and evidences whereby we may distinguish between the enjoyments that strengthen our faith and those that are but delusions and fancies. Primarily, do these enjoyments humble you? Although Christ's free grace exalts you, yet you can sit down low in the dust in your own estimation. If this is your experience, that is an evidence that your enjoyments are real, and no delusion. This is clear from Isaiah 6:5, where Isaiah, when he saw God, was exceedingly humble and debased in his own sight and apprehension. He said, "Woe is me! for I am undone; because I am a man of unclean lips, and I dwell in the midst of a people of unclean lips: for mine eyes have seen the King, the LORD of hosts." Isaiah's humility was evidence that his enjoyment was real.

A second evidence by which you may know if your enjoyments are real and not a delusion, is this: do the enjoyments that you encounter encourage you to seek after more enjoyment of God—to seek after God as newborn babes, desiring to drink the sincere milk of the Word? Then they are real; but, the enjoyments that we have here are not satisfying; they are rather to stir up our appetite and desire than to satisfy our appetite. The first day of a Christian's satisfaction shall not be until the blessed morning of the resurrection from the dead; "I shall be satisfied, when I awake, with thy likeness" (Ps. 17:15).

A third test whereby we may know whether these enjoyments are real is to examine yourself to discover what strength you have through your enjoyments for the mortifying of your lusts and pulling down of the strongholds of corruption. If your enjoyments do not help you much in this duty of mortification, then you may suspect that they are but fancies and delusions. Fourth, do you exceedingly long for and desire that all those that do not know God may be partakers of that same enjoyment? Do you exceedingly desire those who are without Christ to be partakers of that same enjoyment with yourself? Do you exceedingly long for and desire that those who are yet far off may be brought near? Then it is real; but certainly, if that is not your desire, you may suspect your enjoyment to be but a vain delusion.

Another evidence whereby you may distinguish between a real enjoyment and a delusion is to answer this question: are you more taken up in thinking upon the Giver of your enjoyment than upon the gift itself? If it be so, then it is a token that the enjoyment is real. But if you sit down content, and delight yourself with the bare enjoyment, accounting more of it than of Him who is the giver of that enjoyment, then your enjoyment is either not right, or you are misusing the enjoyment. Therefore, you must labor to distinguish between your true enjoyments and those that are but fancies and delusions, by the marks and evidences that we have given you.

Continuing in our observations, we observe in the fourth place that this excellent and matchless love of Christ to you is a great confirmation of your faith, and you ought to take it as such. Here are five considerations which ought to be grounds for our actions and reactions to this grace of faith from the apprehension of the love of Christ to us.

The first observation is that the love of God to us is an infinite love. His love has no bounds; it is both matchless and boundless. May not this provoke you to be in the exercise of faith? I am persuaded that if you could achieve the faith of this knowledge, that His love is infinite, the application of faith would not be so difficult.

A second consideration of His love that will provoke you to be much in the study of the exercise of the grace of faith is to ponder the grace of His love and its unchangeableness; for when we meet with any change of His dispensations, we are ready to draw the conclusion that His love is changeable. But oh, we must believe that He is altogether unchangeable in His love, that there is neither variableness nor shadow of turning with Him. Certainly there is no change in Him; all the change is in us! We are always changeable; we are as unstable as water, in all our ways, designs, and purposes.

Thirdly, let us consider that He fixed His love on us rather than on angels, who were creatures of a far more excellent nature. May not the consideration of that have much influence on us, provoking us to serious living on the grace of faith? "For verily he took not on him the nature of angels; but he took on him the seed of Abraham" (Heb. 2:16). Oh, admire this mystery of the precious and infinite love of Jesus Christ, that He should have condescended so far as to come down from heaven, out of the bosom of the Father, and die upon the earth for our sakes; and that, seeing He did die, He should have died for man, and not for angels! This no doubt is a great mystery. Certainly, if anything in the person had made Him fix His love whereupon He did fix it, no doubt it would have been the fallen angels and not us; for we were lying in our own filthiness, unto the loathing of our persons, and were wholly defiled and miserable. What a matchless and unparalleled mystery of love!

The fourth consideration of His love which may provoke us to be much in the study and exercise of the grace of faith is the fact that despite all our provocations of Him to wrath and displeasure against us, He still rests in His love toward us. Notwithstanding all our gross abominations and blasphemies against Him, He yet rejoices over us and delights in the exercise of His mercy towards us. May not that provoke our desires and stir us up to pursue after Him?

The last consideration of His love that may provoke us to be much in the study of the exercise of faith, is that the love of Christ is an everlasting love; it is even as old as Himself. This love is old as the Ancient of days; even before the mountains were brought forth, or the cornerstone of the world was laid, His delight was with the sons of men and His love was towards them. Then certainly the consideration of the eternity of His love would put away many grounds of unbelief.

Now, first, let those that are groaning under their sins and spiritual ignorance of God be much in the consideration of His love, that He has now, and has had to them from all eternity. Seeing He has such a respect for them and has perfected all their works, He will likewise perfect the work of their redemption, and will bring them safe through this wilderness and land of darkness. I say, they may comfort themselves that such a day is approaching when that shall come to pass. Second, if you desire to know the rise of your unbelief and distrust of God, you are all the more ignorant of Him. Oh, that damnable ignorance that is among the professors of this generation! I think there was never more practical ignorance of God than now. You must study to know more closely Him with whom you have to do, lest He overtake you in the midst of your ignorance, and like a roaring lion, tear you in pieces when there shall be none to deliver you. Oh, remember your Creator in the days of your youth, lest you perish from the way!

Fifth, let us observe that our blessed Lord Jesus Christ does sometimes condescend so far to a sinner as to give them sense for the ground and confirmation of their faith; is not that low condescension? Here are some results that flow to such a person whose foundation of his faith is only built upon sense:

1. Such a person lacks the notable commendation and testimony that is given to one that believes on the promise, as Christ here says to Thomas, "Because thou hast seen me, thou hast believed: blessed are they that have not seen, and yet have believed" (John 20:29). Then encourage yourselves in knowing that you may believe on the absolute and simple promise of God, as well as on sense.

2. I would say this to those whose foundation of faith is only built upon sense—your faith is of shorter continuance than the faith built on the absolute promise and Word of God. Furthermore, you would labor and endeavor to have your faith settled, fixed, and built upon God, that you may find Him to be a shield unto you in the day of your visitation and sore calamity.

Therefore we would recommend this to you as a noble practice, and exceedingly useful, that you would be persuaded to walk more by faith than by sense; for certainly, the foundation of sense is most unsure, and is but a sandy foundation of faith. It is also alterable and subject to change; therefore, it would be in your best interest to build your faith upon Christ Himself. We desire to believe that that day is approaching and drawing near when faith shall flee away, and shall be no more; in this day, we shall walk no more by faith, but by sight and vision; faith shall vanish into fruition and hope into possession, and sight shall sit down and eternally solace itself in the victories and triumphs of faith and hope. Oh, be persuaded that there is such a day approaching, and comfort yourselves in the hope and expectation of it!

The day is at hand when death shall be swallowed up unto life, the grave unto victory, and you shall be taken up above to that higher house, there to remain forever, throughout all the ages of eternity, to behold the beauty and glory of the Lord. Will not that be a joyful and pleasant day, when we shall walk no more by faith and hope, but by sight and sense? Will you not rejoice when you shall be admitted eternally to delight yourselves in Him and He shall delight Himself in you? Certainly tongue cannot express the excellence of that life which is above; but believe it, sense shall instruct you in it before long; we doubt when we speak of this, by multiplying words, that we darken knowledge. Comfort yourselves in the knowledge that it shall not be long until by experience, you will know the sweetness and excellence of that life. Let now your desires run out in affections after it. We shall say no more, but shall desire that Christ would fasten these words in your hearts, as a nail in a sure place. May He alone who is able, do it. Amen.

SERMON 11

Jesus Christ's Preciousness to Believers (1)

Unto you therefore which believe he is precious.
—1 Peter 2:7

Dearly beloved of the Lord, how long will you halt between two opinions? If Christ is precious, then let your soul embrace Him; but if your idols are precious, then may your soul embrace them and delight in them. We may say that eye has not seen, nor ear heard, neither has it entered into the heart of man to conceive and ponder the endless and precious perfections that are in precious Christ. We shall never be able to comprehend the excellence and transcendent comeliness and beauty that is in His face. "My beloved is white and ruddy, the chiefest among ten thousand" (Song 5:10). "Yea, he is altogether lovely" (v. 16). He is precious! Certainly if the angels and the saints were asked the question, "What do you think of Christ?"—all those who are around the throne would venture this answer to the question: Christ is excellent and exceedingly precious and rather a subject of admiration than of speech. I shall say these six things, all of which explain the doctrine of Christ's preciousness.

First, do not all the excellent graces of the Spirit preach that Christ is precious? Does not that noble grace of faith preach the preciousness of Christ as well? For by it we are partakers of communion and fellowship with Him. The excellent grace of love preaches the same doctrine, for love is the grace that unites the Christian's soul to Christ. Christ's preciousness is also clearly seen in the grace of mortification and the grace of patience.

Next, you must read His preciousness through the enjoyment of God that the saints in former times have experienced. Does not their enjoyment tell you that Christ is precious? To be brought under the shadow of the tree of life and to be dandled on His knees—all the enjoyments that a Christian encounters are streams of sweetness that flow from God's ocean and fountain of everlasting pleasure. Do not all these enjoyments preach the preciousness of Christ?

Third, we can see the preciousness of Christ through the lovesickness of the saints of old under absence and distance from Christ (though we confess these diseases are rare now). Then, oh, must He not be precious, whose absence for an hour is as an eternity and whose presence for a thousand years is but as a short moment? Oh, deserted Christians, have you ever seen Him whom your soul loves? I fear that the presence and communion with God is a mystery to most of us.

Fourth, you may clearly see the preciousness of Christ in the unspeakable sorrow and grief that the saints have experienced under their absence and distance from Christ. During these times of waiting for Christ, their souls refused to be comforted, put on their mourning apparel, and ate their bread with ashes in the heaviness of their spirits. Why is Christ so little precious to you? Is He less precious in Himself now than He was under the dark Mosaic dispensation of the gospel? Certainly not! He is no less precious now than He was then.

We may further view Christ's preciousness in the blessed names that are given to Him in the Scriptures: He is called "the desire of all nations"; the "plant of renown"; and "the light of that city above"; the "express image of the Father's person"; the "bright and morning star"; and the "flower of the tribe of Jesse." Do not all these blessed names of His proclaim that He is indeed precious?

Finally, Christ's preciousness is seen in that the most unpleasant thing in Christ (if there is any unpleasantness) is more joyful and precious than the choicest of all created comforts. This is clear when we hear of Moses: "Esteeming the reproach of Christ greater riches than the treasures in Egypt" (Heb. 11:26). Oh, if His reproaches be so excellent and precious, what must His blessings and favorable manifestations be! Dear Christians, do you not desire the tongue of an angel, that you might be fit to express the praises of that Plant of renown, Jesus Christ? Christians, under the sense of your enjoyment of God, cry out, "It is good for me to be here: let me make tabernacles, and a place of abode." Oh therefore, account Christ precious.

Now, examining this verse, we have three things to consider. First, we have a Christian described from that which is his noblest and cardinal characteristic: believing. Second, we see the three precious advantages that flow to a Christian from the noble and excellent grace of faith:

1. Faith makes Christ precious unto the soul.

2. Faith will keep a soul under the impression of Christ's preciousness. The believing soul will always account Christ exceedingly precious.

3. Faith keeps divine reasonableness in its exercise. Faith is not blind; it looks to the former verse, which says that because He is a cornerstone, faith counts Christ precious.

The words in this verse describe a Christian, a *believer*. We have spoken of faith before, so we shall not now insist on it; we shall only propose these three considerations to enforce your pursuit after this noble grace of faith.

First, faith is the grace that gives a Christian the most broad and comprehensive sight of Christ. It draws aside the veil from the face of Christ and presents His beauty to the soul. This is clear in the words, "For he endured, as seeing him who is invisible" (Heb. 11:27). Faith allows the soul to see the invisible God just as clearly as if it did visibly behold Him. Through this faith, a Christian sees four principle parts of Christ's body. First, faith will let the Christian see Christ's heart. Sense will say of Him, and to Him, "Thou hast the heart of an enemy"; but faith will cry out, "I know the thoughts of His heart to be good toward me, to give me an expected and blessed end." Second, faith (if so I may speak) looks to Christ's feet. It takes notice of the actions and motions of Christ; it cries out, "His feet are like pillars of marble set in sockets of silver." Third, faith beholds the smile of Christ's countenance. When sense can read nothing in His face but wrath and displeasure, then faith draws back the veil from His countenance and reveals love. Fourth, faith lets a Christian see the hands of Christ. It beholds all His dispensations; it sees infinite love shining in all the actions of Christ. Faith is an intelligent grace. The believer can clearly see this love, as the scriptures say, "That their hearts might be comforted, being knit together in love, and unto all riches of the full assurance of understanding, to the acknowledgement of the mystery of God, and of the Father, and of Christ" (Col. 2:2).

The second consideration to enforce your pursuit after this noble grace of faith is this: Faith is the grace by which a Christian keeps most communion and fellowship with God. The prayer that Paul has for believers is "that Christ may dwell in your hearts by faith" (Eph. 3:17); it is as if he had said, "By the exercise of all other graces, Christ is to you as a sojourner that turns in to you but to remain for a night; but, by the exercise of faith, Christ becomes an indweller in your house." Faith will entertain communion with God in crosses, in promises, and in all duties. The believing Christian can keep fellowship with God under His most sad and bitter afflictions.

The third consideration is that faith is the mother of a Christian's fruitfulness. "He that abideth in me, and I in him, the same bringeth forth much fruit" (John 15:5); that is, he that *believeth* in me will bear much fruit of the Spirit. This relationship is likewise clear when we read 2 Peter 1:5 which states, "And beside this, giving all diligence, add to your faith virtue; and to virtue knowledge." Here, he puts faith in the first place; faith is always fruitful, and never barren. I would say two words concerning this. First, I confess, though there be a great and marvelous barrenness amongst us, there is not great barrenness in gifts, but in fruitfulness. What is the reason for our unfruitfulness? Surely it is because of the much abounding evil of unbelief. Secondly, I would say that a Christian may have much visible fruitfulness, although there may be much unfruitfulness in his soul, and so may be a barren Christian. By visible fruitfulness we mean the exercise of outward duties, when within there is nothing but barrenness in the exercise of inward duties.

To further this thought, let us look at four ideas concerning a natural conscience.

1. A natural conscience will challenge more for the lack of outward sanctification than for the lack of inward sanctification. It will challenge more for pollution in the outward man than for pollution of the inward man.

2. It will challenge more for the neglect of the outside of a duty than for the neglect of secret prayer.

3. A natural conscience will challenge more for the commission of sin than for the omission of duty. If he swears,

it will challenge him more for that than if he had neglected secret prayer ten times.

4. A natural conscience will challenge a person more for the lack of sanctification than for the lack of justification.

Now to close our discourse on this subject, I ask you, Christian, can you read the Scriptures and not be constrained to blush? Do you not blush when you read of holy Enoch, Abraham, David, Paul, and patient Job? When you look unto their holy walk and conversation, do you not blush? Do you think that the way of heaven was easier when they lived than it is now in our days under the glorious manifestation of the gospel? Certainly it was not. It is reported of the heathen when reflecting upon the famous acts of their predecessors, that they were bereaved of their night's rest; ought not the famous acts of our predecessors bereave us of our sleep as well? I must say, if Christ brings many of the Christians of this generation to heaven, surely there must be a stranger exercise of His power directed toward us than it was before.

Second, I must say that faith is the predominant grace of a Christian while he is here below, and love shall be the predominant grace when he shall be above. Faith and hope fight the battle, and love divides the spoil. Faith may be called *Asher*, meaning, *royal dainties*, and it may be called *Joseph* in respect of its mother, that is, *fruitfulness*.

Thirdly, there are three idols that Christians find very hard to mortify, namely, the applause of the world, the pleasures of the world, and the reproaches of the world. Applause is far from being a blessing; on the contrary, it is a woe: "Woe unto you, when all men shall speak well of you!" (Luke 6:26). The applause of the world is an inconstant thing; it cries, "Hosanna" today, and "Crucify him!" tomorrow.

Now, we will discuss the advantages that come from the exercise of faith. As we mentioned, there are two advantages. The first advantage is having Christ precious to our souls. We conceive that it comprehends three ideas. First, it imports this for a Christian—to have a high account and estimation of Christ above all things in the world, and to cry out, "Whom have I in heaven but thee? and there is none upon earth that I desire beside thee" (Ps. 73:25). In addition, it imports to the soul to be much in the exercise of love to Christ and that is, to have Christ precious. Thirdly, to have Christ precious to your soul is to have communion and fellowship with Him.

Second, we shall discuss how faith makes Christ precious to the soul. A primary way faith makes Christ precious is that it takes a sight of the comeliness and beauty of Christ and it cries out, "Thou art fair, my love" (Song 1:15); and presently on the back of that, Christ is precious. The second way faith makes the soul take up Christ as precious is that faith is the grace that makes up our interest and communion with Christ. It is the believing Christian that has most communion and fellowship with Christ. There is a third way whereby faith makes Christ precious to the soul. Faith is the grace that believes the promises that God has made to the soul—this makes Christ precious to the soul. When a Christian shall read 1 John 3:2, and faith believes it sweetly, you shall be constrained to cry out, "Oh, what a matchless one is Christ!" We shall be constrained to wonder at the love that He has had towards us. A fourth way faith makes Christ precious to the soul is by presenting to the Christian the crown of glory and letting him see all the joys and excellencies of heaven. A broad sight of that crown, even of that glorious and immortal crown, would exceedingly commend Christ unto your souls. A last way faith describes and makes Christ precious to the soul is that it reveals and presents to you the absolute necessity of embracing Jesus Christ.

We would also like to propose some evidences and marks whereby you may know whether Christ is precious unto you.

A first evidence whereby you may try your faith is that those to whom Christ is precious will have a desire to bear His image—that is, they will have a desire after holiness; "Create in me a clean heart, O God, and renew a right spirit within me" (Ps. 51:10). Dear Christians, do you not desire to bear the image of the second Adam as you have borne the image of the first Adam?

A second evidence is that those to whom Christ is precious will desire to make a continual and constant use of Christ for justification, that they may be purged and have the precious lineaments of Christ drawn upon them. They will make use of Him for wisdom, so that they may be directed aright through the wilderness of this world. They will make use of Him for redemption, so that they may be set free from their spiritual enemies. Oh, Christians, do you dare say that ever an idol did assault you that you did not embrace? Oh, I fear there are many that may assent unto this truth.

There is a third evidence of those to whom Christ is precious. They will have a desire after more fellowship and communion with God: "Let him kiss me with the kisses of his mouth: for thy love is better than wine" (Song 1:2), and, "Draw me, we will run after thee" (v. 4). Does it seem an eternity when you are absent from Christ? If so, it is evidence that Christ is precious unto you.

Fourthly, those who love Christ are exceedingly burdened under Christ's absence and withdrawal from them. The spouse vented her respect to Christ in Song of Solomon 3, where she sought Him whom her soul loved; she sought Him, but she found Him not, and she continued seeking until she found Him. The spouse vented her respect to Christ in these three respects:

1. That she should have undervalued angels, as "they say unto her, Woman, why weepest thou? She saith unto them, Because they have taken away my LORD, and I know not where they have laid him" (John 20:13). She, as it were, turned her back on the angels because there was none for her but Christ. The happiness of a Christian lies in the words: "My Lord," if He is taken away from them.

2. A Christian's anxiety is shown as there will be dissatisfaction with all the graces if Christ is missing. This is clear in Song of Solomon 3:1-3. There she had the graces of faith, love, diligence, patience, and submission; yet, there is One absent that she desires.

3. A Christian has a low esteem of all things under Christ; such that, "In the day of my trouble I sought the Lord: my sore ran in the night, and ceased not: my soul refused to be comforted" (Ps. 77:2).

A fifth evidence of those to whom Christ is precious is their spiritual observance and Christian record of the motions of Christ under absence; and when He is present, they take notice when they are admitted to taste of the apples of the tree of life, whereof if once you eat, you shall be as gods, as the devil (or serpent) said to Eve.

A sixth evidence of those to whom Christ is precious is that they will be in some measure saddened for grieving and offending Christ. I fear I may say this to the confusion and shame of most of us, whose sin was never a burden. Oh, Christians, can Christ be precious to you and yet it does not pain you to offend Him?

A seventh evidence of those to whom Christ is precious is that they will have a high estimation and account of union and fellowship with Christ. Oh, what does the heart of a Christian most run after? I fear it is not after Christ. There are some whose hearts are upon the world; there are others whose hearts are upon the pleasures of the world. Still others have hearts set upon the applause of the world, and there are others whose hearts are on the covetousness of the things of the world. This is clear when the prophet says, "For with their mouths they shew much love, but their heart goeth after their covetousness" (Ezek. 33:31). Oh, therefore, strive to embrace Jesus Christ. The devil will let you give all your members to Jesus Christ, but he says, "Give me your heart." He will let you give your eyes, ears, hands, and feet to Christ; but, says he, "Give me your heart."

I shall describe three sorts of persons to you that are not right in heart.

1. There are some that have a divided heart. Certainly the devil possesses the hearts of such. In James 4:8, we read the last words, "Purify your hearts, ye double-minded."

2. There are some whose hearts are not divided, namely, atheists; their hearts are wholly given to the devil. This is clear: "Ephraim is joined to his idols: let him alone" (Hosea 4:17); or, as we may understand, he "is married to his idols." Then surely Christ is not precious to one of these persons. Oh, Christians, has not the world your first thoughts when you rise in the morning, and your last thoughts when you go to bed at night? I fear our idols always have more of our thoughts than Christ.

3. There are some whose hearts are wrestling against their predominant lust, although I may say, there are not many such among us who make and count it their main business to wrestle against the devil and his temptations. Yet, they do not prevail, but fall under them.

I shall add a last evidence of one to whom Christ is precious. They will have some delight in duties by which communion and fellowship with God may be attained; "By night on my bed I sought him whom my soul loveth: I sought him, but I found him not" (Song 3:1). She seeks Him from principles of delight, faith, and necessity. Oh, Christians, why do you go to prayer in such a state? I think most of us go to prayer only to satisfy a natural conscience. I will end our discourse at this time; only let me say that this is an evidence of one that has real delight to duty; he has a low estimation and account of all things below Christ, and he has a high esteem only of Christ Himself.

Now, before I close, I would ask the unbelievers of this congregation these four things. First, is Christ precious to you? Yes, you say? Then how is it that you hate the saints and people of God if Christ is precious to you? For surely you may be persuaded that you cannot love God if you do not love His people: "If a man say, I love God, and hateth his brother, he is a liar: for he that loveth not his brother whom he hath seen, how can he love God whom he hath not seen?" (1 John 4:20). Second, do you count Christ precious to you when the exercise of religion is your greatest cross and affliction in the world? Do you not cry out in the morning that prayer is your greatest burden; and in the evening, it is your greatest cross? And surely there are these two evils that follow such in their prayers: they speak to God as to one of their companions, but they want that divine reverence that they ought to have in their approaches to God. The other evil is that they count that time exercised and spent in prayer an exceeding long time; they tire in God's company, and may not many of us identify with these two? Third, I would say, do you think that Christ is precious to you, whose sins were never your burden? You may be persuaded of it—He is not precious to you! The fourth question I would ask is this: Do you think that Christ is precious to you, who never knew what it was to distinguish between the absence and presence of God in prayer? Oh, Christians, are there not many here who never knew what it was to distinguish the absence of Christ from His presence? Are there not some here who have an unchangeable communion with God which never alters, but still is the same; surely, such may question the reality of their communion.

Oh, atheists and traitors to the Son of God, study this day to make peace with Him; and you that desire your eternal well-being, study to have Christ precious to you, otherwise He will be exceedingly terrible. Has not Christ been offered to you, and have not many of you rejected Him and His offer? Oh, know that matchless fullness and excellence that is in Jesus Christ! What can you desire that is not in Christ? What can you want that is in Him, and have Him? He is altogether lovely; He is all desires; He is all-sufficient; He is all in all. Oh, be persuaded to fall in love with Christ and His offer; believe in Him who is the Desire of nations, the Flower of the tribe of Jesse, the Lion of the tribe of Judah. What can we say to persuade you to embrace Christ, to lay hold on His offer? Surely, when we shall be sifted before the tribunal of God to receive our sentence of perpetual condemnation, it shall be thought our everlasting concern to have embraced Christ. We shall say no more, but know with certainty that above the clouds, Christ is precious. In that place, all are crying, "Blessing, and honour, and glory, and power, be unto him that sitteth upon the throne, and unto the Lamb for ever and ever" (Rev. 5:13). Amen.

SERMON 12

Jesus Christ's Preciousness to Believers (2)

Unto you therefore which believe he is precious.
—1 Peter 2:7

Such is the universal stupidity and hardness of heart that has overtaken the people of this generation that if Christ should come from heaven, being there glorified with majesty, and should invite us to partake of that promised land, there are people that would stop their ears, as with their finger, lest they should be overcome and led captive there and be charmed with the enchanting voice of that blessed charmer. To these that sell Christ at so low a rate, we say, "All the days wherein the plague shall be in him he shall be defiled; he is unclean: he shall dwell alone; without the camp shall his habitation be" (Lev. 13:46). When we consider the contrary practice that is between the higher house and the lower house, how we must blush and be ashamed! The practice of the higher house is still to be singing, "Holy, holy, holy Lord God of hosts"; our practice in this lower house is to undervalue Him. Our complaint should be the reproach of Him. If prayer could be exercised in heaven, the first prayer that we would raise when our feet were within the New Jerusalem would be, "Oh, precious Christ, pardon our undervaluings of Thee while we were below." Have you ever been constrained to say, "Who can shew forth all his praise?" (Ps. 106:2). David summoned all the angels in heaven, the souls of men, sun, moon, stars, beasts, and birds to show forth His praise. Have you ever known what it was to be convinced of the remissness of that duty? Have you seen the coldness of your love? The love of Christ involves an everlasting obligation of angels to praise Him. The grace of love in a Christian is under a twofold sweet mistake; it conceives every hour's absence from Christ to be an eternity, and an eternal presence to be but an hour. In Psalm 13:1, David questions, "How long wilt thou forget me, O LORD? for ever?" Let us also notice the words of Psalm 90:4: "For a thousand years in thy sight are but as yesterday when it is past, and as a watch in the night."

The words of our text describe a Christian with the dignity that is of more value than if he derived his pedigree from a thousand kings without an interrupted line. The word "therefore" in the text relates to the preceding verses. There are two sweet proofs and advantages of faith that make Christ precious to the believer. It is not said unto you, "He was precious," but "He *is* precious." There is a relative preciousness of Christ; He is precious to the believer. Yet, although you are not a believer, it is bad theology to conclude that you are not within the compass of the decree of election. Christ's preciousness to the believer is the foundation of our faith. I shall not dwell long on the excellent and royal dignity of a Christian—let me only say that there is one main excellence. Faith keeps a soul in constant communion with Christ, as we see in Ephesians 3:17: "That Christ may dwell in your hearts by faith." By the exercise of the grace of faith, Christ becomes our husband, our householder, and indweller with us.

It is a most sweet and desirable thing to have Christ dwelling in our hearts by faith and our souls dwelling with Christ by love; that is a sweet connection. Faith renders Christ more precious to a Christian than sense. This may be shown from faith's estimation of Christ; faith is built on His person. Sense looks on Christ's feet, hands, and His outward parts, but faith looks to His person. Faith looks to what Christ was before the world began, or before a cornerstone thereof was laid; sense alone looks to what Christ is at the present time. The grace of faith looks to the love that is in Christ's heart; sense alone looks to the smiles of His face. The estimation of faith is more constant than the estimation of sense; when Christ withdraws, sense loses its opinion. When faith would have wisdom, it consults with Christ, whose name is Wonderful and Counselor. Faith is as a sinew; when our sinew is cut, all our strength goes from us. Faith is a heroic grace; the crown of martyrdom is set upon the head of faith. A Christian that is under the excellence of this grace is a most humble Christian. By what law was boasting excluded? It was excluded by the law of faith. Paul presses this doctrine upon a Christian. Faith reveals to a Christian the excellence of God and makes the Christian take up his dwelling in the dust. Faith makes a Christian have two contrary motions—one to ascend, another to descend, so to speak. It keeps all the graces of the Spirit in motion (Eph. 3:17). Faith is the messenger of the soul; it reveals what Christ is. When faith sees Christ, it cries out, "It is good for me to be here!" Then love cries out, "Let us make a tabernacle."

Faith likewise mortifies corruption. Faith has a sweet influence on the work of mortification in a Christian. When Christ is revealed to a soul, the soul will cast away its idols as a menstruous cloth, and will cry out, "Whom have I in heaven but thee?" (Ps. 73:25). The soul is more where it loves than where it lives. Being justified by faith, we glory in tribulation. Faith holds out the crown on the right hand to a Christian, having this motto written on it, "He that persevereth to the end—shall be saved." We think Moses was never at rest until he was on the top of the mount, where he saw the Promised Land. Faith makes out the promises to a Christian. Faith is a life-sanctifying grace. When faith goes abroad in the world, good works are the handmaidens that accompany the queen. Faith has Rachel's eye and Leah's womb (Rom. 7:4). Faith has a sweet influence on our fruitfulness to Christ: "He that abideth in me, and I in him, the same bringeth forth much fruit" (John 15:5). (See also 1 Peter 2:5.) Faith is the spouse-like grace that marries Christ, and good works are the children which faith bears. Faith is superior; at the motion thereof all the rest go. Faith is an intelligent grace; it is called the "mystery of God" (Col. 2:2). Faith raises the soul to the highest pitch of reason. Faith is a heart-pacifying grace and peace is the daughter of faith (Rom. 5:1). Faith is the dove that brings the olive branch of peace in its mouth. Faith is an empty hand that receives the precious alms out of Christ's merits, and it is the instrument, or the channel, through which the blessed streams of life flow to us from Him. Faith is a heavenly plant, which will not grow in an impure heart. Faith is a heart-purifying grace (Acts 15:9); it is a virgin grace of a pure and heavenly soil.

Now, is faith truly such an excellent grace? Be pursuing after it. There is more guilt in the sin of unbelief than in the sin of murder: "It shall be more tolerable for the land of Sodom in the day of judgment, than for thee" (Matt. 11:24). The only sin mentioned is the sin of unbelief. If once you had the divine plant of faith engrafted in your souls, it would have a kind of omnipotence. Unbelief passes under the veil of humility, and so we embrace it rather than define it as a sin. Now the effects of the grace of faith make Christ precious to a soul; it reveals to a sinner the extract of His pardon and that He has been loved from all eternity: "Her sins, which are many, are forgiven; for she loved much" (Luke 7:47). A Christian that believes shall see Christ as He is.

Faith lets a Christian see the accomplishment of the promises. Faith is a sicker grace; hope is patient; love is impatient. Faith and hope are two sisters, but they differ in that hope looks at the excellence of the promise, faith at the certainty of it. Faith can suspend fruition, but love cannot. When Christ and a Christian are trifled together, faith and love grow apart. The best way to improve your necessity is to believe, although your faith be but in the swaddling clothes or rags, is to be content to wait a while, until you have gotten such a vigorous faith as will carry you with full sails to heaven. We have the reversion in heaven, when the lease of life is run out. A weak faith may be fruitful; the thief upon the cross had but a weak faith, yet how many precious clusters grew upon that vine (Luke 23:43)? Here was a young plant, but very fruitful. Faith is a grace that puts a commentary upon all the actions of Christ: when Christ seems to frown, faith will cry out, "I know the thoughts of His heart are not war, but grace to me." Faith can prophecy at midnight. Let a Christian yield to the premises of unbelief, but deny its conclusions. This may seem to men to be bad logic, but it is Christian theology. Did you not know what it was to use this medium for pardon: "Lord, pardon our iniquities, because they are great"? Christ strengthens love by revealing Himself. Faith reveals the period of our afflictions; love is written in illegible characters upon the cross, but if you consult with faith, you may read it. Faith and love are pleasant in their lives, and in their death they are not divided. Faith and love are the jewels wherewith Christ's bride is adorned. "Charity never faileth" (1 Cor. 13:8). In one sense, love is more excellent than faith. The spouse, when she goes to heaven, shall put off her jewel of faith, but shall never put off her jewel of love. In heaven the smoke of desire shall be ever bathing itself in the pure and pleasant fountain of glory. That which gives the higher house such an aroma is that the floor and windows are strewed with the leaves of the rose of Sharon. What joy shall we experience when Christ shall take us to His banquet house and kiss us with the kisses of His mouth!

When we shall come to heaven, we shall not know which of our senses shall be most taken up. Shall it be the eye? What joy to see there the orient brightness in the face of Christ; there you may see the lily and the rose mixed, white and ruddy (Song 5:10). Perhaps the ear shall be most taken up! The ear shall be filled with melody; what joy to the spouse, to hear Christ's voice, and to hear Him say, "My love, my dove, my undefiled" (Song 5:2). The smell shall be filled with sweet savor; what joy to smell that fragrance and perfume that comes from Christ! All His garments smell of myrrh, aloe, and cassia; the sweet breath of His Spirit blows on you and gives forth His scent as the wine of Lebanon. The taste shall be filled; oh, what joy there is to drink in the fountain of Christ—that is the water of life! The touch shall be filled; the saints shall be ever in the embraces of Christ! "Behold my hands and my feet, that it is I myself: handle me, and see; for a spirit hath not flesh and bones, as ye see me have" (Luke 24:39). That will be our work in heaven, when we shall arrive between the sweet arms that were once stretched out upon the cross. There shall be no such inhibition as that to Mary, when Christ said, "Touch me not" (John 20:17). If Christ's sufferings are so full of joy, what are His embraces?

What joy will there be at the saints' coronation, when they shall be eternally united to Christ Jesus! When we are in the glorious inheritance, what joy, what glory we will experience in the chambers of His presence! If the streets of this inheritance are of pure gold, what are the furniture and hangings? What is the cabinet of jewels? What are all the rarities of the world, the cost of pearls, yea, what are all things to this place? What a rich place must this be, where God will lay out all this cost! This is a purchase worth acquiring. What a spring that will be—a spring that will never dry up! I think I see the morning star appear; it is break of day already; who would, for the indulging of a lust, forfeit so glorious an inheritance? Lay the whole world in the scales with it—it is lighter than vanity. There is the vine flourishing, there are the pomegranates budding (Song 6:11). While we are sitting at the table, Christ's spikenard will send forth His smell (Song 1:12). There is the bed of love, there are the curtains of Solomon; there is the mountain of spices, and streams from Lebanon; there are the cherubim, not to keep out, but to welcome into paradise; there shall the saints be adorned as a bride with pearls of glory; there God will give us abundance of all that we can ask or think (Eph. 3:20). Such is the excellence of that celestial paradise, that if the angels would attempt to delineate it, they would stain and eclipse the glory of it. When you were sailing to hell, for we have both wind and tide to carry us there, did the north wind and south wind awaken? Have the gales of the Spirit blown upon you, and turned your course? Are you sailing to a new port? Then I am speaking to you all this while; this glorious inheritance shall be given to you. But if you are an old sinner, be assured Christ will never put the new wine of glory into old bottles.

We shall add no more. Now, unto the King eternal, immortal, and invisible, be everlasting praise. Amen.

SERMON 13

A Call to Improve the Brevity of Human Life

Behold, thou hast made my days as an handbreadth; and mine age is as nothing before thee: verily every man at his best state is altogether vanity. Selah.

—Psalm 39:5

It is a great point of Christianity for a man to consider himself; but surely it is an unpleasant exercise to accomplish a diligent search in that duty, so that before we find any reason to boast in ourselves, we recognize ourselves lying in sackcloth and ashes. Oh, how suitable and how convenient it is for all men to keep correspondence and fellowship with God, who is all-sufficient and self-sufficient! Among the many things that a Christian should know, he should know this main and advantageous thing: the brevity of his life, and of his appointed time upon the earth. We must study to know this more!

David, in the former verse of this psalm, was praying and sending up his supplication unto God; he desired to know the brevity and shortness of his life. "LORD," says David, "make me to know mine end, and the measure of my days, what it is: that I may know how frail I am" (Ps. 39:4). And here, in these words, he receives a return and answer to that prayer: "Behold thou hast made my days as an handbreadth" (v. 5). We conceive this handbreadth is the breadth of one of our hands; it is one of the measures we carry about with us; it is the breadth of four fingers, which relates to these four times of man's life: his infancy, his youth, his middle age, and his old age. It may also relate to these four times: his morning, mid-day, afternoon, and evening, all of which but amount to one day. "One generation passeth away, and another generation cometh: but the earth abideth for ever" (Eccl. 1:4). From that, David draws this conclusion: "Verily every man at his best state is altogether vanity"; and that every man is more in appearance than in reality. Furthermore, he puts a note of assertion to it, saying, "Selah," that he may let us see how important an affair this subject is to us, to know the brevity of our time.

The first observation we can make from the words is that as David is studying the brevity of his life upon the earth, he observes that the distinct knowledge of the brevity of our time on earth is a strong encouragement to us to bear the cross and afflicting dispensations we encounter with much patience and submission unto God. We must walk with Him, as it were, one hour, and have tribulation ten days (Rev. 2:10). "For here have we no continuing city, but we seek one to come. By him therefore let us offer the sacrifice of praise to God continually, that is, the fruit of our lips giving thanks to his name" (Heb. 13:14-15).

There are two reasons why the consideration of the brevity of our life puts us to the patient bearing of the cross. First, let us consider the approach of everlasting life and eternal happiness. We shall remember that before long we shall be admitted to sit down under the blessed shadow of the tree of life, with all the blessed company of holy angels and all the redeemed of the Lord, and we shall be there for all eternity. There, we shall perfectly enjoy all manner of soul-comforting pleasures and satisfying delights; certainly the hope of this will make the Christian sit down under his saddest afflictions and crosses and bear them with exceeding great patience and soul-submission. He will comfort himself in his darkest night. Oh, Christians, the day is coming and the time is approaching when all these fetters shall fall from your hands and these chains of iniquity shall fall from your feet, and you shall be set free. Then you shall be bidden to come and enjoy these soul-ravishing pleasures and delights that are above.

A second reason why the consideration of the brevity of life is an encouragement to us in cross-bearing is that a man, seeing the shortness of his time and the brevity of the afflictions he is bearing, will look to that precious day when his sun shall rise and never go down again, but shall be a perpetual and everlasting day. May not this encourage a Christian to bear his afflictions with much patience, seeing he can look through them all to that blessed day when he shall be afflicted no more, but shall rejoice with joy unspeakable and full of glory? Then, he shall not be under darkness at all, but shall dwell in light inaccessible. Do not be impatient under your sad afflictions and cross dispensations; the day is approaching and at hand when all your afflictions shall vanish and disappear. Oh, what a day shall it be when all these shadows shall be gone, and you shall be admitted to see God as He is, face to face! All your mourning and sorrowing for sin shall be heard no more; instead of the voice of mourning shall be heard the voice of joy and gladness! Dear Christians, prisoners of hope, and anticipators of the crown, comfort yourselves under your saddest crosses and afflictions with the hope and expectation of the approaching and drawing near of that day, even of that blessed day in which morning shall be far exalted above the reach of your unbelief, and all hypocrites shall be depressed low under the reach of their faith. In that day, the natural man shall be depressed low beneath the reach of his presumptions. Then let your desires be set upon; long for that day! Dear Christians, be persuaded that though all your days should be spent in heaviness and in the bitterness of your spirits, yet there is a day coming that shall make up all our losses; then there shall be a cup of everlasting joy and gladness presented to you and put in your hand. That day shall be an excellent day! Certainly the joy of that day shall be unspeakable.

A second observation concerning the words of the text is that a Christian may obtain the knowledge of the brevity of life even while here on this earth. David makes this clear when he says, "Thou turnest man to destruction" (Ps. 90:3); furthermore, what is man? He is as the grass of the field, which "in the morning it flourisheth, and groweth up; in the evening it is cut down, and withereth" (v. 6). This truth is likewise clear from Jacob's practice (Gen. 47:9). But perhaps some will say, what need is there to press that so much; for who does not know that their days upon the earth are short? Yet I say, if the thoughts of it were deeply engraven on our hearts, as with a pen of iron, or the point of a diamond, such that they might rise with us in the morning and lie down with us at night, it would be a spur in our side, putting us to the working out of that work that is of our everlasting soul-concern.

We shall briefly propose to you the advantages that come to a Christian by carrying about with him the thoughts of the brevity of his life.

First, it would provoke and stir up the Christian to a heavenly mindedness, minding those things that are above. It is clear, says the apostle, "Here we have no continuing city" (Heb. 13:14); and what effect has that wrought? "By him therefore let us offer the sacrifice of praise to God continually, that is, the fruit of our lips giving thanks to his name" (v. 15). Certainly the consideration of the brevity of our lives is good for this very same respect. If there were no other considerations to remind us of eternity, it would be more than sufficient to prove that the thoughts of the brevity and shortness of our time would be good. Therefore, since it is so, we should be longing and setting our affections and desires on the things that are above, and setting our whole hearts upon that glorious and precious pearl that shines so brightly; as in 1 Thessalonians 4:17, where we read, "Then we which are alive and remain shall be caught up together with them in the clouds, to meet the Lord in the air: and so shall we ever be with the Lord." Oh, long for that day, and let your hearts covet the excellent things that are above in heaven.

A second advantage that comes by engaging the thoughts on the brevity of time is that it will cause great sobriety and moderation in a Christian's pursuit after the worldly pleasures and delights of this present life. This is clear from that command given in 1 Thessalonians 5:8: "But let us, who are of the day, be sober, putting on the breastplate of faith and love; and for an helmet, the hope of salvation." If the thoughts of the brevity of our life were engraven upon our hearts, why then would we vex ourselves with the torturing cares of this life that do not at all profit us? Oh, why do we weary ourselves in the fire, which is but vexation of spirit and vanity? Oh, Christians, let now your moderation in the pursuit of the things of this world be made known to all men; for behold, the Lord is at hand to take vengeance on the wicked with furious rebukes of flaming fire and eternal excommunication from the righteous Judge.

A third advantage that comes to a Christian by having distinct thoughts and apprehensions of the brevity of his life is that it provokes him to much seriousness and diligence in going about his duties; it urges him to be diligent and watchful in his going toward that blessed rest that is prepared for all the redeemed of the Lord.

It was the argument of our blessed Lord Jesus: "I must work the works of him that sent me, while it is day: the night cometh, when no man can work" (John 9:4). Then, dear Christians, while it is called today, stir up yourselves for the working out of your salvation. We do not know how suddenly the shadows of that everlasting evening may be stretched out over us, when we will receive that summons from God to remove hence and be gone. Are you not afraid lest you be banished? Do you not fear that the night will approach before your work is perfected? Yea, I am afraid that many shall have to begin that great work of their souls' salvation when death shall summon them to appear before God's terrible tribunal and judgment seat. Oh, be afraid and stand in awe, lest the night be hard by and at hand.

Then, "Let us eat and drink, for tomorrow we shall die," say the Epicureans, who make use of this argument to stir up their delights after their lusts; but let us be watchful and diligent, for we know not if tomorrow we must die. Furthermore, be more in consideration of the things that are before you than of these things that are already behind. Think more on what is before than what has passed, and "press toward the mark for the prize of the high calling of God in Christ Jesus" (Phil. 3:14).

There is a fourth advantage that comes to us by the consideration of the brevity of life. With this knowledge, the believer comes to the knowledge of that state wherein man was once created. Surely he was created after a most glorious image, a most noble pattern and copy, even according to the most blessed and glorious image of God; but man, having a woeful and cursed design to be as God and like to Him, fell from that blessed state, and all his posterity in him, and he made himself and us subject to God's wrath and eternal indignation for evermore. But blessed be God eternally, for He has revealed a new and living way for us to escape the curse that has lain upon all mankind for sin.

There is also a fifth advantage that comes when we consider the brevity of life engraven upon the heart. It is a great help to mortify three deadly idols that have great power over us. First, it is an excellent help to mortify the great idol of faith. Second, it will help you to mortify the idol of love that rules in you. Finally, it is a help to mortify the idol of fear. The idol of faith is when we trust in anything more than in God: "Put not your trust in princes, nor in the son of man, in whom there is no help" (Ps. 146:3). The idol of love is when we love anything more than God: "Cease ye from man, whose breath is in his nostrils" (Isa. 2:22). The idol of fear is when we fear anything more than God: "Who art thou, that thou shouldest be afraid of a man that shall die, and of the son of man which shall be made as grass?" (Isa. 51:12). The thoughts of the brevity of our life and appointed time will mortify these great idols.

There is a sixth advantage that attends a person who has thoughts of the brevity of his time engraven upon his heart. He may win to a holy admiration and divine astonishment at the condescending love of Jesus Christ. We read in Job 14:1 that "man that is born of a woman is of few days and full of trouble." Oh, what a wonder is it to see God delighting Himself in the dust of His feet and making them the object of His love, who dwell in the dust! Surely this is a mystery which we cannot comprehend.

A seventh advantage is that God makes use of this argument to provoke Himself to have compassion and mercy upon a believer. Surely this is God's way; and we must rather wonder at it than inquire and debate why it is so. This is clear from Psalm 78:38, which says, "But he, being full of compassion, forgave their iniquity, and destroyed them not: yea, many a time turned he his anger away, and did not stir up all his wrath."

There is a third observation that you must notice from these words. The brevity and shortness of our days and appointed time are surely determined by God so that we cannot at all go beyond the time appointed for us. This is clear in Job 4:14-16: "If a man die, shall he live again? all the days of my appointed time will I wait, till my change come. Thou shalt call, and I will answer thee: thou wilt have a desire to the work of thine hands. For now thou numberest my steps: dost thou not watch over my sin?" From these words, we understand that the brevity of our time is a great advantage unto us; for who can charge their Maker with folly? Surely, He does all things well, and to purpose. Though we question this dispensation, yet we must believe that the day is coming when we shall subscribe this to them all: "He hath done all things well" (Mark 7:37). Oh, long for the day when that shall come to pass. Certainly there are none before His throne but those who desire to justify Him and acknowledge that He has done all things well. Oh, that we could learn to be silent and acquiesce ourselves in the performance of all

His dispensations! Oh, that we could learn to put our mouths in the dust, whatsoever God doth to us; for we may be persuaded that "all things work together for good to them that love God" and delight themselves in Him (Rom. 8:28)!

The brevity of our lives displays the great love and matchless delight that God has toward sinners. He is longing for the day when all the redeemed of the Lord shall be with Him, to remain with Him forever and ever, to enjoy all delights and all manner of soul pleasures. Oh, when shall that day come, when we shall be brought out from this earthly tabernacle of clay and shall enter our possession in that blessed tabernacle not made with hands? Oh, we long for that day! Yet, we should be submissive unto God's dispensation and good pleasure; we should not challenge Him for the brevity of our lifetime here. Many of us may say that we have not received a short lifetime from the Lord, but that we have made a short life unto ourselves; for it is said that wicked men shall not live half their days. Certainly, these may think their life and appointed time short, whose heaven and joy is ended when their lives are ended. But those who have made use of their lives for this end, to entertain communion and fellowship with God—surely these shall rejoice with joy unspeakable and full of glory. Now we shall desire to have our eyes failing with looking up, until that day shall come, when our blessed Lord Jesus shall come in the clouds. Oh, remember the excellence of that precious and blessed day, when we shall be exalted above all our infirmities; then there shall be no unbelief following us. Let the thoughts of that precious and blessed day comfort your hearts under all your afflictions, and wait with patience for your eternal redemption. Amen.

SERMON 14

The Christian's Case and Exercise in the Night of Desertion

By night on my bed I sought him whom my soul loveth; I sought him, but I found him not.

—Song of Solomon 3:1

Never-interrupted fellowship and communion with God is a fruit of the land above. There is no constancy of our fellowship with God while we are here below, by reason of the corruption within us. There is not one day that passes wherein we are not in the same frame and temper of spirit, but you can comfort yourselves with the song in Isaiah 30:26, where it is said, "The light of the moon shall be as the light of the sun, and the light of the sun shall be sevenfold, as the light of seven days, in the day that the LORD bindeth up the breach of his people, and healeth the stroke of their wound." You may cast up your eyes to heaven and long for the day when these shadows shall be over. Then you shall enjoy perfect and full communion with God.

Now this inconstancy of communion and fellowship with God while we are here is clear if we compare this verse with the previous chapter, where the spouse was "sitting under his shadow," and had communion and fellowship with Him. "He brought me to the banqueting house, and his banner over me was love," and she was sick of love to Him (Song 2:4). But behold, here is a remarkable change of the blessed lot and condition that she was in; she is in a most sad condition, deserted. Christ is not only away, but He is so far away that she cannot find Him and she does not know where to seek Him.

Now the first thing that we shall observe from our text is this: as long as we are within the borders of time and traveling in these tents of mortality, we will never obtain a constant and uninterrupted fellowship with God. We need not take much time to prove this; it is clear from many sad experiences. We shall propose some reasons why there is no constant fellowship with God here. First, His people may be provoked to long for that endless and blessed life when time will be swallowed up by eternity and our corruption shall put on incorruption, and this vile body of ours shall be raised a glorious body. Then eternity will be spent without one moment of interruption. Oh, Christians, comfort yourselves in the hope and expectation of the approach of that blessed day, when you will enjoy complete and full communion and fellowship with God. You will be admitted to eat of the apples of the tree of life that grows in the midst of the paradise of God, of which, once you eat, certainly you shall never hunger any more. If we did enjoy one moment of real fellowship and communion with God, surely we should be ready to cry out, "It is good for us to be here: and let us make three tabernacles" (Luke 9:33). Dear Christians, did you ever enjoy communion and correspondence with God so much that you were constrained to long for the day when you will enjoy full fellowship with Him without any interruption? But Christ draws a veil to cover His own face, so that we cannot enjoy Him fully, with the intent that we may long for the day when we shall see Him as He is, without any veil.

There is a second reason why God orders that the Christian should not have constant fellowship with God here. Some graces in the Christian most eminently appear when they are under such a case, while they know not where to find Christ. These graces are the grace of faith, the grace of patience, and the grace of love. These three graces would not well appear if it were not so. As we used to say, stars appear most in darkness; so these graces appear most when the soul is under desertion, knowing not where to find Christ. In this situation, faith is put to exercise; it appears most when it lacks light. The graces of patience and love are also put to exercise, and shine most brightly in such a sad dispensation.

A third reason God orders it so, is that we may value communion and correspondence with Him at a higher rate and put a greater elimination upon it. This is clear from the spouse's practice, as he says "I opened to my beloved; but my beloved had withdrawn himself" (Song 5:6); He withdrew Himself from her so that she would learn to put a greater account upon His presence.

Fourth, we must be strongly convinced of the freedom of His grace toward us, in bestowing these things upon us. Oh, Christians, study more to know that all that you receive is out of His free love, and for no merit and deserving in us. We have nothing to commend ourselves of but infirmities, but be assured that He with whom we have to do is God, not man.

There is a second observation from the words, and it is this: there is an insufficiency in all things here below, even in the graces of the Spirit, to satisfy the Christian when Christ is away. This is clear in the bride's practice; she had the graces of love, faith, seeking, and patience, and much of the grace of hope; yet, there is a *Him* whom she misses. "By night on my bed I sought him whom my soul loveth: I sought him, but I found him not" (Song 3:1). Oh, but there are many here who may sit down in shame and cover their faces, because they do not show an insufficiency in the things of this present world! Ah, such are not much in the pursuit after Jesus Christ. I am persuaded that most of our pursuit is only after the things of this present life. Oh, we do not know what it is to miss Christ, because we never knew what it was to have His presence! But surely it speaks much of that blessed exercise, to see much of the excellence that is in Jesus Christ—an exercise that makes Christians undervalue all earthly things and all things other than Christ. Oh, the excellence that is in Christ Jesus makes the Christian not rest upon the graces of the Spirit until they obtain Christ, though they put a high estimation on them. All our desires ought to be set on Him who is the uncreated, and not on things created. This is clear in Mary's practice—there is a *Him* whom she misses, and was pursuing after; "They have taken away my LORD, and I know not where they have laid him" (John 20:13). Oh, what will satisfy a Christian's love, if it is real in his heart? Nothing will satisfy him but the noble object Jesus Christ, who is the desire of nations, and the bright and morning star.

Third, a mark and evidence of one that is a real seeker of God is one's sensibility when he misses Christ's fellowship and company. A real seeker of God can give a direct account of Christ's motions, of His comings and goings; he can distinguish well between His absence and presence.

There are two things that make Christians undervalue the enjoyment of Jesus Christ. The first is the lack of the absolute necessity of having Christ. I think there are many here that were never persuaded of the necessity of embracing Jesus Christ. Oh, are there not many of us whose heart-language is this: "We are lords; we will come no more unto thee" (Jer. 2:31)? The reason is because we do not see our necessity of having Christ. Oh, if your eyes were opened, you would see and be convinced that it is your concern and to your advantage to have Jesus Christ as your advocate at the bar of justice.

A second thing that influences our undervaluing of the enjoyment of Jesus Christ is the lack of faith in the precious, endless, and unsearchable perfections that are found in Christ. Oh, if a Christian knew what a one He is, how glorious and how beautiful He is, surely he would fall in love with Him more and would put a higher estimation and account upon communion and correspondence with Christ! He is a lovely and desirable object. He is altogether lovely and all true spiritual desires are in Him. Oh, what a one is He! Certainly we cannot tell; He is "white and ruddy, the chiefest among ten thousand" (Song 5:10). Angels and men could not describe such a glorious object as He is, but, alas, we must lament that He is unknown to many of us. Oh, if we were wise, we would behold the Almighty; if we were conscious of our great need of Him, we might embrace His offer of peace to us and delight ourselves in Him.

The fourth thing we shall observe from the words is that a Christian may seek things from God, and yet not get a return to his prayers; according to the words in Matthew 7:7, "Ask, and it shall be given you; seek, and ye shall find; knock, and it shall be opened unto you." But this observation is far different from these Scriptures. We shall not give the reasons why it is so; we only say that God is wise and righteous in all His doings, and knows the reasons for His actions. However, one reason why many have sought and yet have not been heard, nor met with an answer and return of their prayers from Him is because they undervalued the enjoyments and precious manifestations of His grace towards them. We conclude that He does all things well, according to that testimony of Him in Mark 7:37, "And were beyond measure astonished, saying, He hath done all things well." Surely, when we shall be about to pass over the lintels of the doors of everlasting eternity, when we shall be standing on the farthest line of time, ready to step into eternity, we shall be constrained to leave on record that He doeth all things well. We shall then be deeply convinced of the fact that He has done all things well.

"By night on my bed I sought him." These words may be understood that even in the night she sought Him on her bed, or it may be otherwise understood that she was seeking Him, holding out her affliction; and so the words may be rendered, in the sad time of affliction, "I sought him whom my soul loveth." Love will make Christians break off their night's rest for pursuing Him whom their soul loves; there will be a holy impatience and restlessness in their spirits until they are brought to embrace Him. Oh, Christians, I ask you, even all your consciences: have you ever known what it was to have your night's rest broken off because you found Christ absent and were put to an earnest pursuit after Him? Was your spirit ever restless within you until you found Him whom your soul loves? I fear I may say upon good grounds that this is an unknown thing to most of us; most of us do not know what Christ's presence and fellowship mean because we never had it and we never enjoyed it. Therefore, we cannot tell what it means. Is that not a sad evidence and forerunner of the fact that we shall never at all be acquainted with His fellowship?

Be afraid, you who are secure-hearted, and stand in awe against sin, lest God be upon you before you are aware, lest He tear you like a lion in pieces, with none to deliver you out of His hand. I think many of us may say that we never pursued one night after Jesus Christ, but we always pursue after our idols. We need not make much search of the number of days that we have been pursuing after Christ; we need make no search of the number of nights that we have been in that suitable exercise. But make it your main design and upshot of all your accounts to pursue after Jesus Christ and to study, by all means, a blessed conformity to His image. What will provoke your hearts to close with Christ and His offer? What can persuade you to make your interest sure in Him? Oh, be assured, one day you shall regard it as your everlasting concern to be Christians indeed, not only in the *letter*, but in the *spirit*. Believe it, the day is approaching when you shall rue the day that you were born, if you are not found among those who have received the offer of Jesus Christ. You must count it as your main design in this day to account Christ precious. I am afraid that there are many here to whom Christ was never truly precious.

Oh, that you were provoked and stirred up to make peace with God so that He may make peace with you! Oh, that you were provoked to seek after God! Dear Christians, this exhortation to seek God shall not be given to you for long. It is not long before this treaty of peace will be broken up between God and you, and you will no longer have access to make peace with Him. It is not long before we shall all be gone; we shall be sifted before God's tribunal and judgment seat and shall there receive a just sentence, according to our doings here on this earth. Oh, then study to seek after God while you are here. I think it would be more suitable for us to seek after Him than for Him, even God, to take so much pain in seeking after us. Oh, what admirable love is this that He, even He, should take so much pain for our conversion, as if He should obtain advantage to Himself by so doing. It is a mystery that the cedar of Lebanon should say unto the thistle therein, "Come and suit me!" Is this not a mystery, that the precious Christ should be pleased to suit wretched sinners? Surely it is a matchless mystery; and surely if we would have seven days to behold it, and to search it out, we would be as wise at the beginning of these days as at the end of them.

Furthermore, I would say this to all those that have not been seeking God all their days: there is a day coming when the almighty God shall come with ten thousand of His angels, to take vengeance on all those that know Him not and obey not the voice of His gospel that is now offered freely unto you. Unbelievers, you must embrace this precious offer and delay your repentance no longer! What a dreadful thing it will be when you see the Son of God clothed with fiery indignation against you! You shall see Him who has pronounced blessings upon so many, ready to pronounce that sentence of eternal exile and banishment "from the presence of the Lord, and from the glory of his power" (2 Thess. 1:9). "Depart from me, ye cursed, into everlasting fire, prepared for the devil and his angels" (Matt. 25:41). Then you will be compelled quickly to obey that sentence. There shall be no access for you to delay that sentence. Oh, you must believe that a few days, or at least a few years, will bring you to an unalterable and unchangeable state; it shall not be long until we shall all have taken up our lodging and all of us must either abide in an eternity of pain or in an eternity of joy; there is no other place for any of us; we must go to heaven or to hell. We shall say no more; but since it is so, it would be wise to pursue Him in the enjoyment of whom you will have life everlasting. Amen.

SERMON 15

The Time of Life: A Time of Trouble

Man that is born of a woman is of few days and full of trouble.
—Job 14:1

What a multitude of fears and desires possess the spirits of men since man lost that original unity of affection wherewith he was beautified, having all his desires concentrated and confined upon that blessed and precious object, God! However, since he lost that unspeakable dignity, his desires and hopes have been divided into many channels, he being taken up in these endless and irrational pursuits after unprofitable things. If men who are thus exercised would cast their eyes towards the words that we have now read, "Man that is born of a woman is of few days and full of trouble," it would no doubt abate much of that vigor and strength which he has in the pursuit after such things. It would likewise extenuate his zeal, but without knowledge. For to what end shall men vex themselves in the very fire, for that which is vanity? Furthermore, if it were possible that the whole creation should conspire to give unto you complete satisfaction and that perfect delight which is theirs, yet in the fullness of your sufficiency in these things, you would be in straits. A short moment of time will make an everlasting divorce between you and these things; for when you shall be passing into your long and unchangeable home, then these things wherewith you solace yourselves so much, shall take wings and flee away. It is an undeniable truth that in all points, as we came, so shall we go. What profit is there that we should labor for the wind? We think all things that are within time have no doubt so much vexation, toil, and turmoil accompanying them, both in the pursuit and possession of them, that if such a supposition were possible, men could live an eternity with them; yet, would we not be miserable creatures?

This no doubt condemns the vanity of many in these days, notwithstanding their days are but few, man being but a passing and transient shadow. These things after which we pursue have much anxiety in them, and so little satisfaction; but how much of our time is taken up in scraping together something whereon we may build our hope and satisfy our appetite? But we may say, what a poor thing is it to behold living shadows? Is it not a wretched pursuit to seek after dead shadows, as a man walking in a long gallery, delighting himself with images; but oh, when that image shall be presented, the image of death, when it shall begin to sit down upon your eyelids, then how shall all those idols that were portrayed upon the walls, wherewith you used to solace yourselves, lose their luster? "Also when they shall be afraid of that which is high, and fears shall be in the way, and the almond tree shall flourish, and the grasshopper shall be a burden, and desire shall fail: because man goeth to his long home, and the mourners go about the streets" (Eccl. 12:5). Even they whose hearts are most wedded to the world shall then be divorced from it, when they shall be convinced that all things here are but labor and vexation of spirit.

There is nothing that can satisfy the immortal spirit of man; nothing here below can satisfy. God has so ordered it in the depth of His unsearchable wisdom, that all things below Himself are unable to produce satisfaction in man. He has made all these lower springs to run dry and has famished all the gods of the earth. This is a part of His blessed and precious designs, that the poor of the people may delight themselves in Him, the eternal admiration of angels, and that blessed object upon whom all the desires of our brethren above are confined. Oh, that we were persuaded to put our amen upon that glorious cloud of witnesses who have gone before us, confessing that "here have we no continuing city" (Heb. 13:14). They were made under a divine impression of that one truth, that their days upon the earth were as a shadow and that they must suddenly vanish and pass away. Then, what is man's life? It is but a handbreadth, as David says, which is one of the least of the geometrical measures. The four-finger-breadth takes up the whole life of man, which either relates unto that four-fold estate of man (infancy, youth, manhood, and old age) or to that four-fold condition of man (morning, noon, afternoon, and night), which all amount to one day; for in the morning man flourishes and is green; but at evening, he is cut down and flees away. Yea, the life of man is so short in continuance that, in comparison with the duration of the world, it is nothing. The duration of the world, which is not much, is a little eternity in comparison with the duration of man. This is clear from Ecclesiastes 1:4, which says, "One generation passeth away, and another generation cometh: but the earth abideth for ever." The life of man is so short that in comparison with the endless eternity of God, it vanishes into nothing, as is clear from Psalm 39:5: "Thou hast made my days as an handbreadth." They seemed to be something when they were nothing, in comparison with his days; but when he constructed a comparison between the *eternity* of God and the duration of his life, he adds that his days are "as nothing before thee"; and, as one said well, "Man's life being but a point, is drawn in that immense line of eternity past unto eternity after." There is not one among a thousand who are living under a divine impression of these two truths: the brevity of our life, which is shown in the words of our text, and the woeful and unspeakable anxiety wherewith the life of man is accompanied as long as he is in the valley of Baca.

We confess that Christians should have these truths engraven upon their own spirits as "with a pen of iron, and with the point of a diamond" (Jer. 17:1). Oh, what a divine underestimation of all things here below might he attain? It is easy for a man that meditates much on this point, the brevity of life, to see an end of all perfection here. There is not much that will take up that man who expects shortly to be seized by death, the universal king of terrors. Do you shortly expect to hear the truth confirmed with the oath of an angel, with his hand lifted up toward heaven, that "time shall be no more"? Were you not frustrated that you have been taken up in a pursuit after the things that do not satisfy?

But before we speak about the advantages you have by meditating upon these two great truths, we shall only say, as the scope of this holy man here who makes use of this as an argument with God to provoke Him to this, that he would not enter into judgment with God.

His first argument is in these words, "Man that is born of a woman is of few days and full of trouble." He seems to ask the Lord, "Why shouldest Thou enter into judgment with such a person?" The strength of his argument no doubt lies in the words—as if Job would have said, "Man, who is such a frail and brittle creature, is not a fit object to contend with omnipotent power. If Thou wouldst enter into judgment, Thou must choose to Thyself some convenient party; but what is man, before Him who is infinite? Oh, it would be but a poor honor to overcome such a worm; therefore, do rather condescend to execute mercy, than to persevere in the exercise of justice." Second, man is such a miserable and frail creature, compassed about with so many necessities and wants, that Thou mayest not enter into judgment with him, to render him more miserable. Man is miserable enough in himself, without adding to it the fact that God should enter into judgment with him. Third, it is convenient and necessary that to those that are in misery, their friends should show them pity. He then desires to have his recourse to Him, as to his best friend, wishing "the blessing of him that was ready to perish came upon me," that He, on whose head all the blessings of those that have been separated from their brethren have come, might likewise bless him.

Now we would press this upon you: it is attainable to acquire a distinct knowledge of the brevity of life and of the many anxious evils wherewith life is compassed, as is clear from these words in the text. Job attained a full persuasion of this truth, and so may we. But to proceed, we think if we could give a perfect definition of man, we could give it in no terms more suitable than this: "Man…is of few days and full of trouble." Therefore David, when proposing the question, "What is man?" (Ps. 144:3), gives this as the most suitable answer, "Man is like to vanity: his days are as a shadow that passeth away" (v. 4). Here is the complete motto of man; he is short in continuance and large in possession of trouble; though we confess God has manifested much of His infinite love to us in joining these two together. If man's days be full of trouble, He has made them short in continuance. In this, no doubt, He has given unto us a divine confirmation of the blessed truth that "he doth not afflict willingly nor grieve the children of men" (Lam. 3:33).

Now that you are persuaded to advance in the knowledge and assurance of the brevity of your life, we shall propose several advantages. First, the believer lying under an impression of the brevity of his life, knowing that before long the pins of his tabernacle must be loosed and that he shall be constrained to call the dust his mother, and the worms and corruption his brethren and sisters—how diligent will he be in making his peace sure, through Christ's atoning blood! Epicureans did improve this notion of the brevity of life to persuade people to a more earnest pursuit after their sensual lusts, saying to themselves, "Let us eat and drink, for tomorrow we must die." Might not they that have hope of eternal life, who know that they have a spirit of eternal existence, ought not they rather say, "Let us watch and be sober, for the end of all things is at hand, and we know not but tomorrow we must die"? Oh, that you were taught so much divine policy as not to boast yourselves of tomorrow, for you know not what a day may bring forth.

This night may make a separation between you and time. Some of you, before the dawning of the next morning, may pass into eternity, either with pain or with joy; and no doubt we have but twelve hours wherein we may work, and then, night comes wherein no man can work. Yea, our blessed Lord Jesus who did indeed improve His time to notable advantage, that He was to continue but a short time, made Him diligent in the accomplishment of that great design. He said, "I must work the works of him that sent me, while it is day: the night cometh, when no man can work" (John 9:4). There was a divine necessity upon Him, "I must work"; the reasoning He gave was, "The night cometh, when no man can work." Oh, why do you stand idle at the eleventh hour of the day? There are many of you that have not yet begun to accomplish that great and serious work of the salvation of your souls. If that voice should be heard sounding in your ears this night, "Awake ye dead, and come to judgment," would not your knees smite one against another? With what confidence and hope could you appear before Him, who is that impartial Judge, who judges not after the seeing of the eye, and reproves not after the hearing of the ear, but judges righteous judgment? Who speaks of Him, who is made quick of understanding, in the fear of the Lord? I conceive that which makes that grand idol of ease to be so much adored and that we proclaim so much indulgence to ourselves, being loath to do violence to ourselves, is that we do not live in the consideration of the words, "Man that is born of a woman is of few days and full of trouble."

The second advantage that a Christian may have by considering the brevity of life is that it would be a compendious way to acquire much submission under our most sad and bitter dispensations to be living, knowing that we must soon die. We may spend our forty years in a wilderness, in the bitterness of our spirits; yet shortly our life must come to a close, and we shall have a universal and everlasting separation from all our miseries. David comforted himself under his trouble with the consideration of the brevity of his life; and the apostle Paul, in the consideration of the same, said, "Yet the time is short," and, "The fashion of this world passeth away" (1 Cor. 7:29, 31). This is compared with the third verse, where he says, "They that weep, as though they wept not" (v. 30); this is a mystery that men of the world do not understand, that men should weep, and yet should weep as if they were not weeping; for all their sorrows are mitigated with hope. The very hope and expectation of heaven infinitely compasses the most sad and bitter things that they encounter while they are traveling here below.

It was indeed a notable saying of old—a person who willingly dissolved or bestowed all his inheritance and gave away all his possessions, when asked what he did reserve to himself said, "No more than *hope*"; he had no more reserved to himself than the hope of eternal life and the everlasting fruition of God. With this knowledge, he could solace himself in the midst of all his anxieties. What more could he desire? We desire that you "comfort one another with these words" (1 Thess. 4:18) under all your afflictions, that there is a glorious result and issue of all your travail here below. Heaven shall be a sweet recompense for all your toil. We can scarcely commend it until we are there, sense and enjoyment being better resolvers of the blessedness of heaven than faith and hope, which sees things but through a prospect, and darkly through a glass.

A third advantage that a Christian may have from the consideration of the fact that our days are short, is this: we may be persuaded to much moderation in our use, and likewise in our pursuit after these things in a present world. This is clearly supported in Philippians 4:5, "Let your moderation be known unto all men." He gives this reason for it: "The Lord is at hand." This is likewise clear from the text, "But the end of all things is at hand: be ye therefore sober, and watch unto prayer" (1 Peter 4:7). This is a little water which we must mix in our wine, lest the ferment thereof disturb our heads. But when we have most affluence and abundance of the things below, and when the world and pleasure thereof smile upon us, if a Christian would keep himself free from the snares of the world and be taught that divine gospel mystery, so that he may use the world, but not abuse it, he would be much in reflection upon the fact that his time here is short. If this precious and critical truth were solidly believed, certainly we would understand more of a holy apathy and divine indifference in having and possessing things, or in lacking all things below, to use but not to abuse them. We must ever strive to keep a loose grip of all our possessions, so that we may freely let them go whenever it shall please God to call for them. Surely, if we exercised ourselves more by faith in the knowledge of the brevity of our lives, our hearts would not be so addicted to the world and the things that are in it. We must lament through all eternity that we do so often delight ourselves in the lying vanities of this earth.

Fourth, consider that it is an excellent and compendious way for a Christian not to have his confidence of hope reposed or fixed on man, neither to fear him nor love him above that which is convenient. If we were living with the constant knowledge that man is a passing and transient creature, why would we put our confidence and trust in him? The Psalmist expresses this in Psalm 146:3, 4, saying, "Put not your trust in princes, nor in the son of man, in whom there is no help. His breath goeth forth, he returneth to his earth; in that very day his thoughts perish." David gives a perfect account of all men when he says, "Surely men of low degree are vanity" (Ps. 62:9). There are many that will not debate that men of low degree are vanity, focusing on empty things; but then he adds, "And men of high degree are a lie: to be laid in the balance, they are altogether lighter than vanity." Any advantage that high men have over low men consists in this, which indeed is no advantage, that a poor man is "vanity," but a rich man is "a lying vanity," being something in appearance, but nothing in reality. Therefore, we should not hope in them, neither need we fear them, for "why shouldest thou fear him, whose breath goeth out, and doth not again return," and who shortly must be made as the grass of the field? And why would you love him who is but a flower and a vanishing shadow? "Cease from man, whose breath is in his nostrils; for wherein is he to be accounted of"; and believe it, if we were more in the study of these precious truths, I am persuaded that it would be exceedingly conducive to our advantage and our soul's everlasting concern.

A fifth advantage that a Christian may have from considering the brevity of life is that it is an excellent way to attain spiritual mortification of all things here below; the Christian ought to be dying daily to all things that are within the borders of this short time, which only are of momentary concern and advantage. What advantage does a rich man have over a poor man? "When goods increase, they are increased that eat them: and what good is there to the owners thereof, saving the beholding of them with their eyes?" (Eccl. 5:11). The man that is a passer-by may have the satisfaction of beholding an increase of riches, though he is not a possessor and enjoyer of them; then what advantage can they afford to you, seeing they are but passing and transient, and not permanent? Before long you shall be constrained to part with them; there shall be an everlasting separation between them and you. You may delight yourselves in them while you are here, but it is impossible for you to carry any of these things with you beyond your grave. If the Christians of this generation were persuaded of this reality, they might lose many of the infinite and insatiable desires they have for the things of this world. Most of humanity are like horse-leeches, who always cry forth, "Give, give"; they are like "the grave; and the barren womb" (Prov. 30:16), which can never be satisfied. We do not know whether a rich man has a greater fullness than a poor man; we read in Proverbs 23:5, speaking of riches, "Wilt thou set thine eyes upon that which is not?" Will you look upon these things which do not have a being? Certainly, they take to themselves wings and quickly vanish and pass away, and are not found. Why should these vanities and passing trifles that are of no continuance be so much taken up in the spirit and souls of men?

Now we shall speak a word concerning the complete and full vexation, wherewith the life of man is encompassed, as long as he is here below, traveling in these tents of mortality. The words that are here rendered "full of trouble," may be likewise rendered, "satisfaction with commission"; man is in a perpetual agitation, tossing to and fro. Now, since it is appointed by a divine decree and sentence which cannot be repealed, that man's life is full of trouble, we would once for all persuade you to derive blessedness and satisfaction from these higher springs, and not from any of these lower springs. The things that are here below are full of trouble. Surely I cannot utter it; that unspeakable vexation of the world compensates that unspeakable satisfaction that is in God! If you could see Him in His beauty, surely we would not need much oratory to persuade you to divorce these unprofitable worldly things; there is such an attractive and unspeakable virtue in the glory and transcendent beauty of the face of our blessed Lord Jesus that no person, be who they will, even his greatest enemies, would not dare but love Him when once they truly beheld Him. Dear Christians, since your life is so short and so full of trouble, then study earnestly to walk, with much divine submission, under every cross dispensation that you encounter. It is so ordered and appointed of God that we cannot reverse it or call it back again; but no doubt, when we cast our eyes upon these words, we are constrained to propose that desire to God.

If only it were with us as in the days of old. Man was once placed in such a blessed and perfect estate that he had exemption from common miseries; but the opening of a door to sin did likewise open a door to misery, these being two inseparable companions; we may say that they are unpleasant in their lives, though in their deaths they are not divided. Believe it, if you want to crucify sin, God will graciously condescend to give unto you a suspension from misery, a suspension which will never be recalled, and make you the adopted children of His Father; He will present you holy, without any spot or blemish, before Him in love. There will be no access for any misery to come near you, for all sighing and sorrow is wiped away from the eyes of those that are in heaven. Believe it, there shall be no reduction of that blessed decree which shall pass upon us, in which we shall be declared heirs of the grace of life, and shall be ordained to enter into the inheritance of that everlasting rest that is purchased unto us through the blood of Jesus Christ, who is the mediator and days-man between God and man.

Oh, that we were breathing more after that blessed state of life! Most of you are walking from one degree of misery to another! Your life indeed is full of trouble, but it is only the forerunner of the intolerable pains that are approaching you, except you make your peace with God; and, once your peace is made sure in Him, you need not complain of the brevity and shortness of your time, nor of the troublesomeness of it. It is a great complaint among those that are strangers to God, that their life is so short; no doubt, we may give you a dispensation for this. You may think your life short, or rather, you may think your heaven, that petty and dreary heaven, short; though, we confess those that are well-employed do groan under nothing so much as the length of their life. As Seneca said, "We have not received a short life, but we have made it so." Oh, be persuaded once to flee from the hazard wherein you stand, that, before the strong man shall fail and the keepers of the house wax weak, before the shadows of death shall sit down on our eyelids, and our eye-strings begin to break, we may be sure that we are taken within the bond of the covenant. Now to Him who must persuade you, and who only must drive these things, as a nail, in your hearts—let Him who is the great Master of assemblies do it, and take the praise to Himself. Amen.

SERMON 16

The Believer's Love to an Unseen Christ

Whom having not seen, ye love; in whom, though now ye see him not, yet believing, ye rejoice with joy unspeakable and full of glory.

—1 Peter 1:8

Among all the debates and controversies, this is a statement without debate or controversy—godliness is a great mystery, and we conceive that it would be to your advantage to study it. The truths of the gospel are not only mysteries to our judgment, but much more mysteries to our practices. We conceive they are so elevated above sense and reason that the depths of these truths are not easily undertaken. Consider a natural man who, in things human, has his knowledge and understanding enlarged as the sand by the seashore, who has attained unto an eminent pitch of knowledge of things natural and moral, above even those that are endued with a more divine light in things that are more sublime in their nature and useful in their knowledge; yet bring him to search out the mysterious truths in the gospel and there he is as an infant of days, without understanding in these things, they being spiritually discerned. What a mystery it is for flesh and blood to love Him whom they have never seen.

The first words of our text are a riddle, almost impossible to understand—how can we love an invisible object? But he that is spiritually enlightened does embrace that precious object, Jesus Christ, with these two glorious arms: faith and love. Though He is now entered into the holiest of all, and is set down at the right hand of the Majesty on high and exalted out of our sight, yet faith travails above the clouds to embrace and encircle that invisible object whose name is Immanuel.

There are two great riddles in the words which we have read; though a natural man had seven days to unfold them, he would be no wiser at the close of those seven days as he was at the beginning, as these mysteries are above sense and experience. What a mystery it is for a natural man to see Christians exercising themselves in the grace of love—having love for Him whom they have never seen, and beholding Him whose bodily face they never beheld! This holds forth, no doubt, that divine and sublime action of a Christian soul, elevated above sense and all outward appearance, the glorious and excellent piece of the soul of man, which is of a divine offspring, deriving its generation from the Ancient of days and that which must return unto Him again, God being the first immediate cause and the last immediate end of this noble piece of the creation. What subtle abstraction and divine speculation will it have upon every subject? Yea more, it will be raised up by an attractive virtue of an eminent object, to exercise eminent acts of love and joy, as we see here in the words of our text. Oh, that we were persuaded to be more in the exercise of that first and great commandment, "Thou shalt love the LORD thy God with all thine heart, and with all thy soul, and with all thy might" (Deut. 6:5). Did you ever see Him? It would be impossible for you not to love Him once you had beheld Him; however, though you see Him not, yet you love Him. It is no blind bargain to take Christ by unseeing faith. Oh, if you had such a glorious and excellent discovery of that noble Plant of renown, you would be content to take Him alone, though He should bring none of these great and comprehensive donations that He commonly gives unto His own. If such a supposition had been possible, you would have condescended rather to be in hell with Christ than to be in heaven without Him, as a pious minister once said.

However, lacking the grace of love is a great problem. Other sins have slain their thousands; but this sin, no doubt, has slain its ten thousands. Oh, when shall Christ have dominion, and sit as king in the temple of our hearts? When shall He be commanding the faculties of our souls, saying to one, "Go," and it goes; and to another, "Do this," and it does it? What do you conceive could be the reason that moved Christians, in primitive times, to adhere so closely to the owning of a crucified Christ, though not seen? All torments imaginable could not break these precious cords of love and faith. They were twisted about by an unseen Christ. "They loved not their lives unto the death" (Rev. 12:11); the bonds of their afflictions could not break these precious bonds of love. No doubt they received that precious reward, though their souls went up in the flame of sacrifice, which they offered up to God by giving their bodies to be burnt. They went to heaven in a fiery chariot, and are now resting above the reach and noise of all these toils wherewith we are encompassed; they have spent more than a thousand years in the blessed contemplation of Him whom they did not see while they were here below, and yet they loved Him; but now they both see Him and love Him.

We shall come and speak a little more particularly concerning the words of our text; you have in them the apostle Peter setting forth the excellence of these two cardinal graces from the object about which they were exercised, Christ unseen, the invisible and glorious Majesty, "whom having not seen, ye love." There is a sweet emphasis on the word "yet"—notwithstanding the love was at such a disadvantage, not seeing Christ, yet love overcame it. The object of faith, likewise, is Christ unseen, "in whom, though now ye see him not, yet believing."

Second, the apostle commends these two graces because of the precious fruit which accompanies them: these graces make the Christian "rejoice with joy unspeakable, and full of glory"—that is, with joy that could not be expressed in language. The most divine orator could not describe this joy. Likewise, it is a joy full of glory, which we conceive points at the constancy of the joy that flows to a Christian through a Christian's faith and love for Christ, the invisible object. Where these two are knit together, that is, unspeakable joy and permanent delight, what do they lack? These are two sweet flowers that flow and spring from the roots of faith and love. They shall remain green throughout all the ages of eternity. If the joy of a Christian, while he is here below, is unspeakable and full of glory, what joy must the saints that are now made perfect have, in the immediate contemplation of Jesus Christ? If the love of Christ not seen produced such precious effects, how much more now when they are admitted into His presence, shall they rejoice? If you ask the name of the joy that the souls of just men now made perfect have with God, we could give it in no term so suitable as this—it is a joy without a name. It is a nameless joy, not because of what it is not, but because it is what it is.

Furthermore, we are persuaded that if you could pose the question to any who are now above, "What is the joy that you have in Christ now seen?" I believe they would give you no other answer but that which is in 1 Corinthians 2:9. In this verse, the apostle Paul, by an excellent gradation, holds forth the excellence of that blessed and glorious estate of life that the saints have above. He speaks of the *eye*, the most comprehensive sense, which can take up many various and different objects, and can see such things at a distance; yet it can neither take up nor behold the invisible glory of that estate of life. He also speaks of the *ear*, an even more comprehensive sense than the eye, but it cannot take up the blessedness of that estate; for the ear, says the apostle, has not heard. Furthermore, the *mind* of man, which is more comprehensive than the eye or the ear, and can take up many more things than both the eye and ear, which can in one moment of time run through all the four cardinal points of heaven: west, east, north and south; yet, "neither have entered into the heart of man" to understand that blessed and glorious estate of life.

Sense and fruition shall best resolve that question, and we must delay its answer until we shall have the enjoyment of it; but you may know what these upper springs must be, since the lower springs are such. If a Christian rejoices here below "with joy unspeakable and full of glory," oh, how shall they rejoice in Him, when all these veils that are between Christ and them shall be rent from the top to the bottom? We shall not spend long debating why love here gets the precedence over faith. We think indeed faith is first in order to the begetting of love in the heart; faith is that which goes forth and discovers the invisible things of God. Love sits down and solaces itself in the discoveries of faith. Faith cries forth, "It is good for us to be here," and love cries forth, "Let us make…tabernacles" (Mark 9:5). However, we shall not speak upon the priority of the graces of the Spirit; but we are sure that the Spirit of grace does keep a divine and wise method in putting one line of Scripture before another, though we are often ignorant of the causes of it. We shall not spend long describing to you that divine and pleasant confession that is between the two graces of love and faith. Each one of these helps the other in their exercise; we think the grace of faith only helps the grace of love in its exercise, in the respect that it does reveal unto love objects for it to exercise itself about. Faith is the discerning and comprehensive grace of the Christian which takes up most of God; it reveals the invisible things of God unto the Christian. Love is then provoked to exercise by the large and spiritual discoveries of faith. Faith, likewise, helps love, in that when we meet with some sad and anxious dispensation, then our love begins to call into question and debate the reality of God's good will, not knowing how to reconcile together His good will and His dispensations. I say faith there must eminently help love; faith can read the thoughts of His heart, and can behold His countenance under a veil. Though He seems to frown, yet He loves. We confess these characters, by which love is engraven upon a sad and anxious dispensation, are not easily read; only faith can read them.

Second, faith helps love in the way that it reveals unto the Christian the accomplishment of the most precious and excellent promises that are given unto him. The knowledge of these promises provokes the Christian eminently to love Him who gave such precious and excellent promises, by which we are made partakers of His divine nature. I conceive, if Christians could attain to such a length as to behold the accomplishment of all these promises that are given in Scripture, their spirits would long after Him. Oh, what a divine necessity should that impose upon our spirits to love Him who has thus loved us?

Third, faith helps love in that it goes to Jesus Christ, upon whom our strength is laid, and draws strength and furniture from Him for the exercising of all the graces of the Spirit. We conceive that love helps faith in some respect; for the apostle Paul says, "Faith…worketh by love" (Gal. 5:6). It is impossible for the Christian to be in the divine exercise of faith and not to exercise love. When love has priority, then faith increases with the increase of God. I confess that the languishing of the grace of love makes faith groan within us, with the groanings of a mortally wounded man. Keep love in exercise and you will keep faith also in exercise; likewise, keep faith in exercise and you will keep the grace of love in exercise.

Now that which we intended to discuss at this time, upon the first ground and consideration, is that which the apostle Peter commends concerning these two graces, namely, that they act and exercise themselves about an invisible object, "a Christ not seen." We conceive that this expression, "whom having not seen, ye love," shows that they exercised the grace of love, despite the lack of His presence. We confess that the eye is the serious messenger of the mind; likewise, it has a great influence upon the affections. Herein their love was excellent, that notwithstanding the lack of His bodily presence, yet they did love Him; though they had not known Christ, and Him crucified, according to the flesh, yet their souls were bound to this spiritual object by a threefold cord, which is not easily broken.

This fact shows that they did not, in their exercise of love, seek for an eminent and sensible discovery of the divine power of Christ in some miracle and extraordinary thing; their love was more modest and sober than to seek for a sign and miracle to maintain it. They would clasp about an unseen Christ, notwithstanding the lack of these discoveries.

Furthermore, we believe that they did exercise love for Christ unseen, even in the sensible and gracious declarations of His presence and favor toward them; that though He did sometime turn about the face of His throne and veil Himself with a cloud, and so was not seen in this respect, yet they did love Him. It is, no doubt, the eminent commendation of a Christian, that, let Christ alter His dispensations as He will towards them, they will never alter in the exercise of love; let Him frown, yet they will be persuaded to love. This was the exercise of the spouse (Song 3), where under all her anxious disappointments in her pursuit after Christ, yet four times she gives Him that glorious and loving epithet: "Him whom my soul loveth." A Christian has no will to injure the noble object of His love, even so much as to call in question the reality of His love, because of His dispensations. This, we do not doubt, is an eminent act of love, to love an overclouded Christ, when wrath seems to look out from His eyes and when He hath put on a change of apparel, coming with dyed garments of blood towards you.

We want to consider, finally, this phrase: "Whom having not seen, ye love." It shows that in all our enjoyments of Christ here below on this side of time, we may engrave this inscription upon them: "This is not Christ seen, but Christ looking through at the lattice." In this respect, we do enjoy an unseen Christ, in respect of that complete and immediate fruition of Him which those that are begotten unto a lively hope shall once have, in the immediate contemplation of Him. Oh, what a sight that shall be, when your eyes shall be admitted to behold the King in His beauty! I confess that it is impossible to determine what joy a Christian shall have in that day, when he shall receive the first immediate sight of God. In a manner, all your former enjoyments shall then appear as nothing to your soul; your soul shall be wrapped up in a holy admiration at such an enjoyment. Oh, blessed are those eternally who are living in the lively expectation and hope of such a day; He whom you do not see here, you shall then see.

We shall speak concerning some considerations that commend the exercise of the grace of love toward Christ unseen. I am afraid that we speak as strangers to most of you, and we speak in an unknown tongue when we speak of the exercise of love for an unseen Christ.

First, let us consider that the act of the Christian is most durable. If your love to Jesus Christ only exists when you see Him, certainly your love will not endure long. I must confess, if this is your love, it does not deserve much thanks. Christ, who was the head, did remove Himself from the members, knowing how prone we were to idolize His bodily presence; therefore, He said, "It is expedient for you that I go away" (John 16:7). He went up, thinking it was best to remove Himself, and not to let us have the enjoyment of His bodily presence, until that blessed day shall be, which we desire to believe is not far off, when we shall have the enjoyment of His bodily presence. There we shall not be in danger of idolizing Him, though we confess Christ is the most suitable and divine idol for a Christian soul to have; however, that love is most divine and pure, that originates not from outward sense and appearance. It is the soul, as it were, closing both door and window, and retiring into the inner room of divine contemplation, solacing itself with the sweet and desirable thoughts of Christ unseen; it is the soul of a Christian in a composed and divine frame, studying to have his love taking fire, beholding Him who is far off, that he may meditate upon Him until he loves, love until he wonders, and wonder until he rejoices.

There is a second consideration by which the grace of love is made commendable and eminent, and it is that love that is thus exercised is most contrary to our inclination and disposition. It is the natural disposition of all to love sense and sensible things, to have our eyes and our hands teaching us; no doubt, it must be an eminent attractive virtue of an invisible object to make this impetuous current of our natural inclinations to turn back and to provoke us to exercise love for that which we have not seen. We think Satan knew well what a strong desire men have for sense and sensible things. He brought those things down us; therefore, his precepts, the worshipping of idols and graven images, have been well taken off his hands. We think the way of our worshipping God by sensible types, signs, and figures under the law had more likeness to our nature than the pure and spiritual way of the gospel and of loving Jesus Christ now in the fullness of time. It is one of the most eminent contradictions of our natural inclinations and disposition to love an invisible object.

Third, let us consider that the grace of love is a love that is most pure and divine. We think our love that has its rise from outward sense and appearance has most mud and dreg at the bottom of it. It was, no doubt, a blessed dispensation to Him; but herein is the eminency of the grace of love manifested: to love Christ when He is under a veil, or when He is not seen. It is certain that we cannot persist long in the exercise of love if our love flows and ebbs, as His dispensations do; oh, to be kissing and loving the veil, or an absent Christ, when we are not admitted to behold His face! We pray that our souls might always be breathing after an immediate conjunction, a divine union, between our souls and Him. I think that which is heard in schools is eminently verified of a Christian, *anima magis est ubi amat, quam ubi animat,* meaning, "the soul of a Christian is more where it loves than where it lives." We believe that the soul is acting in its proper element and sphere when it is breathing out love for Jesus Christ, though unseen. Oh, this is truly a mystery to many of us. Our love is full of jealousies, when His dispensations do not suit our disposition. If Christ were as changeable as we are in the exercise of love, the contract of marriage between Him and us would soon be broken! But oh, blessed are changeable creatures in that they have to deal with an unchangeable Christ, whose love admits no variableness nor shadow of change! Who could ever engrave that imputation upon that living and gracious Person, that He changed? He keeps His grip on us when we lose our grip on Him.

There is a fourth consideration by which we commend the grace of love acting itself upon an invisible object, Christ unseen, and it is this: it is a love that does not rise upon any outward motive or extrinsic consideration. It is a love rising from the exercise of a gracious frame of spirit, as the result of a union between the head and the members. It would love Him, although as long as it is within time, it never beheld Him. A Christian that is thus in the exercise of love, if he have the promise of the eternal enjoyment of Him, will suspend all these enjoyments if it seem so fit until it be exalted above the reach of all diversion and interruption of that blessed fellowship. It will grant an indulgence to our blessed Lord Jesus to be arbitrary in the dispensation of love, if so be that once he be persuaded that his Beloved is his, and that he is His. You know that the members ought to love the head; it is a conjugal motion, and it is most suitable and proper. Now love that has its origin from this union, and not from an extrinsic consideration, no doubt is most eminent and excellent.

Fifth, the grace of love can never be brought to perfection until we are brought to love Christ yet not seen, this invisible object. I think that which makes love to be under such a woeful and remarkable decay, even in the most serious and exercised Christians, is this, that when Christ is veiled, and they do not behold Him, their love begins to decay and languish. Believe it, if your love is not exercised when He is away and absent from you, as well as when He is present and condescending to manifest Himself unto you, it is certain that your love can never increase with the increase of God.

Finally, let us consider that it is that love which makes the Christian rejoice with joy unspeakable and be full of glory. This is a paradox and mystery unto many of the Christians of this generation—the loving of Christ unseen should make them thus rejoice, even with joy unspeakable and full of glory. If the words of our text had said, "Whom seeing, ye love," and then, "Rejoice with joy unspeakable and full of glory," no doubt, you might then have closed with it. Now certainly here is a mystery, that the exercise of the grace of love for Christ unseen should make the Christian exceedingly rejoice. It is certain that when a Christian exercises love under absence with Christ, that love is most eminent and most complete. It is impossible to determine what strange and most inexpressible actions of the grace of love a Christian receives when he is exercising this grace and duty of love in Christ not seen.

Now we shall only press this upon you, so that you will be persuaded to confine your love and all your desires upon Him. Dear Christian, love Him, though He be in a far country; for it is not long before you shall see Him. That is the sweet period and result of the sweet exercise of the grace of love for the unseen Christ. You may comfort yourselves in this: shortly, it shall be your eternal exercise around the throne ever to love Christ, who will then be seen. You shall also enjoy Christ seen—may not that provoke you while you are here even to love that invisible object and unseen Christ? Oh, let your love always be traveling above in that higher land, embracing Him who ought to be the object of all your loves.

Are there not many here among us who never knew what it was to exercise love upon this precious object, Jesus Christ? Oh, be persuaded, the day is coming when He, even He whom you would not love, shall tear you in pieces, when there shall be none to deliver you out of His hands; you shall see Him coming with ten thousand of His saints to take revenge upon those who would not obey the voice of His gospel. Believe it, you will then, with all the families of the earth, mourn for Him whom you have pierced, and make bitter lamentation, as one for his only son. This day we do, as the ambassadors and messengers of Christ, entreat you to love this blessed object; and if you deny His desire and command to you, it shall be the matter of your eternal anxiety and torment, that you were invited to love Him, but you would not. The day is approaching when you would be content to love Him, but then He will not be loved by you; and no doubt it is a suitable retaliation from that person, that if you will not love Him while you are here below, when you will desire to love Him elsewhere, He will deny you your desire.

We shall likewise speak a word to the commendation of this grace of faith, upon this same account. The grace of faith is exercised towards Christ not seen, that invisible object. We think the grace of love and the grace of faith are indeed different in their habits, but are hardly distinguished in their exercise. All the graces of the Spirit are so inseparable and interwoven one with another that when one grace acts, all the other graces seem to move; they are like the wheels in a clock; at the motion of the upper wheel, all the lower wheels begin to move. Certainly, these two graces, faith and love, are two inseparable twins; these graces are pleasant in their lives, and in their death they are not divided.

Now the apostle here points out faith, not only in its nature and properties, but even in its object. In its nature, faith is here pointed forth, that it reveals the invisible things of God, and it is the evidence of things not seen, as likewise the substance or rather the subsistence of things hoped for; faith gives a life and being in things before they be, and brings them near to the Christian's eye, even while they are far off. Christians, be much in the exercise of the grace of faith, even about things that are not seen; for believe it, before long, faith shall die and vanish out into the exercise of the grace of love, and love shall be your inseparable companion in heaven; there you shall both love and be loved eternally, even without all intermission.

Now the object of love is here made evident: Christ unseen, or Christ, though not bodily enjoyed. We shall shortly point at some things by which the grace of faith may be kept in exercise when you meet with such a dispensation as this, having Christ unseen unto you, and when He is veiling Himself from your eyes and, as it were, casting at you.

The first piece of advice that we would give as a help to a Christian to keep his faith in exercise and to exercise it in this estate is to look upon all the disadvantages and impediments that you have in the exercise of the grace of your faith as opportunities and occasions given unto you to glorify God. That will help to keep your faith in exercise. When faith has the most impediments in the way, then there is the greatest occasion given for us to glorify Him by being strong in the faith. Furthermore, faith is never in its native exercise until sense and reason contradict the accomplishment of the promises; faith then is deeply exercised, and is in its native place. Know this, the most adventurous acts of faith have had the most sweet and precious results. Now, I say, though all His dispensations that we encounter may seem to be impediments in your exercise of the grace of faith; yet do not, because of these impediments, desist from the exercise of these graces. I think a Christian has then a most spiritual view of all these obstructions that were laid in the way of the exercising of the grace of faith, when he looks upon these impediments as occasions given unto him whereby he may glorify God.

A second help that we would give to one desiring to exercise the grace of faith under such a dispensation, when Christ is veiled and is hid from your eyes, is to look upon all these difficulties and improbabilities as commands given unto you to exercise faith. Look upon all your difficulties, whatsoever, as so many voices, proclaiming aloud the duty unto you—believe in God, and in His Son Jesus

Christ, whom He hath sent into the world. This was the practice and divinity of David, in Psalm 56:3, "What time I am afraid, I will trust in thee." He thought no time so suitable for the exercising of the grace of hope as then, when he was encompassed with difficulties; and we think it altogether impossible for a Christian to exercise the grace of faith upon Christ not seen, except he look upon all the improbabilities and difficulties that lie in the way of the exercising of his faith as exhortations and commands given unto him to believe, and adhere even more strongly unto God.

A third piece of advice for the Christian to exercise the grace of faith upon Jesus Christ absent is to be much in the consideration of the unchangeable nature of God. He is the same yesterday, today, and forever; though He may alter His dispensations, yet you know surely that He cannot alter His love toward you; for as He is, so is His love. He is unchangeable; therefore, His love must be unchangeable also, even according as He is in Himself.

Let us conclude our discourse with this, desiring that those precious and excellent mysteries which, no doubt, are hid from the eyes of many of this generation, to exercise those two spiritual and noble graces, faith and love, about an unseen and invisible object, so that you may once be prepared to set about that blessed exercise. We shall speak nothing to the encouragements that are proposed to the ones that set about this blessed and divine exercise; only I say, they do "rejoice with joy unspeakable and full of glory." Oh, Christians, do you desire to know the most fit and compendious way for one to obtain delight and perfect satisfaction? Then be much in the exercise of these two excellent graces, faith and love. The grace of faith will provide much joy and consolation unto the Christian when all things that are here below seem to be threatening ruin and destruction, when the foundations of the world are out of course, and when all things seem to be overturning; surely I would give the Christian no better counsel or advice than this: by the grace of faith and love, be settling yourselves, even upon this invisible object.

Certainly it is a great mystery to the men of the world to see Christians rejoicing in the midst of all their straits and anxieties, to see them always flourishing and green under the saddest and most crushing dispensations; but here, no doubt, is the Christian's life. He who is planted by that living fountain and well of life shall be a branch that shall spring over the wall. I confess, if a Christian complain of the lack of joy and delight in God, you may reduce it to this cause: lack of the exercise of the grace of faith in Jesus Christ unseen. Believe it, you may have your treasure kept safe, when all other things may be robbed and taken from you. I think of the words of a philosopher, when the city wherein he dwelt was robbed and spoiled. He was asked if he had lost anything. He answered saying that all that he had, he carried with him: *omnia mea mecum porto*. I think a Christian may keep all his treasures within him and may be free from the robbery and spoil of the men of the world. This is a treasure which does not admit any sequestration; neither can it at all be exposed unto theft. Make it your own by the grace of faith, and delight yourselves in Christ as your own in love. Let love rejoice in Christ appropriate unto you.

To conclude, I shall say only this: we need not commend Christ to those that know Him; but we are certain that all we can say on His behalf is infinitely below that which He is. Therefore, come and see this precious invisible object Jesus Christ, and it will best resolve this question concerning His excellence. The angels and the souls of just men made perfect never beheld such a One. His countenance is like Lebanon, and excellent as the cedars. Now to Him who is love itself, who only must persuade us to love Him and to have our hearts driven by this nail of love, to Him, we desire to give praise. Amen.

SERMON 17

Hope Producing Holiness

And every man that hath this hope in him purifieth himself, even as he is pure.
—1 John 3:3

Self-deception has taken impression upon the hearts of many who are not living under the apprehension of these words: "Whatsoever a man soweth, that shall he also reap" (Gal. 6:7). Can such a delusion overtake you, that you should reap grapes of thorns, or figs of thistles? But, alas, there are many of us who intend an impossible union of inconsistent things, conceiving that though we sport ourselves with our own deceiving and take so much liberty and indulgence to ourselves, counting it pleasure to riot in the daytime and to follow after our idols without fear, thinking that yet, at last, you shall have a place to enter into that holy city, into which no unclean thing can have access. There is such a woeful incongruity and disproportion between your walk and your hope that a passer-by may take up the vanity of it. Your conversation so little resembles this precious and spiritual hope, that we may, without breach of charity, cast your horoscope, so to speak, or read your fortune, that your hope shall vanish as a dream and be cut off as a tree, and flee away as a vision of the night. There are many of you here that have the hope of heaven and of seeing God as He is; but if you seriously read over the words of our text, you would reject your confidence and be convinced that you have been walking with a lie in your hand and that a deceived heart has led you aside.

But this is a lamentation, that this delusion has not only possessed the elder sort, whose judgment is so darkened that they count gain godliness, and walk in those vain ways which they received by tradition from their fathers, even of those that are more refined in their walk and have cleansed the outside of the platter, having a form of godliness. They are regarded by others as living at the gates of heaven, deceiving and being deceived; their profession shall be once ashamed of them. It would be to the advantage of many Christians in this generation if they were more disciples like Nicodemus, coming only to Christ in the night. The sound of their feet was not much heard in those ways that are beautiful, lest they begin to build and not be able to finish; lest they, intending that holy warfare of Christianity, not being temperate in all things and not having fully resolved, not having sat down and consulted with themselves, whether or not they with ten thousand were able to meet Him that came against them with His twenty thousand. They do succumb and faint in the day of adversity, and so prove their strength to be but small by their yielding that which they have gained in appearance; thus, they offend the generation of the just, who are as the light that shines more and more unto the perfect day.

Many take up Christianity before Christianity takes them up; but you that would demonstrate the reality of your hope, and desire to hold fast your confidence, and the reviving of your hope, firm unto the end, so that each day you may without difficulty read your names in the book of life, be much in the study of holiness and of purifying yourselves even as He is pure. Thus, you may be always prosecuting that divine and high design of being made like unto Him, which is not your ambition, but your duty. As God did not take rest in all these works of creation, though there were many wherewith He might have satisfied Himself, until He had created man after His own blessed image, in righteousness and true holiness, so you may entertain a holy disquietedness in the midst of all your other enjoyments, until you are made partakers of the divine nature, to have the lively and spiritual lineaments and characters of His own image impressed and engraven upon your own hearts and expressed in your conversations. If those things were more your study, you would be steadfast and immoveable in the work of the Lord, and bring forth even in your old age. Certainly herein godliness is great gain; that is, it is the evidence of the reality of your hope. These two are inseparably linked and knit together by a divine decree which cannot be repealed: the hope of heaven and holiness. What God hath conjoined, let no man separate. Do not put forth your hand to any forbidden fruit and hate even the garments that are spotted with the flesh; if any man keep himself from these, he shall be a vessel fitted unto honor, for the Master's use. Oh, since you have tasted of the tree of knowledge of good and evil, study so much divine understanding as to covet earnestly the best things, and approve these things that are most excellent; since your everlasting advantage and infinite gain do lie in this blessed hope, you may be persuaded after it. Since your access to the enjoyment of this hope is through the beautiful paths of holiness, let the sound of your feet be always heard there. If it were possible that heaven should not be the reward of holiness, holiness is still so beautiful and excellent a thing in itself, that it would be to us both our work and our reward. What greater dignity imaginable, than for the dust of your feet to be so far elevated as to be conformed unto Him who made them? But you undervalue most that which is the greatest part of your happiness.

Now the apostle, in the former verse, had discoursed most divinely of the excellence and eminency of a Christian's hope—that we shall see Him as He is and have an intuitive vision of this incomprehensible Majesty. This is a sight of infinitely more value than the fruition of all things that are within the compass of the globe and those things that are most valued by men. We cannot comprehend what this is. Faith is too dark a resolver of this; sense and fruition shall best resolve it. We conceive, if Abel (who of all men has had the first and longest possession of this hope, to see God as He is) were sent to preach upon it to you, he could not tell you what it is; but when he should begin to speak of this, he might speak the words of Hebrews 11:32, "And what shall I more say? for the time would fail me" to speak of this, and your hearts and patience would fail you to hear of it; yea, rather, we conceive, he should be a barbarian unto us, speaking in an unknown tongue, it being a language which the most part of us would not understand. We conceive that this hope is so mysterious in its nature and so high and excellent, that as long as we are here below, we will not comprehend it.

He likewise did point out the Christian's hope that we should be like Him. I think, if the infinite excellence that is in God and the uncreated beauty and majesty that is in Him were more believed, and the unsearchable deformity and great dissimilitude that is now between God and us were more known, we might cry out in admiration, "How can such a thing be?" We might be wrapped up in holy astonishment at this inconceivable dignity and blessed exchange which shall be made. If any of you who did behold a saint while he was here, traveling in those tents of mortality and made subject to those various alterations unto which all men are made subject, having his garments spotted with the defilement of the world, when he shall be made like unto God, you would not recognize him. There is such an infinite difference between that which they are now and that which they were then. This hope of a Christian, being made like unto God, is so far above a Christian's merit, that often times it is above his hope and expectation; we conceive that there is nothing to satisfy unbelief in this but the faith of His omnipotence and the freedom of His love. This love can make those which have been among the pots to be like the wings of a dove, covered with silver, with feathers of yellow gold; this love can make those who are black, whom the very daughters of Jerusalem did despise, to shine as the sun in the kingdom of their Father. Oh, that you were persuaded to lay hold upon this precious and immense hope! If such a thing were possible and there were a messenger of peace sent to the souls that are reserved in everlasting chains to proclaim this hope to them, it is difficult to determine whether joy or obedience would be more in exercise. Oh, would there be any of them that would cast this hope behind their back? No doubt, they would bind it as a chain of gold about their necks and make it as an ornament unto their heads. We think joy and admiration (if anything could interrupt their obedience) would be this; for, no doubt, they would suppose that they were in a dream and that they had seen a vision, if such a command and decree came unto them.

But lest any should too presumptuously lay hold on this hope, he sets down the characterizing and distinguishing property and mark of him that does have this hope. He purifies himself. This is the motto engraven in great letters on a Christian's forehead: HOLINESS UNTO THE LORD. Yea, furthermore, he does not satisfy himself with a small measure of holiness, having one part and lacking another part; but it is his aim and endeavor to be pure, even as Christ is pure. This is a high design, but is not easy to prosecute. We must not conceive that we can attain to such perfection in this endeavor, to be altogether made like unto Him. We conceive rather that there is a similitude of holiness that is held forth, not an identity of holiness—rather *as* such a thing, than *really* such a thing. We must study a conformity to Him in the quality of holiness, rather than in the quantity and perfection of it. We confess that much of the Christian's attainment in this endeavor, while he is here below, does rather consist in his desires to have it to truly attain it. It is marked by a Christian's lament over his shortcomings, both as to his affliction and his sin, and his groaning for the day wherein he shall be made like unto Him, when that beautiful conformity with God shall be complete. Finally, that light shall be so highly advanced that it shall come to the day of its perfection, from which there shall be no declining.

Let us consider the proposal that there is a possibility of attaining this divine and precious hope, being made like unto God, and the hope of seeing Him as He is; no doubt, herein God hath manifested much infinite love to the heirs of the promise, that they might even have strong consolation while they are in this valley of Baca. Oh, with what excruciating and tormenting fears would they here spend their days if they did not have this hope! Likewise, with what horror would they have entered into eternity, walking with a holy indifference and uncertainty where they should abide, if this divine persuasion had been denied? No doubt, it ought to be our study, that since such a thing is attainable, we must daily be taken up in that holy debate, to prove and examine ourselves, whether we be in the faith or not. If this were more the debate in these days, it would silence the noise of all other debates. Surely this is a controversy worth studying; this does not engender strife, but godly edification, which is in faith. We desire to press you more to follow on to attain that divine persuasion and hope, which is the superior wheel which turns about all these lower wheels; hope is that which engages the sower to sow, for he sows in hope. The merchant traffics through many difficulties because of the hope of gain. Hope is the spring and origin of all our intentions, and makes us prosecute them with much alacrity; though we may say that the joy of our hope in these secular things is often more than the joy of our fruition. However, it is not so here in this Christian and divine hope, for the joy of our fruition is by many degrees above the joy of our hope and expectation.

It is impossible to determine what joy a Christian shall have when faith and hope shall cede to sense, when faith shall vanish into fruition and hope into possession, when all his prayers shall be turned into songs of praises. The very reflecting upon this will make a Christian to rejoice "with joy unspeakable and full of glory" (1 Peter 1:8). The apprehension of that blessed change, of faith into sight, of hope into enjoyment, and of all our tears into divine hymns and songs of everlasting praise; in those blessed deeps, we may drown all the thoughts of our present miseries. We may satisfy ourselves in this, that there is such a blessed and glorious period of all our battles within and without, that when we shall be passing through the lintels of the doors of our everlasting rest, we shall forget our misery as waters that pass away. Then all those tormenting and excruciating fears of unbelief shall vanish. Then the toil and labor which we have had, subjugating all things within us unto the obedience of Jesus Christ, shall sweetly be made up in that complete victory which we shall have over all these things. Then, we shall be admitted to sing that triumphant song, "O death, where is thy sting? O grave, where is thy victory?" (1 Cor. 15:55).

Now to persuade you to seek more after this divine hope, we shall propose these advantages that a Christian has in this endeavor.

First, it keeps many of the graces of the Spirit in exercise and vigor. It keeps the grace of patience under suffering eminently in exercise, as we see in 2 Corinthians 4:10 and 18. With what holy equanimity and joy have some endured the most sad and anxious dispensations, considering that there was a sweet side to their sufferings, like being in heaven, being eternally with God, when all the rivers of their sorrows shall sweetly vanish into that ocean of unspeakable joy. Furthermore, there is so sweet an uptaking of all those disadvantages that they have here, as the believer is reminded of heaven and the hope of it. It was a saying of a king in the east, who having given away all his possessions, one of his courtiers asked him what he did keep to himself. He answered, "Hope." A Christian may rest satisfied under all his wants with the hope of eternal life. Here we are exposed to much labor and toil in wrestling against our corruptions; these twenty years that you have been in the house of your pilgrimage, you have been consumed with the drought of summer, and sleep has departed from your eyes; yet when the twenty-first year of your age is come, and your minority has expired, you shall enter into the possession of these new heavens wherein dwells righteousness. Righteousness, in a sense, is a sojourner here; its proper home and mansion is above; there they shall have a universal and everlasting suspension from sin. If you are exposed to wandering through dens and caves of the earth, without a constant dwelling place—which has been the lot of these of whom the world was not worthy—you may rejoice in the hope of that day, when you shall be made a pillar in the house of your God, no more to go out. Then you shall enter into that glorious mansion which our blessed Lord hath gone before us to prepare. What do Job and David know now of all the sufferings which they had while they were here below? They are now vanished, as though a thousand years have passed; they have forgotten their misery, and remember it as waters that pass away.

Second, hope of heaven is the way to attain mortification to the world. One hoping for heaven will be, through the Spirit, waiting for the righteousness of faith, discovering, off the top of mount Pisgah, the inexpressible and inconceivable joy that is in the enjoyment of that land, which is the glory of all lands. Beholding that sweet and excellent fruition which they shall have of God and the holy and blessed Trinity, all things here below appear tasteless, as the white of an egg. Such a person takes up vanity in the choicest things here below, and vexation in every vanity. This is clearly seen in 1 John 5:4. It is no wonder we see many focusing their delight in things here below, because they know nothing so precious with which to solace and content themselves; but once the eyes of your understanding are enlightened to know the hope of your calling, which is the riches of the glory of your inheritance in the saints, you will see an end of all perfection. Even that which was made glorious shall have no glory compared to this that excels; that, no doubt, is divine and constant mortification, which is derived and deduced from so high and excellent a spring.

A third advantage is that this hope keeps the grace of love eminently in exercise. Hope of heaven and love are so conjoined and linked together that they live and die together; they wax strong and increase together. When one is admitted to behold the New Jerusalem, of which glorious things are spoken, then love increases with the increase of God. Hence are these songs of love, which Paul and Peter have founded upon the consideration of the hope of heaven (Col. 1:5; 1 Peter 1:3). If we remove our hope as a tree, and through the slothfulness of our hands do darken our evidence and obscure our hope, then our love begins to languish and groan within us, with the groans of a mortally wounded man. When is love shed abroad in our hearts? Is it not when we attain to that hope that "maketh not ashamed" (Rom. 5:5)? We conceive that among all the causes that there is so remarkable a decay of the grace of love, no doubt it is from that woeful uncertainty under which many Christians live. Two cardinal and comprehensive evils do exceedingly interrupt the exercise of love: the woeful indifference that we have of attaining divine persuasion and divine hope. The fruit and effect of this is the woeful uncertainty and indistinctness with which many are clothed, concerning the everlasting hope of seeing God as He is.

Fourth, the hope of heaven keeps the grace of peace and joy, which passes all understanding, eminently in exercise. Oh, what a serenity and calmness of mind do we acquire by this hope? What joy in the Lord, which is our strength, do we attain by this hope? These anxious and dividing cares, with which the hearts of many are filled and possessed, with these fightings without and fears within, would all of them sweetly vanish if this divine plant of hope were ingrafted in us. This hope would be as the anchor of the soul, both sure and steadfast, to keep us from these restless agitations unto which men are exposed. What is it that occasions joy unspeakable and fullness of glory? Is it not the hope of glory (Rom. 5:2)? Some may laugh at calamity when it comes, knowing that He will deliver them in six troubles, and in seven no evil shall come near them. This hope of heaven is that comfort with which we must delight ourselves in the midst of our innermost thoughts. He may behold, through the dark clouds wherewith his heaven is overspread, and look to that morning wherein he shall be satisfied with His likeness, when that Sun of righteousness shall arise from the east, and shall refresh these prisoners of hope.

Fifth, the hope of heaven gives a strong provocation and motivation to study holiness (1 John 3:3; Heb. 12:28). The person that has this hope within is endeavoring to be found in Christ, without spot and wrinkle, in the day of His appearance; this person will daily have his recourse to Him who, through the eternal Spirit, offered Himself without spot to God, that He might purge our consciences from dead works. These two are the daughters of a living and a spiritual hope: consolation and sanctification. He that has this hope of seeing Christ as He is looks about him upon the vanities and miseries of the world, and is comforted; he looks within himself and is purified. He compares this immense and glorious hope with the tossing and vain appearance of the world, and he rejoices. He beholds the holiness of that hope and how much abstracted from all iniquity, and he discovers the necessity of studying conformity with it. Hope has a conforming and transforming nature. A Christian, knowing that it is the ornament and livery of all those that attained this hope, and whose hope has vanished into fruition, to be holy as He is holy, covets the conformity between the expectants of this hope and the enjoyers of it; thus, there is a pleasant uniformity and symbolizing between these exercises of his and these that are above, who are now entered into the everlasting possession of this hope, that shall never be cut off.

A sixth advantage is submission to these dark discoveries that we have of God while we are here below. The consideration is this: though we know only in part and are children while we are here below, yet the day is coming when we shall put away childish thoughts and shall be made perfect in knowledge; this knowledge may make us with patience endure these dark and cloudy discoveries of that precious and incomprehensible majesty. The question which was once presumption for Jacob to ask, "What is thy name?" is now no mystery to him (Gen. 32:27). He is now admitted to unfold fully the endless mysteries, and mysterious endlessness of that name of God, *Immanuel*. That name to him is neither secret nor wonderful; he now asks for it without presumption and receives clear satisfaction to that which was his doubt. If we could reflect with what distinct and comprehensive knowledge the souls of just men now made perfect are beautified of God, we would desire to be admitted to that high pinnacle of honor and to be made capacitate of so high an elevation, as to stand eternally before the throne to unfold Him. These two great veils which do hinder our complete discoveries of God, the veil of our iniquity and the veil of His incomprehensive glory, are now rent, as it were, from the top to the bottom. John and Daniel, who could not behold His glory without falling dead at His feet, who could not with direct eyes behold that Sun of righteousness—their eyes are now made like the eyes of an eagle, able to behold the sun; their eyes are not now darkened, neither do they fall dead at His feet, but they admire and rejoice in their clear spiritual discoveries of Him.

Seventh, the hope for heaven does exceedingly help us to resist sin and those temptations that are most dangerous. Therefore the apostle Paul, when he presents the armor of God, gives us that to guard our head (1 Thess. 5:8). The hope of salvation is that which must keep us from fainting in the day of adversity, and so proving our strength to be but small. It is the hope of heaven that must make us rather to endure affliction with the people of God than to enjoy the pleasure of sin, which lasts but for a season; and that respect unto the recompense of reward. Oh, what a great and persuasive restraint from the commission of sin is the lovely persuasion of the hope of heaven? No doubt, it has so much influence in holding us back from eating any forbidden fruit and from polluting ourselves with idols, that we have taken up a holy indignation against all those things, and have been entertaining a divine antipathy, a holy enmity against everything which lifts up their hearts against Him. They have studied the accomplishment of that precious and first promise of grace, that there should be an enmity between the seed of the woman and the seed of the serpent, and that they do not attain to victory over these things. They desire to attain to these things in their longings after them, waiting for that day when they might talk with the enemies in the gate, and not be ashamed. Then they might be as Judah, returning victor after war, wrestling against principalities, powers, and spiritual wickedness in high places, that they might study a closer conformity both unto God and unto this lively and spiritual hope.

An eighth advantage to hoping for heaven is patience under Christ's veiling Himself and turning about the face of His throne. This is clear in John 14:1-2, where, in order to comfort His disciples, whose thoughts were filled with grief because of His departure, He gives this to compose and quiet their spirits: the hope of heaven that is in His Father's house, where remain many mansions. No doubt, a Christian is under most long and sad retirements of His face from us, when he proposes that complaint, "Hath God forgotten to be gracious? Hath He in anger shut up His tender mercies?" (Ps. 77:9). Therefore, our hope of enjoying of Him shall be deferred until our hearts are sick; yet, when there shall be an accomplishment of our desire, it shall be an accomplishment of it indeed, and shall be as a tree of life. They may be persuaded that though their hearts know their own bitterness, yet no stranger shall intermeddle with their joy. The day is not far off when there shall be no delays, when they shall so enjoy as never not to enjoy, when they shall possess and never lose possession. It is a question that we shall not now determine—

whether a Christian, when he shall be admitted to stand before the throne, shall have utter contentment and satisfaction in the conviction of that divine impossibility to lose communion and fellowship with God, or in his present enjoyment and fruition of Him? No doubt, both of these conspire to make him blessed and concur to make that happiness more complete and perfect; for if there were a possibility of losing Him made known to those above, this, no doubt, would be more water mixed with their wine. Their sorrow in losing their joy would so diminish their perfect satisfaction that almost it would be nothing; but oh, blessed are they in this, that this remains eternally impossible, since it would be an everlasting contradiction for them to lose that blessed fruition of God.

There is likewise found in this text a connection and conjunction between the two graces of faith and holiness. We shall not spend long pointing out the influences that hope has upon holiness, nor what influence holiness has upon hope—each one of these does intimately conspire the increase of the other. But, no doubt, hope is subservient unto holiness in several ways.

First, faith is the instrument by which we must increase in this beautiful and divine conformity to God. It is no wonder that our deformity is enlarged, because we are not much in the exercise of faith, through which we must have strength conveyed to us from that golden candlestick, which is full of oil for the fulfillment of all His commands.

Second, herein is faith subservient to holiness: it reveals to a Christian the beautiful comeliness of that grace. Faith is the noble spy and messenger which does not only reveal the invisible things of God, but the visible perfections of piety. It is impossible for a Christian to know the beauty and necessity of holiness, to know the equity of it, its comeliness, its luster, and dignity, except he be much in the exercise of faith; faith is the evidence of things not seen; and, in some measure, it reveals these things not seen.

Third, faith is subservient to holiness; it shows the Christian the precious advantage that a Christian has by being much in the exercise of that grace. It indeed proves a mercenary spirit to be much in the accomplishment of this duty of holiness because of reward. We confess that it should not be the ultimate and cardinal reason of our undertaking; but, no doubt, it may come in its proper place to persuade and constrain us to the accomplishment of these things. Paul had no mercenary spirit, yet the hope of heaven constrained him to the faithful discharge of the ministry of the gospel; this is clear from 1 Corinthians 5:1-3. There are many here whom we wish were endued with such a mercenary frame of spirit, which the men of this generation so much disclaim; we wish that those that do disclaim it so much would study holiness upon a higher and more divine consideration—that the enjoyment, or rather obedience to Jesus Christ and love to His commandments might persuade you to obey these things which He has spoken. Oh, that Christians had such desires in their hearts!

Holiness is likewise subservient unto faith and hope, in that it reveals the reality of our hope and demonstrates that it is no delusion that we are entertaining, but also in that it is the gift of God which has been given unto us.

Furthermore, holiness is herein subservient unto faith and hope. It always keeps a Christian under the distinct knowledge of his hope; for once we take liberty to commit iniquity with greediness, holiness becomes wearisome to us, our hope is darkened, and we begin to walk in the dark. Our woeful indulgence of our own selves and our love to those things with which we cannot dwell, have often constrained Christians to draw the conclusion that there is no hope. In this state, they wish for no greater degree of holiness than to believe that there is a possibility of attaining hope, and that which they have much longed for, that their case might come the length of a doubt. They sadly become positive in the opinion that there is no more sacrifice for sin, since they had sinned willfully, even after receiving the knowledge of the truth.

Likewise, holiness is subservient unto faith and hope in this: it is that which makes all other duties pleasant and easy in their exercise. If a Christian is not constant in the exercise of holiness, it is impossible for him to call wisdom's ways pleasant, and all her paths peace. Herein, no doubt, godliness is gain: there is no man that has so much delight in the performance of these things to which he is called (such as faith, holiness, mortification and the like, against which there is no law), as the man whose daily aim and endeavor is to climb up to that high bench of honor, to be made like unto Christ. There is no one so happy as he who desires to attain that ancient and primitive dignity with which man was once endued; he entertaining that holy ambition and spiritual generosity, studying a conformity with all these things that are above; he thinking it below him who is endued with an immortal and rational soul, to rest satisfied with anything that is in the lower springs of the earth. Therefore, he derives his satisfaction from that higher spring and divine fountain of consolation, which shall eternally flow out. Now, a Christian ought not only to be active in this work of the study of holiness, as it is shown to us in the text: "he that purifieth himself," he must not be as the sluggard, whose hands refuse to labor. On the contrary, the Christian must be subservient to our blessed Lord in the accomplishment of the work of holiness; but a Christian must be likewise constant in this blessed work. Likewise, a Christian ought to have a universal detestation for all ungodly things, and all things which God doth hate and detest, as is shown to us in the words, "even as he is pure."

Certainly, if we were more diligent concerning these three matters: activity in this blessed work of the study of holiness, constancy in the accomplishment of it, and the divine universality of hatred for the things which God hates, we might daily have the joy of reading our names enrolled amongst the blessed society and assembly of the firstborn that are now standing with the Lamb before the throne. However, the defects of a Christian, in some of these, makes him sometimes to walk in a spirit of heaviness, with sackcloth upon his loins and mourning all along the way. However, for you that desire to hold fast your hope and confidence in God and desire to keep always a distinct persuasion and assurance of where you shall rest at night, where you shall take up your lodging, and the place of your everlasting abode, you must seriously endeavor the prosecution of this blessed design of holiness: "to purify yourselves even as he is pure." This is so excellent, sublime, and divine a thing, that if we had so much knowledge and understanding as to take it up in its nature and in its effects, certainly we should commend it as the main and principal spiritual endeavor, and should dig for it as for hidden treasures. I am persuaded that if more people truly and solidly believed that "without holiness, no man shall see the Lord," we would not be so satisfied with ourselves; neither would we sleep easily, nor slumber, until that which might give us a sure evidence and token of seeing Him as He is, were made ours in possession. We would be impatient in ourselves, until that question was put out of doubt, and put beyond the reach of all debate and question, that we had an interest in Christ, and that we would see Him as He is, and when He appears, would be made like Him.

We shall not point out many differences between the two cardinal and principal graces of faith and hope. These are so closely related that they are often promiscuously used in Scripture; no doubt, the resemblance is great, both in the objects upon which they are fixed, and upon that fountain from whence they arise—Jesus Christ, in whom dwells all the fullness of the Godhead bodily, and from whom we do receive grace for grace, from Him who is the express image of His Father's person. However, it is important that we point out these differences and distinguishing characteristics between faith and hope.

First, faith lays hold on the word of promise—of His truth and His omnipotence, which are the golden pillars upon which faith leans; for certainly, if either the truth or omnipotence of God is hidden, our faith can neither stand nor persevere. However, the grace of hope lays hold on the object of the promise. The difference is evident in 1 Corinthians 13:13, "And now abideth faith, hope, charity, these three; but the greatest of these is charity." Faith lays hold upon the promise, and hope lays hold upon the thing that is promised; but love, which is the principal grace there commended, lays hold upon Him who makes the promises, Jesus Christ. Christ is the most immediate object; therefore, that grace is of a more heroic, stately, and spiritual nature.

Second, faith looks upon things that are far off as if they were near at hand; it brings those things that are promised within the view of acquisition. Therefore it is said in Hebrews 11:39, "And these all, having obtained a good report through faith, received not the promise." But having seen them afar off, they were persuaded of them; furthermore, they embraced them and confessed that they were strangers and pilgrims on the earth. As it were, they saluted the promises given unto them, bringing them in so near a propinquity to themselves. But hope, on the contrary, looks upon these things that are promised, as is clear from the words, "For we are saved by hope: but hope that is seen is not hope: for what a man seeth, why doth he yet hope for?" (Rom. 8:24).

The third difference between these cardinal graces, faith and hope, is that the object of the grace of faith, properly, is that which is truth, abstracted from all other considerations; but the object of hope is God. Surely it is most certain that a man does not hope for that which is evil, though he may believe those things that are not pleasant, nor yet are suitable unto him. Also, he may believe those things that are most contrary and opposite to his own blessedness and eternal happiness.

But alas! We are afraid that there are many of you in this place to whom the exercise of the grace of hope is not only a mystery to your judgments, but much more foreign to your practices. Are there not many who never knew what it was to exercise the grace of faith or hope? Are there not many who do not know what it is to believe, or to fix their confidence and hope on Him, Jesus Christ, who is the eternal rock of ages? But I am persuaded, if these words in John 3:18 were more deeply believed by you, "He that believeth on him is not condemned: but he that believeth not is condemned already, because he hath not believed in the name of the only begotten Son of God"; if you were persuaded what condemnation and banishment from the presence of the Lord were, no doubt you would walk with more fear and with more holy jealousy over your own selves. But your conscience is seared with a hot iron, so that if God should speak reproof to you, you cast your reproofs behind your backs; this, no doubt, is the beginner and forerunner of the sad and woeful dispensation God pronounces towards unbelievers. He will laugh at your calamity and mock when your fear comes upon you. Oh, what a terrible and sad dispensation and sight it shall be to hear Him, even Him whose compassions have been so often willing to have been moved within you, and that He who hath called Himself the Father of all mercies, that glorious title and attribute, which you have not valued, that He should rejoice in your eternal destruction and condemnation, take delight and pleasure in your ruin, and count it a relief and refreshment to be liberated of such adversaries as you are? What shall that be to you? We wish that He who is the Master of assemblies would engrave this in your hearts, that so you might be persuaded to be obedient to that which is the upshot and conclusion of the whole matter: to fear God and keep His commandments. This is the sweet epitome of a Christian's duty, as that wise man in Ecclesiastes 12:13 says, "Let us hear the conclusion of the whole matter: Fear God, and keep his commandments: for this is the whole duty of man." Amen.

SERMON 18

The Blessedness of Forgiveness

Blessed is he whose transgression is forgiven,
whose sin is covered.
—Psalm 32:1

Sanctification is not much in exercise among Christians in these days. There is only a small correspondence that Christians keep between Moses and Christ, between Mount Sinai and Mount Zion. We do not often behold the just sentence of condemnation passing against us because of our iniquities, nor do we subscribe unto the equity of that divine sentence; and withal to have our recourse to Him, into whose hand that blessed power is committed, to repeal and reverse our due sentence. Since the time He took the guiding of the posterity of Adam, how many just and equal sentences has infinite grace repealed! Oh, that you would be persuaded to be more engaged in the study of yourselves, that so you may go to Him for the pardon of your iniquities. We stand and wonder at the unspeakable folly that is among many, that they rest with so much contentment under the unsupportable yoke of their iniquities, which, no doubt, before long shall depress them into the lowest hell. Is not your blessedness found in the pardon of your iniquities? Why do you not long after it? Before long, He shall deliver up the kingdom to His Father; then, all hope of returning from these everlasting pains, unto which you shall be sent, shall be cut off from you. There shall be an impassable gulf fixed between heaven and you, so that those who would desire to pass from the one to the other shall not be able. We would strongly commend you to have your transgressions covered; and if you would only listen and take heed, no doubt, you might be persuaded to begin to set about this. There are not many who have ever seriously attempted this unknown work of having recourse unto

God through Jesus Christ for the pardon of iniquity; it is a mystery even to the practice of those who pass under the notion of saints. But there are many who are now walking down to the everlasting prisons, with a strong delusion in their right hand, whose hope shall be cut off as the spider's web, vanish as a dream, and fly away as a vision of the night.

But we must ask, "What is it to have our iniquities pardoned?" One that has attained this, whatever lot he has in the world, were it never so sad or anxious, may comfort himself. This is clear, "Son, be of good cheer; thy sins be forgiven thee" (Matt. 9:2). Oh, what divine consolation may the soul of a Christian reap, by reflecting upon the fact that his iniquities are pardoned? This is clear likewise, "And the inhabitant shall not say, I am sick" (Isa. 33:24); the reason of it is given: "the people that dwell therein shall be forgiven their iniquity."

A second reason we commend seeking forgiveness is that every affliction that befalls the Christian that has obtained the pardon of iniquity is a mystery for one that does not have that pardon. He might have said he had been undone, except he had been undone. Sampson's mystery is no mystery to a Christian: "Out of the eater came forth meat, and out of the strong came forth sweetness" (Judg. 14:14). God makes up their afflictions with this, that He knows their soul in adversity.

The third thing which may persuade you is that one that has obtained pardon of sin may drown all his anxious thoughts within the endless depths of enjoyment of Him through all eternity. This is clear: "Being justified by faith, we have peace with God through our Lord Jesus Christ: by whom also we have access by faith into this grace wherein we stand, and rejoice in hope of the glory of God" (Rom. 5:1-2). All your rivers of sorrows shall sweetly dissolve in that endless ocean of unspeakable joy. It is not long before you shall have a universal and everlasting suspension from all these things that so much encompass you; sorrow and sighing shall fly away, for they will be afraid to seize upon you.

The fourth thing to commend seeking forgiveness is this—a Christian that has obtained pardon of iniquity has peace with God through Jesus Christ. Surely it would require the tongue of an angel to commend the precious advantage that flows unto the pardoned Christian: peace with God. What could be desired more than to have that "peace of God, which passeth all understanding" (Phil. 4:7); or, as the word may be rendered, "quartered in your hearts and minds"? What a gracious God He is; it should be our greatest ambition and most earnest suit to obtain peace with Him. This is clear from the words which we cited from Romans 5:1: "Therefore being justified by faith, we have peace with God through our Lord Jesus Christ."

Fifth, if our iniquities are pardoned, we attain unto divine submission and learn patience under the most sad and bitter dispensations. It is impossible for one either walking in uncertainty concerning his estate, or for those who have been of old ordained to condemnation, to walk with patience under the rod; but one that is sure of his pardon, oh, with what patience will he endure the most bitter experiences in life! Is he afflicted with reproaches? He will make it up with the knowledge that he is pardoned. Yea, if he should multiply his losses, he has nothing with which to make them all up, except for the knowledge that he has obtained mercy and pardon from God through Jesus Christ.

Now that which makes people seldom engage in the divine pursuit after the pardon of our iniquity is first, because we are not much living under the apprehensions of the insupportable burden of the yoke. This made David commend the blessedness of the man who was pardoned, because he felt the burden of his iniquity; for the word that is here rendered "forgive," does likewise signify this: blessed is the man whose iniquity is "lifted up," implying that iniquity is a burden which no man can remove but the everlasting arms of our blessed Lord Jesus. If you were ever under the apprehensions of this truth, you would travel in pain until Christ was formed in you. But behold how it may astonish many to look upon people walking so lightly under such unsupportable burdens! Our blessed Lord, when He was walking under that deplorable yoke of our transgressions, found it so heavy that He was put to a possibility of the passing away of that cup; His soul was "exceeding sorrowful, even unto death" (Matt. 26:38); yea, that burden did put Him to an holy *nonplus*, when He was put to ask, "What shall I say?" Furthermore, if He who upholds all things by the word of His power, and who was sustained by all the fullness of the Godhead, groaned under this burden, shall not that which made Him groan, crush and ruin us? No doubt, if your own estate were revealed unto you, you would utter such complaints that the open fields should be more fit for you than the most secret retirements. This was the practice of this most holy man in Psalm 32:2; when his iniquity was revealed unto him, we read, "When I kept silence, my bones waxed old through my roaring all the day long." He did not mourn as a man, but he complained as a beast.

The second thing that makes us put so little account upon this excellent blessing, the pardon of our iniquity, is that we do not discover how abominable iniquity is. It is so odious that, as the Psalmist says, it stands in need of a covering: "Whose transgressions are covered." He who is of purer eyes than that He can behold iniquity has a blessed antipathy against everything that is evil. There is nothing that has such incongruity with His nature as sin; though we may say without question, that there is nothing that has such a congruity with our nature as iniquity.

There is a third thing which uncovers why we seldom strive for the forgiveness of our sins. We too seldom consider the infinite justice of God. He will, as Enoch the seventh from Adam prophesied, come with ten thousand of His saints to execute vengeance on those that know not God, and that delight in unrighteousness. If we believe that God is just, and that He will in no way acquit the guilty, how do we dare to walk so confidently under the yoke of our iniquities? There are many of you who shall go down to your grave with your bones full of the iniquities of your youth. You have wrapped a yoke around your neck that no hand can untie but He who has the divine art of untying the bond of our iniquities.

We are not much under the exercise of the law. Were we but ten days seriously in the school of Moses, we would long to be disciples of Christ. Has the law entered to reveal your iniquity, to make it out of measure sinful unto you? Oh, what a holy impatience and longing would you entertain, until you had obtained pardon for your iniquity! Heaven and earth cannot cure the distemper, but only Him who hath taken that blessed name to Himself, having the tongue of the learned, to speak a word in season to the weary.

A final consideration why we are so little taken up after the pursuit of the pardon of our iniquity is that we are neither much involved in the study of these advantages that we might have by the pardon of iniquity, nor do we study the disadvantages that we have by remaining at enmity with God. Consider the man that stands at a distance from God; what can we say more to declare his misery than that he is not at peace with God? He is the perfect hieroglyphic and compend of all misery. Blessedness, yea, all imaginable delight, is confined in that one divine sentence: to enjoy God; and we may likewise say that all misery is experienced in separation from God.

Now that you may be regulated to make use of Jesus Christ for the pardon of your iniquity, and so that you do not weary yourselves with debates, we shall only propose a few considerations.

First, a Christian may make use of his iniquity and of the greatness of his transgression as one argument with God to obtain pardon. This is clear in Psalm 25:11, where the psalmist begs, "Pardon mine iniquity"; he gives this reason: "for it is great." This is a reason, no doubt, which could not hold in schools; but it holds well in the heavenly court, where grace and love are judge. This is clear likewise in Psalm 40:11-12, where he desires that God would preserve him with His lovingkindness, and would not withhold His tender mercies from him; his reason is this: "For innumerable evils have compassed me about: mine iniquities have taken hold upon me, so that I am not able to look up." What a mystery must this be, that Christ is taken with such arguments! We confess that we have no stronger arguments whereby to reason our cause with God. We have shut ourselves out from all reasons of equity, and we must take ourselves to this, which grace has made the reason. This is clear, likewise from the words in Psalm 41: "I said, LORD, be merciful unto me: heal my soul; for I have sinned against thee" (v. 4).

Second, we may make use of our necessities as an argument with God to obtain pardon. If you can call yourself needy, you have a sufficient ground to make your recourse unto Him who hath proposed Himself as the everlasting rock of ages, upon which you may rest and repose yourself. Entertain a holy correspondence and divine fellowship between our unspeakable necessity and His unspeakable fullness. Let your unspeakable inability to save yourself drive you to have your recourse in Him who is sufficient and able to save all those that come unto God through Him.

Third, we may make use of our imperfections as arguments with God to obtain mercy and pardon of iniquity; because we are frail, and the dust of His feet, He should pardon us. This is clear from Psalm 78:38-39, where God gives this reason of His compassion: He remembered we were flesh.

A fourth consideration, one which is most wonderful, is that we may make use of the argument to plead for mercy with God, which God hath made use of for pleading justice against us. This is clear from comparing Exodus 33:3 with Exodus 34:9, where God gives this reason why He would not go up among them: because they were a stiff-necked people. Moses, in his pleading with God, uses this same argument, and pleads thus with Him, "Go among us; for it is a stiffnecked people" (Ex. 34:9): This is a divine art of retorting of arguments—an art which grace has taught the Christian.

Now certainly it would be to your advantage to make sure that you have obtained a good hope through Christ, and that you have received a discharge of all your iniquities, ratified and confirmed unto you. It is the duty of those who desire to come within the reach of this mercy to be convinced of these, which, no doubt, would prove to you that you are in the way of obtaining pardon. You must be convinced of the utter inability wherewith you are clothed to satisfy the infinite justice of God. This is the first great lesson that you must learn, to receive the sentence of death in your own bosom, so that you may take your shelter in Him who raises the dead.

Likewise, be convinced of this: the only way to obtain pardon of iniquity must be through the grace of Christ. You must leave all your merit behind you; though, we confess, we need not bid you do so, if we knew ourselves well, for we have nothing that can pass under this name. Let the first lines of your petition run upon this tenor: all my righteousness is as filthy rags. You must have nothing to commend you unto Christ but emptiness, and you must walk under that, as the most suitable argument to provoke Him to have pity upon you. Certainly, those who have obtained pardon from God and have a discharge given out of all their iniquities will, no doubt, have a high and eminent account of Him that is the Pardoner. This is clear from Micah 7:18: "Who is a God like unto thee, that pardoneth iniquity, and passeth by the transgression of the remnant of his heritage?" When we would commend Him, we take no other thing to be so suitable for the subject of our commendation as that He has pardoned our iniquity. No doubt Christ is precious to those to whom He has pardoned their iniquity, except they be living in unbelief, and have lost the sight of their discharge. Those who are pardoned will walk humbly with God.

Third, a man who has obtained pardon from God is so much in reflection upon what he was and how far he falls short of what he should be, that in a sense, he forgets what he is. This is, no doubt, a holy oblivion.

Fourth, the Christian whose iniquities are pardoned cannot look upon those sins, even which are pardoned, without detestation. Certainly, you may question your pardon if you can without resentment and grief, look upon these sins wherewith you have solaced yourselves. Oh, with what contentment do many look upon the seven abominations of the heart! Many are not constrained to weep in secret places because of these.

Fifth, it is the endeavor of a pardoned Christian to have the letters of his discharge always kept legible, that he may read it. In a sense, it is his charter and right of his inheritance; it is the first-fruits of the Promised Land. If we look, whether in reality or in our apprehension, it is no wonder, though we sit down seven nights and days, and do not speak a word because our grief is great.

Let us close our discourse with this; be more under the exercise of the law so that you may give the gospel more employment. Make a diligent inquiry into the idolatrous temple of your hearts, beholding these great and monstrous abominations. I think God has manifested much infinite love and wisdom toward man, that He hath reserved the royal prerogative to Himself to be the searcher of hearts; for if we knew all that is within us (as He who is greater than our hearts does know), we would find it even more difficult to believe. I think if there were a window opened for each one of us to behold one another's hearts, we would loath and shun conversation with one another! If a part of that mystery of iniquity that is within us were engraven on our foreheads, we would be made a curse and reproach in all the earth. Amongst all the eternal trophies and monuments of the victory of our blessed Lord, if ever we shall be made pillars in the house of our God, we doubt we may be put in the highest room. All the mysteries that He has manifested in saving others might vanish in the one mystery of saving sinners. We can desire no more, but we have access unto the holiest of all, through Him who by the eternal Spirit has offered up Himself a spotless sacrifice for sin and iniquity. Now to Him who was that blessed Lamb slain from the foundation of the world, even to Him, we desire to give all praise, glory, and honor, both now and evermore, world without end. Amen.

SERMON 19

The Constant Necessity of Christian Watchfulness

And he cometh unto the disciples, and findeth them asleep, and saith unto Peter, What, could ye not watch with me one hour?
—Matthew 26:40

Most of Christ's visits to His own, while they are traveling here below in these tents of mortality, are rather surprises than the fruit and birth of their hope and expectation. Hence it is that Christ came to His own here, even when they were asleep. The visit that Christ ever gave to sinners was a gracious surprise. When Adam, our forefather, had broken God's command, and had fallen from his former estate and blessed condition wherein he was first created, surely he thought that he should have been made the object of God's wrath and eternal indignation; yet, Christ gave him a sweet and blessed disappointment to his expectation—Christ arose with healing in His wings to Adam and to his lost posterity. He could have risen up against them with wrath and fiery indignation; but certainly, this is our unspeakable advantage, that ever He should have condescended so, as to publish such glad tidings of great joy unto us. It is our eternal advantage that He should have found out that blessed and living way whereby we who were debarred from fellowship and correspondence with God, might have access again to Him, through His own blood.

Now in the chapter we are studying, Christ is drawing near the brink of the intolerable sufferings that He was to undergo for our sakes. He was not to be offered up a spotless sacrifice to the divine and spotless justice of God; He was traveling into the death that sinners would have endured throughout all the ages of eternity, if He had not undertaken it for us. He was put to such infinite pain and trouble that He was constrained to cry out, "My soul is exceeding sorrowful, even unto death" (Matt. 26:38). We have here the practice of the disciples when their Master was in such a sad exercise: they were asleep when He was under all this pain; they were secure, they were overcome with security, while Christ was undergoing such grief and infinite labor. Yet, notwithstanding their fatigue, Christ, while He was under this sad exercise, speaks out much infinite wisdom, that the glory of the redemption might be given to Him alone. There was not one person with Him when He was in this unspeakable and infinite pain; He trod the winepress of His Father's wrath alone, and of the people there was none with Him. If the consideration of this, for whose cause He suffered such infinite and intolerable pain, and that He should have condescended so low as to come from heaven, out of the bosom of the Father to dwell thirty-three years with men on earth, that we might dwell through all eternity in heaven with Him; I say, if we were more in the study of this consideration, surely we would have a more divine and spiritual exercise than we often have.

Next, we have in the text the gentle reproof that Christ gave to the disciples, because of their false security. He says, "What, could ye not watch with me one hour?" It is as if He had said, "Oh, Peter, if you cannot watch with me one hour, how can you suffer with me?" The reason why He directs this reproof and expostulation toward Peter is because he had said before that he would not leave Him: "Though all men shall be offended because of thee, yet will I never be offended" (Matt. 26:33). Likewise, He directs it to Peter because of all the disciples, Peter was at this time to be assaulted most with the temptations of the devil. He also directs this reproof to Peter because, of all the disciples, Peter was in the most secure and most presumptuous frame; therefore Christ directed this unto him by name.

Now, as for the condition and exercise that the disciples were in at the time of Christ's unspeakable sufferings, it is described that Christ "found them asleep again" (v. 43). The text may also be rendered, "They were fast asleep, or, in a deep sleep," similar to the words in Isaiah 29:10, which say, "For the LORD hath poured out upon you the spirit of deep sleep." Certainly, I know no evil so predominant among us as the evil of security and laziness; we are like those that sleep upon the top of a mast, and are not afraid. Oh, beware and stand in awe to continue in this security! Beware lest it be perpetual, and lest the Lord give you over unto the evil of security, whereof you cannot be healed. Be persuaded, a Christian may lose as much by being under the spirit of security but for an hour, as he can make up in many hours, yea, in many days. This is clear from the practice of the saints of old; David lost as much by his security as certainly made him go mourning to his grave.

We would like to point out the times and seasons wherein a Christian is most ready to fall in this woeful and predominant evil of false security.

The first time we believe a Christian is prone to fall into the evil of false security is presently after he has met with some signal and divine enjoyment of God. This is clear from the bride's exercise in Song of Solomon 5:1 compared with verse 2, where the bride meets with the excellent enjoyment of God, "I am come into my garden, my sister, my spouse." She is then bidden eat and drink abundantly, yet, in the following verse, she is under the spirit of security and laziness. "I sleep," says she (v. 2). It is likewise clear from Zechariah 4:1, "And the angel that talked with me came again, and waked me, as a man that is wakened out of his sleep."

There is no time that a Christian falls into this evil of false security, wherein he has so much disadvantage, as after he has met with the enjoyments of God. Let us look at Revelation 19:10, where John falls down to worship an angel after his most divine and signal enjoyment of God. He says, "And I fell at his feet to worship him. And he said unto me, See thou do it not: I am thy fellowservant, and of thy brethren that have the testimony of Jesus: worship God." There is no stroke that is so discouraging to a Christian than to fall into the sin of false security after he has experienced the enjoyments of God.

Likewise, I would say something which may provoke you to watch after your enjoyment of God, lest you fall in that woeful and cursed evil of false security: if you fall into this sin after you have met with enjoyments of God, you will then call in question the reality of your enjoyments. Oh, then be persuaded still to watch and to be upon your guard at all times, because of the subtlety of your adversary, the devil.

Third, yielding to an idol or temptation is the most dishonorable affront that you can give to Jesus Christ; it is to prefer the idol before God. Surely it is an evil for which a Christian shall have most difficulty receiving pardon before the Lord. It is a most terrible and dreadful iniquity to embrace presently after our enjoyment of God, and certainly it shall be known once to be so. You who will not believe it now, be persuaded that before long, you shall know it by experience and trial. Therefore study watchfulness at all times, lest God surprise you unawares, and lest He tear you in pieces like a roaring lion, when there shall be none to deliver you.

A final consideration that may provoke you to watch embracing your lusts and idols after your enjoyment of God, will be that which will break off the holy familiarity and divine correspondence that you have with Him. Christians, make it your earnest care and desire to be more watchful in all your doings. Do not angels, as it were, laugh you to scorn because of this pernicious evil of false security?

A second time that a Christian is incident to fall into that woeful sin of false security is when Christ is willing to bestow His dispensations on them; then often their response is false security. This is clear from that place which we cited above, Song of Solomon 5:1. After the bride had met with the kind dispensation and enjoyment of Christ, when He desires her to open unto Him, even then, she is asleep. Is it not just and also right that Christ should put you to seek Him, when you put Him to seek you? Oh, do not continue any longer under your dreadful false security!

There is a third circumstance under which a Christian is ready to fall into that woeful snare of security: when a Christian is in great hazard of being assaulted with the temptations of the devil—then he is readiest to fall into false security. Peter was never in such great hazard as at this time. It is likewise clear from Jonah's practice, in Jonah 1:6, when he was asleep, he was in great hazard by the tempest of the sea.

A fourth time that Christians are likely to fall into the evil of false security is when they have many duties which they are called to perform. When a Christian has most duties that he ought to go about and perform, then it seems that he is desperate in the performing of these duties. Upon that account, he sits down, holds his hands, and falls in that woeful snare of false security, because he thinks it a very hard thing to go about these duties of his. Surely, nothing has so great influence upon this sin of false security as the apprehension of difficulties in our way of going about our duties;

certainly it proceeds from that indulgence and pampering we give our own flesh, being loath to do violence unto it.

The second point we shall address concerning the text is the following question: What are these things that have influence on a Christian's false security, and what are the causes that conceive it? First, we believe it proceeds from discouragement, or anxious unbelief. The reason of it is that one who is under unbelief does not take up the excellent and matchless reward given the Christian on the last day. There a second rise or cause of our false security—having a full exercise of gifts only, and not of grace, and resting on these, according to that word, "I was great" (Eccl. 2:9). In that state, he was increased in the things which made him too secure; surely, having these outward gifts is the origin of false security because we trust too much in them. A third cause of false security is lofty thoughts and apprehensions of ourselves, as in Revelation 3:17, which says, "Because thou sayest, I am rich, and increased with goods, and have need of nothing." Therefore, we would press humility upon a Christian, that he may eschew false security, which we fear will be the eternal ruin and destruction of many in this place.

In the third place, I would address some disadvantages that come to a person by being under the exercise of woeful security.

First, false security interrupts the divine enjoyments of God that the Christian might experience. This is made clear in Song of Solomon 5:2, where the bride interrupts her enjoyment by her sleep. Likewise, such a person loses much of the apprehension of the excellence of Christ Jesus and makes them lose all their high thoughts of Him and of His excellence; also, the self-secure Christian loses much of that unspeakable sweetness that is to be reaped in communion and fellowship with God while here below, dwelling in these tents of mortality. False security is a universal evil among the Christians of this generation; believe it, it is a most disadvantageous and hurtful evil. It benumbs the conscience of a Christian so that he does not know how to awake out of it.

A second disadvantage that attends the falsely secure Christian is that ordinarily the temptations of the devil prevail most against such a person. Without contradiction, the devil has an arbitrary dominion over secure persons; he has, as it were, a permission to tempt them at his own free will and pleasure. Now since security is so prejudicial, beware to entertain such a woeful evil within your bosoms.

There is a third disadvantage that comes to one by being under that woeful evil of false security. False security brings all the graces of the Spirit to a most low and languishing estate; the grace of love, the grace of faith, the grace of mortification, and all the rest are brought low, to a decaying state. They are like to die within them by reason of this woeful security.

The fourth disadvantage that attends the person that is too secure is that it procures much hardness and impenitence of heart to the person who entertains it. False security will make the heart of the person who entertains it internally as hard as a piece of the nether millstone. Study to guard against false security and delay not that any longer, lest these things which now belong to your peace be hid from your eyes.

We shall only say this unto you, dear Christians: watch with Christ but one hour and you shall reign with Him in heaven, above the clouds, throughout all the ages of eternity. Oh, watch your own hearts, lest you enter into temptation; for "the heart is deceitful above all things, and desperately wicked; who can know it? (Jer. 17:9)" Know that it is a matter of everlasting concern—watch over yourselves, lest the devil prevail against you. Certainly it shall be one day known to be so, when you shall be sifted before the tribunal and judgment seat of Christ Jesus, there to receive according as you deserve. Let this provoke you to watch: you have an excellent companion wherewith you may watch; "Watch with me," says Christ. Now to that excellent One, we desire to give praise. Amen.

SERMON 20

The Sinner's Extremity, God's Opportunity

Then washed I thee with water; yea, I throughly washed away thy blood from thee, and I anointed thee with oil.
—Ezekiel 16:9

The words of our text may humble a person who has the grace of God in him; these words may plainly show unto him how much he is indebted to Christ, and how much he is obliged unto Him because of the free love that He has so abundantly shown towards sinners. Let us examine the words of our text in four points.

First, persons who have experienced the grace of God do not need to spend time examining their descent, neither do they need to study their ancestry. Why is this? Perhaps your father was an Amorite, and your mother a Hittite; this matters little. You do not need to measure your worth by your ancestry, for Christ says in our text, "When I looked to you, I saw no one who would do good to you; and the more that angels and men were neglecting you, I did not neglect you; I took you by the hand, washed you with water, and anointed you with oil."

Second, consider this thought: you must not boast yourselves and say that you had any religion before Christ gave it to you. No person has ever heard any true religion come from your mouth before Christ put it in you; you were wholly alienated and estranged from God. You were polluting yourselves in your own blood until Christ passed by and pitied you; then He washed you with water, cleansed you from your blood and filthiness, and anointed you with oil.

Third, you may not boast that you have ever truly prayed to God. You never bowed your knee to Him until He poured upon you the spirit of prayer and supplication. You can plead grace from neither your father nor your mother, nor from kin, friend, or ally; you can expect nothing from them. You deserve only just wrath and condemnation. When Christ passed by you, you were filthy, naked, and bare—no eye would have pitied you. Yet, He washed you with water, anointed you with oil, and spread His skirt over you.

Fourth, consider that you were cast forth as an unclean thing, not worthy to be let into the house of a stranger. Yet, it is as if the Lord found you and said, "Despite your filth, I will not leave you in your sin; I will wash you, and I will enter into covenant with you and you shall become mine. If that will not content you, you shall take my oath on it. However, despite that covenant, yet you broke the covenant with me, but you do not dare say in your heart that I ever broke my oath to you. I swear in the eternal oath of God above your head, no sooner had I covenanted with you than I made a proclamation through heaven and earth and said, 'Who dare lay anything to the charge of God's elect, and my covenanted people?' I anointed you with oil; I oiled every limb of your body and made it supple for running, with fullness, without fainting." Of His chosen people, we read, "They shall mount up with wings as eagles; they shall run, and not be weary; and they shall walk, and not faint" (Isa. 40:31). For this purpose, He has anointed you with oil.

In Ezekiel 16:8, we read of the covenant itself: "Now when I passed by thee, and looked upon thee, behold, thy time was the time of love; and I spread my skirt over thee, and covered thy nakedness: yea, I sware unto thee, and entered into a covenant with thee, saith the Lord GOD, and thou becamest mine." In the following verse we see the substance of the covenant: "Then washed I thee with water; yea, I throughly washed away thy blood from thee, and I anointed thee with oil." This is the substance of the covenant of grace—washing away blood and guiltiness. In Psalm 51:2 we read, "Wash me throughly from mine iniquity, and cleanse me from my sin." By washing, the author is referring to the grace of God's Spirit; this is how the Lord makes you fit for spiritual grace and prepares you to receive that grace. It is as if He would say, "I gave you grace when neither your father nor your mother had it to give you. I gave my best surety for your love; I sware to you in my covenant."

Certainly, before this covenant was contracted, there was enmity and hatred between you and God. It is as if Christ had said, "You would not have dared to look God in the face before you came through my hand, before I washed you with water and made you clean." From this, let us observe several things.

The first observation is that those who have been washed are those who had as much guilt on their souls as they were able to endure. They were so laden with guilt that they were cast out upon the open fields. It is to such guilt-laden people that Christ says, "I will wash you with water and cleanse you from your blood and filthiness."

Second, consider that the person by whom they were thus highly favored—Jesus Christ, Savior of the lost world, the judge of the families of the earth—took pity on them. "Now when I passed by thee, and looked upon thee, behold, thy time was the time of love; and I spread my skirt over thee, and covered thy nakedness: yea, I sware unto thee, and entered into a covenant with thee, saith the Lord GOD, and thou becamest mine" (Ezek. 16:9). It is He who has power to cover iniquities; it is He who washed you with water and anointed you with oil; it is His prerogative to pardon iniquities, transgression, and sin, which is altogether impossible for the sons of men to do.

The third thing that we would like you to notice are the privileges and favors that are conferred upon these persons. The first privilege is the washing with water. He says, "Then washed I thee with water." Second, we see the privilege of the remission of sin from the soul. He continues, "I throughly washed away thy blood from thee." The third privilege is the anointing with oil, which is the grace of the Spirit. You are the person favored of Christ; you were under extraordinary guiltiness, and you were altogether void of the grace of God; yet, Christ washed you and anointed you with oil.

Now, our Lord Jesus Christ has skill to heal the most desperate cases and dangerous diseases; were the case never so guilty and desperate, yet our blessed Lord Jesus Christ finds no difficulty in curing it. He knows how to heal the most desperate case in the world. This would be sufficiently known if it were sufficiently believed. He is the eternal wisdom of the Father; He is the power of God; His will is perfect, and He has the most seasonable remedies for any disease. He has more than enough skill and experience to handle the most sad and desperate case that a Christian can be under at any time. He has cast out many a devil, and He has conquered many a soul. Let us examine three desperate cases in which a child of God may find himself.

First, a believer may find himself in the desperate state of extraordinary unwillingness. No one has ever repented in that condition. Such a condition has never bereaved any of their night's sleep. However, Jesus Christ knows well how to begin to cure such a condition. He is a Prince, exalted to give repentance to Israel; for it is He, Jesus Christ, who works repentance. "Alas," a sinner may object, "my sins are gross—they are double-dyed sins!" The Lord has an answer to this objection: "Although your sins are gross, let us work together. Though your sins be great, even double-dyed sins—though they be as scarlet sins in a great measure, let them be never so great and grievous—I will make them as white as snow." Now, friend, although you may not know what to do in such a condition, yet our blessed Lord Jesus has skill to cure such desperate cases. "Come now, and let us reason together, saith the LORD: though your sins be as scarlet, they shall be as white as snow; though they be red like crimson, they shall be as wool" (Isa. 1:18). "Him hath God exalted with his right hand to be a Prince and a Saviour, for to give repentance to Israel, and forgiveness of sins" (Acts 5:31).

The second desperate case that a believer may find himself in is this: when a soul finds nothing in his experience, nothing between his poverty and nature's poverty; when he finds great wars and divisions between his mind and spirit, and even when he finds a law in his members which rebels against the law of the mind; when he finds within himself one party for Christ, and one party for the devil, fighting against one another; when he finds that he desires to do the things which he would not, and leave undone that which he should do—in this desperate condition, a Christian may feel he is far from obtaining victories over the body of death. God's people may find themselves in such a condition that grace may seem to disappear and corruptions win victories over them, but surely Christ has skill and expertise in dealing with such a case and condition. He can sow the seed of division in the heart of His own people for their good, making an enmity between their flesh and their spirit. He keeps just enough of His grace in our hearts to keep us needful of Him all our days.

Third, a believing soul may be convinced of his sin and clearly see his guilt; in his conviction, he may receive the light of God's free grace, and may see imputed righteousness through Jesus Christ. Once he receives this justification, he may become sluggish in the battle of mortification; he may think that he need not pray as often, now that he has received God's grace. Certainly, this condition is desperate in the eyes of the world, and it is a very dangerous place for a child of God to be. Surely it is one of the deep pits into which Satan drags us, and I am persuaded that many of us know this condition by experience. But fear not, for our blessed Lord Jesus has perfect skill to handle this wretched condition. Although it may seem to be desperate in our eyes, it is not so for Him. He is infinitely exalted above all, and His understanding does not fail. He can cure such seemingly desperate cases with one glance; and, after curing a condition, He will make sure that the patient sees the gospel. He will make it clear that free grace must be wrought in the heart by faith. Faith is the only remedy whereby any case may be truly cured; along with faith comes all the power of God (Hos. 12:3). After you have freely received imputed righteousness through Jesus Christ, dear believers, do not think that you have the liberty to grow secure and lazy. Rather, you ought to be diligent, watching unto prayer. You must fear God and His goodness! If you have received free grace, keep it diligently, and do not abuse it.

Some may object, "Alas! My case is so desperate, that I do not think I will ever be saved!" We say to you today, there is hope concerning your salvation if you put your case in Christ's hand! Deliver your condition over to Him, so that He may plead it for you, even He who is the advocate of the righteous, who continually makes intercession at the right hand of His Father in heaven for the acceptance of His people. Therefore, let this comfort and encourage you regarding the desperateness of your condition—no case or condition, however sad it may be, is desperate in the eyes of Christ Jesus. There may be some who cry, "Alas! I do not know if I dare to put my case in Christ's hand!" To you I would say this: Yes, you may do it! You have warrant to put your case in His hand. You may surely lean the weight of your eternal salvation upon Him; He is a sure foundation, and whosoever builds on Him will not be ashamed. I say then, you may trust your condition with Christ. To all persons who are thinking of venturing upon Christ, let me say these words: there is yet hope concerning your salvation. I pray you, do not mistake me. I do not attempt to make any desperate case seem light unto the person; surely, that is not our intention; for I pity the Christian, whosoever he may be, who is in a dark condition and knows it not. We pray that Christ Jesus may get employment, and that you will employ Him with the work of your eternal salvation.

There are three particular points concerning these words of our text: "I washed thee with water." First, Jesus Christ is an excellent physician; He knows each cure, for He knows the disease itself. He can take spiritual diseases into His hands. Further, Jesus Christ, if we may say so, is not lordly in His skill; He is easily entreated. Oh, may not these properties commend this excellent physician unto us? He is so good, for no case or disease can be too desperate for Him, yet He is also easily entreated and employed. He takes great pleasure in employment. When He saw the children of Israel wallowing in their blood, He said unto them, "Live." A good physician is disposed to take notice of His patients' symptoms and cases, even when they are in a case of desperation. Our blessed Lord Jesus says in John 6:37, "All that the Father giveth me shall come to me; and him that cometh to me I will in no wise cast out." There was never a person born who dared to say that He has ever given him an answer of refusal on the back of their petition and bill. Here is the reason: Christ knows that no one else will take their case. No one will so much as notice them. They will meet with hard handling if He forsakes them. He knows that if He does not have pity on them, the devil gets leave to lodge in their bosom.

The second point to consider in the words, "I washed thee with water," is this: in these words, we see Jesus Christ taking in His hand those who have given Him many affronts and disgraces. He says to the bride in Song of Solomon 5:2, "Open to me, my sister, my love, my dove, my undefiled: for my head is filled with dew, and my locks with the drops of the night." And how does she answer Him? "I have put off my coat; how shall I put it on? I have washed my feet; how shall I defile them?" (v. 3). Oh, what a crude answer He receives from her! Oh, lazy spouse, could you not stir yourself to go the length of your own house? Do you think that He should ever call upon her again?

Third, notice that the Son of God is willing to take on the case of those who have wringed His gospel and service, who have wasted many a good prayer, and who have slighted many a good preaching. There are a number of murderers and profane persons seeking to take the life of the Son of God, and conspiring against him. In Matthew 26:55, He says, "Are ye come out as against a thief with swords and staves for to take me? I sat daily with you teaching in the temple, and ye laid no hold on me." But still He cries to those who are seeking His life, "You who were seeking my heart-blood yesterday, if you will this day take the grace of God, I am now willing to give you life."

Christians, put your case in His hand; He will hear you and He will hearken unto the voice of your supplication. When men will weary to hear you, then go to Him and He will hear you—He is never weary. When all the ministers of the whole land are too weary to hearken unto you, He will be content to take your case. Know that today, Christ is willing to take your case in His hand, however desperate it may be; and we pray that you are likewise willing to give it to Him. Christ shall get all my change, and you shall never find a wrong thought in Him, nor a wrong look in Him. There shall never arise any vain lust in your heart, but it shall make you have an errand to the throne of God; there you shall lie still until you get that lust mortified and subdued. Certainly, the best among you all is still very unwilling to go to Christ. We entertain such indulgence to ourselves and we have no desire at all to crush our indulgence. Oh, might we not tell our case to Christ, during the many hours of the day that we spend idly? Oh, but it is a great difficulty to believe this, truly and solidly in our hearts, that Jesus Christ shall get all our change.

Let us now consider the next part of our text: "I throughly washed away thy blood from thee." You must observe from these words that it is the privilege and dignity of believers, not only to have guilt removed, but also to have the intimation of pardon written in their own bosom. Surely that is a glorious privilege of the child of God: having a free remission of sins.

A second noticeable point concerning these words is that the believer has remission of sins in the heart of this pardon. There is a perfect peace and joy in the bosom of a forgiven sinner, as we see in Isaiah 26:3: "Thou wilt keep him in perfect peace, whose mind is stayed on thee: because he trusteth in thee." Secondly, the intimation of pardon gives them a peace of conscience. They have great peace of conscience, which flows from the covenant of grace. They also have the joy of the Holy Spirit; they have everlasting consolation, which is a sweet and blessed condition. Those who receive this peace also receive the white stone and the new name, which is pardon of sin and intimation of that pardon. Believe it, there is no perfect peace at all without this intimation of pardon; once you get this peace, you need not be afraid. Yes, then death may come in and terrify the child of God; but, ultimately, neither death, hell, the law, nor anything can frighten the man whose sin is pardoned.

Death can not bring true fear to the pardoned man. Death may threaten you, believer, with its finality. Then you shall conquer that threat saying, "Through Christ I shall triumph, and shall sing that triumphant song: 'O death, where is thy sting? O grave, where is thy victory?'" (1 Cor. 15:55). The grave may say to the pardoned man, "I shall rot you in the dust." "Oh," says the pardoned man, "my head, Christ Jesus, is risen and I shall rise likewise. I defy you, death. What can you do? And grave, what can you do?" For, "Who shall lay any thing to the charge of God's elect? It is God that justifieth. Who is he that condemneth? It is Christ that died, yea rather, that is risen again, who is even at the right hand of God, who also maketh intercession for us" (Rom. 8:33-34). And then we read, "Who shall separate us from the love of Christ? shall tribulation, or distress, or persecution, or famine, or nakedness, or peril, or sword? As it is written, For thy sake we are killed all the day long; we are accounted as sheep for the slaughter. Nay, in all these things we are more than conquerors through him that loved us" (Rom. 8:35-37).

It is as if the pardoned man would say to death, "You may threaten now, but beware, for once I shall come to judgment, and it shall be said unto me, 'Well done, thou good and faithful servant: thou hast been faithful over a few things, I will make thee ruler over many things: enter thou into the joy of thy lord'" (Matt. 25:21). The Christian is under no law, but under grace. He is content to have grace, not only for the rule of his obedience, but the man or woman that has the gospel's pardon defies it also for the condemning power of it.

A third point to notice concerning the pardoned man's duty is that it is taken off his hands kindly and affectionately. You may never have been so poor in the eyes of the world, yet Christ passes His word for you in heaven, and Christ raises His service more than those who offered sacrifices upon the golden altar. When Christ finds defects in the prayers of His own, He helps them; and when He finds the heart of the Christian out of joint in the exercise of prayer, He binds heart and prayer back together.

Finally, there are two desperate cases that often befall a Christian. The first is a self-secure case. The second is an altering case, which is subject to change.

First, let us consider the secure case—a man who was never put to exercise faith, and is still long bound in the bands of death. Such a man has never been troubled enough by his sin to make him check his conscience. He never looked his guilt in the face to see what he truly deserves. "Oh," says the weak believer, "if you knew what I endure! I find the apprehensions of God's wrath hanging over my spirit, as if I were hanging over the brink of the bottomless pit." I say, it is but God's disposing upon you before the intimation of pardon; but in the end, it shall be said to you, "Well done, thou good and faithful servant," and "Son, be of good cheer, thy sins are forgiven thee."

Now, let us consider the following thought. When the terrors of God most frighten you in your mind, it is the time for intimation of pardon and remission of iniquity. When intimation of pardon is proclaimed, He puts them on as noble exploits, as His ministers. He will make them look in the face of the highest man in the world and tell him that he is nothing but vanity—he is vanishing vanity and vexation of spirit.

The second and last case of a believer is one who is in an altering case. The wavering person may say, "I was once in such a state that I could have exercised faith." Look back to that case and learn to keep a better bridle on that which is in your hand. There is nothing that can make the soul happy except Jesus Christ; He can allure the soul, bring her into the wilderness, and speak comfortably to her.

Now you must examine yourselves, but do not be overly anxious about your condition, and do not despair. Christ's blood can pardon sin after conversion as well as before. I would recommend unto you to revise your case and entrust it to Christ's charge. To Him, no case or disease is too desperate, though it may seem desperate to us. Amen.

SERMON 21

A Christian's Exercise under Desertion

But Zion said, The L*ORD hath forsaken me,*
and my Lord hath forgotten me.
—Isaiah 49:14

The former part of this chapter is a large discourse to the nation, showing how Christ was called to the office of a mediator, king, priest, and prophet. You have Christ's acceptation of the covenant; He sets down the bargain on behalf of you. He will have mercy on His afflicted church, in which He resolves many fair promises in the covenant.

First, by virtue of the everlasting covenant, all things are made sure, and all things are removed that contribute to the hurt and prejudice of believers; this is evidently clear in Romans 8:28, "And we know that all things work together for good to them that love God, to them who are the called according to his purpose." Certainly if He has given Jesus Christ unto you, all other things shall soon come to you. Christ is the standing party. To testify to this assertion, He calls heaven and earth to witness and rejoice, in the thirteenth verse: "Sing, O heavens; and be joyful, O earth; and break forth into singing, O mountains: for the LORD hath comforted his people, and will have mercy upon his afflicted." He does these, whereby He expresses His full satisfaction; He does it because heaven and earth were servants of the house.

In the rest of the chapter, there ensues a holy contest and debate between God and Zion. She objects and He answers; she instances and He replies. Zion's first expression is in the fourteenth verse, which at this time we have read: "But Zion said, The LORD hath forsaken me." In expressing her jealousy, she says, "The Lord hath made me desolate"; or, the Lord has left me alone; the Lord has ruined the most part of His people. She looks as if she were in present captivity, although it is not long after she was in captivity. Her first expression is, "The Lord hath forsaken me."

The second expression is much worse than the former; in the latter part of the fourteenth verse, she says, "My Lord hath forgotten me." He answers her objections with an argument taken from the creature: "Can a woman forget her sucking child, that she should not have compassion on the son of her womb? Yea, they may forget, yet will I not forget thee" (v. 15). You may still observe and take notice that in the altering and changing of dispensations, jealousies and suspicions breed; they begin to grow jealous of themselves because of the altering of their former dispensations. You may see it clear in the practice of Gideon, a godly man. The prophet says to him, "The LORD is with thee" (Judg. 6:12). Then he answers again in Judges 6:13, "Oh my Lord, if the LORD be with us, why then is all this befallen us? And where be all his miracles which our fathers told us of, saying, Did not the LORD bring us up from Egypt? But now the LORD hath forsaken us, and delivered us into the hands of the Midianites." It is ordinary for God's people to reason from dispensation to relation. If their dispensations alter, then they conclude that their relation alters also. When the poor soul of a believer is brought to that, alas! My soul is scarcely in a consistent temper for three hours; then, presently, alterations of his dispensations begin to breed jealousy. This is jealousy's language, when things are going that way; and when the person's dispensations begin to change, jealousy says, "I do not know if God purposeth to do me any good or not." In this state, they begin to grow suspicious of Him. I would say to you that this same jealousy and suspicion is very common among the people of this generation, even among the people of God's own bosom. They are very ready to conclude with jealousy over Him, and to resist the covenant and free grace of God; yea, they are glad to pass a challenge on the covenant of free grace.

Second, take notice, if jealousy and suspicion get room in your heart, it will not rest until they bring you under the sin of blasphemy. Let it but once into the nook of your house and it will take the chair. It will sit, rule, and have the entire house in a stir, because the people of God are often jealous and suspicious of Him without cause or reason; then, they resist noble truth that makes God plague them with jealousy, which ruins and brings the house under the sin of blasphemy.

Third, you should observe and take notice that when suspicion and jealousy travel at their own will, true faith enters its protestation, and maintains some entries one way or other. When jealousy and suspicion think to cut off all that you have, the Lord will answer that jealousy. This latter doubt and jealousy of hers is more desperate than the former; but the Lord does not keep that over that which Zion keeps, for her latter doubt was desperate. Whatever the doubts and jealousies God's people have, almost desperate doubts befall them, as you may see in Psalm 3:1, "Lord, how are they increased that trouble me! Many are they that rise up against me."

The fourth thing that you should notice is that this is the desperate doubt of many that are here, saying of their soul, "Is no help for me in God?" Certainly it is but lost labor to debate another doubt, until this desperate doubt be addressed. This may serve both for the use of the public and the private condition of believers. As for the public use of it, there are many who say that the work is full of difficulties. No doubt, if ever we shall get it done, we will win through it loosely; that is a desperate doubt. Also, if you enter into a desperate jealousy, it shall arise to such a height that it shall obstruct and blindfold both your wit and your judgment. For we see many enemies sporting on the one hand malignants, and on the other hand, loose and desperate doubting. He shall remove this out of the way, for private folk's condition. When desperate doubts arise in your heart, and you begin to say, "I fear His secret decree does not reach to me," then I tell you that is a desperate doubt. Once you entertain the doubt that cuts you off from Christ, you lack entrance to Him, and it stands between you and your promise. Without making use of Christ and His promises, you can answer no desperate doubt.

Those who are debating their doubts and have fear in their hearts that the secret decree does not reach them, let them beware of it. Take this doubt out of the way, for it is desperate; it labors to cut you off from Christ and His promises. Christ here uses an argument to divert you from that doubt: "Can a woman forget her sucking child, that she should not have compassion on the son of her womb? Yea, they may forget, yet will I not forget thee" (Isa. 49:15). You are engraven upon the palms of My hands, so that it is not possible for

Me to forget you. He takes the argument from a woman, a creature-argument; you walk continually before me, in my sight; therefore I cannot forget you. It is as if the Lord had said, "I have a great care of my children, and as much compassion upon them as a mother has over her children, even over her sucking children." He pities them the more they fear Him. Look to the care the mother has for the child; she cares for the child when the child cannot care for itself. The mother cares and provides for the child, when the child cares not for the mother; so does God with His people. He cares for them when they cannot care for themselves; "Yet, nevertheless, I am still with thee." He cares for us when we are sleeping, "his eyes behold, his eyelids try, the children of men" (Ps. 11:4). He cares for us when we think not of it. He, like a mother, cares for His children. This is but a borrowed speech from the creature, for He is God over all, blessed forever. He sees more of our dangers than a mother sees the dangers of her children; therefore He cares more for us. The mother of the child knows not the dignity of the child. If she knew that they would be kings and queens, she would never sleep soundly. But, the Lord knows the dignity of His own—that they shall be kings and queens; therefore, the point is clear, that He cares more for His people than a mother for her child. This reproves those who will not give that undeniable respect to God, that is often given to the creature, either in His love, in His faithfulness, or in His power. I think this is an evil incident to many of us, that we trust the creatures too much and that we lay too much weight upon them, even more than we do upon God. You should beware doing this, since all things below God are but vanity, and subject to changes and alterations.

Now when we see means, it is easy for us to believe; but what if the Lord blast all these means? It is then most difficult for one to believe. If you do not believe when you are destitute of means, when there is not a man on your side, as well as when you have twenty thousand armed men; certainly if it be not so, you do not know what it was to believe, that dispensations may alter. We are bound to believe that God can destroy His enemies with few, as well as with many. Look to the argument itself that God uses. Is it taken from the creature? Is it taken from the mother to the child? The point is this: when His people are jealous, He will then set down a complete pattern to answer all their doubts. He will use reasons taken from the creature to prove the doubts that arise in their minds; from experience, you shall make creature-arguments against jealousies. For these that have the managing of the public work in hand, they certainly may reason from creature-arguments. For instance, when ungodly atheists go along in arms, managing that public employment, no argument will satisfy their eye but creature-arguments, such as, "He is a brave Scotsman, he is a good resolute man, and a brave soldier."

Experience, however, has often shown that an honest countryman with a blunt sword, has achieved as much speed as a trooper with guns and pistols rattling. You may reason from experience, when you have much ado with jealousy about the love of God in your soul. You may look to David, how he uses creature-arguments (1 Sam. 17). It is true, David reports. I was but a scoury poor lad keeping the flock. In the meantime, there came a lion and a bear, and took a lamb out of the flock; I went after them, preserved the lamb, and slew the attackers. In verse 37, David continues, "The LORD that delivered me out of the paw of the lion, and out of the paw of the bear, he will deliver me out of the hand of this Philistine." This is David's reasoning from experience; he confirms himself in his faith and experience from it, when he had to confront the uncircumcised Philistine. It is a remarkable text: "David said moreover, The LORD that delivered me out of the paw of the lion, and out of the paw of the bear, he will deliver me out of the hand of this Philistine." The Lord will do this. David, in this condition, had his eye upon God, and looked unto Him by faith, and so he quieted himself

The question may be asked: what if the arguments from the creatures should fail? In answer to this question, I say, even the arguments from the creature may fail, but in such a condition, the Christian should cast his eye upon God by faith. No doubt shall remain then and confirm his heart, even when arguments from the creatures fail. You desire to labor to maintain and keep up your faith in that condition. This was David's practice, in Psalm 73:26, "My flesh and my heart faileth: but God is the strength of my heart, and my portion for ever." God never fails me, and the reason is that the good will of God is a greater ground than the argument from any creature, to maintain our faith in Christ Jesus. Certainly, this ground reproves two sorts of Christians. First, this reproves those that can dispute well enough as long as they can argue from the creature. We have parliament, assemblies, and armies on the field, and we look up no further, but rest upon these. No doubt, these may presently fail whenever unbelief comes in; they can no longer be arguments to maintain a Christian's faith. A second sort of person reproved are those that can argue well enough, as long as they can pour out their hearts before God, and can pray and seek His face. They stay until God closes up their mouth and hardens their hearts, so that they cannot speak a word, neither can they entertain a thought of God. Then, presently, they conclude that they are gone forever.

We shall say no more to you at this time, but make it your exercise to fear the Lord and to have an interest made sure in Jesus Christ. Seek to be in a believing state of life, for "he that believeth shall not make haste" (Isa. 28:16). The day of the vengeance of God is at hand, when the wicked shall be as stubble to the fire, and His wrath shall consume them together. He shall eternally crush them in the lake that burns with fire and brimstone. Amen.

SERMON 22

The Intercourse of Divine Love between Christ and His Church

I am the rose of Sharon, and the lily of the valleys. As the lily among thorns, so is my love among the daughters.

—Song of Solomon 2:1-2

What makes heaven so pleasant a place and so glorious and joyful a habitation? Is it not because all the streets, windows, and porches thereof are sprinkled with the leaves of the Rose of Sharon and the Lily of the valleys? It would be an endless work to set out all the praises of Him that is the noble Plant of renown. It is above the excellent oratory of angels. The bride had been commending Christ in the last verse of the former chapter, but it is indeed most suitable for Christ to commend Himself.

In this chapter we have two important points. First is Christ's speech, which is contained in the first and second verses. Second is the bride's speech, where she sets forth the noble dispensations of love that she encounters; in doing so, she sets out the commendations of Christ. However, there are several things in her speech that are the words of Christ; yet the bride is the immediate speaker of these words, so they fall under the bride's speech and discourse.

First, then, let us consider the excellent speech of Christ. Christ is the master speaker; none can speak like Him. This was the testimony that He received: "Never man spake like this man" (John 7:46).

Now in His discourse you have two things to consider. In the first verse, Christ sets forth and commends Himself; in the second, He commends the bride and sets forth her condition. As for the commendation Christ gives Himself in the first verse, He says, "I am the rose of Sharon, and the lily of the valleys." Let us consider the importance of these words. First, let us consider the person commending, as well as the person commended; both are Jesus Christ, the noble Plant of renown, both commending and commended. Secondly, we have the commendation that Christ gives to Himself, "I am the rose of Sharon, and the lily of the valleys." He was that rose of Sharon, which was a most fruitful and excellent thing; and He is the lily of the valleys, which no doubt were most pleasant, most fair, and excellent lilies. These two expressions hold out a sevenfold excellence in Christ; they hold out the matchless comeliness and surpassing beauty He embodies.

First, is there anything as beautiful as a rose? Is there anything that has such comeliness as a lily? Although these are but dark shadows, they point out the unsearchable beauty and the inexpressible comeliness that is in Christ.

Second, they hold out the savoriness and refreshing nature of precious and matchless Christ. Is there anything more savory than a rose? Is there anything more refreshing than a lily of the valley? These are but shadows to point out the savoriness in Christ, who is all perfumed with the powder of the merchant.

Third, they point out Christ's inexpressible glory and majesty. Is it not said by Christ in Matthew 6:28-29, "Why take ye thought for raiment? Consider the lilies of the field, how they grow; they toil not, neither do they spin: And yet I say unto you, that even Solomon in all his glory was not arrayed like one of these"? Christ being compared unto a lily or a rose points out the inexpressible and matchless glory and majesty that is in Him. Do you not think that Christ must be glorious, with an excellent robe of majesty? "Who coverest thyself with light as with a garment" (Ps. 104:2). Must He not be a glorious One who has such a throne of state to dwell in light that is inaccessible? Must not Christ be a glorious One that has such an excellent frame? As it is said, He "inhabiteth eternity" (Isa. 57:15).

Fourth, these two flowers are examples of the usefulness of Christ. Both the rose and the lily are most fit for medicine's use. Thus, we can conclude that these flowers show forth Christ's healing.

Fifth, these two expressions point out that Christ provides free and easy access to the Father. The word may also be rendered, "I am the rose of the fields," as if Christ would have said, "I am not enclosed in a garden, but I am in the fields—everyone that passes by may have me."

Sixth, these point out Christ's humility and condescension. When He says, "I am the lily of the valleys," it is as if Christ had said, "Do you desire to know the place where I dwell? I dwell in the valleys. I am not a lily that grows on the mountains, but a lily that grows in the valleys." The vision in Zechariah 1 is a comparison of this comment. It says, "I saw by night, and behold a man riding upon a red horse, and he stood among the myrtle trees that were in the bottom." The myrtle trees are lowly trees.

Seventh, these two expressions in Christ hold out His unsearchableness and inexpressibleness. Surely, if Christ should speak to you Himself, as He is in Himself, He would seem to be a foreigner, speaking to us in an unknown tongue. In this life, Christ has revealed Himself to us under a shadow. Despite the shadow of His revelation, however, we understand two things. First, we see Christ's inexpressible greatness; second, our inexpressible ignorance. Oh, the blessed angels are now singing sweetly to His praise! Certainly, though we heard them, we would not understand them because of our ignorance. Must it not be an excellent thing to dwell eternally under the pleasant and comfortable shadow of the rose of Sharon? What a life must it be to have our heart solaced by the beholding of Him, and to take Him in our arms and to cry out, "Are we not eternally made up?" It is the unchangeable joy of these in the higher courts.

Third, let us notice the language that Christ uses in expressing the commendation of Himself. He says, "I am the rose of Sharon, and the lily of the valleys." It seems as if He had said, "I am not like the lily, but I am the same." This form of expression points out that there is no beauty and excellence in any creature of God; but there is eminent beauty in Christ. We may read of the beauty of God in the heavens, on earth, and in ourselves; but when we come to see the beauty of Christ, we must look at the comeliness of the saints. Oh, must He not be beautiful, if He makes His bride to be without spot? In Him there is no guile. Notice this commendation that Christ gives Himself, "I am the rose of Sharon." From it we would have you take notice of three things. First, there is none in the heavens or in the earth that can commend Christ to purpose but Himself. Let angels and all the saints keep silence when He speaks of Himself. I shall give you these grounds why neither angels nor saints can commend Christ rightly; He alone is found worthy to do it.

First, we do not hear much of Christ; and if there be much heard, there is but little known of that which is heard. We see this in Job 26:14: "Lo, these are parts of his ways: but how little a portion is heard of him? But the thunder of his power who can understand?"

Second, we do not entirely believe that which is spoken of Christ, or that which is known of Him. Oh, had He not need of an excellent tongue that can express the greatness of Christ? Had He not need of an excellent heart that can tell the beauty of Christ? The best oratory in commending Christ is silence and admiration. When you desire to commend Christ, be silent, wonder, and admire. You are never at the height of your thoughts of Christ until your tongue is stuck to the roof of your mouth, and until you cry out, "What shall I say?" Yea, although you know where to begin, you and all the angels in heaven know not where to end. Surely it is an excellent work to commend precious Christ, the excellent rose of Sharon, and the lily of the valleys.

We notice a second point regarding Christ's commendation of Himself. Often Christ commends Himself to the saints. This is clear from Luke 24:27, "And beginning at Moses and all the prophets, he expounded unto them in all the scriptures the things concerning himself." He spoke these words to the two disciples that were coming from Jerusalem, on the road to Emmaus. It is also clear in the second and third chapters of Revelation, where Christ insists much on commending Himself. He says, "I am the offspring of David, the bright and morning star." I shall give you these six grounds why Christ does insist so much on commending Himself.

First, there is not a subject that is so worthy to be commended and spoken of as Christ. What can we speak more of than Christ? What is the endless exercise of angels and of all saints? Is it not to speak of the excellence of precious Christ? There is not a word heard in heaven but this, "Worthy is the Lamb that was slain to receive power, and riches, and wisdom, and strength, and honour, and glory, and blessing" (Rev. 5:12). Oh, must He not be excellent, as all the angels and saints in heaven are taken up in commending Him?

Second, the worthiness and excellence in Christ is not soon commended. It is an endless work to tell all that is in Christ. May not a Christian, when he begins to speak, close his discourse by saying, "What shall I more say?" (Heb. 11:32); eternity would fail me.

Third, Christ's commendation of Himself points out that the excellence in Christ is not quickly believed. Thus, we read in Isaiah 53:1, "Who hath believed our report? and to whom is the arm of the LORD revealed?"

Fourth, there is an absolute necessity that we should have the knowledge of Christ; therefore, He insists on commending Himself. What are all the sermons that are preached? Are they not deep draughts of the beauty of Christ? What is this excellent volume of the Scriptures? Is it not the portraiture of Christ that is sent to a strange land, that His bride may behold His beauty?

Fifth, Christ insists so much in commending Himself because by this, the faith of a Christian is increased. By this, the patience of a Christian is increased, and the life of a Christian is increased. When once the soul gets a broad sight of Christ, he is constrained to cry out, "What have I to do any more with idols? I have heard him, and observed him: I am like a green fir tree. From me is thy fruit found" (Hos. 14:8).

Last, Christ insists so much in commending Himself so that strangers may come unto Him. Oh, shall ever our cursed eyes look to Christ and not be constrained to love Him? We conceive our eyes ought to affect our hearts, and the heart follow the eyes. Shall it ever be told that there are some within the visible church that do undervalue matchless and precious Christ? I allude to 2 Samuel 1:20, which says, "Tell it not in Gath, publish it not in the streets of Askelon; lest the daughters of the Philistines rejoice, lest the daughters of the uncircumcised triumph." Shall it ever be preached that there is some within the visible church that undervalue Christ, the matchless one, that noble Plant of renown?

A third comment we would make concerning Christ's commendation of Himself is that all created beauties and delights are but dark shadows and draughts of the uncreated beauty and comeliness that is in Christ. What would you give for one sight of Christ? I think if it were possible that for an hour there could be a veil drawn between Christ and the saints above, they would sit down and lament, crying, "Oh, will you sell Christ? Will you sell Him at such a low rate, as for thirty pieces of silver?"

Let us consider the second part of Christ's speech in the second verse, wherein He commends the bride, saying, "As the lily among thorns, so is my love among the daughters."

We have here Christ setting forth the beauty of the bride. The exposition may run thus: "There is as great a difference (says Christ) between my love, my bride and spouse, and the daughters, these that are strangers and hypocrites, and the rest of the world; there is as great differences between my bride and these that are strangers to me as there is between a lily and a thorn." Or, the exposition may run thus: "As a lily growing among thorns is obstructed in its growing by these, so is my love among the profane daughters, that are as thorns to her, and trouble her" as is clear, "My mother's children were angry with me" (Song 1:6). These that were mother's children and not father's (if so we may speak) were of the church, but not of Christ.

Take notice of these things from the words: first, that the discovery of the excellence of Christ may be a help out of afflictions; so Christ sets out the excellence of Himself before He sets out the bride's condition. Second, take notice that often the condition of the bride and spouse of Christ while she is here below, is an afflicted and assaulted life; she is as a lily among thorns. It must be so that a Christian had a sad and afflicted life in this Baca. However, I shall propose these six considerations that may press a Christian to be in a divine frame under sad afflictions.

First, the sufferings of the bride are a gift from Christ. Every bit of suffering that a believer encounters is a real gift from Christ; "For unto you it is given in the behalf of Christ, not only to believe on him, but also to suffer for his sake" (Phil. 1:29). It is a gift that He has given to you.

Second, the sufferings of a Christian are as many workmen, fitting him for heaven. Did you ever see a mason polishing a stone for a building? Afflictions are as many workmen to fit us for heaven, to be excellent cornerstones of heaven. So it is that the stones of Solomon's temple were hewn in the wilderness, then were brought to be stones in the temple; so we must be hewn in the wilderness, and then we must be brought to heaven.

Third, the afflicting times of a Christian are his enjoying times. This is clear from Psalm 112:4, which says, "Unto the upright there ariseth light in the darkness." There are excellent benefits that are given to a Christian at that time.

Fourth, afflictions help a Christian's sanctification progress. This is clear from Job 23:10: "But he knoweth the way that I take: when he hath tried me, I shall come forth as gold."

Fifth, the sufferings of a Christian are part of his conformity to Christ: "That I may know him, and the power of his resurrection, and the fellowship of his sufferings, being made conformable unto his death" (Phil. 3:10).

A final consideration that will encourage you to endure afflictions is that it was the way by which Christ went Himself. It was the way whereby He brought about the work of our redemption; will you not follow the way that His precious and blessed feet went? He never stepped a step, but what was in the way of sufferings; He was a lily among thorns.

Next, take notice from the words that the commendation Christ takes to Himself, He gives also to the bride. He calls Himself a lily among the valleys; and He calls her a lily, "as the lily among thorns, so is my love among the daughters." This, no doubt, speaks two truths. It speaks the matchless beauty in the bride, she having some conformity and likeliness to Christ. Also, it points out the high esteem that Christ has for His bride—she is as a lily among thorns.

We desire that you are living with an expectation of heaven, longing for the day when you shall be no more lilies among thorns, but shall be trees planted by the rivers of water. You then shall dwell in a land where there is neither thorn nor briar. A discovery of heaven might constrain us to long to be there! What a pleasant thing it must be eternally to sit down under the pleasant shadow of Him that is the tree of life, that bears twelve varieties of fruits every year. Oh, what a pleasant life it will be to drink of these rivers that come out from under the throne of God, and what a life it will be when our cursed, polluted feet shall tramp upon the rock of His glory! They shall sing, "My soul shall awake early and sing the praises of Him that sits on the throne and that hath gone up with the shout of the trumpet." Let it be your exercise here, that which shall be your eternal exercise above, when you shall hang your harps no more on the willow tree, because you are in a strange land, but you shall be singing constantly these excellent songs, the melodious songs of praise that shall be sung to Christ. Oh, what a life will it be to hear David, the sweet singer! How sweetly he sings now! There is a remarkable difference between David on earth and

David in heaven. What a life will it be to hear Solomon, who penned the excellent song of Christ! There is now a great difference between Solomon here and Solomon in heaven. What a life it will it be to be amongst these thousands, whose songs no man is able to learn!

Oh, long for the day when there shall be no more weeping, and all tears shall be wiped from your eyes! There shall be no more ignorance, no more desertion, no more distance from precious Christ; but you shall bathe yourselves eternally in the excellent streams of unspeakable joy, when these tongues that never praised Him aright here shall be as the pen of a ready writer. I think the Christian shall inquire, when he first enters heaven, "Is it I? Christ-despising I? Is it I that was living among the pots, that am now made white as the wings of a dove, covered with silver, with wings as of yellow gold?" What is the exercise of the saints in heaven? There is not one look in heaven that is not fixed on precious Christ. There is not one thought in heaven that is not taken up in thinking on Him; there is not one desire that is not fixed on Him; and there is not one movement of the foot in heaven that is not taken up in following the Lamb. Their ears are not satisfied with hearing, their eyes not satisfied with seeing, and their hearts are not satisfied with enjoying.

From the third verse of the chapter to the close, we read the bride's speech of Christ. There are four parts to this speech. First, notice the bride's matchless estimation of Christ; we read in the third verse, "As the apple tree among the trees of the wood, so is my beloved among the sons." Second, from the latter part of the third verse to the eighth verse, the bride sets out several eminent enjoyments that she had of Christ, under various expressions. Third, from the eighth verse to the tenth, she sets down her enjoyments of Christ in a remote and more distant condition than she had before. Last, from the tenth verse to the sixteenth, the bride sets out condescending terms and good words that Christ spoke to her when she was under this remote enjoyment of Him. In the last verses of the chapter, she closes her discourse with the faith of her interest in Him and a prayer that He would return.

First, we see the bride's matchless opinion of Christ in the first part of the third verse, as she says, "As the apple-tree among the trees of the wood, so is my beloved among the sons." By this statement, the bride means, "There is as great a difference between my beloved and the rest of the sons of men, even the great ones of the earth, as there is between the apple tree and the trees of the wood"; or, in briefer terms, "My bridegroom is matchless." Christ is compared to the apple tree for three reasons. First, for the refreshment that is found in Christ from the wrath of God, as well as from hurt and persecution. A believer may rest and solace himself in this knowledge. Second, Christ is compared to the apple tree because of the excellent fruits that are found in Christ; the apple tree is the tree that bringeth forth good and excellent fruits (Rev. 22:2). This tree, which grows in the midst of the paradise of God, bears twelve types of fruits every year. What fruits of joy and apples of everlasting delight grow on this apple tree! Third, He is compared unto an apple tree because there is much savoriness and refreshment to be found in precious Christ. Is there anything so refreshing as Christ? We may say of these apples that grow on the apple tree, that which Satan told once to Eve, they are good for the body, pleasant to the sight, and good to make one wise; it is by means of these apples that grow on the tree of life that we must become as God, knowing good and evil. From this part of her discourse, take notice of these three things.

First, notice that the soul of a Christian usually has the highest and most eminent uptakings of God under crosses. This is clear by comparing the second verse with the third; she was a lily among thorns; yet, here in the third verse, Christ is as the apple among the trees of the forest. Christ is matchless to the bride, even under her straits and afflictions. There are two grounds for this statement: first, because God often communicates to the soul excellent sights of Himself under affliction; so it is that they have most eminent conceptions of Him when they are under such a case. Second, when the soul of a Christian is most mortified, it is denied to all the idols that it has.

Second, notice that when the beauty and matchless excellence in Christ is revealed to a soul, the soul sees the emptiness of all other things. When Christ is taken up as the apple tree, then all the rest of the things of the world are taken up as trees in the wood in comparison to Him. We think it is the best way to read the vanity and emptiness of our idols in the face of Christ. It is a blessed mortification that comes from beholding Him; we suppose that if you had gotten a sight of Christ, you would never desire to be parted from Him.

Third, notice that Christ's matchless and singular transcendence is far above all things that can be found. There is nothing comparable to Christ. This was David's divinity, "Thou art fairer than the children of men" (Ps. 45:2); there is none in heaven that can be likened to Christ.

There is a sevenfold sight of Christ that will demonstrate to you the matchlessness of Christ. Take a sight of Him in His natures, and this will prove Him to be matchless. There is more in Christ being the Son of God than all the angels can make language of. He is God and man in one person. Oh, take a sight of the humanity and divinity of Christ; this would make Him exceeding matchless in the soul! Sinner, take a view of the highness of Christ, as He is God, and of His lowliness as He is man, then you will see love, condescending love, eminently shining and appearing. First, take a view of Christ in His offices. Is He not a king to rule over us? Is He not a prophet to teach us? Is He not a priest to offer up Himself to us? These three offices in Christ demonstrate both His highness and His condescendence. Oh, that He who is a king should be a prophet, and that He who is a king should be a priest! We conceive that the kingly office of Christ deals with our disobedience, which the prophetical office of Christ responds to our ignorance, and the priestly office of Christ, speaks out our sinfulness.

A second sight and view of Christ that makes Christ exceedingly matchless and precious is the sight of Him administering and going about His offices. Three excellent qualifications of Christ appear in His going about these offices. First, we can see Him as infinite wisdom. According to Isaiah 52:13, which says, "Behold my servant shall deal prudently," he has much infinite wisdom in going about these offices. Second, there is infinite tenderness in Christ going about His offices. We see this in Isaiah 42:3: "A bruised reed shall he not break, and the smoking flax shall he not quench." Third, infinite love and condescension appear in His going about these offices. This is shown by Isaiah 40:11: "He shall gently lead those that are with young."

A third sight that will make Christ singular and exceeding matchless to the soul is the sight of Christ in these enjoyments and communications of love that He gives to His own. Is not communion with Christ an excellent thing? Is not enjoyment of Christ a desirable thing? Yet, He Himself must be much more desirable. What are all our enjoyments? What are all our communications of love? Are they not all streams that run from this precious fountain, which is precious Christ?

Fourth, a view of Christ in His promises will render Him most matchless and singular. Oh, what a matchless One He must be, who has promised us eternal life! Oh, what a matchless One He must be, who has promised us that we shall see His face, and shall be made like unto Him! Every promise in the everlasting covenant has this engraven on the head of it: Christ is matchless!

Fifth, observe Christ and the excellent grants and donations of favor that He has given to His own. Are there not many excellent things that He has given unto us? He has given us peace; is this not an excellent thing? He has given Himself unto us; what more can we say?

Last, a view and sight of Christ in His dispensation of grace to us will exceedingly commend Him and make us cry out, "Whom have I in heaven but thee? And there is none upon earth that I desire beside thee" (Ps. 73:25).

A next observation we make concerning the text is that it is impossible for Christ to be matchless to the soul, until it wins to the distinct assurance of its interest in Christ. When was it that Christ was as the apple tree among the trees of the wood? Was it not then when she could say, "So is my beloved among the sons" (Song 2:3)? It is impossible for you to have high thoughts of Christ except you can say, "He is mine." You cannot truly admire Christ unless you take Christ in your arms in the morning, at mid-day, and at night, saying, "He shall be eternally mine."

I shall not say much more on the first part of this discourse, but these two points: first, matchless Christ was never so much undervalued by a generation as He has been by us. Cursed be the persons that will not yield up their hearts to this matchless and singular one, Jesus Christ. Also, do you think the day is approaching when He that is the flower that grows in the upper garden, He that ought to have had your hearts, shall be satisfied with you?

Now, for the second part of her discourse, which continues from the latter part of the third verse to the eighth verse, we have four things. First, we have the grounds set down which were the rule of her matchless opinion of Christ. "I sat down under his shadow with great delight, and his fruit was sweet to my taste. He brought me to the banqueting house, and his banner over me was love" (Song

2:3-4). Second, we have here the bride hinting her desire and earnest longing after more eminent enjoyments of Jesus Christ. She says, "Stay me with flagons, comfort me with apples: for I am sick of love" (v. 5). Third, we see the matchless tenderness He had of her when she was under this sickness of love, in the sixth verse, "His right hand doth embrace me."

Fourth, we have the endeavor that she had to remove all impediments and anything that might put Him from her. We read in verse 7, "I charge you, O ye daughters of Jerusalem, by the roes, and by the hinds of the field, that ye stir not up, nor awake my love, till he please."

The latter part of the third verse reads, "I sat down under his shadow, and his fruit was sweet to my taste." Here we can observe the grounds for the sincere and matchless opinion that she had of Christ. In her words, we see that Christ was unto her as a shadow in four ways. First, there is something to be required of a Christian in his coming to sit under His shadow; there are five things to be required of a Christian in his coming to sit under this shadow.

First, He must believe that there is neither rest nor satisfaction to be found in anything without Christ. The bride could not rest until she came to Christ. Secondly, he must know the great disadvantage and hazard he is in before he comes to this shadow. Thirdly, he must have some knowledge of the excellence of this shadow. Fourthly, he must have some desire to come to this shadow; thus, the word is rendered in the original: "I desired and delighted to go under his shadow." Fifthly, the Christian must understand the necessity of it, even of Jesus Christ, so that he may feel the need to go under the shadow. We cannot take up Christ except we be weary and heavy laden, and then need to go under the shadow.

A second observation is the way in which the bride comes to make use of this shadow—by the exercise of the grace of faith. The exercise of the grace of faith, in Scripture, is pointed out sometimes under the notion of Christ.

A third observation is the excellent shadow which Christians must come and sit under. I shall describe eight parts of this substantial shadow. First, there is a piece of this shadow we call profession; once a Christian is under this shadow, he is free from the stroke of all iniquity. Second, there is a piece of this shadow we call confession; once a Christian comes under this shadow, there is much of his own constancy known, and more challenges than he had before. The third piece of this shadow is consolation; once a Christian comes under this shadow, he has the excellent influences and consolations of the Holy Ghost. The fourth piece of this shadow is called delightfulness; even when a Christian is in a longing condition, once he comes under this shadow he is so refreshed with it that he springs forth as the trees of Lebanon. The fifth piece of this shadow is help; let a Christian be under ever so many diseases and distempers, but once he comes under this shadow, he will be without all these diseases. The sixth part of this shadow is light; a Christian may be under many occasions of unbelief, and ever so much darkness, but once he comes under the shadow of Jesus Christ, he shall have abundance of clearness to answer all objections. The seventh part of this excellent shadow is growth; once a Christian comes under this shadow, then he begins to grow and spring as a tree planted by the rivers of waters. There is nothing but joy to be found by sitting down under this excellent shadow. The last part of this shadow is safety; this is safety from outward and inward troubles, which is to be found only in Christ. When a Christian abides in Christ the shadow, in the weariest day, when the tempest beats on you as a storm against the wall, then you can sit down under this refreshing shadow.

Next, it is necessary to point out the properties of this shadow. First, the shadow is a substantial shadow. There is no contradiction against the fact that Christ is a substantial shadow. Secondly, He is an eternal and enduring shadow. If you were once under this great shadow, you would never have come out again. It is not like the shadow of Egypt and Heshbon under the soul, that whosoever shall trust in it shall be ashamed. Thirdly, Christ is a broad shadow. There is room enough under this excellent shadow to receive all that are weary; if there were a thousand times more persons given to Christ, there is abundance of room to be found under this broad shadow, under which we may compass ourselves.

The second ground of Christ's estimation is in the latter part of the third verse: "And his fruit was sweet to my taste." By fruit is meant all the graces of the Spirit of God going out to a Christian, by giving over the heart of a Christian, closing by faith, and making application of Him, and of these graces.

With respect to the third ground of the bride's estimation and opinion of Christ, I would only ask you four questions. Be persuaded of it, you that could never answer any of them are strangers to God and aliens from the covenant of grace.

First, did you ever desire and take up a necessity of going to Christ's shadow? Was ever the necessity of Christ borne in upon your spirits, that there was an absolute necessity either to go to Him or else be undone? I am persuaded that there are many here that never took up their need of this shadow; although they have been under the scorching wrath of the almighty God, yet they never saw the need they had to go to the shadow of this great rock in a weary land.

Second, did you ever believe, or were you ever convinced that there was not a way under heaven by which you might escape the wrath of God, except through this substantial shadow? The spouse was convinced of this and she never got rest until she came to this shadow; and that all other things, beside Christ, were but empty shadows compared with this singular and substantial shadow.

Third, did the great distance of this shadow ever interrupt your joy? There are some whose distance from this shadow has been line upon line; yet, their distance never constrained them to be much in the exercise of sorrow, to endeavor to be out from it.

Last, was Christ's fruit ever sweet to your taste? Was He ever pleasant to you? Was justification ever sweet to you? Were sanctification and adoption ever pleasant to you? Were the gifts and graces of prayer ever pleasant to you? I conceive there are not many that make use of Christ thus. To such people, I would say two things. I suppose, the day is approaching that some shall curse the day they were born and professed godliness with the power thereof. There are some that sit down under the shadow of hypocrisy, and will not come under the shadow of Jesus Christ. Oh, what a blessed thing it would be to sit down under that shadow!

I would also warn you that the day is approaching that many shall curse the day that they prayed so much, heard so much, and were so much at communions; not that these things are not commendable in themselves, but you shall curse the day that you were at such ordinances, but made such little use of them. Oh, when you shall meet with death, how many formal sermons and how many slighted Sabbaths shall come then in remembrance? Believe it, religion is another thing than most of us take it to be. I confess, if it is not much to be a well-spoken Christian, or a gifted Christian, it is worth much to be a real and exercised Christian. There are some that take up religion at their feet; they never knew how it came, nor when it came. I think it is much to love religion when it is sent; but it is much to love a dying Christ. Unfortunately, most of us follow Him because of His miracles. Oh, for one sight of Christ, before we go hence and be no more!

We have told you in the preceding verse that the bride had high and precious thoughts of Christ; that He was to her "as the apple tree among the trees of the wood." She sets down three precious grounds for the high and matchless opinion and esteem she had of Christ; the first two grounds are in the latter part of the third verse. First, He was to her as a shadow. "I sat down under his shadow" (Song 2:3). Second, she continues, "His fruit was sweet to my taste." The third ground of the high and matchless opinion that she had of Christ, is set down in the fourth verse, where she says, "He brought me to the banqueting-house, and his banner over me was love." In this statement, we will consider three things.

First, the excellent condition and estate of the spouse; she was brought to the banqueting-house. We understand this to mean a most intimate, familiar, and sweet correspondence with Christ in ordinances and duties of immediate worship.

Second, the person to whom she ascribes the praise and honor of this condition she was in: "He brought me to the banqueting-house." My cursed feet would never have gone such an excellent way if Christ had not brought me: "He brought me to the banqueting-house." This implies acknowledgment of her inability to bring herself to this condition, but this also, that she is willing to engrave this on the head of every one of her enjoyments: Christ brought me here.

Third, consider the real and excellent way that Christ takes to bring her to the banqueting house: "His banner over me was love." You know the banner or sign is used to gather together soldiers to their colors; so love was the thing that gathered her here. Here we have Christ's real and excellent commendation of Himself to her while she was in the banqueting house.

Finally, I would exhort you to sit down with great delight under His shadow, and His fruit will be the sweetest that you ever tasted; however, if you do not sit down with great delight, His fruit will be the most sour that you ever tasted. Amen.

SERMON 23

The Appropriating Nature of Saving Faith

My beloved is mine, and I am his.
—Song of Solomon 2:16

We have in these words the description of a sweet discourse that passed between Christ and His bride in which He makes many feasts. These feasts are His singular tokens of love for the bride; she is overcome and transported with these lovely expressions of Christ. The two last verses of this chapter contain the bride's discourse, in which she means much of the exercise of faith; she means much of the grace of prayer. Let us study her words, so that we too shall take up the meaning of these words, as several exercises of the bride. In Song of Solomon 2:16, we have two points to consider.

First, we have the spouse's persuasive assertion: "My beloved is mine, and I am his." With these words, she casts the knot between Christ and herself very tight. The second consideration in the sixteenth verse is the assertion upon which she walks, or that which led her to her persuasive assertion and confidence; the answer is set down in these words: "He feedeth among the lilies." The meaning of this may be to point out Christ's care of His church; the meaning may also be that Christ feeds His people in a most pleasant or fruitful place, and so this is her condition. It is as if the bride had said, "Why need I question Christ's love to me, since He takes such a care of those that are committed to His charge?" No doubt, Christ's feeding among the lilies is teaching people and admonishing them in His ways. These words may also point out the great love that Christ has to His people. Christ takes as much delight in His saints as a man does in His necessary food. Christ's delight points out three things:

first, the greatness of His delight in His saints, even as a man delights in His necessary food. Second, the great delight of Christ points out the constancy of His delight in His saints. Third, Christ's delight points out the fullness of delight that His saints ought to have.

Now, because this place is the substance of the gospel, I shall dip a little further into this verse, to discourse concerning the soul's conclusions regarding God. The bride, we conceive, has these seven things held out in her words, "I am my beloved's, and my beloved is mine" (Song 6:3).

First, between Christ and the believer there is a mutual covenant and relation in these words. This is clearly imported in the words, "I am my beloved's." Christ assures her back again, "I am the bride's." There is a mutual relation between Christ and the believer.

Second, there is a mutual owning relation between Christ and a believer; Christ thinks no shame to call a believer His, and a believer thinks no shame to call Christ his.

Third, there is a mutual joy arising from this covenant and relation of the believer with Christ; for the bride rejoices that Christ is hers, and Christ rejoices that the believer is His. Therefore, the words hold out a glorious conversation between Christ and His believer; it is as if Christ had said, "Would you know the world that I most rejoice in? It is this, that believers are mine."

Fourth, the bride uses a particular method and order in her conclusion, saying that Christ is hers. "My beloved is mine," says she; notice that first Christ becomes the believer's, before the believer becomes His; the kindness always comes on Christ's side first.

Fifth, the bride casts such a great knot between Christ and her heart that no difficulties or impediments can break it; here she joins and links her heart to Christ, more than she ever had before.

Sixth, take notice of the words as they relate to Christ's former discourse to the bride; here you may observe that the fruit of the gospel is that which brings the soul to an owning interest and relation of Christ only.

The seventh and last thing is the clearing of the bride's assertion to look upon Christ as the fountain of peace with God; and so, by the way, it is an excellent mark of a Christian that before he seek great things of God for himself, he would come and make sure, and fasten his interest in God that Christ is his, and he is Christ's.

Now, having made clear unto you these words, there are seven observations from the text that we shall briefly address.

The first observation is that a Christian, while he is here below, may surely attain a soul's persuasion and assured interest and confidence in Christ; therefore, the bride wins to this length, saying, "My beloved is mine, and I am his." This is attainable to all believers; they may attain a certainty and confidence of their interest in Christ. Now I shall not speak long upon this at this time; I would have you observe and take notice that there are four things which a Christian does exceedingly slight and undervalue.

A Christian exceedingly slights this excellent jewel of attaining the confidence and solid assurance of his interest in Christ. You who have a name among the number of the living in Jerusalem, since the first day you took on the name "Christian," as a follower of Christ, did you ever spend many hours in the search and trial of your faith in Christ? Did you seek to determine whether you were in a believing state or not? Did you seek to find out whether you were in Christ or not? But, oh, I fear that there are many of us here whose hearts are as dead as stones within them, who were never affected with their interest in Christ or their assurance in Him. However, such persons may dreadfully suspect that they are not Christ's, and that Christ is not theirs.

Second, a believer does exceedingly slight the return of his prayers; for although there be many that have prayed often, yet they cannot say that they ever waited for the return and answer of one of their prayers. Such prayers are more for the satisfaction of their own consciences than for the finding out of the certainty and assurance of their interest in Jesus Christ.

A third thing that a believer does exceedingly slight is communion and fellowship with God, which is a most precious and excellent thing in itself, and has been so accounted of by all that have gone before us. They have left this upon record, that fellowship and communion with God is a precious, singular, and most excellent thing; but there is a generation among us who pass under the name of believers, and who put an estimation upon Christ and fellowship with Him; yet it may be said of them that they care not whether they get Christ or not. They care not to make sure of their interest in Christ, and they do not value communion and fellowship with God. It is to be feared that there are many such persons among us, who hereby do declare that they do not value communion with Him.

Fourth, many believers slight the exercise of self-examination, which is as much slighted by us as any of the former; for many Christians are as great strangers to their own hearts as if they were a thousand miles distance one from another.

Regarding the text, we shall make a further observation: many Christians divide the covenant of grace. Some cry out that Christ is theirs; but they cannot nor dare not say that they are Christ's. They will embrace the one half of the covenant, but not the other. Hence, we read the text in Luke 15:18-19, in the parable of the prodigal son, where he says unto his father, "Father, I have sinned against heaven, and before thee, and am no more worthy to be called thy son: make me as one of thy hired servants." Here he divides the covenant; he calls him father, and yet he dares not venture to call himself his father's son. But it is the commendation of the spouse here, that she embraces the whole covenant, and does not divide it. She fills up both her own part and Christ's part of the covenant; she says, "I am my beloved's, and my beloved is mine."

Many Christians divide several parts of the covenant. They divide the law, as well as the gospel; they refuse to have it wholly. But they will have none of it, who will not have it all. It cannot be divided. They also divide the dispensations of the covenant, as well as the heart, giving the half of it to their idols, and the other half of it to Christ. But Christ shall have none of it if He does not have all of it. Either Christ must have all your heart, or the devil must have it. Christians divide the law in four different ways:

Some look to the letter and outward meaning of the law rather than to the spiritual and saving meaning of the law, and so they divide it. Some look to the second table of the law, but neglect the first table of the law; for example, some persons thank the Lord that they are not murderers, backbiters, and adulterers; yet, these same persons are careless about taking the Lord's name in vain, or profaning the Sabbath of the Lord. Some Christians guard against the sins forbidden in the second table, but not against the sins forbidden in the first table. Such people think that they keep the law; but, to them I say that they do not, for whosoever offends in one point is guilty of the breach of the whole law. The author of the first table of the law is also the author of the second table of the law. Finally, some look to the commandments and promises of the law, but will not consider the curses of the law that are pronounced against the least transgressor or breaker of the law.

Second, some divide the gospel. By this I mean that these persons do halve the covenant of grace; they subscribe to the one part of the covenant, but not to the other part of the covenant. There is a second sort of people that divide the gospel; they are those who look to the promises of the gospel, but not to the commandments and warnings of the gospel.

Third, some divide God's dispensations when they look at the outside of dispensations only, and not at the inside, at the inward and real meaning of them.

Fourth, many divide the heart. Many persons would be content to give Christ one half of their heart, but would fain give the other half of it to the world, that it might solace and delight itself with the pleasures thereof.

A third observation is that Christ and all His benefits are the believer's; and the believer may, with God's allowance and approbation, lay claim and right to them. They may say with good reason, and on good grounds, "Christ and all His benefits are mine"; to say this is a greater word than to say, "All the kingdoms of the world are mine"; yea, all the kingdoms of the world are not comparable to this precious and excellent benefit. Always, believers in Christ, whatever your difficulties, crosses or sad afflictions may be, you may comfort yourselves in this, that Christ, the matchless and singular One, He, that noble Plant of renown, is yours. Before long, He shall sweetly recompense and make up all your losses in Himself, and you shall sit down at the mouth of the river of consolation and drink abundantly, remembering your poverty no more. If Christ is yours, you have chosen the better part, which shall never be taken from you.

I will tell you how Christ is a believer's; He is the believer's by a three-fold right. First, Christ is the believer's by the Father's grant and gift. Hence, He is called, "the gift of God" (John 4:10), when Christ is talking with the woman of Samaria. Believer, comfort yourself in this, for Christ is yours by the grant and gift of the Father. He is a royal gift, given by the Father unto you. Second, Christ is a believer's by His own gift and His own grant; for Christ makes a resignation of Himself over to a believer. The third way Christ is a believer's is by the covenant and relationship that stands between them. He a believer's by the estate of marriage whereby He joins His people to Himself, never to be forsaken; He joins them to Himself in a perpetual covenant never to be forgotten.

Fourth, let us observe that as Christ and all that He has is the believer's, so likewise all that the believer has, ought to be Christ's. Christ has a right to believers for five reasons.

First, Christ has a right to believers by the Father's own gift and grant. Hence we read in John 17:6, "Thine they were, and thou gavest them me; and they have kept thy word." There is also support given in John 6:37, which says, "All that the Father giveth me shall come to me; and him that cometh to me I will in no wise cast out." Christ has a right to believers by His Father's grant unto Him from eternity, even before the foundations of the world were set in place.

Secondly, He has a right to believers by His own purchase, in that respect, that He has purchased them by His precious blood. Hence is that word, "For ye are not your own, ye are bought with a price" (1 Cor. 6:20); wherein He clearly affirms, that Christ's purchase is the ground why believers are not their own but His. Therefore, seeing He has given such a price for us, let us study to give our hearts to Him.

Thirdly, Christ has a right to believers by His own choice: "I have chosen you out of the world, therefore the world hateth you" (John 15:19).

Fourthly, Christ has a right to believers by the covenant of grace. Believers make a resignation of themselves to Christ, which is clear from their first engaging to be Christ's. This is found in Ezekiel 16:8, which says that the Lord "entered into a covenant with thee, saith the Lord GOD, and thou becamest mine" (Ezek. 16:8).

Fifthly, He has a right to believers by the Father's promise to Him, wherein He has covenanted with Him in that blessed contract of redemption, that there should be given to him some of the fruits of all the earth. We see this in Isaiah 49:6, "That thou shouldest be my servant to raise up the tribes of Jacob, and to restore the preserved of Israel: I will also give thee for a light to the Gentiles, that thou mayest be my salvation unto the end of the earth." Therefore, since Christ has a right to you by so many ways, oh Christians, be persuaded to give over your hearts to him.

The fifth observation that I shall name from the words of our text is this: a believer may attain a solid persuasion of his interest in

Christ, and yet may be convinced of distance from God, and may be waiting for sensible manifestations of Him. We can see this when we compare Song of Solomon 2:16 with verse 17. In verse 16, we read, "My beloved is mine"; and in verse 17 we read, "Turn, my beloved, and be thou like a roe or a young hart upon the mountains of Bether." We can see that the bride was waiting for the manifestation of Christ, yet she cried out, "My beloved is mine, and I am his."

The sixth observation is that Christ has a most constant delight in His saints. We see this in verses 16 and 17: "He feedeth among the lilies. Until the day break, and the shadows flee away."

Finally, let us observe that Christ's delight in His saints, and His care for them, is the very great foundation upon which Christians may build their interest in Christ. It is the reason why the bride cried out, "My beloved is mine, and I am his," because, "He feedeth among the lilies." Now, I would request you to be provoked at length to make a blessed contrast between Christ and yourself; blessed is the person who can cry out upon good ground, "I am my beloved's, and he is mine!"

To conclude our discourse, let us discuss three false assurances that many take for real assurances.

First, you must be persuaded that an assurance that is easily had and attained is most certainly a false assurance. There are many that take up their assurance of faith, even at their foot; but, I may say to such, that their assurance is a false assurance. Secondly, if you have never had difficulty keeping your assurance, it may be a false assurance. Thirdly, beware of the assurance that does not estrange you from your idols. There are some who will say that Christ is theirs; yet their affection will be as great towards their idols as before. If your hearts still feel affection for your idols, your assurance may be false. Therefore, search and try yourselves, lest you go down to the grave with this mistake in your bosom and a lie in your right hand. There are thousands in hell today, the smoke of whose torment ascends before the throne, who have been dreadfully disappointed, thinking that they were indeed Christ's. Yet on that day, Christ said to them, "Depart from me" (Matt. 25:41). Oh, what a dreadful mistake it would be to be falsely assured of your interest in Christ; therefore, we must be diligent to determine whether we are in Christ or not. Amen.

SERMON 24

The Sincere Christian, God's Peculiar Favorite

Behold, an Israelite indeed, in whom is no guile!
—John 1:47

If Jesus Christ, who is the impartial Judge, were coming to pass sentence upon each one of us that are here, I am afraid that there are none of us upon whom He might engrave this precious testimony, "Behold, an Israelite indeed, in whom there is no guile!" Oh, hypocrisy is a violent epidemic and universal disease in this land, and in these days! We covet more to be Christians in the letter than in the Spirit; we are more taken up about needless pursuits after gifts than after this precious grace of sincerity. Other graces may come with more pomp and observation than this precious grace of sincerity; but this grace comes always with most advantage and reality. "A false balance is abomination to the LORD" (Prov. 11:1). We weigh ourselves in the balance for our conceit, so that we appear to ourselves impressive, but Solomon says, "Whoso boasteth himself of a false gift is like clouds and wind without rain" (Prov. 25:14). We think this is, and shall be, for a lamentation, that there is such a woeful distance and incongruity between our walk and hopes, between our profession and our practice. Do you not know that as face answers face in water, so should a Christian's walk be answerable to his hope? I am persuaded that none may, with great assurance, judge our hope by our walk.

We conceive that sincerity is here commended as a thing that is much strengthened by reason and much confirmed by nature; so that religion, reason, and nature all eminently unite to proclaim the excellence of the grace of sincerity. If we will but cast our eyes upon the beasts of the field, we will behold this grace commended; for does not their outward carriage, their voice, and external workings, evidently speak what is their inward nature? That which nature expresses in this outward walk should be from a principle within. Does not reason also confirm the excellence of the grace of sincerity? For ought not every man to have a sweet harmony between his outward expressions and inward thoughts, words being indeed the proper signification of the mind of a man? We have inverted reason, nature, and religion by that woeful and damnable hypocrisy, wherewith we are clothed in these days.

But to come a little more particularly to the words of our text, we see our blessed Lord Jesus commending this man, Nathaniel; Christ does not say that the man was without sin, for that is a perfection which we cannot attain while we are below, but Christ commends the sincerity of this holy man. If we will cast our eyes upon the preceding words, we will see that this man is grossly ignorant of the fundamentals and precious fruits of God. This shows us that that sincerity may consist with much ignorance, if that ignorance be not affected. Listen also to the expression of Solomon: "Also, that the soul be without knowledge, it is not good" (Prov. 19:2). This is to be understood surely of one that endeavors not to remove his ignorance, but holds it fast. But Christ looked on such a man as sincere, notwithstanding his ignorance. Although his inside had been turned out, he has always appeared the same. We fear that if our insides were as conspicuous as our outside is, each one of us would be a terror to each other. If that mystery of iniquity that works effectually in our bosoms were engraven on our foreheads, we would be made a curse and a reproach in all the earth. I am persuaded that if we were as well-known to men as we are known to God, most people—at least a great deal of the professors of this generation—might be ashamed to have the sound of their feet heard in the ordinances and ways that lead to life eternal; for we have inverted the nature of religion, thinking it consists in the making of many long prayers and in the keeping of some public assemblies; but believe me, there is more true and unspotted religion in one grain of sincerity, and it is of more value and worth, than if you would pray during half of your time, and weep during the other half of it. Certainly, it is a most rare grace. Oh, this precious and excellent grace of sincerity!

Now, in these words, Christ holds out only the excellence of sincerity, which is clear, and He mentions this grace to commend Nathaniel; for no doubt, Nathaniel had other excellent things for which he might have been commended; but Christ pitches alone upon that grace of sincerity, which speaks of its preciousness and excellence; it is the mother and substance of true religion in the eye of this precious and impartial Judge. Christ knows well what it is that deserves commendations in us; His commendation of sincerity here might exceedingly commend it to us.

There is this advantage of sincerity; ordinarily a sincere believer meets with much assurance of his interest in Christ, as these two are sweetly conjoined, Nathaniel's sincerity and Christ's giving unto him that blessed testimony. I say that the sincere Christian lies nearest to the assurance and persuasion of his interest in Christ. Be persuaded that our little sincerity does often occasion our many debates and questionings about our interest in Christ; and you may identify your lack of sincerity by your unbelief.

Christ's words also show the difficulty of this precious grace, and how singular a thing it is to be sincere. Hence Christ makes this the subject of admiration, "Behold an Israelite indeed, in whom there is no proven guile!" This says to us that sincerity must be a singular and rare grace, not easily attained, that even Christ is constrained to wonder at it, that there should be such a one found.

We also see in the text how much the grace of sincerity in religion may be personated and counterfeited. There is a sweet emphasis in that text, that speaks strongly to us, that there are many in Israel who are not Israelites indeed, and in heart. Now, before we speak to the excellence of this grace of sincerity, that Christ here so much recommends, we shall speak briefly concerning what this sincerity is.

We conceive that sincerity is conformity between our profession and our practice; it is a woeful evil among us that our profession is of a far larger extent than our practice. This was the fault of the hypocrites mentioned in Matthew 23:5, "But all their works they do for to be seen of men: they make broad their phylacteries, and enlarge the borders of their garments." I think that most of us come very short of what we ought to be; we also come short of that which we seem to be.

Secondly, sincerity necessitates that a Christian should be as much in the exercise of his duties when he is alone as when he is in company. Believe me, if many of us were tried in this, we might no doubt find ourselves amongst those that are full of guile. Many may breathe out much abroad and speak to the commendation of Jesus Christ; yet, if the stones of the walls of their houses could speak, and the ceilings of their chambers could declare, they would give a greater testimony about this than their sincerity could do. They may say that you do not watch unto prayer; surely, there is much praying abroad, where there is little or no sincerity. This was an excellent testimony of a heathen, who persuaded men to be as religious alone as in company. We also read a mark of the hypocrites, about whom it is mentioned, "They love to pray standing in the synagogues and in the corners of the streets, that they may be seen of men" (Matt. 6:5). We suppose that these persons love not to pray much in private; therefore, they could not be sincere.

There is a third thing that sincerity includes: there should also be a sweet conformity between our heart and our words. Our blessed Lord Jesus commented that in his mouth there was no guile. It is a farther commendation than to say that in his spirit there was no guile. He spoke nothing but that which appeared in his heart; he spoke nothing with his mouth, but that which was really in his heart. A fourth observation is that sincerity necessitates that a Christian, in the exercise of duties, ought not only to act from a divine principle of faith and love, these two being the precious principles of a Christian's duty, but he also ought to himself act in a divine manner and to a precious end in the exercise of his duties. These duties must tend to the glory of God and to our advantage; also, they must go about these duties in a suitable and divine manner. We conceive that these three do truly show the nature of sincerity. Thus, in short, sincerity is a sweet conformity between a Christian's profession and his practice, between his heart and his walk, and between his walk and his hope.

We shall not discuss much to prove that the exercise of the grace of sincerity is a Christian's glory; it is made sufficiently clear in 1 Chronicles 28:9, where David gave his counsel to his son Solomon, that he should walk before God with a perfect heart and with sincerity. We are persuaded that if Christians will reflect on these things, they will be convinced that it is their duty to be in the exercise of the grace of sincerity.

First, there is not a grace in a Christian's life, really, but a hypocrite may counterfeit and impersonate it. This is not only clear in the exercise of the grace of faith, that a hypocrite may counterfeit it, as Psalm 106:12 says, "Then believed they his words; they sang his praise"; but it is subjoined in the next verse, which reports that "they soon forgat his works" (v. 13). The possibility of hypocrisy is likewise clear in Psalm 78:35, where these hypocrites say that the Lord was their rock; and it is subjoined, "Nevertheless they did flatter him with their mouth, and they lied unto him with their tongues. For their heart was not right with him, neither were they stedfast in his covenant" (v. 36).

The grace of love may also be impersonated and counterfeited; even the grace of love, which a Christian really acts out, even this grace, a hypocrite may counterfeit. In Romans 10:2 we read, "For I bear them record that they have a zeal of God, but not according to knowledge." Now what is zeal, but a great measure of love? It is likewise clear from Ephesians 6:24, "Grace be with all them that love our Lord Jesus Christ in sincerity"—importing that there are some that love Him not in sincerity.

We think also of the grace of repentance; a Christian really experiences this great blessing, but hypocrites may counterfeit and impersonate it. This is made clear in Esau's practice (Heb. 12:17), where it is said of his repentance that he sought the blessing with tears, but it is also mentioned that "he found no place of repentance." The possibility of insincere repentance is also clear in Judas's practice in Matthew 27:4, where he repented that he had betrayed innocent blood; he showed much sorrow in his repentance, yet he hanged himself. His repentance was neither real nor sincere, he himself being but a hypocrite.

We think also the graces of self-denial and humility may be counterfeited by a hypocrite. This is clear in 1 Samuel 10:22, where it is said of Saul, when they were going to make him king, that he ran to hide himself; and yet he had used all means whereby he might have been made king, and would fain have been king.

We think also of the graces of patience, and of suffering under crosses, which a Christian really learns to enact. These also may be counterfeited by a hypocrite, not only in his suffering for Christ, but also when he is put to some personal affront. This is clear from 1 Corinthians 13:3, where the apostle Paul says, "And though I bestow all my goods to feed the poor, and though I give my body to be burned, and have not charity, it profiteth me nothing." It presupposes that there is a possibility that a hypocrite and reprobate may even give his body to be burnt for the cause of Christ. Many hypocrites counterfeit this grace of patience in their suffering for Christ.

The hypocrite not only counterfeits this grace of patience in his sufferings for Christ, but likewise counterfeits this grace of patience when he is put to some personal affront and reproach; this is clear from 1 Samuel 10:27, where he makes some mention of those that were the sons of Belial, and undervalued Saul when he was made king. The Scripture says that he held his peace, which requires a great measure of patience. It is the same word in the original that was used to describe Aaron in Leviticus 10:3: Aaron "held his peace" when his two sons were devoured and cut off.

Surely all this tells us that the exercise of the grace of sincerity ought to be studied. These examples also demonstrate the safety of the study of this grace—God is an all-seeing God, and He does behold the thoughts and imaginations of our hearts. This is clear from 1 Chronicles 28, where David pressed sincerity on his son Solomon, upon this account, that God searches the heart and tries it. It is certain that God who judges not according to outward appearance and sees not as men see, can reject an Eliab but choose a stripling like David.

Another reason that points us to sincerity is that whatsoever truly professing Christians have, or can have, is vain, and to no purpose, except they have this precious and excellent grace of sincerity. For example, let us look at the gift of prayer, discourse, and the talking of religion and the covenant. If we lack sincerity, all these will be as precious pearls upon a swine's snout. They shall not be as ornaments of gold unto you, or as changeable chains about your neck, for God shall bereave you of them. This is described in Luke 8:18—a man by hypocrisy provokes God to take these things from him which he seems to have: "From him shall be taken even that which he seemeth to have." Hypocrisy exceedingly provokes God to wrath, and it obstructs much of a Christian's peace and access to Jesus Christ. In Job 36:13, we read, "But the hypocrites in heart heap up wrath: they cry not when he bindeth them." In some measure this is verified of a Christian, while he is under hypocrisy, he cannot win to groan under his bonds. I am persuaded that until sincerity be put in exercise, it is altogether impossible for a Christian even to come to that holy and divine contrition of spirit, that when his bonds are laid on him, he can neither cry, nor lift up his voice. We think also of the words in Job 13:16, "An hypocrite shall not come before him"; in some measure, this is verified of a Christian—that which mars your access to God is the lack of sincerity; hypocrisy is so much your predominant evil. I think many of the Christians that are here might seal that truth with their blood, that hypocrisy has been the strongest bar that ever was drawn between them and access to God.

Consider the words in Job 27:9; they are in part verified of a Christian: "For what is the hope of the hypocrite, though he hath gained, when God taketh away his soul? Will God hear his cry when trouble cometh upon him? Will he delight himself in the Almighty? Will he always call upon God?" I think it is impossible for a Christian to be very eminent in these two precious graces—the grace of delight and love, and the grace and duty of prayer—until he attains to the grace of sincerity. Hypocrisy interrupts our delight in duty; and we may say that hypocrisy amongst Christians abridges much of that sweet fellowship we should have with God. What makes us pray so little when we are alone, but woeful evil of hypocrisy? These things being considered, let us examine the necessity of the study of this grace of sincerity.

The first aspect we propose to discuss is the excellence of this grace of sincerity. Christ makes it the subject of His commendation. We will pause briefly to point out to you the commendation of this precious ornament of a sincere spirit. But surely, sincerity is a noble grace; see that noble testimony given to Jacob, "Jacob was a plain man, dwelling in tents" (Gen. 25:27).

Secondly, the grace of a Christian's sincerity makes him shine. If we may make use of that allusion, we may say that the grace of sincerity is to other graces as the sun is to the planets. Without the sun, the planets will not appear. So it is with this grace of sincerity; it exceedingly adorns all the other graces that Christians have, and all other graces are but shadows if they lack this grace.

A third thing that commends the grace of sincerity is that amongst all other graces of the Spirit that a Christian possesses, there is most peace from the exercise of the grace of sincerity in the day that the Christian passes through death to his everlasting rest and eternal home. Oh, but the reflex thoughts of hypocrisy, when we shall look eternity in the face, will make many of us go down to our graves, having our hands hanging upon our loins! Verily, religion will go to little bulk when death looks you in the face; that which makes it go in so little bulk is this—we have not been exercising the grace of sincerity. Believe me, it is certain that there is not a duty that a Christian now performs that will last when it looks eternity in the face, but the duty which is performed in sincerity. All duties will pass away as a cloud. Multitudes of prayers will afford you no more comfort in those days than the white of an egg; they shall become tasteless, and vanish away from us.

Fourth, it is through sincerity that a Christian begins to resemble the image of God, who is his maker. Is not God also sometimes in Scripture called the God of truth, in opposition to these false gods? So a Christian, from this, may be persuaded to study this duty and divine excellent grace; it is a piece of the nature of God. Further, I am persuaded that the exercise of every grace of a Christian is founded upon the attributes of God, and has somewhat thereof engraven upon them. From hence, be persuaded to search and exercise this grace of sincerity. Oh, that we had the tongue of an angel, to commend this undervalued grace of sincerity! I may ask Christians—that is, true believers—when have you spent one hour in the serious and earnest pursuit after the grace of sincerity? I think Christians spend more of their time in the pursuit of the graces of faith, love, repentance, and mortification than they spend in the pursuit of sincerity. We would only say to those, they invert the divine and comely order. We would have all your graces thrive; and, believe me, all your other graces will not thrive, if they do not spring off this ground, that is, sincerity and reality.

A second point we would make is that there are several advantages that flow to a Christian from this precious and excellent grace of sincerity.

The first advantage is that that grace capacitates the creature most to receive intimation of his peace and interest in God. I shall explain why your debates about your interest are so strong, and why your janglings of unbelief are so many: because you are not sincere. We think it is most true that the grace of sincerity capacitates a Christian most to receive intimation of his peace, because a Christian that is sincere knows best what it is to abuse the intimation of peace and interest in God. Christ knows this well of us, that we can better bear our janglings and our disputings than the intimation of an interest in God because of our lack of sincerity. But the sincere man knows best how to improve it, how to improve the intimations of his peace; therefore, study well the exercise of the grace of sincerity if you would attain to the intimation of peace, and have your interest in Jesus Christ cleared.

A Christian's second advantage that flows from the exercise of the grace of sincerity is that grace engages the Christian most to wrestle against his predominant lusts. I am persuaded that there is no grace that puts a Christian more to the exercise of mortification of his predominant lusts than this grace of sincerity, "I was also upright before him" (Ps. 18:23); and he subjoins these words: "And I kept myself from mine iniquity." There is an emphasis on these words. David claimed relation to any iniquity in him; indeed, Christians may engrave this title upon their iniquity: "It is mine." Now, in a manner, while iniquity is in life and the Christians are under it, while it is yet unmortified, Christ has not much access to the soul. Thus, He is forced to remain under secret of the stairs, and He has only the corner of the Christian's heart.

There is a third advantage that a Christian possesses by the grace of sincerity—it may be an excellent evidence of his interest in God, and that he has obtained pardon of sin. Christians are often taken up in that debate that argues: how shall I know if my iniquity be pardoned? I shall but give you this one mark of it, how you may know it—it is this: if you are sincere, then your sins are pardoned, and you will see David, Psalm 32:2, where he gives out the mark of the man whose iniquity is forgiven, it is he in whose mouth there is no guile.

A fourth advantage that moves the sincere Christian is the excellent way to attain to the mortification of all his lusts, wherewith a Christian is beset and encompassed. And their blessedness is set down in Psalm 119:1, "Blessed are the undefiled in the way, who walk in the law of the LORD." It seems as if he had said, "Would you ask wherein consists their blessedness? It is in this, they hate every false way, and their feet turn not from the commandments of the Lord. I am persuaded of this, that the little exercise of sincerity that is amongst us makes the grace of mortification lag so far behind." It is clear from this, that when an insincere Christian sets about mortification, there is never proposed a divine and spiritual end in such a way as a Christian ought to do. Oh, Christians, is it not often your end in going about prayer to win to more establishment and to quiet your consciences? Know you not what it means to mortify your idols? Is it not that you may attain peace? Is it not that you offend not against the generation of the just by your walk? Do not your hearts propose such ends to you in going about duties? Surely, these are occasioned through the lack of the grace of sincerity; we love not to do violence to our own flesh, and to be spent, until we have beaten down our bodies and held them in subjection to Christ Jesus, and have crucified the old man that remains in us.

A fifth advantage that comes to the Christian by the exercise of sincerity is that the sincere Christian is the one to whom all the promises of the covenant of grace are given. The sincere Christian is the one that meets with the most accomplishment of these promises. I am persuaded that unto the Christian that has been most in the exercise of sincerity, God has manifested most of His faithfulness. This is clear, "For the LORD God is a sun and shield: the LORD will give grace and glory: no good thing will he withhold from them that walk uprightly" (Ps. 84:11). That uprightness, we conceive, consists much in his faithfulness. Now, to whom is God's faithfulness exercised? Is it not to them that are sincere? Who are these to whom the Lord is showing favor? It is to them that walk uprightly; Christians who, with their whole hearts, delight in God's law.

A sixth advantage that comes to a Christian by the exercise of the grace of sincerity is that sincerity is the grace that capacitates a Christian most to receive communion and fellowship with God. This is clear from Psalm 73:1, "Truly God is good to Israel, even to such as are of a clean heart." Who are these that receive divine influence from heaven? Would you have their names? In short, it is they that are sincere.

The seventh advantage that comes to a Christian by the exercise of sincerity is that the sincere man is he who shall press on to the end, who shall endure to the end of his fight and spiritual warfare, without the least spot and blemish upon his walk and conversation. Solomon says, "He that walketh uprightly walketh surely" (Prov. 10:9).

Eighth, it is impossible for one to improve the dispensation of sense and the sensible enjoyment of Christ's face, without this precious and noble grace of sincerity. The only way for Christians to improve the dispensation of sense is to strengthen sincerity in their way to heaven, as also to strengthen sincerity by the mortification of their lusts; certainly, without sincerity you cannot attain to these things. There is a remarkable word to this purpose, in Proverbs 10:29, "The way of the LORD is strength to the upright." We are certain it may conclude that even the ways of mercy and the dispensations of grace are strength to the man that is sincere. Do you desire to know why Christians do not advance in the improvement of their enlargement? It is this because they are insincere.

Now that you may be persuaded to pursue after this grace of sincerity, we would have you consider the difficulty of attaining of it. I am persuaded that these that have paused to try this exercise will find it most difficult; for a Christian must be first under the faith of the omniscience of God before he attain this precious jewel of sincerity.

A Christian must also be mortified to the evil of pride before he can attain sincerity; this is according to Habakkuk 2:4, which says, "Behold, his soul which is lifted up is not upright in him." Furthermore, a Christian, before he can attain to sincerity, must have the glory of God as the ultimate end of all his actions or discourses. Jesus Christ must be the object upon which all his desires must be terminated. Finally, without the exercise of diligence, and without the noble exercise of the graces of faith and hope, you cannot attain to the grace of sincerity, to the precious and lively exercise of that grace.

Now we desire that these things that are so precious and desirable in these days, would persuade you more to follow after them. Oh, Christians, do you think you can win heaven without this royal and excellent grace of sincerity? I am persuaded that if we truly believed the worth and excellence of this grace of sincerity, surely it would not be so slighted and undervalued. Oh, study sincerity! I know no reason why the apostle, in 1 Peter 2:1, speaks of hypocrisy in the plural number, but for this—anything whatsoever a Christian does may be mixed with this ingredient of hypocrisy; hypocrisy may be sown in the root of all a Christian's actions. I confess that there is a difference between doing things with hypocrisy, and doing things in hypocrisy. One may have hypocrisy, and yet not be a hypocrite; for the most precious and mortified Christian that is in the world may have some of this woeful evil of hypocrisy sown in his heart, and we think it is not fit to call such hypocrites. But, by all appearance, hypocrisy was never more universal than it is now; sincerity is at a stand, and faith and love are at a stand in many of our professing Christians.

Oh, Christians, covet this excellent ground. Be not faint-hearted, but fear. Let the excellence of it provoke your desires and affections after it. Oh, that you might be clothed with this precious and excellent garment of sincerity, as with a robe, by which you might obtain a testimony from God and from man, that you were indeed Israelites in whom there is no guile! Surely they received a sweet fruit with blessed effect, of this communion day that you have had. Oh, that you might once be persuaded sincerely to pursue after this precious and excellent object, Jesus Christ, the desire of nations, who is white and ruddy, the chief among ten thousands. Oh, when shall these heavens and earth meet together, and be burnt up with vehement fire? When all the weary travelers of hope shall be exalted, by infinite degrees, above the reach of all these corruptions wherewith they are now beset. Then we that are clothed in filthy garments shall be clothed with this holy robe, made of the holiness of God. This one word I say, "Light is sown for the righteous, and joy for the upright in heart." Oh, let the blessed harvest day of such a precious seed time come, and let all other harvest days pass away! Amen.

SERMON 25

Overcoming Believers Crowned with Glory

To him that overcometh will I grant to sit with me in my throne, even as I also overcame, and am set down with my Father in his throne.

—Revelation 3:21

Behold what a great mystery is it that the dust of His feet and those that are infinitely below Him should be exalted to so high an estate of life as to sit with Him on the throne! Beggars who are sitting on the dunghill are exalted to sit with God. This is God's own doing; oh, that it would be marvelous in our eyes! We think if we consulted with our own baseness and the huge distance that is between God and us, we should blush and be ashamed to appropriate so glorious a condition. We may certainly use that question, with holy admiration, "But will God in very deed dwell with men on the earth?" (2 Chron. 6:18). We may ask, and not without admiration, "Shall men indeed dwell with God?"

Now, before we attain this blessed estate, there is a holy warfare to be accomplished and we have many enemies to overcome. Much of the Christian's life consists of two factors: wrestling and overcoming; then, we receive a free-gifted reward. We live in debate here; but there is a glorious period to be reached at the close, when we shall be exalted above sin and misery. Though we had neither privileges nor advantages by our overcoming but victory and dominion, it would be enough; for it is that which affects men in the world much. Ought not the Christian to be ambitious of it? This is the privilege and advantage of our overcoming: it leads us to a throne. The way may seem unpleasant; but "our light affliction, which is but for a moment, worketh for us a far more exceeding and eternal weight of glory" (2 Cor. 4:17). We shall enjoy this glory before long. Within a little space, the depths of our present sufferings shall be swallowed up in the immense depths of infinite glory. If we did not have this promise and command to sit down on this throne, it would be presumption to desire much to do it; but having this command for it, it is more humility to obey than to refuse. Once it was man's sin to desire to be like God; but now, it is an ambitious design and commendable to aspire to that.

Now this verse describes the duty and exercise of a Christian. We see this in the words, "He that overcometh." Second, a rich reward is promised and proposed to the Christian that is thus exercised: "He shall sit with me upon my throne." Third, there is a confirmation of the blessed promise held forth in the following words: "Even as I also overcame, and am set down with my Father in his throne." It is as if He had said, "As certainly as I was set down on the right hand of the Majesty on high, after I had overcome, so shall you, after you have overcome and completed your victories." The words may also be taken up as an amplification of the promise; as if He had said, "Do you believe what exceeding glory I received after I had completed the victory? Such glory shall be given to you, after you have completed yours." We do not dare conceive of the excellence of glory with Christ; it is only a similitude and likeness.

As for the first part, the exercise and duty of a Christian—which may be understood of the Christian who is in the way of overcoming, or who has overcome—the promise relates to both. From this we would observe that there are many impediments and enemies that lie in the Christian's way to eternal glory. This is implied in the words, "He that overcometh." There is neither victory nor overcoming without a re-encounter with enemies, as Matthew 7:14 says, "Strait is the gate, and narrow is the way, which leadeth unto life." We may wonder at those who look at the way to heaven as so easy a journey, and we think it a mark they are strangers to it. Those that know it best are convinced of the great difficulty in it. Once there was an insuperable impediment laid in our way by our first parents; had not Jesus Christ broken down that partition and removed that impediment, there would not have been any entry for us into that heavenly kingdom. Blessed be He eternally, that has removed that impediment and has taken it out of the way, and consecrated unto us a living way, through the veil, that is His flesh, to the holiest of all. After the way of keeping the law was made void and rendered impossible, our blessed Lord found out an easier way, through faith in Him. After the law could make nothing perfect, He brings in that better hope. Blessed be that noble invention! Blessed unity that found it out! It could never have entered into the breasts of angels or men: all His ways are unsearchable, like Himself, and we can render no reason for it. But it is our happiness that we have such a way to walk in; and it is to His glory that He forged it. I shall here name a few impediments that lie in the Christian's way to his heavenly rest.

First, Christians are hindered by the lack of solid faith that there is a heaven and a rest prepared for the righteous. We think that most people look upon heaven as a notion of man's imagination; but surely, if we had the faith of it engraven on our spirits, we would move more swiftly in our way to it.

A second impediment is the lack of solid faith in the blessedness and happiness of heaven. We cannot speak of the blessedness and reality of it as our actual possession of it, when we shall behold with our eyes that which we have heard with our ears. This will be the commentator on it, and will incline us to resolve the question. But if the faith of it were more in our souls, we would be made as the chariots of Aminadab and we would move quickly toward it; oh, the dark apprehensions we have of it! We shall say no more concerning this; but glorious things are spoken of this city of God, where the redeemed are living. We should be longing for the day when we shall enter into the ports of it. Oh, that your hearts were enlarged as the sand upon the seashore, to comprehend what is prepared for them that love Him!

Third, Christians are hindered by the lack of a solid faith in the everlasting kingdom that cannot be shaken. We are, by our heartless discouragement and anxious unbelief, retarded in our motion. If we truly believed our interest in that immense happiness that Christ purchased, we would be strengthened to walk on freely, from strength to strength, without any wearying. But we may comfort one another knowing that we have a right to such a blessed and precious rest above.

The fourth group of impediments are the afflictions and tribulations the believer has to undergo in his pilgrimage to heaven. These impediments will fall away from those who have obtained some faith in their interest in the kingdom, for such a Christian is filling his eye with the recompense of reward, such that he has no desire to think on his difficulties.

A fifth impediment for Christians on the road to heaven is the threefold enemy of sin, Satan, and our own evil hearts. This threefold impediment is a heavy burden that holds us back in our progress. We must confess, it is a great difficulty to overcome these impediments; however, we may be more convinced of the happiness we are going to, when Christians meet with such oppositions in the way.

The second observation is that it is the duty of the Christian to be wrestling and fighting against all his impediments and enemies; this is implied in the words, "To him that overcometh"; for there is no victory without fighting. We should not be discouraged by the conviction of impediment; but our love should be set on edge by opposition: "Many waters cannot quench love" (Song 8:7). We shall propose a threefold encouragement to the wrestling Christian against all impediments he may encounter on his way toward his blessed rest.

First, we may make use of His omnipotence. He has overcome, and helps us also to overcome. The Christian is allowed to make use of the power that raised Christ from the dead; is not that an excellent encouragement to the wrestling soul?

We may also be certainly persuaded of the victory before we overcome, if we do not become weary in well-doing; in due time we shall reap, if we faint not. We may carry along with us a lively hope that we shall not perish by the way. Our glorious Head is exalted above all impediments and enemies, which may be an earnest of exaltation to those who are the members; for where the Head is, there the members shall also be. He looks on Himself as imperfect until the time that all the scattered sons of Zion shall be brought home to Him.

Another encouragement to the Christian wrestling against all impediments and difficulties that he encounters on his way toward his blessed rest is that Jesus Christ has weakened the strength of all the enemies against whom we wrestle and fight. He has triumphed openly over them all upon the cross, and has spoiled principalities and powers, becoming victorious over them all; the Christian, now, has only to wrestle and fight with defeated enemies that have been already vanquished and overcome.

There is a third observation from the words of our text, and it is this: we ought to persevere and continue in the fight against our enemies until we overcome them. This is implied also in these words, "To him that overcometh will I grant to sit with me in my throne." Certainly there is no discharge in this war at all, until we overcome. Death is the first period of our warfare; after death, we shall have no enemies; we shall have no occasion for war, but we shall sit down and enjoy the sweet fruits of our victory. Yet, before we lay hold on the crown, as we are within time, we must endure hardness as good soldiers, and be followers of the Captain of salvation who was made perfect through suffering. After He had triumphed over all enemies, He ascended on high, where He sat down until the restitution of all things.

A second lesson in this text concerns the rich reward promised to the Christian who is thus exercised in wrestling. Speaking of this, we are afraid to darken your encouragement; for we think it speaks about a great matter that man cannot describe; and that beloved disciple John, was put to a non-plus, saying, "It doth not yet appear what we shall be" (1 John 3:2). All that John could say was that it passed his understanding to declare it; he could not reach nor comprehend it. The exceeding and great joy that believers possess, even while on this side of time, is unspeakable, according to 1 Peter 1:8: "Whom having not seen, ye love; in whom, though now ye see him not, yet believing, ye rejoice with joy unspeakable and full of glory." But how much more unspeakable shall the happiness of believers be when they shall stand with Him before the throne! Certainly, it imposes impossibility on us to speak of this; yet, we ought to admire and stand amazed at this truth.

I shall speak briefly concerning the promise that there is a rest and a repast prepared for those who overcome. The promise is this: to this one, "I grant to sit with me in my throne." After we have wearied and toiled ourselves battling corruptions and other enemies, we shall enter into a blessed rest that admits no interruption: "There remaineth therefore a rest to the people of God" (Heb. 4:9). Oh, what a blessed journey it is that leads to such a rest! We think heaven to the saints is a rest without a rest: "And they rest not day and night, saying, Holy, holy, holy, LORD God Almighty, which was, and is, and is to come" (Rev. 4:8). However, there is a holy quietness in that blessed motion.

The second thing in this promise is the stability and steadfastness of those who overcome, which is shown as the Lord says, "I grant to sit with me in my throne." The happiness of believers is firm and stable: "Him that overcometh will I make a pillar in the temple of my God, and he shall go no more out" (Rev. 3:12). For those that overcome, rest is beyond the reach of change; they shall eternally dwell under a dispensation of love. Changeableness is the motto of believers in time, but unchangeableness is the motto of believers in heaven. There is a promise of this, "Moreover the light of the moon shall be as the light of the sun, and the light of the sun shall be sevenfold, as the light of seven days" (Isa. 30:26)—not only holding out a greater degree of light in the life to come, but also showing the unchangeableness of that estate of life: it shall no more be as the moon, waxing and waning; but it shall be as the sun, in a uniform tenor.

Now from this promise, observe thirdly that those who overcome shall have fellowship in heaven with Jesus Christ, the Mediator of the new covenant; they shall sit down with Him upon the throne. This is the precious diamond that shines most brightly in the glorious crown of Jesus Christ; this is the crown which is set upon His head, which is all glorious within, and which believers shall one day put on. If this were not in believers' blessedness, how small a blessedness they would have in heaven! But that which completes this happiness is that the Lamb is the light of that city. What is heaven, but to be like Him, and to see Him as He is (1 John 3:2), and to be forever with the Lord (1 Thess. 4:17)? What a pleasant life it is, to be eternally with God, the Judge of all, with Jesus the Mediator of the new covenant, with the general assembly of the first-born, an innumerable company of angels, and the spirits of just men made perfect! All His saints have this honor. We were burdened within ourselves until we were exalted to that high dignity and heavenly fellowship. What a poor thing it is for worms of the earth to be conversing one with another on the earth! But oh, what a pleasant life it is for creatures to be eternally conversing with God in heaven! There is no wearying there; eternity shall look but as a moment in heaven, because it is eternal life to be with Christ there, who is the fountain of consolation.

A fourth observation concerning the promise is that glory and majesty shall be given to the believer that overcomes, in heaven.

He shall sit with Christ in heaven; Christ says of the believer, him "will I grant to sit with me in my throne." The throne of God is called Christ's throne because He has purchased it. He was content to lay Himself low, and to exalt us on high; He made Himself of no reputation, that the dust of His feet might be clothed with majesty. Oh, that we spent our days admiring His love towards us! Furthermore, the throne of glory is called His because He shall be there. He shall sit thereon. If we suffer with Christ, we shall also reign with Him eternally; "If so be that we suffer with him, that we may be also glorified together" (Rom. 8:17). The day that our blessed Lord Jesus fixed His love on His own, they became kings and captains of the crown, according to that word, Christ "hath made us kings and priests unto God and his Father; to him be glory and dominion for ever and ever" (Rev. 1:6). Let us also read 1 Peter 2:9, which confirms this promise, saying, "But ye are a chosen generation, a royal priesthood, an holy nation, a peculiar people; that ye should shew forth the praises of him who hath called you out of darkness into his marvellous light." This promise was given our blessed Lord, "Instead of thy fathers shall be thy children, whom thou mayest make princes in all the earth" (Ps. 45:16); though, we confess, these words may be otherwise explained and interpreted.

Oh, what a wonder it is to see those that have undervalued God so much, exalted to so great a dignity, as to be sons and daughters of the Most High! Certainly this speaks of the exceeding freeness of His grace; for the rule of His procedure with sinners is His good pleasure: "Therefore hath he mercy on whom he will have mercy, and whom he will he hardeneth" (Rom. 9:18). These words speak of His absoluteness and sovereignty over all the works of His hand, but of no worth nor excellence in us. Oh, what a wonder it shall be to see those that have been all their days amongst the pots, made like unto doves, whose wings are covered with silver, and their feathers with yellow gold! We cannot say much of this now; but when we shall be exalted on high, we shall know that fully and thoroughly, which now we behold darkly and afar off.

A fifth observation we draw from this promise is that there is a certainty of the performances of these things that we are now addressing. Has He said, "To him that overcometh will I grant to sit with me in my throne"? Has He promised it, who is the Amen and faithful Witness? Then He shall also accomplish it, for He cannot deny Himself: "God is not a man, that he should lie; neither the son of man, that he should repent: hath he said, and shall he not do it? or hath he spoken, and shall he not make it good?" (Num. 23:19).

A sixth observation that you should notice concerning the promise is this: though the overcoming Christian shall receive all these things from God, yet he shall receive them as a free gift, not of merit. After we have completed our warfare, we can plead nothing by debt; when we have finished with all our warfare and wrestling, we must cry out, we are unprofitable servants. Our obedience puts no obligation on God to do us any good; but it puts an obligation on us to bless Him for the good with which He furnishes us, so that we obey His commands. It is sufficient reward to us, though we should get no more. Now we shall briefly point out these reasons why our obedience deserves no reward.

First, there is an infinite disproportion between the worth and the reward of our obedience. Surely, if our obedience deserved any reward, it would be a reward of lower worth than to sit on the throne with Christ. We need not much arithmetic to cast up the worth of our obedience.

The second reason is that our obedience is God's gift to us; therefore, it deserves no reward. We are His workmanship, created in Christ Jesus unto good works; can anything that He has given us be an argument to plead for such a reward? We ought rather to bless God for that which we may have done rather than ask a reward for the doing of it.

Thirdly, our obedience is imperfect. All the good we do is so defiled by us, that in strict justice, it should be rather a matter of our condemnation than grounds for advancement and glory. Paul has nothing to glory in, save in his own infirmities (2 Cor. 12:9). We can use no argument to plead for mercy from God but our miseries.

Lastly, from the connection that is between the exercise of a Christian and the blessed reward that is promised to him, observe this: there is a glorious period and issue of all the contests and warfares to which the Christian is exposed: "For our light affliction, which is but for a moment, worketh for us a far more exceeding and eternal weight of glory" (2 Cor. 4:17). "Light is sown for the righteous, and gladness for the upright in heart" (Ps. 7:11).

Now let that glorious harvest day of such a precious and blessed seed time come, and let all other harvest days pass away. Dear Christians who are fighting and wrestling against your own spiritual corruptions and enemies, be persuaded to endure your fight; for it is not long before you shall overcome and be made conquerors, and shall be set down with Christ on His throne of glory. Wait for Him; He who has promised to come, will come, and will not tarry. Let us live here in the faith of His appearance, when we shall be taken home to the King in raiment of needlework, and shall be made glorious within. Let your souls be continually longing for the dawning of that blessed day when Christ shall rend the clouds that hang above your heads and shall fetch you home to Himself. So shall you be forever with the Lord, from henceforth and forever. Amen.

SERMON 26

The Great Efficacy of the Grace and Duty of Prayer

But withal prepare me also a lodging: for I trust that through your prayers I shall be given unto you.
—Philemon 22

If the substantial worth and real excellence of this everlasting gospel, which is a blessed charter, were believed by us, there might be more hope in our latter end. But we lament that the world has taken up our hearts, and that we do not value those things that are of our souls' concern and everlasting advantage.

Now, in the words that we have read, there are two things to be considered: first, the apostle Paul's message to Philemon—he trusted, through *their* prayers, that he would be given unto them. Second, as Paul was to be given to people, so likewise Christ is to be given to Christians by prayer, if they will pray to the Father for Him.

Now, more particularly, there are four things here to notice. First, Christ Jesus is given of the Father generally. Secondly, as Christ is given, so likewise is the gospel given to us. Thirdly, pastors are also given to us. Fourthly, we should desire that the blessing should be given unto us likewise. The words, "That I shall be given unto you," mean that the blessing should be given to them. The reason I say that this signifies a blessing is because He was given unto all men generally, and He was free to all. A second reason is found in the eighth chapter of Romans, where it is said that Christ gave Himself to all. Now then Paul took himself and said that he gave himself to none but to those who gave themselves to him again. Thus, we clear the point, and make it out in this: we conceive, he offered life to all through a Mediator, if they would come to Him; but he gave not the blessing to all, but to those who gave themselves to Him. Was that the first of His blessings to them? No, but His blessing of them was the motive that makes them give themselves away to Him. Then, why did He not give the blessing to all? "As I live, saith the Lord GOD, I have no pleasure in the death of the wicked; but that the wicked turn from his way and live: turn ye, turn ye from your evil ways; for why will ye die, O house of Israel?" (Ezek. 33:11). The Lord takes no pleasure in the death of the wicked. But I say, it is love, it is love! Now, prayer is an excellent help to people regarding the blessing. I will give you ten excellent commendations concerning the grace of prayer.

The first excellent step of the grace of prayer is that it brings down many strong walls between heaven and us; it brings down many high mountains, or else brings Christ over these mountains to the soul. Song of Solomon 2:17 speaks of this: "Until the day break, and the shadows flee away, turn, my beloved, and be thou like a roe or a young hart upon the mountains of Bether."

The second excellent step of prayer is that it will bring Christ again, when He is away; it is the grace that a Christian should have in exercise when Christ is away. Was not this exercise of the bride most to be understood as the grace of prayer: "I sought him whom my soul loveth: I sought him, but I found him not" (Song 3:1)?

The third excellent commendation of the grace of prayer is although we do not get Christ at first, yet we shall get Him at length; does not that say, dear Christians, be much in the noble exercise of the grace of prayer?

There is a fourth excellent commendation of the grace of prayer, and it is this: prayer is the grace that is to be exercised under desertion. This is clear from Paul's practice (2 Cor. 12:8), where thrice he besought the Lord for the departure of the messenger of Satan; yet he got a sweet answer to his prayer. Does this not say unto you, dear Christians, that you must be much in the exercise of the grace of prayer?

A fifth excellent commendation of the grace of prayer is that it is the grace that God puts on Christians in a special manner. He says, "Call upon me in the day of trouble: I will deliver thee" (Ps. 50:15). He gets not an answer in particular, but in general. So we see these two points: first, God has a high estimation of prayer, so that He recommends it to the Christian, saying, "Call on me in the day of trouble." Secondly, Christ has a precious respect for this duty of prayer: He gave him more than He promised. God promised to deliver him out of that estate for the present, but yet He delivers him out of all trouble.

Now we come to the sixth excellent commendation of the grace of prayer: it is that duty which Christ made use of Himself, when He told His disciples to stay behind while He went to pray. Oh, Christians, does this not tell you that prayer is most excellent, since Christ made use of it Himself?

The seventh excellent commendation of the grace of prayer is that Christ made use of this duty during a time of sadness and grief; as He prayed, did He not sweat drops of blood? Dear Christians, does this not show you that prayer is an excellent grace?

An eighth excellent commendation of the grace of prayer is that He did not only pray once, but He prayed thrice; as it says, "And he left them, and went away again, and prayed the third time, saying the same words" (Matt. 26:44). Oh, Christians, as Christ used it more often than once or twice, I say to you also, be much in prayer.

The ninth excellent commendation of the grace of prayer is that it keeps people from joining with temptations; this is clear in Matthew 26:41, which says, "Watch and pray, that ye enter not into temptation: the spirit indeed is willing, but the flesh is weak." Now, it is not said that temptations shall enter into you, but "that ye enter not into temptation." That shows two things: first, the man that is not much in prayer is the man that knows not where he goes. The words are, "That ye enter not." These words imply that danger is near; for is it not a danger to enter into temptations? Secondly, the text says unto us that the man that is much in prayer is the watchful man; for watchfulness and prayer are put together in the words, "Watch and pray."

Now we come to the tenth and last commendation, and excellent step of the grace of prayer, and it is that all that are now on the top of Mount Pisgah, and are removed out of their tents of Mount Tabor, have been much in the exercise of prayer. Oh, Christians, was not Adam much in prayer? Was not Moses much in prayer? I do not question that when he fasted forty days and forty nights, he was much in prayer. Was not Elijah much in prayer? Was not Aaron much in prayer? Was not sinful Manasseh much in prayer at his conversion? Were not David and Daniel much in prayer? Was not Job and poor Hezekiah much in prayer, when he chattered like a swallow?

Now, I think, if Adam were going to give you counsel, it would be this—be much in the exercise of the grace of prayer. If Moses and Aaron were going to give you counsel it would be this—be much in prayer. If David were going to give you counsel, it would be this—be much in prayer. If all that are now above, were going to give you counsel, it would be the same—be much in prayer. If the four beasts were going to give you counsel, it would be—be much in prayer. If the twenty-four elders were going to give you counsel, it would be—be much in prayer. If all the angels that are standing on the sea of glass were going to give you counsel, it would be—be much in prayer. If all the spirits of just men made perfect were going to give you counsel, it would be—be much in prayer. Now, dear Christians, obey the counsel of those that are above. I do not question that if all the condemned in hell were going to give you counsel, it would be the same message—oh, be much in prayer.

Prayer accomplishes three excellent things. First, it brings down a woefully light heart, and grants it to have Hadadrimmon's song in the valley of Megiddon in their mouth: for "they shall look upon me whom they have pierced, and they shall mourn for him" (Zech. 12:11) A second benefit of prayer is that when faith fails, and when hope languishes, prayer goes up to the Captain of our salvation and brings down strength from Him. Third, when we are not in a fit and suitable frame for exercising the graces of the Spirit, then prayer makes our requests known to God, that He may give us the grace of tenderness. Then, I say, oh Christians, be much in the exercise of the grace of prayer.

The grace of prayer keeps many other graces in exercise and life. First, the grace of prayer holds in life the grace of faith. This is clear in Luke 22:32, where Christ says, "I have prayed for thee, that thy faith fail not"; therefore, Peter's faith did not fail. Second, prayer keeps the grace of love in exercise. A Christian that is much in prayer has much of heaven with him. Then, will not that Christian be much in love? Third, prayer keeps a Christian in the exercise of tenderness. Is not a praying Christian a tender Christian? Fourth, praying Christians are humble Christians. Fifth, prayer keeps the grace of experience in a believer's life. Is it not the salted Christian that is the praying Christian? Is it not the praying Christian that is the experimental Christian? Sixth, prayer keeps the grace of strength in a Christian's life. It is known by experience that often when strength has failed the Christian, prayer has gone up to the Captain of salvation, and brought down strength from Him to the soul. The praying Christian is the strong Christian.

Another excellent commendation of the grace of prayer is that if prayer is non-existent, all the rest of the graces will prove useless. Is not ancient experience the coffer that holds all the graces? Is not the grace of faith the lock of that coffer? Is not love the key of that lock? Is not the grace of prayer the hand that opens that lock? Now what would signify either the coffer, or that within it, or the lock of faith, or the key of love, if the grace of prayer were not to open the lock of the coffer? Do you not know that when the key of a chest is lost, all that is within the chest is of no use until the key is found?

Now I shall tell you what I mean by the key, the coffer, and all that is within it. First, these symbols represent an experienced Christian having all the graces of the Spirit within him. Second, except he exercise the grace of prayer, he can make use of none of these graces. Is it not clear that when all the graces fail the Christian, prayer must go up to the Captain of our salvation, and bring down strength again?

The grace of prayer is also very useful. Prayer is that which makes Christians overcome their temptations. Christians, is not this the way for you to overcome temptations—to be much in the exercise of the grace of prayer? Certainly it is the only way for you to prevail over the temptations that assault you, to be in the exercise of prayer to God, making your requests known to Him. I shall briefly show you how prayer overcomes temptations. First, prayer will go and cry out, "Oh, precious Christ, keep me free of secret temptations; for it is known by Christian experience, that secret temptations are more dangerous than those that are known." Second, prayer can help overcome secret temptations by watching and prayer, as it is written in Matthew 26:41, "Watch and pray, that ye enter not into temptation." As a Christian prays, he ought to take notice of his watchings and of his walk in prayer, according to that word, "I would order my cause before him, and fill my mouth with arguments" (Job 23:4). People should take notice that their walk be constant, and they should also guard against known temptations.

Now, dear Christians, be much in prayer. Prayer is a most excellent and noble grace. I shall tell you what the grace of faith does; it is this that overcomes idols by naming Christ more precious than many idols. Then, says the person, oh why love I my idols any more? Oh, if Christians knew the sad advantage that they sustain by their idols!

Those that never knew what it was to suffer anything under the hand of an idol shall never reign with God in glory above the clouds; that is, they that never wrestled, nor resisted their idols, shall never inherit that life above. They that never overcame an idol, or obtained victory over it, shall never triumph with Jesus Christ in His triumphing. You may ask, what is the reason for this, that all my idols prevail over me? I say, the only reason is because we are not taken up in the exercise of the grace of prayer. Another may ask, what is the reason for this, that there is never a temptation that assaults me, but it overcomes me? There is no other reason but this, our slothfulness in the exercise of the grace of prayer. This is made clear in Proverbs 22:29: "Seest thou a man diligent in his business? He shall stand before kings; he shall not stand before mean men." Likewise, "The hand of the diligent shall bear rule: but the slothful shall be under tribute" (Prov. 12:24).

There are many aspects of Christians' lives that are in a sad decay, and they all flow from the lack of the exercise of prayer. Are there not many Christians that are complaining of the decay of their graces? I will discuss ten things in decay due to lack of prayer in a Christian's life.

First, Christians lack the grace of delight in duties, which proceeds from the lack of this exercise of the grace of prayer. Second, Christians lack the grace of joy. Third, there is a decay of the grace of faith. Fourth, the precious grace of love is much in decay. A fifth grace Christians lack is the grace of tenderness. Sixth, the grace of mortification is in decay. A seventh grace in decay is that of humility and self-abasement. Eighth, the grace of strength is in decay in Christians. Ninth, Christians are lacking the exercise of the grace of sympathy. Finally, Christians are greatly lacking the grace of patience and suffering under crosses. These are ten examples of the decay of grace that a Christian will undergo when he lacks the exercise of the grace of prayer.

We have discussed ten excellent commendations of the grace of prayer, as well as ten examples of the decay of grace which arise from a lack of prayer. Dear Christians, do you not know that prayer is the post that goes between a Christian and heaven? It carries news from the soul to Jesus Christ, to the highest court, and brings down strength from Him for the exercising of all the graces that a Christian possesses. For when faith fails, must not prayer go up to the Captain of our salvation, to bring down strength again? Do you desire to know the Christian that is strong in faith? It is the praying Christian. There are four things that a praying Christian possesses.

First, the praying Christian has much of heaven and Christ's company with him; he solaces himself in Christ's company, even while he is here below upon earth. Second, the praying Christian has much enjoyment of God's presence. It is the praying Christian that is admitted to behold the King's face. The praying Christian never says, "but I have not been called to come in unto the king these thirty days" (Esth. 4:11), for he beholds the King daily. Third, the praying Christian has much clearness concerning his interest in Christ. Do you desire to know the Christian that is walking within sight of his interest, with intimation of the pardon of his iniquities? It is the praying Christian. Fourth, he has peace of conscience and joy in the Holy Ghost. Last, he will be the humble Christian. The praying Christian is he who sits lowest, even in the dust, and is nothing in his own eyes; is not that a precious thing?

There are three noble respects that Christ puts upon the praying Christian. First, Christ says that He will look unto that man. To whom will He look? To him that is of a broken and contrite spirit. He will look unto that man with the eyes of delight, and the soul will look unto Christ with the eyes of faith.

Second, Christ says that He will come unto the praying Christian. Unto what man will the Son of God come today? Is it not to the man that is of an humble spirit? That is, Jesus Christ will come unto him in the robes of condescension.

Third, Christ says that He will not only look unto that man and come unto him; but more, yea, that He will dwell with him. With whom wilt Thou dwell? Even with the humble and contrite ones. Do you desire to know, dear Christians, where the omnipotent, compassionate and spotless, omniscient and great King dwells? It is with the humble man. Furthermore, where is the humble man brought? It is clear from Song of Solomon 2:4, "He brought me to the banqueting house, and his banner over me was love." The humble man is most often admitted to the chambers of presence, and to that sweet fellowship and correspondence with God.

Now dear Christians, may not all these excellent and precious things provoke you to the exercise of the grace of prayer, this most soul-enriching duty?

I shall propose five considerations to provoke you to the exercise of prayer.

First, all the good of it will be your own; like that word in Proverbs 9:12, "If thou be wise, thou shalt be wise for thyself: but if thou scornest, thou alone shalt bear it."

Second, consider that if you do these things, you shall dwell in the King's chambers, to behold the beauty of the Lord in His temple and rejoice in His company. Then be a praying and humbled Christian; for prayer and humility are put together.

The third consideration to provoke you to the exercise of prayer is this: a praying, humble Christian is beholden of the great King. Now, is there a person here today that desires the Ancient of days to take notice and behold him? Then let him be much in the exercise of the duty of this noble and excellent grace of prayer.

The fourth consideration to provoke you to the exercise of prayer is that the praying person shall be admitted to stand with these 144,000 men that stand upon mount Zion, singing songs of praise to Him that sits upon the throne, and to the Lamb, forever and ever.

Fifth, the praying person shall have three of the great guests and courtiers of heaven to accompany him. This is clear from Isaiah 57:15, "I dwell in the high and holy place, with him also that is of a contrite and humble spirit, to revive the spirit of the humble, and to revive the heart of the contrite ones." Also, John 14:23, which says, "If a man love me, he will keep my words: and my Father will love him, and we will come unto him, and make our abode with him" (John 14:23).

Christians, will you not dwell with the Father, the first person of the glorious and blessed Trinity today? Will you not dwell with the Son, the second person of the blessed Trinity? What do you think of His fellowship? What do you think of Christ's company? Is He not unto you comely and beautiful, yea, and all your desire? Is He not altogether lovely, and fairer than the sons of men? Is He not white and ruddy, yea, the chief among ten thousand? Dear Christians, what do you think of Christ and His fellowship? What do you think of Him? Are you not provoked to seek after Him and His fellowship? Oh, Christians, seek for Christ's company while you are here below, that when you go hence, you may have it also. Is not Christ's company the sweetest and most excellent and matchless company, that you have ever been in? Long to be above, when you shall meet with your lover, your husband, and your friend; there, Christ shall meet you and say, "Welcome, oh, my love; welcome, my spouse and undefiled!" Christians, are you not longing for that day?

In the first moment that the Christian shall set his feet within the door of heaven, within the ports of that blessed and precious city, whose windows and streets are all paved with transparent gold, he shall attend to four exercises.

The first exercise of a Christian will be to cry out, when he enters into the threshold of heaven, "Is it I? Is it this Christ-persecuting I? Is it this miserable polluted and Christ-undervaluing I? Is it this Sabbath-breaker I? Is it I?"

Second, will not a Christian cry out, "Is it they? Is it they that sinned with me? Is it they that persecuted Christ with me? Are these they that broke the Sabbath with me? Are these they that undervalued Christ with me? Is it they?"

Third, when first a Christian shall enter within the walls of that blessed city, he shall cry out, "Is this He of whom all these precious things were spoken? Is this He? Is this precious, excellent, matchless, unknown, and undervalued He? Is this He that is the noble Plant of renown? Is this the Ancient of days? Is this He?" We would never believe the half of the things that were spoken of Him, but now we see Him.

Fourth, Christians in that day shall be taken up in this exercise, and shall say, "Is this the glory of the higher house? Is it even this? Is this all the glory that was spoken to us of that blessed land? We would never have believed the half of it, which now we see with our eyes." Believe it, you shall have the queen of Sheba's language in your mouth. The half of that now we see, was never told us. There is one great question I would ask, and it is this: there are five senses that are fully satisfied and filled in heaven; which of them is fullest and most satisfied there?

The sense of the eye shall be filled in beholding the Lamb whithersoever He goes, and beholding the blessed troops of angels and the souls of just men, now made perfect, following after Him. The sense of smell shall be fully satisfied with the savor of that precious ointment, wherewith He is anointed, and with the savor of that precious fruit that grows in the garden of the new Jerusalem, the leaves of whose trees are for healing of the nations. The sense of hearing shall be satisfied with hearing the blessed melody and precious harmony that is among believers in heaven, each of them having a harp in their hand, singing praises, most sweetly to Him who was dead, and is alive again, and now lives for evermore. The sense of taste shall be filled and fully satisfied when they shall sit down at the well-head of consolation, and shall drink of these rivers of pleasures, until they can drink no more. The sense of touch shall be filled in heaven when they shall be admitted to take precious Christ in their arms, and they shall enfold that blessed object at their pleasure; He shall lie all night between their breasts as a bundle of myrrh.

All these senses shall be alike fully satisfied, for the sense of seeing shall yield itself to the sense of smelling, and the sense of smelling shall yield itself to the sense of hearing, and the sense of hearing shall yield itself to the sense of tasting, and the sense of tasting shall yield itself to the sense of touching; so all of them shall yield themselves to one another.

Now dear Christians, are you not longing for the day when you will have these five senses filled and satisfied? Is there a person here today that desires to have these senses filled? Then, I say, let him join himself unto this duty of prayer, for the praying Christians shall have some of them full, even while they are below, traveling in these tents of mortality.

Now, strangers to God, these are five senses that you shall have filled in hell; which of them all do you suppose shall be fullest and most satisfied? Shall your sense of sight be most satisfied in hell? Your eyes shall behold the devil, and that innumerable company of the sons of damned men and women, gnashing their teeth and gnawing their tongues; they are eternally cursing God because of their unsupportable torment, the smoke whereof shall ascend up forever; their worm shall never die and their fire shall never be quenched. Or shall the sense of smell be most filled in hell, in finding the smell of that extreme heat that flows from that intolerable torment that you shall experience? Shall the sense of hearing be most satisfied in hell, with hearing the howling and crying that will be there amongst that miserable company? Each one of them shall cry and bewail their case unto others; but they shall be physicians of no value one unto another, for their case shall be desperate. Or shall the sense of taste be most tormented in hell, when they shall drink of that river of fire and brimstone, and shall drink the cup of the unmitigated wrath of God? Shall the sense of touch be most filled in hell, when the devil shall meet you with a chain to lay about your neck? Then the devil shall go over you and you over him. All these senses shall be alike filled.

Now, unbelievers, as you desire to be free of this, go and engage yourselves in this duty of prayer. You know we have been speaking of the good of prayer, and of the sad disadvantage of not praying; but let us discuss six reasons why we do not pray as we ought.

First, we know not all the advantage that is to be had in prayer; for if we truly knew that it was the convoy of heaven, or the post that goes there, or that it is the way how consolation is to be gotten, we would be more often engaged in prayer. Second, we know not the sad case we are in, and the way how to get it recovered. "This kind can come forth by nothing, but by prayer and fasting" (Mark 9:29). A third reason we do not pray is because we are not aware of the temptations that are ready to befall us; we see this in Matthew 26:41: "Watch and pray, that ye enter not into temptation." Fourth, we lack the noble grace of love; for certainly, if we had the grace of love, we would be more often alone, conversing with God in secret prayer. Fifth, we are slothful. Too much indulgence to our own flesh is a great reason of our being so little in prayer. We shove off all our prayers until another time, being loath to do violence to ourselves. A sixth reason we are so seldom in prayer is that our sad case has not made us return unto the Lord; for certainly, if we had returned unto the Lord, we would be much in the exercise of this grace of prayer; as is clear from Hosea 6:1, "Come, and let us return unto the LORD: for he hath torn, and he will heal us; he hath smitten, and he will bind us up."

There are three ordinary temptations that the devil uses to plague people, to distract them from the duty of prayer. First, he plagues us with laziness, so that we desire not to pray. But, secondly, if we overcome that temptation, he will plague us with a more desperate temptation, an indisposition, and an unfit frame for prayer, so that we cannot speak. Third, if perchance we overcome that temptation also, he will plague us with the lack of delight in prayer. Christians, did ever the devil plague you with any of these temptations that he proposes for the obstructing of our duties?

We have been proposing some reasons why we do not pray, and why we are so little in this present exercise; now we shall here propose these four excellent helps to provoke you to be much in this exercise of prayer.

The first help is this: you should study to understand your sad case and to understand your desperate condition. This is clear from Hosea 14:2, "Take with you words, and turn to the LORD: say unto him, Take away all iniquity, and receive us graciously: so will we render the calves of our lips."

A second help to the grace of prayer is to study the knowledge of the many evils that are within you; for you are full of gray hairs here and there, according to Hosea 7:9, which says, "Strangers have devoured his strength, and he knoweth it not: yea, gray hairs are here and there upon him, yet he knoweth not." The ignorance of the evils that dwell in our hearts makes us guilty of that sin of omission of the duty of prayer.

The third help to motivate the successful exercise of prayer is to be much in entertaining love towards the brethren; for, when sad cases befall them, it will put you often to this duty of prayer, in praying for their delivery out of these sad cases.

A fourth and last excellent help to prayer is a holy, tender walk, still to be walking within sight of these seven abominations of the heart of man. It would make you go seven days sorrowing, and you would bewail yourselves with the weeping of Jazer. You would cover the altar of God with tears, and would be constrained to long for the day when our forty years' pilgrimage, and our many years' captivity, should come to a sweet and precious end.

I shall conclude my discourse at this time. However, I say, one sight of Christ in His beauty shall make you forget all your nine nights' watch, and your three days' sorrowing, in the seeking for Him. Christians, the day is coming when you shall be admitted to stand with these 144,000 upon mount Zion. Comfort yourselves in this: although your beginning be but small, yet your latter end shall be great. That is clear from Job 8:7, "Though thy beginning was small, yet thy latter end should greatly increase."

Before long, praying Christians shall be praising Christians; then they shall be set upon the well-head of consolation, to drink until they can drink no more. Now, pilgrims on earth, prisoners of hope, expectants of the crown, long for that day when you shall be above the clouds. Then, Christ shall say to you, "Come up hither, and I will give you a new name; your name, while you were here below upon the earth, was a praying and groaning Christian; but now I will give you a new name. Your name shall now be a praising Christian." Oh, what a life shall it be when you will cry out the words, "Awake up, my glory; awake, psaltery and harp: I myself will awake early!" (Ps. 57:8). Oh, what an excellent life it shall be, when you will cry out, "Awake, O my soul, and praise precious Christ! I shall praise Him, for He is most excellent and precious!" What a sweet life do you suppose it will be when you shall hear Solomon, the master of experience, who penned many a sweet song, having now changed his tune, singing a more sweet song of praise to the Lamb! What an excellent life it will be, when you shall hear David, who spent his nights in the bitterness of spirit! He has now changed his tune; he is singing a sweet song of praise, singing and praising without any wearying or any mixture of interruption.

There is no wearying in heaven; there is only joy and pleasures forever. I am persuaded of this; if you would ask David if he desires to change his place and his company, he would not return an answer to such an absurd proposition. There is no wearying at all around the throne of heaven; there is not one such desire in heaven among all the innumerable company of the souls of just men now made perfect, as to change their place, or their company, for the least juncture of time. I would only say this unto you, dear Christians—in the first moment you set your foot within the door of heaven, and within the ports of those blessed mansions above, you will be constrained to cry out, "Is it I?" Yet, I say to you, it shall even be you. Oh, what shall we say to provoke you to engage your hearts in the exercise of this precious grace of prayer, which is the path in which we ought to walk? What will persuade you to this noble exercise? We know not; but let him who has the tongue of the learned, do it.

Now, I shall say no more; but, if you saw that sweet communion that is between Christ and the saints who are now above, you would cry, "Oh, send a chariot, Sir, and fetch me!" Now, dear Christians, continue to long for that day when you will meet with an ever-present Christ. Amen.

SERMON 27

A Solemn Charge to Hearken to the Voice of the Son of God

This is my beloved Son: hear him.
—Luke 9:35

If we would reflect more upon our sad case and of the seven abominations that dwell in our hearts, it would make us sit seven days, sorrowing and bewailing ourselves with the weeping of Jazer, covering the altar of God with tears. It would make us sit three days sorrowing, and long for the day when our forty-year pilgrimage and our captivity should come to a sweet and precious end; when our nine-night watch and our three-day sorrowing should come to an end. Christians, do you not long for that day when you shall have Christ's company? Oh, if you knew the sweet life that is above! Will you study to overcome, so that you may enjoy Him?

There are three things that say that we shall never overcome. First, for all the time we have been in fighting with our idols, we have never yet overcome any of them. Second, we never study to overcome our idols; and that tells us that we shall never overcome them. Third, we will not overcome our idols because of the great connection that is between our hearts and our idols. If there were a hole through which one might look into our hearts, they would see our afflictions creeping upon our idols. That says unto us that we are not likely to overcome.

We would like to consider three points concerning the text. First, let us consider the duty imposed on a Christian to hear Christ. Second, we need to consider the author by whom this exhortation is given, that is, by the Father of eternity, the Ancient of days. Third, we must consider to whom the exhortation is given; that is, to all the saints.

This command is relevant and important because out of it are the issues of life and death. This is clear from Isaiah 55:3: "Hear, and your soul shall live." In not giving obedience to this command, the issues of death flow from it; this is clear in the words, "The Lord spake, but they would not hear; therefore the Lord brought on his wrath, and they perished." Now, will you hearken to the voice of the Lord, oh Christians? There are two great reasons why Christ gives this exhortation.

First, there is much advantage that comes to the soul by hearkening to His voice; this is clear from Revelation 3:18. When the people are in a sad case, then He declares, "I counsel thee to buy of me gold tried in the fire, that thou mayest be rich; and white raiment, that thou mayest be clothed, and that the shame of thy nakedness do not appear; and anoint thine eyes with eyesalve, that thou mayest see."

The second reason Christ gave this exhortation is because a most sad disadvantage comes to the person who does not hearken to His voice. Jeremiah 3:19 declares, "But I said, How shall I put thee among the children, and give thee a pleasant land, a goodly heritage of the hosts of nations?"

Christ sends us four messages with His words. Dear Christian, will you hear them? The first message is for the ignorant. Is there not an ignorant person here today? Then let him come to Christ. The benefit is made clear in 1 Corinthians 1:30: "But of him are ye in Christ Jesus, who of God is made unto us wisdom." The second message is for the unrighteous. Is there an unrighteous person here today? Then let him hear Christ, and come away, for in Christ he shall get righteousness. This is clear in the same text: "But of him are ye in Christ Jesus, who of God is made unto us…righteousness" (1 Cor. 1:30). The third message is this: is there any unclean person longing for sanctification here today? Then let him hearken unto Christ's voice and come away, and He shall get sanctification. This is also clear, "[Christ] is made unto us…sanctification" (1 Cor. 1:30). A fourth message that Christ has is this: are there any persons here today that lack adoption? Do they have their hands bound up and their liberty straitened? But do they not have a right to all the privileges of the people of God? Then let such people hearken to His voice, and hear Him, and come away. Then they shall find adoption, and their bonds will be loosed; then they will arrive in among the number of the children of God. This message is clear in the same verse: "[Christ] is made unto us…redemption" (1 Cor. 1:30).

"How long, ye simple ones, will ye love simplicity?"(Prov. 1:22). Will you not come away unto precious Christ, and be wise? Unrighteous and unsanctified persons, will you not come away, and get your spiritual wants supplied in Him, who is all in all unto you? Will you hear Him? Are there any here today who will not hear precious Christ? Dear Christians, behold a wonder! Is not the wonder this; that the great, and high, and holy, and lifted-up One, the Father of eternity, requests miserable, polluted man to hear His Son! Hearken unto precious Christ. Oh, Christians, will you not hear Him? Oh Christians, will you hearken to neither of the two persons of the Trinity? Will you refuse to hear precious Christ? Will you refuse to hear the noble Plant of renown, and the Ancient of days? I shall say one sad word unto those that will not hearken unto His voice in the lower house: they shall never hear the precious voice that shall be with those 144,000 that stand upon mount Zion. I charge you, oh Christians and expectants of the crown, as you do not wish to be guilty of the breach of the command, "This is my beloved Son, hear him." Hearken unto His voice.

Now, unbelievers, what excuse will you have, you who are perishing for lack of wisdom? Is not Christ made unto you wisdom? This is clear from 1 Corinthians 1:30; but you are covered with the veil of ignorance. What excuse will you have who will not hear Him? Did He not offer to counsel you? He makes it clear: "I counsel thee to…anoint thine eyes with eyesalve, that thou mayest see" (Rev. 3:18). Christians, will you not be provoked to hearken unto the Son, the second person of the blessed Trinity?

There are eight valleys in which all men are caught; Christians will only be strengthened in these valleys, if by them they are more provoked to hear the voice of Christ.

The first valley that all men are in is the valley of ignorance. All men are naturally born in this state. The second valley that all men are in is the valley of iniquity; our eyes are the windows by which it is conveyed into our hearts. Third, all are in the valley of unbelief. Our own hearts prevent us from believing; this shows that all men are naturally in that valley. The fourth valley is that which is above our heads, and which shall there remain until it be rent by Him who alone was found worthy to open the book. The fifth valley that all men are in is the valley of Baca, a dry and a wearisome valley. Sixth, all are caught in the valley of Megiddo, a valley of mourning and bitter lamentation, according to Zechariah 12:11. The seventh valley that all men are in is the valley of decision, which is interpretation. The eighth valley, into which only Christians arrive, is the valley of Berachah, the valley of joy.

Dear Christians, were you ever aware of these valleys? Unbelievers, were you ever in these valleys? If you were never aware of these valleys, you will never be admitted to the valley of Berachah; you shall then be put down in the valley of oblivion, in the land of forgetfulness.

Let us further examine these valleys in detail. The first valley we proposed was the valley of ignorance; we were all born in that valley. There are four mistakes in the state of ignorance.

First, we think ourselves blessed when we are actually miserable. This is clear in Revelation 3:17, which says, "Because thou sayest, I am rich, and increased with goods, and have need of nothing; and knowest not that thou art wretched, and miserable, and poor, and blind, and naked."

Second, we think ourselves clothed with the righteousness of God, when we are actually naked. This is also clear in Revelation 3:17.

The third mistake that flows from ignorance is that we think we have the knowledge of God, and are spiritually enlightened into the mysteries of heaven, when we are blind, and see nothing. This is likewise clear in Revelation 3:17.

The fourth mistake that flows from the valley of ignorance is that we call ourselves wise, when we are foolish. This is clear from 1 Corinthians 2:6, "Howbeit we speak wisdom among them that are perfect: yet not the wisdom of this world, nor of the princes of this world, that come to nought." Now, by the way, do you not know that all these worldly things pass away, and the fashion of them changes?

Now we come to a second valley, which is the valley of iniquity. All men are in this valley naturally. Do not our eyes behold iniquity? They are windows through which the devil conveys his temptations into our hearts. This is clear from Genesis 3:6: "And when the woman saw that the tree was good for food, and that it was pleasant to the eyes, and a tree to be desired to make one wise," then, presently, she joined with the temptation. So the devil conveys his temptations into our hearts through our eyes. Christians, guard your eyes from evil.

Now we come to a third valley, and it is the valley of unbelief, in the heart. There are three things that flow from ignorance, which cause unbelief.

First, we do not know that we are unbelieving, as we read in Malachi 3:7-8, "Wherein shall we return? Will a man rob God? Yet ye have robbed me. But ye say, Wherein have we robbed thee?"

The second thing that flows from ignorance is that we know not the evil of unbelief. Oh, if we knew the evil of it! Unbelief makes four things null and of no effect. 1. Does it not call the Father a liar? This is according to the word, "He that believeth on the Son of God hath the witness in himself: he that believeth not God hath made him a liar; because he believeth not the record that God gave of his Son" (1 John 5:10). 2. Does it not call the Son, the second person of the blessed Trinity, a liar? 3. Does it not call the Spirit, the Holy Ghost, the third person of the blessed Trinity, a liar? 4. Does it not call the gospel a liar? What do you think of unbelief, of which you are so guilty? When the Spirit works in believers by His motions, then unbelief calls that work a delusion.

Now the third thing that flows from ignorance is that it puts strong bands on our spirits and renders us more unsuitable to anything, giving the devil greater advantage over us.

The fourth valley is that which is above our head and that shall remain, until it be rent by Him who is the Judge of the whole world. We shall speak no more about this valley, except to say that Christians may long, until He who is the bright and morning star, shall be the morning-star of their blessed day, and shall cause them to ascend up thither, and partake of that sweet and blessed communion that is with Him above, for whom they longed so much.

The fifth valley that all men are in is the valley of Baca. Christians, were you ever in that valley? Christians, while they are here below, traveling in this valley of Baca, may call themselves *Ichabod,* meaning that their glory is departed. Also, in bringing forth of their duty, they may call themselves *Jabesh,* which means with much pain do they bring it forth. Christians, is not this world the valley of Baca to you? When Christ hides Himself from you, do you not sometimes cry out, "Oh, what a wearisome life is it to be living when Christ departs from me"? A Christian will see so much of the ways of heaven, that he will be so weary of his life in the valley of Baca.

Now unbelievers will be in this valley of Baca also: but I shall show you the differences between Christians and unbelievers being in this valley. When a Christian is in this valley, there are two things to be understood. First, when a Christian reflects upon all the seven abominations that are in his heart, and of that great love to sin that is within him, and when he laments treading with his feet in the path of iniquity, he becomes weary of his life here below, and so cries out, "Oh, to be above, where I would sin no more!" Secondly, this is to be understood of a Christian in this valley of Baca: when he gets a broad sight of the joy of heaven and of that sweet communion that is between Christ and His saints, he is then weary of his life, longing to be above, where there is complete fellowship with Christ. The Christian then cries out, "Oh, send a chariot of fire, and fetch me thither!"

There are likewise two ways that unbelievers behave in this valley of Baca. First, when some outward loss or disadvantage of some worldly concern befalls them, then will they be weary of their life, and say, "We wish we were far away from this false world." The second way unbelievers behave in this valley of Baca is that when some cross providence befalls them, and when they are under a cross, then they say, "It would be good for me to be away." But there is nothing that presses them to that desire, but anxiety and ignorance; for if they knew where they were going, they would have no such desire. Hence you may see the difference between unbelievers and Christians being in the valley of Baca.

Let us consider the sixth valley, the valley of Megiddo. This is a valley of lamentation and "great mourning" (Zech. 12:11). Christians, have you ever known anything of that valley? Did you ever set yourselves apart to mourn for Him whom you pierced? Oh, Christians, there is a sweet connection between the valley of Megiddo and the valley of Berachah. Did you ever sit three days sorrowing because of His absence? Our little sorrowing while we are here absent from the Lord will make us go three years to the mountains, to feed with the wild beasts there. It is much for the advantage of the people of God to be in the valley of Megiddo. As there is a connection between a cross and a crown, so there is a connection between the valley of Megiddo and the valley of Berachah; and the person that was never in the valley of Megiddo, shall never be admitted to the valley of Berachah.

Oh, Christians, when did you ever mourn apart one day for the sin you have committed against God? It is a mystery to some to set apart an hour to mourn in secret before God, for the great and heinous abominations done to Him; and oh, is not that very unlike Christianity? We shall say no more concerning the valley of Megiddo; but he that is in that valley, there is hope in Israel concerning him.

Now we come to the seventh valley that all men are in, which is the valley of interpretation. What will you say, unbelievers, in the first moment that you shall see Christ? Oh, what then will you do? Will you not cry out, "Oh, for ten thousand worlds to give for Him?" Upon seeing Christ, the unbeliever will stand before the throne of God, and his knees will smite one another. There will be two books opened unto him: the book of conscience and the book of life, wherein all our iniquities are written. The Lord will say, "Unbeliever, did not I say unto you, come unto me and receive life? But you would not come up. Now, depart unto death." Oh, what will an unbeliever say in that day?

In that day the unbeliever will have three prayers. First, he shall say, "Oh, if only I had ten thousand worlds to give for Him!" Secondly, he shall pray, "Oh, for another day on earth, so that I might recover strength and repent for all the iniquities done against God!" A third and last prayer the unbeliever will have is this: "Oh, to be above the reach of His power, so that I might not be under the reach of His wrath for my sin!"

In that day, an unbeliever will proclaim four curses against himself. First, he will curse the day that he was born. He will cry, "Let the day perish wherein I was born, and the night in which it is said, there was a child conceived!" Second, the unbeliever will proclaim, "Oh, cursed be the day that ever I heard tell of Christ that He came unto the world to save lost sinners!" Third, he will curse the day that ever he heard of the gospel, that ever the report of these glad tidings of great joy was published unto him. The fourth curse that he will proclaim against himself is this: "Cursed be the day that ever I lived in the place where the gospel was preached!" In that day, a hypocrite shall be made to mourn for all the days that he did rejoice. A sight of precious Christ shall be one of the saddest sights that ever he saw.

Now, unbeliever, do you desire to be free from all these curses and sad threatenings that have been pronounced against you? Then, I say, hearken unto the Son of God today and give obedience unto that precious and soul-concerning commandment: hear Him, and in so doing, your soul shall live. But, I am afraid, yes, I am persuaded, that there are some of us that are here today, who shall never hear Him but once; and that shall be in the day when He shall bid you depart from Him into eternal torments, unto that unquenchable fire that shall never be extinguished, which burns with fire and brimstone, and with the unmixed wrath of God. Whose hearts shall endure? Whose hands shall be strong in that day, when the Lord shall contend with the hypocrites of Zion? They shall then cry out, trembling, "Who can stand before the devouring fire? Who can dwell with everlasting burning?" We shall say no more, but there is yet hope, if you will take with you your guilt and acknowledge it, and take Christ to be the guide of your old age.

Let us consider the eighth and last valley we proposed, into which only Christians arrive: the valley of Berachah. Christians, are you not longing for the day when you shall only walk in that valley of Berachah? Then you that are now standing on Mount Tabor shall be admitted to stand on the top of Mount Pisgah; and shall get leave to convey the Lamb from the valley of decision unto new Jerusalem. There you shall enter unto your everlasting habitations. Are you not longing for the approaching of that blessed day? Believe it, one sight of Christ shall make your hearts to leap within you for joy. A broad sight of an absent Christ shall, in that day, make up all your nine nights' watch and your three days' sorrowing, and all the anxiety and trouble that you have had while you were here on earth, in attaining to communion and fellowship with Him.

In the first moment a Christian shall see precious Christ, he shall proclaim four blessings to himself. First, in that day, a Christian will exclaim, "Oh, blessed be the day that ever I was born, and the night in which I was conceived!" Secondly, the Christian will proclaim, "Blessed be the day that ever I heard of precious Christ, that He was come unto the world to seek and to save those that were lost." Thirdly, the Christian will say, "Blessed be the day that ever I heard tell of the gospel, and of these glad tidings of great joy." Fourthly, he will say, "Blessed be the day that ever I lived in that place where the gospel was preached, and where the report of these offers ever came." Blessed eternally be that day!

Are you yet convinced, oh unbelievers and strangers to God, to hear Him who calls you today? I shall propose seven considerations further to provoke you to hear Christ, and hearken to His voice.

First, all the good of it will be your own. If you will but hear Him who calls you today, all the advantage that will result from that exercise shall be yours, according to that word, "If thou be wise, thou shalt be wise for thyself" (Prov. 9:12).

Second, all these persons that will hear His voice and hearken unto His commandments, while they are here below, shall be admitted to hear that precious melody and sweet harmony that is above. They shall be admitted to hear that comely and beautiful concord of praise that shall be in the higher house, amongst all these innumerable thousands of saints, and of souls of just men now made perfect, that are round about the throne, with their harps in their hands, singing most sweetly songs of praise to Him that sits upon the throne, and to the Lamb forever. Oh, what heavenly music and pleasant harmony shall there be in heaven, when the mystical body of Christ shall be perfected, and when all His brethren and sisters shall be where He is, when each of you shall get a harp put in your hands, when you shall come there? Oh, may that allure your hearts, and provoke your consent to hear Him!

A third consideration to provoke you to hear Christ is that it is commanded of God. This is confirmed in Isaiah 55:3, "Hear, and your soul shall live." I recommend to you one thing: "I counsel thee to keep the king's commandment" (Eccl. 8:2). Will you not hear Christ, since it is the commandment of the great King to you today?

Fourth, consider that there are many persons that have sinned by not hearing Christ or hearkening unto His voice. Ezra 10:13 says, "For we are many that have transgressed in this thing."

Fifth, there is not a person within this church door to whom this command is not spoken: "Hear him, hear him." Yes, it is spoken to everyone in particular by name, "Oh, hear Christ, hear him"; this is a main issue of great and weighty concern, and it belongs unto you, according to Ezra 10:4: "Arise; for this matter belongeth unto thee." Now since this duty is of most great and weighty concern to you, even the eternal well-being of your immortal souls; since it is so, and since it belongs to you, will you refuse this blessed offer? Will you be so unwise as to reject the counsel of the Lord against yourselves? Are there any such presumptuous people here today? If there be any such here, let them take warning in time; for yet salvation is being offered to them, if they will embrace it.

There is this sixth consideration to provoke you to give obedience to the precious command of hearing Christ. It is the great proclamation and desire of heaven to you today to hear Him. It is the Father's great desire that you would hear Him. I am also persuaded that it is the desire of all our fellow brethren that are now above about the throne, that we would hear Christ who calls upon us.

Seventh, consider that if you desire to do the Father one of the greatest pleasures and courtesies you can, then hear His Son, whom He has sent into the world to take away the sins of the elect. The Father accounts it a great favor from sinners; will you not be content to do the Father, the first person of the blessed Trinity, such a favor? Is not this marvelous? Yes, there is nothing more pleasant to Him than for sinners to hear and welcome the Son. Certainly, there will be no advantage to hear Christ report to the Father, saying, "I came to mine own, and mine own received me not" (ref. John 1:11). Shall this report be made of us to the Father today that Christ came and offered Himself to us, but we would not receive Him? It shall be sad to have that reported of us. Therefore I entreat you, old and young, every one of you that hears these glad tidings preached, as you would hazard yourselves upon the despising of the pleasure of the Lord and desire of heaven today, that you would hear Him. Oh, is there not one of us that are yet provoked to hear Him?

Now for further encouragement, I shall propose a few aggravations for those who do not hear Him. First, not to hearken unto Christ is a sin against all the wit and contrivance of heaven; it is a sin against the manifold and unsearchable wisdom of God; it is a sin against that blessed purpose and design of the Father, in sending of His Son into the world to save sinners; and it is a sin against the desire of the Son's coming into the world, suffering such hard things, and enduring such an unpleasant life. It is a sin against the Son's coming and traveling upon the earth, and making His abode and resort with us, being only all for this end, that you would "hear him." Now, how does that aggravate the sin of not hearing Him!

A second aggravation of it is that it is a sin against many precious invitations of the gospel and exhortations of the Father to you today. Has He not said, "This is my beloved Son, in whom I am well pleased; hear ye him" (Matt. 17:5)? Will you sin against all those invitations and precious exhortations that the Father has sent to you? Surely, if you do so, it does greatly aggravate your sin of not hearing Him; for He not only says, "This is my beloved Son," but, "This is my beloved Son, in whom I am well pleased." Then, if there be any further aggravations, will it not be in refusing to hearken to the beloved of the Lord, in whom He is well pleased?

A third aggravation of not hearkening to Christ is that there are so many Scriptures given which may prove to us that it is our duty to "hear him." Are there not many Scriptures to prove this? Wherefore are all these excellent promises that are in the Scriptures? Are they not to provoke you to "hear him"? Wherefore are all these warnings written? Is it not to make us "hear him"? There is not one warning of the law written by Moses that says not unto you, "hear him." There is not a command in all the Bible that has not this language unto you, oh, sinners, "hear him." There is not a dispensation to His own that has not this language, oh sinners, "hear him." There is not a cross that befalls His own, but this is the language of it: "hear him." We think it is His great end in coming down from heaven to earth, that you would "hear him." Is it not the great end of the entire Bible? It all drives at this, that you may "hear him." Then, as you do not desire to undermine that great design, both of love and of the gospel, "hear him" today.

The fourth aggravation of not hearing Him is that it is called, "Despite done to the majesty of God"; it is also called, "a rejection of God," "frustrating of the grace of God," and, "turning the grace of God into wantonness"; and it is called, "a resisting of the power of the Holy Ghost." It has also been called, "despite done to the Spirit of grace," "a turning of the back on Him," "a running from Him," "a stopping of the ear," "a hardening of the heart against God," or "a refusal to be converted." Now what do you think of the sin of not hearing Christ? What do you think of it, since it is presented as such a desperate, abominable, and heinous iniquity! Then, unbelievers, as you do not desire to hazard yourselves upon the guilt of all these abominable, blasphemous sins, do not slight the duty of hearing the Son.

The fifth aggravation of the sin of not hearing Christ is the fact that it is such an easy commandment to obey. There is no more required for the accomplishment of it but a lifting up the ear and hearkening to His voice; in Isaiah 45:22, Christ says, "Look unto me, and be ye saved." Is it not a great aggravation to resist this command which may be received upon such easy terms?

There is this sixth aggravation of the sin of not hearing the Son, and it is this: because it is so near, it is come unto you. It is not said only that it is near you; but it is even in your mouth and in your heart. Since it is so near unto you, will it not be a great aggravation of your sin if you refuse these precious offers of the Son of God?

A seventh aggravation of the sin of slighting the voice of Christ lies in the fact that Christ has passed by many nations in the world, but has come unto you. Is it not said, that "many prophets and kings have desired to see those things which ye see, and have not seen them; and to hear those things which ye hear, and have not heard them" (Luke 10:24); yet, you refuse these precious things. What marvelous folly it is to refuse them! I entreat you, by all that boundless compassion that is in Him, that you would refuse Him no more, and that every one of you may say, "If I have done, I will do so no more." Christians, I say, it is the desire of heaven to you today that you would hearken unto the Son! Now he that is wise will hear counsel, but a fool will go on and be punished. Now, I think it is a mystery to some to bid them hearken unto the voice of the Son. There are other persons that think that they have heard Him all their days and have never so much as a challenge upon their conscience. But I never like an unchangeable faith, nor shall I ever like it. I think a Christian, while he is here, is like the moon—subject to change and alterations, and as unstable as water; but that day is coming when they shall be as pillars fixed in the temple of our God, and shall go out no more.

There are some who err, thinking that they have hearkened to the voice of the Son, and yet are mistaken.

First, there are some who think they have obeyed that command all their days, since ever they knew good from evil; but they would think it blasphemy for anybody to tell them that they hearkened not to the voice of the Son. But surely these persons are mistaken.

Second, some are brought to more length and they have some change of conversation; and, since that day forth, they think they have given obedience to that command of hearing the Son.

Third, they have some sort of delight of hearing the Word preached, and some touching of their affections. They like the preaching of the Word as a well-sung song, as did Herod, when he heard John preach gladly; yet these persons wrongly think they give obedience to that command of hearing Him.

The fourth mistake is that under preaching they will be brought to some sort of hatred and detestation of their idols, but when they meet with their idols outside of worship, they embrace them with both arms. Such was the tenderness of Hazael, that he cried, weeping; and yet he went on in his sin.

The fifth mistake in hearing of the Son, is that because it has made them abandon some idols, and has made them to have some reformation in the outward man, and has made their life something like the outward letter of the law, then they think they give obedience to that command of hearing Him; yet they never put their idols out of their hearts.

A sixth mistake is that under preaching, some will take resolutions and vows upon them; but they do not know that a deceived heart will lead them aside, and that the Lord will have occasion to utter that word, "O that there were such an heart in them" (Deut. 5:29).

Seventh, some think they have a natural liking of the truths of God, and that they have love for the people of God; but I say that they follow religion so long as it is accounted of by many of the world, and so long as it is in a blessed condition; but they will soon forsake it when it is of no account and estimation. There are not many that will follow Christ unto Caiaphas's hall. Most of us follow Christ not because of the excellence that we find in Him, but because of the loaves. Now, I say, all such persons are mistaken, and shall one day know themselves to be so.

An eighth mistake of some is that they will listen with the ear and hearken unto Him, and yield obedience unto Him; and will come along with the ear, and with the eye, and with the tongue, and with the hand, and with the foot. There are some persons that will give Christ their ear, that they will not hearken to the voice of a temptation; and yet will not give Him their heart. There are some that will give Christ their eyes, that they will not look upon sin; yet, they will not give Him their heart. There are some that will give Christ their tongue, so that they will speak nothing unsavory; yet, they will not give Him their heart. There are some that will give Christ their hand, that they shall do no unrighteousness; and yet will not give Him their heart. There are some persons that will give Christ their feet, so that they will not walk in ways that are unacceptable to Him; and yet will not give Him their heart. Yet, I say, all these persons are self-deceived, because they have not given Christ their heart.

A ninth reason is that there are some that will be so affected with the hearing of a sermon, that it will make them put their hand to a duty that they are called to, and make them study a sort of performance, though they walk in sadness many days; yet, for all these vain shows and appearances, they will not be brought so far as to yield solemn obedience to that command, unto that precious and most soul-concerning command, unto that precious exhortation that the Father has for us, that we would hear His Son, and that we would hearken unto His voice. Now, will you hearken unto Him today, who calls and invites you to this exercise? I say, it is possible that persons may take all these nine steps in religion, yet be guilty of the breach of this excellent commandment—of not hearing the Son and listening to His voice.

We shall say no more, but we desire that all of you here today would be persuaded to hear Him, and that you would take it as a duty lying on you to hear Him. Listen to His voice, and you will know that you have chosen the better part. Amen.

SERMON 28

Humility: The Christian's Best Ornament

Be clothed with humility.
—1 Peter 5:5

The beauty, excellence, and blessedness of a man consists in a well-ordered subordination and subjection unto the will of God as his maker; and the high dignity of a Christian consists in a sweet and divine complaisance and obedience unto the will of God and the command of God as his Father. God's command has not only an impression of everlasting righteousness, but likewise an impression of beauty and sweetness, of delight and pleasures, engraven upon it to the spiritual beholder; for it is said of wisdom's ways, that "her ways are ways of pleasantness, and all her paths are peace" (Prov. 3:17). He who has walked and looked into the perfect law of liberty, wherein an immortal spirit may expatiate, take sweet solace, and delight himself in the obedience of His commands, by which he may climb up to that high pinnacle of honor and conformity with God, and partake of His divine nature.

Now, being intended to begin our discourse to you concerning the several graces of the Spirit, in the exercise of which a Christian ought to walk while he is in time, we have made choice of these words, to speak somewhat of the grace of humility. Though it has a low name, humility has a high nature. Though in reputation and form, it appears to be but a servant, yet it accounts it no robbery to be equal with the highest, most divine, principle graces of a Christian. Other graces may come with more pomp and observation, but this comes always with more reality and advantages. The exercise of it is much in request in these days. One that would ascend high in the estimation of God and in reputation among men should first descend low in the estimation of himself, and must exercise this low, yet exalting grace of humility. One that maintains and walks all his life with this motto of humility, observing that he is less than the least of all saints, and is not worthy to have his name in that roll of that blessed company, it is not long until he shall shine most brightly in the kingdom of his Father. Such a humble one shall be a cornerstone fashioned after the similitude of a palace; he shall be made a star different far from many other stars in glory, in that higher orb and celestial sphere of immortal glory and dignity.

Oh, how much is the grace of humility slighted in these days! It is a grace that is liable to manifest misconstructions of lowness and baseness of spirit, though we think it is liable to the most eminent expressions of honor from God, and is the forerunner and harbinger of divine reputation; for a wise man says, "Before honor goeth humility." We are confident that if there were no other thing to commend humility to us but that Christ, who is the great prince of pastors, never proposed Himself with words so much a pattern of any Christian grace as this, that it would be more than sufficient. Christ commended humility twice, first in Matthew 11:29, "Learn of me; for I am meek and lowly in heart"; He also commended it to His disciples and followers in John 13:12 through the special lesson of washing their feet. Who would not accept instruction from Him who was the prince of pastors? He pressed this duty earnestly in His doctrine, and preached it in His life. Though He was one who received the Spirit without measure, and in whom the fullness of the Godhead dwells bodily, He did not think it below Him to walk in the paths of humility. Oh, that the same mind was in us which was in our blessed Lord! Though it is not sufficient to have an outward show of this grace, we must not only lodge it in our outward man, but if we are followers of Him, we must lodge it in our hearts; for, He says, "Learn of me; for I am meek and lowly in heart."

This grace is not below them that are of the highest gifts, nor above them who are of the smallest abilities. We think pride is the last enemy a Christian battles and subdues, though humility in part is the first grace wherewith a Christian is clothed and adorned. Pride is the last enemy that opposes a Christian, and does ordinarily gather strength upon the ruins of our corruptions, and all other things that oppose themselves against the Christian. Thus, when a Christian falls, pride rises up and renews the battle; and it often springs up in a spiritual state. We think that it is spoiled in the valley of the shadow of death; and when we are to receive our fatal stroke, it will receive its fatal blow. We may call pride "Shammah," of whom it is reported, that he stood and defended the fort, when all others fled (2 Sam. 23:11-13). So it defends the field when all other corruptions have fled! We think one that is returned victor after war, over this idol of pride, may be called Judah; for who will rouse him up after he is returned victor from his prey? He may then speak boldly in the gate with his enemies, and not be ashamed.

We do confess, however, that it is difficult to be humble in our humility, and to be nothing in our being nothing. Pride will not only erect to itself a throne in the highest step of our exaltation by grace, and tempt us to think of ourselves above measure, but likewise will erect to itself a throne in the lowest step of our descension by humility, in the sense of our sin and infirmity. Then, when we are lowest in our estimation, pride comes and binds us up into her wings, until much of her substance is dissolved, and the soul certainly that is lifted up, is not upright. Oh, how this sin creeps into the most sublime and divine actions from the choicest graces and most eminent advancements! We conceive that there is no sin a Christian falls in that he should battle more, after he has been lifted up to the third heaven, and has been admitted to detain and hold the king in his galleries. It may be said of pride, as is spoken of the whore, "For she hath cast down many wounded: yea, many strong men have been slain by her" (Prov. 7:26). So pride has wounded many strong, and brought many mighty under its feet.

But humility is an exalting grace, though among men of this world, it is reputed baseness, and lowness of spirit; yet there is no spiritual generosity but in the man that has much humility. He is liable to the highest expressions of favor with God and estimation amongst men; for in Proverbs 15:33, we hear that "before honor is humility"; and Matthew 18:4, "Whosoever therefore shall humble himself as this little child, the same is greatest in the kingdom of heaven." Oh, what a monstrous thing it is to see a proud man! However, there is also nothing more ordinary than a proud man. There is a lie in every sin; but the grossest is pride. It is an attribution upon that erroneous conception and vain confidence of our own excellence and worth.

There is no sin we should more abominate and loathe, for it is that which opens the door at which all other sins enter in. If we would reflect upon the woeful evils which have descended on the sons of men through the sin of pride, and examine what a door it has opened to all the miseries under which we groan, how we would abominate and abhor it! It was the sin that threw our first parents out of paradise, and brought them down from their honor to become like the beasts. It brought down an angel from heaven, who was once as Lucifer, the son of the morning. Ought not this to ingratiate humility, and make you fall in love with it? Oh, that exalting exercise of humility! Although it be low in the ground, yet it descends that it may ascend. It is like Jacob's ladder, the foot of it is fastened to the earth, though the top of it reaches to the heavens. Humility is the ladder by which a Christian ascends to God, and by it also, God descends to the Christian; when this is removed out of the way, this fills up the influences of heaven, and makes the Eden of the Lord into a wilderness.

Now, this expression of being "clothed with humility," holds forth to us several points. First, how suitable and convenient a thing it is to have humility, and to be in the exercise of it. Likewise, how unbecoming a thing it is for a Christian to lack it. It is as suitable for him to have it as for a man to have his clothing and apparel; and what a breach of modesty it is to see a man without apparel! So unseemly is it for a man, much more for a Christian, to lack this ornament of humility, which is of great price in the sight of God. Garments are used for ornaments, and how great an ornament is the garment of humility!

Secondly, humility reveals the great advantages that a Christian may have by exercising this grace. It covers the infirmities and other imperfections that are unseemly in one's walk, as a man's clothing covers those unseemly parts of his body, which naturally men shun to behold. Oh, how soon will the imperfections of a man appear who is proud! How obvious they will be to an indifferent beholder!

Thirdly, humility is that grace which we should take pains to put in exercise, maintain, and hold fast, as a jewel of great price; for to be clothed means not only to put on, but to bind and tie fast. It is of such great concern, and is so easily lost, that we should keep it as the apple of the eye, and bind it about with that knot of watchfulness and self-examination. It is no great wonder that the shame of our nakedness appears, because we are not much in the exercise of humility; pride did not only issue in nakedness, but likewise made it appear.

Fourthly, the expression imports that humility should be most eminent among a Christian's graces, shining most in the perfect manner of our duties, as a man's clothes are outmost and most obvious.

Now, in handling this grace of humility, we shall not insist nor dwell long in pointing out what it is. It is that whereby a Christian man descends in his low estimation of himself, and ascends in a high account and estimation of others, preferring them to himself in love. There are several characteristics that humility does not contain.

It does not, first, consist in a complimentary condescendence and estimation of others above ourselves; we often exercise humility only if others are truly above us, or so in the estimation of the world; but we do so in wrath and indignation.

Neither, secondly, does it consist in that external show of humility, either in voice or gesture, under which we often palliate and hide much pride, vice, and filthiness. These are most ugly when they appear under the color of virtue.

Thirdly, it does not consist in a verbal undervaluing of ourselves unto others, speaking these evils of ourselves which we would not have them believing, to whom we speak them, but rather that they would commend us for the contrary. When they seem to believe them, what indignation we have against ourselves for speaking those things to them! What a lack of love we then have in their believing them! Oh, how few are there that, in their undervaluing of themselves, do speak as they think! Or, if they think it so, how loathe are they that others should believe and think so with them! What inconsistency there is between our speech and our thought, and between the intention of the speech and the intention of the speaker! The intention of our speech may be sometimes to undervalue, when our intention is that we may be set on high. Oh, what fearful, hideous hypocrisy lurks under our undervaluing ourselves; yea, in our bowing our knee to God before others! We may complain of these things of ourselves to Him, which we would not have those that hear us believing concerning us, which is certainly the highest pitch and step to pride. Furthermore, when you are clothed with such a spirit, you cannot pray with that divine fervency and holy indignation against yourselves for these things. It is a strong demonstration of unbelief, that you place more value on having yourselves hidden from the world, and are loathe to let them know your sins; yet you are not ashamed and confounded to make them known to God. How we lie to the Holy Ghost when we speak these things we do not desire to have others believing! Among all the graces of the Spirit, there was never one so precious as the grace of humility; we may say that of all the sins that ever entered into the world, there was never one of them acted so much as pride. We believe that when the books shall be opened, out of which we shall be judged, among all that black and infinite roll of transgressions, especially of those who are within the visible church, this item shall be often set down: pride, pride, pride. We may say that if that item of pride were not in the books, our sins should not amount to such a high number. We shall only say this: it is impossible for a natural man to be humble, or for a Christian not to dally under the exercise of the law, or under the exercise of the gospel. We think among all the sad fruits of our interrupting our exercise in these things, pride is a primary sin. Oh, to be much at home into our hearts and less roving abroad!

We need not insist long in proving that it is your duty to study humility. Any person who will read Matthew 11:29, where Christ commends it, will be convinced that humility is the ABC of Christianity, and the first lesson we must learn. Some might have thought that he who was endued with all the treasures of heavenly wisdom, and was the great counselor of heaven and earth, would teach unto his scholars the deep and profound mysteries of art and nature, about which the world has plotted ever since the first tasting of the tree of the knowledge of good and evil. Who would have thought that the One who came from high should have taught such a low lesson as this is, to be lowly in spirit? May not men pause and wonder? "But let it be the hidden man of the heart, in that which is not corruptible, even the ornament of a meek and quiet spirit, which is in the sight of God of great price" (1 Peter 3:4). "If I then, your Lord and Master, have washed your feet; ye also ought to wash one another's feet" (John 13:14). "With all lowliness and meekness, with longsuffering, forbearing one another in love" (Eph. 4:2). Now since this excellent grace of humility is a commanded duty, a Christian ought to spend his time in the exercise thereof. If you desire to attain it, you should take these helps.

First, be much in the spiritual meditation of the wonderful humility of our blessed Lord Jesus, who was God; Christ says, "Learn of me; for I am meek and lowly in heart" (Matt. 11:29). This command has a strange emphasis in it. Christ is saying, "If I be much in it, how much more ought you?" In Philippians 2:5, when he is pressing humility, he proposes the humility of Him who thought it no robbery to be equal with God; and though He had the gift of the Spirit above measure, and in Him dwelt the fullness of the Godhead bodily, yet He thought it not below Him to have the sound of His feet heard in the low paths of humility. If so, it is not above the highest, nor below the lowest, to walk in these paths. It may be exercised by those on the dunghill, as well as by them that sit on the throne.

Oh, how we should blush and be confounded, to be proud! If He, who was so high, humbled Himself out of charity and love, how must we, who are so low, humble ourselves, both out of charity and necessity. We believe that serious meditation upon the unsearchable mystery of the high One would provoke us to humility, we who are so low. One main cause of our pride is our lack of meditation on that inexpressible humility of the Son of God, who clothed Himself with this robe out of charity and love to us. It is impossible that a Christian who is much taken up with the lowest step of His condescension by humility, will not be constrained to cry out that it is a suitable thing that the servant be no greater than his Lord. Example often teaches more than rules; this example has taught many, and if we solidly believed, it might teach us.

Secondly, be much in the consideration of the holiness, and absolute and immaculate purity that is in God. This knowledge will reveal to you such ugly and monstrous imperfections in yourself that you will be provoked to sit low in the dust before Him. When Isaiah gets a sight of God's holiness, he cries out, "Woe is me! For I am undone; because I am a man of unclean lips, and I dwell in the midst of a people of unclean lips: for mine eyes have seen the King, the LORD of hosts" (Isa. 6:5). It is also displayed in Job 25:4-6, where we read, "How then can man be justified with God? Or how can he be clean that is born of a woman? Behold even to the moon, and it shineth not; yea, the stars are not pure in his sight. How much less man, that is a worm? And the son of man, which is a worm?" I say, little meditation on the holiness of God makes us to have high pretensions of innocence, which is the mother of pride. Oh, but when men are once admitted to behold Him in whose eyes the heavens are not pure and clear, and whose saints and angels He charges with folly (Job 4:18), it makes them sit down, loathe themselves, and walk humbly with God. It is a token they never saw one higher than themselves, that walks under this ill of pride. Oh, but one sight of Him that is without spot, whose countenance is as the sun shining in its strength, would provoke us to be much in the exercise of this grace of humility!

A third help is to study your own imperfections and wants, and that which is amiss in you. Know the areas wherein you are defective. Be more faithful in learning what you lack than what you have attained. One reflex look on what you lack, and have not attained, may keep you from boasting. It would be more suitable to sit down and mourn for our shortcomings than to sit down and exalt ourselves in our imagined progress. A Christian should be so consumed with that which is before his hand that he should have no leisure to sit down and search his own glory; for a man to search his own glory is no glory.

Oh, if humanity would believe what infinite defects we contain, and how much we come short of that which is required, we would be constrained to weep more over that which we want than to boast of what we have attained. We see ourselves as defective in so many ways that we cannot boast of what we have attained. Although we may reflect upon what we have received, yet we must not do it in order to exalt ourselves, but to be thankful to the Giver. We think a man that is proud has lost sight of that which he once was by nature; he has forgotten the rock he was hewn out of, and the hole of the pit from whence he was dug, which makes him cry out, "I am, and there is none like him."

Fourthly, compare yourself more often with those that are above you rather than with those that are below you. What secret pride fails by looking on the infirmities of others rather than on their graces? Humility makes a man compare himself with the best, that he may hide pride from his eyes, and see how bad he is; but pride makes him compare himself with the worst, that he may hide his own imperfections. Humility, on the contrary, looks on the best things of others, to discover its own lack, for its humbling. If our comparisons ascended, we would descend; we would descend in humility and all the different degrees of persons would meet in one center, lowliness and meekness of spirit. How we increase and foster our pride by a secret complacency in ourselves, beholding the infirmities of others! But in this, we are not wise, measuring ourselves and comparing by those who are below (2 Cor. 10:11-14). That which makes humility have so little growth, when we behold them that are above us, is our sinful emulation and woeful envies. What a helpful means to humility would this prove if upon the discovery of the perfections of others that are above us, we would sit down and bless Him who has given to men gifts? There cannot be much progress made in this, by reason of this deplorable emulation that is among us. It is impossible that we can reap advantage, except we sit down and bless God, that He has given gifts to men.

Lastly, think seriously about the woeful state we were once in by nature, before we were in Christ. We should look to the rock whence we were hewn, and the hole of the pit from which we were rescued. This sort of meditation led Paul to deem himself less than the least of all saints (1 Cor. 15:9). When we do not meditate on this, we sit down, having such high thoughts, and boasting our own excellence. It is a promise in the covenant of grace for one to be humbled upon their remembering their ways (Ezek. 16:63). By the advantage of humility and disadvantage of pride, a man beholds such excellence in humility that he is forced to conclude that "better it is to be of an humble spirit with the lowly, than to divide the spoil with the proud" (Prov. 16:19). To say amen to that is that blessedness which is pronounced upon the poor in spirit (Matt. 5:3). A man that is much here shall both find favor in the eyes of God and man. We may call humility "Gad," for it comes forth a troop; *chorus virtutum*, a troop of virtues. It is a fruitful womb, always bearing twins. Every sin has a lie in it, but the grossest is in the sin of pride. The foundation of pride is an erroneous conception of our own excellence. It would be good if we did look less and more fully consider what we were when we met first with the surprise of grace. It is a token that we are not either really converted, or else we are not reflecting on what we were before conversion, when pride binds us up in the wings of the wind, and makes us to ride until our substance be dissolved.

Now, to provoke you to study and pursue humility, consider briefly the advantages of this exercise. First, it keeps all the graces of a Christian in exercise. It keeps patience in exercise, even in the most afflicting cross dispensations. It preserves from murmuring and makes the soul sit down and wonder that it is not worse dealt with. It walks through the darkest dispensations, and keeps the motto of patience still before the Christian's eyes, with these words in his mouth: "Wherefore doth a living man complain?" (Lam. 3:39). A man that is much in the exercise of humility—will he not possess his soul in patience? What quiet frame of spirit he will have! He sees so much ground of contentment that instead of murmuring under what God has inflicted, he is taught by humility to sit down and sing that sweet and pleasant song in his night of affliction; he sings, "It is of the LORD's mercies that we are not consumed" (Lam. 3:22). Impatience is a fruit of pride. Oh, what a change! What a sweet change of murmuring, and of saying against him, who accepteth not the person of men, that he does no iniquity. To sit down and wonder, these are conjoined in Lamentations 3:20-22.

Humility likewise keeps the Christian in the exercise of love to others. Humility is the strongest bone of peace and sinew of love. Pride makes contention and discord amongst brethren, but humility makes each prefer others to himself. Therefore Paul, while he is pressing that the same mind may be in us which was in Christ, and commanding that we have the same love, adds this: "Let nothing be done through strife or vainglory; but in lowliness of mind let each esteem other better than themselves" (Phil. 2:3). Why is a Christian's love in such decay? We lack love because we lack humility. Pride subordinates all to the high idol of self, but humility goes out for others' good. If there is any sin that makes love wax cold, it is pride.

Humility helps forward mortification to the applause and report of the world. It sits down when it has the world's approval, discovering that the world's applause has so small a foundation that humility says, surely "all men are liars" (Ps. 116:11). Likewise the humble man, when he lacks this applause, thinks so lowly of himself, that there can come none behind him who undervalue him so much as himself. What anxieties does the lack of the airy applause and the hosanna of the world occasion to the proud man! He is pierced through with many sorrows.

Humility also keeps dependence on God in exercise. The humble Christian does not lean much on his own understanding; instead, he desires to acknowledge God in all his ways. But, oh, how little are we taken up in this exercise! Another quality of humility is that it keeps love to God in vigor and exercise. It discovers so much imperfection in itself that the humble Christian, reflecting upon what he is, wonders that the infinite love of God should have condescended so low as to have fixed His desire and respect on him. Infinite love is a mystery to the humble man; it makes him cry, "I am less than the least of all saints!" Though God has dignified the Christian with that incomparable dignity through adoption, when the Christian's soul reflects upon its unspeakable lowness by humility, and its unspeakable lowness by faith, it cries, "Oh, the height of the love of God! It is a wonder if you know it not, but it will be a greater wonder, if you know it." Likewise, obedience solaces itself in wondering about the mysteries of infinite love—wondering that He, whose countenance is as Lebanon, should condescend so low as to love sinners.

A second advantage is that humility disposes and fits the Christian's spirit of receiving most divine influences and manifestations of the spirit. "God resisteth the proud" (1 Peter 5:5). Those that sit low in their own estimation are high in God's estimation. He knows no mansion on earth but the humble spirit; highness delights most to dwell with those that are lowly. We may regret these interruptions of divine correspondence with God, which our pride has occasioned. Pride makes many clouds between Him and us. Pride is the vapor which creates many thick clouds; though it be but a little cloud, like a hand-breadth at first, yet at last it fills the whole face of our sky. Grace visits none but those that sit low in the dust; that high and lofty One who inhabits eternity dwells with none but those that are of an humble spirit, with "him that is poor and of a contrite spirit, and trembleth at my word" (Isa. 66:2). "Before honour," says the wise man, "is humility" (Prov. 15:33).

A third advantage of the exercise of humility is that a man may attain divine contentment under every call he encounters; he has sweet peace. He develops a sweet undervaluing of the world's applause; he is not taken up with it, for he sees nothing of value in it. He sees in the world's approval nothing on which any worth can be founded; he walks with a sweet and composed frame of spirit, even under affronts; he can sit down and possess his soul in patience, laughing at all those things that are fluctuating. The lack of humility creates anxiety when we are resisted. It is impossible for a man to be one day in peace who lacks the exercise of this grace; whereas having humility brings him to a divine and settled frame. This grace teaches the Christian, under sad and anxious dispensations, to cry out, "Why should a living man complain, a man for the punishment of his sin?" He compares God's dispensations with His merits, and cries out, Lord, "what is man, that thou art mindful of him?" (Ps. 8:4). What is man, that Thou shouldst visit him every morning and try him every moment?

Fourth, humility cannot retain any sore blow by the hand of his iniquities; for he entertains always within himself a holy despair of his own strength, without any despondency of spirit. The humble Christian desires to rely upon Him alone whose name is an everlasting strength; He can make him walk on like David, and David like the angel of the Lord. It is a great mystery in Christianity that when we are weakest in our own apprehensions, we are strongest in reality.

Now to encourage you to shun the ill of pride and to study humility, take notice of these disadvantages that come through a lack of humility.

First, a proud man can receive no advantage by either private or public praying; he subordinates that exercise to his own exaltation. One in whom pride bears sway, when he is enlarged with others in praying, sits down and sacrifices to his own net, kissing his own hand. What numerous breaches of the first command are involved in the evil of pride? With what self-idolatry are men clothed? How is the idol of jealousy set up, and incense offered to it? The vigor of pride is much abated when humility is in exercise. The same holds true in private prayer. Hence, we more often in our secret retirements study the ornaments of the grace of prayer than the grace itself. It is our woeful design, in our private devotion and secret retirements to prayer, that we may be filled with something to come abroad. Often with others, our gifts pray but not our graces. This evil is so prevalent that we think that many, even if they had liberty in public, their secret prayer would be cut off.

Secondly, hypocrisy is an inseparable companion to pride. Men study such a high pitch of dignity that they personate many things of necessity, lacking the reality of humility; this may maintain a uniformity between their profession and their sincerity, or between their outward show and their inward attainments. If we walked with a low estimation of ourselves, and others did esteem us according to our reality, we would lack much of that we seem to have. When pride prevails, and we cut off the exercise of humility, it withholds the divine influences that God is otherwise willing to communicate; yes, it provokes God to be our enemy and to oppose us with a strong hand. He resists the proud, but by humility, a Christian ascends and is admitted to converse with God. God will then descend to him; however, when a Christian lacks the exercise of humility, the doors of access are stopped and closed upon him, and he has neither access to God nor fellowship with Him. We might multiply disadvantages. Without humility, it is impossible to walk tenderly with inward peace; so soon pride prevails, and makes the graces of the Christian to wither. Pride is the dead fly that causes the ointment of the apothecaries to stink. You would make great progress in the course of Christianity if you would once learn the excellent lesson of humility. If a Christian, in eternity, reflected on his carriage in time, there is no sin he would blush so much to think upon as upon the sin of pride. Ignorance is the mother of this devotion to the creature when it is puffed up in itself, not walking in the low path of humility before the Lord. If we spent more of our time unfolding what God is, and what we are ourselves, we would not be so taken up in this mystery of self-conceit. Their fall is great who sit high; but the humble sit so low that their fall cannot be great. That which makes us receive so many stripes is because pride has bound us up in her wings; therefore, when we fall, our ruin is the greater. As the exercise of humility has peace in the lives of Christians, so it is that wherein we will have great peace when we walk through the valley of the shadow of death. As for those that are without humility, we need not press humility upon them; for it is impossible for the natural man to be in this exercise at all. Amen.

SERMON 29

How to Prevent Spiritual Pride During Special Manifestations (1)

And lest I should be exalted above measure
through the abundance of the revelations.
—2 Corinthians 12:7

If the Christians of this time were to write a chronicle of their lives, it would be long before they should come to such a thing, or mark such a dispensation, as that with which this chapter begins: "I will come to visions and revelations of the Lord" (2 Cor. 12:1). Must not these words be engraven upon the forehead of all the religious duties that we go about: "Christ is gone, Christ is gone"? Many may mark and put upon record the dispensations of a silent Christ, of an absent Christ, and of a frowning Christ, which have now become like our ordinary food; but oh, those soul-raptures of love, those ravishing and overpowering enjoyments of Him, which were the lot of the saints of old! Have they not become mysteries unto us? When we speak of those precious depths of communion and fellowship with Christ that are recorded in Scripture, they seem foreign unto you and ourselves, speaking in an unknown tongue that we do not understand. But oh, if we could divinely preface our discourse with these words: "That which was from the beginning, which we have heard, which we have seen with our eyes, which we have looked upon, and our hands have handled, of the Word of life" (1 John 1:1). We would then speak with more advantage and hear with more gain, but had he not need to taste of the abundance of revelations, who would preach upon this text? All of us that are here may say, "That which we know not, teach thou us, oh Lord."

There are six types of visits that Christ gives to His own in this valley of Baca, in these tents of Shechem. First, He gives some standing and transient visits to His own, when He gives them a passing sight of Himself, turning aside as a stranger and pilgrim, to stay but for an hour. Second, there are more abiding visits of Christ, when He continues to rest in His love, and to sit at the table with His own (Song 1:12). Third, there are some ordinary visits, which Christ will commonly manifest to His own people. Fourth, there are some extraordinary visits of Christ's, as when He visited Paul, where there is a high spring-tide of consolation, joy, sight, and life. Then, the gate of access is cast open, and His people are brought into the banqueting house, and are fed with angels' food. Another type of visit is that where Christ is expected and anticipated (Luke 2:25). These visits are like noble birds of hope. Finally, there are some surprising visits of Christ's, when He comes to His own before they are aware, according to that word, "The wind bloweth where it listeth, and thou hearest the sound thereof, but canst not tell whence it cometh, and whither it goeth: so is every one that is born of the Spirit" (John 3:8). It is hard for a Christian, under the night of desertion, to tell what hour of the night it is, and to know the approaching of the morning, when the shadows shall fly away. I think this is a sweet word. It is no wonder, however, that the disciples will be glad when they shall see Jesus (John 20:20). Oh, but it is sweet to feast on Christ, and to taste of that honey of divine consolations that are in Him and be enlightened to taste of the finest of the wheat and of honey out of the rock, and to be satisfied.

But, to come to the text in particular, let us examine three ideas: first, his condition and case, set down in the seventh verse. Second, consider his divine and spiritual carriage under that case, in the eighth verse. Third, consider the sweet and noble period he obtains from that condition. Oh, infinite wisdom can wisely regulate our way to heaven and lead us in paths that we do not understand!

Concerning the first point, take notice of these five ideas: first, there are some times when a Christian meets with singular enjoyments and eminent manifestations of God. This is clearly presupposed. Second, the most eminent enjoyments of God, the most soul-refreshing manifestations of Himself, are readily abused. Paul was in danger of being exalted above measure, through the abundance of revelations. Third, God has a glorious and excellent design of love in even the darkest and most bitter dispensation that a Christian encounters. This is clear in Paul's meeting with a messenger of Satan, a thorn in the flesh. It was the end of that dispensation: "Lest I should be exalted above measure" (2 Cor. 12:7). Fourth, a Christian should take notice of those sweet designs of love and goodwill that God has in even the darkest dispensations. Paul is so affected by the precious end that was proposed in these temptations, that he takes notice of it in one verse twice: "And lest I should be exalted above measure through the abundance of the revelations, there was given to me a thorn in the flesh, the messenger of Satan to buffet me, lest I should be exalted above measure" (2 Cor. 12:7). Fifth, there are some special seasons when the devil does most strongly assault and buffet a Christian. The devil knows the times and seasons; there is a time of peace and a time of war with him.

There are two questions we would answer to further explain the text. First, when did Paul meet with such enjoyment and divine manifestation of God? When was it that Paul was caught up into the third heaven, and heard words that were unspeakable? This he makes clear in the first verse of the chapter, saying, "I knew a man in Christ above fourteen years ago, (whether in the body, I cannot tell; or whether out of the body, I cannot tell: God knoweth;) such an one caught up to the third heaven" (2 Cor. 12:2). This point in time, if many be not deceived, was shortly after his conversion. Christ intended to send him forth to the ministry, and to put him to sore and hard travel, but He desired to give him a feast before He sent him on his journey.

The second question I shall propose is this: what is meant by the thorn in the flesh and the messenger of Satan? We shall not trouble you with the various opinions of men in expounding the meaning of the messenger of Satan and the thorn in the flesh. But, in short, it was some spiritual and inward temptation; whether pride or uncleanness, or such, we shall be loathe to determine. We would only have you to take notice of these four characteristics of this temptation: first, Paul calls it "a thorn in the flesh"; this means that this temptation was a most painful thing to him. The second thing that Paul says describing this temptation is that it hindered his spiritual motion and walk; it was a thorn in the flesh, which you know is something that exceedingly impedes one in his way. A thorn in one's foot mars one's progress in his way. Thirdly, Paul says that it was a messenger of Satan. Paul thus means that Satan is the principal actor in all assaults on a Christian. Last, Paul says that the strength of this temptation did buffet him; this points to the strong assault and the violent incursion that this temptation made upon Paul's spiritual life.

Now let us discuss the first point. Sometimes Christians, on this side of eternity, meet with remarkable manifestations. Christ allows His people manifestations of diverse kinds, as is hinted in Scripture, where the spouse takes notice that "the king hath brought me into his chambers" (Song 1:4). There is not only an enjoyment of Christ in the outer chamber, but there is also an enjoyment of Christ in the chambers of presence, which was the enjoyment the spouse met with. In Numbers 12:8, God promises signal and extraordinary manifestations to Moses. Accordingly, in Exodus 34:6-7 Moses meets with a most extraordinary, soul-refreshing enjoyment of God, the glory of the Lord passing before him. Only take notice that the extraordinary enjoyments of the saints are but transient enjoyments, according to Exodus 33:19: "And he said, I will make all my goodness pass before thee." In other words, the Lord is saying, "I will give you, Moses, a passing sight of My goodness, but you must not dwell within sight of it; it must pass by before you."

Regarding such meetings with Christ, let us discuss first what it means to meet with extraordinary manifestations of Christ. We conceive that it comprehends three things. First, a soul meets with more than ordinary discoveries of Christ and a piece of the veil is taken aside; by this, the soul is admitted to behold more of Christ than it did before. Second, it imports having the impression of these discoveries deeper upon a Christian's heart, so that when Christ reveals Himself in His beauty to them, their soul is more than ordinarily affected with these discoveries. If Christ then draws aside the veil, they are constrained to cry out, "Is that most pleasant Christ?" Their heart is, as it were, put to a non-plus—they cannot speak. Third, these encounters mean that the soul is under more than ordinary impressions of love and joy. Thus, they meet with extraordinary manifestations of Christ when their soul is burning within them, when Christ speaks to them, when the soul through the beholding of His face is constrained to "rejoice with joy unspeakable and full of glory" (1 Peter 1:8). Is it not known that sometimes a Christian, when he meets with some eminent enjoyments of God, is constrained to cry out, "Call me no more Mara, but call me Naomi, because the Lord hath dealt plentifully with me"?

Secondly, we would like to propose eight times in which the Christian ordinarily meets with extraordinary and eminent enjoyments of Christ, and when the soul is overcome with the love of Christ and His beauty. The first time that a Christian experiences extraordinary and eminent enjoyments of Christ is ordinarily at his conversion, when Christ and he first engage together. This is clear in the instance of Paul; he met with this enjoyment soon after his conversion. This may be also seen in Jeremiah 2:2, where we read of the love of espousals and the kindness of youth. It is not always so that a Christian meets with signal or extraordinary enjoyments of Christ at conversion, but it is certain that souls often meet with the sweetest and most comfortable day in Christ's company upon earth, when Christ and they first meet together. Some have a pleasant morning in their way to heaven; the same may have a dark afternoon and a dark night. Some will have a pleasant morning and a pleasant night, but the midst of the day may be overcast and gloomy. However, the Lord Jesus ordinarily dispenses Himself in large degrees to souls when they first trust in Him. He does this for several reasons: first, so that the soul may be much united to Christ by the excellent cord of faith; second, so that the soul may be much united to Christ by the constraining cord of love; third, Jesus shows Himself to the newly converted so that their souls may be much united to Christ by the beautiful cord of profession.

The first ground of it is that a Christian may be thoroughly convinced that godliness is great gain, and that no one is comparable to Christ. This is Christ's great design—to bring the soul to break forth with this conclusion: who is like matchless Christ?

The second reason is that when a Christian meets with dark temptations and dismal dispensations on the way to heaven, he may submit with patience to this providence. A Christian may comfort himself in his darkest night by thinking, I had a pleasant morning, and I shall have a pleasant night; my sun is now under a cloud, but behold, after the night comes the day.

A second time that Christ manifests Himself is when His people are much in the precious exercise of prayer. When they are most spiritual and most importunate in that duty, the soul is lifted unto the third heavens to hear words that are unspeakable. This is clear in Genesis 32:24, when Jacob wrestled like a prince with God. When was it that Jacob held Christ and would not let Him go? Was it not when he was much in the exercise of prayer? "Yea, he had power over the angel, and prevailed: he wept, and made supplication unto him: he found him in Bethel, and there he spake with us" (Hos. 12:4). There Jacob, as a prince, prevailed and had power with God. This is clear from Acts 10:2, where it is recorded of Cornelius that he "prayed to God alway," and, that while he was fasting and praying, he beheld a vision. It is clear in the ninth, tenth, and eleventh verses of the same chapter, when Peter, while he was praying, "fell into a trance, and saw heaven opened."

I shall only give you these four grounds on which Christians meet ordinarily with eminent enjoyments in prayer. First, the prayers of the saints are the dictates of the Holy Ghost, and their bills and petitions are penned by Him; therefore, their desires and prayers must have a noble and perfect proof of His love. Since the Father hears the Son always, will He not hear the Spirit always, too? A second ground is that the prayers of the saints are backed in heaven by the intercession of Christ; Christ, as the great angel of the covenant, stands before the altar perfuming the prayers of the saints with His incense. If the Spirit makes intercession in us, and the Son of God makes intercession for us, must not our prayers have noble proofs of love? A third ground why the saints meet with eminent enjoyments in prayer is that there is a promise annexed to prayer, of tasting the sweetness of God, according to the words of Psalm 22:26, "They shall praise the LORD that seek him: your heart shall live for ever." A fourth ground is that prayer is the duty of a Christian that ascribes the most glory of his enjoyments to Christ. A Christian's prayers acknowledge that Christ is able to give, and the praying of a Christian acknowledges that Christ should only be thanked when he meets with any enjoyments of Him; but let me say, dear Christians and expectants of heaven, may not these words be engraven upon your secret prayers: "Christ is gone; Christ is gone"? May not these same words be engraven upon your family prayers and public prayers also? Yet few are lamenting after an absent Lord.

The Lord also manifests Himself signally to His people during a time of persecution for Christ. He then uses His presence to allure them with the tokens of His love; He "brings them into the wilderness, and speaks comfortably" to them there (Hos. 2:14). The apostle found it to be his experience that "as the sufferings of Christ abound in us, so our consolation also aboundeth by Christ" (2 Cor. 1:5). Likewise, the martyr Stephen found it so when the Jews were persecuting him to death, and the stones were flying about his ears; it was then that Christ gloriously revealed Himself to him, as "standing on the right hand of God," pleading for him. Jacob, when obliged by Esau's persecution to fly from his father's house, having nothing with him but his staff, no roof to lodge under but the heavens, and no pillow to lay his head on but a stone; yet, in that destitute case, God wonderfully manifested Himself to him by the ladder that reached between heaven and earth. Thus he called the place "Bethel," or "the house of God" (Gen. 28), for there God spoke with him. Afterwards, when both he and his whole family were in danger of being cut off by his persecuting brother Esau, who came against him with four hundred men, God manifested Himself to him the night before, wrestling with Him in prayer (Gen. 32); He blessed him, and gave him a new name; thus Jacob called the place "Peniel," or "the face of God," to remind him that there he had seen God face to face. When the children of Israel sighed because of their bondage in Egypt, God heard their groaning and remembered His covenant with their fathers; He sent Moses to comfort and deliver them (Ex. 2). God is pleased to give His people signal manifestations under persecution because He knows their strength is small; He knows that all their stock of grace and experiences, and their strongest resolutions, would not be able to hold out against the violent shock of malicious persecutors, without extraordinary aid and support from heaven; therefore, Christ makes singular visits to His persecuted flock, to harden and encourage them to endure the trial.

A fourth time is when believers have sorest conflicts with Satan's temptations, and with the corruptions of their own hearts—these have been times of God's special revelations to them. Paul found the same truth when the messenger of Satan buffeted him very sore (2 Cor. 12), then God seasonably stepped in, and said, "My grace is sufficient for thee" (v. 9). Even when Peter was laid upon his back by Satan's tempting him to deny his Master, and seemed likely to be wholly overcome and to turn into an apostate, the Lord graciously turned and looked to him, and restored him to repentance. Also, when Thomas was almost overcome by temptations to infidelity and apostasy, Christ appeared to him and showed him

His wounds, thus restoring his swooning faith. Upon this sight of Christ, Thomas was made to cry out in rapture, "My LORD, and my God" (John 20:28). Since the apostles' days, this has been confirmed by the frequent experience of believers—when Satan has sorely harassed them with blasphemous injections, atheistic thoughts, misconstructions of God and His providential dealings with them, and sometimes has tempted them to gross sins, and at other times utterly to despair of mercy—in this distressed condition, Christ has many times come in with special aid and furnishings, and has given them a glorious victory. Thus our compassionate and kind-hearted Lord is pleased to arise and step in at the time of His people's greatest need, to prevent their complying with temptation to sin, and to keep them from despairing thoughts and conclusions under shaking dispensations, and from razing foundations, which they would be ready to do, if the Lord did not appear remarkably for their help. But, by His seasonable succor, He restores and strengthens their sinking faith, whereby they are enabled to put the enemy to flight and triumph over him.

A fifth time is when the Lord calls His people to enter upon difficult work or great trials, He then manifests Himself to them; as when He called Abraham to leave his native country and kindred, and to sacrifice his only son. He also manifested Himself to the apostles by the outpouring of His Spirit before He sent them forth as sheep among wolves, to preach to and convert the nations. He appeared graciously to Moses and Joshua before the great and difficult undertaking to which He called them; also to Paul, before his shipwreck. He took Peter, James, and John to see His transfiguration on Mount Tabor before He called them to behold His agony in the garden of Gethsemane, that by seeing the one, they might be strengthened to endure the sight of the other. This method the Lord takes with His people to show that He will send none to warfare upon their own charges. When He called Elijah to extraordinary work and great trials, He provided a double meal for him beforehand. Before the Lord calls His people to bear a heavy cross, He often provides for them a feast of fat things full of marrow and of wines on the lees well-refined. In Genesis 28:10, and the following verses, before Jacob entered into afflictions and calamities, He gave him a feast. This is also clear from 1 Kings 19:4-5, where, before Elijah met with anxiety, toil, and travail, there was a sweet feast of heaven given unto Him: "Arise and eat"; for in the strength of that meat, he had to go and walk forty days. This speaks forth much of God's wisdom—before He gives us a cross, He will give us furnishings to bear our cross; before we engage in our trials, He will give something to make them sweet unto us. I shall only give this reason why God reveals Himself before a Christian engages in trials: the soul under afflictions is ready to change its love. God, by revealing Himself, keeps the soul under the constant exercise of love, even through afflictions, for the Lord gives to the soul, in the entry to the cross, an eminent discovery of Himself.

A sixth time that a Christian meets with excellent discoveries of God is when he goes about the sacrament of the Lord's Supper in a spiritual and believing way. That is a time when the soul meets with eminent discoveries of God; on this day, they are brought to the banqueting house and His banner over them is love. Now it is clear that a day of communion has sometimes been to a Christian a day of matchless enjoyment. This is clear in 2 Chronicles 30:21-26, where it is observed that the seven days of the Passover were kept with exceeding great joy and gladness. The great joy that was had at that feast of love was the occasion that all of them resolved to keep other seven days unto the Lord. It is observed of them, that they were kept with gladness. Such was the spiritual joy that was at that communion and Passover, that there was not such a day of joy since the days of Solomon (v. 26). This also is shown in Luke 24:35, where it is said that Christ was made known to them in the breaking of bread; which, we believe, without wronging the text, may be speaking of communion. There was an eminent revelation of Christ made to them when He broke bread with them. Christ communicates five acts of love to a believer's soul in communion times.

First, Christ will sometimes say to the soul, "Reach hither thy finger, and behold my hands; and reach hither thy hand, and thrust it into my side: and be not faithless, but believing" (John 20:27). This is the language that Christ speaks to His own in that banqueting day of love; as if He would say to them, "Come, and let the wounds in My hands answer your objections, and let the precious wounds in My side silence your disputations, and make you believe"; for there is not a wound that precious Christ received, but this is the voice of it, "Believe in Him! Oh, believe in Him!"

A second blessed act of love that Christ will dispense to His own in communion days is that He will give to them eminent discoveries of Himself, so that He will satisfy their eyes by beholding Him; He will satisfy their touch by handling Him; He will satisfy their taste by letting them taste His sweetness; He will satisfy their smell by letting them smell His garments that are perfumed with all the powders of the merchant. Sometimes the soul will cry forth, "Is this not 'a feast of fat things, a feast of wines on the lees, of fat things full of marrow, of wines on the lees well refined'?" (Isa. 25:6).

A third act of love that Christ dispenses to His own at communion is to sweetly loosen their bands and make all their fetters fall from their feet. Has not the table of the Lord been the burial of a Christian's bands, so that he has been constrained to cry out, "I have been in bondage, but now I am free; I was a captive before, but now the prison doors are cast open, and I am come forth"?

A fourth transcendent act of love that Christ dispenses to His own in the day of communion, when they are taken to the banqueting-house, is to give them a little emblem of heaven, a little taste of the joy of the higher house. The sacrament of the Lord's Supper is a little taste of the feast of those that are above. Is it not known that sometimes the table of the Lord has been, to the Lord's people, the place of so much enjoyment, that they have been constrained to cry forth, "This is the gate of heaven; the Lord was here, and I knew it not"?

Finally, Christ dispenses to the soul this transcendent act of love on communion day: He makes the soul to find delight in duty. He makes the soul to have hatred against her idols; He makes the soul to desert her arguments. Oh, but a communion has sometimes been to the saints a day of many excellent things! What is heaven? It is the eternal celebration of the Lord's Supper, of His precious sacrament. This is the table of the lower house; and the table that all the spotless spirits are sitting about, is the table of the higher house. What do the saints above feed upon? Is it not upon a crucified Christ? What do the saints of the lower house feed upon? Is it not upon a crucified Christ, who was pierced for our iniquities?

To return to our points, a seventh time when a Christian meets with real enjoyments of Christ is immediately before his death. Often a Christian's night is pleasant, though not always. This is clear, in Luke 2:29-30, where old Simeon has a pleasant night when he takes

Christ in his arms, and cries, "Lord, now lettest thou thy servant depart in peace, according to thy word, for mine eyes have seen thy salvation." Moses, when he was about to die, was taken up to Mount Pisgah, to behold the promised land (Deut. 34:1-5). Sometimes a Christian, before his death, meets with some excellent glimpses of heaven, and is constrained to cry out, "Glory is approaching!" Yes, sometimes a Christian, when he has been walking through the thresholds of the doors of death, has been constrained to cry, "I will pray no more, I will sigh no more." Some have begun the eternal song before they have gone hence. Be sure of it, from the Lord, there are not many Christians of this time that shall go thus down to their graves; by all probability, they shall have an unpleasant entry into heaven.

There are three signs which show that you shall have an unpleasant night. First, you do not have a spiritual walk suitable to your hope. Secondly, you are walking far from the distinct knowledge of your interest in Christ; for it is certain that our not making sure our interest in Christ makes our death most unpleasant. They have to seek for their hope when they should seek their crown. Thirdly, you will have an unpleasant death if you are not much in the exercise of mortification. Believe that one unmortified lust, with death and eternity meeting together, are most sad and dreadful company. An unmortified lust speaking to a Christian, when he is standing upon the borders of eternity, will make him afraid; the very thoughts of eternity will be sad and most dreary for a Christian who has not brought his idols low. Furthermore, if the Christians of this time go to heaven, they shall be as Samson; they shall kill more at their death than they did in all their life; they shall kill more of their lusts when they shall stand upon the borders of eternity than ever they did in all their life.

The eighth time that a Christian meets with eminent enjoyments of Christ is after long and sad desertions. When Christ has been long absent from the soul, then He makes up His absence with excellent manifestations of Himself. When Christ makes mention of a winter, He also makes mention of a night; He cries out, "My beloved spake, and said unto me, Rise up, my love, my fair one, and come away. For, lo, the winter is past, the rain is over and gone; the flowers appear on the earth; the time of the singing of birds is come, and the voice of the turtle is heard in our land" (Song 2:10-12).

There is a pleasant day that follows upon a Christian's night; there is a precious harvest that flows from a Christian's sad springtime. That is faith's divinity; I now mourn, but before long I shall laugh; I sow in tears, says faith, but before long I shall reap in joy; I am now under distance from Christ, says faith, but soon all veils shall be taken out of the way. Faith is an excellent prophet—it prophesies good things to a Christian in his darkest night.

Finally, a Christian meets with eminent enjoyments of Christ when he is under the deepest, most spiritual and excellent conceptions of Christ. When the soul has high thoughts of Christ, then that soul has high enjoyments of Christ. It is clear that the spouse has a high esteem of Christ: "As the apple tree among the trees of the wood, so is my beloved among the sons" (Song 2:3). Then this is immediately subjoined, "He brought me to the banqueting house, and his banner over me was love" (v. 4). A Christian meets with these eminent enjoyments when he has high and excellent conceptions of Christ for two reasons: first, Christ says to the soul, "I will confirm your faith." You may say, Christ is such a thing, and Christ will give you a proof of this; come, behold and see whether it is true. A second ground is that Christ takes great delight in manifesting Himself to those that are much in the exercise of faith and love, and are constrained to cry out, "Whom have I in heaven but thee? and there is none upon earth that I desire beside thee" (Ps. 73:25).

I shall end our discourse at this time, with some evidences of those who have communion and enjoyment of Christ. I shall give you some marks and evidences by which you may know if ever you met with any enjoyment of Christ, or if you have ever tasted of the sweetness that is in Christ. I give these evidences because there is something in a hypocrite that closely resembles communion with Christ, when they are admitted to taste of the good Word of God, and of the powers of the world to come. I shall give unto you six evidences by which you may behold whether or not you have met with enjoyments or communion with Christ.

First, have your enjoyments ever increased your thought and opinion of Christ? Was this ever the fruit of your enjoyment, that when you met with small discoveries of Christ, your heart elevated your thoughts of Him? This is evidence that you have experienced communion with Christ. A soul that never knew what it was to improve his enjoyments of Christ, for heightening his thoughts of

Him, such a person may be sure his enjoyments shall not long endure, and he is in danger of being eternally shut out from Christ.

Also, have your enjoyments ever strengthened your delight in duty? I know it is often the complaint of a Christian that this must not be real enjoyment, because my delight in duty is not strengthened by this enjoyment. Yet, be sure of it, one that never knew what it was to go about duty with more delight after an enjoyment of Christ gives evidence that this enjoyment is not real. The soul will sometimes be constrained to cry, "When I am enlarged, I will run the way of thy commandments"; when I meet with liberty and enjoyment, I will be much in the exercise of obedience—I will delight in it. It is as if he would have said, "Under desertions, I will walk in the way of Thy commandments; but under enlargements, I will run in the obedience of Thy commandments." This is also clear in Song of Solomon 1:4, in which the bride cries, "Draw me, we will run after thee."

Third, has your enjoyment of Christ ever strengthened your hatred against sin? Was this hatred for sin ever the blessed fruit of your enjoyments? Could you ever say that a sight of Christ made you loathe iniquity? Could you ever say that beholding the Lamb made you cast out the works of darkness? Then you may know that your enjoyment was real, and no delusion. I fear that there are many here who, if they would examine their enjoyments, would see their hatred against sin was never strengthened by their enjoyments.

Fourth, has the strength of your idols ever decayed? Were they ever weakened by your enjoyments? When was it, dear Christian, that beholding Christ made your idols fall as lightning? When was it that beholding Christ made your fingers experts at war, and made you wrestle with much power and strength against your idols? You may question the reality of your enjoyments if this has not been the fruit of them. This is the practice and case of many: they have their enjoyments, but their idols are as strong and vigorous as ever. It is certain that there are some whose idols feed upon their enjoyments; their idols are strengthened by their enjoyments. Are there not some for whom the great use of their enjoyments is the strengthening of their idols?

Fifth, you may know whether or not you have met with enjoyment of Christ if your enjoyments have ever humbled you and brought you low. That is the evangelical fruit of real enjoyment of

Christ; it makes the Christian to descend in estimation of himself. Surely a soul that has once gotten a right sight of Christ will cry out, "I have heard of thee by the hearing of the ear: but now mine eye seeth thee. Wherefore I abhor myself, and repent in dust and ashes" (Job 42:5-6).

A sixth evidence of true enjoyments is a love to Christ that increases after your enjoyments. Some go from their enjoyments with as little love to Christ as before. That is doubtless an enlargement in your light, but not in your heart. Sometimes a Christian meets with enlargement of gifts, not of grace, which is the most common way in which we mistake our enjoyments. Also, there may be enlargement of the head when there is no enlargement of the heart; that is, a Christian's light and judgment may be enlarged in prayer when the heart is under bonds. Therefore, study to know whether your enlargements are the enlargements of grace or the enlargements of gifts.

A seventh evidence of real enjoyment of Christ is if your enjoyments have ever constrained you to long for the day wherein you would experience the endless and unchangeable enjoyment of Christ. Has the tasting of the streams made you cry out, "How sweet must the fountain be"? What a day shall it be, dear Christians, when you who have tasted of the sweetness of Christ shall sit down at the fountainhead and drink abundantly of the sweetness that is in Christ, and shall pen songs of eternal praise forevermore. We may say of Christ, that which is said in John 4:11: "The well is deep," and we have nothing to draw with. There are, no doubt, most sweet and excellent things to be found in Christ.

I shall say no more but this: some think they have communion with Christ here, but truly, they shall never have communion with Christ hereafter. There are some that shall go down to their grave thinking that they have walked with Christ, but they shall never walk with Christ after time is past. Oh, blessed is the Christian upon whose grave it may be written, "Here lies a man or woman that walked with God. Here lies a person that spent his time conversing with God." What is heaven? Is it not a more immediate enjoyment of Christ? If you knew Christ, you would long to be with Him.

Must not heaven be an excellent place? If you would ask the reason why it should be so, I would answer that there are five things, even in the enjoyment of God, that make heaven an excellent place.

First, in heaven a Christian has the immediate enjoyment of God; all veils are taken out of the way. Must not heaven then be an excellent place? Second, the Christian has an unchangeable enjoyment of God. There is not such a complaint heard in heaven as this: Why dost Thou stand afar off from me? There is not a deserted Christian in heaven; there is no interruption of fellowship and communion with Christ there. Third, must not heaven be an excellent place because there a Christian meets with enjoyments of God that cannot be abused? A Christian here, when he meets with abundance of revelations, is in danger of being exalted above measure, but all the great and soul-refreshing enjoyments of a saint in heaven shall not occasion one thought of pride. There we cannot abuse our enjoyments; there we shall eternally enjoy; and there we shall eternally make good use of our enjoyments. Fourth, must not heaven be an excellent place because the enjoyments of a Christian are satisfying enjoyments? There is not a visit a Christian receives from Christ here that is satisfying, but the Christian may say, "As for me, I will behold thy face in righteousness: I shall be satisfied, when I awake, with thy likeness" (Ps. 17:15). Oh, David, were you never satisfied with His likeness? Were you not satisfied when you sang that song, "My soul shall be satisfied as with marrow and with fatness" (Ps. 63:5)? Nay, here he says, "The first day of my satisfaction is in the blessed morning of the resurrection; for then 'I shall be satisfied with thy likeness.'" The first fully satisfying sight of Christ is in the morning of the resurrection. Fifthly, must not heaven be an excellent place because the enjoyments of God there are eminent and excellent enjoyments in regard to their degree? Here a Christian does but taste, but there he shall drink; here a Christian does but taste of the streams, but there he shall be drowned in a sea of love and an ocean of everlasting delight. Amen.

SERMON 30

How to Prevent Spiritual Pride During Special Manifestations (2)

And lest I should be exalted above measure through the abundance of the revelations.
—2 Corinthians 12:7

If we could thus divinely preface our discourse, "That which was from the beginning, which we have heard, which we have seen with our eyes, which we have looked upon, and our hands have handled, of the Word of life," there would be no question we would speak with more faith, and you would hear with more spiritual joy and advantage (1 John 1:1). But we lament that when we speak of the deep mysteries of communion and fellowship with God, we may certainly cry out, "We are a barbarian unto you and we are a barbarian to ourselves, speaking in an unknown tongue." Is it not certain that when we speak of the blessed depths of communion and fellowship with God, there are many of you that may cry out those words that Peter spoke to the maid, "I know not what thou sayest" (Luke 22:60)? It is no wonder so many are ignorant of the blessed depths of communion with Christ; for even His disciples proved themselves to be ignorant of these two great depths of communion with Christ (John 16:17-18)—of presence and absence with Him; they were constrained to cry out, "We know not what thou sayest." There are only two things we will point out before we further pursue that which we spoke of in the forenoon.

First, there is a threefold communion with God. There is a communion with God by sense, when a Christian is admitted to cry forth these words, "I look after Him that doth behold me." There is also communion with God by faith, when a Christian is admitted to cry out, "Whom having not seen, ye love; in whom, though now ye see him not, yet believing, ye rejoice with joy unspeakable and full of glory" (1 Peter 1:8). There is also a communion with God in ordinances, when Christians are constrained to sing in the great congregation of the saints, and lift up their voices, and cry out, "How goodly are thy tents, O Jacob, and thy tabernacles, O Israel!" (Num. 24:5). "The shout of a king is among them" (Num. 23:21).

Secondly, we would have you notice that there are four times that a Christian is put to a non-plus. First, when a Christian is under eminent enjoyments of God, he is put to a non-plus. This is clear from the name that Paul gives to this enjoyment in the fourth verse of this chapter. He remarks that he "heard unspeakable words" (2 Cor. 12:4). This seems to be a strange contradiction, to hear words that could not be spoken; but this is the meaning of it: I heard such eminent discoveries of God that I could not put them into words if I were to begin to speak of them. There are times that Christians meet with so much of God that they cannot make language of their enjoyment; they are constrained to cry out, "I have found Him, but I cannot tell what I have found."

A second time a Christian is put to a holy non-plus is when he is under the deep exercise of desertion; during this time, the Christian turns silent, knowing not what to speak: "I am so troubled that I cannot speak" (Ps. 77:4). He could not make language of his desertion, but he only breathes forth the words, "My desertion is beyond expression."

A third time a Christian becomes silent and cannot speak is when a Christian is under deep apprehensions of the wrath of God, but he is standing in his own strength. We see this in the book of Job, where Job sighs, "Oh that my grief were throughly weighed!" (6:2). It is so great that my words are swallowed up; the wrath of the Lord lies so heavily upon my spirit that I have become silent and cannot speak.

A Christian is also put to a non-plus when he meets with the fulfillment of promises; the sweet and remarkable words in Isaiah 38:15 report, "What shall I say? he hath both spoken unto me, and himself hath done it: I shall go softly all my years in the bitterness of my soul." The accomplishment of the covenant rendered Hezekiah speechless in a holy and excellent manner. He could not put into words the thoughts of his heart, but was constrained to wonder and stand astonished.

Let us deal more particularly with the text. We were speaking in the morning concerning the first part of the text, which states that sometimes Christians meet with special, eminent, and excellent discoveries of God, so that there will be some choice and excellent manifestations of love communicated to them. This is clearly presupposed in the words of our text, "Lest I should be exalted above measure through the abundance of the revelations." I shall not spend a long time confirming these words; only consider this text: "And there was no day like that before it or after it, that the LORD hearkened unto the voice of a man" (Josh. 10:14). This teaches that there are some choice and excellent enjoyments of God communicated to His own at various times.

Now having spoken to you of the several times when a Christian meets with enjoyments of God, and some evidences by which you may know whether or not you have met with enjoyments of God, I shall now propose these nine considerations to move and persuade you to be much taken up in pursuit of enjoyment and communion with God. Before I shall speak of these considerations, I shall give you a description of communion with God. It is the soul of Christ dwelling in the soul of a Christian by faith, and the soul of a Christian dwelling in the soul of Christ by love. That is communion and fellowship with Christ.

Now the first consideration is that enjoyment of Christ and communion with Him is a growing thing; therefore, be much in pursuit after this noble and excellent thing. This is clear in Malachi 4:2, where, speaking of an eminent discovery of Christ, He says, "But unto you that fear my name shall the Sun of righteousness arise with healing in his wings." That is, Christ shall rise. It is subjoined, "And ye shall go forth, and grow up as calves of the stall" (Mal. 4:2). When the Sun of righteousness arises in the soul, it is a growing and fruitful time. We may say that desertion is an unfruitful time for a Christian. We may allude to the words, "Thou makest darkness, and it is night: wherein all the beasts of the forest do creep forth" (Ps. 104:20). When it is a night of desertion, all the beasts and idols that are within our heart creep forth and grow apace.

Enjoyment with God has influence upon growth in four different ways. First, when the soul is under choice discoveries of Christ, then the soul delights itself most in the exercise of duty. When is it that the soul runs as the chariots of Aminadab? Is it not when the soul is under the soul-conquering discoveries of Christ? No doubt, when a Christian is much in the exercise of duty, then spiritual growth goes on apace. Secondly, when the soul is under the discoveries of the beauty of Christ and enjoyment of Him, then the soul has a low esteem of all things that are here below Christ. It is an evidence of a growing Christian, when one has a high esteem of Christ and a low esteem of himself, and of all things below Christ. No doubt, it is an excellent piece of growth for a Christian to look upon all his idols and created pleasures of the world, and undervalue them. Thirdly, when the soul is enjoying Christ, then he has much spiritual strength for mortifying his lusts. Let us allude to the words in Proverbs 27:17, where we find, "Iron sharpeneth iron; so a man sharpeneth the countenance of his friend." No doubt, the precious face of our dear friend Christ strengthens a Christian for his duty and for the mortification of his lusts. Fourthly, the eminent discoveries of Christ have great influence upon growth. There are many spiritual influences of heaven by which our branches are made green, and we spread forth our roots. Is it not known that the soul grows most when it is admitted to nearest fellowship with Christ, and springs forth as the cedars of Lebanon and shoots forth its branches to the top of the clouds? I confess, he is a blessed Christian that can grow under desertion; he makes progress when Christ is away and is gone. I think we must remember the words which say, "When the spirit moved, then the wheels moved; and likewise when the spirit stood still, the wheels stood still also." These words mean that the soul under the spiritual influences of heaven moves swiftly; and that when these excellent, quickening influences of heaven are restrained, then he stands still, making no progress to heaven.

A second consideration to move you to be much taken up in pursuit after communion with Christ, and to have eminent enjoyments of Him, is that that time is the time in which a Christian gathers much excellent store of experience. Do you desire to know the experienced Christian? He is the Christian that has fellowship with the Father and the Son, Jesus Christ. This is clear in 1 John 1:3, where John expresses his experience and gives the foundation of it: "Truly our fellowship is with the Father, and with his Son Jesus Christ." I shall give you three advantages that the experiences of the saints have which are the fruit and birth of much communion with God.

The first advantage is the experience of the saints. Is it not an excellent pillar of faith that a Christian has some experience given to him through much communion with God? It is an experience that will uphold his spirit when he is brought exceedingly low by the power of temptations. A second advantage of experience is the noble birth of communion with Christ. Oh, but Christians, when they speak of their experiences that are the fruit of communion with God, these experiences are most savory and refreshing to them. A third advantage is this, that these experiences that yield communion with Christ are experiences that will exceedingly strengthen the noble grace of love. When a Christian is constrained to set up the place of Ebenezer and to say, "Hitherto hath the Lord helped us" (1 Sam. 7:12), then at another place, he is constrained to set up a *Jegarsahadutha,* the heap of witness, that he is obliged to God.

A third consideration to move you to pursue communion and fellowship with Christ is that it is a time in which love is eminently in exercise. We see this in Song of Solomon 1:4 where we read, "The king hath brought me into his chambers: we will be glad and rejoice in thee, we will remember thy love more than wine: the upright love thee." It is as if she would have said, "My heart never has the strong actings of love so much as when I am under the sweet discoveries of Christ." Sometimes a soul, when Christ has condescended to visit it, has been constrained to cry out, "Oh, for a heart to love Him!" Is it not known that sometimes a Christian, when he has met with a surprising visit of Christ, has been constrained to cry out, "Who would not love Him, who is the king of saints?" The spikenard that you pursue much after communion and fellowship with Christ is that it is the time when the soul has much spiritual joy.

Do you desire to know when the heart of a Christian rejoices? It is when there is a blessed correspondence between him and heaven. Would you know the time when the heart of a Christian leaps within him for joy? It is when there is no cloud between the precious face of Christ and him; but he is admitted to cry forth, "Behold He is mine! Behold He is mine!" Then, he takes Him in his arms; that is the time of much spiritual joy, as we read, "I will see you again, and your heart shall rejoice" (John 16:22). Furthermore, your joy shall be full: "and your joy no man shall take from you" (v. 22). You shall have a complete and unchangeable joy when I reveal myself to you. What is the reason Christians walk so often deserted? What is the reason that the complaints of Christians are so abundant? It is because we live without sight of a crucified Christ! What a pleasant life is it every morning, before we go forth, to take a broad sight of Christ, and to cry out, "He is mine!" and before we go to bed at night, to take a broad sight of Christ, and to cry out, "He is mine, and shall be eternally so!" This would make a Christian walk with much spiritual joy.

To continue to persuade you to be much in the pursuit of fellowship with Christ, consider a fifth point. It is during this communion that the soul has most high, majestic, and excellent thoughts of Christ. This is clear from Song of Solomon 1:4. When was it that the bride called Christ a king? Was it not when the Lord was sitting at the table with her? When was it that the spouse was, as it were, boundless in her thoughts of Christ? It was when Christ condescended to be kind to her. It is a great difficulty for a Christian to maintain the same thoughts of Christ under desertion that he had of Christ under enjoyment. Sometimes a Christian under enjoyment will cry forth, "Oh, He is pleasant!" Then, under desertion he will cry forth, "Once I had a high account of Christ, but now I have changed my mind." Therefore study, when Christ is absent from you, to kiss Him through the veil, and change not your thoughts of Him; believe on an absent Christ until He condescends to draw aside the veil, and give you a discovery of Himself.

A sixth consideration to move you to pursue after eminent discoveries of Christ is that these three things are exceedingly spiritually performed well when Christ is present. Is not the duty of prayer a pleasant duty when Christ is there? Is not prayer a Christian's delight when Christ is there? The reading of the Word is also a most pleasant duty when Christ is present with the soul. I know not two commentaries that are more choice and excellent upon Scripture than prayer and communion with Christ, for these are the keys that will open the deepest secrets that are in the volume of the Bible. The duty of meditation is also most pleasant to a soul when Christ is present. Oh, how sweetly will a soul meditate; how refreshing will that duty be to them, when Christ condescends to visit them and to satisfy them with His consolations!

A seventh consideration which I offer to move you to pursue after communion with Christ is that all the graces of the Spirit are then in life and exercise. According to the words, "while the king sitteth at his table" (Song 1:12), that is, when Christ condescends to keep communion and correspondence with me, "my spikenard sendeth forth the smell thereof." Then all the graces of the Spirit are in life and exercise. Is not faith in exercise when Christ is present? Do not all the clouds vanish? Does not a Christian then silence all his disputes when Christ is present? The soul that could never believe before, when Christ condescends to be present, will cry forth, "I am my beloved's, and my beloved is mine" (Song 6:3). Are not the graces of watchfulness, tenderness, and fear then in exercise? No doubt, communion with Christ would make us grow into excellent Christians, and before long, once we could attain this, we could live some days in fellowship with Him. When Moses lived for forty days in the mount with Christ, his face did shine; when the three disciples lived scarcely one hour with Christ upon Mount Tabor, they were constrained to cry out, "It is good for us to be here: if thou wilt, let us make here three tabernacles" (Matt. 17:4).

An eighth consideration to provoke you to pursue eminent enjoyments of Christ is that it is a time in which the soul rises to a blessed conformity with Christ. Do you desire to know the time when a Christian is made a partaker of the divine nature? Do you desire to know the time when the blessed draughts of the image of Christ are engraven upon the soul? It is the time when Christ condescends to manifest Himself, according to the words of 2 Corinthians 3:18, which read, "But we all, with open face beholding as in a glass the glory of the Lord, are changed into the same image from glory to glory, even as by the Spirit of the Lord." Communion with Christ has an assimilating virtue; it makes us grow in conformity to Him.

A final consideration to move you to be much in pursuit of fellowship with Christ is that this is the time when a Christian has most excellent discoveries of heaven and is constrained to long to be dissolved. When did Paul cry out, "For I am in a strait betwixt two, having a desire to depart, and to be with Christ; which is far better" (Phil 1:23)? It was the time when he had communion with Christ. Oh, these are wonderful discoveries a soul has under communion with Christ: the joys of heaven and the excellent things that are purchased for the saints!

Now, that which, fourthly, we would address concerning our text are some impediments that hinder a Christian from attaining these excellent enjoyments of Christ. First, let us discuss some sovereign causes and impediments. Second, let us then discuss some sinful hindrances and impediments.

There are several sovereign causes. First, Christ knows that our old and weak vessels would not always contain the new wine of consolation. Christ knows that we are not able, while in these tents of mortality, to bear much eminent enjoyments of Himself. Christians, when they are brought near Christ, fall ordinarily, either into the sin of pride, the sin of security, or the spiritual sin of roving; these are often the fruit of most immediate communion with Christ and access unto Him. Therefore, since we are not able to bear these excellent enjoyments, He keeps them until the day that we shall be able to bear them, when we shall drink of the wine new in the kingdom of our Father, and shall be satisfied with these excellent consolations.

A second sovereign cause of it is that God does so dispense that the freedom of His enjoyments may more eminently appear. If a Christian had not a night as well as a day, the freedom of the manifestations of Christ would not so eminently appear; but Christ gives a Christian a night as well as a day, that a Christian may go down to his grave knowing that enjoyment is the free gift of love.

Third, a Christian is not always admitted to these excellent enjoyments of God because if we were evermore under these excellent manifestations, we would not think of flitting from place to place; but Christ, by absence, does teach us that we are pilgrims; we are not at home.

Fourth, Christians are not always under these eminent manifestations of Christ because Christ knows that it is not for our spiritual advantage to continue under such an excellent lot. Christ knows that if we were brought to the bed of love and were kept there, we would fall asleep; therefore Christ often mingles our day with a night, so that we may be kept in the exercise of watchfulness. Often, a Christian falls asleep in the bed of love, and there takes his rest when Christ has been most kind to him.

Now, we must speak of some culpable causes that hinder this divine and excellent thing, the enjoyment of Christ, and having manifest tokens of His love.

A first hindrance is security in one's self. Such security is an evil that exceedingly hinders a Christian's enjoyments. This is clear in Song of Solomon 5:2, where we see that laziness and security obstructed an excellent visit which Christ was intending to give; and we do not know if the bride ever received such a visit again, as Christ was about to communicate to her then. We likewise conceive that the sleeping of the disciples hindered the excellent discovery of Christ that was there (Luke 9:32). I shall tell you three reasons why a secure Christian can never have much enjoyment.

First, a Christian who is secure in himself can never be a Christian that puts a high price upon Christ and enjoyments of Him. Once a Christian becomes self-secure, he will write this as a "Zoar," or, "a little and a small thing," upon his enjoyments. It is the tender Christian, the believing Christian, the watchful Christian who places a high value upon enjoyments of Christ.

Second, a secure Christian can never be an enjoying Christian, because such a Christian will never take pains to get the enjoyments of Christ. He can never use diligence to attain to the enjoyments of Christ's face. This is abundantly clear in Song of Solomon 5:3, where the security of the bride made her unwilling to take pains to open to Christ: "I have put off my coat; how shall I put it on? I have washed my feet; how shall I defile them?"

Third, a self-secure Christian can never be an enjoying Christian, because often when Christ desires entrance, such a Christian refuses to let Him in. This is clear in Song of Solomon 5:2; the security of the bride was the great occasion that, when Christ desired to come in, she would not open to Christ, but held Him at the door. It is the watchful Christian that hearkens to the voice of Christ. It is the watchful Christian that condescends to let Christ in when He knocks. If you desire to have eminent enjoyments of Christ, you must study watchfulness. I would charge the Christians of this time, that if they do not desire to prove themselves guilty of accounting the consolations of God small things, they must shake off their own security and stand up, lest they sleep the sleep unto death.

I ask the Christian who is secure in himself—what if Christ should say these two words unto you when He desires to be in, and you will not let Him: "I swear in My wrath, that you shall see My face no more"? Would it not be a just sentence of excommunication that Christ would pronounce against you, if you undervalue fellowship with Him? What if Christ should say to such a Christian that will not let Him in when He desires to manifest Himself, "Sleep and take your rest, for he is at hand that betrays you"? If that were the language that Christ should pronounce against you, it would be most just and equal. If you would love to slumber, Christ should ratify your sleeping with an oath, saying unto you, "Rest, for he is at hand that betrays you."

A second impediment that hinders many Christians from having much enjoyment in Christ is that most Christians do not have many longing after these enjoyments. Why are you so much straitened, and in bonds? You are not straitened by Christ, you are straitened in your inmost being; for He does promise, "Open thy mouth wide, and I will fill it" (Psalm 81:10). I will only say four words unto you concerning this. First, there is satisfaction for the thirsty soul. There is a promise in the covenant of grace that the person that thirsts shall be satisfied; as "For I have satiated the weary soul, and I have replenished every sorrowful soul" (Jer. 31:25). If you are thirsting after righteousness, you will be satisfied. Secondly, I would say that you can never seek from Christ beyond that which He is able to give; your desire to have from Christ can never be above His ability to give to you. Thirdly, your desire to have can never be beyond His willingness to give you; Christ is willing to give to a Christian more than he could ever desire. Do you not know the challenge that is presented to the disciples: "Hitherto have ye asked nothing in my name" (John 16:24)? Is it possible the disciples could have been so long with Christ, and never have sought anything from Him? No, I tell you the meaning of it is this: "You have asked Me nothing in comparison to what I am able and willing to give you"; or, "You have asked Me nothing concerning that which you required." Fourthly, Christ will sometimes condescend to give enjoyments to His own even before they seek. He will dispense enjoyments to them according to that remarkable promise in Isaiah 65:24, which says, "And it shall come to pass, that before they call, I will answer; and while they are yet speaking, I will hear." Is it not strange and remarkable that before a Christian seeks, he shall obtain? However, seeking and longing after enjoyments is an excellent way to obtain much enjoyment of Him.

A third impediment that obstructs a Christian's enjoyment of God are the idols that take up the heart and obstruct the eminent enjoyments of Christ. We read in Ezekiel 14:5, "They are all estranged from me through their idols." "Your iniquities have separate between you and your God" (Isa. 59:17). Of this Jeremiah did sadly complain, "Your iniquities have turned away these things, and your sins have withholden good things from you" (Jer. 5:25). I desire that a Christian who has been living long under the absence of Christ, and has been long deserted, that he would then conclude that he is under the power of his idols; for, no doubt, when the idol takes up the heart, Christ will not condescend to come there. I tell you what our heart is; it is like Bethlehem. When Christ and His mother came there to lodge all night, the entire house was taken up with guests, and there was no room for Christ. When Christ comes to our heart and desires to be in, we must then answer, "There is no room here." Do not our idols rule our heart, and do they not fill our souls so that there is no empty room for that precious guest, Christ? I say to you, keep always the most excellent chamber of your heart for the excellent guest, Jesus Christ, so that when He condescends to visit, you may be in a capacity to let Him in. May not Christ often take up that complaint, "How long shall I stand knocking at your heart? Until My head be wet with the dew, and My locks with the drops of the night!" He is an excellent Christian that can always keep his heart for precious Christ.

A fourth thing that impedes a Christian's enjoyments of Christ is that we are much too engaged to the world. Communion with Christ and love to the world are things that are not consistent together. If you desire to have eminent enjoyments of Christ, you must subscribe a bill of divorce to the great idol, the world. This is clear where, before Ezekiel is admitted to behold the visions of God, the form of a hand takes him by the hair of his head and lifts him up between the heaven and the earth (Ezek. 8:3). A Christian must be up between the heaven and the earth, being elevated above these contemptible things, before he can have these soul-refreshing enjoyments of God. It is impossible for a Christian to serve two masters; it is impossible for a Christian to love two masters. Christ should be our precious master, not the world. Oh, to be a Christian that has the moon beneath his feet! A Christian mortified to the world enjoys God. When the church goes forth clothed with the sun, she then also goes forth with the moon under her feet (Rev. 12:1), that is, trampling upon all created delights, that are like the moon, subject to change.

Fifthly, another hindrance to a Christian's eminent enjoyments is not often exercising those duties by which communion with Christ may be attained. I suppose that there are three duties in which a

Christian often meets with enjoyment of Christ: the duty of secret prayer, the duty of meditation, and the duty of reading the Word. These are the three duties in which a Christian meets with enjoyments of God. The enjoyments a Christian meets by reading the Word—these are the enjoyments in which he more easily denies himself than the enjoyments he encounters in prayer. Do you desire to know whether the enjoyments that a Christian has by prayer or reading most easily promote pride? It is certain, the enjoyments that a Christian meets with in prayer promote pride. This is because the enjoyments by reading the Word, or hearing, seem to be more immediate enjoyments; they have less of ourselves to attribute to ourselves in them as the cause of these enjoyments. Secondly, because these enjoyments that are ordinarily more pure, more spiritual, than those we have by prayer, when we converse with God alone. There is certainly much spiritual dreg in the enjoyments of a Christian, when he converses with God by prayer.

A sixth impediment that obstructs a Christian's enjoyments of God is when he prays without these three qualifications, he shall be unlikely to have any considerable enjoyment. First, we rarely pray with humility; that is the great reason why we do not have much enjoyment of God. Is it not the humble Christian that is the enjoying Christian? Is it not the Christian that sits lowest in the dust that is most often exalted to the third heavens to hear unspeakable words? Is it not the Christian who cries forth, "I am less than the least of all thy mercies," that is admitted to taste of the pure river of water of life that flow from the throne of God? Secondly, when a Christian goes to prayer, he does not make use of Christ as mediator; therefore, he does not have much communion with Him. This is clear from Ephesians 3:12, where the very door of access to God and communion with Him is faith in Jesus Christ. This faith takes up Christ as our Mediator, through whom we must be brought into the chambers of His presence. Thirdly, a Christian that prays with little fervency does not have much enjoyment. I think that if some did overhear us pray, they might say these three things: 1. Surely yonder man cares not for the things he prays for; he is seeking the thing he does not miss, and begging for the thing he does not sensibly want. 2. Yonder man does not have faith in the Godhead; he speaks to God as to his companion, his flesh does not tremble for fear when he speaks to Him. 3. If some were admitted to hear us when we are alone in prayer, they might also say: surely yonder person lives without sight of his necessities—that makes him so formal in his prayers. A main obstruction of our enjoyment of Christ is that our prayers lack a principle of faith. Some Christians, when under a deserted condition, give their answer to themselves before they begin to pray; they shall not find God though they seek after Him.

A seventh impediment that hinders those noble manifestations of love is that a Christian is not often under the impressions of the majesty and dreadfulness of God. Do you desire to know when a Christian is admitted to most excellent discoveries of Christ? It is when he is most under the excellent impressions of the majesty of God. When the spouse was under the impression that Christ was matchless in Song of Solomon 2:3, then it is added, "He brought me to the banqueting house, and his banner over me was love" (v. 4).

We shall, lastly, point out some differences between the enjoyments of a hypocrite and the enjoyments of the truly gracious.

The first difference is that their enjoyments differ both in measure and degree. The enjoyments of a hypocrite are but a taste (Heb. 6:5); even such a taste, as the merchant that sells liquor gives to the buyer, is the great enjoyment of a hypocrite. It is far from the experience of the faithful, of whom we read, "Eat, O friends; drink, yea, drink abundantly, O beloved." (Song 5:1). There is a great difference between a hypocrite's tasting and a gracious Christian's being satiated abundantly with the wine of His consolations. We also read the description of the true believer in Psalm 36:8: "They shall be abundantly satisfied with the fatness of thy house; and thou shalt make them drink of the river of thy pleasures."

A second difference lies in the fruits of the enjoyment. There are different fruits that flow from the enjoyments of truly godly Christians, and the enjoyments of hypocrites. The first fruit of the enjoyment of hypocrites is pride. They do not know what it is to be humbled through the revelations of God. The more they see of God, the more they see themselves; if Christ lifts them up in the dispensations of common mercies, they lift up themselves. The second fruit of the enjoyments of a hypocrite is security in himself; seldom does a hypocrite meet with enjoyments, but he falls secure in himself. Thirdly, a hypocrite is more taken up with his enjoyments than with the person that bestows the enjoyments. A hypocrite never knows what it is to love Christ for the enjoyments that he meets with;

but the thing that takes up the hypocrite's heart is the enjoyment itself. Song of Solomon 1:3 says, "Because of the savour of thy good ointments thy name is as ointment poured forth, therefore do the virgins love thee." It is not said that Christians love the enjoyments that are given them, for all the enjoyments that a Christian meets with increase his love and delight in Christ. There is not an enjoyment a Christian meets with that does not make him to have more love and delight in Christ. The fourth fruit that flows from the enjoyments of a hypocrite is the strengthening of his love to his idols. I suppose that his heart is never more enlarged to his idols than after his enjoyment. I shall not dispute whether such a person has the grace of God or not; but it is incumbent for that person to examine himself.

A third difference is in the origin and fountain of the enjoyments. The origin and fountain of a hypocrite's enjoyments is but common love; but the fountain of a Christian's enjoyment is the love that descends in the boundless and everlasting covenant. There is not a dispensation of love, there is not a discovery of Christ that Christians meet with, that does not eminently speak forth His love for them and His delight to manifest Himself to them. I would desire you, that since there is such excellent sweetness in the enjoyment of God and such excellent advantages that wait upon the Christian that has enjoyment of God, that you heartily take up the pursuit after it.

I shall close by mentioning the most terrible and dreadful words that Christ shall speak to those persons that have constantly undervalued communion with Him.

The first most dreadful word that Christ shall speak to those that have undervalued communion with Him shall be on the day when they shall stand before Him, the Judge of the living and the dead; Christ shall pronounce that sentence upon them, "Depart ye." Then, to you who would not obey that precious command of coming to Christ for an interest in Him and for communion and fellowship with Him, but would constantly depart, He shall give you your fill of it that day. "Depart." That eternal sentence of unchangeable excommunication from Christ shall be ratified, and the soul shall be eternally thrust out from the presence of Christ, and from the glory of His power.

The second dreadful sentence that shall be pronounced against those who have slighted communion and fellowship with Christ is this: since you have slighted and undervalued Me, I will also lightly esteem you. We read in 1 Samuel 2:30, "For them that honour me I will honour, and they that despise me shall be lightly esteemed." Know that if you account little of communion and fellowship with Christ, Christ shall account little of communion and fellowship with you.

The third dreadful and terrible sentence that shall be spoken to you that undervalue fellowship with Christ is that there is a communion between your heart and your idols; there is a separation between your heart and Christ. The marriage between your heart and your idols shall eternally stand in force if you are content to take your idols for your delight. Beware lest it shall be unto you according to the desire of your heart.

Last, there are dreadful days approaching when you shall know that communion with Christ would have been to your advantage. I shall certainly prophesy that the day is approaching, when your eye strings shall begin to break. The king of terrors shall be climbing up upon your walls, and loosening the pins of your tabernacle, and you shall be constrained to cry out, "Oh, for time again that I might spend more of my time with God, and in communion and fellowship with Him!" Know that this shall be the challenge for the choicest Christian living upon earth, when he shall be standing upon the utmost line between time and eternity: "Woe is me, woe is me, that ever I slighted communion with Christ so much!" There shall not be an opportunity for the prayer which he slighted; every formal prayer shall be matter of conviction unto you on that day.

For those who endeavor to converse with Christ and to keep communion and correspondence with Him, there is a five-fold night that shall suddenly pass away before them that are waiting for the appearance of our blessed Lord Jesus. There is the night of affliction that shall suddenly pass away and vanish, when all the troubles which have overwhelmed you shall sweetly pass away and vanish into an endless enjoyment of Christ. There is the night of desertion that shall suddenly vanish and pass away, when all your desertions shall sweetly vanish into those excellent depths of communion with Himself. The night of your sojourning shall suddenly pass away, and the night of your darkness and ignorance shall suddenly pass away. The night of time shall suddenly pass away, when the day of endless eternity shall come, and you shall be possessed of those precious delights that are prepared for the saints. What can you desire, oh expectants of heaven, prisoners of hope, conversers with God? What can you desire that will not be provided for you? Do you not cast up your eyes to heaven and look for the day when you shall be provided, and Christ shall condescend? I would say to you, "We shall ever be with the Lord. Wherefore comfort one another with these words" (1 Thess. 4:17-18). Oh, those blessed depths of eternal fellowship with God; those excellent discoveries of God that are waiting for those who have given their hearts to Christ!

I confess that it is a mystery for us to understand what the life is of the saints that are now living above. It is a mystery for us to comprehend. Your immortal spirits shall eternally enjoy Him, the Father of spirits. It is a mystery for us to comprehend all the endless knots and mysteries of religion. There is no complaint of absence there or of unbelief; there is no complaint of ignorance or of little growth; all complaints are now sweetly vanished. This earth is the house of complaints, but heaven is the house of praise. This is the house of sorrow, but heaven is the house of joy. This is the house of our pilgrimage, but heaven is the house of our abode. This is the house of our misery, but heaven is the house of our eternal solace, divine consolation, and satisfaction, where there shall be no end of our joy and rejoicing. Wait, for behold He comes with ten thousand of His saints.

I desire to say these things to you and then close. Will it not be an excellent day? Will it not be a refreshing day? Your feet shall stand upon the top of mount Zion with these 144,000 that are marked upon their foreheads. Oh, what a day shall it be, when there shall be a general rendezvous of the first-born, when all the saints that have been, or shall be, shall stand before Christ; and what a day shall it be, when Christians shall be entered heirs, having possession of those things they had hoped for. There is not a promise that shall not then receive fulfillment; there is not a good thing that has been spoken unto them that shall not be accomplished in that day. The day of the resurrection shall be the day of accomplishment, deliverance, refreshment, and redemption. Then, all the saints shall stand before Him and shall be conveyed home to their endless and eternal mansions that have been purchased for them. Indeed, they shall be satisfied with the abundance of revelations, and shall have most clear, most precious, and most immediate discoveries of God. Now let that blessed day come, and let all other days pass away. Amen.

SERMON 31

How to Prevent Spiritual Pride During Special Manifestations (3)

And lest I should be exalted above measure through the abundance of the revelations.
—2 Corinthians 12:7

He that goes down into these blessed depths of communion and fellowship with God shall behold the wonders of the Lord; and he that is admitted to taste of the abundance of revelations is constrained to cry out, "Oh, if the day were coming that I should know what that is to purpose, to have communion and fellowship with God." Is not a Christian sometimes constrained to cry out, "Oh, if I might post away as the ship of desire and might at last know what it is to have enjoyments in the higher house, as I have known what it is to have enjoyments in the lower house"? I would only say this before I come to the words of our text: I think this must be engraven upon the posts of our city and upon the doors of our church: Christ is gone; Christ is gone, and has in a great measure departed from us. Is not this engraven upon your prayers when you are alone: Christ is gone? Is not this engraven upon your hearing: Christ is gone? Is not this often, if not always, engraven upon our preaching: Christ is gone? This fact speaks sad things to us from the Lord: we do not mourn after an absent Christ. There are some who do not know how to distinguish between presence and absence; there are some that desire to make earth their heaven. Surely, such persons shall never get to heaven. Some, when they are content in this world, sit down, and cry out, "It is good for us to be here: if thou wilt, let us make here three tabernacles" (Matt. 17:4).

At the last occasion that we spoke upon these words, we told you there were, in Paul's condition, five things to consider. First, there are some particular times that Christ dispenses and gives to His own most eminent and soul-refreshing enjoyments of Himself, which is presupposed in these words: "Lest I should be exalted above measure, through the abundance of revelations." These words show us that Paul had an abundance of revelations and visions of God. The second consideration from our text is that concerning the choicest and most excellent state of the saints, while they are still within time, they are ready to abuse it. This is clear in the words of our text: "Lest I should be exalted above measure." Paul was in danger of being overtaken with pride in this enjoyment. The third thing to consider is that even in the most afflicting dispensation that the saints encounter, there is a sweet design of love, and our advantage is carried on in it. Paul spoke of "a thorn in the flesh, the messenger of Satan to buffet [him]"; and the goal of this dispensation is, "Lest I should be exalted above measure." This was the sweet goal of God's giving a messenger of Satan, a thorn in the flesh. A fourth thing to consider is the duty of a Christian to notice the sweet design of love that God has in His dark dispensations. Paul notices this and leaves it upon record that he was under such a dark dispensation, but he also recognized that the goal of it was, "Lest I be exalted above measure." Fifth, consider that there are times when Satan does more strongly and more violently assault a Christian than at other times. The strongest assaults on a Christian are after their most eminent enjoyments of God. When a Christian is nearest to heaven, Satan endeavors to bring him nearest the earth; Satan never prevails over a Christian so much as at the time when the Christian is nearest God. The stroke that a Christian then receives is a discouraging stroke, and it is a fall that provokes the Majesty of God to hide Himself for a long time. Such a stroke will make him dispute his interest, and if he is a tender believer, to go down to his grave mourning. Dear Christian, watch after enjoyments, for "he that betrayeth [you] is at hand" (Mark 14:42).

God communicates several eminent dispensations of love and manifestations to His own. We have spoken concerning many of these dispensations. We spoke a little of the special times of a Christian's eminent enjoyments. We also discussed what eminent enjoyments of God were. Also, we spoke of evidences whereby we may know whether or not we have ever had any enjoyments of God. Fourth, we spoke of considerations to move you to pursue after such enjoyments. Last, we discussed some impediments that hinder a Christian from having an abundance of revelations and eminent enjoyments of God.

We shall now point out the times when a Christian has the greatest longings and most fervent desires after eminent enjoyments of God. Certainly, some times pass when a Christian has no desire at all after enjoyments of Christ; yea, some times, if enjoyments of Christ were offered to him, he would refuse them, as Song of Solomon 5:2-3 shows. We shall point out six times when a Christian has most excellent desires and longings after Christ.

First, immediately after a Christian's first conversion, when Christ and he first engage together, is the time of a Christian's longing. At this time, communion with Christ will be precious in his eyes. This is clear from Jeremiah 2:2, where there is mention made of "the kindness of thy youth, and the love of thine espousals." In these words, we see that the greatest kindness that Christ receives from His people is when they first meet and make bargain together. Revelation 2:4 says, "Thou hast left thy first love," which tells us that the first love of a Christian is often the most excellent and matchless love. The love will grow much and take root after a Christian's first conversion; but the noble actions and excellent fruits of love appear most presently after the day that the contract of marriage is subscribed between Christ and the soul. Is it not upon this ground that Christians have cried out, "Oh that I were as in months past, as in the days when God preserved me; when his candle shined upon my head, and when by his light I walked through darkness" (Job 29:2-3). I shall give you two reasons why a Christian's desires after enjoyments are most pressing after conversion.

First, after conversion, the soul of a Christian is most abstracted from his lusts; not that the life of lusts is then taken totally away, but the desire after his idols is then much quenched and abated. Having nothing to desire but Christ, he cries forth, "When shall I find Him? Where is the place of His abode?" The Christian, shortly after conversion, takes Christ in his arms in the morning, and cries, "Behold, He is mine!" He takes Christ in his arms at night and cries out, "Behold, He is mine, and shall be eternally so."

The second reason is because after conversion, Christ does ordinarily manifest Himself much to Christians. He gives them marriage tokens; He gives them the valley of Achor for a door of hope; and these sweet manifestations of God make the soul most fervent in desire to have their enjoyments continued and increased. There are many who supposed they had been engaged to Christ, that may be constrained to cry out, "Oh, for my first love! Oh, for my first faith! Oh, for my first mortifications! Oh, for my first tenderness!"

A second time a Christian has most excellent desires and longings after Christ is when his conscience is awake after some gross and eminent sin. Then, God does indeed preach pardon unto them; but they dare not, nor cannot, take hold of it. They desire that the great and broad seal may be put to the pardon, and that they may have the sensible enjoyment of God. I would say that pardon intimated to a Christian after eminent sins can hardly be taken hold of without enjoyments. However, it will be cast at, as we see in 2 Samuel 13:13, where the pardon was granted, yet he prays for confirmation of that pardon, adding, "Restore unto me the joy of thy salvation" (Ps. 51:12). I shall give you four reasons why a backsliding Christian who has obtained pardon, very much desires enjoyment of God and His sensible presence.

First, the backsliding Christian cannot have comfort in his pardon before enjoyments are given to him; he always debates, saying, "It is presumptuous for me to close with this pardoning grace." No doubt, that which must silence the arguments of unbelief and make him look upon his pardon with delight, is the sensible enjoyment of God.

The second reason is that a Christian debates whether God is an enemy or a friend before he sees Him reconciled and beholds the smiling of His face. Yet, the Christian will not be comforted. If His tongue (speaking reverently of Christ) should say, "Be of good comfort, thy sins are forgiven thee," but God casts a veil over His face, a Christian is ready to call God an enemy.

The third ground why a Christian then most longs after communion with God is that he is then convinced of the great advantage that is to be had in communion with God. When is the Christian most convinced of the advantage of enjoying God? Is it not when the conscience is awake, after departing from God? He then cries, "For a day in thy courts is better than a thousand. I had rather be a doorkeeper in the house of my God, than to dwell in the tents of wickedness" (Ps. 84:10).

The fourth reason a Christian is consumed with longing after such enjoyments is because at that time there is much sweetness and excellence in Christ. This makes him cry out, "Oh, if I had Him between my breasts, I would never let Him go." Let a Christian believe his pardon; that is the way to obtain enjoyment. "After that ye believed, ye were sealed with that holy Spirit of promise" (Eph. 1:13).

Third, a Christian does exceedingly long after enjoyments of God when he is under eminent discoveries of the excellence of Christ. When the eyes of his understanding are enlightened in the knowledge of Christ, then his affections take fire and he begins to cry out, "Oh, when will Christ return?" In Song of Solomon 1:3, the bride sets forth the excellence of Christ. In the fourth verse, she pleads, "Draw me, we will run after thee." There are two reasons that a Christian does long after enjoyment of God at this time.

First, the Christian then loses much of his desires for the world. The manifestations of Christ are to a Christian the grave of his lusts; having lost the desire for the things of the world, he begins to desire the enjoyment of Christ.

A second ground is that the discoveries of Christ make a Christian long for the enjoyment of His Person. I am persuaded that if we would draw the conclusion that Christ is matchless, and did believe it with our heart, we would not dispense so well with the absence of Christ. Is it not known that for the Christian who is under the impression of the precious discoveries of Christ, there is not a moment's absence with Him but he thinks it a little eternity? They would deem one thousand years in the presence of Christ as one day, and as a watch in the night when it is past.

A Christian also longs after the enjoyments of Christ when he is under the exercise of faith. This is the time when a Christian longs after enjoyment of Christ, as seen in Song of Solomon 5:6: "I opened to my beloved." Here we see the exercise of faith; further, it is added, "I sought him," or, as the word is, "I truced after him most earnestly." She calls Christ, "My beloved," and she adds, "By night on my bed I sought him whom my soul loveth," and I will rise up and seek Him (Song 3:1). No doubt, living within sight of our interest in Christ would make us long after enjoyments of Him.

A fifth time that a Christian longs after enjoyment with Christ is when he is under the exercise of love. This is clear in Song of Solomon 3:1. She calls Christ "him whom my soul loveth," and immediately she adds, "I sought him." She was in a serious pursuit after Christ. There are three reasons why the soul in love pursues the enjoyments of Christ.

First, to the soul in love, all its duties are pleasant and easy. Do you desire to know what makes duty pleasant? It is love. When the soul is under the exercise of love, it will cry, "Oh, prayer, you are my delight; meditation, you are my recreation."

Second, a soul under the exercise of love must enjoy the object of its love. It is love that makes Christians count any absence from Christ as a long time. Love is a bad arithmetician, and cannot count correctly; for the first hour of absence from Christ will make it cry out, "How long, Lord? Forever?" Love is a bad arithmetician, for when a long enjoyment of God is passed, love cries out, "This is but a moment and a watch in the night!"

Third, nothing can then occupy it but communion with Christ. When does a soul deny all other things, only being taken up with Christ? It is when the soul is under the sweet exercise of love.

A seventh time when a Christian is much under the exercise of longing after these enjoyments of Christ is when a Christian has deep impressions both of the remarkable disadvantages that he has being absent from Christ, and the remarkable advantage that he has when he is present with Christ. Believe it, a Christian will never long after the sweet enjoyments of Christ until he truly believes the faith of these two things. He will write this above the head of his enjoyments: "This is a *Zoar*," or, a little one, until he believes the unspeakable advantage he has by enjoyment of God. Let a Christian sing twelve verses of the first chapter of the Song of Solomon, and his desires will be enflamed: "While the king sitteth at his table, my spikenard sendeth forth the smell thereof" (Song 1:12). While Christ condescends to keep communion with the believer, all the graces of the Spirit are in lively and heavenly exercise.

However, a Christian may be serious and diligent in all the exercises of religion, and yet lack communion with God. He may be a diligent Christian; he may be an active Christian; he may be a serious Christian, and yet, he may be a Christian under desertion. This is clear, not only from Song of Solomon 5:6, where the spouse is exercising faith and love, as we read, "I opened to my beloved"; yet, "my beloved had withdrawn himself, and was gone." Also, the spouse is actively performing her duty (Song 3:2); yet, she is a deserted bride. In Psalm 22:1-2, David is under the exercise of faith, as he cries, "My

God, my God, why hast thou forsaken me?" He is under the serious exercise of prayer: "I cry in the day time, but thou hearest not; and in the night season, and am not silent." Yet, he is a deserted Christian, as is clear from the words: "Why hast thou forsaken me?" Likewise, Psalm 70:1 shows David, deserted and undergoing much trouble and anxiety; yet, he is a Christian taken up in the active and serious performance of duty. He prayed so much, in a manner, that his throat could not speak one more word. This is something that not one in a thousand in these days can say. Concerning this topic, I will discuss two points.

First, let me point out the grounds of such a dispensation, that though we may diligently call upon God, He will still leave us deserted for a time. One reason is that He desires to teach us to trust less in duty; if we found Christ every time we went seriously about the exercise of duty, we would exalt duties too much and deify them. Therefore, He will let a Christian be much in the active performance of duty, yet be deserted, so that the Christian may be brought to write above the head of duties, "These are empty things without Christ." The Christian must learn to write above the head of prayer, "This is an empty thing without Christ," to write above the head of meditation, "This is an empty thing without Christ," and to write above the head of reading the Word, "This is an empty thing without Christ."

A second reason is so that a Christian may be brought to a more immediate dependence upon Christ for enjoyment. Christians will be brought to all these lower cisterns, and they all run dry. What is Christ's design in this? His plan is that they may go to Himself and have the enjoyments of Himself. This is not to bid Christians forsake duty, but is to persuade Christians to go about duty with dependence.

A third reason that Christ will let a Christian pray seriously, lively, and spiritually, and yet be deserted is so that the Christian may be brought low and humble in his own sight. This was the blessed fruit that David had of such a dispensation. Psalm 22:2 shows that he prayed much, yet he was deserted; and this is the fruit of it: "But I am a worm, and no man; a reproach of men, and despised of the people" (Ps. 22:6). He was, as it were, annihilated when he met with such a dispensation as this—to pray and be deserted.

A fourth ground of it is to punish our woeful and unreasonable practice of refusing Christ when He desires to come in to us.

Sometimes Christ will desire to come in to us and we will shut the door; sometimes Christians will desire to come to Christ, and He will shut the door, and will not let them in. This is clear in Song of Solomon 5:2, when Christ desires to come in and He gets the answer in verse 3: "I have washed my feet; how shall I defile them?" In the sixth verse, the spouse cries out, "I sought him, but I could not find him; I called after him, but he gave me no answer."

Fifth, a Christian may be brought to the trial and examination of his way, so that he may discover why He contends with him; there are many excellent flowers of self-examination that have risen from a Christian's desertion, though active in duty, or a Christian's being under a cloud, though most serious in pursuing Christ.

Secondly, I desire to point out a few of the sad conclusions that a Christian draws in such a dispensation, and discuss what disadvantage he encounters with such a dispensation.

First, he begins to call his faith presumption, to call his sincerity hypocrisy, and to call his enjoyments delusions. These are the ordinary conclusions of a deserted, yet active, Christian. He begins to raze the foundations and debate whether Christ and he have ever met together. There is something of this shown in Psalm 77:2, "In the day of my trouble I sought the Lord: my sore ran in the night, and ceased not: my soul refused to be comforted." As it were, all the consolations of God, all his eminent enjoyments had grown tasteless to him; all his thoughts of God were dreadful and terrible to him.

A second disadvantage by such a dispensation is that a deserted, yet active, Christian is ready to give over the exercise of duty and to say, "This evil is of the Lord, why should I wait on the Lord any longer?" Sometimes a Christian is brought to the desperate divinity of Saul, which caused him to lament, "God is departed from me, and answereth me no more, neither by prophets, nor by dreams" (1 Sam. 28:15). Psalm 69:3, where David is under the serious exercise of duty, yet deserted, says, "I am weary of my crying." I will pray no more, because I have no advantage by praying. David's hope begins to fail, for he says, "Mine eyes fail while I wait for my God." He begins to give up his hope, for he thought, do what he may, God had a controversy with him.

Third, a deserted Christian imagines that God has a standing controversy with him; the Christian is then constrained to cry out, "Why is there no hope?" Has not a desertion after activity been the great foundation of a Christian's unbelief, so that he has been constrained through the power of temptations, to cry out, "Why should I wait on the Lord any longer? What is my hope, that I should wait? What is my strength, that I should prolong my days?"

A fourth disadvantage by such a dispensation, is that an active, yet deserted Christian, goes about his duty with much fainting and little hope; he goes about duty most formally and most securely. Once a Christian is deserted while active in duty, it is the ordinary result of that dispensation for him to become formal in the exercise of duty. For, since he cried and was not the better, he will cry no more, because his cry does not have access.

A fifth disadvantage by such a dispensation is that this type of Christian loses much of his esteem of godliness and his esteem of duty; these are ordinarily the fruits of such a dispensation from the Lord. I would not say to you who meet with such a dispensation that you would sit down at the posts of His doors and die depending, waiting, or praying, and know between the first step and the last step on the way to heaven. There is not a grave of any person of whom it may be said, "Behold this person came to Christ, but He refused him." At last he shall cry, and Christ shall speak, "Be of good comfort, the Master calleth thee."

Now the third point we shall discuss concerning a Christian who is deserted, though active in his duty, is that there are five things that such a dispensation says to a Christian.

First, it says that you have undervalued Christ—you have said to Christ, "I have put off my coat; how shall I put it on?" Therefore He will make you read your guilt in your stroke; He will balance your sin and your judgment. You shall be constrained to cry out, "My iniquity corrects me." Sometimes the sin of a Christian is both his sin and his judgment.

Secondly, such a dispensation says that the Christian should depend more upon Christ and less upon the means; he should depend upon Christ for the blessing of the means. When a Christian goes about prayer, but without blessing, let him realize his lack of dependence and faith in Christ. It is a great thing to learn to pray, as though we prayed not; to use the means, as though we used them not; to pray, and not to trust in our prayers.

A third thing that desertion says to a Christian is, "You are still pilgrims in this world." Desertion should teach that lesson, for the day is coming when you shall enter into your Father's house and never again be deserted. The night of desertion shall be gone, and you shall be constrained to cry out, "Now is my day come that shall never have an end."

Fourthly, this dispensation shows the Christian the sovereignty of Christ. It shows that Christ is free and absolute in the dispensations of enjoyment. The enjoyments of Christ are not knit to the serious performance of duties; we may go about our duties, and yet miss Him.

Fifthly, it says to a Christian that he should wait after desertions; though he goes about his duties actively, and misses Christ, still he should wait. I know what sense draws from desertion; it says, "I will wait no more," but the conclusion faith draws from such a dispensation is, "If I cannot find Him by night upon my bed; if I cannot find Him in the broad places of the street; if I cannot find Him at the watchmen—I will yet go a little further." Faith will still go on a little further, after disappointments. Faith's motto is *plus ultra*.

Looking back at the words of the text, let us distinguish first between sense-enjoyment and faith, and secondly between communion with God and union with Him.

First, there are several differences between sense and faith, or enjoyments and faith. 1. The sense of a Christian looks only to things that are present, but faith looks not only to things that are present, but also to things that are absent. Faith looks at both the things that are gone before and the things that follow after; hence faith is called "the evidence of things not seen" (Heb. 11:1). 2. Sense interprets God by His dispensations, but faith interprets God by His Word. 3. Sense will preach nobly of Christ, when dispensations preach excellently of Him; but let dispensations speak nothing of Christ, then sense will sing dumb. Faith interprets God by His Word, so that in the darkest night, faith cries out, "I know the thoughts of His heart." A Christian can be without sense, but he can never be without faith; he must always have the sweet exercise of faith. Faith is absolutely necessary for a Christian, but sense is not absolutely necessary. 4. Sense is only for the comfortable being of a Christian, but faith is for the being of a Christian; sense only makes us go on in our way with joy, but we cannot walk without faith. 5. Sense takes a view of the face of Christ, but faith takes a view of the heart of Christ, and of His hand; sense will look at the face of Christ, and the smiling of His countenance, and will cry out, "How excellent is He 'whose countenance is like Lebanon, excellent as the cedars'" (Song 5:15). Faith will look into the heart of Christ and see eternal love lodging within His bosom. 6. Sense is the birth and fruit of faith; there cannot be much sense, if any at all, without the exercise of faith. This is clear in Ephesians 1:13, which says that after you have believed, then sense comes in apace and cries out, "Ye were sealed with that holy Spirit of promise." Faith and sense are sisters, but they are not twins; they are joined to a Christian, but they do not always dwell together in a Christian. But it is most certain that there may be the exercise of faith when there is not the exercise of sense. Sense may be away, yet faith may be most active, as we see in Song of Solomon 5:6: "I opened to my beloved," which is faith, yet sense is away: "But my beloved had withdrawn himself, and was gone."

Secondly, let us distinguish between communion with God and union with Him. 1. Union with Christ is Christ's dwelling or cohabitation with the soul; but communion with Him is Christ's cohabitation with the soul—the soul of Christ dwelling in the soul of a Christian by faith, and the soul of a Christian dwelling in the soul of Christ by love. 2. Union with God consists of the exercise of faith. Faith is the grace that unites the soul to Christ, but communion with God consists of the exercise of love and prayer. Faith brings in Christ to the soul, and love and prayer entertain Him there; faith unites the soul to Christ—it is the glorious nail that fastens Christ and the soul together, but it is love that roofs the nail to the head. Faith will cry out, "I am my beloved's," but love will make a Christian cry out, "My beloved is mine" (Song 6:3). 3. The union that is between the soul and Christ is an inseparable and unchangeable thing; when union is once made up, it cannot be lost. Communion with Christ, however, is subject to being lost; sometimes a Christian may be under enjoyments, and sometimes under absence. 4. Communion with Christ is more sensible, and often it is a more refreshing thing than union with Him; walking by sight is often more comfortable to a Christian than walking by faith.

The last issue we will discuss concerning our text is this question: what is the reason or cause that communion with Christ, once it is attained, is often quickly broken off and interrupted? Is it not known that sometimes a Christian will be under eminent enjoyments, yet before an hour passes by, his enjoyments are gone? There are a few reasons for this problem.

First, security in self often interrupts a Christian's enjoyments. We see in Song of Solomon 5:2 that security did not only hinder her enjoyment, but also interrupted her present enjoyment, as in Zechariah 4:1.

The second cause that interrupts a Christian's enjoyments is pride. Once a Christian becomes proud through his enjoyments, then he is near a stroke of desertion and absence with God. Hence it is said, "I dwell in the high and holy place, with him also that is of a contrite and humble spirit" (Isa. 57:15); as it were, He is a stranger and passer-by to the proud person, but He takes up His lodging with the humble Christian.

A third cause is that sometimes Christians gaze too much at their enjoyments. Oh, Christians, did you ever know what it meant when Christ was present with you, that you were too taken up with gazing at your enjoyments? In Acts 1:9, we read of an interesting occurrence: "And when he had spoken these things, while they beheld, he was taken up; and a cloud received him out of their sight." Therefore, a Christian should cease to wonder at his enjoyments, and rather wonder at the Person that gives the enjoyment; for a Christian's wondering at his enjoyments is often the great foundation of pride. It makes him cry out, "No doubt I am singular that He does thus singularly dispense to me."

A fourth cause of it is that we do not exercise seriously enough the duties that invite Christ's presence. There are three golden chains by which a soul must keep Christ when He condescends to visit you. You must hold Christ with the excellent cord of faith; you must hold Christ by the excellent cord of love; and you must hold Christ by the excellent cord of prayer. These three must hold Christ and keep Him in His galleries. The little exercise of such duties often interrupts our enjoyments.

A fifth cause of it is that a Christian often idolizes his enjoyments and lays too much weight upon them; therefore Christ absents Himself from them. Christ will teach a Christian to love his enjoyments because of the Giver, and to love the Giver because of the enjoyments. This was the remarkable practice to the virgins: "Because of the savour of thy good ointments thy name is as ointment poured forth, therefore do the virgins love thee" (Song 1:3); that is, because of the excellent dispensations of communion with Christ, therefore the virgins love Him. They terminate their love upon Christ and not upon the enjoyments. All our enjoyments should strengthen our faith, make our love increase, and our hope to wax from one degree to another.

The last reason why it is so much interrupted is that we begin to undervalue our enjoyments. Sometimes a Christian has too high an account of his enjoyments, and at other times he undervalues them. Are not these the great causes that our enjoyments are obstructed (Song 2:3)? When did the spouse sit down under His shadow? Was it not then when His fruit was sweet to her taste? She had enjoyments of God when she had a high esteem of His enjoyments, when His fruit, that is, the sweet dispensations of His love, were pleasant to her taste.

I shall say no more at this time, but I desire you pursue enjoyment of God, since communion with God and enjoyment of Him are such excellent things. There is such an abundance of revelations and visions of God that may be had. A Christian is sometimes constrained to ask, "I have tasted of the lower streams, but when shall the day be that I shall taste of the higher streams?" Is not a Christian brought sometimes to ask, "If this is the sweetness of the streams that fall from the children's table, what must the meat be? When will all the veils between God and me be rent asunder?" There is no immediate communion with God here; there is no satisfying communion with God here; there is no constant communion with God here; there is no communion with God here that cannot be abused; there is no communion with God here, but we should improve it rather for quickening our appetites than satisfying our desires. The more we drink of these rivers, the more we will desire. Oh, blessed is he that will be drunk with the wine of His consolations. What is communion with God? Is it not the summary of the blessedness of heaven? It is, in essence, "to be with God."

Oh, heirs and expectants of heaven and of this excellent hope, the day is coming that you shall be forever with the Lord! Comfort yourselves with these words, and comfort one another with these words. Amen.

SERMON 32

How to Prevent Spiritual Pride During Special Manifestations (4)

And lest I should be exalted above measure through the abundance of the revelations.
—2 Corinthians 12:7

Would it not be a pleasant and glorious sight to behold one in the form and likeness of the Son of man walking in the midst of our solemn assemblies? Would it not be a pleasant sight to behold the majestic steps of princely Jesus in His sanctuary? It is a sad dispensation when, at communions, we feast with a veiled Christ, pray to a silent Christ who does not hearken to the voice of our cry, and walk with an absent Christ. Is it not a sad dispensation to preach of an unknown Christ, and to hear of an unknown Christ? Is it not much worse for Christians to take up Christ as one that is an enemy? I think if the Christians of these days would search their own hearts, they might see four things engraven upon them in legible letters. First, they might see their distance from God and their lack of the ancient fellowship and abundance of revelations that the saints before us have enjoyed. Secondly, a Christian might see engraven upon his heart little desire after the abundance of revelations and choice enjoyments that have been communicated to the saints. Thirdly, a Christian might see little sorrow concerning the lack of such excellent enjoyments that have been of old communicated to the saints. Lastly, when Christ is away, we might see engraven upon our hearts love to the world and delight in the things of this present world. Are there not idols within our bosom that take up His room? May not that lamentation be heard upon the mountains and high places of Israel, "Oh, return Thou, return Thou, whom our soul loves."

At the last occasion that we spoke upon this text, we discussed five things: First, there were some times when Christ did communicate to His own eminent, excellent, and extraordinary enjoyments of Himself. The second thing, which we now discuss, is that Christians are in danger of abusing and ruining the most excellent estate of communion and fellowship with God here. It is clear that Paul was in danger of being "exalted above measure"; pride, as it were, was beginning to spring from that noble and excellent root, the enjoyment of God.

I shall not speak long to make this point. Is it not clear from the practice of Adam, that though he was under most eminent discoveries of God, yet how much did he abuse that estate? Is it not clear in Jacob (Gen. 32:29), who falls into the sin of curiosity when under eminent enjoyments of God? Was it not clear in the practice of the bride (Song 5), as she falls into the sin of security when she was under eminent enjoyments of Christ? Was it not clear in the practice of John, who fell into the sin of idolatry when under eminent discoveries of Christ? All these examples show that a Christian may abuse his nearest and most excellent enjoyment. Furthermore, pride, that desperate evil, is one of the things that does most ordinarily empty a Christian's enjoyments. We would likewise have you notice that there are four things that a Christian is most ordinarily proud of: his gifts, his grace, his enjoyments, and his obedience.

First, the Christian is proud of his gifts. For example, if perhaps he has more knowledge of Christ than others, he may put them down, boast, and begin to be presumptuous about his borrowed feathers. I say to the Christian who is proud of his gifts: beware lest God take from you that which you seem to possess. I would say what Joab said to David: Let God increase your gifts, how many soever they be, an hundred fold more, and do not boast in them.

Secondly, a Christian may be proud of his grace, and what is even more strange, a Christian may be proud of his humility. He may have his humility as the foundation of his pride; therefore, a Christian must be mortified to his mortification, be denied to his self-denial, be humble in his being humble, and be nothing in his being nothing. To you who are proud of your graces, I tell you that it is impossible for grace to grow as long as you are proud; and it is impossible for you to grow by the grace of others as long as you are proud. I say to you that which the young man said to the prophet: "Don't be proud. All that you have is borrowed. Your graces are but the gift of Christ."

Thirdly, a Christian may be proud of his enjoyments. Paul was in danger of being exalted above measure through the abundance of revelations. A Christian often ascends in his own thoughts when Christ lifts him up. Oh, but you must sit near the ground when Christ sits above.

Fourthly, a Christian may be proud of his obedience when he goes about the exercise of any special duty; he is proud when he is honored to suffer for Christ or to do some eminent service for Christ. This was the fault of the disciples who said, "We have left all, and followed thee" (Mark 10:28).

Now, the choicest enjoyments of a Christian may be abused. On this topic, I would first propose some considerations.

The first consideration is that the devil never assaults a Christian more violently than immediately after enjoyments. When a Christian is under eminent enjoyments of God, "the blast of the terrible ones is as a storm against the wall" (Isa. 25:4). Paul was in danger of being overcome by temptations; when he was nearest Christ, Satan was at his right hand, ready to oppose him.

The second consideration is that the devil often gets the most eminent victories over a Christian immediately after enjoyments. This is very clear in the experience of the saints. I will give these three grounds why is it so.

First, after enjoyments of Christ, the Christian is then most independent and presumptuous; therefore, not walking in the blessed way of dependence or in the excellent paths of divine subordination, the devil gets advantage over him. Sometimes a Christian, after his enjoyments, trusts in his own strength, or he trusts in the strength of his enjoyments. Another reason why the eminent victories of the devil over a Christian come especially after eminent enjoyments is that then a Christian is not much in the exercise of watchfulness. Often, when a Christian is admitted to the banqueting house, he falls asleep in the bed of love. It is then that a Christian says to his soul, "Oh, soul, sleep, and take thy rest, thou hast much goods laid up for many years." A third reason is that a Christian does then ordinarily lose the grace of fear. After we have been brought near the King, we sing the triumph before the victory. When we are brought within sight of Christ, we cry out, "He only is my rock and my salvation: he is my defence; I shall not be moved" (Ps. 62:6). Therefore, I say to you, dear Christians, watch, watch! Watch after enjoyments, for he is at hand who is ready to betray you.

Let us also consider a third point: the temptations of the devil, and the assaults that he makes immediately after enjoyments, if they be resisted and withstood, are eminent advantages attending such a frame. If there is a messenger of Satan given to buffet you after enjoyments, there are eminent advantages waiting upon the Christian who resists that temptation. There is more advantage in resisting a temptation after enjoyments than there is in resisting three in desertion. It is then that a Christian kills his ten thousands; but at other times, he kills only his thousands. There are several advantages that a Christian has by resisting temptations after enjoyments.

A first advantage is that it brings much humility. A broad sight of Christ and a broad sight of ourselves will make us to lie low in the dust. This is clear in the practice of Paul in the former part of this chapter; he vented much humility, and we suppose it was the result of resisting temptations after enjoyments. A Christian is never more humble than when he has resisted the devil in the strength of Christ, after enjoyments.

A second advantage is that resisting temptations makes Christ rest in His love, to go on, and continue to rejoice over us with singing. Christians, do you desire to know how to hold and detain Christ in His galleries? Resist your temptations after enjoyments, for giving way to a temptation of the devil is stirring up and awakening your beloved before He pleases. I suppose it is known that enjoyments of Christ that are attended with much spiritual warfare are the longest, the sweetest, and most advantageous enjoyments.

A third advantage is that such a Christian maintains the faith of his interest in God and the faith of the reality of his enjoyments. It is hard for a Christian to give way to the temptations of Satan immediately after enjoyments, and not to be constrained to call into question his interest, or at least the reality of his enjoyments. If you desire to keep the faith of these two things lively upon your spirits, study to resist the devil when he buffets you after enjoyments.

The fourth advantage that redounds to a Christian who is resisting temptations is that this Christian is much in prayer. We see this in the verse following our text: "For this thing I besought the Lord thrice, that it might depart from me" (v. 8). Is it not a noble advantage to have a divine necessity to go about the excellent duty of prayer? By the way, a Christian's prayers to resist temptations are prayers that receive a speedy answer. Paul, immediately after enjoyments, receives the answer, "My grace is sufficient for thee" (v. 9).

A last advantage is that resisting temptations immediately after enjoyments is a notable way for a Christian to attain a proper improvement of his enjoyments.

The proper improvement of our enjoyments lies in four areas. First, it lies in the strengthening of our experience. Every enjoyment of God and each visit from Christ should be put among the records of our experience. Second, our enjoyments should strengthen our faith. Every sight of Christ should constrain us to take assured grips of Him. At each sight of Christ, we should take Christ in our arms and cry forth, "He is mine, He is mine!" Third, our enjoyments should be improved so that our love can be strengthened. Each sight of Christ should strengthen the noble grace of love, so that when we see Him, we may be constrained to love Him, and we may cry, "Did not our heart burn within us, while he talked with us?" (Luke 24:32). Fourth, our enjoyments should be improved for strengthening our delight to duty as well as our hatred of sin. If Christians would attain these excellent improvements of their enjoyments, they would be equipped to resist the temptations which arise after enjoyments.

There is a fourth consideration concerning our text. A Christian encounters the most eminent victories when he resists temptations immediately after enjoyments. I shall give you three reasons why this is so. 1. At this point, a Christian has much strength communicated to him for wrestling with his temptations. An enjoyment of a Christian is as strength to his soul to fight with his spiritual enemies. 2. The Captain of salvation is then present; the Captain of the field is standing at our right hand, and this does exceedingly help to gain eminent victories over the devil. 3. A Christian, in the time of his enjoyments, has a low and undervalued account and esteem of all things besides Christ. There are times when a Christian cannot strike at his idols with force; as it were, there is a piece of his heart that withdraws his strength. It is certain that sometimes one piece of a Christian's heart will cry out to mortify such a lust, and another piece of the heart will cry out not to mortify the same lust.

We would like to propose seven faults that a Christian ordinarily falls into after his enjoyments.

The first is the fault of pride. This is clear from the words of the text, and also from Psalm 30:6. It is easier for a Christian to be denied his grace than to be denied his enjoyments. The graces of a Christian are not so much the foundation of pride as the enjoyments of a Christian. This is clear when we compare Galatians 2:20 with the words in our text, where Paul is denied to his grace, but he is in danger of being proud of his enjoyments.

The second fault that a Christian falls into in enjoyments is curiosity. He proposes questions to God that he should not ask, nor would it be an advantage for him to know. So Jacob, when he was in communion with God, fell into that curious question, "Tell me, I pray thee, thy name" (Gen. 32:29). Manoah also asked, and received the answer, "Why askest thou thus after my name, seeing it is secret?" (Judg. 13:18), or, as the word may be rendered, "It is wonderful." I suppose too much familiarity of a Christian with God corrupts good manners; the Christian then begins to ask a reason for God's actions. He begins to study the incomprehensible essence of God. A Christian in his most eminent enjoyments falls into notable idolatry. Is it not so when you are nearest God? You attempt to bring down the incomprehensible God to some idea or shape; this is damnable idolatry, transforming the invisible God to the image of a visible thing.

The third fault that a Christian falls into during the enjoyment of God is to slight his enjoyments when he has an abundance of the precious revelations of God. This proceeds in the following manner: a Christian may earnestly pursue after enjoyments of God, and when he meets with them, he may undervalue these very enjoyments. Also, he may have a high esteem of an absent Christ, but a low esteem of a present Christ, as we see in Song of Solomon 5. In the beginning, the bride longs for enjoyment of Christ and communion with Him, yet in Song of Solomon 5:2-3, she slights communion with Christ. Furthermore, a Christian may long after communion with God at one time, and refuse communion with God at another time. This is clear when we compare Song of Solomon 4:16 with chapter 5:3. At first, the bride longs after the breath of His Spirit; yet later, in chapter 5:3, she undervalues His condescending to visit. I suppose it is known that it is the great fault of a Christian to undervalue communion with God when he has it.

A fourth sin that a Christian encounters during enjoyment of Christ is valuing the enjoyment more than the Giver of the enjoyment. Thus we are often more in love with the gifts of God than with the Giver; we terminate our love, our faith, and our joy upon our enjoyments, when all of these should end in Christ.

Fifth, we often overlook the sin of security. In Song of Solomon 5:2, the bride is under eminent enjoyments of Christ, but quickly falls asleep in the second verse. When Christ manifests Himself to us, must we then put off our coat and give ourselves to rest?

The sixth fault a Christian commits in the time of his enjoyments is to take advantage of them by being neglectful in his duty because of his enjoyments. Ordinarily, a Christian never slights prayer, watchfulness, or fear so much as after his enjoyments.

A Christian also spends time gazing and wondering at his own enjoyments. Is it not known that sometimes a Christian, meeting with eminent enjoyments of God in prayer, has begun to wonder at what he has attained and forgotten to pursue after more? When a Christian stands and gazes at his present lot and dispensation, he does not pursue after more. A Christian should not reflect too long upon his enjoyments until he is finished with prayer; ordinarily, when a Christian wonders at his enjoyments, he puts himself in a dead and lifeless frame.

Now, we desire to discuss a third point. Since communion with Christ, and the eminent enjoyments a Christian has of Christ, may be abused, we must press that these three things should be a Christian's exercise after enjoyment.

First, we must exercise fear after we enjoy Christ. "Wherefore let him that thinketh he standeth take heed lest he fall" (1 Cor. 10:12). When is a Christian nearest apostasy? He is closest to apostasy when he is far from apostasy in his own apprehension. I do not love a fearless Christian, for he is a Christian that shall not endure long under his own weight.

Second, attempt as strongly to keep Christ when He is present, as you sought Him when He was absent. There is greater difficulty keeping Christ when present than to get Christ when absent. Therefore, when you have gotten the presence of Christ, do not think that your work is done. The greatest work is before you—charge your heart by the roes and by the hinds of the field, that you do not stir, nor awake your beloved until He please. Oh, but it is not simple to keep mere touches with Christ when He is present. Believe it, Christ can dispense with wrongs in His absence that He will not dispense with when He is present.

Third, immediately after your enjoyments, you must see them for the end and use for which they were sent. Every visit of Christ's has a voice and a message. These enjoyments tell us two important things. First, we must mortify our predominant idols. Second, we must love our precious Christ. In a manner, when a Christian sees Christ, he never desires to behold another object. I ask you—did you ever meet with such an enjoyment of Christ that you were constrained to cry out, "Oh, if this place were my grave! Oh, that I might sail away, as the ships of desire!" Have you ever met with the place that you might name the place of "living after seeing"? I think that if the life of communion with God were known, you would not be such great strangers to it.

Now, we also desire to address, concerning the text, that Christ has a purpose with even the darkest and most dreadful dispensations we encounter. The reason God gave a messenger of Satan to buffet Paul was so that he would not be exalted above measure. Even in the darkest, saddest cross and affliction of a Christian, Christ has a sweet design of love treasured up in it.

In further discoursing on this subject, notice that there are five dark and terrible dispensations of Christ to the soul, every one of which has a glorious end and a sweet design of love.

First, God permits the devil, a messenger of Satan, to buffet us. It is sad for a Christian to be under the strong assaults of the devil; sometimes, under strong temptations, he will be forced to ask, "Oh, why am I thus? Why am I thus?" Yet, even this dispensation has a sweet design of love, for the power of grace and love is manifested here.

Second, a Christian may be under desertion and distance from Christ. Sometimes, when Christians go to prayer, Christ draws a veil between His face and them; then, when they come to preaching, Christ stands behind the curtain, and does not manifest Himself to them. When they go to communions, they feast with a veiled Christ; they sit down and feast with one that does not manifest Himself to them. Yet, I say, even in this dark dispensation of desertion, there is a sweet design of love. "All things work together for good to them that love God" (Rom. 8:28). I confess when desertion and distance from Christ is his burden, a deserted Christian has a comfortless life; but the visit that Christ gives after long desertion is a most refreshing visit, for then it has much spiritual advantage waiting upon it.

A third dark dispensation a Christian encounters that has a design of love is when a Christian is put to dispute his personal interest in salvation. Being under a cloud regarding his hope of heaven, he asks himself, "Do I have a right to heaven?" Oh, if only this debate were the lot of many, and were more serious with many! Every dispute concerning your interest and questioning of your peace with God has a noble advantage waiting upon it.

Fourth, when a Christian is denied answers to prayer, it is difficult to pray to an absent Christ. However, it is much more difficult to pray to a silent Christ who does not hearken to the voice of our cry. The delays of the returns of prayer also have a sweet design of love in them. Christ knows well how to dispense His abundance and how to time His gifts.

A fifth dark dispensation is that a Christian, despite all the pains he has taken in mortifying his lusts, cannot conquer them. This is a sad and afflicting dispensation—despite all pains to mortify their idols, yet the idol is as strong upon their hand as before. Christians, continue to fight, for the day of your victory is coming. A Christian must die fighting, not triumphing. I do not think it is unsuitable for a Christian's hope when he shall be standing before the gates of heaven, fighting his corruptions; it is not unsuitable to his hope, even when one foot is within the city, and another without, to have a tear falling from his eyes. It seems appropriate for a Christian to give up the ghost with this cry: "O wretched man that I am! Who shall deliver me from the body of this death?" (Rom. 7:24).

Let us furthermore consider a few points. It is far easier for a Christian to take up infinite wisdom in His stroke than to behold infinite love in His stroke; the darkest dispensations that Christ dispenses to His own may contain infinite wisdom. But they cannot read love in such dispensations. There are three things that a Christian should study in the dark dispensations he encounters. 1. Infinite wisdom: He should endeavor in his darkest dispensations to say that God, in dispensing so, has dealt wisely. 2. A Christian should study spotless holiness and righteousness in his crosses, so that he may say that God is just and righteous. When Christ dispenses a cross to you, you must write this at the foot of such a cross: "Righteous art thou, O Lord, when thou judgest, and just when thou condemnest." 3. A Christian should study infinite love in his cross. It is impossible for a Christian to bear his cross with patience and submission until he sees infinite love in the cross.

Secondly, when a Christian meets with a cross, he may take it in his arms; yet if the same cross be prolonged, he may become impatient. This is clear in the practice of Job: when he first meets with his cross, he cries out, "The LORD gave, and the LORD hath taken away; blessed be the name of the LORD" (Job 1:21). Yet, when the very same cross is prolonged a little, he is constrained to cry out, "My soul chooseth strangling, and death rather than my life" (Job 7:15).

I will propose a third point: there may be much dispute concerning God's way of conveying you to heaven. There may be much repining and fretting at God's dispensations; however, the day is approaching when you will write upon the doorposts of heaven, "He hath done all things well" (Mark 7:37). I think there shall be some part of eternity spent in interrogations and questions. Christ will question you concerning the things you met with. He may ask, "When I sent such a cross unto you, did I not do well?" You shall be constrained to answer, "Yes." "When I sent you out without money, script, or bag, did I not do well?" You shall be constrained to answer, "Yes, precious Christ, Thou hast done all things well."

Fourthly, I would propose unto you that it is hard for a Christian to have the same thoughts of his cross now when he is under it, that he shall have at the day of death. Oh, but a Christian shall be sometimes constrained to cry out, "I had perished, except I had perished, I had been undone, except I had been undone!" For every cross that you meet with, you shall say, "Blessed be the day that I met with such a cross!" I desire you to make your peace once with God, so that all things you encounter may be blessed unto you. Know for certain that there is not one grain weight of affliction in your cup, dear Christian, but infinite wisdom did contrive it to be there, and infinite love did put it there. Is not this a cup that must be drunk, since the precious fingers of Christ did mingle your cup? Therefore, let not your heart say, when you meet with a cross, "Let this cup depart from me!" There is more love in a cross than we often imagine. When are the sweet soul-embracings between

Christ and the soul? When are they admitted to behold the sun in His strength, and to behold Him, whose cheeks are beds of spices beset with sweet flowers? A Christian's midnight without may be his noon-day within. There may be a sweet day within when there is not much light without. Oh, that we were content to go to heaven in a fiery chariot, and that we would take in our arms every dispensation that Christ carves out to us! Oh, prisoners of hope! Oh, expectants of heaven! Oh, heirs of the grace of life! Comfort yourselves in this: Before long, we shall sing comfortably in heaven: "Speak ye comfortably to Jerusalem, and cry unto her, that her warfare is accomplished, that her iniquity is pardoned: for she hath received of the LORD's hand double for all her sins" (Isa. 40:2).

Oh, Christians, Christ is standing at the end of your race with a crown in His hand, crying out, "To him that overcometh will I give this crown of life." Oh, what a day shall it be when the blessed hands of Christ shall put a crown upon our cursed heads! Will we not be constrained to take off the crown which He has put on? All the saints in heaven will think it shameful to wear a crown in the sight of Christ. They that stand round about the throne cast down their crowns at His feet (Rev. 4:10). As it were, they thought it shameful to wear a crown in His sight. They could only say, "Thou art worthy, O Lord" (v. 11). Will you think upon this precious day, when our dark night shall be over and gone, and that blessed morning that shall admit that no following night shall come? What wonderful love, what wonderful joy, what wonderful knowledge shall be in that day. Will you act out heaven now, in your hearts? Think about it, and, as it were, act upon the blessedness in heaven. What will you think to have Christ eternally in your arms? Do you desire to have a description of heaven? Christ is sitting in the midst; the eyes of these precious thousands are fixed upon Him, and yet His eyes are fixed upon them.

In short, the blessedness of heaven consists in these four particulars. First, Christ is looking to the saints, and they are looking to Him. Second, the saints are eternally loving Christ, and Christ is eternally loving them. Third, they are eternally wondering at Christ, and Christ is eternally wondering at them. "When he shall come to be glorified in his saints, and to be admired in all them that believe (because our testimony among you was believed) in that day" (2 Thess. 1:10). Fourthly, the saints are eternally embracing Christ, and Christ is eternally embracing them. Oh, these soul-embracings, these soul-sweet ravishings, and eternally holding of Christ's arms and ours who are begotten to a lively hope! There is no separation between Christ and the soul there. I wish that the desire of the Greeks would be the desire of all that are here today; they said to Philip, "We would see Jesus" (John 12:21). Oh, but if you had one desire to behold, you would get Him for a desire. Shall ever those cursed eyes behold the Sun of righteousness, that noble Plant of renown? Blessed are they that see Him, blessed are they that have the hope of seeing Him, and blessed are they that are walking on in the way to see Him. A Christian, while he is here, is in Christ going to Christ, and out of Christ; a Christian, while here, is in Christ by union; but he is out of Christ in regard to the complete enjoyment of Him. He is going to Christ to have these eternal delights that are at His right hand. Oh, run, run, run, until the day that you shall have Christ enfolded in your arms, when you will cry out, "This is my rest forever: here will I dwell" (Ps. 132:14)!

SERMON 33

How to Prevent Spiritual Pride During Special Manifestations (5)

And lest I should be exalted above measure through the abundance of the revelations.
—2 Corinthians 12:7

In the verse of our text, we may behold these three points eminently shining. First, we behold the precious jewel of infinite love, in giving to His own most eminent enjoyments of Himself, while carving out such dispensations as might most mortify pride. Second, we may behold the unspeakable malice of the devil, who is always ready to mar the most excellent visits that Christ gives to His own. Thirdly, we behold the unspeakable frailty that is in humanity, who is ready to be ensnared and caught through guile, even when he is in most immediate enjoyments of God.

At the last occasion we spoke upon these words, we told you that there were five things to be noticed. First, there are eminent and excellent enjoyments of God that He gives to His own. Next, the soul is ready to abuse even the most excellent and matchless enjoyments. Paul was in danger of being "exalted above measure through the abundance of the revelations." Third, we discussed that even in the darkest and most dreadful dispensation of God, there is always a sweet design of love, which is the purpose of such a dispensation. This is clear in the following verses: "There was given to me a thorn in the flesh, the messenger of Satan to buffet me," and we see the noble end of Paul's affliction: "Lest I should be exalted above measure." This purpose of this dark dispensation was to hide pride from his eyes.

Now we have spoken concerning this truth; there is one more thing we would address concerning this truth. There are eight most glorious and lovely ends that Christ proposes in the darkest dispensations a Christian can encounter.

First, Christ will let Christians meet with dark dispensations so that they may have discoveries and proofs in their own hearts that show their own frailty. In Deuteronomy 8:2 we read, "The LORD thy God led thee these forty years in the wilderness, to humble thee, and to prove thee, to know what was in thine heart, whether thou wouldest keep his commandments, or no." So we see that the purpose of this affliction was to prove what was in the heart of the people of Israel. When a Christian is put through the school of affliction, he will learn many lessons of his own deceitful heart, which he knew not before. There are five great lessons that a Christian learns about his own heart in the school of affliction. These are also five great advantages that he learns through affliction.

First, a Christian will remember formerly forgotten iniquity when he is put into the furnace of affliction. There are many old sins that the Christian forgets; these will be brought to his remembrance. We see this truth in the remarkable words found in Genesis 42:21-22; when the eleven brethren of Joseph are brought to a strait in Egypt, the sin of selling their brother comes to their remembrance. "If they shall bethink themselves in the land whither they were carried captives" (1 Kings 8:47), or as it reads in the original, "If they shall bring back to their heart," which means that affliction is that which brings forgotten iniquities to remembrance. Is it not certain that sometimes when a Christian meets with a cross, there are some sins that were never minded before that will then stare him in the face?

Second, a Christian will also learn through affliction to know the strength of his corruptions and the strength of his idols, which is greater than he supposed it to be. A Christian never knows the strength of his lusts so well as under afflictions. When he is afflicted, he will know the strength of impatience; he will know the strength of the idol of ease, and he will see the idol of love to the world. It is impossible for people to know their love to their idols until afflictions begin to separate their heart and their idols. Then what does love do to an unmortified lust? Do not our living lusts sit down and mourn over the grave of our buried lusts or idols? We often sit down over the grave of our idols and cry the same words that

David cried at the death of Absalom: "O my son Absalom, my son, my son Absalom! would God I had died for thee, O Absalom, my son, my son!" (2 Sam. 18:33).

Third, affliction will also teach us to know that grace is not in such strength and vigorous exercise as we supposed. Afflictions will bring forth the weakness of our faith, love, and patience; we will quickly learn that we are not far advanced in the exercise of grace.

Fourth, through crosses, a Christian will be more convinced of sin than he was before. There are many sins a man will commit in prosperity without much sorrow for them; but, bring him once to the furnace, and the conscience will begin to speak, "As many as I love, I rebuke and chasten: be zealous therefore, and repent" (Rev. 3:19), or, as the original is translated, "As many as I love, I will convince and correct." The convictions of conscience are deepest in the day of affliction, when God calls, as in a solemn assembly, all His terrors round about us.

Fifth, we also learn through the cross to mourn and be humbled for our former iniquities. Manasseh humbled himself in his affliction (2 Chron. 33:12). This was also the fruit of Job's cross, as we read in Job 7:20, "I have sinned; what shall I do unto thee, O thou preserver of men?" I say to you, dear Christian, suspect your cross not to be sanctified that does not give you a broad sight of your own heart. The dross and corruption that is in us never appears as great as when we are put in the fire; then our scum appears.

A second lovely and glorious purpose that Christ proposes in His dark dispensations is that we may be brought low and made humble. This is clear in Deuteronomy 8:2, where we read, "The LORD thy God led thee these forty years in the wilderness, to humble thee." Also, in our text, we see that the purpose of Paul's dark dispensation was that he should not be exalted above measure. "Remembering mine affliction and my misery, the wormwood and the gall. My soul hath them still in remembrance, and is humbled in me" (Lam. 3:19-20); if the cross has humbled us, it has accomplished a great part of its work. But there are many that contend with God in the furnace, and where they should be humbled, they cry out, "Shew me wherefore thou contendest with me" (Job 10:20). A Christian's humility under the cross is shown in three ways. First, it is shown in a Christian's patient submission to the cross and the dark dispensation they undergo. The Christian, as it were, puts his mouth in the dust and cries forth, "It is good for me to keep silence." Second, a Christian's humility under the cross produces a loathing of himself because of his abomination. Thus, if Christ frowns upon him, he will frown upon himself. Third, humility under the cross allows a Christian to take these engagements to himself that are given unto him. It is a notable piece of humility not to refuse to be comforted; for surely, Christ looks upon it as a matchless piece of pride when a man refuses the promises. There is no greater humility than the obedience of His commands and the embracing of His promises.

A third lovely end that Christ has in His dark dispensations is that there are some graces of a Christian that could not be eminently exercised but under the cross, especially the grace of faith and the grace of patience. These two could not be exercised if the Christian did not have a cross. Hence we read in Revelation 13:10, speaking of the sad things there were to befall the church, here is the "patience and the faith of the saints," as if He would have said, here is an excellent field for venting the exercise of the faith and patience of the saints. "Count it all joy when ye fall into divers temptations; knowing this, that the trying of your faith worketh patience" (James 1:2-3); or, "The trial of faith perfects patience," for so the word may be rendered according to the original.

Christ proposes another glorious purpose in His dark dispensations. Through the crosses of affliction, a Christian may have a higher and more majestic view of Christ. The great voice of the cross says that we should increase in our esteem of Christ. This was the notable fruit that Asaph found through his cross in Psalm 73:25, where the wicked prospered, but he is constrained to say, "Whom have I in heaven but thee? And there is none upon earth that I desire beside thee." Do you desire to know what afflictions are? They are, as it were, a little wormwood spread upon the pipes of created enjoyments that may hinder us suck. Every cross a Christian meets with preaches mortification of our idols and increase in our love for Christ. A Christian has most eminent apprehensions of Christ in adversity, as in Song of Solomon 2:2-3.

A fifth glorious and lovely end Christ has in His dark dispensations is that a Christian may exercise more diligence. "LORD, in trouble have they visited thee, they poured out a prayer when thy chastening was upon them" (Isa. 26:16). "In their affliction they will seek me early" (Hos. 5:15). Ordinarily, a Christian has three notable qualifications of his prayer under the cross, which he does not have often during times of prosperity. First, in affliction, he prays from a principle of necessity. Necessity will be the principle that will lead a Christian to prayer under the cross. Second, a Christian under the cross will pray more fervently than he did before. Third, a Christian under the cross will pray more constantly than he did before. Sometimes in prosperity we forget to pray; but when God sends us a cross and afflicts us sore, then we call for Him and make mention of His name.

The sixth lovely end Christ has in sending dark dispensations and crosses to His own is that we may be trained in holiness. In Isaiah 27:9 we read that the fruit of affliction is "to take away sin." This is the fruit of all our afflictions: "That we might be partakers of his holiness" (Heb. 12:10). Every affliction is a workman to fit us for heaven. Have you ever seen many masons polishing a stone for a building? Such is the cross of a Christian; it is like a workman, polishing us for the higher building. These workmen are dinging off our deformities and superfluities; they are polishing us to be pillars in the house of our God, and to be cornerstones fashioned after the similitude of a palace fitted for the heavenly building.

Seventhly, Christ also sends crosses to His own so that they might be taught obedience. Do you desire to know when a Christian disputes the command of God? It is when he is free from any crosses. We see this in Psalm 119:67: "Before I was afflicted I went astray, but now have I kept thy word." Obedience was the noble fruit of his crosses and afflictions.

The eighth glorious goal of Christ's dark afflictions is that a Christian may have renewed experiences of the love, power, wisdom, and justice of Christ. He will put a Christian under such a rod so that he may see His power in delivering him. He will put a Christian under such a rod, so that he may have renewed experiences of His love in delivering him. He will let a Christian undergo such afflictions so that he may have renewed experience of the wisdom of God in contriving a suitable way for his deliverance. Christ will put a Christian under such a cross, that he may have deep apprehensions of the justice of God; he must learn that God does nothing wrong, but does everything upon good grounds.

I would like to point out four things from our text. First, a Christian under a cross may have much love, tenderness, and patience;

yet, upon the first blink of prosperity, his tenderness may be gone. Believe it, it is easier for a Christian to bear his cross than to bear his enjoyments. Next, notice that a Christian should put a blank in Christ's hand when carving out the cross. Oh, but if a Christian had his own cross in carving, he says, I would bear such a cross; but where the cross is in Christ's carving, we turn impatient. Under the cross, we say, "There is no cross but I would have borne it better than this!" But the cross that a Christian's heart carves out is the cross he can least bear; therefore, if you desire to attain spiritual wisdom, let Christ carve out your cross. He knows better how to guide us to heaven than we do ourselves. The third thing I would like to point out is that it is no small difficulty for a Christian to achieve submission and patience under the cross. A Christian may be impatient under his cross one day, and patient under it at the beginning. It is an excellent work to attain thorough submission and patience in our cross. Fourth, take notice that the cross and the manifestations of the love of Christ are not inconsistent together. Some always meet with a cross and draw this conclusion: "He is become my enemy." But know that the cross is the fruit of His love! It is the fruit of the promise of the everlasting covenant, which says, "He can know your soul in adversity."

A fourth point concerning our text is that it is the duty of a Christian to observe the lovely goals of Christ in His dispensations. Paul was also prone to say, "I know there is love in such a dispensation." This was also the practice of David: "It is good for me that I have been afflicted" (Ps. 119:71). He acknowledges that there was advantage in the cross; he knows that there was much love in the cross. There are several grounds why a Christian should study Christ's purposes in the cross.

First, it is impossible for a Christian to be fruitful under the cross until he takes up love in the cross. Much of our time under our crosses is spent in repining and murmuring because of the dispensation. It is often a long time before we come to bring forth the peaceable fruits of righteousness.

Second, thinking of Christ's purposes would hinder a Christian from drawing the sinful and desperate conclusions that he ordinarily draws under the cross. Once a Christian is able to see the love and advantage in the cross, he does not cry out, "I am cut off!" He does not cry out, "Why dost thou chastise me with the chastisements of a cruel one, and with the wound of an enemy?"

A Christian should study Christ's purpose in His dispensations because it is an excellent way to remain patient while bearing the cross. When a Christian takes up wisdom, justice, righteousness, or advantage in the cross, he must cry out, "I will bear the indignation of the LORD, because I have sinned against him" (Mic. 7:9).

A fourth ground why a Christian should take notice of Christ's purposes in affliction is because the love of a Christian to Christ is never so vigorous and lively as when he takes up the lovely ends of His dark dispensations. When a soul takes up Christ's design in the cross, then it begins to kindle with love to Christ. The soul then cries out, "Oh, blessed be He that condescends to take such pains upon me—on unworthy me, self-destroying me, Christ-despising me."

We shall speak no more of this. Now, let us discuss our final point concerning the text: there are some times when the devil does especially assault the Christian more than at other times. There are some remarkable times of the devil's assault on a Christian. This is clear in Paul's words, "There was given to me a thorn in the flesh, the messenger of Satan to buffet me." Here we see that Paul was now notably assaulted by the devil. Let us discuss this further.

There are eight times when a Christian is most assaulted by the devil. First, the devil begins to assault immediately after conversion, when first Christ and the soul yoke together. This is clear from the words of the text, for Paul met with this temptation immediately after his conversion. It is just so with the soul, as it was with the Israelites: once the soul makes mention of going out of Egypt, or going to worship God in the mount, then the devil will increase its bondage and cause it to make brick without straw. As long as the soul is in the bond of nature, the devil will not so much assault it. In the same way, these words ring true: "While the strong man keeps the house, all is at peace." Once the soul begins to come out of the kingdom of darkness, and enters into the kingdom of grace, then he begins to rise. There are three reasons why the soul is most tempted by the devil immediately after conversion.

First, so that a Christian may be put to fear at the way of godliness; also, so that he may think that religion is not so pleasant a thing as he supposed it to be. But I would say this, godliness is an excellent thing; the devil's opposition to it may preach it. Unfortunately, there are many that hear the temptations of the devil, misrepresenting godliness and bringing a bad report upon it, and they believe it. A second reason why the devil especially assaults a Christian after conversion is this: if he cannot bring him back, he will endeavor to give him a discouraged life. The notable falls of a Christian after conversion, if ever he goes to heaven, will cause him to go to heaven in sackcloth; therefore, a Christian should strive to watch after conversion. A third ground is that the afflictions may be means for study to awaken their desires and delight after Christ. I confess, God may be active in this and may have a design in letting a Christian be tempted after conversion. He may desire to try the reality of his religion. There are some who desire Christ because of prosperity; but once Christ and the cross join together, they will say farewell to Christ; the cross will try the sincerity of the religion of many.

A second time the devil tempts a Christian strongly is after long conflicts of interests, when the Christian reaches some new levels of faith, and clear discoveries of interest; at this time, the devil eminently assaults him. Some of this may be pointed out by looking at Matthew 3:17 and Matthew 4:1. When Christ first met with a voice from heaven, telling Him that He was the Son of God, He was immediately led aside to be tempted in the wilderness. Is it not certain that a Christian that has been long under conflict of interest and has gotten faith in exercise, his temptations seem to be livelier than before? This makes him reject his confidence; but know for certain—the devil opposes you. If there were no one left to tell you that your unbelief were a sin, this would be sufficient.

Another time Satan tempts a believer is immediately upon the back of enjoyments. This is clear from the text. When Paul has an abundance of revelations, then there is a messenger of Satan given to buffet him. I will show you three reasons why the devil tempts a Christian most after enjoyments.

First, if the devil overcomes a Christian, then it is a most discouraging stroke for the Christian; it makes him call his faith and his interest into question; it is a stroke that will make him cry out, "I shall one day fall by the hand of one of my enemies!" Second, the devil tempts a Christian most after enjoyments because if a Christian is then overcome, it is impossible for him to maintain the reality of his enjoyments. If we fall immediately after our enjoyments, then we call our enjoyments delusions. The last ground of it is that the many temptations of a Christian after enjoyments puts him from the exercise of love to exercise of war. They distract him from entertaining Christ to going out into the fields to fight with their lusts.

A fourth time a Christian is eminently assaulted by the devil is under a season of self-security. Then behold the devil is at hand, ready to betray you. I think that a sleeping Christian is in danger of being strongly assaulted, as in Song of Solomon 5:2, where the bride is caught sleeping. We also see this in 2 Samuel 11:2, where the origin of all David's sad temptations was his self-security. There are three main reasons why the devil tempts a Christian much in a time of self-security.

First, the devil knows the Christian will not debate to consent to his temptations. A self-secure Christian is prey for the devil. It is impossible for such a Christian to have any strength when such temptations are presented to him. A second reason why the devil tempts a self-secure Christian is because such a Christian lacks that which should guard him from embracing the temptations. Such a Christian lacks a sight of Christ, which would keep him from embracing temptations; a Christian that is self-secure, lacks the exercise of grace that would keep him from temptations, such as the exercise of watchfulness and tenderness. Third, such a Christian, if he is overcome, is in danger of sleeping long in the bed of security.

A fifth time when the devil eminently assaults a Christian is when he is going about duties; the devil knows that the marring of these duties has great influence upon our peace, our faith, and our growth. The devil most assaults us when we are going about duties that are of great concern and importance. There are especially three duties which most invite the assault of the devil: when the Christian is at communion, when he is at prayer, and when he is exercising faith. These are the three duties the devil does especially study to mar, because the right performance of these duties is a foundation of much spiritual joy, and is a noble root of much spiritual growth; therefore, I would say to you when you are about such duties, be much upon your guard, for the devil is at your right hand, ready to assault you. Let us discuss seven temptations of the devil, whereby he studies to interrupt a Christian in the exercise of these excellent duties.

The first temptation is vanity of thoughts; through this, the devil attempts to distract us from serious performance and spiritual exercise. He is a blessed Christian that has such command of his thoughts that he can go about these duties without wandering. A second temptation the devil uses to assault a Christian is to tempt him to go about his duties formally, and not to be serious. He will let us go about the form of a duty, but he hinders us from going about our duties in a spiritual way; if the devil has such victory over us as to hinder us from the spiritual performance of a duty, he will never hinder us from the carnal performance of it. The devil also tempts the Christian to unbelief. He tempts him to say, "I never gained anything by such a duty; God will never hear my prayers, and Christ will never condescend to feast with me." This is one of the devil's strong temptations by which he assaults a Christian in going about these duties. A fourth temptation of the devil is to tempt the Christian to presumption. This is the great design of the devil—when he cannot sail with one wind, he begins to sail another way. Once we seem to have obtained victory, then the devil studies to make us presumptuous. This exceedingly mars the spiritual performance of the Christian's duties.

A fifth temptation of the devil is to bring a Christian to pray in his own strength, to communicate in his own strength, to believe trusting in his own righteousness. It is Satan's great design to hold us in a covenant of works; this is the thing by which he conquers many. It is known that we pray much alone, we preach much alone, we hear much alone. By this we mean that we pray, but we do not pray much with Christ in our hearts, taking Him by the hand; we do not preach upon the strength of Christ, or hear upon the strength of Christ. He is a noble Christian that will not step one step without Christ or pray without Him. We read in Ecclesiastes 4:10, "For if they fall, the one will lift up his fellow: but woe to him that is alone when he falleth; for he hath not another to help him up."

A sixth time when the devil assaults a Christian, and most violently opposes him, is when the Christian is in a presumptuous frame. When did the devil desire to winnow Peter as wheat? It was when he cried out that though all men would forsake Christ, he would never forsake Him. You who walk neither with fear nor dependence, you who pray neither with fear nor dependence, you who read the Scriptures with neither fear nor dependence, you are near a fall. If the devil lets you alone, then you are presumptuous. You may suspect the devil and you are great together; for if there is enmity between yourself and the devil he will tempt. When you are presumptuous, he will assault you. When you claim, "I will never forsake thee," then you are in danger of being strongly assaulted. A seventh time when a Christian is assaulted by the devil is when he is experiencing anxious discouragements. A Christian sometimes has temptations when it is not fit for him to make them known. At these times, I think the devil will cast in some temptations of gross idolatry and atheism, so that a Christian would keep quiet and make them known to God. But oh, how much does the devil not only assault, but overcome a Christian, when under discouragements? What unbelief will such a case bring forth? What wronging of the majesty of God? What disputes of their interest? What spitting in His face will such a case bring forth?

Let us discuss our last point concerning the text. First, it is more difficult for a Christian to be mortified to the temptations of his own heart than to resist the temptations of the devil. The temptations in our hearts are not as easily resisted as the temptations that come from the devil. As for the differences between the heart temptations and the temptations of the devil, we shall speak of them in the following verse.

Secondly, notice that a Christian will never be serious in seeking the mortification of his idols until he is convicted how painful mortification is. When did Paul beseech the Lord three times? Was it not when his temptations were "a thorn in the flesh" (2 Cor. 12:7)?

Thirdly, there are some temptations of the devil that are more easily resisted than others. Some temptations are suitable to our predominant lusts; these are not so easily resisted. Likewise, there are some temptations to entertain invisible idols—these are not so easily resisted. Also, there are some temptations that are not much cross to our nature's light; these are not easily resisted. Some temptations have pleasure, advantage, and honor waiting upon them; these are not easily refuted. I shall tell you three great idols that a Christian has difficulty resisting.

First, Christians have difficulty resisting the idol of reputation among the saints, or the idol of reputation among the men of the world. This refers to the great Diana; most of our labor is spent adorning and sacrificing to the silver shrines of this idol. It is a great thing for a Christian to be denied the pride of life; hence, God often exercises the Christian with the trial of cruel mockings and reproaches. Second, a Christian has difficulty being mortified to his self-opinion. It is hard for him if the world speaks not well of him. Are there not some that lack the applause of the world, and yet they will sit down and commend themselves in the secrets of their own heart? It is as great a difficulty to be mortified to self-examination as it is to be mortified to the estimation of others. A third great idol that is difficult for a Christian to resist is the choice and excellent contentment of the world, abundance of riches, pleasure, and all manner of great delights. We read in Jeremiah 45:5, "Seekest thou great things for thyself? seek them not." There are many that seek an excellent and pleasant way of living. These are the three great Dianas, or idols, that many persons worship and adore.

Now we shall close our discourse at this time. When we look again at our text, we see that there are eight evidences that there is little real godliness and heart-religion among us. I charge you all, as you will one day answer to the Lord Jesus Christ, who is appointed to be the Judge of the living and of the dead, that you would search yourselves by these guidelines to see whether there be many of these evidences in your faith. To you who will not take notice of them, know that it is a poor thing to go to hell thinking that you are going to heaven. It is a poor thing to go to heaven with a lie in your right hand, while all the time you are here, you cry out, "I am in the gate of heaven!" Yet, you will be eternally thrust out.

The first evidence is that you do not work much at discerning the temptations of the devil when he assaults you and tempts you to commit iniquity. You do not take notice of them and say, "This is a temptation." This is known and certain: the devil tempts us without conviction, knowledge, or discerning; we do not so much as know that he is tempting us.

Second, an evidence that we have not much religion, if any at all, is that the temptations of the devil wherewith we are buffeted are not our burden. I would ask you who bear the name of Christians: when was it that a temptation of the devil, and Satan's assaulting, made you to water your couch with your tears? When did the devil's temptations make you walk in the bitterness of your spirit and cry out, "Woe is me"? The joys, contentments, and pleasure you take under temptations say that Christ is not in you.

A third evidence of the little true godliness and religion among us is that there are some that, since the day of their first engaging with Christ, and giving up their names to Him, could never say they mortified one temptation. Will you ask your conscience when the devil returned defeated from you? Was there ever a temptation presented to your cursed heart which you did not embrace? What does that speak? It shows a heart that is much estranged from God, if not totally estranged from Him. I would ask you, dear Christians, when did the ambassadors of peace between you and your lusts ever return weeping because you refused them? Can such a thing be consistent with godliness and real religion, that since our engagement with Christ, we never knew what it was to even endeavor to mortify one temptation? But let the devil assault us at a communion table, and there we yield unto his temptations. I suppose there are many places where we have been, upon which this may be engraven: "Here, at this place, I gave my consent to my idol, and I embraced a temptation." Let the devil assault us in the morning and he has our hearts; let him assault us in the evening and in the silent watches of the night, and are not our hearts ready to embrace him? Oh, where is the eminent wrestling that has been the exercise of the saints? We are estranged from that command, "Resist the devil, and he will flee from you" (James 4:7).

A fourth evidence of little true godliness is that the temptations we encounter do not put us to prayer. I would ask your consciences and search your hearts whether or not the temptations of the devil put you "to beseech the Lord thrice" that such an evil might depart from you? We take little pains for mortifying temptations. I suppose there are some who, though it were certified to them that for one prayer they should get such a corruption mortified, would not pray once; and this shows exceeding heart-estrangement from God.

Fifth, the kind entertainments and the soul-embraces that pass between us and our idols are evidence of a lack of godliness. We pray and our idols remain in our bosom; we communicate, and our idols are still in our heart; we hear preaching with idols in our heart. Nay, go where we will, we may be painted thus: "Behold such a one, and his idols in his heart." Can it be imagined that if the love of Christ were in your heart, you would entertain such soul-love to your idols and give Christ so little of your heart, and so much of your tongue, while your idols have not much of your tongue, but have much, if not all, of your heart?

A sixth evidence of little real godliness among us is that the absence of your idols and your love for your idols affects you more and makes you lament more than the love of the precious Christ could ever do. I ask you in the sight of God, as you shall answer to Christ in the great day: Is it not true that the loss of money has affected many more than the loss of eternal life? Once your idols are gone, however, you will cry out, "What have I more?"

A seventh evidence of little true religion is that you have more joy, more contentment, and more delight in the enjoyment of your idols than in the enjoyment of Christ. Search your consciences to see if this is true: There are some who have been more delighted with the addition of some thousands to their estate, or of some pleasure they had not before, than they ever were with the precious Christ and the things of the everlasting gospel. I fear that this may be engraven upon the foreheads of many: "They have forsaken Christ, and embraced a present world."

An eighth evidence of the lack of true godliness among us is that which has most of our thoughts. Does Christ have most of your thoughts? I may say without breach of charity that if all who are in this house had to answer that question, it is certain that it might be answered that there is not one among twenty of us that Christ has more of our thoughts than the devil has; what does this say? I will not say it means that they are estranged from God, but it does speak that many are distant from Christ, ignorant of the precious excellence of Christ, and totally estranged from the power of godliness. I know Christians, at many times, may have more of their hearts upon their idols than upon Christ. Does it not show a decay in godliness when that is true? Do not your idols have your thoughts when you are in prayer? Do not your idols and lusts control your thoughts at night? I suppose that many of us, if we were asked, "What were you just thinking about?" might answer, "I was thinking about my idol." Oh, the multitudes of vain thoughts that we have in our bosoms, that we do not give up our hearts to Christ! Do you not know that there is not one thought in heaven that is not taken up with Him; there is not one look in heaven that is not pitched on Him; there is not one desire in heaven that is not taken up with Him; there is not one moving of the foot in heaven that is not taken up in following Him; there is not one moving of the hand in heaven that is not taken up in enfolding Him!

The last evidence of the lack of true godliness among us is that we are not taking much delight in the exercise of those duties by which these temptations, wherewith we are assaulted, may be mortified. I would ask you three questions, and I desire you to examine your conscience with them.

First, when did you participate in prayer and faith? When did you go to prayer with faith? When was it that you dared to say, "I go to this duty with much soul-delight"?

Second, when was absence from Christ in the exercise of prayer your burden? I confess there are some Christians who, through the power of feeling secure in themselves, pray always alike; they go to prayer, yet with distance from Christ. They come away from prayer having their distance from Christ increased. Yea, that which is the capstone of our misery, we will come from prayer having bonds upon our love, having bonds upon our light, having bonds upon our heart and having bonds upon our consciences; yet, that is not our burden. We may say, as in Job 23:2, "My stroke is heavier than my groaning." I think that if the groaning of all that are here were suitable to their stroke, there would be a dreadful lamentation among us. We have learned but a damnable submission to these spiritual rods.

Third, I would ask you who never mourned for Christ's absence here, you who were never affected with His presence, who never lamented in secret because of your iniquities, can you cast up your eyes to heaven and think the day is approaching that you shall see Him, and shall stand without spot before Him?

I shall say no more, but it would be an excellent quality, and he is a choice Christian that could walk so with Christ. Such a Christian would be ready, upon the first summons, to appear before Christ and to render Him an account of his way. What if this were the hour, dear Christians, that the voice of the archangel should be heard, saying, "Behold, the bridegroom cometh; go ye out to meet him" (Matt. 25:6)? What would be your exercise? I doubt much if there would be many, if any at all within these doors, who would not cry, "Oh spare a little before I go hence and be no more." Shall Christ find faith in the earth when He comes? Shall He find us watching, or shall He find us sleeping? Shall He find us walking in His way, or whoring from Him? There have been many thousands of messengers of Satan that were never thorns in the flesh to you; you never attempted to wrestle against them. I think it would be a hard work for a Christian, even a Christian indeed, to tell the convictions he has drowned since first Christ and he engaged. It would be hard for a Christian to tell all the bonds and covenants he has broken with God since first Christ and he met; it would be hard for a Christian to tell all his formal prayers since first Christ and he met. I think if some of us get to heaven, all that are there may lay aside their harps; I think Manasseh, who was once among the great sinners, may lay aside his harp; I think persecuting Paul may lay aside his harp, and proud Hezekiah may lay aside his harp, and adulterous David may lay aside his harp, and idolatrous Solomon may lay aside his harp, and let us sing the praises of Him that is seated upon the throne. If we ever come to heaven, we will be convinced that there was never anyone so obliged to the grace of Christ as we are. If we ever get to heaven, we will sing that song: Not unto us, not unto us, but to Him that sitteth upon the throne, be the glory of our salvation. Amen.

SERMON 34

Singular Temptations Call for Fervent and Frequent Supplications (1)

For this thing I besought the Lord thrice,
that it might depart from me.
—2 Corinthians 12:8

Solomon, the master of experiences, remarked, "The highway of the upright is to depart from evil: he that keepeth his way preserveth his soul" (Prov. 16:17). This remark also serves as a lamentation, as the highway on which many of us walk, is the pursuit of our idols, attempting to overtake them. Oh, when shall that blessed time come in which Christ shall find us, who are as wild asses, accustomed to snuff up the wind at pleasure?

In the former verse, you heard that there are times in which Satan violently assaults a Christian. I confess, indeed, while the strong man keeps the house, all is at peace; and when a Christian first marches out from the kingdom of darkness to the kingdom of Jesus Christ, it may be said, "From henceforth thou shalt have wars" (2 Chron. 16:9). There are four great temptations by which Satan attempts to ensnare and catch a Christian.

First, there are temptations of personal advantage, when Satan says to the Christian, "Fall down and worship me, and I will give you all the kingdoms of the world." He lies to the Christian, saying, "Am I not able indeed to promote thee to honour?" (Num. 22:37). Believe it, when temptations come clothed in the robes of advantage and gain, they are extremely difficult to resist. Second, the devil also uses fear and danger in his temptations; he says to the Christian, "If you do not obey my commandments, and embrace my temptations, this will bring you to many sad disadvantages." His reason often says to us, "Pity yourselves." Third, the devil also tempts using pleasure. He clothes our temptations with garments of delight; he brings us low and makes us subject our consent to his will. Fourth, the devil also tempts using the pride of life; he says to the soul, as he spoke in the first temptation, "For God doth know that in the day ye eat thereof, then your eyes shall be opened, and ye shall be as gods, knowing good and evil" (Gen. 3:5). He makes us believe it would be the loss of a deity to disobey his commands. I have two comments to make about these temptations.

First, every time a messenger of Satan buffets you, you should go and beseech the Lord three times. We should pray without ceasing! Do we not encounter many temptations and assaults of the devil in our Christian walk? Yet we never go to God and cry out, "Master, save us, lest we perish!" I would also say to you that a blessed and excellent correspondence with heaven, a conversation within the streets of that city, a heart taken up with the joys of the higher house, would keep us from many snares and temptations. Know for certain that your heart will seek a temptation when temptation does not seek your heart. Do not suppose that if there were not a devil in hell, you would never be tempted to commit iniquity; but I would have you to know, your heart would be a devil, tempting you to sin, as though there were not a devil in hell.

Now, the words of our text are Paul's exercise under his former condition. Let us take notice of seven points concerning the words of our text. First, a Christian may have many spiritual advantages because of the temptations he meets with. This is clear in our text. Paul's suffering from the buffeting of the messenger of Satan brings him often to his knees and makes him a frequent supplicant at the house of grace.

Second, you may notice from the words of our text that prayer is a most noble and most excellent weapon by which a Christian may wrestle with his temptations. This is clear in the practice of Paul; when there is a messenger of Satan given to buffet him, he knows no other way but to acquaint heaven with his case and lift up his eyes to the everlasting mountains whence his salvation comes.

Third, we see in the text that there are some particular temptations and idols that a Christian should especially wrestle against and study to mortify. Paul shows this in 2 Corinthians 12:8: "For this thing I besought the Lord thrice, that it might depart from me."

There is an emphasis in the word *this*. It is as if Paul had said, "I would rather attempt to wrestle against other temptations than to wrestle this temptation."

Fourth, take notice in the text of the great difficulty a Christian has in mortifying a temptation or crucifying a lust. This is clear in Paul's beseeching the Lord thrice that the evil might depart from him. We do not conceive that Paul prayed only three times, but it implies that Paul was frequent and constant in the exercise of prayer, so that he might get his idol brought low, and tread upon the head of it, as upon the mire of the streets.

Fifth, in the text we see that a Christian may be most serious in wrestling against a temptation in prayer, yet have no sensible victory over the temptation. Paul, when first he began to pray, did not receive an answer. When he went to prayer again, he met not with a return. A Christian may wrestle like a prince, yet meet with a silent God who does not give him sensible returns.

You may further notice from our text that neither disappointment nor lack of sensible success in prayer should make him lay aside that duty. Paul, when he first went to prayer, and met with a disappointment, did not cry out, "This evil is of the Lord"; but the disappointment that he met with said to him, "Paul, go and pray again." Then, the second disappointment said, "Paul, go and pray again, more frequently than before."

Seventh, and last, the text shows us that a Christian should not only pray for restraining the acts of temptation and lusts of the soul, but he should pray for the rooting of it out from the heart. This is shown in Paul's words, "That it might depart from me," that it might be gone, and I might see it no more. Alas, Christ subscribes sometimes, if we may so speak, to a divorce between us and our idols, when we will not put to our hand and subscribe amen unto the divorcement.

Let us now discuss the spiritual advantage and gain that a Christian may reap by the devil's assaults. This is clear in Romans 8:28, as well as in 1 Corinthians 3:21-22. Concerning this point, I would first propose six spiritual advantages that a Christian may gain from the temptations of the devil, wherewith he is daily studying to take us.

First, this is a glass in which a Christian may read the freeness of the unsearchable love and grace of Christ; when you shall take a view of your own hearts, and see how much they are defiled, you may be constrained to cry out, "Oh, what a mystery, and what an everlasting wonder is it that Christ should fix His desires upon me." This is clear when Paul, taking a broad sight of the body of death that was in him, subjoins, "I thank God through Jesus Christ our Lord" (Rom. 7:24); as it were, Paul would not look to himself, but he was forced to begin and commend the freedom of the grace of Christ. Oh, but if a Christian could with one eye look to Christ, and with another eye look to himself, he would be constrained to sing, "He who is mighty has done great things for me! Holy and reverend is His name!" Likewise, it is clear from 1 Timothy 1:13-14 that Paul had a great view of Christ and of himself—of his feebleness, and of Christ's grace.

A second spiritual advantage that a Christian may have by his temptations is that temptation puts all the graces of the Spirit that are within to a lively exercise and frame; there is much choice exercise to a Christian's grace in his temptations. We allude to Revelation 13:10, where after meeting with many sore afflictions, John comments, "Here is the faith and patience of the saints." It is as if John would have said, "Here is a notable field where patience and faith may be exercised."

There is blessed harmony and excellent correspondence among these seven graces of the Spirit when wrestling against temptations and maintaining this noble sight; faith is the grace that goes up to the Captain of salvation and lays hold upon His strength; prayer is the grace that goes to Christ, and says to Him, "Pity me, pity me, lest I fall and become a prey." Watchfulness is the grace that stands upon the watchtower, takes heed to the motions of the devil, and gives a Christian warning. Humility is a grace that makes a Christian deny his own strength and trust in the strength of Jehovah, who is the rock of ages; yea, when faith begins to languish, when prayer begins to grow faint, when humility is waxing pale, then hope comes in and says, "Oh my soul…hope in God: for I shall yet praise him" (Ps. 43:5). Hope, as it were, comes in to the wrestling Christian with a crown in his right hand, crying out, "To him that overcometh will I grant to sit with me in my throne" (Rev. 3:21). Likewise, love is a grace that makes a Christian willingly condescend to all the pains that are in his spiritual warfare; and finally, tenderness is a grace that is engaged in this war, so that a Christian is loathe to put forth his hand to iniquity, or to touch or take the forbidden fruit.

All these graces are sweetly engaged in this spiritual warfare. Oh, what a sweet working one to another's hand! When faith begins to decay, prayer comes in and helps faith; when prayer begins to faint and give over, so that it cries out, "Why should I pray any more, He doth not hear me," then faith comes and helps prayer, saying, "I know the thoughts of His heart are 'thoughts of peace, and not of evil, to give you an expected end'" (Jer. 29:11). Yes, we conceive that experience is a grace much engaged in the fight; for when all graces are, in a manner, laid aside in the fight, experience will come in and say to the soul, "I did formerly find Him; in the mount He was seen, and in the mount He shall be seen again." Experience cries out the words of Paul in 2 Corinthians 1:10: "Who delivered us from so great a death, and doth deliver: in whom we trust that he will yet deliver us." The words in 1 Samuel 17:37 are also the words of experience: "David said moreover, The LORD that delivered me out of the paw of the lion, and out of the paw of the bear, he will deliver me out of the hand of this Philistine."

A third spiritual advantage that a Christian may have through his temptations is to make the Christian exceeding humble. This is clear in the former verse, when the messenger of Satan was given to buffet lest he should be exalted above measure. Likewise, we read in 2 Corinthians 1:8-9 that Paul's sore temptations bore the precious fruits of diffidence and humility. In Deuteronomy 8:15, Moses encourages the people to humble themselves when they think of the protection of God through their temptations: "Who led thee through that great and terrible wilderness, wherein were fiery serpents, and scorpions, and drought, where there was no water; who brought thee forth water out of the rock of flint" (Deut. 8:15). There are temptations that assault a Christian so that he may be kept humble. There are many assaults of the devil that eventually cause a Christian to cry out, "I am 'less than the least of all saints' (Eph. 3:8), and the chief of sinners!"

A fourth spiritual advantage that a Christian may have by his temptations is that he may see from them the conquering power of the grace of God and the infinite virtue that is in that grace. The Christian may see that God's grace can maintain itself in the midst of these assaults of the devil; furthermore, a Christian may have temptations in order that they may be a door, at which new experiences of the love of Christ may enter in. This is clear when Paul says, "Most gladly therefore will I rather glory in my infirmities, that the power of Christ may rest upon me" (2 Cor. 12:9). These are many sweet, soul-refreshing experiences of the power and conquering virtue of the grace of Christ, which, if a Christian is not put to war, he will not know or understand.

Fifth, a Christian's temptations put him eminently to the exercise of prayer; believe it, a Christian never improves his temptations so rightly as to make them an errand with which he goes to Christ. In this respect, a Christian may glory in his sinful infirmities in so far as it puts him into a necessity of going to Christ. I think, in a manner, Christ chains us to the foot of His throne by a chain of necessity rather than a chain of love. Necessity is that which makes a Christian to be often at the throne, when love will not make him do so.

A sixth spiritual advantage that a Christian has from the devil's temptations is that he may be constrained to breathe after the day when he shall be assaulted no more, when he shall be tempted no more. It is a divine improvement of our temptations when they cry out, "O wretched man that I am! who shall deliver me from the body of this death?" (Rom. 7:24). When a Christian in the midst of his spiritual temptations sits down and looks out the window of his prison-house, he cries out, "When shall the day of my redemption come? When shall the day come that I shall be exalted above the reach of sin and temptation to sin?"

Next, we shall propose four considerations.

First, a Christian should not be discouraged or exceedingly anxious under the violent and frequent assaults of the devil. There may be much gain by such a dispensation, when the devil is assaulting a Christian most vehemently and most frequently. "Out of the eater came forth meat, and out of the strong came forth sweetness" (Judg. 14:14). I confess, to be tempted is not good, but the end of that dispensation may be love. Christ has an excellent art in bringing our advantage out of these things that seem to be to our great disadvantage. A Christian under temptations should not cry out, "I shall one day fall by the hand of one of my iniquities!" A Christian under temptations should not cry out, "This evil is of the LORD; what should I wait for the LORD any longer?" (2 Kings 6:33). A Christian under his temptations should not cry out, "Who can stand before the children of Anak?" (Deut. 9:2). Let a Christian look to Christ and comfort himself with His strength in the midst of his wars.

Second, let us consider that a Christian should not judge his mortification by the violence and frequency of his temptations. Sometimes idols may greatly lose their power when the devil is assaulting a Christian most vehemently and most frequently. In the history of the gospel, when the devil was going out of the young man, before he came out, he tore him and cast him down as one that was dead. The devil was near taking his farewell; therefore, he desired to leave his last testimony, a final experience of his hatred. So that this may not be mistaken, I propose these eight evidences by which Christians may know whether or not the predominant idol that is in them is decaying, waxing to its grave, and drawing near its fatal period. I would charge you that are here to examine yourselves by these evidences.

The first evidence that an idol is decaying is that it has less of a Christian's heart than it had before. Then, a Christian does not have such fond affections for his idols, as he had before. This is one evidence that an idol is drawing near its grave. It is a sad evidence that our idol is growing when our hearts are increasingly following after it; it is a sad evidence that our idol is growing when, though our way be hedged up with thorns, yet we will pursue after our lovers to overtake them.

The second evidence by which you may know if the strength of your idols is decaying is to ask, do your idols have more of your thoughts than before? There can be a time when an idol sits upon the throne of our heart, that we give it our thoughts in the morning, we give it our thoughts at night in prayer, and out of prayer; that is an evidence that our idol is still strong. But, if our thoughts are not frequently upon the idol, it is an evidence that the idol is decaying in our estimation. But alas! It may be written upon our foreheads that the imaginations of the thoughts of our hearts are only given to our idols. Is it not known that our idols have more of our thoughts than precious Christ has? Is it not known that our idols have more of our thoughts in the morning than precious Christ has? If we may so speak, when we wake, we are still with our idols; in a manner, when our eyes begin to wake in the morning, we may see our idols lying between our breasts.

The third evidence that an idol is decaying is that an idol disturbs the Christian less in the fervent and spiritual way of going about duty. This is taken for a token of good, that the idol is near his grave; for instance, if an idol is still strong, a Christian can hardly speak to God without the idol first speaking to him. It will distract him from the serious exercise of prayer. His idol will let him speak to Christ with his tongue, but it will have the heart of the person speaking. If, when you go to prayer, you are wrestling as a prince with God, and your idol does not so much disturb you or obtain victory over you, it is an excellent evidence that your idol is dying and groaning within you. However, if, as we read in Ezekiel 33:31, your "heart goeth after…covetousness" in duties and it may be said of you, "Yea, in my house have I found their wickedness" (Jer. 23:11), then this shows that your idol is still reigning within you. Is it not known that sometimes in our addresses to God, we speak and converse with our idols? It is certain that when we will be in the acts of immediate worship, we will be conversing with and thinking upon them.

Fourth, if the grace that stands in opposition to the idol is growing, we know that an idol is decaying. If, for instance, pride is a Christian's predominant idol, we may know that this idol is waxing old if humility is growing; for as the grace increases, the idol decreases. If we would more often notice this, we would clear many mistakes concerning mortification. Sometimes you take the silence of your lusts for mortification; when a Christian's lusts are silent and do not assault, you think that those lusts are mortified. When a lust is restrained and is not crucified, you claim that you have mortified your lusts. However, you must test whether the silence of your lusts is actually mortification using this test: an idol is dying if the grace that stands in direct opposition to that lust is growing. Suspect the silence of your idols; if the contrary grace be not waxing strong, the idol is not dead, but only sleeps.

A fifth evidence that an idol is dying is if the Christian is serious in debating with the idol. It is an evidence that the idol is falling down if we are much engaged in a spiritual fight and warfare against the idol. If we pursue it in the morning, pursue it all along the day, and pursue it at night, perhaps the idol is dying. What, dear Christians, is the reason you have so little sensible victory over your idols? You continually interrupt spiritual warfare. A Christian will fight with his idols in the morning, and before night, he will take them in his arms. We are as unsteadfast as water, which does exceedingly interrupt our victory.

An idol is dying and waxing old within you if the objects that formerly used to tempt you and to make your lusts break forth into a flame are presented unto you, and yet your lusts do not take fire. That is an evidence your idol is waxing old and is ready to die. If it is dying, the same temptations do not have victory over you as they formerly did. I think an inclination to sin and a suitable temptation are two bad things to meet together; when we have a heart to embrace a temptation offering occasion to us, when the temptation cries, "Come!" and our heart cries, "Come!" it is a sad evidence we are near a fall.

Seventh, if a Christian's temptations are not so prevalent as they were before, one would know that the idol is dying. We believe that a Christian will sometimes know how to distinguish a strong temptation from a weak temptation. The devil will carry all before him, saying, "Bow down your necks, that I may go over them," when he, with our consent, puts his chain around our necks.

The last evidence that an idol is decaying and waxing old within us is that we endeavor to flee the occasions of that sin, and all appearances to act out that iniquity. Job 3:16 makes clear that this is a noble evidence that the idol is upon the decaying hand: if there is an appearance of committing the sin, you would flee from it as from death; as it were, you would say of every appearance of sin, as the young prophet said, "There is death in the pot" (2 Kings 4:40). So you may say, there is death in such an appearance of sin.

A third consideration that we propose from the text is that a Christian, when he goes out to wrestle against his temptations, would go out being clothed with humility. Do you know the best armor for a Christian who is going to fight? It is self-denial and humility. What is the best armor that a Christian can put on? It is to be weak; for when a Christian is weak, then is he strong; and when a Christian is diffident in himself, then is it that he receives most divine discoveries of the power and hand of Christ. It is a noble command, "Likewise, ye younger, submit yourselves unto the elder. Yea, all of you be subject one to another, and be clothed with humility: for God resisteth the proud, and giveth grace to the humble"

(1 Peter 5:5); also, "Above all, taking the shield of faith, wherewith ye shall be able to quench all the fiery darts of the wicked" (Eph. 6:16).

Fourth, a Christian, when he is assaulted by temptations, desires to mortify temptations in the bud, when they first come to him. We conceive that it is sinful for one to pity his lusts and to spare the king of his idols, so that it may cry out, "The bitterness of death is past" (1 Sam. 15:32). We should do with them as Pharaoh did with the Israelitish children.

Next, let us consider that prayer is a noble and excellent weapon by which a Christian wrestles with his temptations. We conceive that it is clear that prayer is an excellent weapon for a Christian, for these reasons.

First, among all the pieces of a Christian's armor, prayer is placed last as the most binding and most excellent piece of the armor. "Praying," says he, "always, with all prayer and supplication in the Spirit" (Eph. 6:18). In that verse, a Christian may know that he should pray with all manner of prayer; that is, he should pray both in private and in public; yes, it is required in that verse that Christians should seek occasions to pray, especially when, in their own apprehensions, they have none.

Secondly, prayer is an excellent piece of armor to resist temptations. Christians in former times, when they were assaulted most by the devil, went to this piece of armor. Paul makes clear in our text that this is his practice. We also read in 1 Chronicles 4:10 that "Jabez called on the God of Israel, saying, Oh that thou wouldest bless me indeed, and enlarge my coast, and that thine hand might be with me, and that thou wouldest keep me from evil, that it may not grieve me! And God granted him that which he requested." Prayer, in a manner, is a flying cherub, to take our unspeakable necessities to the infinite fullness that is in Christ; prayer is that which goes to Christ and draws strength from Him for the mortifying of lusts.

Thirdly, prayer is an excellent piece of spiritual armor. Christ, when He would resist the temptations of the devil, and have his assaults quenched, makes use of this spiritual weapon in Luke 22:31-32: "Satan hath desired to have you, that he may sift you as wheat: but I have prayed for thee, that thy faith fail not: and when thou art converted, strengthen thy brethren." No doubt, Christ left that as a pattern for us to follow, so that we may walk in the same steps that He walked.

Before closing, I desire to speak concerning two things.

First, let us clarify what influence prayer has upon mortifying temptations and crucifying our idols. We shall examine this point in six areas.

First, prayer is the grace and duty in which a Christian meets with divine discoveries of Christ. Prayer makes him cast out his idols and forsake his iniquity. Prayer is a grace by which a Christian receives a broad sight of the matchless beauty that is in Christ; that makes the soul cry out, "What have I to do any more with idols?" (Hos. 14:8).

Second, its influence may be known in the fact that prayer is the duty in which there is much spiritual strength conveyed to the soul for wrestling with temptations. Do you desire to know what prayer is? It is a divine channel in which the stream of strength, joy, and life flow from the precious fountain that is above unto a Christian. Is it not known that prayer is the duty in which a Christian has received so much strength so as to make him cry out, "God is on my side, Christ is at my right hand, I will not fear what temptations can do unto me"?

Third, we clearly see that prayer is the duty and the grace by which a Christian receives lively discoveries of his temptations and of the subtlety of his temptations. If a Christian who is under the strength of his temptations, goes to God by prayer, and receives no more but a clear understanding of the subtlety of the devil, it is a noble advantage. It is an excellent art for a Christian to be advanced in the knowledge of the subtle devices of the devil.

Fourth, prayer's influence upon mortification may be known because it is the grace that keeps all graces in use. It is the grace by which we must mortify our temptations. Prayer is the grace that keeps faith in life, and faith is the captain of graces of this spiritual fight. Prayer is the grace that keeps hope, love, and experience in life. A notable piece of prayer's help is to keep in vigorous exercise all these graces by which we must wrestle with temptations.

Fifth, prayer is the grace that makes the Christian diffident of himself. This is a noble piece of humility. The Christian is near the victory when he is persuaded to sing, "Without Christ, I can do nothing." I think a Christian is near the spiritual victory over his lusts when he comes to cry out, "I am not able, by myself, to strike one stroke in this spiritual warfare; but thanks be to Him, through whom

I can do all things." As it were, a Christian will look to himself and write upon his forehead, "Here is one that can do nothing"; and he will look to Christ and say, "There is one that can do all things."

Finally, prayer is the duty and grace that makes a Christian to see the sinfulness of his idols and the reward of embracing his idols. Who is the Christian that lives under the impressions of the sinfulness of his idols? It is the praying Christian. Who is the Christian that subscribes the truth of that saying, "The wages of sin is death" (Rom. 6:23)? It is the praying Christian; it is the wrestling Christian. It is hard for a Christian who does not pray much to have any victory over his idols!

We shall briefly discuss some considerations before closing up the discourse.

First, a Christian may pray for the mortification of his lusts, yet not pray for the mortification of his idols. A Christian may go to God and seek that such a lust may be mortified; yet he does not pray that the idol of that lust may be mortified. For example, a covetous person may pray that the lust of covetousness may be mortified, yet he may desire to keep riches, which is the idol. We can see that he who has pride for his idol may pray that the lust of pride may be mortified; yet, he cannot be crucified to the applause of the world and the commendations of all who are around him. A Christian may have something in his idol that may move him to pray for the mortifying of it, yet he may see something in his idol that may make him to hold it fast with both his hands.

Second, a Christian may pray more for the restraint of his idol than for the mortifying of sinful idols. Is it not certain that you pray more for restraining the acts of sin than for mortifying the idol of sin? Though I may say, you shall never have much advantage by praying for the restraint of sin, until you go down to its root, and pray for the mortifying of the idol of sin.

Third, an idol may be mortified to a Christian when a Christian is not mortified to his idol; for instance, these gourds under which we sit may wither above our heads, yet our living lusts may go and lament over the grave of our buried idols. There is a difference between a mortified idol and a living lust; God may draw back our idols from us, and yet our living lust may go over it. Furthermore, a covetous person may lose his riches, which were his idol; yet if we look to the breast of the covetous man and to his living lusts, they are crying, "Ye have taken away my gods which I made, and the priest, and ye are gone away: and what have I more?" (Judg. 18:24). I will tell you how you forsake your idols, even as Phaltiel was forsaken by Michal; he went after her weeping when his idol was taken away. When your idols are taken away, you cry out, "O idol, return, return, for what shall I do, if you go away?"

A fourth consideration we would propose is that there is a great contradiction in a Christian who is mortifying temptations and crucifying his idols. There is a fivefold contradiction in a Christian in accomplishing this work.

First, we will sometimes cry out, "Oh, crucify such a lust!"; yet our hearts, at the same time, will cry out, "Oh, do not crucify such a lust!" Our heads may speak one thing, and our hearts another. Second, one part of our hearts may cry out, "Oh, spare such an idol, and let it change the bitterness of death," and the other part of our hearts may cry, "Crucify this idol." There may be a division in our hearts about crucifying an idol.

A third woeful contradiction in a Christian mortifying his idols is that a Christian may cry out in the morning, "Oh, to be rid of such a lust," and yet, before night he may change his opinion and say, "Oh, I will not quit such a lust, but hold it between my breasts, until I be no more." A fourth contradiction in a Christian is that there may be a contradiction between a Christian's petitions and a Christian's practice. When we go to God, we have not a word so often as this: mortify our idols, crucify our idols; yet, in our practice, we contradict our prayers—we never desire to quit with that which we hold. Fifth, there is a contradiction between a Christian's vows and resolutions, and his performance. Sometimes a Christian at a communion table has said, "I shall forsake this idol, and never take it up again"; yet no sooner than he has gone out of the house of God, when the vows of God have been upon him, he has taken the idol in his arms. Is there not a great contradiction and difference between a Christian's vows and his performances? How many vows have we broken to the precious Christ? What if He should break His one covenant with us, and say, "I will call you no more sons, and ye shall call me no more Father." What would you do?

Let us also consider the following point; wrestling against temptations and crucifying our idols shall afford to a Christian in the day when death shall be looking him in the face, exceeding joy and spiritual consolation. When Paul is near his death, he casts back his eyes and reads the history of his spiritual warfare and all his fights; when he reflects upon all the debates between himself and his idols and corruptions, he breaks forth with these words: "I have fought a good fight, I have finished my course, I have kept the faith" (2 Tim. 4:7). He cannot speak of that fight, but he must commend it. Do you desire to have my testimony of it? It is good, oh, it is good to fight with your corruptions and your idols. The day is coming when there shall be a cessation of arms, but it shall be matter of conviction to you. Do you desire to pass with comfort and consolation through the gates of death? Oh, fight, Christians, fight, fight! The day is coming when you shall triumph, and die fighting. Oh, they are blessed who have now ended this warfare and have entered into the possession of eternity!

A sixth consideration that I shall propose is that the prayers of a Christian, when he is violently assaulted of the devil, are prayers that are ordinarily suddenly heard, and have speedy return; the fervent prayers of a Christian, when violently assaulted, have most speedy returns from God. This is clear, as we read in 1 Chronicles 4:10, when Jabez cried unto God, "And God granted him that which he requested." It is also clear in the words of our text that Paul no sooner besought the Lord three times, but he receives the Lord's answer: "My grace is sufficient for thee" (2 Cor. 12:9). Christ loves to give His own strength in the day of need, to make them to endure their temptations; but let a Christian always ask the question that Nehemiah asked on another occasion: "Should such a man as I flee?" Should such a person as I flee when my temptations assault me? Should the person that is bound so much to Christ flee when the devil tempts? I would say to you, if you faint in the day of tribulation, you prove your strength to be but small; a Christian's yielding to his temptations says, "His grace is not very strong."

Last, let us consider that the devil desires to overcome a Christian; yet, it is above his power and strength, for he has greater desires than he has ability. This is clear from Luke 22:31, "Simon, Simon, behold, Satan hath desired to have you, that he may sift you as wheat." It is not said, "He was able to sift him as wheat"; thus, Satan's desires and power are not commensurable, and are of a little extent, compared to the desire and power of Christ.

Now I shall conclude this discourse by giving three applications. First, a person who never knows what it is to wrestle with his temptations shall never know what it is to triumph and to have the sweet trophies of victory. Do you think you will reign if you do not fight? Second, is it not a sad and lamentable evidence that you are not acquainted with Christ, that you never had a temptation assault you that did not overcome you? You never knew what it was to make your temptations depart and to sing a song of triumph over them. Third, dear Christian, who is even now debating with your idols, you who are beseeching the Lord thrice that this might depart from you, the day is coming when you shall bless Him thrice, and eternally set forth His praises. The day is coming when He shall deliver you from all your enemies and make you overcome. Oh, what a day shall it be when you shall sing that triumphant song, "O death, where is thy sting? O grave, where is thy victory?" (1 Cor. 15:55). Amen.

SERMON 35

Singular Temptations Call for Fervent and Frequent Supplications (2)

For this thing I besought the Lord thrice,
that it might depart from me.
—2 Corinthians 12:8

It is an unchangeable and unalterable decree of heaven that cannot be repealed, that there should be enmity between the seed of the woman and the serpent; it is unchangeable that he should bruise their heel, and that they should bruise his head. However, Christian, be comforted, knowing that in the midst of this blessed warfare, it shall be not long before the waters of Jordan shall be divided and the ransomed of the Lord shall pass through. They shall set up twelve stones of the everlasting remembrance of their precious deliverance. The day is approaching when the fighting Christian shall sing the triumphant song, "Not unto us, O LORD, not unto us, but unto thy name give glory" (Ps. 115:1). God receives all the glory of the Christian's victory. Then a Christian shall seal the truth that "safety is of the Lord" (Prov. 21:31). It would be a pleasant and excellent thing for a Christian to read the history of the wars of the sons of God against their spiritual enemies. What strange vicissitudes are in this blessed war of the saints! A Christian is overcoming today, yet is defeated the next day. What strong subtleties vent themselves in this war! Satan plots a snare for the foot of a Christian, but a Christian, through the wisdom and power of Christ, escapes as a bird out of the snare of the fowler. What strange changes of joy are in this war! A Christian rejoices today in the hope of victory, then he mourns tomorrow in fear that he may lose the field. What a strange change of love is in this war! A Christian is persecuting his idols today, and he will be embracing them tomorrow. What a strange change of faith is in this war! A Christian will cry out today, "Once I shall be more than a conqueror through Christ that loved me!" Yet he will cry out tomorrow, "I fear that one day I shall fall by the hand of one of my iniquities." What a strange change of strength is in this war! A Christian is strong today, and he is weak tomorrow. Let us discuss two points concerning the text.

First, I suppose there are some that may dispute whether the temptations of the devil or the victories of the devil are of greatest number. There are some who never knew what it was to be assaulted without being overcome. Are there not some here who fall to sin every time they are tempted? I conceive it would be an endless and a most lamentable task for some of us to declare all these victories that the devil has obtained over us; there are many trophies of his victories that both we and he possess.

Secondly, the devil is a most unrelenting assaulter of a Christian. He will assault a Christian when he is out of duty, before duty, in duty, and after duty. He will assault a Christian under enjoyments and under desertion; he will assault a Christian under sad dispensations and under prosperity. Know this as well: a Christian may know well how to resist one temptation of the devil, yet when the devil changes his temptations, he will not know how to resist them. A Christian will be helped to resist the devil when he fights upon the right hand; but once the devil begins to fight on the left hand, it will be difficult to wrestle against him. To make this point clear, there are some Christians that will fight against the devil when he tempts them to pride, yet they do not know how to fight against him when he tempts them to covetousness. The devil often takes advantage of the change of a Christian's exercise and the change of a Christian's temptations. I would say to a wrestling Christian that after he has obtained some victory over the devil, he should not sit down, but stand; the enemy will not leave you quickly. We see a most remarkable word in Scripture concerning this point; after Satan had so strongly assaulted Christ, after he had ended all his temptations, we read that "he departed from him for a season" (Luke 4:13). Thus, it was only for a little time, and then he was minded to come again. There may be a cessation of arms for a time, but that is the great design of the enemy, so that he may assault you most strongly.

Now, at the last occasion that we spoke upon this verse, we told you that there were seven things in it upon which we intended to pitch our discourse. We have spoken of the first, which was the spiritual advantage and excellent gain attending the Christian in his temptations; such temptations drove Paul to his knees to beseech the Lord *thrice*.

We also spoke concerning prayer. We said that prayer is one of the most noble and excellent pieces of a Christian's armor, by which he ought to wrestle and withstand all the fiery darts of the devil. When a Christian is assaulted, Christ takes the Christian into His arms and desires to receive the first dint of temptation before it reaches him.

We will now discuss the third point of the text. There are some assaults against which you must especially endeavor to wrestle. This is clear in the words of our text: "For this thing"; there is an emphasis in the words "this thing." It is as if Paul had said, "I would not be so serious about *another* temptation, but about *this* temptation I must endeavor to be serious and wrestle with all my strength." Further, let me mention a few points in discoursing upon this subject.

First, there are some temptations of the devil that a Christian should especially endeavor to mortify and resist.

A Christian should endeavor to resist the temptations of the devil that take place immediately after conversion. This was Paul's practice; for we told you that he met with this temptation immediately after his conversion. I shall not say much to press this point; I shall only propose three grounds to enforce it.

First, it is extremely commended by God to resist temptations immediately after conversion. This is clear in Hebrews 10:32, where we read, "After ye were illuminated, ye endured a great fight of afflictions." You know that it is an ordinary practice among men of war that the soldiers who fight strongly in the first encounter with an enemy should be much commended; so Christ, the Captain of our salvation, exceedingly approves when we resist our first encounter with our spiritual enemies.

A second commendation is that resisting and mortifying temptations immediately after conversion affords a Christian much hope. It affords a Christian much joy, inward peace, and consolation. I am confident that the first victory of a Christian after his engagement with Christ, if it be observed, will make him to cry out, "What a pleasant thing is it to fight with Christ, and to fight for Him." Alas, a Christian often does not observe his victories, which makes him lack many excellent songs.

Third, failing to resist temptations of the devil immediately after conversion may make a Christian go halting to heaven. A victory obtained by the devil immediately after conversion may make a fool go to heaven with sackcloth, weeping all along the way; yea, I suppose the victories obtained by the devil after conversion are a most discouraging stroke. They make a Christian cry out, "Let us make a captain, and let us return into Egypt" (Num. 14:4). It is sad for a Christian to have his blood drawn upon the border of the kingdom of grace.

It is also extremely commended by God that a Christian should resist the temptations that come immediately after enjoyments. This was Paul's practice in this place; he did, no doubt, strongly endeavor to wrestle against this temptation, because it came shortly after his enjoyment. I shall not say much to enforce this duty, as I have spoken about it at several times. I have only two points to share with you.

First, resisting temptations after enjoyments is the way to make Christ rest in His love, and to continue rejoicing over you with singing, if we may so speak. Do you know which cords keep Christ united to the soul under enjoyments? This cord is made of wrestling against temptations when it has met with Christ.

Secondly, the most remarkable and successful victories that a Christian obtains over Satan and his idols is when he wrestles against them after enjoyments. That is the time when the strong corruptions of our heart fall as lightning, and we tread upon the high places of the earth. You know it is ordinary for a Christian to fall asleep in the bed of love; it is ordinary for a Christian to exalt himself when Christ exalts him; it is ordinary that when a Christian is enlarged, the wind of the wilderness binds him up in her wings until all his substance is dissolved.

Thirdly, a Christian would especially wrestle against the temptations that do provoke and kindle his predominant lusts and idols. A Christian's idol may take fire at certain temptations a Christian encounters, that kindle his lust. These are the temptations a Christian should especially battle. This was the practice of David, as we see in Psalm 18:23: "I kept myself from mine iniquity." David is saying that he has endeavored by all means to have the predominant lust within him mortified and brought low. Be assured that the defendant of one idol will never be brought low so long as the idol has much strength.

Fourthly, a Christian should especially wrestle against those temptations that he meets with under afflicting dispensations. This was also the advice of Solomon in Ecclesiastes 7:14: "In the day of affliction consider." Under this advice and command, we conceive, is included a wrestling against all temptations that do then assault us; it also imports there is much advice and spiritual deliberation to be used by a Christian under such a case. I shall give you two reasons why a Christian should especially wrestle with temptations under afflictions.

First, the love of a Christian is often at a stand when he is under affliction. When Christ begins to dispense better things unto us, then we lose much of the spiritual affection we once had to Him; we conceive it is a great difficulty for a Christian to resist temptations when the love of Christ is not constraining him. Second, we should resist temptations under afflicting dispensations because if the Christian shall embrace his temptations when he is brought to such a case, it is both the way to make such an affliction bitter to him, and the way to lengthen the thread of his calamity and sad dispensation. Withal, embracing temptations under such a case is the way to obstruct the blessed correspondence and familiarity that Christ uses to entertain His own when they are under the night of afflictions.

Fifthly, a Christian should especially wrestle against the temptations that assault his faith and his love. These are the two cardinal graces; these are the two pillars of a Christian's consolation; however, these are the two great targets of Satan's arrows. There is something of this pointed out in Luke 22:31, where we read, "Simon, Simon, behold, Satan hath desired to have you, that he may sift you as wheat." Here, we conceive that there are two things pointed out to us.

1. The object that the devil mainly pointed at in Peter was his faith; he was endeavoring to have that excellent sort of a Christian laid in a heap.

2. The second thing pointed out to us in Christ's practice in studying to disappoint the devil, is that when Satan comes to strangle our faith and to shake our love, then we

should stand much in opposition against him. It is certain that once Satan has gained your faith and has defeated your love, there is no difficulty in the rest of the war; he will have the advantage.

Sixthly, a Christian should strive to wrestle against the temptations that assault him when he is going about duties that are of much soul-concern, such as communion. The temptations wherewith we are assaulted at communion are the temptations a Christian should especially endeavor to fight. I shall name only three temptations with which the devil often assaults a Christian at such an occasion.

The first temptation of the devil with which he assaults a Christian at this time is to have his thoughts taken off the thing he is going about; once he can make us to think upon things not fitting, he has gained much of his point. Believe it, vanity of thoughts at all times is sinful, but at that time they are most sinful and also most hurtful.

Another temptation with which he assaults a Christian at this time is that he tempts the believer to diffidence and unbelief. When he accomplishes this he has gained a greater length than that which he had gained before; for once a Christian begins to dispute the love of Christ at communion, once a Christian begins to dispute his interest at a communion, it is sure to be a tasteless and heartless ordinance unto him. Do you desire to know the messenger that the soul sends forth to embrace Christ in that ordinance? It is faith; and faith feeds upon Christ as though He were seen.

A third temptation with which Satan assaults a Christian at that ordinance is that he puts him sometimes to debate and question the nature, end, and use of the sacrament, which is not fitting for the time. I suppose there are some, who, if they would consult with their own heart, would know this to have been their temptation when they have been sitting at the table of the Lord. They have begun to debate how one eats the body of Christ when he eats this bread, and how one drinks the blood of Christ when he drinks of this cup; one may further ponder, "How can I know if there be a real advantage by going about this ordinance?" I would only say that when Satan puts you to such debates as these, you may say to him what Hushai spoke to Absalom concerning the counsel of Ahithophel: Your counsel is "not good at this time" (2 Sam. 17:7). It is much to feast with Christ and have our hearts with Him. I confess that it is sad to feast with a veiled Christ, to sit down at table and eat with an absent Christ. It is a sad dispensation for one to sit down to feast, while the Master of the feast is away.

Now I would like to propose some encouragements that may provoke you to be serious in this blessed war. I wish to provoke you to wrestle against all the temptations of the devil that you encounter.

The first encouragement is that omnipotence is upon your side. Stronger is he that is in you than he that is in the world; therefore, you may be comforted, for though the blast of the terrible one be as a storm against the wall, yet Christ stands upon your side. This is clear, "That ye may know what is the hope of his calling, and what the riches of the glory of his inheritance in the saints, and what is the exceeding greatness of his power to us-ward who believe, according to the working of his mighty power, which he wrought in Christ, when he raised him from the dead, and set him at his own right hand in the heavenly places" (Eph. 1:18-20). It is also clear that His are those "who are kept by the power of God through faith unto salvation" (1 Peter 1:5); the word there rendered *kept* imports such a keeping as in a garrison or in a guard. Omnipotence is upon the Christian's side by the experience of the saints, who in their wrestling with the devil, have been constrained to cry out, "It was some higher hand that helped me to overcome, not my own strength." We notice this especially in Genesis 49:23-24, speaking of Joseph, "The archers have sorely grieved him, and shot at him, and hated him; but his bow abode in strength"; how was that? "And the arms of his hands were made strong by the hands of the mighty God of Jacob." This may comfort a Christian in all his debates with the devil: underneath him are the everlasting arms, and the eternal God is his refuge. There is a fivefold tie and obligation, if we may so speak, upon the power and omnipotence of God, to be forthcoming to a Christian in all his debates and wrestling.

First, love puts a tie upon the omnipotence of God to be forthcoming to a Christian. If a Christian has Christ's heart, he shall also have His hands; if a Christian be beloved of Christ, He will, no doubt, give him the precious outpouring of His power to help him overcome the strong enemies that meet him in his way. Love and compassion in Christ make Him give His hands to us when we are straitened. Love in Christ makes Him strengthen us with all might in the inward man, so that we may be helped to resist the fiery darts of the devil.

Second, these precious interests between Christ and a believer engage His power and lay a tie upon His omnipotence. If Christ be the believer's husband, will He not dispense strength to him in the day of straits? If Christ be a believer's brother, will He not help in the day of adversity? He was born for that very thing; our elder brother Jesus was born for adversity. If Christ be the believer's captain, will He not help him with strength in the day of war? When he is in the encounter with his spiritual enemies, every knot of union between Christ and a believer lays an engagement upon the power of God to be forthcoming to him in all his straits.

Third, the covenant and faithfulness of God lays a tie upon His power and omnipotence to be forthcoming to us in our straits. Is this not the precious promise of the covenant of grace, that when we are without strength, He would communicate strength to us? In Isaiah 40:29, we read, "He giveth power to the faint; and to them that have no might he increaseth strength." Is it not promised, "When thou passest through the waters, I will be with thee; and through the rivers, they shall not overflow thee: when thou walkest through the fire, thou shalt not be burned; neither shall the flame kindle upon thee" (Isa. 43:2)? That is, in all your difficulties, He will always be at your right hand.

Fourth, the necessities of Christians lay a tie upon His omnipotence, to be forthcoming to us in our straits. In Isaiah 59:16, we read, "And he saw that there was no man, and wondered that there was no intercessor." There is a blessed *therefore* that follows: "Therefore his arm brought salvation unto him; and his righteousness, it sustained him." It is as if He would have said, "If I can have no other argument to engage My power and right arm to you, I will take an argument from your necessities."

Last, the dependence of a Christian upon Christ, in all his spiritual straits, lays a tie upon His omnipotence to be forthcoming to him; He will not disappoint the expectation of the poor, nor will He deliver him unto the will of his enemy. Now, if the omnipotence of God be engaged to help a Christian in this spiritual warfare, he need not be much afraid. May not a Christian cry out the word that Elisha spoke to his servant when he said, "There are more with us than against us"? Once a Christian could act in faith upon the fact that the omnipotence of God is upon his side, a Christian might be constrained to cry out, "I care not for ten thousand of my idols, though they should compass me round about, for the Lord does sustain me." It is as impossible for a Christian to be totally defeated as it is to overcome an omnipotent God.

A second encouragement to help a Christian continue in the fight against his temptations is that this fight with his temptations shall be short. Before long, you who are now so taken up in fighting shall once be taken up in triumphing. This is clear in Romans 16:20, where we read, "And the God of peace shall bruise Satan under your feet shortly. The grace of our Lord Jesus Christ be with you." We also read in 1 Peter 5:10, "The God of all grace, who hath called us unto his eternal glory by Christ Jesus, after that ye have suffered a while, make you perfect, stablish, strengthen, settle you." Oh, wrestling Christians, before long there shall be an eternal cessation of arms, when you shall enter into the joy of your Lord and shall eternally sing that triumphant song, "O death, where is thy sting? O grave, where is thy victory?" (1 Cor. 15:55). What is the voice of those that are heard in heaven? Is it not the voice of those that shout for the mastery? Do you not think that it will be a pleasant day when Christians shall go into these precious mansions of eternity, and shall divide the spoil? Do you not imagine that it will be a precious day, when all the sorrows of a Christian shall vanish into endless joy? Will it not be a sweet and pleasant day, when all the debates and fights of a Christian shall vanish into endless triumph? Will it not be a sweet and pleasant day, when the conquering Christian shall have a crown put upon his head, and a palm put into his right hand, and shall be led through the streets of the New Jerusalem, where it shall be cried before him, "Thus shall it be done to the man whom the king delighteth to honor" (Esth. 6:9)? Who has delighted to honor the King? Oh, fighting Christian, what a pleasant day will it be, when all your complaints shall be taken out of your mouth, and you will begin a song that will never have an end! Will you not watch with Christ one hour? Before long your eternal day shall dawn.

A third encouragement to engage a Christian to wrestle with his temptations is the certainty of the victory. We may call a Christian, "Gad," for, "a troop shall overcome him, but he shall overcome at the last" (Gen. 49:19). A Christian is as sure of victory as he is sure that Christ is in heaven. I confess that it is a noble encouragement to provoke you to fight, and you shall certainly obtain the crown and victory. Therefore, we say with Paul that we fight, but "not as one that beateth the air" (1 Cor. 9:26). We fight as those that cry out, "I shall once receive a crown of victory."

There is a fourth encouragement to engage a Christian in this war; there are many precious rewards that attend the wrestling Christian. This is clear in 2 Timothy 4:7-8, where we read, "I have fought a good fight (of faith): henceforth there is laid up for me a crown of righteousness." In the second and third chapters of Revelation, there are many excellent encouragements proposed to the overcomer: "To him that overcometh, will I give to eat of the tree of life" (Rev. 2:7); "He that overcometh shall not be hurt of the second death" (v. 11); "To him that overcometh will I give to eat of the hidden manna, and will give him a white stone, and in the stone a new name written, which no man knoweth saving he that receiveth it" (v. 17); "And I will give him the morning star" (v. 28); "He that overcometh, the same shall be clothed in white raiment; and I will not blot out his name out of the book of life, but I will confess his name before my Father, and before his angels" (Rev. 3:5); "Him that overcometh will I make a pillar in the temple of my God, and he shall go no more out: and I will write upon him the name of my God, and the name of the city of my God, which is new Jerusalem, which cometh down out of heaven from my God: and I will write upon him my new name" (Rev. 3:12); "To him that overcometh will I grant to sit with me in my throne, even as I also overcame, and am set down with my Father in his throne" (Rev. 3:21). Oh, take a sight of the crown, take a sight of the reward, and this will exceedingly help you in the midst of your fights. Do you desire to know the reason why Christians faint so much in their spiritual war? It is because they do not have eyes to behold what is prepared for the one that overcomes. You will never know your reward until you have it. It is beyond expression, these things that are purchased and provided for them that overcome.

A fifth encouragement to provoke you to continue to wrestle against your spiritual enemies and temptations is that all the enemies you have to wrestle with and debate against are overcome and vanquished enemies. Christ has overcome them and taken away much of their strength so that we have no more to do, but to fight with an already defeated army; we are fighting a vanquished enemy. This is clear in Colossians 2:15: "Having spoiled principalities and powers, he made a shew of them openly, triumphing over them in it." Believe it, if Christ had not first fought with principalities and powers, it would have been impossible for us to overcome them; but we must be constrained to ascribe the praise of our victories unto the victory of Christ.

A sixth encouragement to persuade you to fight against temptations is that the things you fight for are of exceeding and eternal soul-concern. What is it you fight for? You fight for your soul; you fight for a crown; you fight for an eternal enjoyment of God. It is clear that "we wrestle not against flesh and blood, but against principalities, against powers, against the rulers of the darkness of this world, against spiritual wickedness in high places" (Eph. 6:12). This may also be understood, "In heavenly things"; that is, your great debate with the devil is for heavenly things—things that are of much soul and everlasting concern. Thus, does that not put you to a serious war with the devil? Oh, the loss of heaven is a great loss, the loss of Christ is a great loss, and the loss of a precious and immortal soul is a great loss. Therefore you should fight and seriously wrestle with all your temptations.

There is this seventh encouragement also: there is more spiritual joy and soul-satisfaction to be found in a serious wrestling against our idols, though with little sensible success, than is to be found in an eternal fruition of our idols. It is impossible to know what soul-contentment, what joy in the Holy Ghost, what inward peace of conscience redounds to a Christian that is serious in wrestling with his idols. You know it—most serious fighters have a continual feast. Now, do you think that you who are engaged in this war are fighting with your temptations? Are you fighting to overcome your idols? I would have you answering all your temptations as Jehu answered the messenger of Jehoram, crying out, "Is it peace?" You may answer, "What hast thou to do with peace? So turn thee behind me" (2 Kings 9:19). I would say to you, if you love your immortal souls, have no peace with your idols. Oh, Christians, why are you under so much dominion and power of your idols? Why do they tread upon you and overcome you at every assault? I shall give you three reasons why our idols obtain much victory over us.

First, we are not diligent and earnest in fighting with our idols and temptations; if we were diligent, we would have something to say, which now we cannot speak. It is clear that "the hand of the diligent shall bear rule: but the slothful shall be under tribute"

(Prov. 12:24); it shall be impossible for a slothful Christian to be an overcoming Christian. It is impossible for a slothful Christian to be an enjoying Christian; it is impossible for a slothful Christian to be a tender Christian. If we were more spiritually diligent, we would be able to sing, "Through God we shall do valiantly: for he it is that shall tread down our enemies" (Ps. 60:12). Slothfulness has been the occasion of many of the devil's victories over us.

Another reason why our lusts and temptations have so much victory over us is that we are not in the exercise of watchfulness and prayer. A Christian does not stand upon his watchtower to behold the motions of the enemy; nor when he beholds them, is he much in the exercise of prayer to overcome them. Oh, for a Christian to go to Christ and cry, "Master, save me, lest I perish!" Oh, for a Christian to groan out his complaints to Christ! When you cannot speak your complaints to Christ, then sigh your complaints to Him.

Third, our lusts and temptations have so much victory over us because we do not exercise our faith. This is a noble piece of a Christian's armor; it is clear in Ephesians 6:16, where we are commanded to above all, take up the "shield of faith," and also in 1 Peter 5:9, where we hear of those who "resist steadfast in the faith." I confess that a Christian who fights without faith shall not fight with much advantage. A Christian must fight with faith for three reasons.

First, faith is the grace that takes hold of the arm of Christ, and of His strength; it is the grace that draws strength from Christ for resisting temptations. Faith says to Christ that which the poor woman spoke to the king of Israel: "Help, my lord, O king, or else I die." If we may so speak, faith would never be put to a *non-plus*. Where discouragements abound, faith can say, "Here is help in Christ." When the enemy grows strong, our faith has an eye that can see strength in Christ, which sense cannot see. If grace be not lively, sense is a most discouraged thing; but faith, though grace be not lively, can take up Christ as mighty to save.

Second, faith is necessary for a Christian to fight because it is the grace that reveals to the soul much of its own weakness. A Christian is most likely to cry out, "I am weak," when he is most believing. A believing Christian is most diffident of himself and at the same time, most confident in Christ. A believing Christian will cast one eye to himself and cry out, "I am undone," and he will cast the other eye to Christ and cry out, "I can do all things through Christ which strengtheneth me" (Phil. 4:13).

A third reason faith is necessary in this war is that it is the grace that most reveals the subtleties and motions of Satan. Oh, study faith, dear Christians, otherwise you shall never overcome. I give you this advice: study to put on the whole armor of God and to have yourselves wholly girt about with it. If any piece of the armor of God is loose upon you, or if there is an opening between the joints of your armor, there may come an arrow, as a messenger from Satan, that may pierce through the joints of your harness and be as death in your bones.

Thirdly, I would like to propose some considerations concerning the text. First, consider that Satan observes a great deal of policy and subtlety in trysting and timing his temptations; he assaults a Christian exactly when he knows there is most advantage to be found. I shall give you these five steps of Satan's policy when he is trysting his temptations.

1. He trysts his temptations and times his assaults when a Christian is in the greatest incapacity to resist. When is it that the devil assaults us most? It is when we are least capable to resist. When did he tempt David? Was it not when he was sleeping in the bed of security (2 Sam. 11:2)? When was it that he tempted Peter? Was it not when he was upon the high pinnacle of presumption, crying out, "Though all men should forsake thee, yet will not I"? Satan knows there is a time of peace and a time of war, he knows when to assault and when to suspend his assaults.

2. Another step of Satan's policy in timing his temptations is that he times his temptations when we have most opportunity to fall into them. When was it that he tempted Cain to kill his brother Abel? Was it not when they were both in the field alone? When did he tempt Achan to steal the Babylonish garment? Was it not when there was no eye to behold him? He can perfectly time his temptations so that both occasion and inclination meet together to invite the Christian to act. These are two dreadful companions, an inclination to sin and the occasion to sin.

3. Satan also times his temptations when he knows there is most advantage to be had by overcoming. The devil mainly assaults when he knows there is an advantage to be found. If we embrace his temptations, he knows how to sail both against wind and tide; when he cannot gain his point at one time, he will attempt to gain it at another. However, when he can gain most by his point, then he is upon a Christian. A Christian often says to himself the same words which Delilah spoke to Samson: Awake, "the Philistines be upon thee" (Judg. 16:20). We must be put to watch, for our enemies are upon us.

4. He times his temptations so they arrive when the temptation seems most beautiful and pleasant. He knows the time when such a temptation is pleasant and when it is unpleasant. He knows the time when such a temptation is clothed with the robes of advantage; then he assaults. When is it that he tempts many to hypocrisy? Is it not then when religion is in fashion? But once religion is out of court and fashion, then he tempts many to apostasy. When religion is baulked up with the feathers of advantage and applause, it is not much then to be a Christian in show; but it is much to love a dying Christ. It is not much to love a dear Christ, when we can get Christ for nothing; it is not much to love Him then. But, when you cannot get Christ except you forsake the world, then it is much to love a dear Christ, a Christ that must be bought.

5. The last step of Satan's policy in timing his temptations is that he ordinarily tempts when his temptations are least expected. He comes upon us when we are unaware; and we, not being upon our guard, are easily surprised and overcome. An unexpected trial is a double trial. If a Christian sees his temptation before it comes, he is ready to resist. Now, is not our adversary subtle? You should have your recourse to Christ, who is the eternal wisdom of the Father. "Wisdom is a defense" (Eccl. 7:12). It is indeed a precious shadow when Satan does assault.

The second consideration that I would propose unto you is this, dear Christians and prisoners of hope. Comfort yourselves that there is no temptation you encounter that is not proportioned to your strength. Christ will not allow you to be tempted above measure. We read that "there hath no temptation taken you but such as is common to man" (1 Cor. 10:13). This may also be understood, "Such as is moderate unto men." There is a moderation that appears in a Christian's temptations; his temptations are proportioned to his strength. When you cannot find out a way to escape, Christ can find out a way to deliver you. He knows how to deliver you out of all your temptations. When you cannot see an escape from your temptations, Christ can see an escape and make it known to you.

Third, consider that one of these two must overtake you. Either you must overcome your temptations, or else your temptations will overcome you. Either you must tread Satan under your feet, or Satan will tread you under his feet. There is no middle ground between these two; you must either overcome or be overcome. All the woeful disadvantages that attend anything, attend the woeful defeats that the devil shall give unto many of you; and all the sweet and precious advantages that attend any victory, attend upon the precious victories that the Christian shall have over his idols. This will be a disadvantage to you. If you are overcome, there shall be an eternal union between you and your idols; if you do not overcome your idols here, you shall never overcome hereafter. This is a disadvantage that attends Satan's victories: that if you are overcome and defeated by your idols and by the messengers of Satan, you shall be eternally shut out from the presence of God and from the glory of His power. He is indeed blessed that fights to overcome his idols. It is most assuredly a pleasant thing to overcome the devil.

Let us close by discussing seven points. First, do not all the saints around the throne say that it is a pleasant thing to fight and overcome your idols? Do not Abel, Joseph, and Abraham agree that it is a pleasant thing to overcome? Do not the twelve patriarchs, the twelve apostles, and all who are around the throne say that it is a pleasant thing to overcome? Do not all these that are taken up in a serious fight with their idols cry forth that it is a beautiful thing to overcome?

Second, if all the angels in heaven and all the saints around the throne were admitted to give you their counsel, it would be to fight the good fight of faith. What counsel would Adam and Eve give you if they were admitted to give it? It would be to resist the devil.

There is none in heaven who would not counsel you to fight against your spiritual enemies. What is heaven? It is an everlasting mansion of the debtors of the love, power, and wisdom of Jesus Christ. What is heaven? It is a precious mansion in which there are many thousands crying out and shouting forth for the mastery obtained. What trophies of the love of Christ are seen in heaven!

Third, there are many sad and telling evidences that few of us shall overcome and sing these eternal songs of triumph that are sung above. I would only beg you to take notice of the six sad and telling evidences that not many of us shall eternally triumph in heaven.

1. The first evidence is that we do not entertain a heart-enmity against our idols. I suppose if there were a window opened in every one of our hearts, we might see our idols keeping up our hearts, and our affections embracing them. Does this not show us that we shall not overcome and triumph? We are joined to our idols and married to our lusts; therefore, we must be left alone. Yea, when Christ desires us to embrace Him, many cry out, "I have married a wife" (Luke 14:20). Many have married themselves to their idols; therefore they cannot come to embrace Christ.

2. Another evidence that many of us shall not overcome is our lack of prayer when we are assaulted by the devil. When did a temptation constrain you to go to Christ, seriously to beseech Him to give you help? I think if some Christians who profess religion would tell when a temptation put them to prayer, the house would begin to wonder, and cry out, "Can such a one be a Christian?" Dear Christian, what do you do with your temptations? I shall only say that when we meet with temptations, we either embrace or forsake our idols. Is this not a dreadful evidence that we shall be overcome in the end?

3. All the idols in our bosom were never the matter of our complaint. I think there are some spirits that would have sunk under the weight that some of us are lying under; yet, there are some of us that may say, "My stroke is heavier than my groaning" (Job 23:2).

4. We are not often refreshed with the hope of the day of redemption. I would ask you who are here: when was it that the hope of a complete victory over, precious end of, and complete redemption from all your lusts and idols did refresh you and make you rejoice? In a manner, we desire no other heaven but that we and our idols should eternally live together; we desire to be pleasant in our life, and in our death not to be divided. If some of us could have the enjoyment of our idols for an eternity, we would cry forth, "It is good for us to be here" (Matt. 17:4). This is but a poor good.

5. Has it not been some time since you professed Christ? Are there many temptations that you have overcome? Are there any that you even wrestled? I may say, the Christians of this time do not love to fight. Be persuaded, he who does not fight against his idols, Christ shall eternally fight against him; furthermore, he shall eternally fight against Christ, and that shall be a dreadful war.

6. Last, we so often have low and undervaluing thoughts of Christ. If we were fighting Christians, if we were overcoming Christians, we would think Christ matchless. With every step, the Christian sits down and cries out, "Who would not love Thee?" With every step of a Christian's victory, he is constrained to sit down and cry out, "Thou hast delivered my soul from death, mine eyes from tears, and my feet from falling!" (Ps. 116:8). With every step of a Christian's victory, he compasses Christ about with songs of deliverance.

Oh, that the Redeemer were come out of Zion, that He might turn our transgressions away! May He teach our fingers to war, so that we might tread upon our idols as mire in the streets. Amen.

SERMON 36

Singular Temptations Call for Fervent and Frequent Supplications (3)

For this thing I besought the Lord thrice,
that it might depart from me.
—2 Corinthians 12:8

It was a noble saying of Solomon's: "Every purpose is established by counsel, and with good advice make war" (Prov. 20:18). I think, in any war, a person should ask advice. Is this not the case, especially in this divine and spiritual war? It is the duty of a Christian to depend much on Christ, whose name is Wonderful and Counselor. Each time a Christian begins to fight, he should ask Christ, shall I at this time go up against the Philistines? No doubt, if we were more in the habit of this, our success would be more palpable. I think a Christian, in his spiritual warfare, should be much more dependent because of the strength and subtlety of his enemies. Is not the way of Satan more subtle than the way of a serpent on a rock, or the way of a ship in the sea, or the way of an eagle in the air? Before I come to what I intended mainly to speak about, I desire you to take notice of these three things.

First, a Christian may be comforted knowing that there is much spiritual advantage in wrestling against the messengers of Satan. Out of this eater may come meat, and out of this strong one may come sweetness. A Christian may know five things by his temptations from the messengers of Satan.

1. He may acquire the knowledge of the strength of his corruptions often before his corruptions meet with a suitable temptation. We do not know their strength, but when

the wood that is within meets with fire from without, then we shall know the strength of our corruptions.

2. A Christian may acquire knowledge of the strength of his grace in Christ. What noble songs must a Christian sing to the grace of Christ by virtue of that noble war that he has with the messengers of Satan! Many precious songs would have been buried in silence if we had not met with the messengers of Satan. We would not have encompassed Christ with songs of deliverance if we had not been tempted.

3. Through his temptations, a Christian may have a distinct knowledge of the strength of his graces. Sometimes a Christian, under the power of discouragement, will never know his own faith until he meets with a temptation; though I confess, sometimes a Christian will also know the weakness of his grace by his temptations.

4. The tempted Christian may also discover the strength of his enemies. Do you suppose that you can be content with a weak enemy? When do we take up the strength of the devil and know that he is a prince of darkness? It is when the blast of the terrible one is as a storm against the wall, and when his arrows are sharp in piercing us.

5. Through his temptations, the Christian will also understand the strength of Christ's love. Oh, what a sea of wondering will this bring the Christian to, when he reflects upon his infirmities within and Christ's love without. Will he not be constrained to cry out, "After whom is the king of Israel come out? After whom dost thou pursue? After a dead dog, after a flea" (1 Sam. 24:14).

Secondly, such is the love we have to our idols—not only the idol itself, but the very emblem of it will make us to fall in love with it. That is a strange place, when Israel and Judah saw the Assyrian portrayed upon the wall (Ezek. 23:14, 15), it is said in the 16th verse, "And as soon as she saw them with her eyes, she doted upon them, and sent messengers unto them into Chaldea." The very beholding of the picture of her lovers made her lust to burn. Do you not know that the very picture of our idols will make our lust to flame? For instance, the man that is given to the sin of lust, the very beholding of the picture of the idol will make his lust to burn. So the man that is given to applause, the very beholding of another enjoying the same will make him cry out, "Oh, when shall I enjoy such a god?"

Thirdly, it is the duty of a Christian not only to put his idols out of his heart, but also to put them from before his eyes. In Ezekiel 14:6 we read, "Thus saith the Lord GOD; repent, and turn yourselves from your idols; and turn away your faces from all your abominations" (Ezek. 14:6). You may ask, "May I not put my idols before my eyes, if I put them not into my heart?" No, says God, you must not so much as set them before your eyes, for that is an appearance of evil, which you should shun. If you are tender, you must not so much as name your idol, as we read in Hosea 2:17: "For I will take away the names of Baalim out of her mouth." You may ask, "Is not Baalim a good name? May I not use that name? It signifies 'my lord,' or 'my husband.'" Because it is the name of an idol, you must not so much as name it. You must not inquire how other men serve their idols. That is a strange command in Deuteronomy 12:30: "Take heed to thyself that thou be not snared by following them, after that they be destroyed from before thee; and that thou enquire not after their gods, saying, How did these nations serve their gods? even so will I do likewise." You must not inquire how another man serves his idols. One may ask, "Might not I inquire?" The answer is that you must not ask; it is the appearance of evil, and you must not encourage the shadow or appearance of evil.

We have, at great length, discoursed to you upon the seventh verse, in which is contained Paul's case and condition. Now we will speak of Paul's exercise under this case and condition. There are seven things which we intend to discuss concerning Paul's exercise. We have already spoken of the first three.

> 1. First, there is noble advantage redounding to a Christian by his temptations. This particular messenger of Satan that Paul met with drove him often to his knees.
>
> 2. One of the most excellent ways to resist temptations is to be much in the exercise of prayer. This is clear in Paul's words: "For this I besought the Lord thrice."
>
> 3. There are some temptations that a Christian ought especially to wrestle against. This is made clear in Paul's

word *this*: "For *this* I besought the Lord thrice." There is an emphasis in the word *this*; it is as if he had said, "Let me not fight against *many* temptations, but against *this* temptation, I must fight and stand in opposition. I will never conclude any peace with this messenger of Satan, but continually war against it."

We intend, then, to speak of the fourth thing in the words which is that it is very difficult for a Christian to crucify these temptations wherewith he is assaulted. Before Paul ever got victory over this messenger of Satan, he is driven thrice to his knees. I hope there is not a person here that is so ignorant of himself, but will seal this truth with his blood: it is difficult to resist temptations. I shall show you this difficulty by way of four points.

First, did not the Christians in former times, engaging all their strength to resist temptation, say that it is difficult to resist temptations? We read in 2 Timothy 4:7, "I have fought a good fight, I have finished my course, I have kept the faith." This may also be rendered, "I have fought as in an agony, and with all my strength, the good fight." Further, in 1 Corinthians 9:27, Paul says, "But I keep under my body, and bring it into subjection: lest that by any means, when I have preached to others, I myself should be a castaway." This is a metaphor that is borrowed from wrestlers, who when wrestling together, employ all their might for defeating the contrary party. Now, does not Paul say that it is difficult to mortify temptations? Paul says, "I could never get my foot on the neck of a temptation, except when I fought as in an agony; since faint fighting could not purchase me the victory, I was forced to fight as in agony."

Secondly, this proves the difficulty of resisting temptation: Christians, while resisting, crave the help of God. "I am oppressed; undertake for me" (Isa. 38:14), says Hezekiah. He means, "If I stand alone in this fight, I will fall. Oh, heaven undertake for me, or I am gone!" We read a similar plea in Psalm 35:2: "Take hold of shield and buckler, and stand up for mine help."

Thirdly, we see the difficulty of overcoming temptations by their name in Scripture: "Principalities and powers, and spiritual wickedness in high places" (Eph. 6:12). The very name of temptations shows the difficulty of wrestling against them.

Fourthly, we see the power of temptations in the many lamentable victories that temptations have had over the most eminent, wrestling saints. Every Christian that has ever gone to heaven has endured and succumbed to many temptations. I think if we were admitted to ask all the saints around the throne, they would agree that it is difficult to resist temptations. Were you to ask David, he would respond that it is difficult to resist temptations. Were you to ask Hezekiah, he would also say that it is difficult to resist temptations. Were you to ask all those who have finished this glorious war, they would say that it is most difficult to resist temptations. Be sure of it, whoever you may be, you have not fought such a battle as this. However, I must say to you, oh fighting Christian, comfort yourself, knowing that God has given Himself the name, "Jehovah-Nissi," which means, "The Lord is my banner."

Now, in discussing this truth more fully, I shall speak a little concerning four points.

First, it is with great difficulty that a Christian has to mortify and resist temptations.

1. It rises from the soul-union and heart-conjunction between his idols and him. Is it any wonder that the devil tempts you, though he captivates you? Your temptations, your idols, and you are married together. I hope you will not find it to be difficult work to persuade a man to love his wife. So it is no difficult work for the devil to persuade many to love their idols, for their idols and they are married together. We see this in Hosea 4:17, where we read, "Ephraim is joined to idols: let him alone."

2. The temptations arise when the devil tempts us to commit a sin, and there is a proctor within us that cries out, "Obey, obey!" Do you not know that when the devil tempts you to commit iniquity, there is something within your bosom that cries out, "Listen to him, listen to him"? Indeed, it is sad when there is an enemy within crying, "Oh, yield," and an enemy without crying, "Oh, yield"; I think it is not long then before the temptation will be victorious. If the devil cries, "Yield!" and your heart cries, "Yield," it will not be long before he will obtain the victory. Every time the devil tempts us, there is something within us crying, "Oh, yield!"

3. Also, we trust too much in our own strength; we go to war upon our own strength and charges. Take notice of the words in Proverbs 28:26: "He that trusteth in his own heart is a fool: but whoso walketh wisely, he shall be delivered." From these words, we learn two things. First, it is an act of folly for one to trust in his own heart. Second, when we do not trust our own heart, we may finally come to victory over our idols. I would have you, when you begin to contend with your idols, recognize and say these two things: without Christ I can do nothing, and I can do all things through Christ who strengthens me.

4. We too often embrace temptation, and this makes overcoming temptation very hard work for a Christian. We are so accustomed to yielding that we do not know what it is to fight. "How weak is thine heart" (Ezek. 16:30); you can barely rid it of the least evil, the weakest temptation that assaults you; and what is the reason? The verse continues, "Thou doest all these things, the work of an imperious whorish woman." We are so accustomed to yielding that we almost never set about to fight. I think the devil seldom needs to tempt more than once, for we yield at the first temptation.

5. We apprehend some sweetness when we embrace such a temptation. You may say when the devil begins to tempt you, "This will be an excellent thing if I embrace it." To you, I would say two words. The bread of deceit may be sweet in your mouth, but afterwards your belly shall be filled with gravel. Do not trust in vanity, for vanity shall be your ruin.

6. You are almost never in a resisting frame. When the devil comes to tempt you, what are you doing? Are you sleeping? Often he finds us sleeping, and therefore he comes and spoils the house. We are like the men of Laish in Judges 18; we dwell securely. Yea more, I think, we are like them that sleep upon the top of a mast. I think it is strange that so many lamentable victories should be obtained by the devil over us, and we never lay it to heart.

Secondly, I desire to discuss how to distinguish between the temptations that come from one's heart and the temptations that come from the devil. I desire you to know that our hearts often tempt us to sin when the devil is not tempting us. Furthermore, our hearts will seek temptation when the temptation does not seek them. In Matthew 26:41 we read, "Watch and pray, that ye enter not into temptation: the spirit indeed is willing, but the flesh is weak." Notice that it is not said, "Lest temptation enter into you," but, "that ye enter not into temptation." Now, before I answer the question, I propose that we consider these four things.

1. It is very difficult to distinguish between temptations that come from one's own heart and the temptations that come from the devil; this is because that which in Scripture is attributed to the devil is often attributed to our own heart. For example, Peter says to Ananias, "Why hath Satan filled thine heart to lie to the Holy Ghost," and, "Why hast thou conceived this thing in thine heart? thou hast not lied unto men, but unto God." Thus that which is attributed to Satan in the third verse, he attributes to the man's heart in the fourth verse.

2. There is much advantage to a Christian by knowing distinctly when his temptations come from his heart and when they come from the devil; for it will, on the one hand, remedy discouragements, and upon the other hand, remedy presumption. There are two great faults among Christians. First, when we charge you with sin, you may blame the devil for that sin. This is the ancient divinity of your mother, when God charged her with eating the forbidden fruit. "No, no, it was not me, it was the devil that beguiled me." Persons often extenuate the sin by saying that the devil beguiled them, and they were against it. To such I say, "Oh, man, if your own heart had not given consent to the temptation, all the devils in hell could not have reached you with one stroke; therefore, you must forsake this excuse!" Also, Christians often cry out that it is "no more I that do it, but sin that dwelleth in me" (Rom. 7:20); they mean to say, "It is not I, but the law of my members

rebelling against the law of my mind. I take heaven as my witness that I protest against such a thing!"

3. When a Christian is beginning to search whether his temptations arise from the devil or from his own heart, it is best to lay the blame upon his own heart.

4. There is a cursed correspondence between our heart and the devil. Some folks' hearts send ten messengers to the devil, when they send but one to Christ. We keep a cursed correspondence with hell, but that blessed correspondence with heaven we often know not.

Now there are these differences between the temptations that come from the devil and the temptations that come from our own heart. Let us discuss six of these differences.

The first difference is that the temptations that arise from our own heart are more difficult for a Christian to resist than those that come from the devil. You must certainly know that the temptations that come from your own hearts are the worst to resist. It is easier to overcome two temptations framed by the devil and sent unto you than to resist one from your own heart. Every man will think internal war worse than foreign war. I think, when the enemy is assaulting from without, he is more easily resisted than when he fights within. I hope that you all will agree that it is better to fight with an enemy that stands outside of the gate than to fight with an enemy that stands within the gate. Furthermore, every saint is a divided party. There is a piece of a Christian's heart, there is a piece of a Christian's sight, and there is a piece of a Christian's will that fights against another piece of him. There is a law in his members that rebels against the law of his mind.

A second difference between the temptations that come from the devil and the temptations that come from a man's own heart is that the temptations that come from the devil have ordinarily some propensity or tendency in them, if not always, to stir up a lust within such a person. For instance, if he tempts David to adultery, he will put a beautiful Bathsheba before his eyes; if he tempts Achan to covetousness, he will put a Babylonish garment and a wedge of gold before his eyes; if he tempts Absalom to pride, he will put a crown before his eyes; if he tempts Zimri to adultery, he will put a beautiful Cozbi before his eyes; when he tempted Joseph, he put a

Potiphar's wife before his eyes. When the temptations come from our own hearts, ordinarily there will be no connection between the temptations that it stirs up. I ask you, is it not true that beholding a certain object provokes such a lust in you, that if you would ask someone who stands nearby, what would such an object provoke and stir up, he would guess a whole year before he would guess the lusts that it stirs up in you. Often, an object stirs up a lust that is only remotely related to it. If lust is your predominant idol, will you draw temptations from every object you encounter? Is there any object you can cast your eyes upon that will not stir up your lust? Whatever your predominant idol or lust is, your heart will almost always draw a temptation from everything to stir it up.

A third difference between the temptations that arise from the devil and the temptations of our own hearts is that the devil's temptations are often more surprising, while the temptations of our own hearts are often exceedingly deliberate. When our hearts frame a temptation, we sit down in council to find out the way to carry out the sin. The temptations that rise from our own hearts are very deliberate. We find several expressions in Scripture that describe our own hearts' temptation: "Forging iniquity," and "devising iniquity upon their beds." The devil attempts to take us by surprise, but our heart deliberates how to commit sin. Some will not spend one hour in prayer unto God, but they will spend ten hours deliberating how to satisfy such an idol. How many hours of sleep have you lost just to satisfy the lust of covetousness, thinking upon the most expeditious way of making yourselves rich? You were never so diligent to satisfy Christ.

Fourth, we often embrace the temptations that come from our own hearts with more delight than the temptations that proceed from the devil. They are our own native birth, and therefore we love them.

The fifth difference between them is that the devil ordinarily tempts us to more gross sins against the light of nature, and our hearts tempt us more to spiritual, refined, and invisible sins. When the devil tempts, he will tempt to gross sins against which the light of nature stands in opposition; but when our hearts begin to tempt, they will tempt to more refined, pleasant, and more spiritual lusts.

The last difference between the devil's temptations and the temptations of our own hearts is that a Christian will more easily take up the temptations of the devil than he will take up the temptations of his own heart. We will take the devil when he begins to tempt us, but we will let our hearts tempt us often; or we recognize that it is a temptation. I am sure that it was not without ground that it was written of our heart, "The heart is deceitful above all things, and desperately wicked: who can know it?" (Jer. 17:9). Oh, a deceitful heart and a deceiving devil meeting together—what would they do if Christ did not stand between them? Oh, precious Christ, how much are we bound to Thee? How often has He stood between your deceitful heart, oh Christian, and a deceiving devil? How often has He said to you, "Whither goest thou?" How often has He told you to return to your first husband; for then was it better with you than now (Hos. 2:7)?

We would like to propose several considerations concerning this matter.

First, consider that when a Christian first meets with a temptation, he may cry out, "Am I a dog's head, that I should embrace such a temptation?" and yet, before long, he will embrace the same temptation. When we are first assaulted, we will shun temptation; yet, before all is done, we will take our idols in our arms and dandle them upon our knees. Never trust your first resisting of temptation. I warrant you, Job, when he first met with his temptations, cried out, "The LORD gave, and the LORD hath taken away; blessed be the name of the LORD" (Job 1:21). He would not so much as open his mouth to speak an ill word of God; but before he finished with the temptation, how many dark words did he utter! Truly, a temptation is a strong thing when it assaults more than once!

The second consideration that I would propose unto you is that there is something in a Christian that may cry out, "Resist temptation!" Yet, there is something within a Christian that will cry out, "Embrace the temptation!" There will be two voices in a Christian's breast—the one crying out to yield, and the other crying out, "Quit yourself, and be strong like a man"; which of the voices do you most often obey?

Third, temptations are often, for the omission of duty, not so seasonably resisted as temptations to the commission of sin. This is clearer when we see that a Christian may be overcome by a temptation to neglect prayer; yet, if he meets with a temptation to swear, he will shun that temptation. It is certain that the temptations that entice us to the omitting of duty are not as easily resisted as the temptations that entice us to the committing of sin.

A fourth consideration that I would propose unto you is this: the temptations that entice you to the omission of duty are more easily resisted than these temptations that entice you to the formal way of going about your duties. The devil sooner overcomes you when he tempts you to pray formally than he overcomes when he tempts you to altogether neglect prayer. When the devil will tempt you to forbear prayer, you may say that you scorn to embrace that temptation; but if he comes to tempt you to pray formally, then you give way to the devil.

The fifth consideration is that it is easier to resist temptations that entice us to the breach of the second table of the law than to resist the temptations that entice us to the breach of the first table of the law. You will resist the temptation that entices you to fornication, but you will not resist the temptation that entices you to pride! The one is a breach of the seventh commandment, and the other is a breach of the first commandment. You will be overcome by the temptations that entice you to pride; yet, if a temptation entices you to uncleanness, you will scorn to embrace the temptation. The reason of it is that nature's light will help us to wrestle with the temptations that assault us to break the commands of the second table, but nature's light is half blind when we are tempted to break the commands of the first table of the law.

Sixthly, temptations to unbelief are not as easily resisted as temptations to sins against the second table of the law. When the devil comes to tempt us to unbelief, we never debate with him; but if he comes to tempt us to swear, you will say, "Get thee behind me, Satan" (Matt. 16:23). The reason is that a Christian looks upon unbelief as his duty; also, He does not know if the hand of Joab is in this. Oh, Christian, know that the hand of Joab is in all your unbelief, as well as in other sins. What can be the reason that a Christian will put his name to all the commands of the law and subscribe, "I am guilty"? He will subscribe to the first command, saying, "I am guilty"; he will read the second command and admit, "I am guilty"; he will read the third command and subscribe, "I am guilty"; yea, he will subscribe guilty to all the commands of the law. But when he comes to the gospel, he will not subscribe to his guilt there. Oh, fool, did you ever read the words, "This is the work of God, that ye believe on him whom he hath sent" (John 6:29)? Have you ever broken this? Often, much of the ruin of a Christian lies in the breaking of the command of Christ to believe in Him.

Fourthly, we desire to propose unto you some aggravations of the embracing of temptations.

First, to embrace a temptation, after you know it to be a temptation, is a mighty aggravation. Will not many here recognize a temptation, and yet will embrace it? What is this? It is even to sin against heaven, to spit in the face of Christ. You who sin with a witness within your breast and a witness in heaven, know that you are laughing Christ to scorn.

Second, when we are tempted to embrace temptations with delight; when we are tempted to sin, we join with the temptation with both our hands. We are so far from resisting it, according to that word, "When thou doest evil, then thou rejoicest" (Jer. 11:15). Are there not such persons here that are only glad when they have committed evil? I would only say this to such people: stand in awe, lest God in His wrath overtake you, when there shall be none to deliver you.

The third aggravation of embracing temptations when we embrace them after resolutions and vows to the contrary is, are there not some of you who have broken communion vows before now? Are there not some of you who vowed to God that you would not embrace a temptation to such an idol again, yet you have embraced it? That is a mighty aggravation. We see a clear example of this in Peter, who forsook Christ after he had vowed and promised the contrary.

The fourth aggravation of the embracing of temptations is to embrace temptations after communion with God; it may be then said of you that you sinned after the Lord appeared to you twice.

A fifth aggravation of this occurs when you embrace a temptation to a certain sin at the same time that God is punishing you for the same sin. Are there not some persons who, even when God is punishing them for such a sin, when a temptation to commit the same sin comes, will embrace it? What is that? It is to fight against heaven and to cry out, "Who is the LORD, that I should obey his voice?" (Ex. 5:2).

The sixth aggravation is that you will embrace temptations when they are neither very strong nor very subtle. Some persons, let the temptation be ever so weak, yet their lusts will take fire at it; this is a mighty aggravation of the embracing of temptations. Sometimes the devil will tempt a Christian as a roaring lion, and sometimes he will tempt a Christian as an angel of light; sometimes he will tempt a Christian upon the right hand of discouragement, and sometimes he will tempt him upon the left hand of presumption. I would only say this to you, if you embrace a temptation when it is not very strong, that is an evidence that Christ and you are very distant one from another.

The last aggravation of embracing temptation is to embrace temptations in the presence of Christ. Are there not some here who will embrace temptations when Christ is kind to them? What does that say? It says that I love my idols better than Christ; it says that you do not value the sweet and precious visits of the Son of God.

Now I have this to say, and I hope I may say it with boldness: I am sent from heaven today to engage you in this spiritual warfare, so that you would give up your names unto Christ to fight against the temptations of the devil. I am sent here today to demand your consent to this blessed offer, so that you would give up your names to Christ, enroll yourselves in His book, and come under His banner and colors. Now, what do you say to this? Are you content? I shall remove seven objections that may hinder you to consent to this blessed offer.

Objection 1: "Oh," you may say, "I would be content to subscribe my name and give up myself unto Christ, but my heart will not let me; I find that my heart withdraws when I desire to consent." I would say to you, "Will you consent with your mouth until your heart comes along at length? Will you consent with your mouth, so that you will be content to fight against the enemies of Christ? Will Christ be content with a consent of your mouth? Yes. He will be content with a consent of your mouth until better consent comes."

Objection 2: You may say, "I would give up my name to Christ and enroll myself in His book to be a continual fighter under His banner, but I cannot write my name." I say to you, desire Christ to write it for you if you cannot write it yourself; desire Christ to lead your hand if you cannot write it alone.

Objection 3: Perhaps you say, "Why must I give up my name to Christ and enroll myself in His book; for I cannot fight at all; I do not have the skill." I say to you, comfort yourself with the words from Psalm 18:34: "He teacheth my hands to war, so that a bow of steel is broken by mine arms." Come under Christ's government and He will tell you all that you must do.

Objection 4: You may argue, "I would come and give up my name unto Christ and enroll myself in His book to fight against all Christ's enemies, but even if I had the skill, I do not have the strength." I say to you that you must give up your name, for "in that day shall the LORD defend the inhabitants of Jerusalem; and he that is feeble among them at that day shall be as David; and the house of David shall be as God, as the angel of the LORD before them" (Zech. 12:8).Yes, I say to you, "Fear thou not; for I am with thee: be not dismayed; for I am thy God: I will strengthen thee; yea, I will help thee; yea, I will uphold thee with the right hand of my righteousness" (Isa. 41:10). We hear, "I will help thee" (v. 14); though you have no more strength than a worm to fight against your temptations, "fear not, thou worm Jacob, and ye men of Israel; I will help thee, saith the LORD, and thy redeemer, the Holy One of Israel" (v. 14). There is more required of you; if you give up your name, you shall beat your enemies as small as the dust of the mountains, and all that stand against you, you shall beat them small as chaff.

Objection 5: Then you may argue, "I would give up my name to Christ to fight, but I fear my idols are so strong that I will not overcome them." I answer, "They that war against thee shall all be as nothing" (Isa. 41:12). Is this not a precious promise? All your idols shall be as nothing if you subscribe your name to fight for Christ. Yes, they will be counted as less than nothing if you give up your name to Christ. Every idol you encounter, you will overcome with the help of Christ. "One man of you shall chase a thousand: for the LORD your God, he it is that fighteth for you, as he hath promised you" (Josh. 23:10).

Objection 6: Another would argue, "I fear that I would turn a coward in the day of war; I fear that I would desert Christ and so dishonor Him, if I engage myself with Him." You who are afraid, and who despair of your own strength, comfort yourself with this: you may wax strong through the Captain. Though you despair of yourself, one sight of your Captain may make you fight with strength. "The righteous are bold as a lion" (Prov. 28:1).

Objection 7: You ask, "What encouragement do you give for me to give up my name? Is there nothing to persuade me to enter into this blessed bond?" Let me give you six blessed reasons to enter into this bond with Christ.

1. Old men, young men, old women, and maids, give up your names to Christ to fight under His banner, and you shall get a crown for your wages. Christ is standing at the end of every Christian's race with a crown in His right hand, crying out, "To him that overcometh will I grant to sit with me in my throne" (Rev. 3:21). What a day it will be when Christ shall put the crown upon your head and say unto you, "Welcome, conqueror!" I think, if we may say so, there is a blessed and yet an orderly confusion of victory between Christ and the believer. Christ overcomes the believer, and the believer (in a manner) overcomes Christ. Let us look at Song of Solomon 6:3, where we read, "Turn away thine eyes from me, for they have overcome me." I say to you, if you knew what an excellent crown this was, you would not refuse to give up your name to Christ.

2. A second encouragement is that Christ's faithfulness is laid in pledge for your victory. You are as sure of victory as Christ is faithful. Once you are fairly entered, you shall at last sing the triumphant song: "O death! where is thy sting? O grave, where is thy victory?" (1 Cor. 15:55).

3. No weapon that is framed against you shall prosper; the gates of hell shall not prevail against you. You may stand with confidence, dear Christian, when you are engaged to Christ. You may stand with confidence and cry out, "Yonder is the Person that will help me tread Satan under my feet!" You may comfort yourself with this: Satan may bruise my heel, but I shall bruise his head. Dear believer, the victory is certain; does this not persuade you to engage in this blessed war?

4. A fourth encouragement to persuade you is, the fight will not last for many hundreds of years. How long are you to fight? It is only for a very short time; before long you shall triumph and put up the blessed trophies of your victory. You who have given your names to Christ, before long you will stand upon the sea of glass, having the harps of God in your hands. Before long, you will be above the

reach of sin; before long, you will be above the reach of temptations to sin. You who are engaged to Christ, before tomorrow, your fight may be finished and your victory may be at hand.

5. I would say this, oh Christian who has given up your name to Christ: what a day it will be when you hear, "Speak ye comfortably to Jerusalem, and cry unto her, that her warfare is accomplished, that her iniquity is pardoned: for she hath received of the LORD's hand double for all her sins" (Isa. 40:2). What a day it will be, when Christ shall command you to rejoice at those who divide the spoil! I confess indeed, faith and hope do fight the war, but love and sight sit at home and divide the spoil. Faith is the grace that fights, but love is the grace that overcomes; or rather faith and hope are the graces that fight and overcome, but love and sight receive the sweet fruits of victory.

6. The sixth encouragement to persuade and engage you to give up your names unto Christ is that all of us here must know and be persuaded that either temptations must overcome us, or we must overcome our temptations. Either you must overcome the devil or he will overcome you. Now, what do we answer? Are you content to give up your names to Christ?

I shall ask the least that I can ask of you, and it is these two things. If you will give Christ no more, at least give Him these two things.

First, if you will not engage to fight with Christ, will you engage not to fight against Him? If you will give me no more today, will you at least say that you will never fight for the devil anymore? Perhaps the next sermon that you hear, you will finally conclude that you will never fight with another than Christ. Is not this the least that can be demanded? Shall it be said in heaven tonight of anyone here that they will not lay down the weapons of their rebellion against the Son of God? This epitaph is given to some: "Haters of God" (Rom. 1:30). Here, Paul is speaking of himself, saying that he did once fight against God. Now, are you content to grant this request unto Christ? Will you lay down the weapons of your rebellion, though you may not grant the other part of the invitation?

Second, this is the least that you should give: if your heart will not consent to enroll yourself into His book, will you consent with your mouth that you will never be for any but for Christ? I hope you will find this reasonable. Oh, shall it be told in heaven, that there is a blessed war concluded in Glasgow this night against the devil and all that will take his part? Shall it be told in heaven tonight that there is a blessed war concluded by you; you have determined and resolved to wage an eternal war against all who stand in opposition to Christ? Oh, what a blessed report would this be! How it would make the heart of Christ rejoice! Now, what is your reply? Are you resolved to give up your name to Christ? Then come away and put your name to this excellent and noble offer that is given to you. I hope you have nothing to say against it.

I desire to remove only one point. "Oh!" you may say, "Is there any so cursed who will not come to Christ, if they had strength to do it? Alas! I lack strength!"

First, when you complain that you lack strength, you may know that what you are really lacking is willingness. Christ knows what the father of our unbelief is better than we do. "Ye will not come to me" (John 5:40). If you say that you are willing to come, but not able to come, then Christ must answer the objection, for it is above the reach of a minister. I defy all the ministers in Scotland to answer this objection: I am willing to come, but I cannot. I would only say to you, comfort yourself, knowing that Christ will compel you, though your will and your ability may both be against it. He will compel you to come and give your consent. I wish no greater blessedness out of heaven than to be under the sweet compelling force of the love of Christ. Are you content to be compelled? Then let Christ and you decide the controversy. Once you reach this point, you are content to be compelled.

Secondly, I say to you who complain that you would come to Christ, but you cannot, I think Christ is engaged to the Father so that He can help you and give you strength. I defy all the persons who shall stand upon Christ's left hand at the last day, to say they were willing to come to Christ, but were not able. If you were willing to come to Christ, you would have strength to come. If you lack strength to engage yourself to Christ, go to Him and plead upon

His own promise. Does He not promise, "Him that cometh to me I will in no wise cast out"? Christ says to you tonight, "Give Me but a hearty consent, and I will give you strength to close with Me."

The third thing that I say unto those who say they desire to come, but cannot, is that I hope if you have indeed come this far, you are not far from closing with Christ. Do you think that when the sinner is willing and Christ is willing, that it is long until the bargain closing? Do you think when you are pursuing to close with Christ and He is pursuing you to close with Him, that it will be long until closing? If Christ cries, "Come!" and the soul cries, "Come!" do you think it will be long before closing? If the gospel cries, "Come!" and your heart cries, "Come!" do you not think they will close before long? You who are willing to come, but unable to come, Christ will help you. He will give you strength. What do you say to this? Is there no one who will enroll his name in Christ's book? Shall the contract be sent back to heaven blank tonight; shall there not be one more name seen on it than was on it before? Every Sabbath day the contract is sent down to you; I suppose there are not many subscribers in Glasgow. Alas! The ministers of Scotland are forced every Sabbath night to send up the contract blank to Christ, just as it came.

Oh, shall we send back the contract to Christ blank with no names on it but Christ? Christ has put His name on the contract, and He has sent it down to you, desiring you to put your name on it. Will none of you put your hand to subscribe? Are you not content with it? Is it not a good bargain? I hope you think Christ is easily got, for you can get Christ for two words—your name and your surname. Oh, cursed be that person who refuses the pen when it is given to him! Oh, will you not subscribe?

I do not want you to have any carnal conceptions of this blessed contract. Heaven is waiting for your answer. There is not a person within these doors that knows, but the persons of the Trinity know whether or not you refuse. You secretly refuse, and you think there is no one who sees you. But there are three in heaven that know and see what you do. Consider that Christ sees whether you consent or not, and all the persons of the blessed Trinity see whether you consent or not. Christ is waiting to see what you will say. He is crying out, "Will you not give Me your consent?"

Fourth, there are two wooers and suitors that have come to Glasgow today; the Prince of heaven has come to woo you today, and the prince of the bottomless pit has come to woo you. You must either close with the one or with the other. Now which of the persons will you take? I think you need not seek advice, for where there is no choice, there should be no deliberation. Though you have never seen Christ, take him blindly. If Christ is not more than you hoped for, quit Him when you see Him. If Christ is not above your faith, you may quit Him when you see Him. If Christ is not greater than our report, quit Him when you see Him. If Christ is not above your desires, quit Him when you see Him. If you could enlarge your desires as the sand on the seashore, if He is not above your desires, quit Him when you see Him. If He gives you no more than your necessity requires, quit Him when you see Him. If Christ is not above your thoughts and opinion of Him, quit Him when you see Him. If Christ is not greater than your report, your faith, your hope, your desires, your necessities, your thoughts and your opinion of Him, then quit Him when you come and see Him. But oh, will you quit Him? Shall He go out of these doors tonight saying, "There is none who will take Me"? Shall Christ return to heaven tonight, saying, "There is none in Glasgow who will take Me"? Is there anyone here who will have Him? Oh, take Him and come away!

Now I shall close discussing the six reports that will be given in response to this message.

First, is there any that will give Agrippa's report tonight? This sad report is, "Almost thou persuadest me to be a Christian" (Acts 26:28). Is this your report? If I can have no more, give me this to report to heaven tonight, that you are almost persuaded to be Christians. I think it is a deficient report; yet, if you will say no more to Christ, say this, "Almost thou persuadest me to be a Christian." Thou hast almost persuaded me to love Thee. Oh, if only the word *almost* were brought to an *altogether*, to make the answer complete! Then we could say with joy, "Oh, Christ, Thou hast *altogether* persuaded me to love Thee, and to embrace Thy offers."

Second, there are some who will give Felix's answer and speak the words that Felix spoke to Paul: "Go thy way," Christ, "this time; when I have a convenient season, I will call for thee" (Acts 24:25). Is there anyone who will send Christ away with this answer? Do you dare to send the Son of God away with this response? "I will call for thee at a more convenient season." Is not *this* the convenient time? Is not His time the convenient time? Oh, shall any be so bold as to give Felix's answer? Is there a person here tonight who desires this report to be carried to heaven of them? I will think upon the business until another time, and I desire Christ to come and woo me at another time. I say unto you, whoever you may be, you know neither yourself nor Christ.

Third, some will give a complimentary answer to Christ, such as can be found in Matthew 20 and Luke 14. When we invite you to come to Christ and to enroll yourselves in His book, your answer is, "Go tell Christ, 'I have bought a piece of ground, and I must needs go and see it'" (Luke 14:18). I say to you that I shall never excuse you. Yes, I shall accuse you to Christ if you come not away. Will I excuse your rebellion? No, I shall accuse you to Christ, and not excuse you.

Some will give this answer to Christ's blessed offer: I will consider it and ask advice. I entreat you to do this, if no more; and if you will not tell me what I shall report to Christ, I pray report to Christ tonight yourself. I shall be content to commit the report to you, but I pray you report your minds. Heaven is waiting for your report. Now you desire to seek advice, then go home and think upon it.

Fifth, there are some who will give this answer to that blessed offer: "Go tell the King of heaven that I will not have Him to reign over me." Are there any here tonight of whom I shall report this? Do you dare bid me tell Christ in your name that you will not have Christ to reign over you? Is there anyone so bold as to give this answer?

Sixth, there are some who will give this answer to Christ when we persuade them to come and take Him: "I will come, but first I must go and bury my father. I will come; and go tell Christ, I will come; but first I must go home and bid farewell to those who are at home. I must first go and set my house in order, and then I will come." I say to you go, let the dead bury their dead, and come and follow Him. Christ waits for your return—for your present answer. Now, what do you say to Him? Are you content? What can persuade you? I shall leave these five further things with you.

First, tell me what you desire of Christ, so that I may report that to Him, to make up the bargain. Is there anything that you desire more than this contract bears? Would you desire an article of the contract to be changed? Or would you have any article put into it that is lacking? Is not the contract complete? Are not all of you here witnesses of the fact that the contract is complete? I hope that none of you here would desire an article annulled from this contract that is complete. Further, I hope that there are none who will venture to add anything to this contract which is not here already.

Secondly, if you do not obey us, if Christ Himself were coming to woo you, you would not obey Him either. I would only say this to you: if Christ would come from heaven and preach in the pulpit of Glasgow, you would shut both your eyes and your ears. You would shut your eyes, lest you should be overcome with His beauty. You would shut your ears, lest you would be overtaken with the sweet enchanting voice of the charmer, when He should charm so wisely.

Thirdly, I would say to you, God forbid the desolation that shall come upon you if you do not embrace this good and everlasting gospel. If you do not embrace the gospel, your houses shall be left unto you desolate, until the day shall come that you shall say, "Blessed is he that cometh in the name of the Lord" (Matt. 23:39).

Fourthly, know that Christ is crying in heaven to you, "Glasgow, Glasgow—how oft would I have gathered thee together, as a hen doth her chickens under her wings, and ye would not?" Oh, Glasgow, why will you not come away? Do you not think that Christ is weeping over this place tonight because you will not know in this your duty, the things that belong to your peace? Is there a heart so cruel here, as to give Christ an occasion of weeping in heaven? Yea, if you do not consent, your words pierce into His bones.

Fifthly, I shall give the gospel at the lowest offer that can be made. Glasgow, you shall have Christ for any one of these four things.

> 1. Glasgow, you may have Christ by simply putting your name on the contract. Here is the contract—put your name and surname on it, and you shall get heaven, Christ, and all. You do not, of course, deserve this, but you shall be freely given all these things. Now, at what lower rate can Christ be gotten, than for this? Now, if you cannot put your name, put your mark for your name, and another for your surname.
>
> 2. You will get Christ for a mere look; will you not give Christ one look? You will get heaven, Christ, and salvation for it. "Look unto me, and be ye saved, all the ends of the earth: for I am God, and there is none else" (Isa. 45:22). Oh, will you begin to look to Christ?

There are two objections I must remove here by the way. First, you may say that you are a great distance from Christ; therefore, you cannot look to Him. You complain that you are far from Christ by many degrees. The verse says that from the ends of the earth we must look to Christ; though you were as far distant from Him as the east is from the west, yet He will be content if you look to Him. A second objection is that you would look to Christ, but you cannot. To you I say that your look is in a promise—the very look for which you shall get Christ. We read in Zechariah 12:10, "They shall look upon me whom they have pierced." Christ says, "Behold Me, behold Me!" Now, is not that a low rate? Yet, the great voice of heaven says, "I am found of them that sought me not: I said, Behold me, behold me, unto a nation that was not called by my name" (Isa. 65:1). Now, is there a person here who will refuse to give Him one look? Your cursed eyes shall never see such a pleasant sight. Christ is here this afternoon; do you dare refuse Him one look? Shall it be said in heaven, "I was here, and there was no one who was aware of it." Oh, that the scales would fall from our eyes, that we might see!

3. I offer Christ to you for this: will you give ear and hearken to the offer, for then you shall get Christ. Is this not a great condescension? You will get Christ for a listening of the ear! I say, hearken to this offer, and you shall get Him. We read in Isaiah 55:2, "Hearken diligently unto me, and eat ye that which is good, and let your soul delight itself in fatness." After hearing this promise, will you be content to hearken to this offer? Oh, will you hear Christ? He will give you Himself upon these very terms, and I hope that you never have to regret your decision.

4. In Christ's name, and at His command, I offer Christ unto you for one desire. Is there not a person here who has one desire for Christ? Heaven declares unto you tonight that you shall get heaven for one desire.

Now, which of the four options will you consider? Will you sign your name to this contract? If you cannot, at least put two marks on the page—one for your name and another for your surname. Will you give Him one look, or will you listen with your ear and hearken to His offer? Will you give Christ one desire and have Him at any of these rates? Is He not offered unto you for a small price? Will you refuse Him? Can you imagine any lower terms to buy Christ? Are you content to take Him? Shall it be declared in heaven that no one would take Christ, though He is offered at so low a rate? Know that Christ will tell your names to the Father tonight; He will tell the Father that such a person would not give Him one desire, not one look, not one listening of the ear, nor would put his name to the contract. I offer Christ for any of the four options. Put down your name; give Him a look, a hearing, or a desire, and you shall not go away without closing the bargain.

Christ never seeks anything from you; you have never seen a contract after this manner. "I promise and covenant to give to My spouse a kingdom and faith and righteousness and a crown; I promise and covenant to give to My spouse sanctification; I promise and covenant to give to My spouse redemption, life, peace, joy, and contentment. I promise them all." Now, where is the thing that He will take from you? What does He require on your part? He seeks nothing from you but that you be content. He desires that you take Him with all things, but come to Him with nothing. That is Christ's word. He says, "Come, take Me with all things, and come to Me with nothing." Is not this a free offer? Have you ever seen such a contract? But shall this contract be sent back to heaven blank? Is there no one here who will put down your name? If you will not, know that the day is coming when you shall know you have forsaken your own mercy.

God forbid that heaven should weep tonight over Glasgow. Is your consent ready? I charge you in the name of my Master Christ, every one of you, ask yourselves: is my consent ready? Ask it now, for I do not wish to leave you without closing with this blessed offer. Therefore, I shall propose five points to persuade you to give up your names unto Christ. I would charge you to consider them.

First, know that heaven and all the Persons of the blessed Trinity are waiting for your answer. This must provoke you to come and to enroll yourself in this book. I hope you would not be content if there were a bad report carried back to heaven of you. Have you not read the words that Solomon wrote? He wrote, "A good name is better than precious ointment" (Eccl. 7:1). A good report of you before all heaven tonight is better than much precious ointment. All heaven is waiting for the coming of your report. Now, give up your name to Christ.

A second persuasion to give up your name to Christ is that I am confident that when you will be made gloriously like Him and shall see Him face to face, you shall be obliged to cry out, "Blessed be the day that ever Christ and I met together! Oh, blessed be the day that He condescended to woo and court me!" I desire not to speak much to you concerning the mysteries of the joys of heaven. Oh, what will you think on that day, when you will be called to the marriage supper of the Lamb? You will go into the eternal bed of love, there to remain with Christ forever.

Third, ask whatever you please of Christ, and He will give it to you. There has never before been a wooer who, when he came to woo his bride, gave such a generous proposal as this. Sinner, ask whatever you desire; Christ will give it to you. There shall be no more between you two if you will take Christ; only ask and have. Is that not sweet and comfortable communing? You have no more worry; you need only send up a messenger to Christ and He will send down your request unto you.

A fourth consideration for you to press closer to Christ is that in the day that you shall look eternity in the face, when the king of terrors shall summon you to go there, you will be able to say, "Welcome, friend." Christ sends death with a letter of love in His hand, and the letter says, "Arise my love, my dove, my fair one, and come away." Death will commend this excellent bargain of closing with Christ.

Another thing that may persuade you is that once you are content to take Christ as your own, you shall have a blessed relation made up between heaven and you. Is it not sweet to look to heaven and say, "Oh, my Father, my Husband, my Brother, and my Redeemer"?

A final point whereby I would persuade you to come and give up your name to Christ is this: if you would give Christ a thousand kingdoms, He would not be so content, nor rejoice, as if you would but give Him your consent today. I defy angels to express the joy that Christ would have if you would be content to take Him. Oh, Glasgow, take Him! This would make Him rejoice with joy unspeakable, and it would be to Him the gladness of His heart.

In closing, do not delay to come away. I fear that I am forced to return a blank report of you by all appearances. I must report tonight that I know not what to say; for what does the appearance of your countenance speak? Does it say that you are content to take Him? If Christ were embraced tonight and the contract were full of subscriptions, our countenances would declare it more than they do. I wish there were more heart-work; though that takes place on the inside, I think it would appear also more on the outside. Now, do you not find it sad that we would go away as much strangers to Christ as when we came? Oh, who will do the favor to Christ as to put to their hand and subscribe, content? If I can have no more, let one come and put to his hand, though he should indeed be striving to be first. Oh, will you not strive for this honor?

Thus, ask yourselves: what will you report? Do you have your report ready to give to heaven? Oh, come away, let us hear it. If you desire to go home, tell Christ your report in secret. I think it would be a report more suitable for angels than for us to commend Christ to you.

Old men, will you come away? Men of fifty years, come away and subscribe; your time is already far spent. Christ's Father is always ready. Are you not content to come and take Christ? Christ is still willing to take you. What do you say, old men? Will you think upon it? Your gray hairs should be a crown of glory, but what if they are not found in the way of righteousness? Now, if you desire your gray hair to be a crown of glory, then come away, old men. I entreat you, by the beauty of Christ, come away. You do not know what a low price He is offered at! Oh, come and subscribe! You have subscribed to many blank contracts; if the devil would present to your view all the contracts that you have signed with him, you would wonder that Christ would ever condescend to subscribe a contract with you. "Thou hast played the harlot with many lovers; yet return again to me, saith the LORD" (Jer. 3:1).

Dear old women, come away, for He is waiting for you. Old women, you will get Christ for one desire. Will you come away?

Young men who are taken up in pursuing youthful lusts, come away! You who spend your years in vanity and your days as a tale that is told, come away. You ask, "Oh, will Christ make me welcome, if I come?" I say He will make you welcome. Oh, come away!

Young women, come away to Christ. Dear young women who look for husbands, come away and be married to Christ. He is the most blessed husband that you could ever find. Oh, young women, will you come away to Christ? I think it would be best if you are married to Christ before you be married to another husband. Christ can give you a fair portion. If a man were seeking a wife, what can he find who has more than this: I have Christ for my husband already? He may say, "I have Glasgow for my portion." Yes, it is more than the kings of the earth can say. I say unto you, young women, come away. You know at what low rates He is given; therefore come away to Him.

Now, are there neither old men nor old women, young men nor young women who will come away? To Him who can persuade you to come away, to Him who waits for your return, we desire to give praise. Amen.

SERMON 37

Singular Temptations Call for Fervent and Frequent Supplications (4)

For this thing I besought the Lord thrice,
that it might depart from me.
—2 Corinthians 12:8

Oh, hopeful travelers and expectants of the crown, do you think that if you shall be in heaven, that it will be a great mystery to all who are there? Will it not be a mystery to wrestling Jacob, who spent so much of his time in praying to God, if such prayerless Christians as we are shall go to heaven? Will it not be a mystery to patient Job, if such impatient Christians as we are shall go to heaven? Will it not be a mystery to heavenly Enoch, who spent so much of his time walking with God, if such Christians as we are, who undervalued communion and fellowship with God, shall go to heaven? Will it not be a mystery to upright Nathaniel, in whose heart there was no guile, if such hypocritical Christians as we are shall go to heaven? May not all these blessed thousands who are now about the throne lay aside their harps and give us leave to sing? We shall be the most precious, the most wonderful monuments of Christ's victory and power that shall be in heaven.

Before I discuss the text, let us consider four points to make our discourse clear.

First, it is a duty incumbent upon a Christian to take notice of and to observe in what part of his prayer he finds most liberty and enlargement. I trust you know that there are three parts of prayer: confession, petitions, and praises. If you have more liberty in confessing to God than in seeking from Him, that is the call of God unto you to be much in confession. Likewise, if in your prayers you have most liberty in praise, it is the call of God unto you to be much in praise while you pray. Take notice in what part of prayer God is seeking your enlargement; for unto whatever part He directs your liberty and enlargement, it is His call unto you to be much in that part of prayer.

Secondly, it is a Christian's duty to observe to which religious duty God directs you. There are some Christians who find most liberty in reading the Scriptures; some Christians find most liberty in meditation; and some Christians find most liberty in prayer. Now in whichever duty you find most liberty and enlargement, be much in the exercise of that duty.

Thirdly, a Christian must observe the most profitable time and season to go about his duty. When is he often in the best capacity to go about a duty? A Christian should observe whether he is most fit for going about duties of religion in the morning, at noon, or at night. Whatever the time that he finds himself in the most suitable frame, he should perform his duty at that time.

Last, it is a Christian's responsibility to be importunate with God, to be wrestling as a prince with Him until he prevails. Where has the exercise of prayer gone? I think that if all the persons within these doors were asked if they had prayed before coming here, and if all who did not pray today before coming would leave, we would have a small congregation. Is there any man here like David, who in morning, afternoon, and evening would call upon God? Is there any man here who would prevent the dawning of the morning and the night-watches to call upon God and to meditate upon His Word? Is there any woman in Glasgow like the precious woman mentioned in Luke 2:37? Oh, women, read this and be ashamed, for I think there are none here who endeavor to be like her. She was a widow of about eighty-four years, and she departed not from the temple, but served God with fasting and prayer night and day. Is that not a noble epitaph of a person wholly devoted unto God? For eighty-four years, she never departed from the temple; for eighty-four years, she fasted and prayed night and day. Oh, if only there were many such women among us!

Now let us consider the text. We told you that in this eighth verse, there are seven things we intended to address. We have already mentioned four of them in the previous sermon, and shall not repeat them.

Thus, a fifth point we would like to make is that a Christian may be exceedingly earnest in the exercise of prayer, and yet not meet with any sensible answer. We can clearly see this when Paul was brought to pray many times before he received an answer. In Psalm 22:2 we read, "O my God, I cry in the day time, but thou hearest not; and in the night season, and am not silent." It is likewise clear in Lamentations 3:8 where we read, "Also when I cry and shout, he shutteth out my prayer." In Psalm 22:1 we hear Christ's prayer, which the Father did not answer: "My God, my God, why hast thou forsaken me?" Yet in the second verse He goes so far as to say, "I cry in the day time, but thou hearest not." In Psalm 69:3 we see David exceedingly serious and importunate, and yet not hearing any sensible answer: "I am weary of my crying: my throat is dried: mine eyes fail while I wait for my God."

Before we speak upon this truth, I shall clarify what it means to be importunate and serious in the exercise of prayer. This practice comprehends five things.

First, a Christian must engage his whole heart in a serious quest for that which he wants, so that when he is seeking anything from God he can say unto Him, "With my whole heart have I sought thee" (Ps. 119:10). I confess that in most of our prayers in these days, half of our heart does not seek the thing that we want from God.

Second, a Christian must be frequent in presenting and renewing his desires to God for such a thing—he must be importunate in prayer. You must be persistent, so that when you cannot get such a thing in the morning, you seek it at noon; and when you cannot obtain it at noon, you seek it at night. You do not rest until you obtain it. To be importunate is never to leave God, but to wait at the posts of wisdom's doors until He shall condescend to answer you. If He will not give you that which you seek, you resolve to die waiting for it. This is the importunity required in prayer. I confess these are not importunate Christians who, if they seek once from God, and He does not give them their desires, they never seek it again, and justify themselves in so doing.

Third, Christians must have a divine restlessness and holy impatience until they have that which they seek; they must be impatient in a holy way until they receive an answer. They must cry out to God, "Lighten mine eyes, lest I sleep the sleep of death" (Ps. 13:3); they cry out, "Hear me speedily, O LORD: my spirit faileth:

hide not thy face from me, lest I be like unto them that go down into the pit" (Ps. 143:7).

Fourth, importunity means that a Christian must wrestle with all discouragements that stand in his way to seeking such a thing. Thus, though one temptation assaults him upon the right hand and another temptation upon the left hand, yet an importunate Christian will break through all these discouragements and will not rest until he obtains that which he seeks. Yes, if you are importunate and serious with God, even if He should forbid you to seek such a thing, you could not be forbidden. Follow the example of Moses: when God said unto him, "Let me alone," yet he would not. He persisted in his desire (Ex. 32:10). So it was with importunate Jacob. The angel said unto him, "Let me go, for the day breaketh" (Gen. 32:26). Jacob replied with much importunity: "I will not let thee go, except thou bless me" (v. 26). Importunity in prayer has a kind of great impudence. It has no shame. Do you not think that Jacob's speech was very bold? Yet, such seriousness and importunity in prayer is allowed by God; yes, I say to you, when God is going away from you, you may take Him by the skirts of His garments and constrain Him to stay all night with you.

Last, importunity in prayer means that a Christian must not be content with a small measure of the returns of his prayer, but to pursue after the full and satisfying answer to his prayer. An importunate Christian, when he receives the first bit of the answer to his prayer, will not rest there until he obtains it altogether.

Now, a Christian may be importunate and serious in prayer, yet have no sensible answer, nor success. Let us discuss this situation.

First, as for the ground of these dispensations, what can be the reason that a Christian should be importunate in seeking something from God, yet not obtain that which he requested? Let us discuss nine reasons this could occur.

> 1. A Christian is often too peremptory in seeking such a particular thing from God. This hinders and obstructs the answer to prayer. Are there not many of us who are like Rachel, crying out, "Give me children, or else I die" (Gen. 30:1)? We go to God and we cry, "Give me such a thing, or I will perish!" Nothing obstructs the return of a serious prayer so much as limiting the sovereignty of God in our prayers. Be as serious as you will, but leave the answer

blank for God's sovereignty to dispense as He desires to give you.

2. A Christian may be importunate in prayer, yet not have a response because we trust too much in our importunity. It is difficult for a Christian to be importunate and serious with God for such a mercy, and not to trust his importunity. Believe it, there is nothing that mars your coming to God speedily so much as when you wrestle for an answer from God, and you believe that God is obliged to give you an answer.

3. God may hearken not to such a prayer because we hearken not to the voice of His commandments. If we were hearkening more to the voice of His commandments, He would give us more answers to our prayers than He does. We read in Zechariah 7:13, "Therefore it is come to pass, that as he cried, and they would not hear; so they cried, and I would not hear, saith the LORD of hosts." Thus, the Lord is saying, "If you will not hearken to me when I command, I will not hearken to you, when you pray." "Then shall they cry unto the LORD, but he will not hear them" (Mic. 3:4); but He will chastise you according to all your sins. God often plagues our disobedience by not giving us sensible returns to our prayers.

4. Often, when a Christian is importunate and serious with God, he will only accept that which he seeks, despising all other answers to his prayer. This provokes God to deny him any answer to his prayer. Some will come to God and say, "Oh, give me such a mercy," and if they do not receive that mercy, they think nothing of all the former receipts of the love and mercy of God. I say unto you, there is nothing that obstructs the returns of prayer so much as when you come and seek a certain thing, despising all the former mercies God has granted you. This was the Israelites' fault in Numbers 11:4. They sought flesh and undervalued all the mercies they had formerly received.

5. One may be serious and importunate in prayer, yet not receive an answer, for God may heighten the esteem of the mercy they seek from God. He will delay their answer

to prayer so that they may have a higher regard for the mercy they seek. When Abraham prays for a son, God gives him the mercy; but, He lets a long time pass between Abraham's prayer and the answer to it. This is often the design of God, to wait before giving you sensible returns of your prayer, so that the mercy you seek gains more importance in your eyes.

6. God sometimes delays His answers to our prayers so that we may know it is free grace that is the fountain and origin from whence the mercies spring. I think if a Christian would receive his answers to prayer immediately, when he is serious with God, he would probably grow proud under such a mercy. But He lets us be importunate in the morning and importunate at night, so that we may know that it is grace that answers all our prayers, not our own importunity.

7. God loves to have us always about His throne. He will keep a Christian with a broken leg or a broken arm so that he may not go far out of His sight. If we did not have necessities to oblige us to pray, I doubt much if love would often inspire us to pray; therefore Christ thinks it fit to keep our necessities and wounds bleeding, so that we do not leave the throne of grace but remain constant supplicants to Him. I say to you, dear Christians, bless God for your infirmities. I doubt if you would pray much if you did not have them.

8. God sometimes denies a return to the importunate prayers of His children because there are some idols within their bosom that they still worship. What hinders our answers from heaven? What hinders the precious extracts that God intends to give regarding the answers to our prayers? There is some bosom idol we dandle upon our knee. This is clear: "If I regard iniquity in my heart, the Lord will not hear me" (Ps. 66:18). If there is an idol within my bosom, I am sure God will never answer my prayers. We read in Lamentations 3:42-43, "We have transgressed and have rebelled: thou hast not pardoned. Thou hast covered with anger, and persecuted us: thou hast slain, thou

> hast not pitied." What follows upon that? "Thou hast covered thyself with a cloud, that our prayer should not pass through" (v. 44). I confess that it is no wonder that Christians do not receive many sweet answers to prayer, for there are so many secret idols set up within their bosoms. Is not the sacrifice of him that despises the law an abomination to God? There are seven abominations in our heart that obstruct our answers to prayer and make us go away without these sweet answers from God.
>
> 9. The last ground why God suspends and delays the answers of the importunate prayers of His own is to test the patience, hope, love, and faith of His own. When you meet with delayed answer to prayer, you may write above it, "Here is the faith and patience of the saints." God will try patience by delaying to answer your prayers. Yes, He will try your love by whether you seek Him for the loaves or for Himself. Have you ever been content to be much in prayer, though you may not get an answer all your days?

Let us discuss five more points. First, it is not a wonder that many of us do not receive answers from God, because we are not serious and importunate with God when we seek things from Him. I will give you a description of many of our prayers: there are many whose prayers are the breach of the third commandment. Their prayers take the name of the Lord their God in vain. Yea, I may say, some of their prayers are as a building in the air. The words they speak come out with so little force that they die before they are halfway to heaven. I think if some heard us praying when we are alone, I am sure they would cry out, "I am persuaded that yonder person is complimenting himself with God; he is not serious." I think if some were privy to our secret devotions, they would say, "I am sure yonder person lacks nothing; he seeks with such coldness from God."

Secondly, when we shall be standing upon the utmost line between time and eternity, and shall look back upon our prayers, it shall be a heartless sight to many of us. I think there are five things in prayer in which we display much hypocrisy.

> 1. We practice hypocrisy in our confessions to God. We often confess things to God that are not our burdens. We will come and confess sins to God, but we are no more

troubled with them than with stones in a wall. We come to God and confess that we are burdened and oppressed with such an idol, yet in truth, our hearts were never troubled with it. I say, it is a damnable thing to lie to the Holy Ghost. Perhaps we do not truly know our own hearts. How often have you confessed your sins to God? You dare not have heaven be your witness, as you have never been pained in your heart for them all. I think that this shows your true heart-belief and faith: you believe that God is an idol, otherwise you would never dare to vent your confessions to God, and you would never be burdened with sin. I may say that some of you are so little moved in prayer that your confession could be mistaken for praise.

2. Some vent much hypocrisy in their desires. We seek things by guess from God. Yes, sometimes when we go to our knees, we ask God for the first thing that comes into our head, though we never thought upon it before. You may seek something from God, but your heart is no more affected with it than if you did not desire it at all. Many have more desires to fill up their prayers than to fill up their necessities. If we knew how to fill up our prayers, we would never confess, pray, or praise. Yes, I would ask you this: when have you, before you went to prayer, taken pains to discover the necessity and excellence of the thing you seek, so that you might be serious in seeking it?

3. We vent much hypocrisy to God in our praises. Some will begin by praising God that Christ died, and that we were purchased from death, when this does not even affect our heart. Sometimes we praise God for things that never affected our heart; some will even praise God for mercies for which they never felt thankful to God in their heart.

4. Many vent much hypocrisy in their action of grace in prayer. Some of us, when we come before God, will begin our prayers saying, "Our Father which art in heaven"; or we will begin our prayers with these words: "My Lord and my God." There are many who will call God their Father, whom He will never call sons and daughters. There are many who call Christ their husband, whom He

will never His call wife. I wonder how some of us can so easily call God 'Father'; what if God should say unto you, "You liar; I am not your Father, and I should stop your mouth and serve an inhibition upon you, so that you could never again have that word in your mouth." It is a significant claim to begin prayers with the words 'My God'; he is truly blessed who can use these words without hypocrisy.

5. Last, we vent our hypocrisy in prayer when we use beautiful expressions. Many speak great, swelling words of vanity in their prayers; in fact, many are more concerned with speaking well than praying well. I think that we imagine that God is an orator who will look to, and be pleased with, fine basking of discourse. Look at Luke 18. The former was better basked than the other, yet the latter was best heard. Believe it, he prays not best that speaks best and most to God in prayer. I say, if you speak with sincerity, it may have more success in heaven than if you would bask your prayers with the finest notions of discourse that can be imagined. I would only add to this that many seek the gift of prayer more than the grace of prayer. If they have the gift of prayer, and can exercise it in prayer, they will not mourn for the lack of the grace of prayer. Pay more attention to the sincerity of your grace in prayer than the show of your gift in speaking. Some Christians, if they are not straitened in the exercise of gifts, never mourn to God when they are straitened in their grace. There may be much enlargement of gifts and expressions, even when there is no enlargement of grace.

If you are serious in the exercise of prayer, these characteristics will accompany your prayers.

First, if you are serious in the exercise of prayer, there shall be no more between God and you. Ask and you shall receive. Old men, is this not a fair advantage? If you pray, there shall be no more between God and you. "Ask, and it shall be given you; seek, and ye shall find; knock, and it shall be opened unto you" (Matt. 7:6-8). I am sure the things of God are worth seeking.

Second, I will commend the duty of prayer, for you must be serious in it! Prayer is the channel through which all the excellent gifts of heaven are conveyed unto your soul.

Third, the wrath and indignation of God will come upon the families that do not call upon God. I know there are some of you who would rather go many miles than be engaged to bow your knees to God before your family. I desire all of you to read Jeremiah 10:25: "Pour out thy fury upon the heathen that know thee not, and upon the families that call not on thy name: for they have eaten up Jacob, and devoured him, and consumed him, and have made his habitation desolate." Jeremiah says that he desires God's wrath to pour upon every family that calls not upon the name of God. Similarly, it is David's prayer in Psalm 79:6: "Pour out thy wrath upon the heathen that have not known thee, and upon the kingdoms that have not called upon thy name." I know Christ will not get much lodging in some of your families. If there is a person in all the family who desires to pray, some may be a thorn in the side of that person and persecute him. But I would say to you who persecute those who pray, that God will persecute you one day. I exhort you who have been slighters of prayer now for a long time, in His name, set about it this night. If you have nothing to say to God, at least say these words: "Lord, teach me to pray" (Luke 11:1). If you make this request to God, perhaps He will give you another thing to say before you rise from your knees again. Even if you only speak six words to God, you are still bound to pray.

To you who slight family worship, know that your conscience shall one day be heavy with the burden of this sin. What will you answer when you are asked, "Where is the honor wherewith you have honored me in your family?" I think there are many families in Glasgow that are emblems of hell; there is much cursing in them and no praying. What is the exercise of them that are in hell, if not to be cursing God and themselves? Do you think that we should try to convince you to be much in the exercise of prayer? Are you not bound to it by all the cords of heaven? Yet you say, "Let us break his bonds, and cast his cords from us."

Let me give you three thoughts that I think certainly concern you. First, I think some, when they have begun to pray formally, have been made to be serious in that duty. You must set about it—whatever way you do it, do not neglect it. Second, there are many who say they cannot pray. But I ask you, can you seek? I am sure that you can seek. Can you not say, "Lord, I cannot pray"? I believe that some of you have rightly evaluated yourselves, for indeed you cannot pray. If you do not believe in your heart and head that you cannot pray, then indeed, you cannot pray. Third, I denounce the wrath of God upon the person who neglects the worship of God in his family. I think I will not say it is a universal truth, but I believe that the grace of God cannot be in the person who totally slights the worship of God in his family. The full force of God's indignation shall enter into the house that does not have a throne for Christ. I think that many who slight family worship bring a stroke upon them and the place where they live. God may thrust you out of your dwellings, when you do not have a throne for Christ in your home.

You may complain that you do not have the opportunity to pray because of strangers. But I say, you did not pray when there were no guests; therefore, God has sent them upon you as a just plague for your neglect of the duty of family worship. The wrath and indignation of God will surely follow those persons who neglect the duty of prayer in their family and in private.

Now, to further discuss the truth that a Christian may be serious in the exercise of prayer, yet not meet with any sensible return, let us consider nine points.

First, it is the duty of a Christian to expectantly wait for the returns of prayer. This is clear in Psalm 85:8 where we read, "I will hear what God the LORD will speak." These should be a Christian's words after he has prayed. The Christian should cry out, "Now I will wait to hear what the Lord will speak to me." We read in Habakkuk 2:1, "I will stand upon my watch, and set me upon the tower, and will watch to see what he will say unto me." Also, in Psalm 40:1 we read, "I waited patiently for the LORD; and he inclined unto me, and heard my cry"; I sought the Lord and I waited for an answer to my prayer. I will give you six reasons why a Christian should wait for an answer to prayer. Let me emphasize this to you, beloved of the Lord, for I know that many Christians will pray a hundred times and will not wait for one answer to prayer. Believe it, it is easier to pray than to wait for returns of prayer.

The first reason is that not waiting for an answer to prayer says that prayer is a needless work, and that it is an ordinance in which there is no advantage. I say unto you who undervalue waiting for returns of prayer, you are saying that prayer is an empty thing. You are saying that there is no advantage to worshipping God. You who slight waiting for returns of prayer, I give you two thoughts: it will come to pass that the person who slights waiting for an answer to prayer will soon wonder what profit there is to walking mournfully with God and pouring out prayer to Him! Also, if you do not wait for answers to your prayers, it will be impossible for you to have much delight in prayer.

The second reason a Christian should wait for the returns of prayer is that refusing to wait for the returns of prayer denies a glorious and excellent attribute of God: that He is the "hearer of prayer," as He has said of Himself. "O thou that hearest prayer, unto thee shall all flesh come" (Ps. 65:5). Not waiting for the returns of prayer denies that God is the hearer of prayers.

Third, once you come to this length, as not to take thought what becomes of your prayers, it is certain that you will render the most formal, the most hypocritical, the most complimenting prayer unto God that is imaginable. If you do not wait for the returns of prayer, it is impossible to keep you from formality or hypocrisy. It is impossible to keep you out of a sinful indifference toward the thing you are seeking from God. I hope this is known to many of us, that our reluctance to wait for the returns of prayer for ten days has brought on a spirit of formality that we will not shake off for twenty days. I say to you, Christian, as you do not desire to take on a spirit of formality, wait patiently for the answer to your prayer. There are many of us who never ask the Lord what has become of our prayers. When did you last wait for the return of a prayer? It is one of the saddest, most lamentable evidences of the decay of godliness among us—there is so little waiting for the returns of prayer. I confess, we pray to satisfy our natural conscience, but we never pray to get our true necessities supplied.

Fourth, one of the most soul-enriching exercises that a Christian can experience is to wait for answers to prayer. The Christian shall truly know that each word he speaks to God has great worth. If we would wait for the returns of prayer, we would be rich in experience. If we would wait for the returns of prayer, we would be rich in confidence and hope, we would be serious, we would be rich in the exercise of love. If we would wait for the returns of prayer, we would have some distinct knowledge of ourselves. I think it is the Christian who can best describe himself who is most taken up in this most precious duty.

A fifth ground to persuade a Christian to wait for the returns of prayer, is that you have God's promise that He will answer you; therefore, wait. A person that does not wait for the returns of prayer in essence says that many promises in the covenant are not true, or at least, he does not value them. Is not this His promise: "Then shalt thou call, and the LORD shall answer; thou shalt cry, and he shall say, Here I am" (Isa. 58:9)? Is not this a sweet return that is promised to a Christian who prays unto God? He shall say unto him, "Here I am." "Thou shalt weep no more: he will be very gracious unto thee at the voice of thy cry; when he shall hear it, he will answer thee" (Isa. 30:19).

The sixth ground is that a Christian's not waiting for the returns of prayer obstructs many precious returns. If we had been waiting for the answers of our prayers, how many sweet returns from God would we have had in comparison to what we do not have? But, alas! Our slothfulness withholds good things from us. Oh, Christians, will you let me expostulate with you concerning this? Is not your conscience convicted that you do not wait for the return of prayer? We will pray ten times and have a hundred desires, and yet we will not wait for the answer to one of them.

Second, let us consider why a Christian may beseech the Lord and be importunate with God, yet, he does not wait for the return of his prayers. Let us discuss four reasons that may be the cause.

First, a Christian is not convinced of the deep necessity he has for the thing that he seeks. If you were deeply convinced of your necessities, you would weep at the gates of heaven night and day until you get a return. But alas, we seek from God, and our necessities are not seen. A needy Christian will be an importunate Christian.

A second reason may be, even if we see our need for that which we seek, our slothfulness hinders our waiting for a return. No doubt, slothfulness murders this duty exceedingly. It obstructs our waiting for the answer to prayers. When we go to God and seek something from Him, we do not take pains to wait for it, standing upon our watchtower. No, like the sluggard, we desire, but we will not wait: "The soul of the sluggard desireth, and hath nothing: but the soul of the diligent shall be made fat" (Prov. 13:4).

A third thing that hinders our waiting for the returns of prayer is that we do not exercise faith in God's ability and willingness to answer us. Therefore when we pray, either lack of necessity or lack of faith obstruct our waiting for a response.

A final obstruction is that we do not live within sight of the matchless beauty of that for which we pray. Some will pray for the mortifying of an idol, but do not wait for the return of it, because they do not know the advantage and excellence of such a thing. It is certain, often we pray by our sight rather than by our necessities; often we pray by our head rather than by our heart; and often we pray trusting upon our own strength rather than upon the promises of God in Christ.

The third consideration that we would propose unto you is that sometimes a Christian may have an answer to prayer, but not know it. It may seem strange to many that a Christian's prayer may be answered without the Christian knowing it. This can occur for four reasons.

First, there could be a lack of watchfulness. If a Christian is not watching for the answer to prayer, God may give him the answer, and he may not notice. Secondly, God may give the Christian something other than that which he seeks. When the Christian is seeking mortification of an idol, God may give him delight in duty. God sometimes changes the mercy that we seek, and we do not recognize the answer to our prayer. Third, the greatness of the mercy we receive often makes us mistake our answers to prayer. Sometimes to a Christian, the mercy of the return of prayer will be so big in his eyes that he will not believe it: "When the LORD turned again the captivity of Zion, we were like them that dream" (Ps. 126:1). It is as if the people of God would have said that it was a dream for them to think or believe that their prayer was answered. Likewise in Acts 12:14, when the disciples were praying for Peter's deliverance, they got the answer to their prayer. The damsel came and told them Peter was delivered; yet, the greatness of the mercy did so surprise them that they could not believe it. Fourth, there are many indirect precious returns of prayer that Christ gives His own. I shall tell you eight precious, yet indirect answers to prayer that Christ gives to His own, which a Christian should notice.

1. Christ may commend to you the very thing for which you are praying. For example, if you pray for the mortifi-

cation of an idol, Christ may commend this to your heart, saying that it is an excellent thing to seek, and that the mortification of that idol would be a great advantage—that is an answer to your prayer. When the thing is commended to your heart more than it was before, it is evidence that your prayer is answered. To make it clear, when you are seeking delight in the duty of prayer, if the duty is further commended to your heart, though you do not delight in the duty, it is evidence that your prayer is answered. In Luke 17:5-6, the apostles ask the Lord to increase their faith. What was His answer? "If ye had faith as a grain of mustard seed, ye might say unto this sycamine tree, be thou plucked up by the root, and be thou planted in the sea; and it should obey you." Now, I say to you, dear Christian, when you pray for such a mercy, if God commends the thing unto your heart, count it as an indirect answer to prayer.

2. A second indirect answer to prayer is when a Christian has faith that the thing shall be granted unto him. We read in Psalm 10:17, "LORD, thou hast heard the desire of the humble: thou wilt prepare their heart, thou wilt cause thine ear to hear." This may also be translated, "Thou hast established my heart"; that is, Thou hast strengthened me in the hope that my prayers shall be heard, which I take for an answer to prayer. Let me explain it this way: when a Christian prays for a specific spiritual mercy, if he has faith that the mercy will be granted, that is an answer to his prayer.

3. A Christian may have great liberty and enlargement in seeking such a thing from God, so every time he goes to God to seek anything his heart is poured forth as water, and he has liberty to tell his mind to God. This is a token that his prayer is heard and will be answered. This is clear where Job conjoins together God's acceptance of him and the beholding of His face (Job 33:26). It is, in many cases, a very strong evidence that your prayer is accepted when you have liberty to bring such a desire to the throne of grace.

4. When a Christian's anxiety about the thing that he prays for is removed, this is a token that his prayer is heard. This was the case with Hannah. We read in 1 Samuel 1:18 that "her countenance was no more sad." Her anxiety about a son was removed; she takes this as an answer to prayer. I say to you, Christian, if the sinful anxiety about the thing you seek is removed, it is an evidence to you that your prayer is heard. For example, if a Christian were seeking his daily bread from God in prayer, and his sinful anxiety is removed, he puts a blank in God's hand that He may do to him as He will; this is an evidence that his prayer is heard and that it shall be answered.

5. When God suits and prepares a Christian for the mercy that he seeks, the prayer is answered. If you desire that God would prepare your heart to receive the mercy you were seeking, you may take that as a door of hope that your prayer is heard and that it will be answered. This was David's conclusion in Psalm 10:17: "LORD, thou hast heard the desire of the humble: thou wilt prepare their heart, thou wilt cause thine ear to hear." Once my heart is prepared, He will answer the voice of my cry.

6. When a Christian is strengthened to persist in prayer unto God, despite delays, it is clearly an answer to prayer. Psalm 138:3 says, "In the day when I cried thou answeredst me, and strengthenedst me with strength in my soul." This means that the psalmist received the answer to prayer, which was the strength to persist in duty. I ask you, Christian, when you are seeking such a mercy from God, and He answers it not, do you have strength to seek it again, and persist in the duty? This is evidence that your prayer is heard; you shall, before long, receive a gracious return.

7. When a Christian prays for such a mercy, and God condescends to give him another in the place of it, the answer he received is certainly for the better. For instance, Moses prays that he might see the Promised Land (Deut. 34:4). God will not answer that prayer, but He gives a better answer in the place of it. He gives him heaven—that is indeed the Promised Land, the heavenly Canaan. What

disadvantage do you have, Christian, if you receive a mercy far better than that which you sought?

8. The eighth precious indirect response to prayer happens when a Christian is wrestling with a predominant lust. A Christian may think that the more he wrestles, the more it prevails against him. It is an answer to prayer when he receives strength from God to hold up the fight against it. What is Paul's answer after he had prayed thrice? "My grace is sufficient for thee." The Father answers that He will give Paul enough to strengthen him for the fight. Oh, Christian who is complaining that you are praying and wrestling against such a lust, yet it prevails even more, do you comfort yourself with the fact that His grace is sufficient for you?

A fourth consideration that I will propose is that a Christian, when he does not receive a sensible answer to prayer, ought not to give up praying, but persist in it. This was Paul's practice in this situation. He went to God at first, sought that the messenger of Satan might depart from him, and received no answer from God. He met with a silent God. Then again he cries, "Oh, let the messenger of Satan depart from me!" Again, he gets no answer. He goes the third time, prays the same prayer, and perhaps he meets with a silent God there also. Yet, he persists in the duty; he does not give up, although he cannot sense an answer to his prayer. We are commanded to "continue in prayer" (Col. 4:2); or, as the words may be translated according to the original, "Be instant in prayer," and continue until you obtain an answer. Romans 12:12 says, "Continuing instant in prayer." This may also be rendered, "Continue wrestling in prayer"; never give up praying until you obtain an answer. This is a word that is borrowed from hunting dogs; once they have found the scent, they never stop until they find the prey. I say to you, when you meet with a silent God in prayer, I entreat you, do not give over until He condescends to you. Here are five reasons to encourage you to continue in prayer, even if you meet with a silent God.

The first is this: there is no way to obtain the thing you pray for, but by prayer; therefore though you meet with a silent God, continue in prayer.

Second, there may be as much love in the dispensation of a silent God as in the dispensation of a hearkening God. I say there may be sometimes as much love to a Christian in meeting with a silent God as in meeting with an answering God.

Third, if you continue in prayer, despite all disappointments, you shall at last have a blessed issue; you shall go but a little further, and you shall find Him whom your soul loves.

The last ground to encourage you to be instant in prayer, though you meet with a silent God, is that there is much precious advantage that redounds to the Christian by going on in that duty fervently, even when he meets with a silent God. Faith, love, and patience are much in exercise when a Christian prays and meets with a silent God. If God should never speak to you, would you still pray?

Fifth, it is the duty of a Christian to mark the answers to prayer. He must not only observe them or watch to make sure that he receives them, but he should mark and record these answers. I encourage you to record them, so that the answer to prayer will exceedingly strengthen your experience and your boldness in prayer. This would so strengthen your faith that you might remark that you presented such a prayer to God, in such a day of the year, and such a day you received the answer. You should also mark the time and place of your answer to prayer. David did this in Psalm 30:2 and Psalm 34:4: "I sought the Lord, and he heard me, and delivered me from all my fears." Here David marks his returns of prayer. You should also mark the day when you receive an answer to prayer because it is God's command to do so. We read in 1 Kings 3:12, "Behold, I have done according to thy words." He bids Solomon take notice and remark that He had answered him according to his desire. Even if there were no more to encourage a Christian to mark the returns of prayer but the command lying upon him, would this not be more than sufficient? Believe it, there are some who, when they shall be looking death in the face, shall remember the many answers to their prayers, and be very comforted.

Let us, in the sixth place, endeavor to engage you to this noble and excellent work of importunate prayer. To that end, I shall propose seven things to encourage you to be importunate and serious in prayer.

1. Do you desire to know a description of prayer? I will tell you what it is. It is the travel of the soul between emptiness

and fullness, between misery and mercy, between inability to help ourselves and complete ability in Him to help us. Prayer is one depth crying out to another depth; it is the depth of our necessities crying out to the depth of the fullness of God. Prayer is the messenger of the soul by which the soul keeps intimate and familiar correspondence with heaven; is not this a pleasant thing? Do you desire to know what is at court? Then, be much in the precious exercise of prayer. There are some persons who are very taken up in asking news from abroad, from the revolutions of states and kingdoms. But I think that it would be a more suitable question to ask what news there is from heaven. If this question were more often asked among us, we would not need to trouble ourselves so much concerning the other.

2. Be much in prayer unto God and be importunate with Him because the day is approaching and drawing near when the most diligent and importunate with God shall be deeply convicted for not being more diligent and importunate. He who was never very diligent in this duty shall cry out, when he is passing through the gates of death, "Woe is me, that I prayed so little!" The day is approaching when every neglected opportunity to pray will stare you in the face. The day is coming when you will be deeply convicted that you have wasted many invitations to pray. It is certain that when the devil does not present a temptation to divert us from prayer, our heart will invent one, and will invent one of the most plausible diversions that we can to satisfy our natural conscience. Sometimes when we find an opportunity to pray, but we can see a plausible diversion, we are very glad.

3. There is an excellent promise that is annexed to the command to pray. There is a sweet gradation in these words of Christ; first He says, "Ask, and it shall be given unto you" (Matt. 7:7). Now if you cannot get by asking, then "seek, and ye shall find." If you cannot get by seeking, then "knock, and it shall be opened unto you." If you cannot get by asking, go to seeking, and it may be you

shall find; and if you cannot get by seeking, go to knocking, and it shall be opened unto you.

4. Dear Christians, be much in the exercise of prayer, for the day is coming when all your prayers shall be turned into songs of praise; the day is coming when you will pray no more. All your sighs and all your prayers shall be turned into songs of praise.

5. When the Scripture is giving a mark of an unbeliever, what mark does it give? It is that they do not call upon God. If there were nothing more to persuade you, this fact may encourage you to pray, lest you be branded with the mark of an unbeliever. Psalm 14:1 says, "The fool hath said in his heart, there is no God." What is a mark of this person? The Spirit of God says that they do not call upon God. This is the most convincing evidence of him. Are there not many unbelievers in Glasgow, if this is the mark of an unbeliever?

6. Neglecting prayer will incline your heart to a fearless frame, so that you shall not stand in awe of God. "Thou restrainest prayer before God" (Job 15:4); but why? "Thou castest off fear," which here means the fear of God. These two are joined together: casting off fear and restraining prayer.

7. If you were much in the exercise of prayer, what an excellent and sweet use you might have. Oh, what a life you might have, if you were much in the exercise of prayer! A Christian who is much in the exercise of prayer may daily be admitted to walk through the streets of the New Jerusalem. A Christian who is much in the exercise of prayer may daily be admitted to behold Him that is invisible. A Christian who is much in the exercise of prayer may be permitted to have his conversation in heaven, and his heart there as well. What will you not have, if you are serious in the exercise of prayer? Now I desire to know and to ask you this question: is your heart engaged in prayer more than it was before? Oh, slighters of private prayer and slighters of family prayer, do you resolve this night to begin the work which you have slighted all your

> days? I desire to know what you are minded to do in this matter. Are you minded to continue as strangers to this blessed work and precious exercise of prayer?

Seventh, every Christian has a duty to improve his returns of prayer aright. When you meet with a return of prayer, I entreat you to improve the mercy as you ought. There are many who use the answers to prayer for the strengthening of their conceit; there are also many who employ their returns of prayer for strengthening their negligence and slothfulness. There are five specific ways in which a Christian may rightly employ the returns of prayer.

First, a Christian must improve the returns of prayer to strengthen his delight in the duty of prayer more than it was before. This is clear in Psalm 116:2: "I will call upon him as long as I live." What ails you, David, to take on that resolution? "I will tell you the reason," David replies: "Because he hath heard my voice and my supplications" (Ps. 116:1). Improve your returns of prayer for strengthening your delight in your duty.

Second, improve your returns of prayer to strengthen your love to God, so that when you receive answers to your prayers, you may sit down and commend God to your heart for such a mercy. This was David's practice: "I love the LORD, because he hath heard my voice and my supplications" (Ps. 116:1). Oh, Christians, there is more love in one answer to prayer than eternity can make language of. I defy the world to search the depth of the love that lies in God's answers to our prayers.

Third, dear Christian, improve your returns of prayer for the strengthening of your experience, so that when you meet with such a mercy, you may bring it to the storehouse of experiences. It may be unto you for an advantage in the day of evil.

Improve your returns of prayer for the strengthening of your confidence, so that when you are put to a new strait, you may cry out, "Now will I go to my God, to my prayer-answering God who will hearken to the voice of my cry." This is hinted at in Psalm 32:6 where David, pressing for an answer to his prayer, says, "For this shall every one that is godly pray unto thee." Yes, it will engage David himself when he is put to a new strait, to be much in the exercise of prayer.

Fifth, a Christian should employ his answer to prayer to strengthen his interest in God or his assurance of it. Every answer to prayer that a Christian receives is a pledge of everlasting love; with every answer to prayer, a Christian may sit down and cry out, "Now I am passed from death to life"; every answer to prayer directs a Christian to cast up his eyes to heaven and cry out, "My Lord, and my God." I say, improve the returns of prayer for the strengthening of your faith and your assurance of your interest in God.

The next consideration we propose unto you is to distinguish between a Christian's importunity in prayer and the importunity that a hypocrite may attain. We told you that Paul was exceedingly importunate in this place. Now, one may desire to know how he may distinguish between a Christian's importunity in prayer and a hypocrite's importunity in prayer. I shall give you these things to distinguish them.

1. The importunity of a real Christian is accompanied by answers to his prayer. By this I mean that he waits for the answer to his prayer. A real Christian is never satisfied until he receives answers to his prayer, but a hypocrite is satisfied with being importunate, though he does not receive any answer. I confess they may suspect their importunity in prayer who never, since they first began to bow their knee to God, knew what it was to be impatient until they received answers to their prayers.

2. The importunity of a hypocrite runs into another channel than the importunity of a real Christian. A hypocrite's importunity runs after temporal things, as we see in Hosea 7:14: "They howled upon their beds: they assemble themselves for corn and wine, and they rebel against me." The importunity of a Christian runs in a more divine channel; it runs most after communion with God and fellowship with Him, increase of love, and increase of faith. You may distinguish between the importunities by the different channels into which their importunities run.

3. The importunity of a hypocrite is often, if not always, in company. Hypocrites are seldom alone. Suspect the importunity that you have when you are not alone. A Christian's importunity will be sometimes in secret as well as in company. Some hypocrites, when they are praying before folk, will attempt to bring up all their

affections and to have their hearts in a tender frame. This is a damnable evidence of hypocrisy, and proof that one was never truly importunate. There is a strange desire that Christ has for the church: "Thou that dwellest in the gardens, the companions hearken to thy voice: cause me to hear it" (Song 8:13). It is as if Christ would have said, "Not only your companions should hear your voice, but I should hear it also." Therefore, when He is speaking to the bride, He describes her from the exercise of private duty: "O my dove, that art in the clefts of the rock, in the secret places of the stairs, let me see thy countenance, let me hear thy voice; for sweet is thy voice, and thy countenance is comely" (Song 2:14). Suspect your importunity in prayer if it is not sometimes in private as well as in public; for it is certain that there may be importunity in prayer from natural abilities, from the love of applause, and from some conviction, when one is in public. But oh, to have secret importunity with God is blessed!

4. The fourth difference between the importunity of a hypocrite and the importunity of a real Christian is that a hypocrite takes his importunity by fits. I will tell you four times when a hypocrite takes on fits of prayer; he will lay aside all his praying every other time of the day but at that time.

First, when he is under sore affliction, a hypocrite will be found praying. A hypocrite that never prayed seriously to God before will then begin to cry to Him night and day. We see an example of this in Psalm 78:34: "When he slew them, then they sought him." They began to seek Him when He began to slay them, but never until then. During affliction, they will enquire early before God. Affliction will put the hypocrite on his knees in a way that conscience never could. Affliction will put a hypocrite on his knees in a way that the commandment of God never could. God may afflict us with such dispensations that the stoutest-hearted slighter of family and private worship may be forced to cry out, "Oh, for a hole to pray in!"

The second time a hypocrite takes on fits of importunity is when the hypocrite is drawing near to his grave and death summons him. Believe it, there are some, yes, many, to whom we speak, that are convicted when they are going down to the grave and when their eye strings begin to break. These will say, "Oh, cursed am I who prayed so little," and they will pray as often as they can.

Third, a hypocrite will pray two or three days before a communion and a day or two after it, but he will leave his religion there until the next communion comes again. He will never be so importunate. Cursed be the person that brings all his religion to the communion and leaves it there.

The fourth time that a hypocrite is sometimes serious in prayer is when he is under some conviction. Sometimes the Word and warnings will reach a hypocrite's conscience, and he will go home and pray for six or seven days, but soon, both his convictions and his prayers die. Some people, when they are under fits of conviction, will be much in the exercise of prayer, like those mentioned in Acts 2:37, where we read that they cry out, "Men and brethren, what shall we do?" When the conviction is over, they are as they were before. A Christian's importunity is more constant and uniform. A Christian will be importunate alone as well as in company, and he will be more constantly serious and importunate.

The ninth consideration that I shall propose, and with which I shall close, is that we have a commission. We are sent unto you this day to engage you in this excellent duty of prayer. We have spoken much to commend this duty unto you. Will you not engage in it? Dear old men, who have slighted family worship so long, will you begin to pray tonight? I take heaven as my witness that you have been exhorted this day to begin to pray. Will you try what this exercise means? I say to you, man or woman, it is not so great a difficulty as you imagine it to be. Do you not think a man is great if he has access to speak to the king whenever he desires? Such a man is esteemed a great courtier. I say, since it is so great an honor to speak to the petty princes of this earth, what a dignity must it be to speak to the King of heaven whenever you desire? Will you begin this night, you who have long slighted private prayer and family worship? Know that I shall be a witness against you if you do it not. Now, do we need to press it any further upon you? How often do we go to our beds as beasts? We go to our beds and sleep without knowing God's thoughts of us. What, unbeliever? What if that word at midnight should cry in your ears, "Behold, the Bridegroom cometh"? You who go to bed without praying, what if you should hear, "Thou fool, this night thy soul shall be required of thee" (Luke 12:20)? It is a dangerous thing to go to bed without distinct knowledge of how it is between God and us. If you slight prayer now, you shall one day pray very earnestly, but without hope.

If you neglect prayer now, soon you shall earnestly pray, "Oh, hills and mountains, fall on us, and cover us from the face of the Lamb." That is the prayer that many unbelievers in Glasgow shall pray if they do not mend their ways; it is a poor thing to pray to them who can neither help nor hear.

You who disregard the exercise of prayer shall one day pray, "Cursed be the day that ever I was born." You shall rue the day when tidings were brought to your father that a child was born unto him. You shall curse the day that you heard this preaching in Glasgow, because this is the day when you are challenged and encouraged to set about the noble and soul-enriching duty of prayer. "Oh, that I had been deaf, that I had never heard preaching!" That will certainly be your prayer as you enter into eternity.

You may also pray that you had never heard the everlasting gospel. You may pray, "Oh, if only I had never heard the joyful sound!" Every preaching of the gospel that you hear shall aggravate your pain one day, if you do not make use of it.

There are many in Glasgow who will cry out, "Oh, if only I had been born in Sodom, and had been a burgess in Gomorrah instead of a citizen of Glasgow!" It would be to your advantage if you had been born in Sodom, if you do not respond to this offer. I entreat you, in this day, study to know the things that belong to your peace.

One day you shall pray, "Oh, if only I were outside the reach of God's justice!" Do I dare tell you to take your account to Him, so that you may amend what is wrong? Will you engage in this? It is for your soul's advantage! Do you not find it pleasant to worship God in your family? Do you not think that it is gainful to have traffic with heaven? Merchants, pray much; it is the best way to make you successful merchants. Be your employment what it will, pray much, and you will be successful. Commend yourself and all that you have to God. Dear merchants, "The blessing of God maketh rich, and there is no sorrow in it." To be rich with the approbation of God, to have a place with the approbation of God is better than to have all the wealth of Glasgow with His curse. I think it would be a blessed thing if you could take Christ to your shops every morning and discourse and talk with Him all the day. Whatever your employment is, you may have most success on the day that you are most serious with God. Godliness has the promise of this life and the life to come. The merchant is blessed who, when all is cast away, can say, "Christ is my stock." When all is cast away, if you have Christ for your stock, you shall have enough. Merchants, will you buy Christ? You never bought a better bargain; shall you not buy Him today? I shall be no merchant to you; I offer Him, if you will take Him. Oh, that we might be induced to take Him! I take the stones of the wall as a witness, and every one of you as witnesses: each one of you is invited to engage in this duty of prayer.

Now, if you are willing to engage in the noble exercise of prayer, I entreat you to try it tonight. Even if you only have six words to say, go to God with them. Alas! I fear there are many of Pharaoh's humor here today; they cry out, "Who is the LORD, that I should obey his voice?" (Ex. 5:2). I will tell you who He is: He is your Creator, He is your Judge, and He is content to be your Savior. We exhort you to serve Him. Oh, do not slight your time; and if nothing more, you shall have peace. Now, to Him who can persuade you and commend this duty to you, we desire to give praise. Amen.

SERMON 38

The All-Sufficiency and Seasonableness of Divine Grace Manifested in the Return of Prayer(1)

God's Time and Way of Answering Prayer Always Best, Though Different Than Our Expectations

And he said unto me, My grace is sufficient for thee: for my strength is made perfect in weakness. Most gladly therefore will I rather glory in my infirmities, that the power of Christ may rest upon me.

—2 Corinthians 12:9

Expectants of heaven, let me ask you the same question which Delilah asked Samson: wherein does your strength lie? Might we not be constrained to answer, "The excellence of our strength lies in God, who made the heaven and the earth; without Him we can do nothing, but having Him, we can do all things." The text that we have read to you is a text that will answer all cases; it is a text that will answer all objections, doubts, fears, and all our disappointments. I pray you, what can trouble a Christian that is not answered by Christ's reassurance, "My grace is sufficient for thee"? It is an excellent cure for all our distempers; oh, that we were wise and would take hold of it.

Concerning the text in the seventh verse of this chapter, we find Paul's case and condition; we have already spoken of this. Second, we told you that in the eighth verse, we can find Paul's divine exercise in this case and condition; he beseeched the Lord three times, asking that this evil might depart from him. In the verse we have read, we find the glorious answer he received from this lamentable exercise. In this verse, we have four things to consider. First, Paul's answer to prayer came in these words: "My grace is sufficient for thee." This was the excellent voice that he heard from heaven. Second, we see the reason that he gives for this excellent answer to prayer; these words may comfort you. The Lord says, "Paul, there is a sufficiency of grace in Me; I am never more ready to help than when a person is weak." Third, Paul makes an excellent resolution upon the receipt of this excellent answer to his prayer; he says, "Most gladly therefore will I rather glory in my infirmities." Last, we see the excellent motive that leads Paul to make this resolution; for he says, "When I am weak, then am I strong" (2 Cor. 12:10).

Now, let us consider the first point: the excellent and glorious answer to prayer that Paul receives. What are we to understand by God's words, "My grace is sufficient for thee"? We conceive that there are two expressions in the words that are both suitable to the place and to the scope. First, by 'grace' we may understand the strength that is in Jesus Christ. His grace is communicable to believers for the mortification of their lusts and corruptions. It is as if Paul is saying that God says to all believers that His strength is sufficient for them: "For my strength is made perfect in weakness." Second, by the word 'grace,' here we understand pardoning grace; by this grace, the Lord graciously pardons all the iniquities and transgressions of His own. It is as if He had said to Paul, "My pardoning grace is sufficient for you, in all the escapes that you shall have in that unpleasant exercise." The word that is here translated 'sufficient' may be also rendered 'enough'; God says, "My grace is *enough*."

Before we discuss the substance of the answer, there are seven general observations that we shall gather from the context and words of our text.

The first general observation is that though the prayers of His children meet with long delays and do not have a present answer, yet in the end, the answer shall come. Furthermore, the Christian shall have a gracious answer. Paul besought the Lord three times, but did not receive an answer. Finally, he receives this excellent answer: "My grace is sufficient for thee." The vision shall at last speak, and will not tarry. This may comfort a Christian; God has not said to the house of Jacob, "Seek ye my face in vain." The day is approaching when the Christian shall meet with a hearing, speaking, and answering God in prayer.

Secondly, it is the duty of a Christian to observe and take notice of the answers to prayer. Paul does this here; he puts upon record God's excellent answer to prayer. Paul says that he shall never forget this answer. It has been the practice of the saints of old to take note of the answers to prayer. There is an example of this in Psalm 116:1 when David says, "I love the LORD, because he hath heard my voice and my supplications." Here David takes notice of a prayer-hearing and prayer-answering God. In Psalm 138:3 we read, "In the day when I cried thou answeredst me, and strengthenedst me with strength in my soul." Paul deliberately takes notice of the answer to his prayer. There are four things a Christian should take notice of concerning his answers to prayer.

1. The Christian should take notice of the time when he receives an answer to prayer; he should note the day and the hour that he meets with such a return. Additionally, I think that there are four times a Christian should notice if he can. First, a Christian should take notice of the time of conversion, if he can, and observe the month of Abib—when he came out of the land of Egypt. Second, a Christian should observe the time of his enjoyments, when he enjoys excellent visits from God. Third, he should observe the time of the answers to his prayers. Fourth, a Christian should take notice of the time of the dispensation of some remarkable mercy, as well as signal manifestations of love to him. If a Christian takes notice of these times, he shall not quickly forget the day when he met with such mercies. Hence, the saints have put new names unto the days upon which their mercies were tasted.

2. A Christian should take notice of the frame of his spirit. Let him notice what frame he is in when he receives answers to prayer. He must take serious notice of his case and temper when God arranges a tryst, with the answer to his prayer. No doubt, a Christian would find much advantage by observing this.

3. A Christian should take notice of his reaction to the answers to prayer. He should notice what use he makes

of them. If we took notice of this more often, we would not waste time and waste answers to prayer.

4. A Christian should take notice of the return of prayer itself. What is the particular return of prayer he receives? I suppose some Christians, if they had met with such an answer to such a prayer as Paul here receives, they would say, "I am sure this is not the return of my prayer." One might ask, "What answer is this to Paul's prayer? He was praying that the messenger of Satan might depart from him, and he receives this as an answer: 'My grace is sufficient for thee.'" Now a Christian should observe the particular answer to prayer he receives. Christians, let me ask you, how often have you prayed since Christ and you first owned one another? You may answer, "Oh, I cannot tell; I have prayed very often." Dear Christian, how many answers to prayer have you waited for, among all these very many prayers? We will pray a hundred times, but not wait for the answer to one of them; this says that we pray, but we do not care whether we get an answer to our prayers or not. It also says that we pray to be respectful toward God rather than to obtain anything from Him. If we did not have a natural conscience to satisfy, we would not pray much at all. Oh, Christians, is this like the conversation of the saints of old? Much of their time was taken up waiting for answers to prayer. This is the ruin of many Christians—they do not expect and wait for the returns of their prayers. I think there are four things that reign in the prayers of many. Many prayers consist of hypocrisy, presumption, formality, and unbelief. These are the four great ingredients that reign in your prayers. That is the great reason why you pray with so little delight, so little advantage, and you wait so little for the returns of prayer. Do you not think that if some persons were admitted to witness many of our secret prayers, that we would blush and be ashamed that anybody should know that we are praying with so much formality and indifference?

Let us consider a third observation. There are many things in the answer to prayer that make it an excellent and matchless mercy to a Christian. There are two things in the words that make the returns to prayer a matchless mercy. First notice the word, 'He,' and then the word, 'me.' It is as if Paul had said, "Transcendent *He* said to unworthy *me*; spotless *He* said unto defiled *me*; infinite *He* said to finite *me*; Christ-saving *He* said to self-destroying *me*, 'My grace is sufficient for thee.'" The consideration of these two—the Person that gives the return and the person to whom the return of prayer is given, would make the return of prayer an excellent and glorious dispensation of love. Therefore, we conceive there is an emphasis in that word *He*, and an emphasis in that word *me*. Might one ask, "Oh, Paul, what is the reason that you speak of God without a style, and say only, '*He* said unto *me*'?" No doubt he would answer, "I know not what to say of Him." He is a nameless God. I know not what He is; He does not lack a name, but I do not know His name. In Proverbs 30:4 Agur begins to catechize himself and he proposes the same question: "What is his name, and what is his son's name, if thou canst tell?" How would you answer this question if it were posed unto you? No doubt, you would trouble your head to find out some excellent description of God; but indeed, you must give Agur's answer to it: "Who can tell it?" Agur would confess that he is ignorant, and cannot resolve that question.

The fourth general observation that we shall consider is that there are many indirect ways that God answers the prayers of His own. No doubt, many might suppose this was not a direct way of answering Paul's prayers. There are many indirect answers to prayer that God gives His own. When we spoke on the former verse, we spoke of seven or eight indirect answers to prayer that God gives unto His own. Moses gets a strange answer in Exodus 33:18-19 when he prayed, "I beseech thee, shew me thy glory." He receives this answer: "I will make all my goodness pass before thee." Is this not an indirect answer to his prayer? In Luke 17:5, 6, the disciples pray, "Lord, increase our faith." They received this answer: "If ye had faith as a grain of mustard seed, ye might say unto this sycamine tree, Be thou plucked up by the root, and be thou planted in the sea; and it should obey you."

Let us consider a fifth general observation. There is a kind of spiritual speaking between Christ and the soul. We see these words in our text: "He said unto me." There is a kind of secret language between God and the soul which the world does not understand. We see clearly in Exodus 33:9: "The Lord talked with Moses." In the eleventh verse of the same chapter we read, "The LORD spake unto Moses face to face, as a man speaketh unto his friend." Furthermore, we read in Numbers 12:8, "With him will I speak mouth to mouth, even apparently, and not in dark speeches." A final example is found in Numbers 7:89 where we read, "When Moses was gone into the tabernacle of the congregation to speak with him, then he heard the voice of one speaking unto him from off the mercy seat that was upon the ark of testimony, from between the two cherubims: and he spake unto him." Does it not seem strange that Moses should have had such a design before him as to talk with God? There is then a language between Christ and the soul that the world does not understand.

A sixth observation that we would have you notice is that the answer to prayer may be as certain to the soul as if he heard a man speaking unto him. We see the proof for this in the words, "He said unto me." Paul explains, "I heard Him speak to me; I am certain I met with such a return."

There is this last general observation we would notice: it is the duty of a Christian to be convinced and persuaded that the answer to prayer he receives is from God. Paul is positive in this fact: "He said unto me, my grace is sufficient for thee." Dear Christian, take notice of these three things that counterfeit the returns of prayer when God does not give it.

First, sometimes our affections counterfeit the return of prayer when God does not give it. Some come to seek light from God to do something, and indeed they beg that God would confirm them in it. Now their affections counterfeit a return and they get something that agrees with their affection. Thus they say, "Now I have gotten my answer, I will go and do the thing." We see an example of this in Ezekiel 14:4 where we read, "I the LORD will answer him that cometh according to the multitude of his idols." They come and say unto God, "Oh, shall we go to such a gate?" Yet, they are almost resolved to go to that gate already.

Secondly, your light may counterfeit the returns of prayer. A Christian's light may sometimes speak something unto him when it is not an answer to prayer. Are there not many mistakes in a Christian's light about the returns of prayer? Is it not known that a Christian has not always received an answer to prayer when his light says, "Now, I have the answer to my prayer"?

Thirdly, your perverse conscience will counterfeit an answer to prayer. Your conscience will speak peace unto you when God is speaking war. Sometimes a hypocrite will go to God to seek clarity concerning his interest and his conscience counterfeits a return unto him, saying, "Heaven is at peace with me," while there is no such thing. Some unbelievers will go to God desiring to be assured of their right to heaven, and their presumption will counterfeit a return unto them, confirming them in their presumption and delusion. When we are disputing such a thing in our consciences, our conscience will answer us as our interest leads us. Therefore, let a Christian examine whether his returns of prayer be from his affections, his light, his perverse conscience, or from God. For that affliction, that light, that perverse conscience may counterfeit the returns of prayer when heaven is silent concerning your case. Furthermore, a hypocrite is ruined by his conscience counterfeiting the returns of prayer; therefore be distinct in this, as Paul is distinct in it: "He said unto me, my grace is sufficient for thee." We shall not insist further upon these points, having spoken about similar things in the former sermon.

Now, let us consider how, in the answer to Paul's prayer, grace is taken for strength. Let us then notice this in these four points.

1. There is a sufficiency of grace and strength in Christ for a Christian to help him in all his straits and conditions. Christ says, "My grace is sufficient for thee." Oh, Christian, what trouble do you have that this text will not answer?

2. Only Christ's grace is sufficient for a Christian to help him through his trials; therefore Christ says, "My grace is sufficient for thee." There is an emphasis in the word *my*; it is as if He would have said, "The strength of angels is not sufficient for thee, Paul; thy own created strength is not sufficient for thee; but My grace and My strength are sufficient for thee."

3. The grace and sufficiency of strength in Christ Jesus is communicable and forthcoming unto a believer in all his straits. We can clearly see this in the words, "My grace is sufficient for thee." God's grace is forthcoming for you, Paul, and also for you, dear Christian.

> 4. Let the case and trial of a believer be never so great, there is something that may answer it in Christ. Is not this imported in the words, "For thee," for you who persecuted, and for you who killed the saints, and had a commission to put to death all that called upon my name—"My grace is sufficient for thee"? Yes, for you.

Now, let us discuss the first acceptation: grace, in this text, may be taken for strength. To clarify this point, let us take notice how there is a sufficiency of strength and grace in Christ Jesus for a believer in all his straits.

First, let us see how this grace is actually strength by looking at eight points. It is clear in Scripture that "of his fulness have all we received, and grace for grace" (John 1:16). Furthermore, in Colossians 1:19 we read that "it pleased the Father that in him should all fulness dwell." If all fullness dwells in Christ, no doubt a fullness of strength must dwell in Him as well. "For in him dwelleth all the fulness of the Godhead bodily" (Col. 2:9). Now, what is the reason that all fullness dwells in Him? We find the answer in the tenth verse: "Ye are complete in him, which is the head of all principality and power."

Secondly, we see this strength in the gift that the Father gave unto Christ when He undertook the blessed work of our redemption. This is clear from Psalm 89:19, "I have laid help upon one that is mighty; I have exalted one chosen out of the people," and Isaiah 42:1, "Behold my servant, whom I uphold." This was one of the great grants and gifts of the Father to the Son, when He undertook this excellent work. The Father furnished Christ with strength for all the cases and conditions of believers.

Thirdly, we can see the sufficiency and fullness of strength in Christ forthcoming unto believers in the confession of believers in Scripture. For example we read in 2 Corinthians 3:5, "Not that we are sufficient of ourselves to think any thing as of ourselves; but our sufficiency is of God." Also, in Philippians 4:13 we read, "I can do all things through Christ which strengtheneth me." Do not these confessions show that there is a fullness and sufficiency of strength in Christ?

Fourthly, the resolutions of many Christians in the Scripture show the sufficiency in Christ. We see the fullness of Christ's strength in Psalm 71:16: "I will go in the strength of the Lord GOD." Also, we read, "I will strengthen them in the LORD; and they shall walk up and down in his name, saith the LORD" (Zech. 10:12). Do not these words show that there is a fullness and sufficiency of grace and strength in Christ Jesus that flows unto believers?

Sixthly, the name that Christ has taken unto Himself declares His power and sufficiency. He has called Himself, "Mighty to save" (Isa. 63:1). Does not that prove it? Furthermore, do not the names that believers often give unto Christ in Scripture prove it? They call Him their rock, their strength, and their refuge. These names clearly show that there is a fullness and sufficiency of strength and grace in Christ Jesus.

Seventhly, we see Christ's fullness in the experiences of the saints. They have met with many excellent outpourings of the strength and grace of Christ; when they have been weak, they were made strong. An invisible strength is conveyed into the heart, and they say, "Of his fulness have all we received, and grace for grace" (John 1:16). These experiences show that there is a fullness and sufficiency of strength and grace in the promises of Christ. We read in Isaiah 45:24, "Surely, shall one say, in the LORD have I righteousness and strength."

Lastly, the commands in Scripture speak the truth that there is a fullness of grace and strength in Christ Jesus. Listen to the command in Psalm 105:4: "Seek the LORD, and his strength: seek his face evermore." All these things preach aloud that there is a fullness of strength and sufficiency of grace in Christ Jesus that is forthcoming unto a believer in all his trials.

To make this clear unto you, I shall name seven glorious steps of the grace and strength of Christ that will prove that there is a sufficiency of grace and strength in Him.

1. The first glorious step of the grace and strength of Christ is that He delivers us from the bonds of nature and from the bonds of the devil, and translates us into the kingdom of grace. He brings us out of darkness into His marvellous light. Is not that a glorious step of His sufficiency and fullness of grace and strength? Is there an angel that can pull a soul out of nature? No, put all the strength of all the angels in heaven together, and it could not pull a soul out of the arms of the devil. It is only the everlasting arms of Christ, who is mighty to save, that can do it. This proves that there is a sufficiency of strength in Christ.

2. The mortification of an idol and bringing low a Christian's corruption is a mighty evidence of the sufficiency of the grace of Christ. Christian, is it possible for you to mortify an idol? Is it possible for all the saints put together to mortify an idol? Only the strength of Christ can do it. There must be an infinite power engaged for a Christian before he can sing the triumphant song, "O death, where is thy sting? O grave, where is thy victory?" (1 Cor. 15:55). Every time any stronghold and imagination within you is brought down, it is an evident proof of the sufficiency of the strength and grace that is in Christ Jesus, forthcoming unto believers.

3. Christ's sufficiency helps the Christian through any duty. This shows that there is a fullness of strength and sufficiency of grace in Christ. We read in Joshua 1:7, "Only be thou strong and very courageous." Might one ask, "Why must we be courageous? Is God pressing Joshua to be stout and courageous in fighting the war?" No, we read, "Only be thou strong and very courageous, that thou mayest observe to do according to all the law, which Moses my servant commanded thee: turn not from it to the right hand or to the left, that thou mayest prosper whithersoever thou goest." Here we see that it is necessary that a mighty power be engaged for the strength of a Christian, before he can do the duty unto which he is called.

4. We see proof of Christ's fullness in how Christians are brought back from apostasy. This is a glorious show of His power and strength. Believe it, it is as difficult for Christ to bring us back from our apostasy as to bring us from the state of nature into grace; therefore, in Luke 22:32, the recovering of Peter from apostasy is called *conversion:* "And when thou art converted, strengthen thy brethren." No doubt he was converted before, but we see that it is as great a work to bring Peter back from his apostasy as it was to convert him.

5. Christ helps the Christian to bear all the crosses that he encounters. It is a wonder that a Christian should be helped so patiently to bear his crosses, but it is Christ who

strengthens him. We read in Colossians 1:11, "Strengthened with all might, according to his glorious power, unto all patience and longsuffering with joyfulness."

6. Our minds are enlightened and our will is brought into a blessed conformity unto Him. Also, our affections are renewed. These three things show the sufficiency of strength and grace that is in Christ; for it is a work above the strength of angels to do any of these things.

7. Christ brings the Christian back from his desertion, from his lack of spiritual life. Christ brings the Christian back from the loss of his mortification and from the gates of his discouragement. All these are glorious steps of the power and sufficiency of the strength that is in Christ Jesus. In this you can see that Christ has a sufficiency and fullness of strength and grace forthcoming to believers; furthermore, it is abundantly true that His grace is sufficient for you.

Now, in examining this truth a little more fully, let us consider several more points.

First, since there is a sufficiency of strength and grace in Christ that is forthcoming unto His own for the mortification of their lusts and idols, why are Christians still under the feet of their idols? Oh, what can be the reason, since Christ "is mighty to save," that you are yet so trodden upon by the temptations that assault you? I shall give you six reasons why you are still so controlled by your idols.

The first reason is that we are too confident in our own strength; this is the greatest reason. Though there is a fullness of strength in Christ, yet we are under the power of our idols. Do you desire to know why you are so often constrained to cry out, "Oh, when shall the day of victory approach?" It is because you are wrestling too much upon your own strength. Let us listen to Hannah's remarkable song: "By strength shall no man prevail" (1 Sam. 2:9); that is, by his own strength shall no man prevail. Believe it, if you were wrestling more with your lusts and idols upon the strength of Him that is "mighty to save," you would, before long, bruise the head of him that has so often bruised your heel.

There is a threefold self that is the ruin of a Christian. There is self-indulgence, self-dependence, and self-worship. These three selves are the ruin of many. Are there not many who are under the power of self-indulgence who, before they miss an hour's sleep, would rather miss twenty prayers? Self-dependence is also the ruin of many. We go out to the war in our own strength; therefore, we often return overcome and foiled. Thirdly, self-worship is also the ruin of many; that is, many persons make themselves their own God. To whom do you pray, dear Christians? I confess, I think we pray often unto ourselves, and not to God.

Secondly, though there is a fullness of strength in Christ communicable unto us, yet we are under the power and feet of our idols because we are not much in the exercise of faith. Faith is the grace by which a Christian must suck strength from Christ to mortify his idols. This is made clear in Isaiah 40:31, where we read, "But they that wait upon the LORD shall renew their strength; they shall mount up with wings as eagles; they shall run, and not be weary; and they shall walk, and not faint." Do you know who is most able to wrestle with his lusts and corruptions? It is the believing person. We may certainly say the words in Matthew 13:58, and no doubt we have much reason to say them: "He did not many mighty works there because of their unbelief." What is the reason that you have never prevailed over any of the idols that ever troubled you? You do not believe! For "all things are possible to him that believeth" (Mark 9:23).

Thirdly, though there is a sufficiency of strength in Christ that is communicable to believers, yet we are often conquered by every temptation that assaults us. I say it is because we are not constant in our dependence upon Christ for the mortification of our idols. Sometimes a Christian at communion will depend upon Christ for the mortification of his idols and for help in his duty. However, it is a mystery unto a Christian to be constant in this, to be constantly drawing strength from Christ for the mortification of his idols and for helping him to do his duty. I confess we rarely depend upon Christ.

There is this, fourthly, that is another reason that we are so much under the power of our idols, though there is a sufficiency of strength in Christ Jesus that is forthcoming unto believers: we do not solidly believe that there is a fullness of strength and sufficiency of grace in Christ. We do not believe it; therefore, though there is strength in Him to be had, yet we do not make use of it. There are three things in Christ that a Christian does not seek after, though they may be easily had: first, there is joy in Christ to be had, but we do not seek after it. We are like Hagar; there is a well of consolation in Christ, but our eyes are not opened to see it. Second, is there not life to be had from Christ for quickening us in our duties and performances? He is indeed the God of our life. Third, there is strength in Christ for mortifying our idols, and if we would come and seek it from Him, no doubt we would obtain it.

Fifthly, we are still under the power of our idols because although we believe in some measure that there is a fullness of strength in Christ, yet we still dispute whether or not that strength and grace is forthcoming to us. Thus, though there is fullness of strength in Christ, our hearts are as weak as water, and we are much subjected to our idols and overcome by our temptations.

Sixthly, Christians are ignorant of the right way to draw strength from Christ for mortifying idols. There is a secret way of drawing strength from Christ which the world does not understand. Many Christians are under the power of their idols because they do not know how to draw spiritual strength from Christ.

Last, believers are still so trapped under the feet of their lusts because the Christian does not often use these duties by which strength and sufficiency of grace are conveyed to the soul. Oh, Christians, if you would pray more, you would prevail more. If you desire to have greater faith, you must mortify your idols. But as long as you are seldom about these duties, by which strength is conveyed to the soul, you will be constrained to cry out, "Oh, when shall my prison doors be cast open and the foundation of my prison-house be shaken?"

A second observation I would like to make concerning the text is that in order for a Christian to be faithful in his walk, he must keep in mind six things.

First, there are many Christians who seek more for righteousness from Christ and pardoning grace than they seek strength from Him to mortify their idols. Many Christians are so taken up in pursuing after pardoning grace that they do not pursue mortifying grace. Christians halve many things that they should not halve; there are five things a Christian should never halve. First, a Christian often halves his love. Often the world has one part of our love and Christ has but a very small part of it. Second, many Christians halve their desires. They desire one thing from Christ and another thing from the world. Third, Christians often halve faith; they will not put their confidence in God, but put their trust in their own righteousness. Fourth, do not Christians often halve fear? Do we not often fear man more than God? This is a great evidence of our unbelief; we do not know with whom we have to do. Fifth, Christians often halve their diligence. How much of our diligence is taken up in pursuit of the world? How little of it is consumed by the pursuit after God?

Second, a Christian often asks strength from Christ for doing one duty; yet in another duty, he will ask no strength from Christ. I shall tell you of three duties ordinarily where a Christian slights Christ and does not seek strength from Him.

Christians often slight Christ in the duty of self-examination. Often a Christian will not employ Christ's strength to help him in going about it; he thinks that he does not need to be in Christ's common for the examination and search of his own self. Surely, says the Christian, he can go about this himself without the strength of Christ.

Secondly, Christians often neglect Christ's strength in the reading of Scriptures. We cast up our books and fall to reading and cry out, "I am sure I can read ten lines, although Christ is away from me."

Third, Christians seldom employ Christ's strength to help in the duty of prayer. How often do we pray upon our own strength? I would only say this further unto you: there are three duties for which a hardened Christian will depend on the strength of Christ; yet, for all other duties he will not employ Him.

> 1. There is the duty of communicating aright; a hardened Christian will say, "I must depend on Christ for doing this, or I will never do it right."
>
> 2. A hardened Christian may depend on Christ for the duty of believing. "I am sure," says one, "I can read on my own, I can examine myself on my own, and I can pray on my own, but I cannot believe on my own." I say, you cannot do anything on your own! Some think that they can do these things alone, but they cannot.
>
> 3. A Christian who is no longer tender may depend on Christ for the duty of meditation. I confess there are some who will go about meditation saying, "Without Christ I can do nothing." Now, is not this true, that there are

some duties for which a Christian will depend on Christ for strength, while for other duties he will not depend on Christ at all?

A third consideration we would propose unto you is that it is much for a Christian to be mortified to any victory over his idols and to give the praise of it to the strength and grace of Christ. Do we not often say, when we achieve a victory over our idols, that our own hands have done it? Do we not report that we have saved ourselves? It is much for a Christian, when he has gained victory over his idols, to sing Psalm 124:1-4: "If it had not been the LORD who was on our side, now may Israel say; if it had not been the LORD who was on our side, when men rose up against us: then they had swallowed us up quick, when their wrath was kindled against us: then the waters had overwhelmed us, the stream had gone over our soul." It is difficult for Christians to sing Psalm 115:1: "Not unto us, O LORD, not unto us, but unto thy name give glory, for thy mercy, and for thy truth's sake." Ascribe strength unto God, and the praise of the victory of all thy idols unto Him.

Fourthly, it is one of the greatest difficulties for a Christian on this side of time to believe the words in John 15:5: "Without me ye can do nothing." This is one of the great mysteries, and we have great difficulty believing it. I do confess that a Christian may be brought to believe that he can never save himself, he can never sanctify himself, and he can never mortify his idols without Christ; but he is still sure that he can do *something* without Christ. He is a blessed Christian who can believe that without Christ he can do nothing. Even when you are speaking to one another, have the faith of this engraven upon you: without Christ you can do nothing!

Fifthly, it is much for a Christian to believe that the sufficiency of grace and strength in Christ, communicable to him, is as effectual for mortification as if it were his own proper strength. There is as much efficacy in the strength of Christ for mortifying his lusts as if it were his own.

The sixth and last consideration that we would offer unto you is that it is much for a Christian to believe that the mortification of his idols, through the borrowed strength of Christ, is as pleasant and acceptable to God as if it were done in his own proper strength. Will Christ give us thanks for mortifying our lusts on borrowed strength? Yes, He will thank you for doing it upon His strength. Is it not strange that Christ shall say to His own at the last day, "Well done, good and faithful servant" (Matt. 25:23)? He never mentions the strength that He gave unto them to help them to obey Him; even more, He calls many things that He has done for them, theirs. He fathers it upon them as their work, and says they have done it. Though believing is His work, and it was He that made them to believe, yet He says of the disciples, "Ye have believed." Is not mortification of our idols and temptations Christ's work? Yet He says that we have done it. Is not patience under suffering Christ's work? Yet He says unto His disciples, "Ye are they which have continued with me in my temptations" (Luke 22:28). Everything you do in Christ's strength shall be as acceptable unto God as if you had never been one bit obliged unto Christ for strength to do it.

To conclude our discourse, we desire you to make use of this sufficiency of strength that is in Christ. Oh believers, what are you doing since there is so much strength to be had, and you are still so weak? I may say unto you that which Elisha said to his servant, that there is more upon our side than there are against us. Why then do we return home foiled by our enemies so often? I would ask you this question, dear Christians: do you think you will die conquerors or conquered? Is the day coming when the devil shall sing a song of triumph over you? Or will Christ sing a song of triumph over you? Why do Christians so often cry out, "My strength and my hope is perished from the Lord; not only I have lost my hope, but my strength also"? Oh, believe the words in Hebrews 11:34: those who "out of weakness were made strong, waxed valiant in fight, turned to flight the armies of the aliens." If you believed, I know not any temptation that should assault you, but you should be able to overcome it.

I shall close with this: there are five excellent resolutions that a Christian should take on, that shall persuade him that Christ's grace is sufficient for him.

First, Christian must say, "I am sure that any duty may be commanded me, and I shall not fear to obey it, for there is a sufficiency of grace and strength in Christ to give me strength for the obedience." What makes Christians tremble when they meet with commands? They think they do not have the strength to do the work. Oh, cast your eyes to the fullness of Christ's strength and say, "I can do all things through Christ which strengtheneth me" (Phil. 4:13).

Second, a Christian must believe that all the strength that he has is from Christ and that there is a fullness and sufficiency of strength in Christ. Such a Christian takes on a resolution never to have a high thought of himself again. What makes a Christian proud when he prays well, communicates well, reads well, and hears preaching well? He believes not that all the strength he has is from Christ, that there is no strength that he has for doing any duty but that which comes from a high hand. If we believed that all our strength was from the high springs, we would cry out, "I believe, yet not I!" We would cry out, "I am the chief of sinners!" We would walk to heaven with these words in our mouth: "I am less than the least of all Thy saints."

Third, once a Christian believed this truth, he would no doubt be resolved never to dispute anymore. What is the reason of all a Christian's disputes? Is it not a lack of faith in this truth, that the grace of Christ is sufficient for him? Believe it, it would cut the neck of unbelief to believe this text.

Fourth, once a Christian believed that Christ's strength is sufficient, he would be comforted, knowing that under all his anxieties and trials, Christ's grace is sufficient for him. In every strait that he encountered, he could comfort himself under it with this knowledge.

A last resolution that a Christian would take on if he believed this truth is that he would resolve never to leave nor forsake Christ, but to hold fast unto Him, since the joy of the Lord is his strength, since the fear of the Lord is his strength, and since the name of the Lord is his strength. Will you come and draw strength from this text, by which you may be helped to overcome? Now, to Him who is the everlasting strength and the rock of ages, we desire to give praise. Amen.

SERMON 39

The All-Sufficiency and Seasonableness of Divine Grace Manifested in the Return of Prayer (2)

God's Time and Way of Answering Prayer Always Best, Though Different Than Our Expectations

And he said unto me, My grace is sufficient for thee: for my strength is made perfect in weakness. Most gladly therefore will I rather glory in my infirmities, that the power of Christ may rest upon me.

—2 Corinthians 12:9

There is a cursed situation unto which we are often subject—at times, three wretched things meet together: strong temptations from without, strong lusts from within, and desertion from God. When these three come together in a person, when temptations from without assault and the heart consents, Christ is often away. Paul received a noble and comfortable answer from heaven: "My grace is sufficient for thee." Be persuaded, Christian, Christ has given you His heart; He will also give you His hand. Once the precious name of His love has been fixed upon you, His strength shall be communicated unto you. I think there are two things that are impossible for a Christian to do: it is impossible for a Christian to tell the debt that he owes to the grace of Christ, and it is impossible for a Christian to pay the debt he owes to the grace of Christ. We may not cry, "Son of God, have patience upon us, and we will pay Thee all," for though He may have patience with us for all eternity, it would be impossible for us to pay all our debt to Him. We must live here debtors to

Christ, we must die debtors to Christ, and we must reign eternally as debtors to the freedom of the grace of Christ. Believe it, Christians—your riches consist in your debt.

There are only three things I shall name before I come to the words of our text.

First, a Christian may comfort himself under all the assaults and temptations he encounters with the knowledge that this is his right. The day will soon break, and soon the shadows will fly away. Do you know, Christians, what Christ is doing now? He is leaping over the mountains and skipping over the hills of Bether. The day is approaching when we shall be set free from our bondage, and the year of our jubilee shall come. Oh, Christians, be of good cheer—it is not long until the breaking of your day. Dear Christians, be comforted, for it is not long until you shall sing that triumphant song: "Death is now swallowed up in life, and mortality has put on immortality."

Second, be comforted that Christ will not plead with you by His great power; He will put strength in you to undergo all your straits and difficulties. We read in Job 23:6, "Will he plead against me with his great power?" No, He desires to put strength in me. Christ is communicable to you for every trial and difficulty you encounter. He is a very present help in the day of trouble, when the blast of the terrible one has been as a storm against the wall. Has it not often been so? Often, when we have been ready to cry out, "My foot is slipping," His mercy and grace have upheld us.

Third, I would say to you that despite all the difficulties and opposition that you meet with now while you are building up your spiritual house, the day is coming when you shall put on the capstone and shall be constrained to cry out, "His grace is sufficient for me." All who have taken Christ in hand are fairly landed. There are none who have committed themselves to Him who are now lost; they are all fairly landed on the other side of time. Christ is able to make that faithful account; of all who were given to Him, He has lost none, except the son of perdition.

We told you the last time we spoke upon these words that there were four things to consider in them.

First, let us consider the glorious and excellent answer to prayer that Paul receives: "My grace is sufficient for thee." We discussed that the word *grace* might also be understood as *strength* and *ability*, which is found in the Son of God. This strength is forthcoming and communicable to believers in all their straits and difficulties. Under this acceptation we have spoken of many things. The word *grace* might be taken for the pardoning grace that is in Christ; this grace is also communicable to believers in all their straits and difficulties. By his words Christ was saying, "Oh, Paul comfort yourself with this: there is not one escape, nor any transgression of which you are guilty that cannot be overcome by My pardoning grace. There is a sufficiency of this grace in Me to answer you."

Now, concerning grace taken under this acceptation, we shall speak of three things. First, there is a sufficiency of pardoning grace in Christ, which is forthcoming to believers. This is clear in the words, "My grace is sufficient for thee." Second, a Christian should be content to take the pardoning grace that is in Christ. This grace is here rendered *sufficient*; it may likewise be rendered *contentment*. It is as if Christ would have said, "Oh, Paul, be content with my pardoning and overcoming grace." Third, this pardoning grace in Christ is able to answer all objections, straits, and difficulties we can encounter. Paul, be your straits ever so great, there is pardoning mercy in Christ to answer them.

Concerning the fullness and sufficiency of pardoning grace in Christ, we see in the words of John 1:14, that Christ is "full of grace and truth." Also, we read in Nehemiah 9:17 that God is "ready to pardon." By this we understand that He grants all sorts of pardon; furthermore in Daniel 9:9 we read, "To the Lord our God belong mercies and forgivenesses, though we have rebelled against him." There is abundance of mercy and forgiveness with God. In Isaiah 55:7 we see that "He will abundantly pardon," or as the words may be understood, "He will multiply pardon." To clarify this, I shall name four things that will abundantly show the fullness and sufficiency of pardoning grace in Christ.

1. There was never a person who came to Christ whom He was not content to pardon. Their iniquities may have been great, and of so deep a dye; yes, they may have been fighters against heaven; yet, He was always willing to pardon. Does this not show that there is an abundance of pardoning grace in Christ? Do you think that there is a person in hell today who can say, "I came to Christ for pardon, and He would not give it me"? Oh, does not Manasseh say that there is a fullness of pardoning grace in Christ? Does not Paul

say that there is abundance of pardoning grace in Christ? Do not all the thousands that are standing on the glassy sea say that there is a fullness of pardoning grace in Christ? What brought all the saints up to heaven? It is pardoning grace. Believe that if you come to Christ, whoever you are, you will not be sent away. There are four properties in Christ that invite you to come for pardon from Him, notwithstanding all your iniquity.

First, Christ can cure all your diseases with a mere look. Is there a person here who is sick with many diseases? One look from Christ will heal you. Do you desire to have all your diseases cured this day? Then give Christ a look. "Look unto me, and be ye saved, all the ends of the earth: for I am God, and there is none else" (Isa. 45:22). Second, Christ is a physician who can cure all your diseases with a *word*; we read in Matthew 8:8, "Speak the word only, and my servant shall be healed." Third, one touch of the Son of God today would heal all your diseases. This is clear from the example of the woman with the issue of blood. We read in Matthew 9:20 that she said, "If I may but touch his garment, I shall be whole." Even a touch of Christ's garments would make us whole from all our distempers. Fourth, the very shadow of Christ passing by would cure us of all our distempers. There is not a sickness in you that the passing by of Christ's shadow cannot heal. Is there a person who has waited thirty-eight years at the pool of ordinances, but has not been cured? I say to you, employ Christ and you shall be healed. Is there a person here who has spent all he had on physicians, and spent twelve years with an issue of blood? I say, touch but the hem of the garment of Christ and you shall be made whole. Believe it: Christ is exceedingly willing to pardon all your iniquities.

2. Though this precious fountain of pardoning grace has been standing open near these six thousand years, and all the saints that are in heaven have drunk of it, yet it is as full as the first day that it was opened. Does not this prove that there is a fullness of pardoning grace in Christ? This fountain cannot be exhausted. This fountain is running over and this is the great commandment of God: come and drink of it!

3. Despite all the escapes of His own, after closing with Him, yet He does graciously pardon them all.

4. Despite all the sins that are committed against resolutions, even upon small temptations, Christ is both willing and able to

pardon. There is not a transgression any man is guilty of, except one, that Christ will not pardon. Therefore, do not cry out, "Thy bruise is incurable, and thy wound is grievous" (Jer. 30:12). Instead, comfort yourself with the fact that there is balm in Gilead and a physician there. Let your case be never so broken, bring it to Christ and He will heal it. He will plead it—commit it to the Advocate who has never lost a cause. Oh, how many broken and desperate causes has Christ pled in heaven? He can invent things for the clearing of our cause that we never could invent ourselves. Now, before we come to speak to anything for use from this, we shall speak a little concerning a second point in the words.

Let us consider that persons should be content to take this pardoning grace that is in Christ. Oh, slighters and dreadful undervaluers of pardoning grace, take it today! You may be encouraged to take it after you hear these eight considerations.

1. The first consideration to press you to take this pardoning grace is that it is entirely free; we see in Luke 7:42 that "when they had nothing to pay, he frankly forgave them both." There is no price Christ craves for pardoning grace, only that you may be content to take that grace. I charge you, in the sight of God, although pardoning grace is free, that you may not undervalue it! Christ offers His pardoning grace in six ways.

First, there is not a person here that may not have pardoning grace for confession. Count fairly, and you will never pay. Now, is not this a low rate? Only confess your debt and Christ will pardon you. I would ask you, if you were set down to determine what God would have you do in order to get your iniquities pardoned, I am sure you would never have fallen upon such an easy way. All you need do is confess your offences. In Psalm 32:5 we read, "I acknowledged my sin unto thee, and mine iniquity have I not hid. I said, I will confess my transgressions unto the LORD; and thou forgavest the iniquity of my sin." Further, in Jeremiah 3:13 we read, "Only acknowledge thine iniquity." Is there no more to do for pardon? No, there is not a person here who will not be forgiven when he confesses his sin to God. Is there a person here who will deny his debt? I say, that person shall be void of pardoning grace. Oh, but is there a person here who will say, "I have sinned and done wickedly"? That person shall be pardoned.

Secondly, I shall go a little further. Be serious in the things that concern your eternal state. Every person that has a real desire to be pardoned shall indeed be pardoned. Oh, is there not a person here that will condescend to have one real desire for pardoning grace? I say, whoever you are, if you have one desire for pardon, you shall be pardoned indeed. This is made clear in Matthew 18:32, "I forgave thee all that debt, because thou desiredst me." Now, since pardoning grace is again offered at so low a rate, for just one desire—will you refuse it? I may say, the eternal curse of the infinite God be upon the person who, for one desire, will not take pardoning grace. If everyone here who has not a desire for pardoning grace were put to the door, I doubt if there would be two hundred that would not be put out.

Thirdly, I shall yet go a little further and ask: Is there a person here who purposes to confess his debt to God? I say, that person shall get pardon, according to the remarkable words of Psalm 32:5, "I acknowledged my sin unto thee, and mine iniquity have I not hid. I said, I will confess my transgressions unto the LORD; and thou forgavest the iniquity of my sin." Now, is there a person here who has a real purpose to take with his debt? I say, if you have a real purpose to do it, Christ is willing to give you pardon. Now, are you not content to take pardon at this rate, slighters of pardoning grace?

Fourthly, I shall go a little lower with you to see whether or not, at last, you will consent to take this pardoning grace. Is there a person here who will but put Christ in remembrance to give it unto Him, and He will give it to him? "I, even I, am he that blotteth out thy transgressions for mine own sake, and will not remember thy sins" (Isa. 43:25); He only requires one thing: "Put me in remembrance." Is there not a person here who will remember Christ in exchange for salvation? Will you not be content to receive His pardon?

Fifthly, I will go a little lower, so that you may be content to take pardoning grace. Is there a person here today who cannot seek pardon from Christ? I say, if you are serious, He will put words in your mouth; we see this shown in Hosea 14:2: "Take with you words, and turn to the LORD: say unto him, Take away all iniquity, and receive us graciously: so will we render the calves of our lips." Blessed be the person into whose mouth Christ puts words. Is there any person who expects Christ will put such a thing in his mouth? These are the words we must take: pardon mine iniquity. There are many who have cursed words in their mouth. Will you once say in sincerity, "Oh, precious Christ, pardon all my iniquity"?

Sixthly, is there a person here who will be content to subscribe to the law of Christ and be content to subscribe to the gospel? Is there not a soul that owes Christ a thousand talents? Put your name to the debt, and Christ will rive the bond. Is not that an easy rate? Now, is there not a person here who can do this? I persuade you, pardoning grace is free and He is willing to give it you. Are you not ashamed that pardoning grace should be brought to so low a rate, and there be no one to take it? Shall Christ pray today, "Father, forgive them; for they know not what they do" (Luke 23:34)? Are there none within these doors who are content to take pardoning grace? Oh, take heed lest the words in Isaiah 22:14 be written in heaven against you: "It was revealed in mine ears by the LORD of hosts, Surely this iniquity shall not be purged from you till ye die, saith the Lord GOD of hosts." Now, are there any here who are content to take pardoning grace at such a low rate? Oh, confess your debt; you cannot pay it, and you shall have pardon for your very confession.

Lastly, I shall go yet a little lower. Is there any person here who is wearying God with his iniquity? I say to that person, if he be content, he may have pardon today. We see in Isaiah 43:24-25 that God charges the people with two sins: they brought no burnt offerings unto Him, and they wearied Him with their iniquities. Yet, He says, "I, even I, am he that blotteth out thy transgressions for mine own sake, and will not remember thy sins." I say, will you take a rope and put it about your neck, knowing that Christ is a merciful king? Will you come unto Him, since He has bidden us forgive our brother seventy times seven times a day; how much more shall He that is infinite, forgive our iniquities? I think, if you had a sight of the roll of all your iniquities, you might cry out, "Oh, will Christ pardon me?" Even if your iniquities were like scarlet and your transgressions like crimson, if you are content, you may come and receive pardoning grace. If Christ cannot find an argument in you to pardon your iniquities, He will pardon you for His own name's sake.

2. A second consideration to urge you to come and embrace pardoning grace is that the pardoning grace which is in Christ is most complete. There are two or three expressions in Scripture which speak the fullness of pardoning grace. The first is Exodus 34:7: "Keeping mercy for thousands, forgiving iniquity and transgression

and sin." Now, why must we read all these expressions, namely, iniquity, transgression, and sin? It shows us that there is no sin of which you can be guilty that Christ is not willing and able to pardon. We also read in Hebrews 8:12, "For I will be merciful to their unrighteousness, and their sins and their iniquities will I remember no more." The repeating of these words says that there is no scarlet transgression which Christ is not able to pardon.

The second word which shows the fullness of pardoning grace in Christ Jesus is found in Jeremiah 33:8: "I will cleanse them from all their iniquity, whereby they have sinned against me; and I will pardon all their iniquities, whereby they have sinned, and whereby they have transgressed against me." Oh, do you wish to have all your debt paid today? Then be content to take this pardoning grace. Is there a person here who has nothing to live on? Come and be content to take this pardoning grace and you may go home and say, "I am richer than the richest merchant in Glasgow." I say to you, if you owe Christ a thousand measures, He will not bid you sit down and write fifty; He will say to you, sit down and write nothing.

3. There is a third consideration: this pardoning grace is bought at a most dear rate. Therefore, come and take it. There is not a pardon for one evil thought that is not purchased by the blood of Christ. Shall pardon that was bought at so dear a rate be so undervalued? I say, you shall get for nothing that which Christ bought with His death. Is it not a precious bargain to get forgiveness for one desire, which was bought at an infinite price? Do you not know that our iniquity was laid upon Christ, and by His stripes we are healed? Do you not know that He is the blessed mediator that must lay His hand on us both?

4. Consider that this pardoning grace is exceedingly abundant, as we see in Romans 5:20: "Moreover the law entered, that the offence might abound. But where sin abounded, grace did much more abound." Oh, will you not be content to take this abundant grace today? This grace shall cover all your iniquities.

5. The pardon of sin is an exceedingly unsearchable grace. It is an unspeakable token of love; therefore, I entreat you, be desirous of it. Do you know what Paul calls pardoning grace? He calls it, "The unsearchable riches of Christ" (Eph. 3:8). The reason why I call it an unspeakable grace is that there are so many different expressions in Scripture which show the nature of pardoning grace. Sometimes this

grace is taken for lifting up our iniquities, as in Psalm 32:1: "Whose transgression is forgiven, whose sin is covered." This may also be understood as sin being "lifted up," which is the same word used in Exodus 34:7: "Forgiving iniquity, and transgression, and sin."

Are there any people here who desire the precious hands of Christ to lift the burden of iniquity off their back? Sometimes it is pointed out under the notion of purging away, "washing away," or covering as in Psalm 32:1: "Whose sin is covered." These words show us that sin is a shameful thing which needs to be covered. Sometimes grace is called a forgetting of iniquity, as in Hebrews 8:12: "For I will be merciful to their unrighteousness, and their sins and their iniquities will I remember no more." Other places it is called the casting of sin behind His back; this shows us that the sin of the unpardoned person is always before God's face, but the sin of the pardoned person is cast behind His back. Micah 7:19 says, "He will subdue our iniquities; and thou wilt cast all their sins into the depths of the sea." This serves to point out that pardon of sin is a precious mercy; one expression is not sufficient to express it. There is much telling in the pardon of sin!

6. God is exceedingly ready to accomplish this blessed work, as we see in Nehemiah 9:17 where He is called a God ready to pardon. Yes, He takes delight in this work, as in Micah 7:18 where it is said of God, "He delighteth in mercy." Now, since you have to do with one who is ready to pardon you, will you be content to take this pardon? Will you not embrace this pardoning grace?

7. This grace is the most excellent, precious, and beautiful thing that you could pursue. Let us consider the practice of Job: "Why dost thou not pardon my transgression, and take away my iniquity?" (Job 7:21). If you had all the mercies in the world, but lacked this grace, you would indeed have nothing at all. Whoever shall go down to the grave lacking this noble and excellent gift of God, the pardon of sin, shall lie in eternal estrangement from the Son of God. Shall this excellent mercy of pardoning grace be so slighted?

8. Even if you could pray and weep for forty years, if you lacked this pardoning grace, you would be eternally condemned. Even if you could preach like an angel and weep exceedingly, if you lacked pardoning grace, you would be nothing; you would be condemned. Now since there is such a necessity lying on you for this, I entreat you to pursue it. Oh, shall a grant of pardon be offered

to rebels, and shall not one of them accept it? Is not this matter of astonishment, that persons who are condemned to eternal death, when pardon is offered unto them, will not embrace it? I think this is one reason: we do not truly believe that there is a hell, a God, or judgment to come.

Now, in prosecuting this further, let us consider three points. First, let us consider eight properties of this pardoning grace, which I desire Christians to observe.

A first observation is that there are many persons who pray more for the pardon of actual sins than for the pardon of original sin. Are there not some persons, if they were asked, who must say that they never prayed for the pardon of original sin? Now, what is the reason folks are more taken up in praying for the pardon of actual transgressions than for the pardon of original sin? I shall give you three reasons for it: first, there are many who think that original sin is not their own; therefore, they do not pray for the pardon of it. Secondly, there are some who think original sin not so great a sin as actual transgression. I confess that original sin will not so much smite the natural conscience as actual sin will, but there is a deep dye of guilt in original sin that is not in actual sin. Thirdly, the sinfulness of original sin is not so easily taken up as the sinfulness of actual sins. He has come a great length who can weep in secret places for the sinfulness of original sin. It is vain to pray for the pardon and mortifying of any sin until you are taken up with the pardon and mortifying of original sin.

A second observation concerning the pardon of sin is that there are many Christians who never pray for the pardon of their idle thoughts and idle words; these are two things that do not often lie within the compass of our prayers. Whoever you are, dear Christian, pray for the pardon of your thoughts and of your idle words. Do you not know that "by your words ye shall be justified, and by your words ye shall be condemned"?

A third observation concerning the pardon of sin is that there are many who are more taken up in pursuing after sense than after pardon. Many Christians are more taken up in pursuing sensible enjoyments of Christ than the pardon of sin. The reason of this is because sense is more obviously felt than pardon.

Fourth, there is a great difference between the intimation of pardon of sin to a man's conscience and the application of that pardon. Sometimes pardon may be intimated to a man, but he does not apply it. This is clear from 2 Samuel 12:13 where Nathan says unto David, "The LORD also hath put away thy sin." Yet in Psalm 51, he prays four times for the pardon of the same sin. Likewise, there is a difference between the intimation of pardon and the grant of pardon of sin.

A fifth observation that I shall give you is that there are many persons who forgive and pardon themselves before God forgives them; many persons forget their sins before God forgets them. I'll tell you two courts out of which many hypocrites and presumptuous persons take extracts of pardon. First, some take the extracts of their pardon from the court of self-love. Secondly, some persons take their extracts of pardon out of the court of an erring conscience. Yet, Christ shall not own either of these pardons; He shall rive them. Therefore, I entreat you, examine whence it is that you have your pardon of your sin. Cursed are the persons that forgive themselves their iniquities before God forgives them. Everlasting woe shall fall upon them that forget their sins before God forgets them. There is an everlasting woe that will light upon that person's back, who is at peace with himself before God is at peace with him.

There is a sixth observation concerning the pardon of sin. Pardon of sin is a gift of the love of God; therefore, pardon is properly the object of faith. I do not desire Christians to question their pardon, because they have it not by sense; we must believe our pardon.

Seventh, a Christian may have the pardon of sin sealed unto him; yet, if all the ministers of the world would come to him and say that he was a pardoned person, he would not believe them. Sometimes when a Christian is under the power of estrangement and hardness of heart, and under the power of temptations, he cannot indeed then make application of the pardon of sin.

The last observation concerning pardoning grace is that there are Christians who may know the excellence of sense; they know the worth of communion with God, but they never knew the excellence of pardoning grace. Pardon of sin is a mercy, the worth of which we do not easily take up.

Secondly, since it is our duty to take pardoning grace, and since there is so much in it, I would only propose unto you a few things that are obstructions to your embracing pardoning grace.

Many persons conceive they are already pardoned; therefore, they stand in the way of pardoning grace. Some persons, when we desire them to come and embrace the pardoning grace of Christ, say, "We need it not; are we not pardoned already?" Oh, there are many who are now in the pit, who thought that their iniquities were pardoned. I shall give you seven evidences by which you may know if you have obtained the pardon of your iniquity.

1. He who is pardoned will have a high esteem of the Pardoner. Now, is there a person here who does not have a matchless esteem of Christ, the Pardoner? This is evidence that you are not pardoned. I would ask you, are there not many things that you value more than Christ? Then you are not a pardoned person. In Micah 7:18 we read, "Who is a God like unto thee, that pardoneth iniquity, and passeth by the transgression of the remnant of his heritage? He retaineth not his anger for ever, because he delighteth in mercy." Once you have received pardoning grace, there is none in heaven or earth that will be like unto the Pardoner, in your account and esteem. Let me ask you, does Christ have the uppermost room in your heart? If He does not, what does this say? It says that you are not a pardoned person. Are there not many persons here who may say that Christ has none of their thoughts? I say, if you had pardoning grace, Christ would be matchless unto you. Do you dare say that He is matchless unto you?

2. The second evidence of a pardoned Christian is that he hates the sin which is pardoned. Some persons can look upon the sin they thought was pardoned with as much delight as before. Be sure of it, as long as you look upon sin with delight, that sin is not pardoned. What kind of pardon is it, that the day after we think we are pardoned of such a sin, we can look to our old sin with delight?

3. A pardoned Christian is a Christian "in whose spirit there is no guile," according to the words of Psalm 32:2. Now, is there a person here who dares to say that there is no guile in his spirit? Are there not many persons who have hypocrisy reigning in their tongues, in their affections, and in their walk? This is an evidence such are not

pardoned. Now, if this is an evidence of a pardoned person, how many of us come short of pardon?

4. A pardoned person will be much in the exercise of praise for such a glorious mercy. This is clear in Psalm 103:2 compared with verse 3. The Psalmist says, "Bless the LORD, O my soul, and forget not all his benefits." What is the reason of that? For it is He "who forgiveth all thine iniquities; who healeth all thy diseases." It is clear, "Take away all iniquity, and receive us graciously: so will we render the calves of our lips" (Hosea 14:2); that is, we shall praise Thee.

5. A fifth evidence of a pardoned Christian is that He will have a high esteem of the pardon itself. He will put a higher account upon that mercy than upon many of the mercies of sense. That is an evidence of someone who has obtained pardon; he puts a high account upon the pardon, esteeming it a singular mercy.

6. A pardoned Christian will have much patience and contentment under every lot and difficulty that he may endure. In Isaiah 33:24 we read, "The inhabitant shall not say, I am sick." Why is this? Because, the verse continues, "The people that dwell therein shall be forgiven their iniquity." Pardoning grace is the thing that shall bring the inhabitants of Jerusalem to say, "I am not sick."

7. A pardoned person is ready to forgive offences committed against himself. When we do not forgive our neighbors the wrongs and prejudices we sustain by them, it is evidence that our sin is not pardoned. Are there not many persons here who cannot name the fifth petition of the Lord's prayer: "Forgive us our debts, as we forgive our debtors"? Listen to the words of Matthew 18:35: "So likewise shall my heavenly Father do also unto you, if ye from your hearts forgive not every one his brother their trespasses." Now, are there not some who have enmity against others? This is evidence that you are not pardoned.

8. There is this last evidence of a pardoned person: there are three things that generally accompany the pardon of sin when it comes home to the soul. First, when

pardon comes home to the soul, there is much inward joy and communion with God. Ordinarily, communion with God and pardon of sin meet together. There is a voice of joy within when that word is spoken from heaven to the soul: "Son, be of good cheer; thy sins be forgiven thee" (Matt. 9:2). Secondly, when the application of pardon is right, there is a heart-detestation of iniquity. When God intimates pardon to a soul, that soul is brought to a real detestation of sin. There is this, thirdly, that attends the pardon of sin; ordinarily, at the time of intimation of pardon to a Christian, there is much delight in duty. These are the three sweet companions of pardon intimated to the soul. Now, let us name some of the reasons why we do not embrace pardoning grace.

The first reason we do not embrace pardoning grace is that we do not truly understand the weight of sin. If we knew the weight of sin, we would cry out night and day, "Oh, to be pardoned!" Our consciences are not tender; therefore, we do not cry out for pardon. When did David cry out for pardon? Was it not when he waxed old with crying, and when he roared night and day? "Blessed is he whose transgression is forgiven, whose sin is covered" (Ps. 32:1). What brought him to these words: "My moisture is turned into the drought of summer" (v. 4), and my bones, which are the pillars of my house, are moldering within me?

The second reason we do not embrace pardoning grace is that we do not mind our sin. Some, in twenty days, will not have one thought of their sin; that is the reason we do not seek much for pardon. When did David plead for pardon? It was when his sin was ever before him, as we see in Psalm 51:4: "My sin is ever before me."

A third reason we do not seek after and embrace this pardoning grace is because we do not know what a loathsome thing sin is. Once you believe what a shameful thing sin is, then you would highly value pardoning grace and pursue after it. If you knew that sin needed a covering and needed to be purged away, you would cry out, "Oh, for the blood of sprinkling, to purify from an evil conscience!"

A last consideration before closing is to discuss the seven great objections that may be answered from this text, all which may give a sufficient resolution to any argument against seeking pardon.

A first objection may be: "Alas! I have so many and such great iniquities that I think Christ will never accept me. I am forced to say that my transgression is great and my sin is infinite." I shall say no more to you but that His grace is sufficient for you. Do you have scarlet transgressions? The tongues of men and angels cannot give another answer than this: "His grace is sufficient for thee." I say unto you today, His grace shall have the victory over your transgressions; therefore, come away.

The second objection may be: "Oh, I have been a professor for many days, and the more I wrestle with my lusts and corruptions, the more they prevail against me." There is an answer to that case in the same words: "His grace is sufficient for thee." There is a fullness of strength in the Son of God to make you overcome.

Third, one may object, saying, "Alas! I would be content to take pardoning grace, but I cannot get my heart to embrace it." I say, there is also an answer to that objection in the words, "His grace is sufficient for thee." He can work in you both to will and to do. Are there any persons here who say that they would take Christ if they could be made willing? I say, Christ has engaged His strength to make you willing.

A fourth great objection may be: "Alas! I never go to prayer, nor any religious exercise, but I weary of it, and it becomes a burden to me." This is also addressed in the words, "His grace is sufficient for thee." There is nothing that you lack that you will not receive in the words, "His grace is sufficient for thee." Do you weary in duty? Do you go about duty with formality and hypocrisy? "His grace is sufficient for thee!"

One may also object thus: "How shall I conquer this evil heart of unbelief? How shall I begin to exercise this noble grace of faith?" There is an answer to this in the text: "His grace is sufficient for thee." Can you not get your heart to believe? This text will answer your objections.

The sixth great objection of some is, "I fear if I come to Christ, I will only dishonor Him and I will leave a stain on the ways of God and a reproach upon His name." There is an answer for you in the words, "His grace is sufficient for thee." He can bring you unto Himself and He can keep you there with clean garments.

A seventh and last objection which some have is this: "Alas! I am under the evil of hypocrisy. There is not a duty I go about in which I do not show a great deal of hypocrisy. There is a contradiction between my heart and my light; between my outward and inward man; between myself when I am alone and myself when I am in company; between my desires and my endeavors; and between my resolutions and performance. Oh, how will I conquer my hypocrisy?" "His grace is sufficient for thee." Oh, be content to embrace this pardoning grace.

I would ask all that are here, though I think there are not many of us who are in any suitable frame, what do you think of the offer of this pardoning grace that has been offered at such a low price to you? I doubt if there is a person within these doors who will go out with more love unto this pardoning grace than when he came hither. Oh, slighters of this precious pardoning grace of God, be afraid, and stand in awe, lest there be a sentence passed in heaven that your sins shall never be forgiven! I confess, we may preach much of this pardoning grace; but this is the ruin of many—they are not convinced of their lack of pardoning grace. I would only say this and charge you to take it home: if you will not come a greater length, come at least this far: be convinced of your need for this pardoning grace! I shall tell you of five things to commend the necessity and need of Christ without which you shall never come to Christ for pardoning grace.

First, necessity and need of Christ are not ceremonious things. If you had a real need of Christ, you would not stand upon all the ceremonies which unbelief makes. Necessity would leave many of these fruitless ceremonies.

Secondly, a real need of Christ raises only one question. It cuts off all the debates and objections toward unbelief. Necessity has no question but this: "Oh, when shall Christ and I meet? When shall I appear before Him?" If you had real need of Christ, you would not dispute any longer.

Thirdly, it makes a person come on the highway to Christ. Unbelief makes a Christian come to Christ, as it were, in a circle, but necessity makes him to come straight forward to Christ, and stands not to go about by those ways that unbelief leads. Believe it, if you were needful, you would make a speedy and hasty voyage to the Son of God.

Fourthly, I would say of necessity that it is a thing that will not allow delay. Christians and those who undervalue this pardoning grace—what makes you delay so much, and some of you to cry out, "Oh, for a delay"? I say, you lack necessity. Necessity would make you impatient of delays. I tell you what necessity would do—it would make you think every hour of your distance from Christ is a year. Necessity, the real need of Christ, would dispossess you of your night's rest until you got Christ. Necessity has only one prayer, and it is this: "Oh, for a sight of the Son of God!" If you had necessity and a real need of Christ, you would not dare admit so many delays as you do. The lack of necessity unveils Christians like Felix; they will say to the minister, "Go your way, and at another time, I will call for thee."

Fifthly, necessity is the best preacher of Christ's beauty of anything I know. Nothing will commend Christ so much as necessity. Necessity would bring up a good report. If there were a person that had the real need of Christ here today, he would be ravished with love of Him. Necessity is that which most commends Christ. What is the reason we have such low thoughts of Christ? It is a lack of necessity. Necessity would preach more of the beauty of Christ in a moment than all the preachers of Christ in Scotland would do in a year. Oh, that soul-conquering preacher of Christ's beauty, necessity!

What makes you cry out, "Christ shall never be my Lord"? It is that you lack necessity. Necessity would make Christ white and ruddy, the chiefest among ten thousand. Believe it, the dreadful undervaluing of Christ that is among us shows that we have no necessity and real need of Christ. I tell you, this necessity makes a Christian diligent in the use of all the means to get Christ. The real need of Christ would make you miss sleep night and day for a sight of the Son of God. I will tell you what necessity is: it is like David's three worthies. It will break through an army of objections to get a drink of the water of Bethlehem's well. Believe it, once you were brought home with a real need of Christ, you would be restless until you get a sight of Him.

I have no more to say, but seek after a real need of Christ. Believe it, need of Christ would make you run swiftly to Him. I am persuaded there would be longing until the day should come that you would cry out, "Christ is mine, and I am His!" Now, to Him who can persuade you to take Him and can give this soul-enriching pardoning grace, we desire to give praise. Amen.

SERMON 40

Precious Remedies against Satan's Devices (1)

Lest Satan should get an advantage of us: for we are not ignorant of his devices.
—2 Corinthians 2:11

Do you not suppose that there has been much joy in hell these many days? Do you not suppose that the devil and his angels have kept a day of feasting and joy, because of the success of his kingdom, and the war that he now has with immortal souls? The words of Revelation 12:3 are coming to pass in these days: "Behold a great red dragon," which is the devil. We see that "his tail drew the third part of the stars of heaven, and did cast them to the earth: and the dragon stood before the woman which was ready to be delivered, for to devour her child as soon as it was born" (v. 4). By these words, we understand that many glorious professors who were once shining in the highest orb and sphere of profession of godliness, have been cast down by him. Thus, we also hear the lamentable words of Isaiah 14:12: "How art thou fallen from heaven, O Lucifer, son of the morning! how art thou cut down to the ground, which didst weaken the nations!" There are many who were once shining lights, who now have embraced this present world and are ashamed of their profession. They make their profession ashamed of them.

I conceive there are three things in the devil that are matter of astonishment unto us.

First, we wonder at the different ways that the devil takes to carry souls to eternal torments. There are some he drives to hell in a more public way, and there are some he drives to hell in a more silent way. In this silent manner, he drives the hypocrite in Zion; some he pursues as a roaring lion and others he pursues as an angel of light.

Secondly, we are amazed at the subtleties and desperate devices by which he catches immortal souls. His way is more subtle than the way of a ship in the sea, the way of an eagle in the air, and the way of a serpent on a rock; he knows well how to catch advantage, and how to deceive the simple who are serving diverse lusts. There are three fundamentals of Satan's kingdom: the lust of the eyes, the lust of the flesh, and the pride of life. These are the common places out of which he draws all his arrows to deceive simple souls.

Thirdly, we wonder at the cursed harmony that is between the temptations of the devil and our deceitful hearts. There is no temptation that Satan presents that does not entice our deceitful heart to fall into it. Even if there were not a devil in hell to tempt you to sin, your heart would constantly tempt you. I conceive that the hearts of many tempt them to sin more than the devil tempts them; you may have this written upon your foreheads: "You have destroyed yourselves."

There are these two things I would press upon you as a subject of study. First, you must understand the desperate deceitfulness of your own heart. Second, you must know the desperate devices of the devil. These are depths that no one has been able to fathom. Certainly, when a Christian reflects upon the devices of the devil, he shall be constrained to cry out, "Oh, the height of the power of him that is prince of the power of the air, and oh, the depth of his subtlety and policy, which transforms himself into all shapes!" He can sail with our discouragements, and he can sail with our presumptions; he can sail with the cross, and he can sail with prosperity to accomplish his ends. Likewise, the Christian may cry out, "Oh, the length of his temptations! He tempts day and night; he goes about continually seeking whom he may devour. Oh, the breadth of his temptations! There are none, from the beggar that sits on the dunghill, to the king on the throne, who are free from his temptations. He assaults all men."

Let us consider our text. You have in the words of our text a threefold character of a Christian who has gone on to much perfection.

First, do not be ignorant of the devices and stratagems of the devil: "We are not ignorant of his devices" (2 Cor. 2:11).

Second, the perfect Christian regulates his walk and conversation so as not to give the devil any advantage over him. This is also clear from the words of the text: "Lest Satan should get an advantage of us." This relates to the former part of the chapter, where Paul presses the Corinthians and himself to walk so as the devil might not get an advantage over them, nor circumvent them.

Third, a Christian who has gone on to much perfection improves his knowledge of the devices of the devil. This is an excellent means and impediment in the way of the devil, to hinder him from getting advantage over the Christian. The last words of our text are the reason of the former: "We are not ignorant of his devices"; therefore, he adds, "Lest Satan should get an advantage of us." We may say, in vain is a net spread before the eyes of a Christian who has a divine understanding of the stratagems of the devil.

Concerning the first noble character of a Christian, we shall discuss several points. First, we shall point out these general devices of the devil, by which he catches immortal souls. Secondly, we shall speak about the devices Satan uses to keep men in their natural state, without moving to Christ. Thirdly, let us discuss the temptations of the devil, by which he assaults a Christian when he is under the exercise of the law. Fourthly, we shall speak about the devices with which Satan assaults a Christian after his first closing with Christ. Fifthly, we shall discuss the devices by which Satan assaults a Christian when he has gone on to some perfection in his way to heaven. Sixthly, we shall discuss how much the perfection of a Christian stands in the distinct knowledge of the devices of the devil.

Primarily, we shall name the general devices by which the devil ensnares all sorts of persons.

First, Satan suits his temptations to our predominant lusts and idols; he knows which lusts and idols within our bosoms our heart follows, and according to those lusts he frames his temptations. The devil has some fiery darts, which are his more public and hellish temptations; he also has some invisible darts by which he takes advantage of us. Now it is clear in Scripture that he suits his temptations to our predominant lusts and idols. He will set a wedge of gold and a Babylonish garment before the eyes of a covetous Achan; he will set thirty pieces of silver before the eyes of a covetous Judas; he will set a beautiful Tamar before the eyes of a lusting Amnon; he will set a beautiful Bathsheba before the eyes of a lusting David; he will set a fair occasion of preferment before the eyes of an ambitious Absalom; and he will set a fair occasion of pride before the eyes of an aspiring Hezekiah. Now, in the further prosecution of this general device of the devil, take notice of these four things.

1. It is difficult to determine whether it is better for one who has an unmortified lust and idol to have the enjoyment of his idol or to lack the enjoyment of his idol. I think it is better to have the enjoyment of his idol rather than to lack it. This is clear in Ahithophel, when he lacks the enjoyment of his predominant idol, his reputation; he will go home and strangle himself. It is also clear in the life of godly Jonah; when he lacks the enjoyment of his predominant idol, he cries out, "It is better for me to die than to live" (Jonah 4:3).

2. Oh, the damnable desires that a Christian will have for succumbing to his lusts and the enjoyment of his idols. It is impossible to determine what unnatural desires an unmortified lust will have for its enjoyment; this is clear in Jonah 4:11. We see that his unmortified lust may be satisfied and he can wish that the whole city of Nineveh were destroyed, that thousands of people might be cut off. This is also clear in the practice of godly David. What monstrous desires he had, that his idol of reputation might be preserved; he will make godly Uriah drunk, and be ashamed among the people. Then at last, he will not hesitate to kill him to preserve his damnable idol of self-reputation.

3. These temptations are not much incentive of themselves to stir up your predominant lusts; yet, through the deceit of your heart, will prove to be temptations to stir up your predominant lusts. I would ask you, is there anything that comes your way that, through the deceit of your heart, does not prove to be a temptation to your predominant idol?

4. Lastly, you must notice that the first sight of a lust or idol is the most beautiful, and the most refreshing sight that you ever shall encounter. Your idols, when first they woo you, appear in their garments of advantage, beautiful robes, and in the sweet garments of delight and pleasure.

Now, there is a second general device of the devil: he suits our temptations to our predominant necessities. This is remarkably clear when Christ, being under the sinless necessity of being hungry, is tempted by the devil. The devil proposes a temptation suitable to that necessity: "Command that these stones be made bread" (Matt. 4:3). It is also clear in the practice of David that the devil will tempt David to go down to Achish when he is in straits and dangers; similarly, the people of God, when they are brought to any outward strait, will go down to Egypt and trust in the arm of flesh. We confess that necessity is an excellent orator; it is easier to answer the arguments of reason than to answer the arguments of necessity. Necessity will make one do things that all the arguments of reason would not influence him to do. I would only say to you, when the devil suits his temptations to your predominant necessity, you must be aware of two things; first, the devil will never provide an escape from your necessity. He may give you an appearance of an escape, but the purpose of it is to enthrall you more unto your necessity. Second, when the devil suits his temptations to your predominant necessity, you must attempt to live more by faith than by sense. You must believe this when dispensations appear not to agree with the word.

There is a third general device of the devil. He takes the fittest time for tempting persons. He knows how to watch for his advantage; he knows that there is a time of peace and a time of war. To make this clearer, there are four things to observe.

1. Satan makes the strongest assaults when a Christian is most secure and least watchful. This is clear in the story of David, in 2 Samuel 2:2. While he is sleeping on his bed and walking on the roof of his house, the devil assaults him and obtains much victory over him. We see in the practice of Peter, that when he is in his most presumptuous frame, the devil desired to winnow him as wheat (Luke 22:31-32).

2. Take notice of the policy of the devil; he chooses to assault us when he conceives we are in the place where we may respond most conveniently to his temptation. When a person is in a convenient place and time for acting out his lust, then the devil tempts to act out that lust. This

is clear in the history of Cain and Abel—when they are in the field together, Cain will be tempted to murder his innocent brother (Gen. 4:8). We also see in Genesis 39:11-12 that when all the servants of the house were out, Joseph's mistress assaults him. This is a remarkable circumstance of Joseph's chastity; when he had such a seasonable opportunity for acting out his lust, he would not. I think there are some of you who engage in secrecy when committing iniquity; also, there are some who sorrow for sins that are known, but they never mourn for sins that are committed in secret. You may be afraid that your sorrow will continue eternally if you sorrow no more than this.

3. We must point out the subtlety and devices of the devil. He chooses the time to tempt to such a lust, when the lust or idol to which he tempts is most beautiful, most inviting, and most commended. For instance, he tempts many to hypocrisy when religion has the applause of the world. Certainly, when our lusts have most beauty and luster on them, he tempts and often prevails. Finally, he chooses the time to assault a Christian when his affections are somewhat warming to the lust or idol; behold, he comes to stir up our lusts the more after it. Once the fire of love begins to burn within your bosom for any idol, Satan increases the fire by his temptations.

The fourth general device that the devil uses to catch immortal souls is to show you the pleasure, the advantage, and the dignity of your idols; but, he does not at all show you the sinfulness, the misery, and anxiety of your idols. This is clear in Matthew 4:8, where we read that He "sheweth him all the kingdoms of the world, and the glory of them." However, it is not said that Satan showed unto Him the misery and emptiness of all the kingdoms of the world. We also see this in the first temptation presented to our first parents; we read, "For God doth know that in the day ye eat thereof, then your eyes shall be opened, and ye shall be as gods, knowing good and evil" (Gen. 3:5); there is not one word about being under the curse of God and eternal sequestration from His presence. Upon this device, we would have you to take notice of several points.

1. Be persuaded that there is more joy in the hope and expectation of your idols than in the enjoyment of them. All the enjoyment of an idolater stands in hope; little of it stands in fruition.

2. When a soul comes to the enjoyment of its predominant idol, God either blasts the idol or cuts short your life ordinarily. We see this in the parable of that fool in the gospel, when he embraces his predominant idol. He says, "Soul, thou hast much goods laid up for many years; take thine ease, eat, drink, and be merry," and then it follows: "Thou fool, this night thy soul shall be required of thee" (Luke 12:19-20).

3. An eternity's enjoyment of your idols is not worthy to be compared to one moment's enjoyment of Christ; for all the pleasures that idols can afford unto you, the loss of one hour of fellowship with Christ is a greater loss than they all can compensate.

4. Finally, notice that when the devil presents you with the beauty of your idols and you embrace these temptations, be then afraid, lest there be a knot of marriage made between you and your idols. There are two knots that will be made between you and your lusts; there is a knot of love and a knot of desire. Certainly, when you cast these knots between you and your idols, God will cast a third knot between you and them. He passes a sentence in heaven, saying, "They are joined to their idols, let them alone."

Satan's fifth general device is the subtle method that he uses to gain your consent unto his temptations; there are two things that show this.

There are five things in a Christian which Satan attempts to gain. He seeks to gain their eyes, their ears, their memories, their affections, and their light. First, Satan attempts (in those that are subject to the idol of uncleanness, or the idol of the world) to gain their eyes, to look upon the object that he presents. Second, Satan studies to gain their ears, to parley and discourse with the temptation. Third, if you open to him your ear and give him the courtesy of hearing him, he goes further on to press unto his victory. He then attempts to gain your memory, to think and reflect upon your idols.

Fourth, he endeavors to gain your light; this is, that you may be convinced of the beauty and necessity of embracing such an idol. Last, he studies to gain your affections; he delights to have the idol dwelling within your heart. I would only say two things concerning this device of the devil.

1. It is a greater difficulty to mortify an idol to a Christian's light than it is for him to mortify an idol to his love. To mortify an idol to his love is to lose his affections to his idol; but for a Christian to mortify an idol to his light is to be convinced and persuaded of the vanity, emptiness, and anxiety of that idol. Second, when an idol has seized upon you, and both light and love come to defend it, then mortification is a most difficult work. Therefore, though your hearts are granted to your idol, beware that you do not betray your light unto your idol.

2. The devil is extremely subtle in gaining your consent unto his temptations. He will tempt a Christian to some sins so that he may have better access to tempt him to that which is his main aim. For instance, he will tempt Sodom to pride, to idleness, and to fullness of bread; but his aim is to tempt them to uncleanness. So we see in Cain: Satan will tempt him to discontent and then he will tempt him to murder, discontentment being the sin that drew him to murder.

A sixth general device of the devil is to tempt a Christian to sin under the veil of virtue and grace. This was most clear in the assault that Christ encountered, when Satan presses Christ to presumption, but does so under the veil of faith. Satan says, "If thou be the Son of God, cast thyself down: for it is written, He shall give his angels charge concerning thee: and in their hands they shall bear thee up, lest at any time thou dash thy foot against a stone" (Matt. 4:6). In essence, Satan says that if Christ will do what he says, it would be an exercise of faith. This is clear in his first temptation to Christ, where he presses Him to perform a miracle to prove His divinity. This principle is also clear in Satan's interaction with Christians; he will tempt a Christian to unbelief under the veil of humility; he will tempt a Christian to hypocrisy under the veil of love; and he will tempt the unbelievers of this age to presumption under the veil of faith. No doubt, this is a subtle device of the devil. Upon this thought, I would like to add two points.

First, always suspect a temptation to be that unto which your affections run without contradiction. You must be persuaded that is a temptation. Also, suspect the temptation that has the least challenges when it is embraced. This is taken home by a Christian under the veil of a virtue. You never challenge your unbelief because you conceive it to be humility. A hypocrite is never challenged for hypocrisy because he conceives it to be love. An unbeliever is never challenged for presumption because he conceives it to be faith.

A seventh general device by which the devil endeavors to ensnare immortal souls is to suit his temptations to the estate you have in the world. If one be in a low estate, he will suit his temptations to that estate; and if one be sitting upon a throne, he will suit his temptations to that estate. This is most clear from the temptations of scriptural persons. Thirty pieces of silver is a suitable temptation for Judas; a wedge of gold is a perfect temptation for Achan; but for Absalom, a kingdom is a suitable temptation.

There is an eighth general device of the devil: he suits our temptations according to our natural disposition. The devil knows there are some spirits which are more refined; they have a natural kind of generosity that would undervalue low temptations. There are also some spirits which are more brutish. Now this kind of policy is clear in Matthew 4:8. The devil never presented such a large offer unto any he has assaulted as he did to Christ, because he knew with whom he had to do. A low temptation, he supposed, would not reach Him; therefore, he brings out the strongest arrow in his quiver. Certainly, there is much of the devil's device that stands in this temptation. Let us consider two points upon this topic.

First, you need to know that to which your natural disposition inclines; whether, as the heathen speaks, it be born to high things or whether you suppose your spirits would be content to walk in a humble sphere. Second, guard your heart well against the temptations of the devil that correspond with your natural disposition. There are some who are naturally proud; therefore, such should guard against the sin of pride. Pride is a predominant sin to some, lust is a predominant sin in some, covetousness is a predominant sin in some; therefore I say, whichever lust is predominant in you, you must work especially to guard against the temptation that suits that lust.

The ninth general device of the devil is that when he tempts us to sin, he will furnish a suitable plot to cover that sin when it is acted out. This is clear in the practice of Absalom; he tempts

Absalom to ambition, but he gives him a cloak to cover it. He tempts Judas to covetousness, and he gives him a veil of charity to the poor to cover it. It is clear in Scripture that Satan tempts Herod to kill Christ, giving him the veil of religion to cover it, for Herod says to the wise men, "Go and search diligently for the young child; and when ye have found him, bring me word again, that I may come and worship him also" (Matt. 2:8).

Tenth, let us consider the last general device the devil employs to catch immortal souls. Satan takes an appropriate season to correspond with the frame of our spirits. When a Christian is discouraged, Satan will press him to despair; when a Christian is secure, he will press him to fall asleep, and not to open to Christ; and when he is under the fits of presumption, he will make him to believe all is right; when he is experiencing jealousy, he will create suspicion between Christ and the soul.

Now that we have spoken upon the general devices of Satan, we desire to propose these six considerations to you:

1. The devil has a limited power over some and he has arbitrary power over others. There are some he cannot tempt without permission; others he can tempt at will. This is clear in Job 1:8 and 2 Timothy 2:26: "And that they may recover themselves out of the snare of the devil, who are taken captive by him at his will." In Job, Satan testifies he does not dare to put his hand to Job until he received a commission; I am afraid that there are many here who are under the arbitrary power and government of the devil, and are the subjects of his kingdom. They shall remain eternally so, except the blessed Lion of the tribe of Judah rescue them from the paw of this destroying lion.

2. There are three things that are deceitful, the deceitfulness of which cannot be known. First, the devil, who is the deceiver of the brethren, is extremely deceitful. Second, sin is an extremely deceitful thing. Third, our own hearts are the princes of deceitfulness. Our hearts are more deceitful than the devil; our hearts are deceitful above all things. The deceitfulness of our hearts is more subtle and more secret than the deceitfulness of the devil. I say unto you, woe to the man when the friends of his own house become his enemies, and when his own heart betrays him. It is impossible for such a one to escape the snares of the devil, since his heart betrays him. I would only here show you the harmony that is between these

deceivers: the first presents the temptation, the second commends the temptation, and the third closes with the temptation, taking it home to himself.

3. All the temptations the devil presents would not overcome you if there were not something within your bosom which betrays you. It is impossible for the devil to tempt one to sin, except the person consents to that sin. We read in Matthew 26:41, "Watch and pray, that ye enter not into temptation: the spirit indeed is willing, but the flesh is weak." Notice that it is not said, "That *temptation* enter not into you," but, "That *ye* enter not into temptation" (emphasis added). The Christian must not voluntarily go into the house of temptation.

4. Christ has a blessed purpose in letting the strong one wrestle with the believer. I shall tell you three reasons why Christ permits the devil to assault you. First, He desires to exercise your graces. Second, He has the goal of provoking you to long for heaven. Third, He desires that the power of His graces may be more conspicuous.

Let us examine these goals a little more closely. First, He desires to exercise grace in you. Temptations keep grace in exercise. Grace is never in more vigorous exercise than when temptations abound. Secondly, He desires to make you long for heaven; this was the apostle Paul's goal in his wrestlings: "O wretched man that I am! who shall deliver me from the body of this death?" (Rom. 7:24). Third, Christ desires that the power of His grace may be made more conspicuous, so that He may be known to be the absolute and irresistible one. He desires it to be known that all His enemies shall fall under His feet as lightning, and that He shall once tread upon them as mire in the streets.

5. There are three damnable properties of the devil that may provoke you to watchfulness; he is a potent, constant, and subtle adversary. These are the three great qualifications of the prince of the bottomless pit. He is potent; hence he is called "the prince of the power of the air" (Eph. 2:2); he is a constant enemy, who goes about continually seeking those whom he may devour (1 Peter 5:8). The devil can never be wearied of tempting; he has an earnest desire for the accomplishment of his designs. He is also a subtle enemy, who can transform himself into all shapes.

6. You who never knew what it was to resist the temptations of the devil, who never knew what it was to wrestle against the prince of darkness, there is an eternal agreement ratified in heaven

between you and the devil, that shall eternally stand in force; God ratifies the agreement of peace that your heart makes with your idols and temptations.

I desire to say three words to you who never knew what it was to wrestle against the temptations of the devil.

First, every battle of the warrior is with confused noise, and with garments rolled in blood; but the war that Christ shall have with you shall be with fuel of fire and with everlasting burnings. It shall be a war that shall never have an end. He shall eternally bruise you in the mortar of His justice and with the pistol of His omnipotence. I shall not ask whether the fire of hell is a material fire or not; I am sure that the pains that are allotted for condemned men are unspeakable. What is most sad is that there is no redemption out of that pit.

Second, in what direction are you traveling? I would desire to know what you propose unto yourselves to be your home and resting place. Will you be at home in an eternity of pain or an eternity of joy? Will you be with the devil and his angels or with the Lord Jesus Christ and the innumerable company of holy angels? Do you ever ask yourselves where you will rest at night, when the long shadows of the everlasting evening shall stretch out upon you? What if in the next twelve hours, the trumpet was heard in heaven, sounded by the archangel, "Arise ye dead, and come to judgment," and you must appear before the tribunal of Jesus Christ? What would be your thoughts?

I am persuaded that those who pass under the name "Christian," and are so indeed, most of them might be forced to cry out, "Oh, spare a little, that I may recover strength before I go hence and be no more." I would tell you what would be the exercise of these damnable unbelievers who have lived all their life in a damnable agreement between them and their idols; their knees would smite one against another, and their faces would gather paleness. They would sing the words of Job 3:3: "Let the day perish wherein I was born, and the night in which it was said, 'There is a man child conceived.'"

Third, consider that you have twelve hours to work, and that you are now in the eleventh hour of your day; only one hour remains for you to work. Be sure, if your day shall come to an end before your peace with God is made, the blessed treaty of peace shall eternally be shut up. Do you think, reprobates and you who are destitute of the knowledge of God, that there is repentance in hell? You who are indeed begotten to a lively hope, oh, slighting and formal Christians, do you think there is repentance in heaven, while you have exercised so little of it here below? You believe that there is a purgatory indeed, that the sins of which you have not repented might be purged away by fire. Once you shall pass this line between time and eternity, there is no hope of change; there is no desire of change to some; and those who are in eternity of pain shall lose all hope to be changed. Those who are in eternity of joy shall lose all desire to be changed.

The last point I would propose is that the devices of the devil may be understood in this manner. As long as we do not resist the devil, he will never flee from us. Satan is bold as a lion when we flee, but the way to overcome him is to be firm in our posture of defense: "Resist the devil, and he will" not only go away, but will "flee from you," as one who is afraid (James 4:7). So that you may better understand this point, I offer unto the Christian these three comforting conclusions.

First, you must remember that "greater is he that is in you, than he that is in the world" (1 John 4:4). Let all the corruptions of hell war against you as in a solemn assembly, yet the party that wars for you is strongest.

Second, remember that Christ stands continually within the holy place to make intercession for you in the day of war. I would compare Christ's intercession to Moses and Joshua; Moses prayed on the mount when Joshua was fighting in the valley. As long as Christ's hands shall be held up in intercession, you shall always prevail, until you sing the triumphant song: "O death, where is thy sting? O grave, where is thy victory?" (1 Cor. 15:55).

Third, remember that all the enemies with whom you have to wrestle are vanquished enemies. You have already subdued them in Christ. Be certain, the devil and the seven abominations of your heart were once defeated by the hand of that noble conqueror. He turned the battle to the gate, and brought all His enemies into subjection.

To conclude our discourse at this time, we shall propose three sad and soul-afflicting thoughts to you who are destitute of the grace of God, and who have never entered into this blessed warfare.

First, unrepentant people, know that every day of your life fills up the cup of the measure of your iniquity until the cup of unmixed wine of the indignation and fury of God shall be presented to you.

Do you desire to know a description of your life? It is an offense to the majesty of God, and it provokes Him to jealousy.

If you will not abandon your idols, be sure this sentence shall be passed against you: "Because I have purged thee, and thou wast not purged, thou shalt not be purged from thy filthiness any more, till I have caused my fury to rest upon thee" (Ezek. 24:13). It is a most sad and a most lamentable state when the wrath of a living God rests and dwells upon you! If you will not bathe your souls in the sweet and precious blood of Christ, you shall be made the objects of the wrath of the Most High. Christ shall come from Bozrah with His garments rolled in blood, traveling in the greatness of His strength, after He has accomplished the greatness of His fury.

Last, consider that there is an approaching judgment when Christ shall sit down upon the throne, and when all the families and tribes of the earth shall appear before Him in the valley of decision; no doubt, that shall be a most sad and lamentable day unto you. I would seriously urge you, by the dreadful sentence that Christ shall pass against the hypocrites in Zion, by all the curses that are within the book of the covenant, by the love that you have for your immortal souls, by all the joys of heaven, and by all the terrors of that everlasting prison, that you would forsake your idols! The wrath of the Most High shall enter eternity with you if you do not make your peace with Him! Therefore, take hold of His strength and make peace, lest His fury shall be kindled against you, and there shall be none to deliver you.

There are three parts of Christ's body that a Christian should kiss. First, you must kiss His mouth, which imports the sweetness of communion and fellowship with Him. Next, you must kiss His hand, which imports subjection. Third, you must kiss His feet, which imports love to Him. Now you who never knew what it was to kiss the feet of Christ in love, nor the hands of Christ in obedience, nor the mouth of Christ in communion, what do you suppose will be the end of your estate? Will you not be afraid that His wrath shall enter the lifts with you? I am sure that if many of us knew how near we are to the brink of eternal destruction, we would be distracted until we would know that our peace is made in heaven. Do you consider an eternity of pain a fancy, that you fear it so little? Do you consider an eternity of joy a delusion, that you will not follow after it? I am sure there are some who will never believe that there is an eternity of pain until the day shall come that sense shall instruct them in it. Sense will once instruct that there is a judgment to come, an eternity of pain, and a resurrection both of the just and the unjust.

Oh, to be provoked before that day comes, that shall burn as a whirlwind without any mixture of mercy! You must embrace Christ, who is the object of the saints' love, the eternal admiration of angels, and the glory of the higher house. Oh, love Him and delight your soul in Him! He is the person who ought to be the object of our love, our hope, our fear, and our desires. Forsake your idols of love, fear, and obedience, and let Christ be the precious center upon which all these graces are terminated. The day is approaching in which you shall commend yourself in that excellent choice you have made. It is a choice that cuts off all repentance that is worthy to be repented of. So now I close with these words: cursed be the person who will not love our Lord Jesus. Let all the congregation say, "Amen."

SERMON 41

Precious Remedies against Satan's Devices (2)

Lest Satan should get an advantage of us: for we are not ignorant of his devices.
—2 Corinthians 2:11

A very wise and judicial law existed in the Old Testament. It said that a man in the first year of his marriage should not go to war (Deut. 24:5). So it is in the first year of a soul's marriage with Christ—the new Christian must not engage in strong debates so that he is not hindered in his progress to heaven. Christ suits a believer's trials to his strength, but Satan suits his temptation to our predominant lusts and weaknesses.

There are four things we desire to tell you before we address the words of our text.

First, notice that a Christian is a compound of many contradictions. A Christian is as "black as the tents of Kedar," yet he is as "comely as the curtains of Solomon" (Song 1:5). A Christian can do nothing, yet a Christian can do all things. A Christian is always sorrowing, yet he is always rejoicing; a Christian is ever poor, yet he is always rich; a Christian possesses nothing, yet he possesses all things.

Secondly, a hypocrite is also a compound of contradictions. There is a contradiction between a hypocrite's hope and his walk; between a hypocrite's profession and his practice; between a hypocrite's tongue and his heart; between a hypocrite when he is alone and when he is in company.

Thirdly, there are four mysterious dispensations that God administers, that may provoke us to a divine astonishment.

1. We may stand in awe that He should have contrived the way to heaven through so many outward trials and afflictions, and through so many inward conflicts; a Christian, through his entire life, has terror without and battles within. Christ could have carried believers to heaven in a valley of roses! Christ might have transported believers to heaven in a chariot on a road paved with love and ease; yet, He deemed it good to carry His own believers to heaven in a fiery chariot. He desires that they go through the Valley of Baca before they should be brought to the Valley of Berachah.

2. Another mysterious dispensation of God is that He has appointed so many outward and inward enemies to interrupt a Christian's progress and motion to heaven. The devil assaults us upon our left hand and our own deceitful heart assaults us upon our right hand. We conceive that the reason God allows these attacks is so that the power of Christ's grace might appear; or else, so that the fainting and weary travelers of hope might one day sing aloud these pleasant songs of everlasting love.

3. We may also wonder that God should permit Christians to fall so often into the snare of the devil; why does God allow Satan to obtain the advantage over them so often? We believe that there is also a reason God allows us to fall in these snares: since there is nothing but sinning against Christ while we are here in this life, Christians might thus be constrained to long for heaven.

4. There are three things that are too wonderful for us, and four things which we cannot understand. First, there are the subtle, yet incomprehensible devices of the devil. His words are softer than butter when war is in his heart. His speeches are softer than oil when he intends them to be sharp swords. We may say of the devil that he becomes all things to all men, so that he may gain some. Second, our own deceitful hearts are a mystery to us. We have never plumbed the depth of their wickedness, nor fathomed the depth of their iniquity. Third, we may wonder

at the incomprehensible love of Christ and the incomprehensible essence of God.

Now, we told you at the last occasion that there was a threefold character of a complete Christian contained in the words of our text. First, a Christian is not to be ignorant of the devil's devices: "We are not ignorant of his devices" (2 Cor. 2:11). A second characteristic of a complete Christian is that Satan should not get an advantage over him. We see this also in the words of 2 Corinthians 2:11: "Lest Satan should get an advantage of us." The third characteristic of a perfect and complete Christian is that he improves his knowledge of the devil's devices as a means to hinder the devil from getting advantage over him. The last words of the text state that "we are not ignorant of his devices"; therefore, Satan shall not get advantage over us. As for the first character of a perfect Christian, we proposed several things to discuss. At the last occasion, we spoke concerning the many devices of the devil, by which he assaults every sort of men.

Now we propose to discuss the devices the devil uses to keep men in their natural state. Before we begin our discussion, we desire you to hear three considerations.

First, when we speak of the devices the devil uses to keep men in their nature, you abstract from the decree and precious purpose of God; for certainly, God has determined in the counsel of His will that many should be eternally the prisoners of the devil. However, this does not excuse Satan for tempting, nor you for embracing his temptations.

A second consideration is that Satan keeps some in their nature by visible bonds, and some he keeps in their nature by more invisible bonds. He keeps hypocrites in their nature as an angel of light; he keeps persons that are more grossly profane in their nature as a roaring lion.

Third, the devil's devices are subtle, profound, and deep. There are several things that show the subtlety and profoundness of the devil's devices. Let us consider some of these examples.

We see that the Scripture clearly shows that most of you are in your own nature; yet notwithstanding all the light of the Scripture, Satan keeps many persuaded that they are in an excellent state. We see this happening in two ways. First, sometimes you are convinced that you are in a natural state and void of the grace of God; yet Satan, by his devices, keeps these convictions hidden and causes you to fall asleep. We see the subtlety of his devices when the conscience of a natural person is convinced of the beauty of religion, yet Satan keeps him in a state of sin, despite that conviction. This is clear in the case of Balaam; he was convinced that it was an excellent thing to die the death of the righteous; yet Satan kept him in his sin. This is also clear in the case of Agrippa, who was almost persuaded to be a Christian, yet his *almost* never became an *altogether*. The last way we see the subtlety of Satan's devices is that he ensnares immortal souls by most woeful temptations. Are not some of you tempted to sell precious Christ for thirty pieces of silver?

A fourth consideration that we propose unto you is to show you the differences between a hypocrite and one that is grossly in a natural state. First, the devil reigns in the hypocrite as an angel of light, but he reigns in a person in a state of gross sin as a roaring lion. Second, the hypocrite crucifies Christ under the veil of love; he that is grossly profane crucifies Christ under the veil of virtue. He supposes his sins are virtues. Third, the hypocrite denies the omniscience of God in his practice, while he that is grossly in a natural state denies the justice of God. The last difference between them is that the hypocrite's sin or hypocrisy is a silent and spiritual sin; but gross profanity is a crying and visible sin.

Now, let us finally discuss that which we proposed to engage: the devices of the devil by which he keeps men in a natural state. Let us discuss this in two points. First, we shall speak concerning the devices by which he keeps hypocrites in nature. Secondly, we shall speak concerning the devices that Satan uses to keep them that are in a gross state of natural sin.

The devil keeps even the most refined hypocrites in a natural state using most wretched devices.

1. Satan makes them mistake the common graces of the Spirit for saving graces. To show this subtle device, I shall make two clarifications.

(1) There are seven grievous steps that a hypocrite takes towards heaven; the devils makes him trust in these steps.

[1] The first grievous step of a hypocrite is that a hypocrite may have the grace of conviction. This is clear in Matthew 27:4, when Judas cried out, "I have sinned in

that I have betrayed innocent blood." This point is also clear in Acts 2:37, where there were some reprobates who were pricked in their hearts. A hypocrite may have deeper convictions than one that shall inherit heaven.

[2] The second step of a hypocrite's progress is this: a hypocrite may have the grace of knowledge, as is clear from Hebrews 6:4, which speaks of hypocrites saying that they were "once enlightened." Furthermore, we see in 1 Corinthians 13:2 that Paul says, "Though I have the gift of prophecy, and understand all mysteries, and all knowledge; and though I have all faith, so that I could remove mountains, and have not charity, I am nothing." Here we see that a hypocrite may attain the length to speak of the truths of God like an angel, and yet be eternally damned. To make this a bit clearer, look at the heavenly discourses of Balaam, and of Nebuchadnezzar in the fourth chapter of Daniel. A hypocrite may have more profound knowledge in the mysteries of God than one that is truly godly; though, we confess that there are some aspects of grace that a hypocrite cannot truly understand.

[3] A hypocrite may have deep sorrow for sin. This is clear in 1 Samuel 24:16, when Saul "lifted up his voice and wept." This is also clear in Hebrews 12:17, where we read of Esau, that "he found no place of repentance, though he sought it carefully with tears." Upon this we would mention two points. First, a hypocrite's sorrow for sin may be deeper, or just as deep as the sorrow of a truly godly person. Secondly, the sorrow of a hypocrite flows from the apprehension of justice, but the sorrow of a godly person flows from the apprehension of justice and of love.

[4] A hypocrite may have sense as well as sensible enjoyments of Christ; we see this in Hebrews 6:4 where we read that hypocrites "tasted the heavenly gift." They tasted of the sweetness of Christ. No doubt a hypocrite may have some sweet motions and some flashings of the Holy Spirit.

[5] A hypocrite may have delight in the exercise of duty; we see in Isaiah 58:2 that hypocrites "take delight in approaching to God." We also read in Job 27:10, "Will he always call upon God?" This is a question that shows that a hypocrite, for a time, may have delight in God.

[6] A hypocrite may have sweet apprehensions of heaven; yes, a hypocrite may even long for heaven. We read in Hebrews 6:5 that even hypocrites "have tasted the good word of God, and the powers of the world to come." Furthermore, we see a hypocrite say, "Let me die the death of the righteous, and let my last end be like his" (Num. 23:10).

[7] A hypocrite may have the grace of patience under sufferings for Christ. We see in 1 Corinthians 13:3, "Though I bestow all my goods to feed the poor, and though I give my body to be burned, and have not charity, it profiteth me nothing." These words tell us that a hypocrite may give his body to be burned, and yet he may be one that shall be eternally burnt with fire.

(2) Let us consider a second point. It is a greater difficulty to convert a hypocrite than to convert one that is grossly in a natural state. Christ says, "John came unto you in the way of righteousness, and ye believed him not: but the publicans and the harlots believed him" (Matt. 21:32). The hypocritical Pharisees were not converted, but the grossly profane were made a prey to the love of Christ. Do you desire to know why it is more difficult to convert a hypocrite than one that is grossly in a natural state? First, a hypocrite lies far from the convictions of the gospel. It will be long before convictions seize upon a hypocrite. Second, a hypocrite is the most presumptuous creature imaginable; he does not know what it means to heed warnings, though he knows what it is to apply promises. A hypocrite desires to make use of Christ, but desires to make no use of Moses. He desires to dwell at Mount Zion, but desires not to dwell forty days at Mount Sinai.

2. The devil also keeps hypocrites, and those who are somewhat refined in their nature, by keeping a hypocrite from self-examination. A hypocrite may embody all graces, but he can never have the grace of self-examination. This is the grace that hypocrites almost never pretend to exercise; this is how the devil keeps them in their sin. A hypocrite has strong faith, strong idols, and strong delusions.

3. A third device the devil uses to keep hypocrites in their nature is to let a hypocrite personate all the graces of the Spirit. There is not a grace of the Spirit which a hypocrite does not feign. A hypocrite may counterfeit the grace of faith, as we see in Psalm 78:35: "They remembered that God was their rock, and the high God their redeemer." Yet the persons that exercised that faith were gross hypocrites. It is said of these hypocrites, "Then believed they his words…they soon forgat his works" (Ps. 106:12, 13). It is said of the hypocrites that they "for a while believe" (Luke 8:13). Likewise, a hypocrite may personate the grace of love; this is clear from Romans 10:2 where we read, "They have a zeal of God." Now zeal is nothing but an intense measure of love. It is clear, "Grace be with all them that love our Lord Jesus Christ in sincerity" (Eph. 6:24). This tells us that there are some that love Christ, but not in sincerity.

A hypocrite may also personate the grace of humility, as we read in the remarkable passage when ambitious Saul was made king; he hides himself among the stuff (1 Sam. 10:22). No doubt he was ambitious for the crown, but hypocritical Saul will endeavor to counterfeit the grace of humility. Likewise, a hypocrite may counterfeit the grace of patience under sufferings; this is clear where there is mention made of the sons of Belial who spoke against Saul, and it is said that "he held his peace" (1 Sam. 10:27). Here we find the same word which is spoken of patient Aaron when his sons were destroyed; he "held his peace" (Lev. 10:3). Likewise, a hypocrite may personate the grace of mortification. In 2 Peter 2:20, we read that they "escaped the pollution of the world" through lust. A hypocrite may go so far as to cry out, "All these things have I kept from my youth up, what lack I yet?" (Matt. 19:20). Certainly this is a strong delusion of the devil.

4. The devil also keeps hypocrites in their nature by making them meet with approbation from the saints; that is a snare to the righteous as well as a snare to the hypocrite. The lack of approbation from the saints has been an excellent help to promote a Christian's motion to heaven. How much did the lack of the approbation of these three saints, Eliphaz, Zophar, and Bildad, make Job go on his way to heaven? Now, concerning this device of the devil, I will mention four thoughts to you who are more taken up in pursuit after the approbation of the saints than after divine approbation. First, this is evidence that you have no faith; we read in John 5:44, "How can ye believe, which receive honour one of another, and seek not the honour that cometh from God only?" It is as if Christ had said that seeking approbation from men is inconsistent with the grace of faith. Second, there are two characteristics of a person who seeks the approbation of saints instead of divine approbation.

[1] He is more religious when he is in company than when he is alone. Trace a hypocrite to his secret retirements, and there he appears in his worldly colors.

[2] Another character of the person that seeks the approbation of the saints more than the divine approbation is that He is more anxious about his public bonds than about his private bonds; that is, a hypocrite will sorrow more for lack of enlargement in company than for lack of it twenty days alone. You who think Christ's absence is a cross when you are in company, and think it is not when you are alone, it is no cross to you at all. Having the applause of the saints is your greatest idol, and the lack of it is your greatest cross. Have not some here mourned more for the loss of reputation with the saints than for the loss of approbation and repute from Christ? You deem the former an indispensable lack, and the other a dispensable loss.

5. The devil also makes hypocrites conceive the ornaments of religion to be the substance of religion. For instance, a hypocrite mistakes the gift of prayer for the grace of prayer; a hypocrite mistakes his knowledge for sanctified and saving knowledge, when it is but common knowledge. Upon this I would only say, pursue the substance of godliness more than the ornaments of godliness. I would add, seek saving graces more than adorning graces.

Let us now consider our second point: the devices the devil uses to keep those who are grossly profane in nature.

1. A first device which Satan employs to keep many in nature is to make us believe that the sins that prevent us from trusting in Christ are indeed virtues; this is Satan's great design. To make this somewhat clear, I shall show you three examples.

(1) When we endeavor to convince a covetous person of his covetousness, he answers, "I am not covetous, but frugal." Thus, with his answer he defends his covetousness. Yes, a covetous person will defend his idolatry using Scripture; a covetous person cites these words from Scripture: "But if any provide not for his own, and specially for those of his own house, he hath denied the faith, and is worse than an infidel" (1 Tim. 5:8). The covetous man draws all his arguments from this verse. But I say to such, oh, ten times worse than an infidel is he that will not provide for his immortal soul.

(2) When we come to convince a prodigal person of his prodigality, he will tell us that he is not prodigal, he is not lascivious but mortified. A prodigal person defends his idolatry using the words of 1 John 2:15: "If any man love the world, the love of the Father is not in him." Thus, he will endeavor to seek that sign and evidence of the grace of God sinfully.

(3) When we attempt to convince a man of his pride, he will answer that it is not pride, but generosity of spirit. You know the words which we have heard: "It is necessary for a man to know himself." Some of us endeavor to

know ourselves too much. This is a strong delusion by which Satan keeps many in their sinful state.

2. The second device of the devil, by which he keeps them that are more grossly profane in their nature is that he misrepresents unto them the way of godliness. The devil casts a fourfold veil over the way of godliness unto a natural person.

(1) There is first the veil of disadvantage. It is clear that Satan made Eve believe that it was the loss of a deity to be religious; this was the delusion by which he caught Eve: "If you do not break the command, you will never be as gods, knowing good and evil." Also, what made Demetrius the silversmith worship the great Diana? "By this craft we have our wealth" (Acts 19:25). If we receive the doctrine of a crucified Christ, our gain will cease. Oh, but it is a poor gain that is reaped by the loss of Christ; the enjoyments of the world are not able to compensate one hour of absence from Christ!

(2) The second veil that the devil casts over the way of godliness is the veil of sorrow. He makes men by nature believe that once they leave their sinful ways and become religious, that they must also leave their joy behind. Friends, godliness is not the way of sorrow! Are the godly not commanded to "rejoice evermore" (1 Thess. 5:16)? There is not such a strong command in all natural books! I desire to ask all that are here: have your idols and all your possessions ever commanded you to "rejoice in the Lord always" (Phil. 4:4)?

(3) A third veil that Satan casts over the way of godliness is that it is a way that is most straight and severe, and extremely limiting. He says that except we keep every punctum required, all is in vain. I confess that the way of Christ is not so broad as the way of nature. But, the bonds that are put upon you by Christ are indeed your liberty. Do you know the description of liberty? It is to be under the precious bonds of Christ, and to have His yoke and commands as a chain of gold around your neck, and as an ornament of grace on your chest. I would only tell you, oh, you who are destitute of the grace of God, if

you are made captive to the love of Christ, after seventy years have passed, you will not cry out, "Turn again our captivity, O LORD, as the streams in the south" (Ps. 126:4). There is not such a voice heard in all heaven as the voice that cries, "Oh, to be exempted from the bondage of serving Christ night and day!" Their bondage is liberty; their servitude, complete liberty.

(4) The fourth veil that Satan casts on the way of godliness is that he makes you believe that it is a most seditious and troublesome thing to be godly. Let us look at what poor Paul and Silas encountered. They are the men that "have turned the world upside down" (Acts 17:6), and the people say, "These men, being Jews, do exceedingly trouble our city" (Acts 16:20). Beloved in the Lord Jesus, there is a sweet conjunction between your cross and your crown; there is a sweet connection between your tears and your joy; there is a sweet connection between the garments of heaviness and the garments of praise; there is a sweet connection between the Valley of Baca and the Valley of Berachah; there is a sweet conjunction between your poverty and your riches, between your shame and your glory.

3. A third device Satan uses to keep men grossly profane in their nature is to make them postpone the time of their being religious. Is not this a device with which the devil keeps many in his grasp? They suppose their old age is enough for Christ, and the first three fingers' breadth of their life should be given to their idols. Oh, unbelievers, have you ever read the words in Ecclesiastes 12:1: "Remember now thy Creator in the days of thy youth"? I say to those who delay their faith until their old age, there is not one of a thousand who are religious when they die, who purposely deferred their being religious until then. Christ may, of course, save a soul when he is standing upon the utmost line between time and eternity. But a sinner who has delayed the time of closing with Christ so that he might be religious when he is old, is not often conquered by Christ. Also, it is much more pleasant to Christ when we are religious in our youth than when we

are religious in old age. Godliness is more esteemed by Christ when it is attained in youth than in old age. "My son, give me thine heart" (Prov. 23:26). I shall give you three reasons why religion at a young age is better than religion at an old age.

First, when Christians give their heart to Christ in their youth, they have more temptations to hinder them from that work; their lusts are strong and their temptations are pressing. It is a commendable work to give your heart to Christ when you are young. Second, one who is converted in his youth has a purer godliness, and his religion is more evangelistic. Certainly, old men strive to be godly to escape hell and the wrath of God, but those who are converted in their youth bring their souls to that high pitch of love—to love Christ for Himself. Third, you who delay repentance until your old age, are you God, that you should have your life in your own hands? Death may cut you off in a moment! When death comes, the pains of sickness may interrupt the exercise of religion.

4. The fourth device the devil uses to keep in nature those who are grossly profane is to make their idols most pleasant to them. He makes the idol of love pleasant unto you, he makes the idol of faith pleasant unto you, and he makes the idol of hope pleasant unto you. By the idol of love, we understand the world, the lust of the eyes, the lust of the flesh, and the pride of life. He makes the idol of love pleasant; he clothes the world with the garments of advantage and with the robes of pleasure. He also makes your idols of faith pleasant; that is, these things upon which men trust, as great men and riches—he makes these things most pleasant unto you. He also makes the idol of hope pleasant; he makes these things, from which you expect consolation, most pleasant unto you.

5. The devil also keeps men by making them believe that it is an easy thing to be a Christian. This is a device that many of you have experienced. He makes people think that it is an easy thing to become religious. I would say to persons who have been so beguiled, you never knew

what it was to be religious if you think that religion is an easy work. Before you become religious, your belief shall change, or you shall eternally perish.

6. He keeps them from the exercise of self-examination. People by nature do not know what it is to sit down, examine, and judge themselves. They conceive all is right when indeed all is wrong. It is a sad disappointment, you who never knew what it was to doubt of heaven, to be eternally thrust down to hell. Is it not a sad disappointment to spend all your days in the gall of bitterness and in the bond of iniquity, and yet to be supposing that you are walking in the path to heaven?

Now, to conclude our discourse, we propose these considerations. They may press the things closer unto your heart.

First, all the devices of the devil would not prove effectual if there were not a secret enemy within your bosom that did correspond with the enemy himself. Do you know who betrays the immortal soul? It is not the devil, but your own heart. Observe the cursed harmony between the devil and your own heart, in tempting you to sin; we shall show you this harmony in a few examples.

1. The devil presents the temptation and there is something within your breast that pleads for the embracing of the temptation. As soon as the devil assaults, there is a proctor within your breast that cries forth, "Embrace, embrace!"

2. When tempting you to sin, the devil clothes his temptations with the robes of advantage and robes of pleasure; your sight closes with the temptation because of the robes of advantage, and your affections close with the temptation because of the robes of pleasure.

3. Sometimes our sight will cry, "Do not embrace such a temptation!" Yet, our love will cry, "Oh, embrace this temptation." Sometimes a Christian's sight will preach the doctrine of resisting the devil when his affections are saying, "Embrace the devil and his temptations."

4. This harmony will lead us to sin when both our sight and our affections contradict it. This is clear in the practice of Herod. His sight and affections forbid him to

behead John; he was sorrowful, yet despite the voice of his affections and the sight of his judgment, he embraces the temptation.

A second consideration that we shall propose unto you is that it is easier for a Christian to resist the devil than to resist the temptations of his own heart. Heart temptations are much more difficult to resist than the temptations that flow from the devil. This is known in the experience of the saints.

Third, the devil may tempt you to that which is good in itself. To make this clear, I will give four examples.

1. The devil may sometimes tempt to that which is good, but most unseasonably; for instance, when a Christian is in the exercise of prayer, the devil will present some good thoughts to divert him from his spiritual seriousness and fervency.

2. The devil tempts sometimes to good so that he may hinder from the exercise of a more excellent good. For instance, he will tempt the Pharisees to tithe mint and anise, but the great end of it is that they may neglect faith, righteousness, and the weightier things of the law.

3. The devil may tempt a Christian to good, but it is a good that is above his strength. For instance, he will tempt a Christian who is not profound in knowledge to dispute this question: how is it consistent with the justice of God to punish man for sin, since He has decreed that man should sin, and man cannot resist His decree? He will tempt a Christian who is not very knowledgeable to study how it is consistent with the mercy of Christ that any should be damned, since He has the ability to save them. He will do this to weaken the faith of a Christian.

4. The devil may tempt a Christian to what is good, but it is always for a bad end. He will tempt some to seriousness in prayer, but only so that they will put their confidence in their prayer. He will tempt a hypocrite to these common works of the Spirit so that they put their confidence in them when they are attained.

Fourth, it is the great design of the devil to promote all along your way and motion to heaven, while really seeking the destruction of your immortal soul.

This is the devil's policy: he bids the hypocrite give Christ his tongue and his outward man, but give the devil his heart. This is the great desire of the devil, that the hypocrite should give the devil his heart and let him give his tongue to whomever he will. Hence, we often give our hearts to our idol when we give our tongues to Christ.

A last consideration that we would propose is that the devil is incessant; he is subtle in his assaults on a Christian. He is incessant, according to that noble description, if so we may call it. God proposes the question unto him, "Whence comest thou?" (Job 1:7). He answers, "I come 'from going to and fro in the earth.'" He is an incessant assaulter, and he is a most subtle enemy. He knows what it is to sail both with wind and tide. When a Christian is under the power of unbelief, he will press him to discouragement; when a Christian is under the exercise or power of security, he will press him to presumption; when a Christian is enjoying carnal ease, he will press him to security; when a Christian is much in the duty of self-examination, he will press him to despair; when a Christian is little in the exercise of Christian duties, he will press him to claim to exercise faith while avoiding duty. Every state you are in, the devil will have a suitable temptation to catch you.

Now, we desire you seriously to ponder and think upon these things. You who are desperately ignorant of the grace of Christ, let me ask you three questions. If you are not able to answer, you are yet in the gall of bitterness and in the bonds of iniquity.

First, have you ever fought against the devices of the devil? Have you ever seen his subtlety in catching advantage over you? If not, then it is undeniable evidence that you have been sleeping in the grave of sin from your birth.

Secondly, have the devices of the devil by which he gains advantage over you, ever pressed you to seek strength and grace from Jesus Christ? Have your temptations ever led you to make use of Christ and His strength? If they have not, it is evidence that the devil needs not much debate with you to overcome you.

Thirdly, have you ever groaned for the day of your redemption, convicted that you are continually under the assaults and temptations of the devil? Have you ever groaned for rest because of the devil's constant assaults? I tell you I can compare the devil and you who live by nature to no other thing, but to the people of Israel when they were in the land of Egypt. Pharaoh never let the people of Israel make mention of the bondage of Egypt, though they had no straw to make brick. Let them never propose that suit; we desire to go out and worship God in the mountains, and they shall have straw to make brick. So, once you mention of going to Christ, then Satan will multiply his temptations and make your life bitter.

The devil, because he knows his time is short, goes about more seriously (Rev. 12:12). The devil's kingdom is now drawing to the last period; and this makes him endeavor by all means to enlarge his subjects and to make many to fall by the strength of his tail. Oh, that you would be persuaded to resist him who seeks to ruin that precious thing—your immortal soul! Will you never be persuaded to fight against him? I think even this is a strange delusion by which the devil catches advantage over us; we believe the voice of his temptations as if they were faithful sayings and he were a faithful witness. The devil will circumvent a man in nature twenty times before the man calls in question his faithfulness. He evermore believes his word, as if it were authentic Scripture.

The day is coming when the deceits of many shall be discovered. I shall close with this thought. The day is coming when a hypocrite shall believe no more, when a person that is grossly profane in nature shall presume no more, when the true Christian shall be no more unbelieving. You will shortly hence be exalted above or depressed below the reach of these temptations. There is no faith in hell, there is no presumption in hell, and there is no unbelief in heaven. If there is any faith in hell, it is upon that truth that out of that pit there is no redemption. This is the sort of faith that you shall eternally exercise when you are eternally in that prison. The motto of your prison, which is engraven upon the doors of the prison is, "Out of this house there is no redemption." The motto that is upon the doors of heaven reads, "Out of this pleasant place there is no going out." Oh, what a life shall this be, to be with Christ eternally, and never leave!

Dear expectants of heaven, which of all the five senses shall be most satisfied in heaven? Will it be the sense of sight, when you shall be admitted to behold Him who sits on the throne, and your eyes shall see completely the beauty of the rose of Sharon, and shall behold the invisible God? Perhaps it shall be the sense of hearing, when the ears shall be admitted to hear the divine songs that are among these daughters of music? Or shall the sense of smell be most satisfied, when you shall be overcome by the smell of Him whose garments are perfumed with all the powders of the merchant? Perhaps it shall be the sense of taste, when you shall be admitted to drink of these pure rivers of everlasting consolation, and when you shall sit down to drink at the well until you are satiated? Shall the sense of touch be most satisfied in heaven, when a Christian shall be admitted to encircle that precious object, Christ? There is no such inhibition in heaven as the words, "Touch me not"; that inhibition is sweetly reduced which is served here. Mary dared not touch Christ because He was not ascended. If we were admitted to behold her exercise in the future eternity, is she not holding Christ in her arms? Now, which of them shall be most satisfied? They shall all be satisfied. The sense of sight shall make the sense of hearing satisfied; the sense of hearing shall make the sense of touch satisfied; and the sense of smell shall make the sense of taste satisfied.

Oh, heirs of wrath, which of the five senses shall be most tormented in hell? Shall it be the sense of sight, when you shall see the devil and the tormenting place? Or shall the sense of hearing be most tormented, when you shall hear the screeches of your fellow prisoners, or when you shall be admitted to hear these lamentable notes that shall be sung by Cain, the first reprobate, and all who have followed after him? Shall the sense of smell be most tormented, when you shall be cast into the place that burns with fire and brimstone? Or perhaps the sense of touch shall be the most tormented, when you who cannot endure the burning fire, shall be eternally scorched in the fire of the indignation of the Lord. Christ traveling in the greatness of His strength shall tread your immortal souls in the wine-press of the fury of His wrath, until His garments are dyed with your blood. Do you suppose that sense of taste will be most tormented, when you shall drink of these rivers of brimstone that are prepared for the devil and his angels?

I would answer this question just as I answered the question before: all your senses shall be tormented. Oh, eternity of pain! Oh, eternity of joy! I would say this, and I desire you to meditate upon it: such is the stupidity that is among you, that if Abraham would come from heaven with a crown upon his head and a palm in his hand, being clothed with these beautiful robes of the righteousness of Christ, and would desire you to embrace the offer of this gospel, you would not hearken to him. If Judas would come from hell, carrying the lashes of everlasting wrath upon him, and having the fire of the indignation of God burning around his ears, and would say to you, "Flee from the wrath to come," most of us that are here would despise his words (Matt. 3:7). We do not believe that there is eternity of pain and that there is eternity of joy; otherwise we would not rest until we knew that we had made peace with God. Amen.

SERMON 42

Precious Remedies against Satan's Devices (3)

Lest Satan should get an advantage of us: for we are not ignorant of his devices.
—2 Corinthians 2:11

Who can comprehend the way of this deceiver, whose way is more subtle than the way of an eagle in the air, the way of a serpent on a rock, or the way of a ship in the sea?

There are two things we would mainly urge you to consider. First, you should know the subtle devices and stratagems of the devil, which he uses to catch immortal souls. Also, we desire you to know and understand the precious, divine stratagems of Jesus Christ, by which He endeavors to catch immortal souls. We read in Hosea 2:14, "I will allure her, and bring her into the wilderness." We may also understand this verse to mean, "I will deceive her." Christ has a divine "deceit," a precious "guile" by which He endeavors to gain the soul of man. He knows what key can best open our hearts. He who has the keys of the house of David knows what arguments will be most effectual to persuade us to embrace Him. Christ knows when is the most suitable time to propose His divine allurement to catch our immortal souls. I ask you, to persuade you to be caught by Him who has been a fisher of men for six thousand years: do you desire satisfaction of all your senses? Then come and embrace Christ. Do you desire to have eternal blessedness? Then come and embrace Christ!

You shall have satisfaction of all your senses. Will not your sense of sight be satisfied when you embrace Him? Oh, what a sight it will be to behold Him, whose countenance is as Lebanon, excellent as the cedars! What a sight it will be to behold Him whose face is as the sun when it shines in its strength! How marvelous it will be to behold Him who is the light of the higher house and the eternal admiration of angels! Do you desire to have satisfaction for your sense of hearing? Then come and embrace precious Christ. Oh, what a life it shall be to hear His voice and to hearken to these pleasant words that He shall speak! If Christ never spoke a word but this, it might satisfy your sense of hearing: "My beloved spake, and said unto me, Rise up, my love, my fair one, and come away. For, lo, the winter is past, the rain is over and gone; the flowers appear on the earth; the time of the singing of birds is come, and the voice of the turtle is heard in our land" (Song 2:10-12). Is not that a pleasant song to satisfy your sense of hearing?

Do you desire satisfaction for your sense of smell? Then come and embrace Christ. Oh, what smell does He cast, who is perfumed with all the powders of the merchant! What a smell does He cast, who is the beautiful rose of Sharon and the lily of the valleys! What a smell does He cast, whose garments smell of myrrh, aloes, and cassia, out of the ivory palaces! Do you desire to have satisfaction for your sense of taste? Then come and embrace precious Christ, and be caught by His deceits. How much shall the sense of taste be satisfied when you shall be admitted to eat of these pleasant apples that grow upon the tree of life, and shall be satisfied with flagons, and be taken into His banqueting house! There is a great difference between the apple that Eve ate and these precious apples that grow upon the tree of life. The eating of these apples shall indeed make you as "gods"; you shall be made partakers of a divine nature.

Do you desire satisfaction for your sense of touch? Then come and embrace Christ. Oh, what a life shall it be, eternally to enfold that precious object, Jesus Christ! What a life it shall be to hold Him as a bundle of myrrh, all night to lie between our breasts! Comfort yourselves in that there is no such inhibition served upon Mary in heaven, as was upon the earth: "Touch me not" (John 20:17). That inhibition is sweetly eliminated in heaven. What will her exercise be forever? She will forever enfold and kiss Him who was the object of her desires.

Do you desire satisfaction for your desires? Then come and embrace Christ. There shall be no end to your desiring once you fix your desires upon Him who has no end. Let Christ be the object of your love, the object of your faith, the object of your desires, and the object of your delight.

Do you desire eternal blessedness? Then let Christ woo you. Oh, blessed are these eternally, whom Christ has caught and taken into the bond of the covenant. I would only ask three questions.

First, have you ever blessed God for giving you the wisdom to choose Christ? Have you ever blessed Him because He did so wisely direct you as to make such a choice? This was the practice of David, as we read in Psalm 16:6-7: "The lines are fallen unto me in pleasant places; yea, I have a goodly heritage. I will bless the LORD, who hath given me counsel." He there sits down and magnifies the Lord that had directed him to this choice.

A second question I would ask you is, will you rather believe the promise of him who is a liar from the beginning than believe the promises of Him who is the faithful witness and the Amen?

Third, do you put a higher account upon fellowship with the devil and his angels than upon fellowship with Jesus Christ and the spirits of just men made perfect? I would seriously desire you to consider Him, for then you will be forced to become His captive. There was never any one that ever saw Him in His beauty that ever turned into His enemy. At the first sight that persecuting Saul ever got of Christ, he asked, "Lord, what wilt thou have me to do?"

We have told you that in the words of our text we may find a threefold character of a complete Christian, of a Christian who has gone on to a great length in godliness. The first characteristic of a complete Christian from the words of our text is that he is not ignorant of the devices of the devil; he is familiar with the devil's stratagems. From this point, we propose seven things to consider. The first is the general devices of the devil by which he catches immortal souls and endeavors to assault everyone. We have already discussed this point. We also proposed to speak a little concerning these devices of the devil by which he keeps men in nature; we have already spoken about these devices. Thirdly, we must become familiar with the devices by which he assaults those who are under the exercise of the law before closing with Christ. We conceive that there are these devices by which he assaults such persons.

A first device the devil may employ to assault a Christian under the exercise of the law is to make him misinterpret three things. Satan makes such a Christian misinterpret sermons, misinterpret providence, and misinterpret Scripture. This is the first device the devil uses to catch and assault those who are under the exercise of the law. As for misinterpreting sermons, we could speak a bit concerning these things.

1. How may a Christian know whether a word that is borne in upon him is from the Spirit of the Lord or from the spirit of delusion? We conceive that there are seven marks by which you may know when a word is from the Spirit of the Lord.

(1) The word that seals a Christian's exercise is from the Spirit of the Lord, not from the spirit of delusion. For instance, when a Christian under the exercise of security meets with a word that awakens him, that word is from the Spirit of the Lord. We see an example of this when the words that are spoken to David by Nathan were blessed; they awakened David from his security (2 Sam. 12:7). Thus, these words were from the Spirit of the Lord. In Matthew 25:6, we read the words of the voice that was raised at midnight: "Behold, the Bridegroom cometh." These words are from the Lord, because they were effectual to raise the virgins from their security. Likewise, when a Christian is under the exercise of unbelief and questioning his interest, if he meets with a word that strengthens his faith and confidence, that word is from the Lord and not from a spirit of delusion.

(2) The words that are borne in upon you from the Spirit of the Lord have a more precious luster and excellence than the words that are borne in upon you from the spirit of delusion. There are three things that point out the luster of a word that is borne in from the Spirit of the Lord. First, it is a seasonable word; it is spoken in season. For instance, when a Christian is likely to give up his hope, he may meet with a word that will strengthen his faith. Christ's words have this property: He has "the tongue of the learned, that I should know how to speak a word in season to him that is weary" (Isa. 50:4), and all His words are fitly spoken, like apples of gold in pictures of silver. Second, the words that are spoken unto you by Christ are spoken with authority; you cannot resist their power. This is clear from

the words of Christ in Matthew 7:29: "He taught as one having authority, and not as the scribes." Third, the words of Christ do exceedingly affect your hearts; there is much tenderness and love that accompanies a word from Christ to your soul, as we see in Luke 24:32: "Did not our heart burn within us, while he talked with us by the way, and while he opened to us the scriptures?" When Christ talked with them, their souls burned within them. Words from a spirit of delusion do not have this quality.

(3) You may be assured that a word that is borne in upon you is from the Spirit of the Lord when the word increases your delight in duty. For example, in the sermon preached by Haggai, it is evidence that the words were from the Lord because it put the people to a more serious building of the temple (Hag. 1:4). In short, the word that moves you from the exercise of duty or makes you lose delight in the exercise of duty is a word from a spirit of delusion.

(4) The word that reveals to a Christian both his sinfulness and his duty is a word from the Spirit of the Lord, and not from a spirit of delusion. In Acts 2:37, we read that the words spoken by Peter were from the Lord because they have these two effects: the discovery of sin, which is shown in the words, "They were pricked in their heart"; likewise, the discovery of duty. They cry out, "Men and brethren, what shall we do?" I would like to mention two thoughts from these words. First, Satan may reveal all your sin unto you and bear down strongly upon you, but he will never send you a word that will encourage you to do your duty. The word that has these two best attendants, the discovery of sin and the discovery of duty, that word is from the Spirit of the Lord. Second, you must question the word to be from a spirit of delusion that reveals unto you your sin, and causes you to give up hope.

(5) You may recognize a word from the Spirit of the Lord by its scope and goal. The words that are borne in upon you from the spirit of delusion, their goal is surely sin; but the words that are borne in upon you that are from the Spirit of the Lord, their purpose is surely duty. For instance, the devil will bear in promises upon a pre-

sumptuous sinner, and he will bear in threats upon a discouraged Christian. The end of both of these is sin. But the end of Christ's speaking unto a soul is one of these two: He will bring promises to a discouraged sinner, so that his hands may be strengthened and not hang down; and He will bring threats to a presumptuous sinner, so that he may see his state.

(6) You may also recognize it by this: the word that removes a Christian's confusions and darkness is a word from the Spirit of the Lord and not from a spirit of delusion. For instance, when a Christian is under debates concerning his interest, or concerning such a truth of the gospel, and meets with a word in a sermon that will make that truth clear unto him and affect the heart with the clearing of it, that word is certainly from the Spirit of the Lord. But, more particularly, if one were questioning concerning the nature of original sin, and had confusion about that sin, and meets with a word in a sermon that would make clear the nature of that sin; that word is certainly from the Spirit of the Lord. Likewise, when a Christian is under confusion concerning the nature of the free grace of Christ, and meets with a word in a sermon that makes clear the nature of the freedom of His love, and makes the Christian's heart to burn within him, that word is certainly from the Spirit of the Lord.

(7) A last way by which you may determine whether a word is from the Spirit of the Lord or from the spirit of delusion is that the Lord's words have a more constant impression upon your spirits than the words that come from a spirit of delusion.

2. Now the second thing we would discuss concerning the misinterpretation of sermons is to point out when the devil applies threats, and when the Spirit of God applies them; for it is certain that the devil may apply threats to a Christian under the exercise of the law. The devil has three goals in applying threats to a Christian. First, he is attempting to make you give over your hopes and confidence, so that you may cry out, "My strength and my

hope is perished from the LORD" (Lam. 3:18). This is the greatest reason the devil applies threats. A second reason he applies threats is to keep a Christian from the exercise of duty and to make the exercise of religion a burden unto him. Third, the devil applies threats so that a Christian may have low and sinister apprehensions of Christ.

Let us also discuss Christ's goals in applying threats. We conceive that Christ has four goals in applying threats. First, He applies threats so that we may awake from our self-security. He desires to rouse us up. When He applies a word of threatening, He challenges the bride, but the goal of that challenge is that she may awaken from her present state (Song 2:10). A second goal that Christ has in challenging and threatening is that a Christian may be motivated to perform his duty. He will apply threats to a Christian that neglects the duty of prayer so that he may be pressed to pray more. Third, Christ applies threats so that we forsake our idols. This is His great purpose in applying threats. He desires to hear us say, "What have I to do any more with idols?" (Hos. 14:8). A fourth purpose that Christ has in applying threats is to impose upon a Christian a divine necessity of making use of Him. There is not one threatening you encounter that does not tell you to embrace Christ. The goal of threatening is to encourage you to make use of Christ.

To conclude this discourse on the misinterpreting of sermons, I shall add two thoughts. First, it is a notable evidence of a complete Christian to take up when Christ speaks, and when temptations and the devil speak. The spouse takes notice of this in Song of Solomon 2:10: "My beloved spake"; and this is "the voice of my beloved" (v. 8), which she knows to be the voice of Christ. "It is the voice of my beloved that knocketh" (Song 5:2); she knows Christ's voice by any other. We read that "the sheep follow him: for they know his voice" (John 10:4). Also, mistaking Christ's voice in prayer or in preaching obstructs much of a Christian's communion with God. Nothing will obstruct a Christian's fellowship with Christ so much as a lack of clarity when Christ speaks, and when the devil and temptations speak. We see this in 1 Samuel 3:7. The Lord appears to Samuel three times and calls him; but the reason why Samuel does not correspond with God is because he did not know His voice, and he was not acquainted with the Lord. Therefore, if a Christian desires communion with Christ, he must know His voice.

Now, as for misinterpreting providence and Scripture, I shall not say much; I have two things to mention concerning the misinterpretation of providence.

1. The first is this: you must judge Christ by His words rather than by His providence. Judge Christ by what He has said of Himself rather than what dispensations say of Him. As long as you build faith upon providence, it will be changeable.

2. The meaning of providence is most dark. I can compare the meaning of providence to nothing so fit as the writing that Belshazzar saw upon the wall. He saw it, but did not know the meaning of it. It would require the spirit of Daniel to understand the meaning of providence. It is easy to know that there is something intended in such a providence, but it is hard to know the particular intention of such a particular providence. It would require a spirit very well acquainted with God to interpret providence. There are several grounds of misinterpreting providence. Unbelief, sense, and reason often misinterpret providence. All three of these interpreters put a wrong gloss upon the meaning of providence. Unbelief will always read wrath in a cross; sense will evermore read wrath in a rod; and reason will never believe when providence contradicts a promise, but will say, "This evil is of the LORD; what should I wait for the LORD any longer?" (2 Kings 6:33). Therefore, I entreat you, do not misinterpret providence but interpret providence more by faith than by these three bad interpreters. Also, if you desire to rightly interpret providence, do not take providence by halves, but take the whole series of providence together.

The second device that the devil uses to assault Christians under the exercise of the law is to bring those Christians into a spirit of discouragement. Once a soul begins to see its whoring and departing from God, and to see the terrors of the law, then the devil presses that soul into the spirit of discouragement. We see an example of this in 2 Corinthians 2:7, where a soul is "swallowed up with overmuch sorrow." In discussing this device, let us speak a little of these three things.

First, I shall give you some evidences by which a Christian may know when he is under a spirit of excessive discouragement.

1. The first evidence by which a Christian may know he is under a spirit of discouragement is this: when your discouragement leads you to the neglect of duty, then you may be assured that your discouragement is excessive, and you are under the spirit of it. We see an example of this in Jeremiah 20:9, where Jeremiah's trouble, no doubt, was excessive. We know this because it put him from the exercise of duty: "I will not make mention of him, nor speak any more in his name." His discouragement was accompanied with a conclusion that he would preach no more. So then, if you desire to know when your discouragement is above the due limits and bounds, you may know it to be this: when your discouragement makes you neglect the exercise of duty.

2. The second evidence is when your discouragements lead you to refuse the consolations that are given to you and you will not receive them, then you are truly under an excessive spirit of discouragement. This was so in David's case; he says in his sadness, "My soul refused to be comforted" (Ps. 77:2). David would not accept the comforts that were suitable for him to take. Likewise, Jeremiah is under the spirit of discouragement in Jeremiah 8:8. When he should be comforted, his heart is sorrowful, his heart is faint in him, and he could not apply the consolations of God that were suitable for him to take.

3. We may certainly know that a Christian is under discouragement when he casts off his faith and his confidence. This is made clear in Lamentations 3:18, when Jeremiah was under the spirit of discouragement. He cried out, "My strength and my hope is perished from the LORD." Whenever your discouragements lead you to abandon your faith and cast off your confidence, you may know they are excessive.

4. A fourth mark of one that is under a spirit of discouragement is that he has a wrong and sinister apprehension of Christ. This was clear in David's life; when he was under

the spirit of discouragement, he said, "I remembered God, and was troubled" (Ps. 77:3). The remembrance of God was a trouble to David when he was under a spirit of discouragement. It is also clear from the words in Jeremiah 15:18 that Jeremiah is under a spirit of discouragement when he cries out, "Wilt thou be altogether unto me as a liar, and as waters that fail?" His discouragements led him to such a length as to charge God with lying. Discouragement will sometimes speak falsehood, and discouragement will sometimes speak blasphemy, as Jeremiah's discouragement did. His discouragement brought him to such a length that it speaks blasphemy against God.

5. Another sign is when a Christian's discouragements make him lack delight in the exercise of duty. Every duty a discouraged person undertakes bears the words, "This duty is my burden," and, "This duty is my cross." It is impossible for a discouraged Christian to go about duty with delight. Every duty he performs becomes a burden unto him when he is under the spirit of discouragement. He does not know what it means to obey or believe.

A second point we desire to discuss concerning this device of the devil is that discouragement births apostasy and departure from God. There is nothing that so greatly travails in birth of apostasy from God as discouragement. We read in Lamentations 1:8 of backsliding Christians, "She sigheth, and turneth backward." All their exercises are to backsliding, for it is impossible for a discouraged Christian not to backslide and depart from God. Also, discouragement of spirit is one of the most damnable sins that a Christian can fall into; therefore, you will see that among them that are cast into the lake that burns with fire and brimstone, he that is discouraged is put in the first place. We read in Revelation 21:8, "But the fearful, and unbelieving, and the abominable, and murderers, and whoremongers, and sorcerers, and idolaters, and all liars, shall have their part in the lake which burneth with fire and brimstone: which is the second death." The discouraged and unbelieving creatures are first in the roll of those who are cast into the lake burning with fire and brimstone.

Lastly, a Christian will condemn himself rather for presumption than for discouragement; for discouragement seems to be a more gospel and spiritual thing than presumption. But, be sure of it, discouragement is as great sin in the sight of God, if not more, than presumption. Discouragement charges God with lies; it contradicts the truth of the Scripture; it makes a Christian cast off duty.

Now, there is a third device by which the devil assaults Christians that are under the exercise of the law: he studies to kill their convictions. When a Christian is under the exercise of the law, it is impossible for him not to be convicted. Let us discuss six convictions of a Christian that the devil seeks to mortify.

1. When you are convinced of your former evil way, and all your iniquities are presented unto you and set before your face, the devil attempts to mortify that conviction.

2. The devil also studies to mortify the conviction of a Christian's last and desperate state. Once you come to the conclusion, "Woe is me, I am undone," then the devil studies by all means to mortify that conviction and to kill it in its birth.

3. A third conviction of Christians under the exercise of the law that the devil studies to mortify is the conviction of their utter inability to save themselves. Once you sing that first song of gospel, the first line, as it were, of the precious tidings of salvation: "There is no name under heaven by which I can be saved but by the name of Christ," then the devil seeks to mortify that conviction, so that you may be brought back to make mention of your own righteousness and to seek salvation through a covenant of works.

4. A fourth conviction that the devil attempts to mortify is the conviction of the necessity, advantage, and beauty of believing. Once a person realizes, "I will never be made right with God until I believe," then the devil studies, by all means, to have that conviction mortified. When you are brought to this conviction, you are upon the utmost lines and borders of Satan's kingdom and you are stepping into the kingdom of Jesus Christ.

5. The devil studies to mortify a Christian's conviction of how unsupportable a burden of sin is. Once you begin to cry, "Who will bear the burden of iniquity?" the devil begins to make sin to appear very light unto you.

> 6. The last conviction of a Christian that the devil studies to mortify is how sad and woeful an estate, how intolerable a lot it is to live under the wrath of the living God. When a Christian is convinced of the burden of sin and wrath, then Satan tries to mortify and kill these convictions.

Let us consider several points concerning this device of the devil. First, a Christian under the exercise of the law helps to mortify his own convictions. We have a cursed correspondence and harmony with the devil in mortifying these convictions, for when we are convinced of the excellence of believing, we mortify that conviction through the apprehended difficulty that is in the exercise of that grace. Once we begin to believe, if it does not immediately succeed with us, we abandon faith and the exercise of believing as something impossible. Second, though a Christian is knowledgeable concerning these six convictions, he can not rest upon these, but he must press forward to close with Christ. He must endeavor to have peace and union with Christ.

A fourth device of the devil that we will consider is to darken the freedom of the gospel and the offers of the everlasting covenant. He makes you believe that the gospel requires more of you than it does. You who are assaulted with the darkening of the freedom of the gospel, please take along with you these five things by which you may consume all your temptations.

First, know that there is no impediment put in your way of closing with Christ except the lack of willingness. If you are willing to have Christ, you may have Him. The gospel requires no qualification, only to have a willing mind. Here the gate of the gospel seems to be cast open; the gospel is proposed in these terms: "Let him that is athirst come" (Rev. 22:17). However, lest this should be the subject of discouragement, Christ casts the gate open a bit farther, saying, "And whosoever will, let him take the water of life freely" (v. 17); if you have a desire to close with Christ, you may close with Him.

Second, you must recognize that your unbelief proceeds from a lack of willingness rather than from a lack of qualifications. I know that some Christians will not close with Christ because they were never in such a measure under the exercise of the law. They never knew what it was to mourn for sin, and they never knew what it was to sit down and lament over themselves because of their sinful state; therefore, they will not close with Christ. Know this, you may blame your unbelief on a lack of willingness, and upon no other thing. Christ blames unbelief upon that very point, saying, "Ye will not come to me" (John 5:40). He does not say, "Ye are not able to come to me," but, "Ye will not do it." If you so desired, then certainly you would come to Christ.

Third, know that all the promises of the gospel that hold out the qualifications of those that come unto Christ, are to be interpreted this way: they hold out the qualifications of those who will come, but do not hold forth the qualifications of the people who should come. In Matthew 11:28, we read, "Come unto me, all ye that labour and are heavy laden, and I will give you rest." It is not to be supposed that weariness and being heavy-laden are the qualifications of those that should come to Christ. Rather, they are the qualifications of those who do come to Christ. It is as if Christ would have said, "There are none that I need bid come, but only these who are weary and heavy-laden; for it is only these people who will come." If you would come in another state, He would not insert you.

Fourth, I have never read in Scripture (which may make the disputers of this age ashamed) of any, who after they were invited to come to Christ, stood up and disputed, saying, "Wilt Thou embrace me? Am I fit to come?" Are there any such disputes as this recorded in all those converted at the preaching of the gospel in Acts 2, or anywhere else in Scripture? Have you read of anyone who said, "I am not fit to come to Christ; I have not been humbled for my sin, and I have not been under such a measure of sorrow for sin." No, they embraced Christ without debate. I would ask you who delight so much in disputing if you have seen such practice of any of the saints in Scripture before their closing with Christ. Did the three thousand Jews ever mention such a dispute? Yet, some of them did consent unto the killing of Christ. But when the gospel is offered unto them, they do not debate their qualifications, but they close with Him who is offered unto them in the gospel.

Finally, when the devil darkens the freedom of the gospel unto you and taunts you saying, "You dare not close with Christ because you are such a sinner," you must make use of this very argument of the devil; he uses it to hinder you from closing with Christ, but you can make it a ground of your closing with Him. Do you know how to improve aright the discoveries of your sin? You must lay upon yourselves a necessity of closing with Christ. Would you like to improve the discoveries of the multitude of sins? You must cry in faith, "For thy name's sake, O LORD, pardon mine iniquity; for it is great" (Ps. 25:11). That divinity will not hold out at the court of men, but it holds out well here, where love sits as arbitrary judge. These words are a strong argument at the court of love: "Pardon mine iniquity; for it is great." It may not be a strong argument at the court of justice; justice would surely cast this argument away, but love will take hold of such an argument.

Let us now discuss the fifth device the devil uses to assault Christians under the exercise of the law. He attempts, by all means, to make you fall asleep. The great scope of all his temptations is to bring you from a spirit of discouragement to a spirit of security. This is a most ordinary and most fruitful device of the devil. If you do not improve your discouragements for making use of Christ, your discouragements will end in self-security and in hardness of heart. Therefore, you would be wise to dwell long in the place of the breaking forth of children. But when Christ gives you the first summons to go out of the land of Egypt and to go into the land of Canaan, you must obey the summons.

Let us now conclude our discourse with five final thoughts.

First, it is the duty of a Christian, if he can, to observe the day, month, and year when Christ brought him out of the land of Egypt. A Christian should observe the day when love first began to overcome him, when he was made a captive unto Christ. In so doing, we may fitly apply the words of Deuteronomy 16:1, which read, "Observe the month of Abib, and keep the passover unto the LORD thy God: for in the month of Abib the LORD thy God brought thee forth out of Egypt by night." Keep it in perpetual record. I confess it is undeniable that there are some Christians whom Christ overcomes while they are unaware; if you would ask them when they began to believe, they might say with that blind men, "One thing I know, that, whereas I was blind, now I see," (John 9:25). However, they may not know the time.

Second, the observation of the month and day when Christ brought you out of the land of Egypt will be a notable help to answer many temptations to unbelief. Let me tell you about the mother of much unbelief among Christians: they can never pitch upon the day when first they began to trust in Christ. If that day were well-known, we might better battle the temptations to unbelief. We might say, "I know Christ was once kind to me, and He took upon Him my iniquity." Do you know the first song of a Christian when he is planted in that pleasant land? That Christian will sing, "Thou art stronger than I, and hast prevailed" (Jer. 20:7). Oh, to be a captive of Christ is a noble captivity. Even after seventy years are accomplished, you will not cry out, "Turn again our captivity, O LORD, as the streams in the south" (Ps. 126:4).

Third, let us be concerned, Christians, as we desire not to wrong our own peace and satisfaction, that we do not needlessly dwell at Mount Sinai. There are some whom we cannot persuade to touch Mount Sinai, and some who once they have touched Mount Sinai, they will not venture to touch Mount Zion. Though Christ holds forth to them the scepter of His love, they will sit down, and say, "He has a controversy with me; I dare not adventure to go unto Him." I must ask you, has Christ ever killed a contrite soul? Were there ever any that could say that Christ is a hard master who will not easily condescend to take in these that are strangers unto Him?

Fourth, do you believe that it is good theology to say that because you are sinful, that you will not close with Christ? Will you not go to a physician because you are too sick? This was Peter's theology, as he said to Christ, "Depart from me; for I am a sinful man, O Lord" (Luke 5:8). But I must ask you, do you believe that it is good reasoning to say, "Because I am filthy, I will not go to the fountain; because I am sick, I will not go to the physician"? Do you believe that it is a good argument to say that because you are under bondage you will not go to Him whose name is the Redeemer of His people? Do you believe it is good theology to say that because you are held captive by your own lusts, you will not go to Him whose name is Jesus, who saves His people from their sins?

A fifth point that I would make is to seriously challenge you to not be found despisers of the precious offers of this everlasting gospel. I wish that some were no surer of heaven than some, if not many of you, may be certain of hell, eternity of pain, and seclusion from the presence of the Lord.

Before closing, I will only say these five words unto those that despise the precious offer of this everlasting gospel, and who account the blood of the covenant an unholy thing.

1. You who despise and never knew what it was to lay hold upon the precious offers of Christ, know that Christ

is either your best friend or your worst enemy. The vengeance of a crucified Savior is the most terrible vengeance, just as the love of a dying Christ is the sweetest, the most conquering, and the most refreshing love. Do you think that you will be able to endure that war, when Christ shall enter the lifts with you? Every battle of the warrior is with confused noise and with garments rolled in blood, but the noise of this battle and war that Christ shall eternally wage against your immortal souls, shall be with scorching and everlasting pain.

2. Behold, the day is approaching when instead of the doctrine that you now hear, which invites, saying, "Come unto me, all ye that labour and are heavy laden, and I will give you rest" (Matt. 11:28), you shall hear the sad words from heaven, "Then shall he say also unto them on the left hand, Depart from me, ye cursed, into everlasting fire, prepared for the devil and his angels" (Matt. 25:41). You who will not obey that precious invitation, "Come unto me," shall of necessity obey that sad sentence, "Depart from me." There is no delaying of that command; you may ignore the precious offers and invitations of Christ, but that sentence you cannot ignore.

3. Despisers of this gospel, what will be your exercise when you shall behold Christ sitting upon a white throne? I will tell you four things that will be a reprobate's exercise when he shall behold Christ upon the throne.

First, he will suddenly be much in the exercise of prayer. There are two prayers he shall pray most fervently: the first is, "Oh, call one more time! Oh, call just one more time!" Oh, reprobates, what would you give for an hour in that day when you shall appear before the dreadful tribunal of Jesus Christ, and shall see Him passing sentence upon you, whom so often you have dishonored? What would you give for one hour? "Oh," you will cry, "ten thousand worlds for one hour! I would give ten thousand worlds for one sermon to embrace Him, whom so often I have despised!"

The second prayer that you shall pray in that great and terrible day of the Lord is this: "Hills and mountains fall on us, and cover us from the face of the Lamb, and from Him who sits upon the throne!" You who never knew what it was to pray seriously, you shall pray seriously, and with much zeal in that day. Oh, to hear your prayers in that day of the Lord! How you will lament over your abuse of sermons and the precious invitations of the gospel, and how you sold your time into the hands of your enemies!

Shame and confusion of spirit will also be your exercise. Let me ask your consciences, what will be your thoughts of Christ when you shall see Him clothed with majesty as with a robe and with righteousness as a garment? What will you think when you shall see the same Christ to whom you have often spoken the wretched words, "We will not have this man to reign over us" (Luke 19:14)? Will you not condemn yourselves for folly in that day that this precious Savior should have been so often despised by you?

You will also be full of fear. In that day your knees shall smite one against another and you shall fear the dreadful sentence of separation from God that shall come out against you. Did you ever see the leaves of a tree shaking in a windy day? So shall your knees and all the joints of the most stout-hearted sinner in Zion shake on that day, when Christ shall render up the kingdom unto His Father.

4. You shall be full of hope in that day. Yes, you shall be full of the exercise of hope and expectation. You will be waiting at His throne until the sentence is passed against you.

5. Know that within threescore and ten years, you shall judge and determine whether you did right in refusing Christ or embracing Him. Oh, if you could hear the screeches of the souls that are in everlasting chains! If a minister of the gospel could possibly go down to hell and preach the doctrine, "Upon the embracing of Christ, ye shall win out," we conceive if they could exercise any grace in hell, there would not be one inhabitant of that place that would refuse these offers. Believe it, we do now summon you in His great name, who is the great master and author of this gospel. We invite you to take Him and

embrace Him; therefore, this shall meet you in the day of the Lord, if you do not take Him; He has been offered unto you, and you would not embrace Him.

If you do not embrace Jesus Christ, it would have been better for you if you had never been born. The curse of all the three blessed persons of the glorious Trinity will light upon you. The curse of the Father, the first person of the blessed Trinity, the curse of the Son, the second person of the blessed Trinity, the curse of the Holy Ghost, the third person of the blessed Trinity will be upon you. The curse of the four beasts, the curse of the twenty-four elders, all the angels that are in heaven, all the patriarchs, and the curse of all the blessed apostles of our Lord Jesus Christ will light on the head of them that undervalue Christ. Will you refuse Christ, although you may have Him for just one glance? For one look, you shall receive an infinite object—Christ. Will you not give one look unto Christ? You shall get Him for one look, which we see in Isaiah 45:22: "Look unto me, and be ye saved, all the ends of the earth: for I am God, and there is none else." Oh, take precious Christ at such a low rate. Now to Him who can persuade you we desire to give praise. Amen.

SERMON 43

The Christian in Complete Armor; or, The Devil Resisted and Put to Flight (1)

Resist the devil, and he will flee from you.

—James 4:7

It is a tragedy that this most excellent command, to resist the devil, should be so little obeyed by the majority of us. I suppose that there are some who know not whether the temptations of the devil or his victories be of the greater number, for there are some who must say that they have never resisted the devil's temptations. Might not a serious reflection upon the many dreadful victories the devil has had over us provoke us to call for those who are skilled in lamentation, that they might help us mourn? It is a wonder that some of us have not lost the hope of victory. We must ask ourselves why we should contend anymore. Must we say with Jeremiah, "My strength and my hope is perished from the LORD" (Lam. 3:18)? I ask you, do you think it is a small matter to be subdued by him who is the enemy of your salvation, and to allow him to trample upon your neck and crush your soul under his feet? The cursed correspondence between strong lusts within and an assaulting devil without, is that which often causes our ruin. Not only is there something outside of us that cries out, "Oh, embrace such a temptation!" but there is something within us that cries out, "Oh, embrace this temptation and subject your soul unto him who is the prince of darkness." We must confess that a Christian's enemies are those of his own house.

Let us pay particular attention to the words of our text; we will consider two points. First, we have an excellent command in the words of our text: "Resist the devil." The word that is rendered *resist* is most emphatic in the original language; it signifies such a resistance as not to yield a hair's breadth to the devil, but to oppose him with all our might and strength. This word is so strong that when the apostle says, "Resist the devil," he says that we are not to yield to the devil even a hair's breadth. Second, we find in the text a notable encouragement and motive to encourage a Christian in the exercise of this duty, in the words, "And he will flee from you." Face the devil and you will overcome him.

Now, from the words themselves, take notice of four important things.

1. It is every Christian's duty to engage in serious, diligent, and active resistance of the devil. This is imported in the force of the words in our text.

2. Notice that resisting the devil is attended with many excellent victories over him: "Resist the devil, and he will flee from you."

3. Notice that drawing near to God and living within sight of the Almighty is an excellent help for a Christian resisting the devil. We may gather this by connecting the seventh verse with the beginning of the eighth; the apostle, pressing them to resist the devil, immediately subjoins, "Draw nigh to God" (James 4:8). The apostle is saying that the best way to practically obey this command is for you to draw near to God; that is, never live outside of the sight of the invisible God if you desire help resisting the devil.

4. Humility and submission of spirit are excellent ways for a Christian to resist the devil; therefore, these two duties are put together in the verse: "Submit yourselves therefore to God," and then the apostle adds, "Resist the devil, and he will flee from you." Thus, humility and active effectual resisting of the devil often go together. Nothing more incapacitates a Christian to resist the devil than pride and presumption of spirit.

Let us examine each of these points in detail. First, a Christian ought to oppose the devil. I shall not take long to clarify this: it is clear from the words recorded in 1 Peter 5:9: "Whom resist stedfast in the faith." Here we find the same word; it signifies not yielding a hair's breadth unto the devil. We also read in Ephesians 4:27 that we must "neither give place to the devil," or, as it may be rendered, "Do not yield place to the devil." Likewise, this is clear in the remarkable words of Hebrews 12:4, "Ye have not yet resisted unto blood, striving against sin." These words tell us that a Christian ought, through his life, to resist temptations. Thus, a person should never be taken alive as a captive in this war. Before I can proceed any further concerning this truth, let me discuss the four things needed to resist the devil.

First, do not yield or give place unto the devil. When the devil comes to assault you and to purchase your heart's consent to sin, it is your duty to stand against him and give him no place. In this way, if he comes, you can with much indignation cry out, "Get thee behind me, Satan" (Matt. 16:23).

Secondly, a Christian must use all the means that are prescribed for resisting the devil. Paul, in the sixth chapter of the Ephesians, makes mention of the "spiritual armor" that a Christian should put on. A person who desires to resist the devil must exercise himself in the use of all of the pieces of spiritual armor.

Thirdly, a Christian should not faint or give over, notwithstanding the strong assaults and temptations that he encounters from the devil. This is clearly shown in the force of the words which the apostle uses: do not yield even a *hair's breadth* to the devil, but oppose him with all your might.

Fourthly, a Christian must put forth his utmost strength in resisting the temptations of the devil. We see that we must "resist" him with all our might, so that there should not be a bit of strength in a Christian's heart that is not engaged in resisting the devil's temptations. Every bit of the Christian should be engaged in the war.

Now, having thus examined this truth, I would like to discuss six points concerning our text. I suppose that the things we will discuss are common to many within these doors.

First, why does Satan so often obtain such a victory over us? Why do his temptations become so forcible and prevalent that he prevails over almost all he tempts? Are there not some Christians here who would have said once a day, "Blessed be the LORD my strength which teacheth my hands to war, and my fingers to fight" (Ps. 144:1)? Sometimes the Christian may say, "We are more than conquerors through him that loved us" (Rom. 8:37); but at other times, the same Christian may lament that all his temptations now have victory over him and the devil now digs his feet upon him. Let us discuss nine reasons for the rise and victory of the devil's temptations.

There are many persons who, in wrestling with temptations, use a wrong method to overcome them. Some, when they meet with a temptation, dare not but resist; however, they resist it wrongly, and they are still overcome by the devil. There are many improper ways for Christians to resist their temptations, none of which will succeed and do the turn on their own. I entreat you, search your hearts; if any of these are the ways of your resisting, abandon them.

1. Some attempt to overcome their temptations by forgetting them; that is, when the devil casts such a temptation into their minds, they think that they may overcome it by shutting the temptation out of their thoughts. Forgetting temptations does not mean victory over them. I confess that shutting temptations out of a Christian's mind is a part of his duty; but never think that this is a mortification of your temptations. Is this an ordinary method that you use to mortify your temptations?

2. Some think that an excellent way to resist temptation is to embrace it for a little; in this way, embracing the temptation just a little might further deaden their heart to that temptation. Is it not common for some Christians, when they are assaulted with such an idol and lust, to use this method to mortify it? Thcy think that once they indulge in the lust, they will forever deaden their heart unto it. This is a most dangerous path. It is for a man to think he will quench fire by casting fuel into it; likewise, it is for one to take fire into his bosom and not be burnt, or to handle trash and not be defiled. You must never take this path to resist your temptations. If you indulge in them once, you will be forced to grant them more.

3. Some endeavor to resist their temptations using their own strength. This is also a wrong way. If you desire to effectually oppose your temptations and mortify your idols, you must wrestle against them in the strength of Him whose name is *Jehovah*. A Christian can never fight

effectively without borrowed strength. Therefore, whenever you endeavor to wrestle with your temptations, you must go to Him who is the Captain of salvation, and seek strength from Him. A Christian, when he goes out to fight, should cry to Christ, "Master, save me, lest I perish!"

4. Some think that they will overcome their temptations through the strength of reason; they try to reason away their temptations. I confess, indeed, there is a godly, spiritual, and holy reasoning against temptations which I do not condemn. A Christian may cry out, "Shall I do this and sin against God? Shall I do this and lose the company and fellowship of God? Shall I do this and lose the company and fellowship of angels? Shall I do this and wrong my peace?" Never think that the strength of your reason will overcome your temptations. Therefore I say unto you, it is always good to reason against your temptations in Christ; that is, you must stand upon His strength, and then reason your temptations away. Never trust upon your reason, though it may seem entirely clear; for your reason shall never help you to overcome without the strength of Christ.

5. We may not attempt to overcome temptations by granting them a part of our will, but not the whole. This is a distinct thing from that which we named formerly. Some, when they are tempted to such a sin, will go so far with the temptation, but they will not do all it desires. They think that granting their temptation only a part of its desires will mortify it; but I say to such people, you are only plunging yourselves into a ditch; it is a most foolish way.

6. Some attempt to leave the place where they meet with temptation. For instance, some, when they are tempted to uncleanness, will embrace a solitary life. Now, leaving the place where your temptations meet you is lawful, but do not rest upon that as a first resistance of your temptations. I say to the person that rests upon that, even if you never see an object to tempt you, your heart would present you a thousand.

7. When some Christians are tempted, they attempt to guard the outward ports, which the devil takes in, and which have great influence upon the embracing of their temptation. Hence some persons, out of a stupid vanity, have plucked out their own eyes, so that they do not look upon the object of their temptations. Some, out of such a senseless conceit, have plucked out their tongue, so that they will not curse or swear. Oh, but even if some lacked eyes, they would still break the seventh command; even without a tongue, some would break the third command. Though their tongues were out of their mouths, they would curse God in their hearts. Though their eyes were out of their heads, they would lust after their neighbors' wives in their hearts; for there may be a lusting heart where there is not a lusting eye.

8. Some attempt to overcome their temptations more than they resist their lusts; when their temptations assault, they concentrate on resisting them and not the lusts upon which the temptation works. I tell you what it is to resist the temptation and not to resist the lust—it is for a person to dam up the stream and let the fountain run, which is an act of extraordinary folly.

9. Some people attempt to resist temptations through their natural inclination and antipathy against such a thing; but I may say unto you that this shall prove a defense of lies. I shall say no more of this first reason, but read the words of 2 Timothy 2:5: "And if a man also strive for masteries, yet is he not crowned, except he strive lawfully."

A second reason why Satan has such great victory in this war is because we do not have sobriety of spirit regarding the things of the world. I say, it is impossible for any unsober Christian to be a conquering Christian. This is clear in 1 Peter 5:8—when Peter is encouraging them to resist the devil, he adds this as a necessary qualification of one that would resist: "Be sober, be vigilant; because your adversary the devil, as a roaring lion, walketh about, seeking whom he may devour." Likewise, we read in 1 Corinthians 9:25, "And every man that striveth for the mastery is temperate in all things." A lack of moderation in our pursuit of the things of this world is often the very occasion that the devil has such great victory over us. It is impossible for a worldly Christian to be a conquering Christian. Alas! Think of the words of Ecclesiastes 3:11, which I believe ring true of many professors: "He hath set the world in their heart." The very world is in the midst of your bowels and affections; the pleasures and allurements of the world are as many cowards that obstruct a Christian's victory.

A third reason for Satan's victory is that we are not aware of our own inability when we go out to fight. It is suitable for Christians, when they go out to fight, to cry out, "I can do nothing," but when a Christian goes out to contend with his enemies, he must cry, "I can do all things through Christ which strengtheneth me" (Phil. 4:13). A Christian is never stronger to resist his temptations than when he is most weak in his own apprehensions. We see this in 2 Corinthians 11:9, where Paul writes, "When I am weak, then am I strong." A Christian's strength depends upon the apprehensions of his own weakness. It is much for a Christian to pray upon borrowed strength, and it is much for a Christian to walk upon borrowed strength; it is even as much for a Christian to fight upon borrowed strength. But, you must never go out to fight without Christ in your arms; put Him in the front. He is indeed a blessed Christian that can fight in the strength of Christ.

A fourth factor that has influence upon Satan's victory is our lack of faith and the power of unbelief, which is present in many wrestlers. The apostle says, "Above all, taking the shield of faith, wherewith ye shall be able to quench all the fiery darts of the wicked" (Eph. 6:16). We may take notice of two things from the verse. First, of all the pieces of a Christian's armor, most especially he ought to put on faith; therefore it is said, "Above all, taking the shield of faith." Second, faith is a universal conqueror. Nothing is able to stand before the excellent champion of faith; therefore it is said to be able to quench the fiery darts of the wicked. There is not a temptation that you will encounter that faith will not be able to dampen. In 1 Peter 5:9 we read, "Whom resist stedfast in the faith." From this we may gather that a lack of faith is that which will indeed ruin a Christian when he is assaulted. I am persuaded that there is nothing which makes the devil victorious more than unbelief; unbelief ruins a Christian.

Fifth, Christians are often overcome by temptations because they are inconstant in maintaining the fight against their temptations. Do you know why a Christian is so easily overcome by his temptations? He fights with them in fits. We are not constant; we do not always oppose ourselves against our temptations. We read of an excellent qualification of a Christian's resistance in 1 Peter 5:9: "Whom resist steadfast in the faith." We must not resist the devil only in fits; we must resist him steadfastly. Will not a Christian often, upon a Sabbath day, be fighting against such a lust and idol; yet before tomorrow comes, he embraces the same lust and idol. We pierce such an idol today, and we kiss and embrace that idol tomorrow. The inconstancy of a Christian's resisting of the devil does mightily obstruct his victories. Beloved in the Lord, we exhort you to be more constantly engaged in this war against temptations. He is an excellent Christian who is always in a fighter's posture. Though he is not always in a fight, yet he is always in a frame for fighting. Satan is often successful in this war because we do not constantly oppose ourselves against him.

A sixth reason for Satan's success is our lack of observation and Christian watchfulness and circumspection. In Mark 14:38 we read, "Watch ye and pray, lest ye enter into temptation." 1 Peter 5:8 records a similar command: "Be sober, be vigilant." A Christian ought to stand upon his watchtower and observe all the motions of his enemies. There are three things, the motions of which, a Christian ought especially to observe. First, a Christian ought to observe the motions of Christ. Second, a Christian ought to observe the motions of the devil. Third, a Christian ought to observe the motions of his own heart. A Christian who is much taken up in observing the motions of these three shall be an excellent Christian; not in the letter only, but also in the spirit. Satan often steals his victories; he overcomes us before we even know that he is warring. Frequent experience proves that the devil is often within our hearts before we are ever aware of his coming.

A seventh influence upon Satan's victories is Christians' lack of resisting sin in its bud, and temptations in their first assault. It is clearly easier to mortify sin in its bud than when it has taken root. It is easier to mortify the first assault of temptations than the second; for the more often temptations do assault, the stronger they are, if they are not resisted. Take notice of these two points: the first offers of temptations are most pleasant, but the first assault of temptation is also the weakest. You must resist it the first time.

Eighth, the cursed correspondence between our living lusts from within and our strong temptations from without are a large influence on Satan's victory in temptation. The temptations from the devil always have a friend within our hearts. When the devil assaults you with a temptation, does not your heart cry out, "Open, open," to the temptation? No doubt, these desperate lusts of ours are mighty procurators for the embracing of temptations. They plead like advocates the cause of the devil. There is a treacherous Sheba within which betrays our hearts. Until the cursed harmony between temptations and lusts is cut off, it is impossible for us not to be overcome.

A ninth ground for Satan's victories is that a Christian is so easily overcome by his temptations. It is hypocrisy, lacking truth in the inward parts, and lacking the grace of sincerity. Hence the apostle brings in the rest of the pieces of a Christian's armor: "Having your loins girt about with truth" (Eph. 6:14). This is no other thing but being clothed with the grace of sincerity. As long as hypocrisy reigns in our hearts, the devil shall not have much difficulty overcoming us and treading us under his feet.

At this time, let us discuss some temptations that the devil uses to divert a Christian from the exercise of duty, especially from prayer. Since, I suppose, the neglect of secret prayer is a thing frequent among us, I would desire you to search yourselves whether or not any of these temptations have had victory over you.

1. The first temptation whereby the devil studies to put a Christian from duty, especially prayer, is this: "Oh," says a Christian, "why must I pray? If I be an elect person, whether I pray or not, I will be in heaven; and if I be a reprobate, even if I would pray all my days, I would never be the better." This is a strong temptation by which Satan sequestrates and puts a Christian from his duty. I would only say to you who meet with this temptation, how will you answer it? I think this is the best way to answer it: as for your election or your reprobation, that is not your rule to walk by. The Word of God is the rule of your walk. The decree of God and the secret will of God are not your rule. There is a line in this Bible that says, "Pray without

ceasing"—you must obey it although you were reprobates to your own knowledge (1 Thess. 5:17). I will tell you what this argument of Satan is: it is the same as to bid a ship sail without sails, or to bid a man go up a ladder without steps. Are not prayer, mortification, holiness, patience, and humility the steps of the ladder by which we must ascend unto the holy place?

2. A second temptation the devil uses to discourage a Christian from duty is to bid a Christian cease praying for a while, saying that when he goes to prayer the next time he will have more liberty. Some Christians think that if they let prayer alone two days, which is their temptation, they would have more liberty in their next approach unto God after the two days of omission than if they had prayed all three days. The devil will tempt some to desist from duty upon this account: do not pray today, and you will have more liberty tomorrow. If a Christian observes the motions of his own heart, he will see this to be a temptation of the devil.

3. Satan also keeps a Christian from his duty by saying, "Oh, do not pray now, because you are not in a good and spiritual frame." He would have you laying aside duty; why? Because you are not in a spiritual frame; your heart is under bonds and you are distant from God. Now when you encounter such a temptation, you must ask the devil, "What poor argument is this? A man is sick, and therefore he must not go to the physician? A man is in necessity and therefore he must not go to beg? A man is wrong and therefore he must not go to be righted? If a man is deadly diseased, must he not make use of the thing that must heal him?" Are you not in a good frame? Now, what will bring you to a good frame more than prayer? You must even pray for a good frame when you are lacking it; therefore, it may not be an excuse that you must let alone prayer because you are not in a spiritual frame. It is as if a man would say, "I am full of spots, and therefore I must not wash."

4. A Christian may also say, "Alas! I must not go to prayer because I sin more in duty than when I neglect duty; it

would be better for me never to bow my knee, for I think I never offend God more than when I pray. Ought I not then to desist from prayer?" I confess that this is a strong temptation. I will oppose it with three points. First, never abandon prayer because of your temptations in prayer. Should you abandon your prayer because you are not such in prayer as you should be? I am sure that this is not good theology. Second, perhaps you see your sins better when you pray than when you are not praying. Therefore, Christians, guard against such a mistake. Some think their hearts are never so light and whorish as when they go to prayer. I say, perhaps it is not so, but you think it to be so; perhaps in prayer, you see your whoredom more than when you do not pray. Third, I charge you in His name, do not give up; for though you should never have advantage by your prayers, I say, it is your dignity to pray. I tell you, the day is coming that you shall pray no more.

5. Perhaps Satan will tempt a Christian to say, "Alas! I should never go to prayer because I find neither profit nor advantage by it. Every time I go to prayer, I come away a greater unbeliever and more ignorant of God than I was before. Every time I come away from prayer, my lusts and idols have greater power over me than before; ought I then to pray?" Yes, I say, notwithstanding that, you ought to pray. I would only say this to answer the temptation that you find no advantage in prayer: now, is it good theology to reject prayer because, by your fault, you find no advantage in it? It is just as for a man to condemn a doctor for lack of skill because, through some neglect of the patient's self, he has made the treatment ineffectual. Though you never had advantage by prayer, yet you must pray. We may not have a word to say to God in prayer but, "Lord, these are bad days; but we look for better. Oh, that it were with us in the days of old, and as in the years of ancient times." Even then, we must never give up prayer. Though you find no advantage in it, yet in time you shall learn that "godliness with contentment is great gain" (1 Tim. 6:6).

6. A sixth temptation the devil uses to divert a Christian from duty is to tempt the Christian to say, "Alas! I fear I have no right to do that duty; I fear I am not warranted to do that duty." This is an ordinary assault to impede a Christian from the exercise of faith. "I would dare to believe, but I fear that I do not have the right!" I will tell you what gives you a right: do you have a necessity? "Yes," you answer. Then, that gives you a right to the promise. Do you have a desire to have Christ? "Yes," you say, "I would fain have Him." I say, that gives you a right to the promise. Now, if necessity and desire give you a right to the promise, then who lacks the right? There may be some who lack the right by desire, yet all have right by necessity.

7. The devil casts in our way some diversion, lawful in itself, to divert us from the exercise of duty. He will cast in some occasion to tend to some lawful calling, just when we are going to prayer. I am afraid that we are glad and cheerful to have lawful diversions to hinder us from the exercise of prayer. This is a desperate treachery of our hearts.

8. The last temptation, which is a most subtle one, is this: sometimes the devil will keep a Christian from prayer by making him believe that he has more liberty praying in his thoughts, walking up and down in any room, than when more purposely he goes to his knees. Some Christians think that when they pray walking up and down, they have more liberty than if they should go to their knees and make a more deliberate and solemn approach unto God. This is often the experience of many. Though I dare not deny that there are some Christians who are thus guided, yet suppose that your liberty be tied to your prayer in your thoughts; if that hinders you from going to your knees, you may fear there is some temptation in it. I think it is a necessary and useful question, though we cannot enter upon it at this time, to ask: what is the reason that some Christians can never have liberty when they bow on their knees before God, and yet have some liberty and refreshment when they pray in their thoughts, walking up and down? Perhaps on another occasion we

shall speak a little to this case, as the time is now spent, and having much prevented us, I shall not insist longer to speak to many things concerning this text.

I shall now come to make some applications concerning that which we have said. The first thing that I would press upon you from what we have discussed is this: I charge you by all the promises and by all the warnings and curses that are written within the Bible, that you would this night, this very night, give up your names unto Jesus Christ, that you may be soldiers under His banner and colors. This is the great substance of all I have to say. Oh, lift yourselves tonight, you who have been fighting against Christ, against heaven, and against God. I entreat you that this night, even tonight, you would let the weapons of your rebellion drop out of your hands and seek quarters from God. Do not fight any longer under the cursed banners of him who is the prince of darkness, but come and fight under the banner of Him who is the Prince and Captain of our salvation.

Do you intend to be soldiers under the Son of God? No question all of us would respond, "Who could be so cruel to themselves as to refuse to fight under Christ's banner?" Oh, I pray that indeed there is not a person so cruel to himself here tonight. In Job 15:25-26, Job is speaking of a wicked man. He points him out under three characters, which, I suppose, is the practice and frame of many. First, "He stretcheth out his hand against God." Is not that a mighty act of boldness, for a person to stretch out his hand, as it were, to fight and contend against God, and to proclaim open war against the exalted Prince of Israel? There is a second expression that points out the wicked: he "strengtheneth himself against the Almighty." Is this not a strange expression? Not only does he stretch out his hand against God, but he endeavors to fortify himself in his opposition against God. He, as it were, endeavors to put on his harness, so that he may effectually contradict the Almighty. The third expression, which is yet more wondrous and strange than any, is next: "He runneth upon God" (v. 26). We conceive that those words are also spoken of the wicked. Do you not think it to be a horrible and unknown act of opposition for a person to run away from God? Could any of us imagine a person who is thus demented and out of his wits, who will not only stretch out his hand against God, but fortify himself against God; yea, who will run away from God?

I would say no more to such a man, but, "It is too hard for you to kick against the pricks." I would ask of you all here, do you intend, through the strength and grace of God, never to join up with your corruptions and idols again? Ask your own hearts, do you intend tonight never to side with temptations or the devil anymore? I say, blessed is the person who has taken this intention.

A second point I would make by way of application, is this; dear Christians, be comforted and let your hearts rejoice, for your victory is certain. Wrestle with your corruptions and manage a spiritual war against them; the victory is certain. The certainty of a Christian's victory is founded upon seven golden pillars.

1. The first thing upon which the certainty of a Christian's victory is founded is the unchangeable Word and promise of God. Oh, Christians who have engaged in this war, comfort yourselves, for there is a word passed from the mouth of Him who is unchangeable which says that you shall overcome. "The God of peace shall bruise Satan under your feet shortly" (Rom. 16:20). It is as impossible for a Christian not to be a victor as it is impossible to make God a liar. Oh, Christians who are engaged in this war, do you not have the Word of God laid in pledge for your victory so that you shall overcome? It is as impossible for the devil to foil and overcome a Christian as to make this book, the Bible, a book of lies.

2. The second golden pillar on which the certainty of a Christian's victory is founded is the intercession of Christ. Christian in warfare who is taken up in wrestling against the devil, the certainty of your victory is founded upon Christ's intercession. What is the exercise of Christ in heaven, Christians who have "Christ in you, the hope of glory" (Col. 1:27)? I will tell you His exercise: He prays night and day that our faith fail not, when Satan desires to winnow us as wheat. We see this in Luke 22:31. Now, Christ cannot come short of His intercession; therefore, a Christian cannot come short of victory. Shall Christ be praying and shall you not be triumphing? Shall Moses' praying upon the mount have influence upon Joshua's victory in the valley? Shall not the prayers of Him who

is the spiritual Moses have influence upon your victory? Christians, you may sing the triumph before victory.

3. The certainty of a Christian's victory is founded upon Christ's victory over our temptations. Has Christ overcome the devil? That is a pledge that you shall overcome him also. Be sure of it, as Christ has overcome principalities and powers, so likewise shall you be helped to overcome your temptations. Hear the sweet words in John 16:33: "Be of good cheer; I have overcome the world." You shall also overcome. Christ's victory is the foundation of a Christian's victory.

4. The fourth golden pillar of the certainty of a Christian's victory is the unchangeableness of Christ's purchase and the utter impossibility that He can come short of anything for which He laid down His life. Has Christ died, and shall you not overcome? I would comfort a Christian with this: Christ's death is the foundation of the certainty of your victory. Christ's resurrection and ascension is the foundation of your victory. Has Christ paid the price for you, and for your soul, and is it possible that He can be disappointed? Yes, the day is coming when Christ shall see of all the travail of His soul.

5. The certainty of a Christian's victory is also based on the certainty of the omnipotence of God, which is engaged on a Christian's behalf; who can overcome Him? What devil, what temptation, what lust can overcome you who have omnipotence on your side? The omnipotence of God is engaged on a Christian's behalf: "Who are kept by the power of God through faith unto salvation ready to be revealed in the last time" (1 Peter 1:5). It is impossible for you to be totally overcome because omnipotence is on your side. Hence we read in John 10:29, "My Father, which gave them me, is greater than all; and no man is able to pluck them out of my Father's hand." Christ reassures His children, saying, "Greater is he that is in you, than he that is in the world" (1 John 4:4). I confess that the devil will sometimes tempt a Christian as a roaring lion and sometimes as an angel of light; yet, comfort yourself,

saying that you shall at last overcome. Why is this? For "when I am weak, then am I strong," through the omnipotence that is engaged on my behalf (2 Cor. 12:10). Oh, Christian, do not fear; you shall one day tread upon the heads of your enemies because you have a second standing at your side, whom none can overcome.

6. There is a sixth golden pillar of a Christian's victory: Christ's faithfulness, His truth, and His honor are laid in pledge for a Christian's victory. Christ is faithful. There is a commission given to Christ to keep all the gifted ones; He is to render this account to His Father: "Those that thou gavest me I have kept, and none of them is lost" (John 17:12). If I may say so, without reflection upon precious Christ, it would be a stain upon Him if any of the ransomed ones would be lost. Christ's honor is laid at stake for the victory of the saints. Hence, Christ has that excellent report to make in the day of the Lord.

7. A seventh and last pillar and excellent foundation of a Christian's victory is the constant influence of heaven that is promised to a Christian for helping him when he is put to a strait. Do you have a trial? You may, as it were, look to such a promise. Every trial and temptation a Christian encounters is a promise in the covenant of grace, to which he may go to resist such a temptation.

Now, since the certainty of a Christian's victory is founded upon these seven golden and excellent pillars and foundations, Christians, will you not rejoice? Is not this good news from a far country, and should be as cold water unto a thirsty soul? There is such a decree passed in heaven that it is impossible for you to be overcome. Now, is it not a comfort to you to be sure of your victory? Will you not be engaged in this war, even tonight? I charge you, since the victory that attends this war is certain, come and let the weapons of your rebellion fall out of your hands. A Christian may say, though all the devils in hell did assault him, "There are more with me than there are against me." He may say with much spiritual boldness and confidence, "Though thousands do assault me, yet I will not fear, for the Lord is with me." Oh, will you fall in love with this excellent condition and state of life—to be a fighter under the banner of the Lord Jesus? Do you intend to fight against Christ any longer?

If there had been time, I would have pointed out to you several evidences that many of us here are fighters against God. You shall never fight for Christ if you are never convinced that you were once fighters against Him. You must first be convinced that it is impossible to get you engaged in this war. I may say, to press you to it, the day is coming when you shall say, "Oh, that I had stood to my knees in blood, striving against my lusts!" I pray you, what a day shall it be when you and all your lusts shall be standing before the tribunal of Christ! Oh, Christians, what an excellent sight it will be to see all your idols and lusts bleeding at your feet and gasping out their last! Would it not be life and resurrection from the dead? When shall the day come when there shall not be a Dagon within our hearts, which shall not fall before Him who is "the Prince of the kings of the earth" (Rev. 1:5)? On that day, every idol that was within these cursed hearts of ours shall give subjection to Jesus Christ. There shall be an eternal and universal subjection of our hearts unto Him. Oh, that I had the tongue of an angel, that I might commend this excellent war unto you! Oh, be engaged in this battle, I entreat you! Will you consider the words that shall be spoken to you at the close of the war? Will you take the testimony of dying Paul of the fight and warfare: "I have fought a good fight, I have finished my course, I have kept the faith" (2 Tim. 4:7)?

You shall never regret that you fought a stroke in this war; it is a brave fight. I must say, the day is coming when you shall be standing on the utmost line between time and eternity; at that day, saying the words, "I have fought a good fight," shall afford you more consolation than if you had been a possessor of all the kingdoms of the world. Oh, believe it, and take it for your duty and work; "Resist the devil, and he will flee from you." If you face the devil and refuse to embrace his temptations, he shall prove to be but a coward.

Now unto Him who can persuade you to engage in this blessed war, we desire to give praise. Amen.

SERMON 44

The Christian in Complete Armor; or, The Devil Resisted and Put to Flight (2)

Resist the devil, and he will flee from you.
—James 4:7

As long as a Christian is traveling in these tents of mortality and is a stranger to his Father's house, his life will be a constant warfare between the flesh and the spirit. There will be constant battle between the law in his members and the law in his mind. There are many who are called Christians of whom this may be said: "They have ceased to contend with their idols and are not much taken up in that excellent work of resisting the devil." I shall now discuss the text; there are four things we wish to notice concerning these words.

First, it is the duty of every Christian, effectually and with a great deal of zeal, to oppose and resist the devil and his temptations. The word translated *resist* implies such a resistance so as not to yield a hair's breadth to the devil, but to oppose him with all our might. It is the duty of a Christian effectually to resist the devil and his temptations.

Let us point out some mistakes among persons who think they have overcome the devil and his temptations, but who have not indeed overcome. Are there not many who think the devil is already defeated and the bitterness of death is past? Is it so with them as they suppose?

They may be mistaken on many grounds. One reason some people believe that the devil and their lusts are overcome, but are mistaken, is because their lusts and idols are sleeping. Thus, they think all these evils are overcome. However, there is a way to distinguish between defeated evils and sleeping evils. An idol or lust may be sleeping in a person's heart when it is not mortified or subdued; often, that is the reason for our mistake. We do not know how to distinguish between a sleeping lust and a mortified lust.

There are four ways a Christian may know whether his lusts are sleeping or mortified.

> 1. If your lusts are subdued and mortified, you will have a great abhorrence against a lust and idol; but if it is only sleeping and quiet for a little while, you will, at most, have but a kind of indifference toward that lust and idol. You may, however, slight it in those ardent actions of love.
>
> 2. If your lusts are mortified, then your delight in and estimation of Christ will increase; but, if they are only sleeping within you, then your estimation of Christ will neither increase nor grow upon your hand. This becomes clear if there is a part of your heart that has been engaged to such an idol, and that idol is now dead to your affections, you will give that part of your heart unto Christ. Is your estimation of Christ growing? If not, your lusts and idols are only sleeping, and are not dead.
>
> 3. Is your delight in duty increased by the mortification of your idol? Now, if your idol is indeed mortified, delight in duty is an unquestionable attendant; but if your lust is sleeping, surely your delight in duty is decaying. By this point, you may measure whether your idol is sleeping or mortified.
>
> 4. You may test whether your idols are mortified or sleeping by your growth in sanctification; for growth in mortification is attended with growth in sanctification. If your conformity to precious Christ does not increase, that is evidence that your idol is not mortified, but sleeping. I would have you take notice of these words: "When a strong man armed keepeth his palace, his goods are in peace" (Luke 11:21). If you find your idol sleeping, be afraid that the strong man is now keeping your house more strongly. Yes, sometimes the devil will be within

our heart and will make so little din, that we can hardly discern he is there.

A second ground for mistake is that many people think their idols and lusts are overcome because they are restrained. Now, there is a difference between an idol and lust when mortified and when restrained; for a lust may be restrained in its actions when not mortified in its root. Now, do not think that your idol is always mortified when it is restrained. As for the differences between these two, I have spoken about them upon another occasion.

A third ground for mistake is that many people think they have overcome their idols and their lusts because their lusts have gone out. Now you must know there is a difference between a lust and an idol when it goes out and when it is cast out. It is certain that the devil will sometimes go out with his own consent, even when he is not cast out by force. I will tell you two times when the devil leaves by consent, not by force. First, the devil leaves when there is a change in a person from a visibly flagitious, wicked man, to a moral walk and conversation. The devil goes out by consent when a man changes from open profanity to a more refined moral walk and conversation. Secondly, the devil goes out by consent when there is a change from profanity to hypocrisy, and the man owns Christ by a bare profession. The devil will never stand to endure such a change. Oh, search your own hearts to see whether the devil has been cast out, or whether he has willingly gone out.

Fourth, many are mistaken by thinking that they have overcome the devil because they have put him to flight. You must distinguish between a fleeing devil and a defeated devil; when the devil assaults a Christian, he flees either to make secure, or to come back with the greater advantage and force.

The fifth ground of mistake is that many believe their victories over the devil are greater than indeed they are because of the lack of watchfulness and self-examination. Some are such great strangers to their own hearts that they do not know what great progress the devil and his works have made in them.

Now, I shall address ten of the most subtle arguments that our hearts use to persuade us to embrace temptations when we are assaulted. If you search yourselves, you will find that when you are assaulted by the devil, your heart will often make use of one of these arguments to move you to embrace temptations.

The first subtle argument that our hearts use to persuade us to embrace temptation is this: our hearts try to embrace one temptation to shun another. Let me make it clear: if a person is called to pray in public among his fellow Christians, he will decline the call to prayer because he is concerned whether he prays well or not. He may think, "I will be liable to temptations; for if I pray well, I am liable to the temptation of pride; and if I do not pray well, I am liable to the temptation of fretting and anxiety." Therefore the heart, to shun these temptations, falls into the temptation of neglecting the duty. This is a subtle device of the heart of man, to make him embrace one temptation to shun another.

The second subtle argument the heart employs to persuade us to embrace temptations is to present a spiritual reason why we should embrace such a temptation. To make this a little clearer unto you, I would propose these two instances. First, when a Christian is tempted to embrace the riches of the world and love of them, the heart will move him to embrace such a temptation on this spiritual ground: you may love and pursue the world so that when you have abundance of it, you may minister to the necessities of the saints and be helpful to those who are of the household of faith. Therefore, we give way to that temptation, because the heart seems to have a spiritual end in desiring the riches of the world. Hence some will say, "If I desire the world, it is for no other end than to help those in need." This is to embrace temptations upon spiritual grounds. Here is another example: some, when they are assaulted with the temptations of love to the world, say, "I may give my heart leave to pursue a little after such things, because if I had such abundance of the things of the world, I would pray much and wait upon God without interruption. I would go to every communion and fast." This is a subtlety of the heart of man to press a person to embrace temptations through spiritual designs. Do you think that Absalom was approved when he covered his treason saying, "Let me go and pay my vow, which I have vowed unto the LORD, in Hebron" (2 Sam. 15:7)? Do you think that Jeroboam was justified when he feigned concern for the comfort of his people to justify his idolatry, saying that it was too much for the people to go up to Jerusalem twice a year? I say to the person under such a temptation, do not succumb to evil hoping that good may come of it; though your temptation may be backed with a spiritual end, do not embrace such a temptation.

The third subtle argument is that the heart, when under temptation, concludes that there is a consistency between that sin and a state of grace; therefore he may do it. Hence, when the devil assaults us, we have this refuge: though we do this, yet we shall not be shut out from having a place in Christ's thoughts and His heart. We believe that it is consistent to embrace such a temptation and remain in a state of grace.

A fourth subtle argument of the heart is to persuade us to embrace temptations to purchase tenderness. Sometimes when temptations assault a Christian, he will embrace them, thinking that he will have tenderness as his lot and frame. Many have sought to purchase contrition of spirit by embracing temptations. They fall into some gross iniquity so that the grossness of the sin might waken their conscience and make their hearts tender.

The fifth subtle argument of the heart of man is that the heart will say, "Embrace such a temptation for once, and that will forever deaden your heart to the temptation." Often, those being assaulted with temptations have taken this way to escape it, that after embracing such a temptation just one time, they might forever be free of it.

Sixth, the heart may make the person believe that the temptation is his duty. Sometimes when the devil assaults a man, the heart will persuade him that it is his duty to succumb to the temptation. This is clear when the devil tempts a Christian to unbelief—the Christian sits down and thinks this may be his duty. Also, when the devil tempts some to presumption and carnal confidence, their hearts make them believe that it is their duty to believe and have confidence in God; therefore they do it. Hence, temptations have such victory over some, so that they think the very killing the apostles of Christ good service unto God (John 16:2). We read in Jonah 4:9, "I do well to be angry, even unto death," where his heart pleads that his temptation is his duty.

The seventh subtle argument the heart makes is to persuade us to embrace temptations so that we may purchase experience. A Christian, if he examines his own heart, will find he has embraced temptations to purchase experience.

An eighth argument is to present the advantage that waits upon the embracing of such a temptation. The devil and our own hearts luster and varnish the temptation with such excellent colors that we must, because of our corruptions, embrace it.

The ninth subtle argument which our hearts use to move us to embrace temptations is that sometimes we embrace temptations so that grace may abound; we will do such a sin that the grace of Christ in pardoning may super-abound, being made conspicuous and evident.

A final subtle way is by presenting to us the danger and disadvantage that awaits us if we do not embrace such a temptation. At times when our lives come in competition with our owning of Christ, temptation seizes the moment. Oh, spare yourself, and these temptations will press so forcibly the danger and disadvantage that waits for us if we do not embrace such a temptation, that we immediately begin to consent and embrace it.

Now, I would like to consider eight ineffectual ways of resisting temptations. These methods are commonly used, but they will never fully help us reach obedience to the excellent command, "Resist the devil."

1. First, it has been thought that a Christian could resist the devil with his desires. Some persons, when they are assaulted and tempted by the devil, will sit down and cry out, "Oh, that I were free of this temptation!" Now, your resistance is but the sluggard's resistance, for the "the soul of the sluggard desireth, and hath nothing" (Prov. 13:4). I ask you, does your resistance of the devil consist only of desires? Do you desire to be free of such a temptation? I say to you, that is but the coward's resistance. Unless you add force to your desires, you can never win the victory over your idols.

2. A second sort of ineffectual resistance is the resistance of the devil by resolutions; this resistance will not prove effectual. This type of resistance occurs when some persons take on resolutions after the temptation has already overcome them. They confirm that they will never embrace the temptation again. I say to you that resisting the devil by resolutions is never an effectual and successful resistance. I think if there is any resisting of the devil's temptations among the professors of this age, it is either a resistance by desires or resolutions. I shall make clear what I mean by resisting the devil by resolutions. Sometimes when the

devil assaults a Christian to desist from prayer, he yields to the temptation with this resolution: "If I were in such a place, and I had different opportunities and accommodations, I would not neglect prayer." When a Christian meets with this temptation, when he is in a house where there is no room to pray, he takes on this resolution: "I may now desist from prayer, but if I were in a house where I had accommodation, I would pray much." Now, this is indeed to yield the cause unto the devil. It is found that a Christian who has given way to a temptation on this account, even when he does have the proper accommodations, his heart has been estranged from the duty.

3. Another ineffectual form of resistance is that of formal prayers. Sometimes when the devil assaults a person, out of very conscience and custom, he goes to his knees and speaks two or three words to God with much formality. I say, resisting the devil by formal prayers is no successful resistance. You think that you are resisting the devil, but when you are pressed to resist, you cry out, "The Lord save me from the devil, and all his works." I say, you may cry that out a thousand times and yet be a subject of the devil. It is but a poor resistance to resist the devil in this manner; perhaps we even take the Lord's name in vain when we employ such an expression. Prayer is a part of a Christian's resisting the devil; as it were, a Christian should sit down and weep at Christ's feet until He condescends to send him forth strength to overcome his temptations. If we exercised the duty of prayer more when we are assaulted by the devil, we would have a greater victory over him. Do you know what Paul did when there was a messenger of Satan given to buffet him? He went and "besought the Lord thrice, that it might depart" (2 Cor. 12:8). But, there are many professors who will meet with a hundred temptations before they will go to their knees to seriously ask God to send them strength to wrestle against their temptations. I am sure that if every messenger of Satan sent us to our knees, we would pray without ceasing. There are some that the devil tempts, not only when they wake, but when they sleep; not only when they are not at duty,

but when they are immediately engaged in duty and after duty. Thus, there is no time in which we are set free from his temptations. The word which Satan said concerning himself is true. When the Lord asked him where he was coming from, he responded, "From going to and fro in the earth, and from walking up and down in it" (Job 1:7).

4. Another ineffectual resistance is a partial and divided resistance. Some persons will resist one idol and embrace another; some will embrace one temptation and fight against another. This is much like Saul's practice; they will spare the fat goats among the flock, and they will kill those that are not so pleasant to them. Now does this partial resistance seem to be effective against the devil? A covetous man will resist the temptations to prodigality, but will embrace those to covetousness. A proud man will wrestle against temptations to lust, but not against those to pride. A man that has the pleasure of the world for his idol will embrace these temptations that lead to his predominant idol, but will wrestle against temptations to covetousness. If you desire to be wrestlers indeed, then oppose yourselves to every temptation and idol that assaults and opposes itself against you.

5. Inconstant resisting is not a way to fight the devil's temptations. Some persons wrestle against the devil by fits; but a constant wrestling against the devil is foreign to them. I do not say that a Christian is always engaged, or is always earnest in managing this blessed war; but I would say that it is the duty of a Christian to be constantly fervent and not interrupted in accomplishing this blessed fight. Some persons, when they go to communion, will resist some temptations; but for a whole year again, they will not resist a single temptation. Only if you are constant in the excellent work of resisting the devil's temptation is it impossible for you to attain any sensible or remarkable victories over them. I suppose if all of us who are here were searched, we would find this to be true—we resist the devil in fits, and we exercise those fits only occasionally.

6. Let us also examine a presumptuous resisting of the devil. Some persons engage to resist the temptations of the devil in their own strength; for often they are foiled when they go out to fight with their idols. Therefore, when God is pressing them to resist the devil here, immediately they must attend unto the words of James 4:10: "Humble yourselves in the sight of the Lord." If you ever will be a successful resister of the devil, do not be too confident in your own strength and ability. You may say, "I can do nothing as of myself"; yet, "I can do all things through Christ which strengtheneth me" (Phil. 4:13). There are some of you, when we desire you to resist the temptations of the devil, who cry out, "I defy the devil and all his works." I say, it is a token that you will not obtain victory when you know so little of your strength. I confess, it is suitable for a Christian to follow Christ with confidence of victory; but it is hard to wrestle with your temptations when presumption has victory over you.

7. A seventh ineffectual way of resisting the devil is doing so when you are alone. This is not the resisting spoken of in the text; for when he impresses the importance of resisting the devil, he also says that you must "draw nigh to God" (James 4:8). It is as if he would have said, "Never enter the field with your corruptions, except if Christ is in the field with you." Therefore, it is good for a Christian to engage Christ always in his quarrel, and to make Him his second in all his oppositions that he makes to his corruptions. Know this, Christian who is taken up in wrestling: you shall not overcome if you are left alone. It is hard for a Christian to pray alone, to hear alone, and to meditate alone. It is much harder for a Christian to fight alone.

8. We will not succeed when we resist the devil with discouragement. When a person being tempted is discouraged and heartless in the fight, he fights, but loses hope of overcoming. This resisting will never prove successful. It is much indeed for a Christian to keep a middle ground between presumption and discouragement—neither to be puffed up with pride nor cast down with a

> sense of his own inability. I think he is a blessed Christian who, when he goes out to fight, can take these two graces along with him: the confident grace of faith and the self-debasing grace of humility. These two graces may suitably balance a Christian's spirit under all the temptations he encounters.

Now, does not all your resistance to the devil and his temptations fall under one of these eight sorts? Does it go any further? I shall no longer speak about this text; I shall only give some words of application before closing.

First, observe the subtlety that the devil uses in pressing home his temptations. Our hearts are all too ready to concur with his plots. Take notice of the four subtle steps of the devil's assault on a Christian.

First, the devil will often suit his temptations to a Christian's present frame. If a Christian is in a believing frame, he will tempt him to presumption; and if he is in an unbelieving frame, he will tempt him to sinful anxiety and despair. Whatever the present frame of a Christian may be, Satan will suit his temptations unto it.

Second, he times his temptation when a Christian has opportunity to act upon the temptation. When did Satan tempt Joseph to uncleanness? Was it not when there was no one in the house but he and his mistress? When did Satan tempt Cain to murder? Was it not when he had occasion to act upon it? If some persons will search their own hearts, they will find Satan times his temptations to arrive exactly when the Christian has greatest opportunity to act on the temptation.

Third, there is the subtlety which we named the last time: he suits his temptations to a Christian's predominant lust and idol. Whatever your predominant lust and idol may be, the devil will often study to stir up a temptation to that lust.

A fourth step of his subtlety which often appears is that Satan suits his temptations unto a Christian's predominant necessity and strait. Whatever your strait is, your temptations will be suitable to your strait. To make this clear, if a person is reduced to poverty the devil will present a temptation suitable to that strait. Let your strait be what it will, you may expect temptations suitable unto your straits.

A second application I shall give is this: because it is God's commandment to resist the devil and to stand in opposition against him, then be much in this precious work and exercise. Oh, Christians, will you blush and be ashamed of the fact that so little of your precious time is taken up in resisting the devil and his temptations? I suppose that if the danger that awaits our embracing temptations were known, we would wrestle more and debate with our temptations. The day is coming when those who have been consumed by their lusts and idols shall cry out, "Alas! For evermore, that ever I embraced these temptations."

Last, Christians, since it is certain that you are appointed, as long as you are alive, to endure and fight this blessed fight, take these three excellent motives to persuade you to be involved in this blessed war.

The first motive and encouragement that I would propose is that every Christian who has ever seriously engaged in this blessed fight, who has truly given up his name to fight under Christ's banner, has either already received the sweet fruits of victory, or is on the way of overcoming. Not a single person now in hell can have this lamentation: I gave up my name to Christ to fight under His banner, and I was defeated and overcome. No, all who have ever enlisted themselves under His colors are now sweetly rewarded, and have entered into the possession of the reward of the war. Now I suppose if all the conquerors around the throne were admitted to give their advice, they would say, "Oh, resist the devil!" Yea, I am sure, if there are thousands in hell, as no question there are, if they were admitted to give us their advice, it would be, "Oh, endeavor to resist the devil!" All who have effectually resisted the devil are in heaven this day.

The second encouragement is, "Resist the devil, and he will flee from you"; face him and stand to it, and as the Lord is true who has promised it, the devil shall prove himself to be a coward. Oh, stand and face your temptations "and he will flee from you." It is good that the righteous are as bold as a lion, and sometimes have occasion to sing, "Blessed be the LORD my strength which teacheth my hands to war, and my fingers to fight" (Ps. 144:1). He has not allowed your enemies to prevail over you. If the rock upon which your confidence is built has not sold you, then one of you shall put a thousand to flight, and ten of you shall put ten thousand temptations to ruin (Deut. 32:30). This may be an excellent fight: if you will but stand your ground and not yield a hair's breadth to the devil, he will soon flee from you.

The last encouragement to move you to seriously engage in this blessed fight is that there are many who are watching your behavior. Every embracing of every temptation is known to Christ. Are not angels spectators? Are not the persons of the Trinity spectators? Are not the saints about the throne spectators, beholding how you acquit yourselves in this blessed war, and how you carry yourselves in resisting the devil?

The word which Christ shall speak unto you in the day when you shall fairly land on the other side of time, shall sweetly make up all the loss you have sustained on this side of eternity. Welcome, conquerors! His precious hand shall put the crown upon your head and His blessed hands shall deliver unto you those excellent harps of God; His hands shall deliver unto you the palms that you shall carry, those excellent robes of righteousness. When Christ Jesus shall take you and embrace you in His arms and cry out, "Welcome, you who have overcome the devil!" shall it not be a sweet restoration for all the losses that you may sustain while you are here?

Now to Him who is able to persuade you to remain faithful in fighting this blessed war, we desire to give praise. Amen.

SERMON 45

The Christian in Complete Armor; or, The Devil Resisted and Put to Flight (3)

Resist the devil, and he will flee from you.
—James 4:7

It may be said of some of us that we have ceased to contend; may it not also be said of some of us, reflecting on all the victories that Satan and our corruptions have gained over us, that it is with consent of our own hearts? I think there is such a cursed correspondence between the devil and our hearts that the very shadow of a temptation will overcome us. Every condition of our lives becomes a temptation to us. Is not a wife a temptation? Are not riches a temptation? Is not poverty a temptation? Are not children a temptation? Is not lack of children a temptation? Whatever some persons encounter in life, whether alone or in company, whether in married or in single life, it may become a temptation to them. I think that Ham's curse has become the curse of many of us. We have become servants of servants. That which ought to be our servant, we have made our master, and we have become servants unto it. I would ask each of you seriously, do you intend to overcome and be placed with those blessed thousands that shall possess the sweet fruits of their fight against their enemies and the great adversary?

There are three great delusions that have overtaken many of us in these days. First, many think they will reach heaven without wrestling against their corruptions. I say to you, if you do not fight with Christ, you shall not reign with Him. Second, many are deluded and think that they will reach heaven without repentance. There are some who have gone that length of hardness, believing that they could get heaven without repentance. Yes, there are some who have been so hard that if they could get heaven with one tear, they would not shed it. Oh, the dreadful impenitence that has overtaken many in these days! Third, many believe that they may reach heaven without any mortification. "Be not deceived; God is not mocked: for whatsoever a man soweth, that shall he also reap" (Gal. 6:7).

Some, when they have reflected on their spiritual enemies, and seen the weakness of their own hearts, are constrained to cry out, "Oh, to be gone and to depart from this life!" There are many strait passes between you and glory; before you enter, you must pass through these gates. Is not faith a strait gate through which you must enter? You will see hundreds lying before the gate of faith who are buried there; they never passed through the gate. There is also the strait gate and pass of mortification. You will see hundreds of thousands lying before the gate who have been attempting to go through, and were never able. Is not sanctification a strait gate? You will see many lying before that gate who have been attempting to go through and were never able. I say, you must wrestle as in an agony, and strengthen yourself to it; if I may say so, Christ is standing at the end of the race with a crown in His two hands, crying out, "To him that overcometh shall this crown be given."

In the forenoon, we spoke a little concerning the duty of a Christian effectually to resist the temptations of the devil; we discussed several points. Let me now speak a little concerning three points.

First, let me propose some considerations that may move and persuade you to be much in this blessed and excellent work of resisting the devil.

> 1. The first consideration I shall propose is to resist the devil. When you shall be standing on the final line between time and eternity, and shall be entering in through the first and second gates of death, this shall afford you much spiritual joy and contentment—that you have been taken up in this blessed work of resisting the devil. I would say that next to faith, which is the very hinge of a Christian's comfort, this shall be the second thing that will prove most consolation to him. This is clear from the excellent words of Paul, who, when he had one foot in heaven and the other out of it, comforted himself with this: "I have fought a good fight, I have finished my course, I have kept

the faith" (2 Tim. 4:7). Paul says, in essence, "I have been taken up in that blessed work of resisting the temptations of the devil. Would you like to have my testimony? I am now going to die, and if this were my last word, I would never regret my time spent resisting the devil." Why do most Christians die with so little joy and spiritual confidence? It is because they have not been taken up in this work of resisting the devil; while a Christian is traveling here, he is like those who built Jerusalem. He has a sword in one hand and a building instrument in the other. Oh, blessed is he who, when death comes, can take it in his arms and cry out, "Welcome, friend." Believe it, death shall not be the friend of any one of us here if we do not trust in Christ and resist the devil.

2. A second consideration to encourage you to practice this duty of resisting the devil is that there are four things a Christian will come to fully understand by practicing this duty. First, a Christian will more fully understand the sinfulness of his own heart. Secondly, he will more fully understand the subtlety of the devil. Thirdly, he will gain understanding concerning the strength of his corruptions. Fourthly, a Christian will come to understand that without Christ he can do nothing in the overcoming and wrestling against his temptations. What is it that makes so many of us have such a good opinion of our own hearts? We do not often wrestle against our temptations and corruptions; for if we did, we would change our very thoughts about our hearts.

3. A person who wrestles with the devil and his temptations meets with much divine communion and fellowship with God; he is often taken into the chambers of God's presence, where he is fed with the finest wheat and honey from the rock, and is satisfied. This is clear from Revelation 2:17, which says, "To him that overcometh"—that is, to him who is in the way of overcoming and taken up in wrestling—"will I give to eat of the hidden manna," which is nothing else but the hidden, immediate, sweet consolations that flow from Christ. Do you know why there is

a veil drawn between the face of Christ and us? Do you know why Christians must often walk in their dole weed and mourning apparel because of their absence from Christ? They do not often wrestle with their corruptions and resist the temptations of the devil. If every one of us who has the hope of heaven were asked, "When did you last see Christ?" we might answer, "I know not the time, or else I question much if ever I saw Him." Do you know when Christ visits His own? It is when they are in the heat of war, taken up in vigorous persecution of their idols.

4. It is an excellent way for a Christian to have peace of conscience and quietness under every lot and dispensation that he encounters. What will quiet a Christian's conscience so much as this—he has been resisting his temptations and buckling with his corruptions?

5. A person who resists and wrestles against the devil and the corruptions of his own heart is the person who receives intimation of his peace from God. Do you know why Christians are not living within sight of these words: "I am my beloved's, and my beloved is mine" (Song 6:3)? Do you know why a Christian is not admitted every morning to take a view of heaven and cry out, "Yonder is my inheritance, and yonder is my hope"? Do you know why a Christian is not admitted to daily embrace Christ in the promise and cry out, "He is mine, and shall be eternally so"? We do not often contend with our lusts and idols. This is clear from Revelation 2:17, where this is promised to the one who is in the way of overcoming: I will "give him a white stone, and in the stone a new name written, which no man knoweth saving he that receiveth it." By the white stone and the new name, we conceive is understood adoption and the intimation of it to the soul; the white stone is the sign of absolution and the new name the sign of adoption, intimated by the Spirit of the Lord. Some complain of their darkness and desire nothing so much as to be clear concerning their state and right to heaven; to such I say, be obedient to this text, and "resist the devil."

6. A great danger awaits those who do not resist the devil. There are five cardinal hazards that await those who are not concerned with resisting the devil.

First, if you do not resist the devil and his temptations, the devil shall surely be your conqueror for all eternity. You must either resist him now or he will overcome you and tread you eternally under his feet. Now, do you not think that is a notable danger? Oh, what do you think it will be to be eternally the prisoners of the devil? Yes, you will pass under the name of servants and slaves. Be sure of it, those who do not resist the devil shall be his slaves for evermore. We read in 2 Peter 2:19, "While they promise them liberty, they themselves are the servants of corruption: for of whom a man is overcome, of the same is he brought in bondage." This verse speaks of the victory of our corruptions; if they shall overcome us, they shall keep us in bondage and eternal slavery. Now, as you do not desire to be the slaves of the devil, I say, "Resist the devil"; for the day is drawing near when all the persons who would not strike a stroke against the devil and his temptations shall be brought out of the everlasting pit with the chains about their neck. They shall have that sentence passed against them, "I never knew you: depart from me, ye that work iniquity" (Matt. 7:23).

A second hazard is that he who will not resist the devil shall be the eternal enemy of God. It is certain that he who will not resist the devil is resisting God and the Spirit of God; therefore, this is the day we make intimation unto you—either you must make the devil your enemy or God your enemy; but it is too hard for you to kick against the pricks. If all the persons that are among us who are not fighting against the devil were asked to leave, we would have a small assembly. Yes, you must either have the devil or God for your enemy. I know there is not a person here who will not say, "I hope never to strike a stroke against God." I am afraid that there are many here who, by all appearances, shall die as enemies of God. Oh, will you consider what it means to state yourselves to be in enmity against heaven?

Third, you who do not resist the devil and his temptations, you shall be eternally shut out from communion with God. You may be as sure of this as the light shines. Every person that shall go to heaven has begun and perfected this blessed work of resisting the devil and his temptations. Heaven is at stake, and if you do not fight for the crown, you shall never have it.

The fourth danger you encounter if you do not resist the devil, is eternal separation from God. You shall be eternally separated from God, the Judge of all, and from Christ, the Mediator of the new covenant. You shall be separated from the innumerable company of angels and from the general assembly of the firstborn; and you will certainly meet with a sentence of everlasting exile from the presence of the Lord if you do not resist your lusts and corruptions.

There is a final danger that awaits the person who does not wrestle with his lusts and idols: if none of these things befall you, but you are a Christian indeed, yet you continue to omit this duty, you will break your peace, break your fellowship, weaken your graces, or be halt on your way to heaven. All of these are disadvantages that await a true Christian who does not resist the temptations of the devil. To propose considerations to hearts to engage in this blessed fight is no more effective than writing upon the sand or trying to plough upon a rock.

Before I continue in the study of this text, I charge you by all the mercies that are in Christ Jesus, by the boundless compassions that are lodging in the heart of precious Christ, by all the joys in heaven, by all the terrors in hell, and by the love you owe to your immortal souls, as you would not prove yourselves enemies to God and to His Son Jesus Christ, that today you would resolve and engage your hearts to resist the devil and his temptations. You must take on this excellent bond; God forbid that I should be a friend with my lusts so active as they have been.

A second thing I shall discuss at this time is eight excellent helps by which you may be enabled to wrestle with, yes, even to overcome the devil and his temptations. When the blast of the terrible one is as a storm against the wall, and when the devil is standing at your right hand, do you know the best way to overcome? At this point, I desire that you may so march up, and as it were, thus order yourselves in opposing this enemy.

1. Let this excellent grace of faith lead the way to all the graces of the Spirit, and the spiritual army that marches against this prince of darkness. Let faith be Christ's lieutenant general, marching just at His back, with Christ always coming in front. Let faith buckle with the devil and

his temptations. Do you not know the words of Ephesians 6:16: "Above all, taking the shield of faith, wherewith ye shall be able to quench all the fiery darts of the wicked," and the words of 1 John 5:4: "For whatsoever is born of God overcometh the world: and this is the victory that overcometh the world, even our faith"? Faith never turns its back upon a temptation; faith is a beaten soldier that knows how to buckle with the devil in his strongest assaults. Many other graces will be crying, "Surrender!" but faith will cry, "Stay a little and hope in God, for He will help you." The best way is to buckle faith and your temptations together.

Yet, one may ask, "How can faith defeat the devil and his temptations?" First, faith reveals the beauty of Christ, which makes a Christian have a strong enmity to his idols. No idol can present itself to such a Christian, but the beauty of it is darkened and obscured with the transcendent loveliness in the face of Christ. Faith says never to take another object for your love but Christ, for you shall never find His match. Secondly, faith takes hold of the strength of Christ and uses that strength in battle. Faith can do nothing with its own strength; the strength of faith lies in Christ. Thirdly, faith exercises itself upon the promises; those promises convey spiritual life and strength, by which Christians are made more than conquerors. To conclude this point, I will only say, though all the graces of the Spirit may be engaged in this blessed fight, if faith is missing, there will be a great void.

2. That which marches next to faith is watchfulness. Faith may grow presumptuous if watchfulness is not with it; let therefore watchfulness be engaged so that you do not take up the motions of the enemy. "Watch and pray, that ye enter not into temptation: the spirit indeed is willing, but the flesh is weak" (Matt. 26:41); it is not said, "Lest temptation enter into you," but, "Lest you enter into temptation." This tells us that we often enter into temptation before temptations enter into us. In 1 Peter 5:8, among the rest of the things that he requires for an effective resisting of the devil, Peter tells us that we must be "sober, be

vigilant; because your adversary the devil, as a roaring lion, walketh about, seeking whom he may devour." If you desire to enter this excellent war, you must be watchful, taking a circumspect look of the motions of your own heart, as well as the motions of the enemy.

3. Third, we must be aware of the excellent grace of prayer. Sometimes faith will begin to faint, watchfulness will begin to sleep, hope will begin to languish, and prayer will go up to Him who is the Captain of salvation to cry for help. Prayer is the messenger of the soul that goes up to Christ to seek strength; therefore, let prayer be kept in exercise for overcoming your temptations. "Praying always with all prayer and supplication in the Spirit, and watching thereunto with all perseverance and supplication for all saints" (Eph. 6:18); this is one piece of a Christian's spiritual armor by which a Christian must be helped to withstand all the temptations of the devil. Likewise, "Watch and pray, that ye enter not into temptation: the spirit indeed is willing, but the flesh is weak" (Matt. 26:41). A Christian will not overcome, nor can he have much victory over his idols, except he be a praying Christian.

4. Another help to overcoming temptations is for a Christian to live within sight of the dreadful power of God. Once a soul begins to embrace its temptations, then he shall make omnipotent God his enemy, and that he must not do. It was the dread of God that kept Job in awe; when speaking of the things that kept him from embracing his temptations, Job says, "For destruction from God was a terror to me, and by reason of his highness I could not endure" (Job 31:23). The dread of God kept him from committing sin and posting in the way of iniquity. I would only have the soul, when it is tempted to commit such a sin, say unto the temptation, "Do we provoke the Lord to jealousy? Are we stronger than he?" (1 Cor. 10:22).

5. The faith of the omniscience of God is an excellent help to keep a Christian from committing sin. This is clear when comparing Job 31:1 to verse 6. Therefore, Christians, as you desire to be helped in the fight with your temptations,

consider the omniscience of God whose eyes are as a flame of fire; He sees how you behave yourselves.

6. Also, endeavor always to live near God. If you desire to effectually oppose and wrestle with your temptations, then be never outside of the sight of God. We see this truth when we compare the words of the text with the following words. First we read, "Resist the devil," and then he subjoins, "Draw nigh to God." It is as if he had said, "You who did not walk near to God, nor entertained much communion and fellowship with Him, it is impossible for you to observe your temptations." There is a twofold nearness between the soul and God; that is, nearness with respect to a Christian's state and frame. Now, when we present nearness to God as an effectual help to resist the devil, we do not only mean nearness to God in respect of state, but also nearness to God respecting frame; thus, the frame of your spirit may breathe forth that which is indeed your case. For it is most certain that when a Christian's mindset is far from God, his spirit is not near unto God.

7. Resist temptations by endeavoring in all things, and above all things, moderation in the things of the world. Nothing gives the devil so much advantage, and makes him so often a conqueror, as our ardent and earnest pursuit after the things of the world. This is clear from 1 Corinthians 9:25 and from 1 Peter 5:8, where sobriety is proposed as an excellent piece of armor by which we may be helped to oppose the devil and his temptations.

8. You may also be helped to wrestle with your temptations and corruptions by endeavoring to crush your temptations at their first assault, and to crush your lusts in the very bud. Study, by all means, to crush temptation's first assault. When your sin is in the very bud, you must subject it unto the obedience of Christ. Resist the very beginnings of evil, for then your corruptions will be most easily subdued.

Third, let us discuss five false principles that lead folk to resist their temptations; these principles shall not be approved by God. Before I speak of them, I would have you know that a hypocrite, and one that shall never get heaven, may resist his temptations; yet his resistance shall not be approved by God.

1. The first false principle that leads many to resist their temptations is this: resist the temptations of the devil to keep the natural conscience quiet. In this case, when a temptation affronts them, they stand and oppose it, not so much because it is a sin, but because the doing of it would break the peace of their natural conscience. The hypocrite would rather be at peace with his conscience than be at peace with God. Now, if this is the principle that leads you to resist your temptations, I say, a person that is a stranger to God may even go that far. The preservation of the peace of his natural conscience may lead him to resist the devil and his temptations.

2. Some persons resist their temptations because they fear that if such a sin were done, it would come to light. For instance, a person may be tempted, but he does not dare to embrace the offer; what hinders him? He fears if he embraces the temptation, it will come to light. He does not hate the sin, but the knowledge of the sin. If he were sure the world would never know about it, he would be very slow to deny his soul the pleasure such a temptation affords. Does this not often hinder some from embracing their temptations? They fear that if they do it, the world shall discover it.

3. Some wrestle with their temptations; they fear that if they embrace the temptation, the sin will break forth, and they will lose their name and credit. However, I fear that this hinders many professors from embracing their temptations, not so much because they hate the sin but because they fear that if they embrace it, it will come to light, they will be reproached, and be made the object of the discourse of many. Some would rather lose their soul than lose their name; this is a damnable religion. I confess, a Christian ought to keep his name and his garments without spot; but if you resist temptations because you fear that the sin will come to light and that you will lose your name and respect among the saints, your principle shall never hold its feet.

4. Some resist temptations because they oppose their predominant idols and stand against them; however, they do so not because they are sins, but because they stand in opposition to their predominant idols. For instance, a prodigal man can resist the temptations that are against his predominant idol; a covetous man can resist the temptations that seem to cross his idol. When a covetous man meets with a temptation to prodigality, he may fight that temptation—why? Because it seems to be an enemy to his great idol and predominant lust. To make this clear, consider this: a proud man who loves the applause of the world will resist temptations to many outward acts of iniquity; however, he does not hate the sin, but he has no will to crush and oppose his predominant idol.

5. Many oppose their temptations because they are exceedingly gross. Now this, in some cases, is a lawful principle; yet, to make it a sole principle of resisting temptations is most unsound. Some persons will embrace temptations, thinking, "This is but a Zoar, a small thing"; but when they meet with gross temptations, their natural conscience stands, and they will not embrace it.

I shall conclude our discourse at this time. I suppose that there are many of us who may question whether or not we were ever secretly engaged in this blessed war of contending and fighting against our lusts and idols. I need not point out the reason why many persons do not resist the devil and his temptations. I think that in short, there are strong lusts within that keep a correspondence and harmony with strong temptations from without. I will give you three thoughts, in closing.

First, be persuaded that you must either be the ruin of your iniquities, or your iniquities will certainly be the ruin of you. Secondly, you must wrestle and resolve to overcome the devil's temptations, or you must resolve eternally to be the devil's servant, for there is no middle ground between these two. Either you must be a conqueror or be conquered. Thirdly, you must either resolve to be a friend of God or resolve to be His enemy, for there is no compromise between these two. Either you must be a friend to God and an enemy to the devil, or a friend of the devil and an enemy of God. I fear that most of us shall be enemies of God if He does not prevent it; shall not that be a dreadful word to be written upon our graves: "Here lies one who spent fifty years in fighting against God; and here lies another who spent eighty years in fighting against God"? Shall it not be a dreadful amazement in the great and notable day of the Lord, that you have spent so much of your time fighting against heaven and against God? Oh, will you take His advice? Let the weapons of your rebellion fall out of your hand and cry for quarters from God. If you have been fighting against God, you may now let your weapons fall out of your hands and cry out, "If I have done iniquity, I will do so no more!" Believe it, God is willing, and He waits to be reconciled to you, if you will be content to take and embrace Him.

Now, to Him who is able to help us to resist the devil, that so he will flee from us, we desire to give praise. Amen.

SERMON 46

Strangers Called to Behold Christ (1)

I said, Behold me, behold me, unto a nation that was not called by my name.
—Isaiah 65:1

Would you like to know what is the exercise of the saints above? They are giving obedience unto the command of the Lord: "Behold me, behold me." There is not an eye in heaven that is not beholding and contemplating Him who sits upon the throne, the Lamb, forever and ever.

The text that we have read is one of the greatest mysteries that exist. Is it not a mystery that we should be invited to behold one who is invisible? Who can resolve such a mystery? But, oh, to behold Him and touch Him, who calls us to behold and draw near unto Him! If we would attain a satisfying look of Christ, we would be content to depart and be gone from this world. Believers and expectants of the crown, are you not longing to be away, so that you may have these precious, immediate, and uninterrupted sights of Christ? If that were possible, you would take the hourglass of time, shake it, and cry out, "Oh, time, flee away!" Is there this desire among you? Do you cry out, "Oh, when shall my night be gone, and all my shadows flee away? When shall I enter in through the blessed gates and walk upon the streets that are paved with gold?" Old men, are you longing to have the immediate light of Christ? You who are nearest eternity, are you longing to be carried home? Old women, are you longing for the immediate sight of God? Young men and maids, do you long for the day when you shall be above all these veils that are between us and Christ? Then you shall take Him in your arms and cry out, "He is mine, He is mine!" Oh, the draughts of love that are among the saints above! May we not say, "Oh, time, haste and flee away!" I am sure that if you knew Him, you would count the hours and days of your time; you would desire Him to rend these clouds and cry out, "Arise, my love, my fair one, and come away" (Song 2:13). Do you know why it is said of those around the throne, that they are full of eyes within and without, but they are not said to be full of tongues? I think that the saints round about the throne are more taken up in looking than in speaking; they are taken more up in admiration than expressing their thoughts of God. Each one of you must ask yourself, "Oh, am I longing to be gone and have the sight of Christ that shall never have an end?" Believe it, there is no wearying in heaven.

But, let us look more closely at the words of our text: believe it dear Christian, Christ's heart is with them who fear Him, and they are perfumed with love. You may find two things in those who fear Christ.

First, you have the excellent desire that Christ presents to sinners; He says, "Behold me, behold me" (Isa. 65:1). He desires no more from you but that you give Him one look. Do you think this is a poor desire? Yes, it is both the poorest and richest desire Christ has to present to you. Oh, Glasgow! Do you desire to satisfy Christ? Then, I say, behold Him! Old men in Glasgow, would you like to satisfy Christ? Then, you must behold Him. Young men and maids, would you like to satisfy Christ? Give the Son of God one look before you go away. Do you resolve to give Christ a look before He goes? Believe it, once we see Him, we will never part with Him. I cannot tell you what He is, neither do I think that angels could tell you what He is. Oh, come and see for yourself; that will best resolve the mystery.

Second, in the words, you see these considerations by which He presses home this desire and command upon you who are here.

1. The first thing we must consider is the word *Me*: "Behold me." This consideration is taken from the excellence of the object that we are invited to behold. It is as if Christ should say, "Behold transcendent *Me*, behold spotless *Me*, behold beautiful *Me*, behold dying *Me*, behold compassionate *Me*, behold glorified *Me*." Yes, I think all the rhetoric and oratory of heaven is comprehended in that word— *Me*. Yet, will you not take a sight of this precious and excellent object?

2. The second consideration is that Christ is exceedingly serious with you this day. Oh, Glasgow! His seriousness is pointed out as He doubles and repeats this command, "Behold me, behold me." It is as if He should say, "Behold me; and, if that will not serve you, I will even say it over again, *Behold me.* I have such love for you that I truly desire you to obey." Believe it, Christ is serious with you; cursed be the person who will not be serious with Christ.

3. The third consideration in the words to press home this command is that Christ has interposed much of His authority for bringing you to the obedience of this command; therefore, He sets this preface before it: "I said, Behold me, behold me." It is as if He had said, "Omnipotent I said, *Behold me*. I, who cannot be resisted said, *Behold me*; I, who will in no ways acquit the guilty said, *Behold me*; I, who will tread in the winepress of my fury all those who do not value this command said, *Behold me, behold me*." Oh, blessed are we to hear this blessed sentence that proceeded out of the mouth of Christ: "Behold me, behold me!" Now, will you not stir up yourselves to obey? Do you not think that this is a most excellent command? What word of Christ will relish your heart?

4. A fourth consideration is taken from the freedom of this offer; for the offer is given to persons who were not "called by his name."

5. The fifth consideration from the words is that there is strength covenanted for those who resolve and endeavor obedience to this command of beholding Christ. Are there any persons within these doors who resolve, before they go home, that they shall get a sight of Christ? I say, there is power covenanted for you; you shall get a sight of Him. Do you not know the words of Ecclesiastes 8:4, "Where the word of a king is, there is power"? The word of the king is here; therefore there *is* power. I have this word to say unto you; in fact, if this were my last word, I would say this unto you: Christ is serious with you, but you do not know how long He will be so. Therefore, I beg you, by all the blessings of the everlasting covenant, be serious

> with Him. If we could preach the heart of Christ as it is, I think we could persuade even stones to love Him; but know that we cannot commend Him half enough.

Oh, precious Christ, commend Thyself, for we cannot commend Thee aright. I think that if we do not commend Christ, if He were to come here Himself, He would not commend Himself. We undervalue the offers of Christ; it is as if He were here Himself, entreating you to behold Him, and you say unto Him personally, "We will have none of Thee." Now, we say to Him, "Persuade this people that Thou art serious." Christ is precious company; will you take a sight of Him?

Last, let us consider the command given to "a nation that was not called" by his name; that is, to a people who neither knew Christ by name nor surname. These are the persons who are invited to take Christ; I say to you, whoever you are, even the greatest adulterer within this house, I charge you in His name to behold Him. Before we speak to any of these things fully, let us consider two questions.

First, what is meant by "beholding Christ"? We conceive that beholding Christ is understood to be nothing else but faith; and there are three grounds why faith is called "beholding Christ."

1. Faith is a thing that may be exercised on Christ at a distance; therefore, faith is called beholding. You know that a person may look at a thing far off before he comes to take hold of it; so a Christian, when he cannot get a grip of Christ, may still get a look of Him. When Christ departs, cast a greedy eye upon Him; that is the best way to bring Him home.

2. Faith is also called beholding because the discoveries of faith and of Christ are as certain and sure as the discoveries of sense. Every word that faith says of Christ is as certain and sure as if you had seen it.

3. Faith is the grace that has sense waiting upon it; sense is the excellent and inseparable companion of faith. For that cause, faith is called a beholding of Christ.

The second question concerning the text is this: what is the reason that Christ doubles this command, saying, "Behold me, behold me"? Might not one word have served? No, I say, we are so desperately wicked that a thousand words will not serve the turn; though Christ should cry unto you until the breaking of the next day, there are hundreds here who would not give Christ a look! There are several reasons why Christ here doubles His command.

1. The first reason He doubles the command is to point out that a Christian should not be satisfied with one look of Christ; therefore He cries, "Behold me"; and when you have done that, you must even then take another look. He desires you to give Him a look and then another look.

2. He doubles the command to point out the cursed frame that is among many. We are content too soon with the looks we get of Christ; some of us are content with half a look of Christ. Christ says that we must not be content until we get two full and broad looks of Him.

3. Christ uses two commands to point out the unwillingness of the greatest part of gospel-hearers to give Christ one look. Christ is, as it were, constrained to cry out unto you twice, "Behold me, behold me!" Yes, we may as soon persuade the stones of the wall to look unto Christ as persuade some of you to do so. When we cry unto you to give Christ a "behold," the devil stands at your elbow, crying, "Oh, give *me* a behold!" Oh, that you would obey Christ as quickly as you obey the devil's desire. Now I entreat you to ask yourselves, "Shall I go away and not get a *behold* of Christ? Shall I not get one look of Him?"

4. Christ doubles the command to point out Christ's exceeding seriousness and earnestness in this thing. We must behold Him! Know it, oh Glasgow, Christ is not complimenting with you; therefore He says, "Behold me! behold me!" Old men, do you think that Christ is complimenting with you? I charge you, old men, know and believe that Christ is not complimenting with you. If you will not believe and obey this precious saying, you shall one day obey that terrible command, "I never knew you: depart from me, ye that work iniquity" (Matt. 7:23).

5. Christ doubles this command to point out the excellent advantages that lie in the duty of beholding Christ. Christ says, "Oh! Take a look at Me. Yes, again, take a look at

> Me; I cannot tell what advantage lies unto you in this." I entreat you, dear friends, what do you think you will do before the half hour is over? Are you resolved to obey this command? Oh, sleepers, awake and study to obey this command. I would say this to you, oh Glasgow, if you disobey this command today, I defy all the ministers of Scotland to assure you that you shall meet with another "behold." Therefore, do not harden your hearts in this day, as in the provocation; since Christ entreats you to behold Him, I entreat you, do not close your own eyes.

Let me make one proposal regarding this exhortation. It is the duty of all those that hear this excellent gospel, to whom the glad tidings of salvation are preached, to behold Christ. This is clear, as Christ urges this home with a twofold command, "Behold me, behold me." It is also clear from Song of Solomon 3:11, where we read, "Go forth, O ye daughters of Zion, and behold king Solomon." I shall turn over this command and say unto you, "Go forth, oh daughters of Glasgow, and behold the greater King Solomon." This is Christ's command to you today. You must go forth and behold Him. It is clear in Isaiah 42:1, where we read, "Behold my servant, whom I uphold." Also, in John 20:27, the same is pressed upon Thomas. To the end that this may be pressed home upon your consciences, I shall propose eight considerations.

First, it is His command that we should look unto Him; therefore, I say, behold Him. Where the commandment of the king is, there is power, no doubt, to revenge them that disobey Him. Listen to Ecclesiastes 8:2: "I counsel thee to keep the king's commandment, and that in regard of the oath of God." This is the commandment of the great King, that you should give Christ one "behold." Who will refuse Him? Oh, that we could make a covenant with our eyes, that we might never look upon another object but Christ. I would give you that counsel which Abimelech gave unto Sarah in another sense: let Christ be the covering of your eyes among all you meet. Is this not a pressing consideration, as it is Christ's command? Oh, will you take this excellent command and kiss it, and then send it home again?

A second consideration to press you to look unto Christ is that you shall get salvation for a look. Is there a person here that desires freedom from the wrath of God? If you would have it, give Christ one "behold." Is not salvation offered unto you at an easy rate? Give Christ but one "behold," and you shall get salvation. Christ says in Isaiah 45:22, "Look unto me, and be ye saved, all the ends of the earth." The gospel—the eternal, full, complete, ravishing, transcendent salvation—is offered unto you for one look. Oh, Christian, do you desire to have all the purchase of the death of Christ? Then come and take but one look of Him, and you will have it. I am sure that it is an easy market; you shall get all the wares of the everlasting gospel for a look.

I shall yet go a little lower; you shall get salvation for half a look. Is there a person here that cannot look unto Christ with both his eyes? I say, look unto Christ with one of your eyes, and you shall get salvation. Listen to Song of Solomon 4:9: "Thou hast ravished my heart, my sister, my spouse; thou hast ravished my heart with one of thine eyes, with one chain of thy neck." I say unto every person, will you give Christ but half a look? You shall get all the riches of the everlasting covenant. I charge you, as in His sight, you must not despise His offers.

Third, if you could pray and weep for forty years, if you could make your eyes dim with weeping and your knees weak with fasting, if you had been at all the communions that ever were in Scotland, and if you could be at all the fasts, preachings, and meetings in Scotland, it would be for no purpose if you do not give Christ one look. Your forty years weeping and praying shall be but the aggravation of your punishment if you do not give Christ a look. Therefore, this may provoke you to give Christ a look; for whatsoever is not of faith is sin. All the actions of those who are out of Christ are abominations.

A fourth consideration to press you to look to Christ is that there are many sad disadvantages that attend those who will not look unto Christ and behold the Son of God. Oh, every curse written within the book of the covenant (and there are many broad and everlasting curses in it), from the first of Genesis to the end of the Revelation, shall come upon the head of the person who will not behold the Son of God. Oh, what will you do when Christ shall begin to read the curses in Leviticus 26 or Deuteronomy 27 and 28: "Cursed be he that confirmeth not all the words of this law to do them. And all the people shall say, Amen" (Deut. 27:26)? I ask you, what will you do when Christ shall be sitting upon the throne and shall judge and say, "Cursed shall be the undervaluers of Me"? There shall be a saint on His right hand, in that blessed congregation that shall say, "Amen." Oh, friends, consider this!

Do you desire to have heaven upon earth? Then, behold Christ! For what is heaven? Is it not the beholding of Christ? If you desire a heaven upon earth, then give obedience unto this command, "Behold Christ." Oh, know it for a certainty; there is not an unbeliever here who shall not give Christ one look. You shall get one look of Christ, all you who are here. Yes, even you who are strangers to Christ shall get one look of Christ, and then you shall wish that you were blind and did not see Him. In that day when He shall sit upon the white throne, you shall lift up your eyes and see Him whom you have pierced. You shall then cry out, "Oh, that I had no eyes to see Him whom I have pierced so often!" The greatest unbeliever here shall get one sight of Christ. But, oh, pass not beyond death without taking a look of Him.

Sixth, you must look to Christ because of all the exercise of a Christian, none has so great advantage waiting upon it as looking to the Son of God. I shall name seven advantages that await those who look to Christ.

> 1. The first advantage of beholding of Christ is that it is the most excellent way to increase the grace of love. Oh, Christian who is crying, "How shall I get my love increased?" I say, give Christ a look. It would make your love burn as a fire if you would only take a broad sight of Christ. "At that day shall a man look to his Maker, and his eyes shall have respect to the Holy One of Israel" (Isa. 17:7). When you look unto Christ, your heart shall follow your eye, and your eye shall affect your heart. Oh, if only this were Glasgow's day of looking to its Maker! Perhaps this is your last day of looking to your Maker! Oh, will you be provoked, as you desire to have the excellent grace of love increased, to give Christ one look? Oh, shall Christ be here, and shall there be none of us who will take one look at Him? I pray you to consider it. Oh Glasgow! What if Christ shall report this in heaven? "I came to two great congregations under one roof in Glasgow, and there was none that would behold Me." I charge you, give Him one look. Old men, will you behold

Him? Did you never desire to see a wonderful sight? Oh, come and take a sight of the Son of God.

2. The second advantage that awaits those who look unto Christ is that it is the most excellent way to promote the mortification of our idols. A compendious way to mortify your lusts is to give Christ one look. This is clear in Isaiah 17: "At that day shall a man look to his Maker," (v. 7) "and he shall not look to the altars, the work of his hands, neither shall respect that which his fingers have made, either the groves, or the images" (v. 8). Once you have a sight of spotless Christ you will cry out, "What have I to do any more with idols?" (Hos. 14:8). Paul says, "While we look not at the things which are seen, but at the things which are not seen: for the things which are seen are temporal; but the things which are not seen are eternal" (2 Cor. 4:18). What ails you, Paul? May you not take a sight of the world? "No," says he, "I look for better things that are not seen." The looking unto an unseen Christ made him forget to look to the transient vanities of the world. Is there a person here that is complaining that he cannot get victory over his idols? Give Christ one "behold," and you shall have victory.

3. A third advantage that accompanies beholding Christ is that it is the most compendious way to win to repentance. Impenitent Glasgow, I think we are indeed a generation of impenitent people. Do you desire repentance? Then give Christ one "behold." In Job 42:5-6, we read, "I have heard of thee by the hearing of the ear: but now mine eye seeth thee. Wherefore I abhor myself, and repent in dust and ashes." The first sight that I got of God made me repent, sit down in the dust, and abhor myself. "And they shall look upon me whom they have pierced, and they shall mourn for him, as one mourneth for his only son, and shall be in bitterness for him, as one that is in bitterness for his firstborn" (Zech. 12:10). I think if we were looking to Christ at this time, there would not be a person within these doors who would not be weeping for Him whom they have pierced. I charge you, if you desire repentance,

then look to Christ. One look at Christ would make our frozen hearts melt; one look at Him would make all our bonds break; one look of Him would break all the bars on our doors that hinder us from repenting. Do you desire repentance? Then give Christ a look—"behold him."

4. If you look to Christ, you will have a victory over the grand idol of pride. Are there any persons here who are complaining that they do not have low thoughts of themselves? I say to such, give Christ a look. "Mine eyes have seen the King, the LORD of hosts," we read in Isaiah 6:5; and what of that? The response: "I am a man of unclean lips." In Job 42:5-6, we read, "I have heard of thee by the hearing of the ear: but now mine eye seeth thee. Wherefore I abhor myself, and repent in dust and ashes." We read further in Job 7:8, "The eye of him that hath seen me shall see me no more: thine eyes are upon me, and I am not." Just one sight of Him who is invisible would cause us to make our dwelling place in the dust, and never to have high thoughts of ourselves any more!

5. After beholding Christ, you would recover from your apostasy and desertion from God. Are there not many Christians who lament, "Oh, to be as in the days of old, and as in the months past"? I say to you, give Christ but one look. One look to Christ is as a cord about our necks that draws us home to Him. A look to Christ makes a person cry out, "I never had a good day out of Christ's company, therefore I will return again to Him." One look to Christ will make a Christian forsake his lovers, after whom he has followed, and return again to Him. Do you desire to recover from your apostasy? Then give Christ a look.

6. Beholding Christ is the most excellent way to conquer your discouragements. Is there a person here who is under the feet of discouragement? If you desire to be done with discouragement, then behold Christ. One sight of Christ would make us a city of joy: "They rejoiced when they saw Jesus." Yes, one sight of Him would make us "a city of praise." Is there any person here who would like

to have the garment of praise instead of the garment of heaviness? Then look unto Christ and obey this text.

7. A seventh advantage that attends the beholding of Christ is that it is an excellent way to have steadfastness of spirit. Are there not some persons here who cry out, "I am unstable as water, and that mars my excellence; how shall I attain to a composed way of serving God?" Look unto Christ; that is the way to attain steadfastness. What strange words we find in Psalm 16:8: "I have set the LORD always before me: because he is at my right hand, I shall not be moved." My stability depends upon having God always within sight. If you are not within speaking range of God, oh, be within looking range of Him. Is there a person here that is not within gripping or speaking range of God? Yes, be within looking range of Him; though He is far off, you may take a look at Him.

8. Give Christ a look—that is an excellent way to cultivate tenderness. Peter's heart, in a manner, was like a rock before Christ gave him a look; after looking to Christ, Peter's heart might have melted to water. Oh, tenderness! Where has it gone? What is the reason we are so hardened? It is because we are not much taken up with looking unto Christ. If there is a person here that has gotten a look at Christ, he will be brought to say, "I water my couch with my tears" (Ps. 6:6).

9. Christ is exceedingly earnest and desirous that you would behold Him. What was the first morning salutation to Adam? It was, "Behold me." A look at Christ is both law and gospel; a sight of Christ would be both Mount Sinai and Mount Zion; a sight of Christ would both help us to believe and to obey.

10. The look you get of Christ here is but the forerunner of a more excellent, transcendent, and permanent look at Him hereafter. Any person that has given Christ a look here shall have a satisfying look of Him hereafter! Let us look at nine differences between the look that a Christian has of Christ here upon earth and the look that he shall have of Him in heaven.

First, the look of Christ that a Christian has here is but a look through the veil; but there we shall see Him face to face.

Secondly, the look of Christ that we have here admits of interruption, but the look of Him which we shall have above shall never be interrupted. A Christian will get a look of Christ here, but presently a cloud comes in between and interrupts the enjoyment; but there is no cloud in heaven to interrupt. Blessed is the congregation that stands around the throne, where they never cease to behold Him.

Thirdly, a look that a Christian has of Christ here does not complete his joy and satisfaction, but the look that he shall have above shall fully complete his joy and satisfaction! All the looks a Christian gets of Christ here are rather to provoke his appetite than to satisfy it. Do you desire to know the first day of a Christian's satisfaction? It is in the morning of the resurrection. This is clear, "I will behold thy face in righteousness: I shall be satisfied, when I awake, with thy likeness" (Ps. 17:15). Might one ask, "Oh, David, were you never satisfied? Were you not satisfied when you sung Psalms 63, 147, and 148?" "No," says David, "I shall never be satisfied until the morning of the resurrection."

Fourthly, here a Christian gets a look but of Christ's back parts; but there he shall see face to face. All these excellent sights we have of God here are but a beholding of His back parts; but there we shall see Him face to face.

Fifthly, all the looks of Christ that we have here are but the beholding of the picture of Christ; but there, we shall see Him as He is. There is a great difference between the picture of Christ and the real substance of Him. All the sights of Christ that a Christian has here are only His likeness. In Numbers 12:8, we read of Moses' beholding of God; "The similitude of the LORD shall he behold." Ezekiel, giving account of the sight he saw, says, "It was the appearance of the likeness of the glory of the LORD" (Ezek. 1:28). But there we shall have a sight of a real, discovered Christ.

Sixthly, the look that a Christian gets of Christ here may be abused; but the look that he gets of Him above cannot be abused. Do we not often abuse our looks of Christ through pride? Do we not often abuse our looks of Christ through formality? Do we not often abuse our looks of Him through security? But these looks of Christ that are above cannot be abused; there is no abusing of enjoyments in heaven.

Seventh, all the looks of Christ that a Christian has here do not complete his conformity; but the everlasting and broad immediate look of Christ that a Christian shall have above shall complete his conformity. Our beholding of Christ in a glass makes us to be "changed" in some measure, "from glory to glory" (2 Cor. 3:18), but when we shall have an immediate sight of God, we shall be completely conformed to His image; there shall not be a spot in all our souls.

The eighth difference between them is that all the looks of Christ that a Christian has here never discourage him from saying, "Give, give." This is the language of a Christian; once he shall get a sight of Him above, he shall be forced, in a manner, to cry out, "Hold Thy hand, for I have abundance now." Do you not long to get the looks of Christ that are above?

The last difference between them is that the sight of Christ that we have here does not complete our love; but the sight of Him which we shall have above, shall complete our love. Then hope and faith shall leave us, and light and love shall walk in with us and divide the spoil.

There is this ninth consideration to press you to look to Christ: I entreat you to think about what you will do. Oh, what do you intend to do? Do you intend to let Christ go away, and not give Him one look? Shall it be told in heaven of you, "I came to Glasgow, and Glasgow would not give me one behold"?

Tenth, once you look unto Christ and behold Him, there shall be a knot of marriage made up between you and Him, which all the world shall not be able to untie. Oh, young women, I entreat you, come and give Christ one look; this shall be an eternal and excellent marriage-knot that shall be cast between you and Him. I will tell you five things that may break the nearest and most intimate relations imaginable, but which cannot break this knot of union.

> 1. Many people have very close relations, but cannot the pain of ingratitude break their knots? Two brethren or intimate friends may say, "Will I love an ungrateful friend any more?" But, be you never so ungrateful, it shall never break the knot of union between you and Christ; it may well get you many strokes from Christ, but it will never break the union.

2. The second thing that will break knots of union is sin. It will break the knot of union between man and wife; adultery will break the marriage-knot; but no sin shall break the knot between you and Christ. If you should play the harlot for many hundreds of days, that will not break the knot. Blessed are we in this, that no sin shall break that knot of marriage.

3. Distance of place breaks knots of friendship between persons, but it will never break the bond between Christ and a soul. Once we are long out of sight of a friend, we forget him; but oh, blessed be precious Christ; though He be living in heaven, distance of place does not make Him forget us. Blessed are we in this—distance of place does not break the knot of union with Christ. His heart is in Glasgow, if your hearts would be in heaven.

4. Passions and anger often break the knots of union among persons. Nothing would divide two friends sooner than passion and anger. However, Christ may be angry with you, but He will not break His covenant. Let Him be angry at you, and you at Him, yet it shall not break the marriage-knot. Yes, if you would take both your hands to break it, it should not be broken.

5. Prejudice and jealousy often break a knot of union, but it will not break the union between Christ and you. Is there anything that makes persons more heartless with one another than to have a suspicion and jealousy that such a person does not really love them? But blessed are we in this, for Christ has no jealousy; as for us, He has no suspicion. Though it may even be our desire, we shall never come so far as to break the knot. Although you may even desire to break the knot and scrape your name out of the marriage contract, Christ would say, "You shall not get leave." Many persons that have been married to Christ have been brought to say, "Give me a pen, and I will scrape out my name out of Thy contract." "No," says Christ, "You shall not get leave; it shall stand there." What do you have to say to this? I entreat you to think what

> you shall answer concerning this bargain. Being loathe to leave it without gaining your consent to this excellent bargain, I shall tell you these four things, and I charge you to remember them.

First, remember that you heard this once preached in Glasgow pulpit: "Behold me, behold me." The day is approaching when that verse shall come to your mind, and you shall cry out, "What was I doing that I would not give Christ a look?" Yes, know it of a certainty, that when you shall be passing through the threshold of the doors of your everlasting prison, this text shall come to mind, and you shall lament, "Once I was bidden to look unto Christ, and now where am I going?" You shall then cry with a dreadful lamentation, "Where are undervaluers of Christ now going? Oh, I would never disobey that preaching if I heard it again."

Secondly, all the persons within this church shall be witnesses against one another if they do not embrace Christ. Perhaps you are the person to whom Christ will say, "What was the reason that you would not give Me one look?" I pray, what would you say if Christ would come here tonight and ask every one of us, before we depart, "What is the reason that you would not give Me one look?" I pray you, what would you say? Think of it; what shall you answer unto Christ in that day, when He shall ask you this question?

Thirdly, I would say this: there are two times approaching when you shall cry out, "Oh, for a sermon upon Isaiah chapter 65:1!" Shall not that be a day when you shall cry out, "Oh, for a look of Christ"? You shall be standing near the gates of death and you shall cry out, "Oh, for a command to look unto Christ!" The second time that you will long for these words is when you shall be standing before your judge. I know that a multitude of words will not persuade you. There are four things that I would say unto you; there are four sorts of persons that I fear are within these doors; now the broad and everlasting curse of the eternal God will be upon the person, be he who he will, that is among these four.

> 1. There are some of the Gadarenes among us, who cry out, "Oh, Christ, depart out of our coasts!" Are there not many here who would be content to give Christ a bill of divorce? I say, cursed are you, whosoever you may be.

2. There are a second sort of folk here today who will cry out, "We care for none of these things; you press us to look to Christ, and what of that?" I say, cursed is that person that is of Gallio's frame, who, as much as Christ and the minister will press you, will not give Christ one look. I say to you, be it according to your desire. You shall never get a look of Christ.

3. I think there may be many of Pilate's spirit here today. They cry out, "I know nothing against the man whom you press us to behold." But, at last, you will consent to crucify Him. Oh, even if you know nothing against Christ, you will consent to crucify Him!

4. There will be some here today of an Athenian frame, that will say, "This man feigns to be a setter forth of strange gods." I tell you, I am no setter forth of strange gods; it is Jesus of Nazareth that I preach unto you, oh Glasgow! Unpersuadable Glasgow! Will you not be persuaded to give Christ one look?

Let me tell you one last point to press you to give Christ one "behold." If you would ask all the angels in heaven and all the saints round about the throne, they would all say, "Oh, give Christ one look!" Do not all that are around the throne say that it is good to behold Him? Do not Adam and Eve say that it is good to behold Him? Do not Abel, Enoch, and Noah say that it is good to behold Christ? Do not Abraham, Isaac, and Jacob say that it is good to behold Christ? Do not the twelve patriarchs, the twelve apostles, and all His saints who have tasted of the sweetness of Christ say that it is good to behold Him? Dear friends, ought not our souls to say, and all in us, to cry out, "Oh, it is good to behold Him"?

Now, will you go away without giving your consent? Oh, speechless Glasgow! Can you say, "I am content to take Him"? Oh, speechless and unpersuadable Glasgow, will you once come to say to Him, "I am content"? Though you cannot say it heartily, you shall never rue it. Those words shall afford to you everlasting joy. Some folks will be ashamed to speak their consent to a husband that is suiting them; but will you speak your consent to Christ with a look, if not with your mouth? Christ desires no more but that you would now speak your consent to Him with a look, if not with your mouth.

Christ desires that you would speak your consent to Him in a broad look, if you cannot do it otherwise. Now, are you persuaded?

I shall say no more, but this book will be a witness against you if you do not heed His command. I am sure it is but a poor work, if you will do no more, to give Christ a look. Shall I use any more arguments? Or shall I take it for granted, that you will not give Christ one look? I do not think Christ is to be beheld with bodily eyes; I think you will do this, as if one desired another to behold a pleasant object, which they desire not to behold; they would put their hands upon both their eyes, so that they might not behold. I am afraid that you will do the same with this intimation to behold Christ. If Christ were coming here Himself tonight, you would put both your hands upon your eyes so that you might not behold Him. Now, if this were the last word that I could speak in the name of the Lord, I might say that Glasgow is an unpersuadable and speechless place. Oh, Glasgow, will you not know the things that belong to your peace, and begin a pursuit after the Son of God? I have three things to say unto you, and shall close with these words.

First, though you have undervalued Christ for forty years, He is content now to take you. Old men, you have your names, old undervaluers of the Son of God—will you be content now to take Him? Though you had never given Christ a look before, you are welcome to give Him a look now. Second, nothing on earth would be pleasant to us once we have given Christ a look. Third, dear friends, if Christ goes away, will we be as great strangers to Him as before? Oh, Glasgow, sing the words of Job: "I have heard of thee by the hearing of the ear: but now mine eye seeth thee" (Job 42:5). If you could say that, then you might indeed cry out, "Now I wish I were blind, so that I could never see another sight."

To Him who can anoint your eyes with eye salve, so that you may see Him, we desire to give praise. Amen.

SERMON 47

Strangers Called to Behold Christ (2)

I am sought of them that asked not for me; I am found of them that sought me not: I said, Behold me, behold me, unto a nation that was not called by my name.

—Isaiah 65:1

We told you that Christ was presenting a great desire to you; are there none of you presenting a desire for Christ? I shall tell you two great desires that you should present to Christ.

The first great desire that you ought to present to Him should be these words: "Lord Jesus, help me to receive my sight."

A second great desire that you ought to present to Him is found in Psalm 13:3: "Consider and hear me, O LORD my God: lighten mine eyes, lest I sleep the sleep of death." Let me give you the same advice that Abimelech gave to Sarah; let Christ be to you "a covering of the eyes," with whom you converse (Gen. 20:16). Christ is willing to satisfy all your senses. Will you come and be satisfied? Will you come and have the sense of sight satisfied? Does not Christ invite you in the text, saying, "Behold me"? Would you like to have your sense of tasting satisfied? This is commanded in Psalm 34:8: "O taste and see that the LORD is good: blessed is the man that trusteth in him." Do you desire to have the sense of hearing satisfied? This is His command, in Luke 9:35, where we read, "This is my beloved Son: hear him." Do you desire to have the sense of touch satisfied? Is this not His great command to Thomas? He says, "Reach hither thy finger, and behold my hands; and reach hither thy hand, and thrust it into my side: and be not faithless, but believing" (John 20:27). Would you like to have your sense of smell satisfied? Come to Him who is "perfumed with myrrh and frankincense, with all powders of the merchant" (Song 3:6).

I am afraid that most of us shall die as strangers of Christ. I think if we would ask the angels, "Who is Christ?" they would say that they could not tell. The saints around the throne and all who have tasted of the sweetness of Christ would say the same. If we were to ask all of them what His sweetness is worth, they would say that they could not tell. If you were to ask about the depth of Christ, as in Job 28:14, the response would be that the price of Christ "is not in me." Yea, all the gold that lies in the bowels of the earth could not buy Christ. With what then could you buy Him? I tell you, friend, with one look you shall get Christ.

Now, in the forenoon, we spoke a little about the first thing in the words, which was the great command given to the Gentiles: "Behold me." Oh, what a wonder that there was ever such a command! What would you think if all that is in this book were framed by these words: "Cursed is every one that continueth not in all things which are written in the book of the law to do them" (Gal. 3:10)? What if all had been like Deuteronomy 28:1 and Leviticus 26? Angels wonder that there ever was such a command; all the saints around the throne wonder, and let all who are here wonder that there ever was such a command.

I have several things to add concerning this command. Let me mention three points.

First, let me point out the difference between the look of Christ that the saints have above, and that which we have below. We are calling you to behold Christ; but they that are in heaven have another look. I shall point out nine differences.

> 1. The first difference is that the look we have of Christ is but a mediate look; but that which the saints have above is immediate. Here we behold Him through the veil—through the dark veil of duties, ordinances, promises, and dispensations. Oh, but above we shall have an immediate look; there, nothing shall intervene between Christ and the soul. There shall be an immediate embrace of the Son of God. These that have seen Him through the veil will be longing for the time when they shall have these immediate looks of Him, when all the veils between them and Christ shall be rent from top to bottom. Are you not longing for the day when you shall behold Him in glory?

2. The look we have here is easily interrupted. The look that we will have above shall have no interruption in it. There is neither cloud, nor night, nor desertion there. There are no such complaints in heaven as, "Why hidest thou thy face from me?" (Ps. 88:14). We shall not hear, "It is thirty days since I did behold the king, and I have lived two years in Jerusalem, and have not seen the king's face." Oh, that look that shall admit of no interruption! It is an endless look that the saints shall have above. Do you not think that our looks to Christ should make us long for that day?

3. Third, the look which we have here may be abused; but that which is above cannot. Here a Christian may abuse his look to Christ through the pride of life. Oh, there is no abusing of that spotless look that we will get of Christ above.

4. The look which we have here is but a beholding of His back parts; but there, we shall behold His face. Here we see only the skirts of His garments, but there we shall see Him face to face. There is a great difference between the two.

5. The look which the Christian has here does not complete his joy. As long as he is here, the Christian spends his life in bitterness. Do you know the first day that a Christian has true, complete joy? It is on the blessed morning of the resurrection. Oh, what joy the Christian shall have when Christ and he meet together, and He takes the Christian in His arms and says, "Welcome, friend!" On that day, Christ and he shall meet together in the streets of the new Jerusalem.

6. The look which the Christian has here does not complete his conformity to Christ; but the look we have above does abundantly complete our conformity to Him! Do you know the words of 1 John 3:2, which say, "Beloved, now are we the sons of God, and it doth not yet appear what we shall be: but we know that, when he shall appear, we shall be like him; for we shall see him as he is"? The look of Him, as He is, makes a complete conformity between Christ and the soul; but all these looks that we have here do not complete our conformity. We must go to heaven

trailing a body of death; but the time approaches when we shall take our everlasting farewell of all our lusts and idols and we shall say, "Farewell," with all our hearts; we shall never meet again.

7. The look of Christ which we have here does not complete our grace; but that which we shall have above shall complete all our graces. Shall not love be complete when we shall get our look of Christ above? Shall not joy be complete? Then that which is in part shall be done away, when that which is perfect is come. Oh, Christians! What a day it shall be when faith shall say to love, "I give my place to you," and sight and love shall be the eternal company of the Christian!

8. A Christian's look of Christ here is not perfect in its degrees. When we shall be able to behold Christ and shall fall into a sight of Him, when we shall first see the Lord, we shall begin a song that shall never have an end. It is an endless look, a satisfying look, and a soul-refreshing look. There is no work so much as this in heaven. Do you know what the saints in heaven are doing? They are said to be full of eyes and not of tongues, because they are more taken up with looking than speaking; more in wondering than expressing. Therefore, they are said to have many eyes, but one tongue.

9. Finally, the look of Christ that we have here is only the look of a largely unknown Christ and an unconceived Christ. But then we shall have a look of a known Christ, of a Christ that shall be well taken up and understood. These are the differences between the looks here and the looks that are above. When shall it be that the exercise of heaven and earth shall be one?

I shall, in the next place, proceed to answer some objections of those who think they have never looked to Christ.

Some may object, saying, "I have never looked to Christ because I know not the day, and some folks can tell the time and place when they have looked to Christ."

To such people, I would give this answer:

First, few attain such knowledge. "Whereas I was blind, now I see" (John 9:25). You can say, "Though I know not the time and place, yet, I am sure that these things were hidden from my eyes before." To you, I would say, it may not be for your advantage to know the time. Christ keeps that in His own hand. It is not always for your advantage to know the times. Also, it is not absolutely necessary for a Christian to know the time when Christ and he first met. There are some who have met with Christ, but they do not know the time, the place, or the first discourse that passed between Christ and them. What more do you need to know than that He has stolen away your heart?

Others may object, saying, "I do not know if I looked to Him, for since I began to look to Him, my bonds are strong."

To this person, I would say three things. First, do not cast off your faith because of that, and do not dispute your love. There is nothing more ordinary to a Christian than to have a spirit under bonds, as we see in Hebrews 10:32: "But call to remembrance the former days, in which, after ye were illuminated, ye endured a great fight of afflictions." Second, the best way to conquer these bonds is not to reject your faith, but to hold it fast. It is a poor thing in Christians, whenever they lose their feet, to let their hands go; when they slip into unbelief, they run out of the land of the living. Third, dear friends, comfort yourself, for the day of the liberty of the sons of God is coming. On that day, these bonds shall be taken off you, and it shall be said, "Oh, prisoner! Come out."

A third objection some may have is this: "I do not have Christian light and joy, as I have read of in Psalm 97:11."

Let me respond by saying two things to you. First, your light and joy may be underground until they both appear together. Perhaps Christ is trying the reality of your faith, to see whether you love Him rather than sense or sight. I will tell you what this says for Christians, if when they do not get all they sought for when they began with Christ, they reject all. The reason is that many think more of sense than of Christ; yea, many professors think more of knowledge than of Christ. Secondly, Christ may be teaching you to love Him more by faith than by sense.

Fourth, some may object, saying, "I cannot pray! Each time I go to prayer, my tongue is still."

I would not have you mistake, for there is a threefold silence a Christian may have in prayer; but you may have greater liberty in them than if you spoke like an angel.

First, there are some who, when they are enjoying God most, then their heart is enlarged with love, and prayer is little upon the tongue. Do you imagine that Daniel was straitened when he saw the angel and stood trembling? In Revelation, was John not full of love when he fell at Christ's feet? Do you not know how a Christian, through a sight of Christ in prayer, will cease speaking and wonder? Sometimes a Christian will not be able to express his love for Christ. Also, there may be divine silence when you have a deep impression of God's greatness and your own sinfulness. A Christian is never more enlarged than when he can only say, "Thou holdest mine eyes waking: I am so troubled that I cannot speak" (Ps. 77:4). Thus, when his heart charged him with uncleanness and his tongue could not speak, sometimes his guilt seemed to be staring him in the face, and he was stricken with dumbness and could not speak one word. Sometimes Christians cannot speak their confession to God; they must roar. Sometimes they are so convicted that though one may put a spear through their heart, they could not speak one word. In Psalm 38:8, we read, "I am feeble and sore broken: I have roared by reason of the disquietness of my heart." Thirdly, there may be divine silence when a Christian is going to commend Christ; then he receives such a silent revelation of Christ that he charges himself with presumption, asking, "Shall I speak?" We must never question Christ thus. There is more expression in a moment's wondering than in ten hours of praying. There is, I confess, a silence that proceeds from a spirit of bondage; and I think that a look of Christ is the way to help it. If your tongues speak no more than your heart thinks, your prayers may oftentimes be short prayers. There are some folks' prayers that are nothing but a lying to the Holy Ghost; in their prayers and confessions they lie, and as for their desires, they care no more for them than the dirt under their feet. It is a wonder we are not stricken dead in prayer, both ministers and professors. It is strange that Ananias and Sapphira were stricken dead for one lie, yet we are not, for so many; yea, we may have fifteen lies in one prayer. Will you examine yourselves, oh Christians?

Fifth, one may say in objection, "If I had ever looked to Christ, I would have had some desires to Him"; no doubt, to such persons who are looking for these immediate looks of Christ, I would say these five things:

First, there may be some Christians that may have ten desires for death, but not one desire for heaven. You may desire death more often in ten days than you desire heaven in a month. What is the reason for this? It is not from our hope, but from the cursedness of our heart, as Jonah desired rather to die than to live; he did not desire heaven, but he had corruption in his heart, and was disappointed by God. Second, I would answer such a person thus: one may have forty desires for death, yet not one for the death of sin. You should desire the death of the body of death more. Third, I think that a Christian may long to go away, and so to escape this world. Fourth, I entreat you, dear Christians, when you get a look of Christ, work to improve it. Do you know what makes Christians long so little? It is because they do not improve their looks to Christ. Fifth, it is no wonder that Christians do not long for a look of Christ. Have you ever thought these three thoughts?

1. Have you thought, "Oh, time, time, that passes not away to let eternity come!" Have you ever been content to shake the hourglass of your time to sooner reach eternity? If it were in your own hand, would you not lay it down upon its side, so that it would not run, or would you shake it?

2. Have you ever longed for your light? "Rise up, my love, my fair one, and come away. For, lo, the winter is past, the rain is over and gone" (Song 2:10-11).

3. Were you ever like Sisera's mother, looking out at her windows and saying, "Why is his chariot so long in coming? Why tarry the wheels of his chariots?" (Judg. 5:28) When death comes, will you take it in your arms and say, "Welcome, friend"? Do you know what death is to a Christian? It is the putting off of your burdens, the day of death to all your sorrows, to all your iniquities, to all your idols, and to all your anxieties; it is the door whereby you must enter into eternal good. It is like Joseph's chariot, which was sent to bring Jacob down into Egypt. Where is your heart, Christians? Ought it not to be up in heaven? Where is your faith? Is it not there?

I have but three things to persuade you to give Christ one look.

First, with what will you send me away? Will you send me away with a blank? Oh, that this congregation, that is much destitute of knowledge, would begin this night! For I defy all the ministers of the world to assure you that you shall live to look to Him tomorrow; therefore look to Him today!

Second, do you know for certain that not one of you will break your neck and face Him this day? Perhaps it will be said this night, "Arise, undervaluers of the gospel and of the Son of God, and give an account in judgment." What would you say if that voice were heard this night? Perhaps it will be! Would you look Christ in the face with that countenance? With such a countenance, you would desire that you were ground into pieces.

Third, will you be content to take Him tonight? What further arguments can be used to persuade you? Is there any argument under heaven that can persuade you to take Him? Oh, you despisers and slighters of the Son of God, I charge you, as you must answer one day, to take Him. Beware, lest you shall hear it said of you, "His blood be upon us, and our children." The curses of one side of this book are able to smother ten thousand worlds. What will you think then, when all the curses in this book shall light upon you? Where shall you flee on that day, when all that is in the 28th chapter of Deuteronomy and 26th chapter of Leviticus shall light upon you, and there shall be no redemption? This night, look unto the Son of God.

Is it no matter wherein you trifle over your time? I say, be serious in this day. Old men, what do you say? You are near your graves! "I have set before you life and death, blessing and cursing: therefore choose life, that both thou and thy seed may live" (Deut. 30:19). Will you refuse or choose? It is Christ that is offered to you! Know this, that be what you will, slighters of the gospel, the words of Isaiah 65:1 shall gnaw at your consciences. You will remember this day when you are crying for mercy; you shall cry out, "Where now is the slighter of the gospel? I shall never again have another offer! The day in which I was bidden to take Christ and give Him one look is now over."

Before you go, close the bargain this night. You do not know if Christ shall ever come again to send His message to invite you to take Him. So again, what is your last report? Speak to Him, for these may be His last words to you. Let us therefore be entreated to take Him now. Cursed be the person that will never see Him all their days. It would have been better if such had never heard a word of Him. Oh, shall Christ in His face, and in His beauty, and in all the excellent offers of heaven, be slighted? Now, the day is approaching when you shall wish that you had never been born. Oh, slighters of the great salvation, you shall cry out, "Oh, that I had never been born!" Therefore, I say, seeing that Christ is being offered, take Him, and take instruments in heaven, so that you shall never have another. Old men, will you take instruments of this, that you shall never have another but Christ? Young men and young women, look to the Son of God, and it shall be one of the days of the Son of man to you. Oh, what a beautiful look Christ shall give to His own children when time shall be no more, when they shall be led with the Lamb to the rivers of living waters! Are you all content? Will you say nothing against it? Then if it be so, blessed be he who embraces the Son of God; and cursed be the man or woman who takes Him not. Since you are standing before the mountain of cursing or blessing, I entreat you, look to the Son of God; He is the Serpent who can heal you from all your diseases and iniquities.

Now to Him who can persuade you, and will one day stand to judge you, be praise for evermore. Amen.

SERMON 48

The Necessity and Advantage of Looking unto Jesus[1]

Look unto me, and be ye saved, all the ends of the earth: for I am God, and there is none else.
—Isaiah 45:22

Solomon once said that "truly the light is sweet, and a pleasant thing it is for the eyes to behold the sun" (Eccl. 11:7). It is even lovelier to behold the Sun of righteousness. Yes, the light of the eyes is better than the wandering of desires. The soul may receive two looks—one is at Christ and the other is at ourselves. Once you have looked at Christ, I might give you the same counsel that Sarah received concerning her husband Abraham: "Behold, he is to thee a covering of the eyes" (Gen. 20:16).

We told you that in the duty commanded in our text, there are seven things to notice. First, notice that it is incumbent for all the members of the visible church to look unto Christ for salvation. Second, all persons, when Christ first begins with them, have their eyes turned away from Him and on something else. Third, we ought to look unto Him immediately. Fourth, it is entirely attainable to look unto Christ immediately for salvation. Fifth, faith is a thing that may be exercised on Christ from a distance. Faith is accompanied with a look, and so it can cast an eye to Christ though He be afar off. Sixth, there are some special times and seasons when a Christian ought to look unto Christ for salvation and seek to be saved by Him. Seventh, the revelations that Christ makes of Himself to the soul are as certain as if we had seen Him with our eyes; therefore it is called a

[1] Preached on the Saturday before the communion at Bothwell.

looking. Now, having spoken about the first three of these, we shall now discuss the remaining points.

It is entirely attainable to look unto Christ immediately for salvation. To make this clear for you, I shall first propose these four considerations.

First, we shall consider that Christ is a noble physician who can heal all diseases and plagues that a soul may have. I will tell you of ten heart-plagues; one look at Christ will heal you and set you free from them all.

1. There is the plague of ignorance; this plague causes you to know nothing of God, nor of Jesus Christ. To remedy this plague, you must labor to get a look at Jesus Christ; one look will clear you and cure your ignorance. We read in Isaiah 32:3 that "the eyes of them that see shall not be dim, and the ears of them that hear shall hearken." We also read in Psalm 34:5 that "they looked unto him, and were lightened: and their faces were not ashamed." One broad look of Christ would make the mist of darkness to flee far away. Now, if this is your errand tomorrow, that you may get your eyes opened, I say, one broad look of the Son of God will be your remedy. One look will cure you of the plague of your ignorance.

2. There is the plague of hardness of heart, which plagues many of this generation; one broad look of Christ will heal this plague. When Christ turned and looked upon Peter, he remembered himself, "and wept bitterly" (Luke 22:62). If you could get one look at Christ, He would make your eyes rivers of water and your head a fountain of tears. In Zechariah 12:10, we read, "They shall look upon me whom they have pierced, and they shall mourn for him, as one mourneth for his only son, and shall be in bitterness for him, as one that is in bitterness for his firstborn." Oh, the embracing of a wounded Christ would melt and wound your heart strongly! Oh, that we could weep tears of blood for wounding the Son of God! Believe it, there are many here who have pierced Him; now see that you do not bring a spear with you, to thrust Him through at this time also.

3. The third plague is that of apostasy and defection from God. Have not our hearts been unfaithful to Him in all things? Will anything bring us home again but one broad look at Christ? Then this sore plague will be healed—when Christ will come and stare you in the face, it will make you come home again. Here is a sad apostasy of Peter, an eminent Christian, both from his spiritual light, his experience, and diligence; what cures all of this unfaithfulness? Just one look upon Jesus Christ cures all (Luke 22:61-62). Christians, your light, grace, experience, and diligence are exceedingly decayed; what will heal all this? One look of Christ's face would do it. Oh, for one look of Christ's fair face today!

4. The plague of coldness sickens us. We exercise little love to Christ; but one look at Christ would cure this. We read in Isaiah 17:7, "At that day shall a man look to his Maker, and his eyes shall have respect to the Holy One of Israel." You have low thoughts of Him today; but oh, if you saw Him, you would wonder and cry out, "Is it He? Is this the undervalued, condemned, and crucified Savior?" Yes, a sight of Christ would kindle a glow of love in our hearts to Him that would not be put out again. Cry to Him to heal this plague of coldness.

5. We also suffer from the plague of pride. The fool says, "Oh, if I could get my pride brought low, then I would sit down and bless Him." One look at Him would do this. What happens when Isaiah has seen the Lord? "Mine eyes have seen the King, the LORD of hosts" (Isa. 6:5). He follows saying, "Woe is me! for I am undone; because I am a man of unclean lips, and I dwell in the midst of a people of unclean lips" (v. 5). In Job 7:8 we find the testimony of Job concerning this fact: "The eye of him that hath seen me shall see me no more: thine eyes are upon me, and I am not." Later, in Job 42:5-6, we read, "I have heard of thee by the hearing of the ear: but now mine eye seeth thee," and later, "Wherefore I abhor myself, and repent in dust and ashes." Believe it, the pride of professors is

evidence of their distance from Jesus Christ. Now, labor to look to Him to heal this plague.

6. The plague of impenitence also ails us. The Christian may say, "Oh, how shall I be set free from this, that I may mourn in secret and take up a lamentation for my wrongs done to Jesus Christ? Oh, for a clear sight of Him!" "Mine eye seeth thee, wherefore I abhor myself, and repent in dust and ashes" (Job 42:5). One sight of Christ would make you go through all the ten commandments, and having read them over, you would weep. When you consider the words of Exodus 20:3, "Thou shalt have no other gods before me," you would sit down and weep over that commandment. What is it that makes us weep so little? It must be that we too rarely have sights of Christ. A look of Him would be both law and gospel to us.

7. We are affected by the plague of lightness and unsteadfastness, so that we cannot focus on one thing but for a moment. We will have some resolutions at night, but by the morning they are as the morning cloud and early dew; they pass away. Yet one look of Christ would heal this. "I have set the LORD always before me" (Ps. 16:8); and what follows this? We read, "I shall not be moved." One sight of Christ would make us cry out in humility. Oh, Christians, unto what can you compare yourselves? There is nothing as unstable as we are.

8. The eighth plague is that of little growth. Believe it, nowadays Christians are like old merchants; Christians are like old traders who have fallen back. They cannot trade—they live upon their old stock. Now, one look of the Sun of righteousness would heal this plague, as we read in Malachi 4:2, "But unto you that fear my name shall the Sun of righteousness arise with healing in his wings." What follows this statement? "Ye shall go forth, and grow up as calves of the stall" (v. 2). I am afraid that if we are asked, "When did you last see Him?" we would not be able to answer one word.

9. There is the plague of worldly mindedness and love for the things of this present life. The Christian may say, "Oh,

> I would fain be like the young woman in Revelation 12:12 that had the moon under her feet!" This moon represents the world; let us desire victory over the world! Also, let us consider 2 Corinthians 4:18: "We look not at the things which are seen." We must ask the apostle, "What ails you, Paul, concerning the things that are seen?" He may answer, "Even I have another thing to look unto—that which is eternal." Christians, your love for things in the world shows your great distance from God.
>
> 10. Last, there is the plague of the dominion of our idols. The Christian may ask, "Oh, what would heal me of the love for my idols?" Even one look of Jesus Christ will do it. Consider Isaiah 17:7: "At that day shall a man look to his Maker, and his eyes shall have respect to the Holy One of Israel." Continue reading in verse 8: "And he shall not look to the altars, the work of his hands, neither shall respect that which his fingers have made, either the groves, or the images." What would make this place the grave of our idols? One sight of Jesus Christ would destroy the school of them; one look to Him would heal all these plagues.

Let me make clear what it means to look unto Jesus Christ. It comprehends these four things.

First, when looking to Jesus, a soul turns away its eyes from all its other idols, and prays that God would turn away his eyes and sight from all other things beside Christ. Second, one must be convinced of his lost state without Christ, and of his inability to help and save himself out of that lost and hopeless state. Thirdly, when the soul is under the conviction of all this, it must cast up its eyes to Jesus Christ, for our eyes pray to Him when we cannot speak. Even tears have a voice unto God; yes, when we can do none of these, even our breath has a voice unto God. He counts it prayer, as we see in Lamentations 3:56: "Thou hast heard my voice: hide not thine ear at my breathing, at my cry." Fourth, looking unto Jesus includes a soul waiting upon God and depending on Him for deliverance from burdens and troubles, either inward or outward. In Psalm 145:15 we read, "The eyes of all wait upon thee; and thou givest them their meat in due season." Oh, will you cast up your eyes to Him, and say, "Oh, Master, Son of God, save me, lest I perish"?

Let us consider some points that may provoke you to look unto Him. First, consider the words of our text: "Look unto me, and be ye saved, all the ends of the earth." Believe me, He calls many to look unto Him; I charge you to answer to your name when you hear it called, as you shall answer to Him at that great day.

First, all who are weary, we call you to look unto Christ. Are there none here who are weary? Do not deny your name; we urge you to look unto Him. Search your bosom and answer the call if this is your name.

Second, are there none here who are heavy laden? Are there any who are called by this name—who are groaning under the power and stirring of a body of death? Oh, embrace this call and look unto Him! Are there none here called heavy laden? Oh, do they not call you so? Old and young, is not this your name? Will you answer? Oh, look unto Him.

Third, are there none here who are naked? Are there none here that lack the righteousness of Christ to clothe them with? Does anyone here have a need for Jesus Christ? Do not mistake your name, but answer to it; as you do not desire to come under the eternal curse of God, we call you to look unto Jesus Christ and embrace Him.

Fourth, are there none here who are called poor? Are there none here who are destitute of grace and all the excellent gifts of heaven? As you would not be declared rebels of Christ, answer to your name and embrace the call.

Fifth, are there none here called foolish, blind, and ignorant? Yea, are there none such here who are destitute of the saving knowledge of the Most High? Come to Him. "I counsel thee to buy of me gold tried in the fire, that thou mayest be rich; and white raiment, that thou mayest be clothed, and that the shame of thy nakedness do not appear; and anoint thine eyes with eyesalve, that thou mayest see" (Rev. 3:18). My counsel to you this day is come unto Him and embrace Him.

Sixth, are there none here called thirsty? Will you answer to your name? "Ho, every one that thirsteth, come ye to the waters, and he that hath no money; come ye, buy, and eat; yea, come, buy wine and milk without money and without price" (Isa. 55:1). Oh, come, you thirsty, to the waters of life; or will you be like Hagar, casting away the child of hope for thirst before the waters? Now, will you answer to your name? Are there none in this side of the congregation, nor in that side of the congregation? Oh, will you not answer? We pray that you will embrace Christ.

Seventh, are there none here called poor folk? Who are they? They are people who have no righteousness of their own, no confidence in the flesh, or in the doing of their duty, in their own light, or in their own gifts. Now, I ask such people, will you look to Christ for salvation?

Eighth, are there none here who are willing? If this is not your name, I do not know what your name will be. We read, "Whosoever will, let him take the water of life freely" (Rev. 22:17). Is not your will to come? Do you not recognize your name in all these?

Ninth, are there none here called strangers to God? Now, if this is your name, you are commanded to look unto the Son of God.

Now, have you seen your name among all these? Cursed be the person in eating and drinking, who does not recognize his name among all these, or who finds his name here but will not answer to it. This is the great proclamation of peace; in the first day of the feast, we have called this roll. Old unbeliever, answer to your name! This is the roll that our Master has sent us to call; who knows if this roll shall ever be called among you again. Every person here has heard his name called. Will you answer me? It shall cost the person dear who will not answer. He shall be forced to answer one day, when he shall hear the words, "Depart from me, ye cursed, into everlasting fire" (Matt. 25:41). Then, the question will be asked of you that was asked of Adam: "Where art thou?" (Gen. 3:9). You shall be forced to answer then, when all these curses shall be read in your hearing: "Cursed be the man that would not take Christ, and serve Him." At that point, the congregation shall say "Amen." "Cursed be the man that despised Me," and all the congregation shall say "Amen." "Cursed be the man that loves anything better than Christ," and all the people shall say "Amen." Oh, do you think that you will escape then? Consider these two verses.

First, read Job 31:14: "What then shall I do when God riseth up? and when he visiteth, what shall I answer him?" Consider what you will do when God rises up and charges you to answer for treading Christ under your feet! Also, in Isaiah 10:3 we read another strong question: "And what will ye do in the day of visitation, and in the desolation which shall come from far? to whom will ye flee for help? and where will ye leave your glory?" Is there any city of refuge to hide you from Christ, when He shall come and reckon with you? If Christ were to come through this house tomorrow and read over all the names of those who have undervalued Him, there would be few left behind. Will you betray the Son of God with a kiss? Shall there be such a traitor at the Bothwell feast to do such an evil turn to the Son of God? Oh, will you look unto Him for salvation?

Perhaps this will provoke you to look unto Christ. Consider that He is the most excellent physician that ever was. He has four singular properties of a physician, that no other physician in the world has.

First, He can cure all diseases with a look; no physician on earth can do so but Him. Will you undervalue such a simple cure as this? Secondly, He can cure all diseases by His Word, as we see in Matthew 8:8, "Speak the word only, and my servant shall be healed," says the centurion. No physician can do so but Christ. Thirdly, He can heal all diseases by a touch of the hem of His garment; faith says, "If I may but touch his garment, I shall be whole" (Matt. 9:21). No physician can do so but Christ. Fourthly, He can heal all diseases by His shadow. There was never a physician in the world who could cure like Him; therefore look unto Him. There must be much begging, but little buying; you must beg much, but you must not think to buy anything from Him, for He cures for no price. If you are willing, you need only to ask and you will receive healing from Him. "Ho, every one that thirsteth, come ye to the waters, and he that hath no money; come ye, buy, and eat; yea, come, buy wine and milk without money and without price" (Isa. 55:1).

Fourth, consider that Christ is exceedingly importunate to have you look unto Him for salvation. We read in Song of Solomon 4:8 the words of Christ to His church: "Come with me from Lebanon, my spouse, with me from Lebanon: look from the top of Amana, from the top of Shenir and Hermon, from the lions' dens, from the mountains of the leopards." Christ is saying, "Come with me from the places of estrangement, from your beastly lusts and natural estates, from the lion's dens." We think again of the words in Isaiah 65:1: "I am sought of them that asked not for me; I am found of them that sought me not: I said, Behold me, behold me, unto a nation that was not called by my name." In this verse the command is doubled, because it is certain. Now, will none of these things move you to look unto Him? Oh, look unto Him for salvation, and let the considerations that we have named move you to this.

Now, in the second place, I shall propose some evidences of the people who have never looked to Christ for salvation.

First, those who have never mourned for sin have never looked to Christ. Those who look to Christ mourn for Him whom they have pierced by their sins, as we see in Zechariah 12:10: "They shall look upon me whom they have pierced, and they shall mourn for him."

Secondly, was Christ's absence ever a burden to you? If your answer is no, then you are a traitor to the Son of God and an enemy to the cross of Christ. Are there any here who have never mourned for the body of death in themselves, or yet for an absent Christ? Then such persons have never looked to Him for salvation.

Thirdly, those who do not give Christ the preeminence in all things have never looked to Christ. Furthermore, the person who loves his idols more than Christ has never looked to Christ. He who looks to Christ has respect to Him above all things, as we see in Isaiah 17:7 and in Acts 7:56. "Behold," cries Stephen, for he could not speak without wondering and crying, "Behold!" What ails you, Stephen, to wonder so? He answers, "I see the heavens opened, and the Son of man standing on the right hand of God" (Acts 7:56). Stephen got a look at Christ, and he wonders at Him. Will many of you see the like of this tomorrow? I say if you get a look of the Son of God by faith, you will esteem Him above all things that you have ever seen.

Fourthly, you have never sufficiently looked at Christ to know how to discern when Christ was present and when He was absent. A person who has looked to Christ can tell these things well; they can write a weekly diurnal of Christ's motion, so to speak. The spouse in the Canticles can write this diurnal well, "I sat down under his shadow with great delight, and his fruit was sweet to my taste" (Song 2:3). This is the news of one time; but what news will come the next week? Oh, sad news and a sad diurnal follow: "I sought him whom my soul loveth: I sought him, but I found him not" (Song 3:1). If you have looked unto Christ, you can say in honesty, "Such a day I was in the spirit, and such a day I sat by the river Chebar, and had such a piece of communion with God." But you who know nothing of this nearness with Christ, you have never looked unto Christ for salvation.

Fifthly, those who have never put off their own righteousness have never looked unto Christ; they that could never be freed from the covenant of works, and could never say, "If I go to heaven, I must sing that song, 'Not unto us, O LORD, not unto us, but unto thy name give glory, for thy mercy, and for thy truth's sake'" (Ps. 115:1). If you have never desired to be dug out of your own righteousness, and to sing this song of Christ, you have never looked to Him for salvation.

Now, in the third place, a person may be very near Christ, and yet not know it. Mary supposed Christ to be the gardener (John 20:15). Now there may be five reasons for it.

First, you may be experiencing anguish of spirit (Luke 24:37). The disciples were terrified, and they supposed that they had seen a spirit when Christ appeared unto them. Likewise when they saw Him walking on the sea, they mistook Him. Fear may make a soul mistake Christ when He is at hand.

A second reason is that such a person would so desire to have Christ that when he sees Him, he cannot believe it is He. Even like a loving wife whose husband has been long absent, when she sees him, she can scarcely believe that it is he; she would fain have it true. Jacob would not believe that Joseph was alive; and it is said of the disciples that they believed not for joy (Luke 24:41). Yes, sometimes they will accuse the news-bearer of being mad, for they would so fain have it true, yet they think it impossible. Those that were in Mary's house said that the maid was mad when she told them that Peter was standing at the door knocking (Acts 12:15).

Thirdly, their mistaking of Christ makes them blind to Him, so that they do not recognize Him.

Fourthly, Christ will sometimes be very near us, and He will close our eyes so we do not recognize Him. It is said of the two disciples that were going to Emmaus that their eyes were "holden that they should not know him" (Luke 24:16).

Fifthly, if Christ alters the way of His manifestations, we are presently mistaken; yes, if He simply changes His clothes, we will mistake Him. The church mistook Christ because He was clothed with red garments, "Who is this that cometh from Edom, with dyed garments from Bozrah?" (Isa. 63:1). There Christ comes very near folk, and yet they knew Him not.

In the fourth place, we shall obviate some objections that might be made.

Some may object, "But I fear I have never looked to Christ, because I do not know the time when I did it." There are several answers to such an objection. First, can you say with the blind man, "I was blind once, but now I see"? If you can say this, you are happy, though you do not know when you first began to see. A second answer to this objection is that perhaps it is not for your advantage to know the times and seasons of it; for sometimes this knowledge steals away the heart and makes the soul to say, "Or ever I was aware, my soul made me like the chariots of Amminadib"; or, "As the chariots of my willing people," as it is in the original. Third, sometimes the kingdom of God does not come with observation, so that folk may discern it. Fourth, perhaps it is your duty to search whether you have really looked unto Christ more than searching the time when you looked to Christ for salvation.

Second, some may object, "Since my coming to Christ, I think that my corruption has gotten more advantage of me than the first day that I looked to Christ; my corruptions stir me more than they ever did before." First I say to you, even as Pharaoh did with the Israelites; he made them and their tasks heavier, to make them fear going away from him. Thus it is with you. The devil puts in your head that you may be tempted to lie in the old security and not look unto Christ for an escape. Do not impute that weakness to your faith, for it may be from some other thing that your corruptions stir more, not from looking to Christ. This is a fault among Christians who cry when anything goes wrong; they impute it to their faith and call it unsound, while it is from some other thing. Third, perhaps your corruption has not grown worse, but your eyes have been opened so that you see it more clearly than you did before you looked to Christ. Therefore, do not mistake it. Fourth, wrestle against your corruption; if you are really wrestling against it, you shall have a period of escape; therefore keep your hands firm and hold a grip with them when you lose your footing.

Third, some may object, saying, "But I have less delight in duty since I looked to Christ than I had before I looked to Him." First, let me answer by directing you to Hebrews 10:32: "But call to remembrance the former days, in which, after ye were illuminated, ye endured a great fight of afflictions." It may be by reason of the sight of affliction that all the duties may grow dry and dreary to you after illumination. It may come to pass that you have less delight in duty than before. Second, the change of a Christian's exercise makes great alteration in a Christian; some Christians who wrestle against absence, will not wrestle against unbelief; they let unbelief overcome them. From this they delight less in duty than before they looked to Christ. Third, let me say this: your lack of delight in duty may proceed from not knowing before you looked to Christ, what it was to delight in duty; it comes from some carnal principle, and now it is abated.

A fourth objection some may have is this: "But since I looked to Christ, I think I have lost my tenderness, and am more gross than before." Now to this I answer two things. First, Christ is trying you, to test if you love Him more than these, if you love Him more than tenderness, and if you will give Him your whole heart, when it seems not to be so soft as it was. Second, Christ does so try your faith; if you come to Him because you are not tender, it may be that you looked not unto Christ when you lost your tenderness. This tells me that you look more to your tenderness than to Christ; therefore He abates it afterwards, so that He may try your faith.

Fifth, some may object saying, "But I have none of these sweet effects that other folks have after they have looked to Christ, such as light, and joy, and comfort, and consolation. I think therefore I am not right." You may comfort yourself with the words of Psalm 97:11: "Light is sown for the righteous, and gladness for the upright in heart"; dear Christian, it is sown for you.

A sixth objection is as follows: "But, alas! I fear I deceive myself in the matter of my looking to Christ, because many have deceived themselves with it. May not I also be deceived?" Fear and presumption do not always work together; sometimes they are contrary one to another. Also, ask for the most direct path to heaven, and go straight forward in it until you are well on your way, beyond the hypocrite. Then, you may be out of all doubt, and not beguiled.

Now what do you think of it? This is the fourth call that we have sent from heaven to you; will you not answer to your name? Will you say, "I am marked four times for non-compliance these eight days"? What do you say to this call? Now, this is the last time that we will preach upon this text; expectants of heaven by profession, shall this be the answer we shall give for you, that you are marked for non-compliance? What is your answer? Will you look to Him tomorrow? As He has given us commission, cry, oh, cry to Him, "Oh, Son of God, come and visit us with thy salvation"; friends, bring Christ with you tomorrow, or else do not come to the communion table.

This will be a pleasant church tomorrow if He comes with you. It is Christ who has made the loaves to multiply. If all the saints in heaven were admitted to give advice to you, they would say, "Bring Christ with you!" Yes, Abraham, Enoch, Noah, the twelve apostles, and all those who were ever in the banqueting house would say, "Bring Christ here!" Oh, Bothwell, shall we say to you that you are sick of love? Is there such a thing among you? If you had this sickness, it would not be unto death; but there are some here who are sick from loathing of Christ, and that is a sickness unto death. Yes, there are some who will be here tomorrow, to whom Christ will propose these three questions.

1. "Friend, how camest thou in hither not having a wedding garment?" (Matt. 22:12). Oh, stand in awe, lest this be your question! This challenge from the Son of God is dreadful; yes, it has been the challenge of many. Oh, lords and ladies, take heed to this call!

2. Do you betray the Son of God with a kiss? You who offer to kiss Christ, what will you answer to this question when Christ asks you?

3. How dare you come here, you who have lifted up your heel against Me?

Search yourselves diligently, and try that it be not so with yourselves, lest He come to you awfully and ask you these questions. It will be dreadful if He must do so. Now, may the Lord bless this word unto you. Amen.

SERMON 49

The Comfort and Blessedness of a Pardoned Sinner[1]

Son, be of good cheer; thy sins be forgiven thee.
—Matthew 9:2

If there were none here to hear this preaching but those to whom Christ might say these words, I fear we would have a small congregation. Has Christ said these words to you? Let each of you ask in your own heart whether Christ has said to you, "Thy sins be forgiven thee."

There is a fivefold debt that Christians owe to God, which they will never be able to pay.

The first debt is that of sin; none of you will ever be able to pay the great debt of your sin. Count fairly, dear friends, and you shall never be able to pay it. Subscribe the law to Christ and He will subscribe the gospel to you.

The second debt is that of duties; you will never get that debt paid. Even if you would sit down, weep, and fast for forty years, you would never get this debt paid. Yes, if we come to heaven, we must step into it with these words in our mouths: "We are unprofitable servants," for all that we have done (Luke 17:10).

Third, there is the debt of love; will you ever be able to pay your debt of love to Christ? You will forever be paying it.

Fourth, Christians owe the debt of resolutions. I fear that many of you will never pay them unto God; God will avenge the quarrel of a broken covenant with many of you. A curse shall come unto false swearers, and consume their house, as we read in Zechariah 5:4.

[1] Preached on the Sabbath after the communion at Bothwell.

Further, Malachi 3:5 says, "I will be a swift witness against the sorcerers, and against the adulterers, and against false swearers."

There is also the debt of praise; do you think that you will ever pay the debt of praise to Christ? Ask Abel if ever he has gotten that debt paid, although he is the first-born among the saved sons of men. He would say that he is only beginning to praise. Christians, do you think you will ever pay this debt to Christ?

In the beginning of this chapter, we read the history of a sick man brought to Christ; the story is more particularly set down by Mark and Luke. There is one thing recorded by them that is not here: "When they could not come nigh unto him for the press, they uncovered the roof where he was: and when they had broken it up, they let down the bed wherein the sick of the palsy lay. When Jesus saw their faith, he said unto the sick of the palsy, Son, thy sins be forgiven thee" (Mark 2:4-6). Observe that when faith cannot win through impediments, it goes above them and mounts over them until it reaches Christ with its errand. This man receives a precious word from Christ: "Son, be of good cheer, thy sins are forgiven thee" (Matt. 9:2).

Let us consider six thoughts concerning these words.

1. Christ sees fit at some times and at some particular occasions, to give believers the intimation of the pardon of their sins; He does so for this sick man at this time, saying, "Thy sins are forgiven thee."

2. Pardon of sin is an excellent ground of consolation; so Christ bids the man "be of good cheer." A person pardoned may sing sweetly, for Christ says, "Rise up, my love, my fair one, and come away. For, lo, the winter is past, the rain is over and gone; the flowers appear on the earth; the time of the singing of birds is come, and the voice of the turtle is heard in our land" (Song 2:10-12). If you were pardoned, you might sing in captivity.

3. There are many sweet attendants that wait upon pardon of sin. I shall mention three. First, there is adoption. Christ calls the pardoned, "Son." Second, there is consolation in the words of Christ; He says, "Son be of good cheer." There is also stability; the word in the original

could also be translated "steadfast." There are these, and other attendants, that wait upon the pardon of sin.

4. Often, Christ is larger in His answers than we are in our desires. A man may seek bodily health; but Christ adds these precious words: "Thy sins be forgiven thee." If it were not so, we would more often be forced to beg.

5. Consider that a Christian who must receive pardon does not improve his pardon for that suitable joy and comfort as he ought to do; therefore, Christ commands this man to rejoice in his pardon, saying, "Be of good cheer."

6. It is a great difficulty for a Christian to attain assurance and full persuasion of the remission of sins; therefore, He bids the man be settled in the assurance of the pardon of sin.

Now, before we consider the words of our text, let us propose seven thoughts concerning the intimation of pardon.

First, there is a difference between the grant of pardon and the intimation of pardon to a person.

Second, there is a difference between the intimation of the pardon and the application of it. A soul may have the experience of David, who had the pardon of sin intimated unto him by Nathan (2 Sam. 12:13); yet, in Psalm 51, he prays for the application of that pardon.

Third, consider that there are many who take pardon of sin for themselves before God forgives them; yes, many forget their sins themselves before God forgets them. Many take a false extract of pardon for themselves from the court of self-love. All the ministers and saints in the world may pardon you; yet, when you come to judgment, you will be asked, "Where is Christ's name?" God will ask you, "Where is my Son's name?" If you do not have this, your case will be sad.

Fourth, once a sin is pardoned, it cannot be recalled to a Christian again. "For the gifts and calling of God are without repentance" (Rom. 11:29); yet, to a Christian's apprehension, the pardon of sin may be recalled, though not on God's account. For we do not walk humbly under the intimation of pardon; pride makes us walk in bitterness of spirit. Remember how low Hezekiah's pride brought him. Also, some gross sins committed after the intimation of pardon will open the grave of buried sins and fill you with apprehensions. Pardon is a tender plant which must be carefully used. A Christian does not often seek a new extract of pardon, but lets the old extract lie beside him. Eventually, it grows very black and unclean and he cannot read it. Further, the power of unbelief and discouragement makes a Christian mistake and think that his pardon is recalled again after the intimation of pardon.

Fifth, consider that the spring and fountain from which all pardon flows is the goodwill of Christ and His purchase (Ps. 68:18). Any pardon is a mercy, but that it runs through the bowels of Christ makes it far better and sweeter.

Sixth, though many of us cannot praise Christ for pardoning, conquering, and electing grace, all here ought to praise Christ for restraining grace. This marks the difference between you and the most profane unbeliever in the world.

Seventh, it is a Christian's responsibility, after the intimation of pardon, to walk very humbly with God. The two greatest enemies to a Christian's thriving are pride and slothfulness. What defaces all resolutions at communions? Pride and slothfulness—they spoil all our duties. What is the reason that we do not grow more? Nothing hinders our growth so much as pride, self-conceit, and laziness.

Concerning our text, let us first consider that sometimes, and at some particular occasions, Christ thinks it fit to give sinners an assurance of their pardon. In Luke 5:20 Christ says to the man, "Thy sins are forgiven thee." There are eight special times when God does indicate pardon of sin.

First, Christ assures a believer of pardon immediately after conversion, when He first takes the soul by the hand. It is the mercy of little children to have their sins forgiven them (1 John 2:1).

Secondly, a Christian receives assurance of forgiveness when he is lying under the spirit of discouragement, and when he is likely to be overwhelmed with it. In Isaiah 38:17 we read, "Behold, for peace I had great bitterness: but thou hast in love to my soul delivered it from the pit of corruption: for thou hast cast all my sins behind thy back." These words are like a star in a dark pit to them, until the shadow flees away. In the multitude of their thoughts, this will delight their souls.

The third time is when the soul is often confessing sin: "I said, I will confess my transgressions unto the LORD; and thou forgavest the iniquity of my sin." (Ps. 32:5). Oh, Christians, can you confess your sins? If you confess them, you shall have pardon.

Fourthly, a Christian shall have assurance of pardon when he is exercising repentance; "Repent ye therefore, and be converted, that your sins may be blotted out" (Acts 3:19). When we do not exercise repentance, we do not receive assurance of pardon.

A fifth time is when a Christian begins to recover from his apostasy, and from going a-whoring from God; then, the Christian begins to say, "I will go and return to my first husband" (Hos. 2:3). Then let us see what follows: "Thou shalt call me Ishi; and shalt call me no more Baali" (v. 16). "Repent ye therefore, and be converted, that your sins may be blotted out, when the times of refreshing shall come from the presence of the Lord" (Acts 3:19). We understand the word "converted" to signify a recovery from apostasy. In Luke 22:32 we read, "When thou art converted, strengthen thy brethren." A soul is said to be converted after apostasy because it as difficult to bring a soul again to Christ after it has been unfaithful to Him, as it is to bring it home for the first time. Thus, in this case, a soul may receive an intimation of pardon.

Sixthly, a soul will receive pardon from the Lord when he seriously exercises prayer. "The prayer of faith shall save the sick, and the Lord shall raise him up; and if he have committed sins, they shall be forgiven him" (James 5:15). Is this not often the lot of a Christian: when he comes from God, he is no longer sad? It is said of Hannah, "And her countenance was no more sad" (1 Sam. 1:18). A Christian may not dare to begin the prayer calling God his, yet he may close with it, calling Him, "My Lord, and my God."

The soul will also receive intimation of pardon after communion; some may have come to the table wishing for assurance of pardon of sin, and have gone out saying, "Lord, keep this pardon in the mind of thy servant, and keep this intimation of pardon in the heart." Are there any here who have come seeking assurance, and have gone away without it? Christ, on such a day, speaks peace to His friends.

An eighth time Christ speaks pardon to the soul is when the Christian is exercising great faith; we see this in our text, "Jesus, seeing their faith said unto the sick of the palsy; Son, be of good cheer; thy sins be forgiven thee" (Matt. 9:2). It is a great error among many to seek more after the assurance of pardon than after the lively exercise of faith; but faith is the means by which we receive assurance of pardon. Now at this, and similar occasions, God does intimate pardon to believers.

Let us now consider a second main point; let us propose some evidences of those who have received pardon for their sin. I charge you to try yourselves with these eight things, because many beguile themselves in this matter.

The first evidence of the pardoned sinner is that he has a high estimation of the Pardoner, Jesus Christ. If there are any who hate the Son of God in their heart, they do not know what pardon is. "Who is a God like unto thee, that pardoneth iniquity, and passeth by the transgression of the remnant of his heritage? he retaineth not his anger for ever, because he delighteth in mercy" (Mic. 7:18). What ails you to cry so, Micah? What is the matter? Micah cries because his Lord pardons iniquity, transgressions, and sin. Is there any person here who loves the creature more than Christ? You have never been pardoned; you are not able to commend Christ. Yes, Christians are forced to swallow up this commendation in silence, wondering in awe at Him for His pardoning mercy.

A second evidence of those who are pardoned is that they love the Pardoner much. We read in Luke 7:47 of Mary: "Her sins, which are many, are forgiven; for she loved much: but to whom little is forgiven, the same loveth little."

Thirdly, a pardoned man will be much in the praise of Him that pardoned him. Have you ever experienced such conversion that you do not dare to praise Him for it yourself, but you needed to call upon others to help you? We see such an experience in Psalm 103:1-3. Blessed is the Christian who can sing this song, in the morning and the evening, upon the ground that all his sins have been pardoned.

A fourth mark of a pardoned sinner is hatred of the sin pardoned. If you can look on your sin with delight, you do not know the pardon of Christ. There are some whose hearts begin to flutter within them whenever they see their sin or even a portrait of it, as we see in Ezekiel 8:10-11. The portrait of their idols is before them, and they bring their hearts in love with them. A pardoned sinner will look upon his sin with hatred and disdain.

Fifthly, a pardoned sinner will weep as much for the sin that is pardoned as he did before the intimation of pardon, if not more. I confess that there is mourning without hope when pardon is not attained. There is also mourning with hope, which occurs after pardon has been received; yet the pardoned Christian may mourn just as much after his sin is pardoned as before.

Sixthly, the pardoned sinner will have a high account of the pardon he has received. Be his estate in the world what it will, he answers all cases and all doubts with the fact that he is pardoned: "Blessed is he whose transgression is forgiven, whose sin is covered" (Ps. 32:1). There is a great debate as to which man is most blessed; but we know that the pardoned man is the blessed man. Pardon of sin is one of the sweetest clusters that grows on the tree of life. Are there any here who have never esteemed the pardon of sin?

Seventh, the pardoned man is of a guileless spirit. Is there no hypocrite here? I fear there is much of painted love, painted fear, painted hope, painted assurance, painted faith, and painted pardon of sin among us. "Blessed is the man unto whom the LORD imputeth not iniquity, and in whose spirit there is no guile" (Ps. 32:2).

Eighth, what was the frame of your spirit immediately after the receipt of pardon? Now there are three things that ordinarily accompany the Christian after the receipt of pardon. First, the Christian receives liberty of spirit and enlargement of heart, so that he is constrained to sing. Second, he also receives much delight in duty accompanying it. Third, he has great hatred and abhorrence of sin. Now was this your experience after you received pardon of sin? Are there any here who have these things attending them?

Our third main task this day is to propose encouragements for you to come and seek pardon of sin from Jesus Christ. We will attempt to stir you up to it, for there are some who will never get their sins pardoned until they die, as we see in Isaiah 22:14: "Surely this iniquity shall not be purged from you till ye die, saith the Lord GOD of hosts."

First, Christ is very ready to pardon: "Thou art a God ready to pardon, gracious and merciful, slow to anger, and of great kindness" (Neh. 9:17).

Secondly, be encouraged by the noble letter of His name: "And the LORD passed by before him, and proclaimed, The LORD, The LORD God, merciful and gracious, longsuffering, and abundant in goodness and truth, keeping mercy for thousands, forgiving iniquity and transgression and sin, and that will by no means clear the guilty; visiting the iniquity of the fathers upon the children, and upon the children's children, unto the third and to the fourth generation" (Ex. 34:6-7).

Thirdly, let the words of Isaiah 55:7 encourage you: "Let the wicked forsake his way, and the unrighteous man his thoughts: and let him return unto the LORD, and he will have mercy upon him; and to our God, for he will abundantly pardon." In the original it says that "He will multiply to pardon." Is it not unspeakable folly that so many continue to lie under the cross, with the Son of God saying unto them, "Here is a pardon for your release"? Yes, with every sermon you hear, Christ sits down on His knees, so to speak, and cries for you to come and be pardoned; but many will come and cry at the great day, "Oh! To have it but once offered!" Yet, they do not receive it when it is so often offered to them! Oh, will you think about this?

Fourthly, let this encourage you to seek pardon: Christ will help you to come to Him, making intercession for you: "If any man sin, we have an advocate with the Father, Jesus Christ the righteous" (1 John 2:1). Oh, if you could hear your prayer after Christ has cleansed it, taken the refuse out of it, and delivered it unto God, you would say, "I never prayed such a prayer!" Oh, how many lines of our prayers does He cross out, putting others in their place, making ours prayers acceptable to God! Let this stir you up to seek pardon from Him.

Fifthly, be encouraged that you may make use of at least four strong arguments to provoke God to pardon you.

> 1. The first argument that the saints have used is, "Pardon mine iniquity; for it is great" (Ps. 25:11). That may seem to be a strange reason; surely, such a reason would not suffice if justice sat as judge. Some of us have great reason to seek pardon; but this reason does suffice here, and it is strange theology to plead so. Love sits as judge, and any reason will be heard with love, as long as it is for the soul's benefit. Yes, love will bear with love, and find out reasons to the soul.
>
> 2. You may also argue, "Withhold not thou thy tender mercies from me, O LORD: let thy lovingkindness and thy truth continually preserve me. For innumerable evils have compassed me about: mine iniquities have

taken hold upon me, so that I am not able to look up" (Ps. 40:11-12). Oh, what a strange argument this is, you may think! If Scripture had not said it, we would not dare to venture upon it! Oh, make use of it, since the medicine is free love.

3. A third sort of argument is, "LORD, be merciful unto me: heal my soul; for I have sinned against thee" (Ps. 41:4). Here, the reason is, "for I have sinned against thee."

4. Compare Exodus 33:5 with Exodus 34:9. In Exodus 33:5, God says unto the children of Israel, "Ye are a stiffnecked people: I will come up into the midst of thee in a moment, and consume thee: therefore now put off thy ornaments from thee, that I may know what to do unto thee." In Exodus 34:9, Moses prays, "O LORD, let my LORD, I pray thee, go among us; for it is a stiffnecked people; and pardon our iniquity and our sin, and take us for thine inheritance." They take the same argument, making use of it to provoke God to pardon them. He had said that He would consume them for a strange and wonderful reasoning; but faith will come to God with strange arguments, yes, it will even come within three feet. So before it stays away from Christ, it will come halting to Him. Now, this may encourage you to come and seek pardon.

Sixthly, be encouraged to seek pardon because of the advantages that attend the pardoned Christian. Oh, what advantages attend the pardoned Christian! What advantages wait upon him!

1. There is peace with God: "Being justified by faith, we have peace with God through our Lord Jesus Christ" (Rom. 5:1).

2. Receiving pardon is an excellent way to attain patience. I know some who, at the intimation of their pardon, have been forced to forget their faith and sit down and sing for joy. The pardoned Christian is the patient Christian (Rom. 5:1-3). One thing works another, until patience is wrought.

3. The pardoned sinner has the most lively discoveries of heaven: "We have access by faith into this grace

wherein we stand, and rejoice in hope of the glory of God" (Rom. 5:2).

4. We find in Scripture three steps to the benefits of receiving pardon. First, they refuse to let Him go. Jacob said, "I will not let thee go, except thou bless me" (Gen. 32:26). Oh, what boldness he had, that he would not let God go, although He had bidden him! That was sweet disobedience. A second step is when they have been forbidden to pray for a thing; yet, they have been bold enough to pray for it. Moses, in Exodus 32:10-11, did so; this was faith and not presumption. Thirdly, when Christ has desired to withdraw Himself, they have kept Him. When the two disciples were going to Emmaus, Christ made as if He would have gone on without them; but they constrained Him to abide with them (Luke 24:28-29). Oh, but these are strange steps of familiarity with Christ Jesus! Let all these press you to seek pardon from Him.

Now, before we close, what do you think of Christ? You heard yesterday that He speaks to those who are wallowing in their sin—He desires to have them embrace Him. Oh, blessed is the person who has a high estimation of Christ; let all the congregation say, "Amen." Blessed is the person who has eaten and drunken worthily; let all the congregation say, "Amen." Blessed is the person who has Christ for his portion; blessed is the person who is an expectant of heaven; let all the people say, "Amen." Now, the blessing of Him, who is one in three, and three in one, the blessing of God the Father, and the blessing of God the Son, and the blessing of God the Holy Ghost, the blessing of the saints militant, and our blessings be upon every one who helps to set and hold the crown upon Christ's head, giving Him the highest glory; let all the congregation say, "Amen."

Now to this God—the Father, Son, and Holy Ghost—be glory from us, and from all the churches, forever. Amen.

SERMON 50

The Indispensable Duty of Giving the Heart to Christ[1]

My son, give me thine heart, and let thine eyes observe my ways.
—Proverbs 23:26

Introduction

Let us discuss two things before we conclude in prayer. First, let us discuss how you can know if you have communicated rightly. I shall give you seven evidences of a proper communicant.

The first evidence is that the soul will be consumed by fellowship with Christ. The person who has eaten and drunken rightly will sing with the bride in Song of Solomon 2:4-5: "He brought me to the banqueting house, and his banner over me was love," and then she prays, "Stay me with flagons, comfort me with apples: for I am sick of love." I am afraid that our desire for fellowship with Christ is now gone. Oh, when did you last see Him? Are there not some here who have gone to bed without prayer last night, and have come here this morning without prayer? I say to you, if that is the case with you, you have not communicated rightly.

The second evidence is that the person who has communicated rightly will have high conceptions of Jesus Christ. We read in Song of Solomon 2:3, "As the apple tree among the trees of the wood, so is my beloved among the sons. I sat down under his shadow with great delight, and his fruit was sweet to my taste." It is as if the bride had said, "I do not know anyone in the world who is as

[1] Preached on the Monday after the communion at Bothwell.

worthy as Christ." I am afraid that many of us would sell Jesus Christ for a pair of shoes, as the prophet Amos records in Amos 2:6.

Third, if you have communicated rightly, the graces in you will be strengthened by this meal. If the graces of love, faith, mortification, patience, and humility are strengthened in you, you can be sure that you have communicated rightly. In Song of Solomon 2:3 we read, "I sat down under his shadow." Before, she stood, but now she sits down in the settled and solid exercise of grace. I am afraid, however, that all our graces are in the same posture that they were in before.

Fourth, the gifts of Christ will be sweeter to you than they ever were before. Song of Solomon 2:3 records, "His fruit was sweet to my taste," but if I may say so, I fear that Christ and His fruits have grown tasteless to many of us. Oh, I fear that there were many tasteless communicators here yesterday.

The fifth evidence that you have communicated rightly is that the strength of your idols and predominant corruptions will be decaying. I think communicants are either the greatest feeders of predominant corruptions or the greatest slayers of them. Now are there any here who dare say that they hate their predominant idols more than they did before? Some of us will go to our graves full of the sins of our youth! A Christian will pray for the mortification of his lust, but not against the idol of his lust. For example, if pride is a man's idol, he may pray against pride, but he would hate to lose his lust for the applause of the world. A man who has covetousness for his predominant idol may pray against it, but he has no true desire to be rid of it, although he would be content to leave the lust. If this describes you, you are not mortified to your predominant idol, and so you have not communicated rightly.

Sixth, he who has communicated rightly will know it by his diligence in duty. I do not love the communion that impairs Christian diligence. Now I suppose if we search well, many of us will be found among those who have not communicated rightly.

Seventh, you will know if you have communicated rightly by your obedience to and delight in commanded duties. Each time some go to prayer, they tell the Lord everything that has happened from beginning to end. Yes, we may say when we go to prayer, the same words that Ahab spoke to Elijah: "Hast thou found me, O mine enemy?" (1 Kings 21:20).

Eighth, you will know it by this: your love for the saints will grow. There is too little spoken concerning this issue, for there are some here who neither love Christ nor His image; yea, they not only hate His image in the godly, but His picture in the hypocrite. If you communicate rightly, you will love the saints.

The second thing I propose to address tonight is this question: what is the best way to recover an absent Christ, since He is gone and returned to His place? What is the best way to find the sweet enjoyment of His presence?

Now, there is a fivefold defect for lack of His presence that we must recover. (1) Regarding His sensible presence (2) Regarding life among us. (3) Regarding joy and comfort. For the most part, we are greatly lacking these qualities as Christians. (4) Regarding faith and other graces; specifically, when a Christian loses his sap and vigor in these graces. (5) Regarding a Christian's delight in his duties. Oh, how many of us are guilty of this defection!

Now the question is, how shall we bring the king back over Mahanaim to Jerusalem? For an answer to this question, let us look at Song of Solomon 3:1-4 and 7:8. In these verses, we find most excellent ways to recover Christ when He is absent. First, you must exercise faith, despite His absence. Second, do not forget your love for Christ. Third, do not disregard diligence. The bride sought Him in secret prayer, in public ordinances, and in fellowship among fellow Christians. Fourth, seek Him in the exercise of patience, so that when you miss Him in one thing, you go to another, as the bride did. Fifth, you must go a little further. By this I mean three things: (1) You must have patient submission under all these disappointments. (2) You must make an immediate application to the Son of God when all other means fail, as the man who brought his sick child to Christ when His disciples could not heal him. You must come to Christ in a diligent use of the means; you must make an immediate application to Christ. (3) You must employ over and over again all the means you went through before. If you are deserted in prayer, seek to become diligent in prayer again. Pray again, and do so with all other duties; when you miss Him in them, perform the same duty again. Now let us go to Him and pray to Him who has gone to His place until we seek Him.

Post-Communion Sermon

How beautiful upon the mountains are the feet of those who bring glad tidings and publish peace! I have glad tidings from a far country to declare to some of you this day. What are these tidings? Two great suitors have come to Bothwell this day. The first is Jesus Christ, the noble Plant of renown. He is suiting you; He says, "My son, give me thine heart" (Prov. 23:26). The devil is also suiting you; to you he says the same: "My son, give me thine heart." Now to which of these two will you answer and hearken? I do conceive that it will fill us with astonishment that He who is infinitely perfect in Himself should suit the likes of us, and that He who lacks nothing should seek our hearts.

Now, let me first ask you three questions. First, have you ever seen such excellence in Christ that you were forced to cry out, "Oh, for a thousand hearts to give to Christ; oh, for a thousand eyes to behold Him, and a thousand hands to do Him service! Oh, for a thousand feet to walk in His ways!" Have you ever cried these words? Second, what do you think of this desire that heaven presents to you today? It is difficult to determine whether this text shows more clearly Christ's love or His condescension; but it breathes forth both. Oh, that such a noble Plant of renown as Christ should suit us, who are sinners! Third, what is the reason that heaven should present such a desire unto you this day?

This is the great petition of the great King to you: "My son, give me thine heart." We will delay no more, but we will woo you to Christ. You must not delay any longer; give Him your heart. Oh, if we could see Him in His beauty, there would not need to be much preaching to persuade us to give Him our hearts!

Now, in the words that are read unto you, there are three things to be considered.

1. Consider the invitation and desire that Christ puts forth to sinners when He says, "My son, give me thine heart."

2. Consider why Christ presents this desire to sinners, that they would give Him their hearts. We conceive that there are six reasons in our text that show why Christ would urge sinners to fulfill this desire.

The first is taken from the excellence of the person that presents this invitation: Jesus Christ. He says, "Give *me* thine heart"; Christ speaks of dying *Me,* crucified *Me,* excellent *Me;* give glorified

Me, thine heart. All that can be said is here said when Christ says, "Give me." There are great reasons for us to give such an excellent Person our heart.

Secondly, if you would give Christ your heart and deliver it over unto Him, He would look upon it as a gift, although it is our debt and duty to do it; therefore, He says, "Give me thine heart." Oh, who will refuse such a gift to precious Christ? Blessed be the Asker, and blessed be the giver of this gift.

Thirdly, consider the smallness of the gift for which He asks. It is your heart. Would He say, "Give spotless Me your spotted heart; give holy Me your profane heart; give glorified Me your foul, loose black heart"? No, He only says, "Give me thine heart." Yet, there is a great difference between "me" and "your," though it is not expressed in these words.

Fourthly, consider the loving and soul-conquering way in which Christ talks with sinners to gain their hearts. He comes not by charge and command, as He might do, but by way of humble supplication, as it were, sitting on His knees, and asking for sinners' hearts.

Fifthly, consider how the sinner who gives his heart to Christ is advanced to a noble dignity: Christ calls him, "My son." Although sinners had been strangers to God before, now they shall have the state of adoption, and shall be God's sons, if they give Christ their hearts.

A sixth consideration is, if we do not give Christ our heart, we must give it to someone else. This is clear in the text, when we compare it with the following verses, where we see that the whorish women will get the hearts of sinners if Christ does not get it. The devil will have your heart and give it to whoredom, if Christ does not get it!

3. The third thing to consider is the time when the heart should be given to Christ; it is in the morning. The word in the original is, "My young man, give me thine heart." Now, we have already spoken of the commendation of believing at a young age; I shall now propose seven considerations to commend young religion and giving the heart to Christ at a young age.

> 1. Consider Christ's earnest desire to have your heart in your youth: "Remember now thy Creator in the days of thy youth" (Eccl. 12:1). This is Christ's earnest request to sinners, to remember Him in their youth.

2. Give your heart to Christ early because your work is great and your journey is long; therefore, give Christ your heart in your youth, so that you may have enough time to take this long journey of faith and sanctification.

3. You have only a short time to a do great work and to travel that long journey; yes, much of our precious time has passed, and little of our work is done. We have scarcely begun it! Yet, I will say the same words that the husbandman said to the vineyard-dressers: "Why stand ye here all the day idle?" (Matt. 20:6). Now, will you give your hearts to Him?

4. Giving your heart to Christ in your youth will help to flee from ills that you and your heart are apt to fall into in time of youth. "Childhood and youth are vanity" (Eccl. 11:10).

5. If you give Christ your heart in your youth, it shall be more acceptable and welcome to Christ than when you are fifty or sixty years old; therefore, do it now, while it is time.

6. The sooner you give your heart to Christ, the sooner you are admitted to the partaking, fruition, and enjoyment of many excellent things in Him and in His company.

7. Consider that if you delay to give Christ your heart today, you shall be even more unfit to do it tomorrow; for with every hour's delay, you are less inclined to give your heart to Christ in the future. Therefore, young men, give your hearts to Christ. I have no better advice to give you all than this. Oh, shall we send Him away with a refusal on the first, second, and third day of the communion feast? Oh, will you refuse Christ all the three days? I charge you to refuse Him not, but give it to Him.

Now, we have finally come to the first main point of our text. Christ puts forth the suit and desires sinners to give Him their hearts. In further discussing this, I shall mention five thoughts.

First, what does it mean to give Christ our heart? I shall explain it in five manners. First, it is to give the thoughts to Christ. There are some that will give the devil their thoughts, but they would give

Christ their affections; but I say, you must think of Christ when you sit down and when you rise up, in the night-seasons and in the day when you walk in the way. I fear, however, that Christ is not in all our thoughts.

Secondly, to give your heart to Christ is to give your desires to Christ, so that your desires that before were running in so many different channels, may now all run Christ-ward. Thirdly, it is to give all your affections to Christ—your joy, delight, love, and patience; yes, all affections to Him. Fourthly, to give your heart means to give Christ your mind, the light of your mind, and all the knowledge that you have, to improve it for His glory. Fifthly, to give your heart to Christ is to give your soul unto Him—your entire soul and all the faculties thereof.

Now, in the second place, we shall propose some considerations to press this home upon you. I charge you, as you would not despise that noble Plant of renown, Jesus Christ, give Him your heart.

First, consider that if you would weep and pray for forty years, yet you do not give your heart, it will be asked of you, "Who required these things at your hand?" It is clear that to love God is better than sacrifice (Mark 12:33); in 1 Corinthians 13:2 we read the telling words, "And though I have the gift of prophecy, and understand all mysteries, and all knowledge; and though I have all faith, so that I could remove mountains, and have not charity, I am nothing." So then, as you would not like to have your prayer and fasting counted as nothing, give Christ your heart.

Second, if you give your heart to Christ, He will give His to you. Is this not a sweet exchange? "He that hath my commandments, and keepeth them, he it is that loveth me: and he that loveth me shall be loved of my Father, and I will love him, and will manifest myself to him" (John 14:21). Oh, these are sweet guests to lodge with you, and they shall lodge with you if you give your heart to Christ.

Third, your heart, which Christ seeks, is not worth much without Christ: "The heart of the wicked is little worth" (Prov. 10:20); I may say the same of all men's hearts; therefore, give it to Christ!

Fourth, consider that Christ is earnestly asking you to give Him your heart. Cursed be the man and woman who will not give Christ his or her heart; let all the congregation say, "Amen." Yes, the broad gospel curse and malediction will be upon such a person.

Fifth, giving Christ your heart will set you free from a great fivefold burden under which you lie. Let us look at this fivefold burden in greater detail.

1. You will be relieved from the great burden of desires; for the desires of one who is a stranger to Christ are like the grave, which cries, "Give, give," but will never be full. The desire of the sluggard slays him; but once you give your heart to Christ, you will say with the psalmist, "One thing have I desired of the LORD, that will I seek after; that I may dwell in the house of the LORD all the days of my life, to behold the beauty of the LORD, and to enquire in his temple" (Ps. 27:4).

2. Giving your heart to Christ would deliver you from the burden of fears. Some persons, as long as they are strangers to Christ, fear such a curse, such a loss, and such a sad dispensation; but if you have given your heart to Christ, those fears will be buried in the grave.

3. You shall be freed from a burden of sorrow; as long as a person is a stranger to Christ, he has no cause to rejoice—he knows only sorrow. But when the heart is given to Christ, you shall rejoice with joy unspeakable and full of glory. The believer may have bitterness indeed, but not for his lot. We read in Proverbs 14:10, "The heart knoweth his own bitterness; and a stranger doth not intermeddle with his joy."

4. You now have a burden of doubts; but if you would give your heart to Christ, you would be set free from all perplexities. Your anxious cares would be sweetly resolved in freedom, if Christ had your heart.

5. You would be set free from a burden of anxious hope. The stranger to Christ has many imaginary and vain hopes; but when he gives his heart to Christ, he has it set free from all such false hopes. So then, stir yourself up to give your heart to Christ, so that you will be set free from all these vain hopes.

Sixth, all the other gifts that you may give to Christ will not be acceptable until you give Him the gift of your heart. There are five gifts that a hypocrite may give to Christ, yet not give Him the heart.

1. A hypocrite may give Christ the tongue; yes, he may speak very excellently to any religious purpose. Now, there are many here who have never given their tongue to Christ; therefore, know that you are a step below a hypocrite if you have never even given your tongue to Christ.

2. The hypocrite can give Christ a profession; he will put on Christ's robe, but not His graces; are there any such persons here? Then you are one step below a hypocrite, and you have never given Christ your heart.

3. A hypocrite can give Christ the show of outward duties; yes, he can pray, communicate, fast, read, and meditate. He may have the show of all duties, yet never give his heart to Christ.

4. A hypocrite may sometimes give his conscience to Christ, and let it act according to His honor, yet he may never give Christ his heart.

5. A hypocrite may give his outward man to Christ—his eyes, hands, and feet. Outwardly, he will do nothing except what Christ bids him; yes, many give Christ their tongue, face, eyes, feet, and hands, yet never give Him their heart. Now, all these gifts are unacceptable to God until you give Him your heart; therefore, let this stir you up to this duty.

Seventh, except you give Christ your heart, the mark between you and a hypocrite is never rightly laid. There may be a change in a hypocrite who has not given Christ his heart. There is a sevenfold change that a hypocrite may attain, even if he has never given his heart unto Christ.

First, there may be a change in his light. In 1 Corinthians 13:2 we read, "Though I have the gift of prophecy, and understand all mysteries, and all knowledge; and though I have all faith, so that I could remove mountains, and have not charity, I am nothing." How many people who have said glorious things of Christ are in hell this day? This is clearly shown in Numbers 23. I doubt if there is a minister in Scotland who can speak of Christ as Balaam did; yet he may be in hell this day. Yes, a hypocrite may solve doubts and cases that a Christian cannot solve; such may be his light, yet he will never give his heart to Christ.

Secondly, there may be a change in a hypocrite's conscience. Believe it, his conscience may challenge him for neglect of duty, and for wrongs done to Christ, as Judas's conscience did. Yes, such persons sometimes come as far as the truly godly, if not further. Now, there is a three-fold change that may occur in a hypocrite's conscience.

First, the conscience may challenge a hypocrite for committing sin, and that very deeply. We see this in the stories of Judas, Saul, and Cain. Saul wept for his sin, and Judas hanged himself on account of it; because of sin Cain cried out, "My punishment is greater than I can bear" (Gen. 4:13).

Second, a hypocrite's conscience may be convinced in such a way that, when he encounters sadness because of his sin, he will acknowledge that God is just in it. Even Rehoboam cried out, "The Lord is righteous" (2 Chron. 12:6); yet he was an unjust man who "did evil, because he prepared not his heart to seek the LORD" (v. 14). Third, a hypocrite's conscience may lead him to dispute his interest in Christ, yet such a person has never given his heart to Christ.

Thirdly, there may be a change in a hypocrite's affections. There are places to prove this; in Isaiah 58:2 we read, "They take delight in approaching to God." Now I ask you, do you dare to say this? If you never delighted in approaching God, you are a step below a hypocrite, and you have not given Christ your heart. Oh, tremble at that! Another place which proves this point is Romans 2:17-19 where Paul says to the Jews, "Behold, thou art called a Jew, and restest in the law, and makest thy boast of God, and knowest his will, and approvest the things that are more excellent, being instructed out of the law." Thus, they knew the will of God, approving that which is excellent, yet it is said that they rested in the law and never gave their hearts to Christ. Oh, that is a fearful thing!

Fourthly, a hypocrite may have a change in his will; this is one of the strangest changes that can be. Yes, he may have a half-desire to take Christ, as Balaam had when he cried out, "Let me die the death of the righteous, and let my last end be like his!" (Num. 23:10).

Fifthly, a hypocrite may have a change in his conversation. Believe it, many of our walks are like painted tombs; they have on Christ's coat, but not His graces. Therefore, let no man judge the outward appearance, but only the giving of the heart to Christ.

Sixthly, a hypocrite may have a change in his expressions. Oh, to hear some hypocrites pray, how beautifully they speak of Christ! Solomon says, "Whose hatred is covered by deceit, his wickedness shall be shewed before the whole congregation" (Prov. 26:26).

Seventhly, there may be a change in a hypocrite's experience; there are some great steps of experience that a hypocrite may attain, although he has not given his heart to Christ.

1. He may distinguish between Christ's absence and His presence. Saul could do so, as we see in 1 Samuel 28:15: "God is departed from me, and answereth me no more."

2. A hypocrite may know when his prayer is not answered. Again, Saul knows such things, saying, God "answereth me no more" (1 Sam. 28:15).

3. A hypocrite may be anxious and sorrowful under the absence of God, when he does not have an answer to prayer. In the fore-cited place, Saul says, "I am sore distressed." What ails you, Saul? What ails you, unbeliever? "God does not answer me," he says, "and that is what ails me." Are there not many here whose lack of answer to prayer never put them to their feet, nor made them sore distressed? If you are so, you are one step below unbelieving Saul, and so you have never given your heart to Christ.

4. He may be convinced of the insupportable weight of sin. Cain cried out, "My punishment is greater than I can bear" (Gen. 4:13). Here is one unbeliever who is convinced of the insupportable weight of sin, yet he never gave Christ his heart.

5. A hypocrite may have some small experience of the joy of heaven. There are some who have tasted of the powers of the world to come, and yet these may fall away (Heb. 6:5). Hence they are but hypocrites who have not given their hearts to Christ.

6. Sixth, a hypocrite may discern between a good preaching and an ill, as those in Hebrews 6. They can discern and tell when they find sweetness in the Word, and when they find it not.

7. This crowns the hypocrite's experiences: he may have some small desires to have Christ, and yet never give his heart to Christ (Heb. 6).

Now since the hypocrite may reach so far, and does so in these days, let this press you to give your heart to Christ, because it is the distinguishing mark between you and a hypocrite. Now how will you answer this proposition? Old and young, have you gone as far as the hypocrite? Oh, vile and profane unbeliever, have you come this far? Oh, stand in awe, lest you be disappointed of your expectation of heaven. I shall now mention three steps that the hypocrite may take. Let me ask you, if you have ever come as far as the hypocrite. If you have not, you are far below a hypocrite who has never given Christ his heart; hear these points, and let them be most convincing to you.

First, have you ever dared to say that you delight to pray and to hear preaching? Do you delight to approach unto God? If you can answer these questions in the affirmative, you may still be a hypocrite, despite all these marks. But if you answer in the negative, you are worse than a hypocrite, and you have never given your heart to Christ.

Second, have you ever mourned when you have not received an answer to prayer? Ask your conscience if you have ever dared to say that you did this in earnest. Will you answer? Did a lack of an answer to prayer ever affect your heart? Although it may have affected you, you may still be a hypocrite in the gall of bitterness and in the bond of iniquity; however, if you dare not say that these things are true, you are one step below a hypocrite who has never given his heart to Christ.

Third, have you ever distinguished in your own condition between the absence and presence of God? If you do not understand this, then you are one step below a hypocrite who never gave his heart to Christ. Now, beloved, since even hypocrites may attain this much, be stirred up to give Christ your hearts, and make a distinguishing mark between yourself and the hypocrite.

Eighth, consider the excellence of the person who seeks your hearts; it is the eternal Son of God that desires to have your hearts. "Lift up your heads, O ye gates; and be ye lift up, ye everlasting doors; and the King of glory shall come in" (Ps. 24:7-8). This is the great argument that He uses to persuade them to open; it is a noble guest who desires to come in—the King of glory. Oh, shall there be a person here who shall keep precious Christ waiting at the door? Oh, let Him in!

Ninth, to provoke you to give Christ your heart, consider that He has waited exceedingly patiently for this, so that you would condescend to give your heart to Him. Christ beseeches His bride in Song of Solomon 5:2, saying, "Open to me, my sister, my love, my dove, my undefiled: for my head is filled with dew, and my locks with the drops of the night." This is His own argument that He uses with her: "Oh, will you open and let Me in?" But let me ask all of you, how long has Christ courted you to get your heart? Now will you not let Him in? For Christ's sake, give Him your hearts, for He has waited well on you.

Tenth, if you do not give your heart to Christ, the devil shall get it. There is a contest, if we may so speak, between the two wooers—Christ and the devil. I fear Christ may return alone from the kirk of Bothwell. Shall the devil prevail more with you than Christ? Shall this devilish courtier prevail with you? I charge you by Him who is white and ruddy, that you would give your hearts to Christ. What arguments can we use with you to persuade you to give your hearts to Christ? I entreat you to give Him your hearts. Though I have spoken much of the length that a hypocrite may come, yet will you also venture upon Christ? He will not put you away if you come to Him and offer your hearts to Him. Oh, will you do it? I beseech you!

Eleventh, consider that if you give Christ your heart, He will look upon that pretty small gift as a reward to Him for all the travail of His soul; yes, He will think it valuable enough recompense to Him for all His sufferings. Now, shall the Son of God be content with such small recompense and reward for all that He has done, and will you not give Him that? Precious Christ, wilt Thou return at this time without dividing the spoil, and taking the prey from the strong? Now, ask your own souls—shall I give away my heart to Christ or not?

Twelfth, until you give your hearts to Christ, all that you communicate, fast, pray, read, or whatsoever you do, is but an abomination unto the Lord. Oh, how much more so when it is done with a wicked mind! Now let all these considerations press you to give Christ your hearts.

In the third place tonight, we shall propose some evidences whereby you may know whether you have given your hearts to Christ or not. We charge you to search and see whether you have done it or not; if you have not done it, make haste and do it.

The first evidence of whether you have given your heart to Christ is that Christ will have many of your thoughts. That which has our heart has most of our thoughts. Now, whereon are your thoughts first in the morning? Are they on Christ? I fear they are on some other thing, when you sit down and when you rise up. In that case, Christ has not yet gotten your heart.

Secondly, those who have given their hearts to Christ will observe His ways. These two are joined together in the text. Now are there not many here to whom commanded duties are a burden? This is an ill token that you have never given your heart to Christ.

Thirdly, for the man who has given Christ his heart, Christ's absence will be his burden. It was Him whom her soul loved who was gone; therefore she mourns for His absence (Song 3:2).

Fourthly, such a man answers all temptations with these words: "Oh, temptations! I am not mine own, now I am in Christ; you must go and seek me from Christ, if you can get me!" That is a noble way to answer assaults from Satan, saying, "I am Christ's, and not mine own."

Fifthly, he is the person who will loathe to offend Christ. "I charge you," says the spouse, "that ye stir not up, nor awake my love, till he please" (Song 3:6).

Sixthly, once this person is admitted to taste of the sweetness of Christ, he endeavors, by all means, to keep Christ and his soul together. "I held him, and would not let him go" (Song 3:4). Now are there any here who lack these evidences, and who are convinced that they have not yet given their hearts to Christ? I shall speak concerning these impediments, which hinder some from giving their hearts to Christ.

1. We are not convinced of, and do not believe, the excellence that is in Christ. Do we dare stand so boldly against this command of Christ's? He commands, "My son, give me thine heart" (Prov. 23:26). Ignorance of Christ is that indeed which hinders marriage with Him; for if we had known the Prince of life, we would not have crucified Him, who is the King of glory. But, He is both unknown and despised among us.

2. The second impediment is the perverseness of our will. There are many who cry out, "We will have none of Christ," like that in Psalm 81:11. But I say to you, perhaps Christ will one day say to you, "I will have none of thee." Perhaps that sentence will be passed against you, according to your word; you shall have none of Christ and He will have none of you. Oh, but what a dreadful sentence that would be!

3. Our hearts chase after things of a present world; such things have taken the heart from Christ. We are greatly hindered from giving our hearts to Christ when our hearts run after the things of this life, and begin to take pleasure in them.

4. We are not convinced indeed of the necessity, advantage, and pleasure in giving our hearts to Christ. Dear stubborn friends who are far from righteousness, will you not give your hearts to Him? There is such a great necessity for it, and a great advantage in it!

5. There is a strong soul-union and heart-conjunction between us and our idols. There are three words in Scripture that speak of this heart-conjunction between us and our idols. "Ephraim is joined to idols: let him alone" (Hosea 4:17). In the original, it reads, "Ephraim is married to idols." Hosea 14:8 and Ezekiel 14:2-5 also show the strong union. Consider these two places at your leisure, for there is such a great union between us and our idols that we cannot give our hearts to Christ.

Will you give Christ your heart or not in this last and great day of the communion feast? What argument will persuade you? What argument has not been used with you? Oh, stubborn creatures, will nothing persuade you? I say this one thing to him who gives his heart to Christ: believe me, he shall never rue it, nor yet have cause to rue it. Oh, Christ is well worthy of your heart! The knot of union between you and Christ, that golden, indissolvable knot, shall never be loosed again.

There are four things that break bonds and loosen knots between dearest friends; yet, these things will not dissolve this knot of union with Christ.

1. The sin of whoredom will break the bonds of friendship; yet, it will not break the knot of union with Christ. In Hosea 2:7, we read, "I will go and return to my first husband; for then was it better with me than now." She says this when she had been playing the whore; yes, she had been married to another lover since she went a-whoring from Christ. Yet, this does not break the knot of the first marriage with Christ; therefore, she is welcomed when she returns unto Him again.

2. Ingratitude will break the knot of friendship among dearest friends. If one friend did a great courtesy for another, and the other friend proved ungrateful, would this not break their friendship? But how ungrateful have we been to Jesus Christ! Yet, it will not loose this knot of union between Him and us; no, as it says in Zephaniah 3:17, "He will rest in his love."

3. Mistakes will break union between dearest and choice friends; yet, this union between Christ and us cannot be broken thereby. Although we mistake Him, it lies not in our power to break this knot, and it is not possible that He can mistake us.

4. Passion and anger, Solomon says, separate the closest of friends; but anger cannot separate Christ from those who have been cast within the knot of His union. Oh, blessed are we, that the knot is in His hand! For any anger will not make Him break it; yes, He will hale us to heaven before He breaks this knot with us.

Now, shall I leave you without giving your consent to Christ? Shall we return to Him and have nothing to say? Oh, will you give your hearts to Christ? He is importunate with you! I think that Christ must steal away your heart before He will get it; but, if you would give Him this gift, it would blind your eyes to all other things. Oh, give your heart to Christ! What do you say to His proposal now? We must leave you and go away; you do not know when you will be wooed so much to Jesus again as you have been at this time. If we have gained our point, we labor not in vain; whether you grant or refuse, Christ will have His honor. Angels and the spirits of just men made perfect will praise and glorify Him, though you may not do so.

I shall close with this thought: let all the angels praise Him; and let all the congregation say, "Amen." Let all the saints in heaven and earth praise Him; and let all the congregation say, "Amen." Let the sun, moon, stars, fire, hail, stormy winds, vapors, frost, grass, fowls in the air and fishes in the sea, old men, young men, old women and young maids praise Him; let the congregation say, "Amen." Yes, let all our souls and all that is within us praise Him who is, by infinite degrees, exalted above all our blessings and praises; to whom be everlasting praise, glory, and honor forever and ever. Amen.

A Word of Exhortation before the Communion of Glasgow

I shall not speak much to you; I would only like to say that there are six evidences that these days will be dreadful days to Glasgow. Before long, the ministers and people shall begin to pray to God saying, "Oh, that we had never had a name!" He who says that these two days shall be seen many days hence, must be rightly prophesying.

The first sad evidence that these days will be dreadful days is the lack of tenderness. I suppose few tears have been shed since Glasgow's communion began. I think that we are as little moved when we are feasting with Christ, as if we were feasting with a stone. The second sad evidence that these days will be dreadful days is that never were there less pains taken for such a solemn ordinance, as have been by many of us. What are we doing? I know that many of us are rushing upon the edge of Christ's eternal displeasure. Third, are there any here today to whom Christ's withdrawing from these solemn ordinances is their burden? May not this be written on all your communion tables: "O Glasgow! Glasgow! Christ is gone, Christ is gone!"? The fourth sad evidence that these days will be dreadful days is the little longing that we have after Christ the crucified Savior. In a manner, I think there are some of us who have lost all the desire which we seemed to have. Christ may seem to come and go without observation of us all. Is there a desire in you to feast with Christ today? I know that if you saw Him, you would not know Him; yea some, I know, know not whether there be a Christ or not. The fifth sad evidence that these days shall be dreadful days is that for anything we may discern or read, we see little exercise of faith, love, or repentance among you. You may think it strange, and I desire to be mistaken, that if it were in my own case, I would we were all presently dismissed from going to the table, for we are not in a feasting frame. Are you content to go? I think that now He forbids us to come to the table. Believe me, I think we shall feast alone today, and then it shall be a sad feast. Are there any here that have seen the Master of the feast? The sixth and last sad evidence, which may speak forth a sad and dreadful day to this place, is that in all the communions that we have attended, and all the ordinances that we have received, we had often said, "Oh, that I had not attended such an ordinance!"

I desire that you may be composed for such a solemn work. Are you ready? Are you ready to come and embrace Jesus Christ? Yes, we think there is a noise sounding in our ears that says, "Inquire not after me." Do you not all miss Him, of whose countenance one look would make this assembly a blessed assembly? Think but a little, whether we shall proceed or stay. We desire not to speak so much of the causes of His departure; I think indeed there are some of us, that it would be better for you that they were away. I think there are some that never were at a communion, but they were a blemish on the feast of love. Now, that may seem a heartless invitation to come to this love-feast. I confess, so it is; it is truly heartless. It is a wonder we are not stricken with silence; and it is a wonder the places you sit on are not made the place of your graves before you leave here.

Let us go on and venture to the end that we may approach to this holy feast—we, in the name of the Master of the feast, debar and excommunicate all them that hate Christ, and all profane and scandalous persons, that they come not to eat and drink their own condemnation. In His name and authority, I debar all strangers to God and enemies to our Lord Jesus Christ. Alas! We fear we have debarred many. He is gone, He is gone, and we care not for Him!

On the other hand, we do, in the name and authority of our blessed Lord, who is the Master of the feast, invite all those who are convinced of their need of Christ. We do, in His precious name, invite all those that desire to have Him, and eternally to enjoy Him; and all His friends, we invite you to come. This is His command, "Eat, O friends; drink, yea, drink abundantly, O beloved" (Song 5:1). Alas! I fear Christ shall not speak that word to many. We will not say but He may, as He has many times, graciously disappointed our fears; He may make this a feast of love, a "feast of fat things, a feast of wines on the lees, of fat things full of marrow, of wines on the lees well refined" (Isa. 25:6). Are you ready? Then come.

If the Master of the feast had come, we would desire to know it. It has been long since Christ spoke the words, "Without me, ye can do nothing" (John 15:5). And, sure I am, you cannot communicate without Him today. There are two visible attendants that Christ the Master of the feast brings with Him when He comes, but I do not see them here this day.

The first visible attendant that Christ the Master of the feast brings is repentance. He brings repentance with Him; is not repentance lacking?

The second visible attendant that Christ the Master of the feast brings with Him is faith. Is not faith lacking? Many of us may question if ever we had faith at all. There is not a step we walk, but we thrust a spear in the side of precious Christ. Now, are you all resolved to eat and drink of this feast? Look to it, sirs, there may be poison in this cup that you are going to drink. We, after His example who appointed this ordinance, read our warrant, "And when he had given thanks, he brake it" (1 Cor. 11:24). Let us bless Him who has prepared such a blessed feast. Let us seek His blessing who has appointed it for our spiritual nourishment. Now the bread is changed; now the wine is changed, not as to their substance, but their use. "He took the bread, and brake it." There are these two things that Christ has taken to commend Himself, which may make us fall in love with Him on this the day of our feast.

First, we shall love Him knowing that before long He shall come again. Christ has a purpose and is longing to come again. He says, "I will give this feast until I come again, and then I will give you a better."

Second, we may fall in love with Him when we see His great condescension. It would be a wonder to see a beggar sit down with a prince—but here is a greater wonder! What a sweet pavilion is love! There was never such a royal pavilion as Christ and His bride in the midst of His love! In the greatest of all His trouble, He looked toward you with love!

Now, where are your thoughts of His love? Do you have higher thoughts of Christ now than when you sat down? Who is like unto Him, the King of saints? Will you carry away with you these thoughts of Him? Who is the crucified among ten thousand? Have you seen Him? Alas! I fear He is gone. Of all the persons that you have ever seen, you have never seen His match! There is a soul-captivating look in the sight of His face, that if you have once seen Him, you would never desire to look on another.

THE PATH OF TRUE GODLINESS

by Willem Teellinck

In nine short "books," this remarkable work by Willem Teellinck (1579-1629) shows believers the character of true godliness and the kingdom of darkness that opposes it. Dr. Joel R. Beeke, editor of the book, has included an introduction that chronicles Teellinck's life and times. This is one of the best books ever written on the subject of sanctification. How does one flee from temptation? What is the best way for believers to open their hearts to God? Packed with scriptural guidance, this book answers these questions and many more about how to live godly in Christ Jesus.

978-1-892777-75-1 Paperback, 303 pages

"A SWEET FLAME"

Piety in the Letters of Jonathan Edwards

Edited and introduced by Michael A. G. Haykin

"A Sweet Flame" introduces readers to the piety of Jonathan Edwards (1703-1758). Dr. Haykin's biographical sketch of Edwards captures the importance the New England minister placed on Scripture, family piety, and the church's reliance upon God. The remainder of the book presents twenty-six selections from various letters written by Edwards, two written by family members at his death, and an appendix drawing upon Edwards's last will and the inventory of his estate.

978-1-60178-011-9 Paperback, 192 pages